The Cavalries in the
Nashville Campaign

ALSO BY DENNIS W. BELCHER
AND FROM McFARLAND

The Union Cavalry and the Chickamauga Campaign (2018)

The Cavalries at Stones River: An Analytical History (2017)

The Cavalry of the Army of the Cumberland (2016)

General David S. Stanley, USA: A Civil War Biography (2014)

*The 11th Missouri Volunteer Infantry
in the Civil War: A History and Roster* (2011)

*The 10th Kentucky Volunteer Infantry
in the Civil War: A History and Roster* (2009)

EDITED BY DENNIS W. BELCHER
AND FROM McFARLAND

*"This Terrible Struggle for Life": The Civil War
Letters of a Union Regimental Surgeon,* by
Thomas S. Hawley, M.D. (2012)

The Cavalries in the Nashville Campaign

DENNIS W. BELCHER

Foreword by James D. Kay, Jr.

McFarland & Company, Inc., Publishers
Jefferson, North Carolina

ISBN (print) 978-1-4766-7599-2
ISBN (ebook) 978-1-4766-3991-8

LIBRARY OF CONGRESS AND BRITISH LIBRARY
CATALOGUING DATA ARE AVAILABLE

Library of Congress Control Number 2020017058

© 2020 Dennis W. Belcher. All rights reserved

*No part of this book may be reproduced or transmitted in any form
or by any means, electronic or mechanical, including photocopying
or recording, or by any information storage and retrieval system,
without permission in writing from the publisher.*

On the cover: *insets* Nathan Bedford Forrest urged his men to
"drive the enemy from our soil" (Library of Congress); James Harrison Wilson
boldly declared, "[W]e shall soon destroy their cavalry and establish the
invincibility of our own" (Library of Congress); *background* "Confederate
Deflection," aka "The Blue and the Gray," by William T. Trego, n.d.,
oil on canvas, 36 × 24 (courtesy Syd and Sharon Martin collection and
the James A. Michener Art Museum; photograph by Joseph Elkhardt)

Printed in the United States of America

*McFarland & Company, Inc., Publishers
Box 611, Jefferson, North Carolina 28640
www.mcfarlandpub.com*

Table of Contents

ACKNOWLEDGMENTS	ix
FOREWORD BY JAMES D. KAY, JR.	1
PREFACE	3

Part One—Prelude

One. The Situation on September 4, 1864	8
Two. Hood Prepares to March to Tennessee	18
Three. The Union Cavalry in the Nashville Campaign	38
Four. The Confederate Cavalry in the Nashville Campaign	58

Part Two—The Advance on Nashville

Five. Forrest Attacks Johnsonville and Hood Prepares to Advance into Tennessee	75
Six. Florence to Columbia	84
Seven. The Armies Move into Position at Columbia	120
Eight. Columbia: Forrest Pushes Across the Duck River	128

Part Three—The Battle for Nashville

Nine. Spring Hill and Franklin	146
Ten. Hood Marches to Nashville	183
Eleven. The Battle of Nashville—December 15, 1864	226
Twelve. The Battle of Nashville—December 16, 1864	248
Thirteen. Hood Retreats	274

Conclusions	311
Chapter Notes	317
Bibliography	355
Index	367

"The old campaign is ended, and your commanding general deems this an appropriate occasion to speak of the steadiness, self-denial, and patriotism with which you have borne the hardships of the past year. The marches and labors you have performed during that period will find no parallel in the history of this war."
—Nathan Bedford Forrest

"I know of no battles in the war where the influence of cavalry was more potent, nor of any pursuit sustained so long and well. The results of campaign ... clearly demonstrate the wisdom of massing the cavalry of an army..."
—James Harrison Wilson

And now I'm going southward,
For my heart is full of woe,
I'm going back to Georgia
To find my "Uncle Joe."
You may talk about you dearest maid,
And sing of Rosalie,
But the gallant Hood of Texas,
Played Hell in Tennessee
—Song sung by Confederate soldiers at the end of the campaign to the tune of the "Yellow Rose of Texas," from *Battles and Sketches of the Army of Tennessee* by Bromfield Ridley

Acknowledgments

Anyone who has ever worked with historical materials knows that the end product is due to the efforts of many people. I am very fortunate to have had the cooperation of many archivists, special collections professionals and librarians as this project was completed. Many individuals went out of their way to guide me to the relevant collections and many personally worked to ensure that I was able to have access to these materials, so I want to thank all the kind people who professionally and efficiently provided their expertise to assist in this project.

In particular, I want to thank Kyle Hovious, University of Tennessee; James Prichard, Filson Historical Society; and Tutti Jackson, Ohio Historical Society, for their assistance in this process. I am ever grateful for the help of Darla Brock, Archivist, Tennessee State Library and Archives. They all have consistently gone out of their way to assist in sharing the materials from their collections.

In addition, I would like to thank Molly Kodner and Dennis Northcutt, archivists at the Missouri History Museum Library and Research Center; Gayle Martinson, Reference Librarian, Wisconsin Historical Society; Brooke Guthrie, Research Services Coordinator at the David M. Rubenstein Rare Book & Manuscript Library; Amy Vedra, Director, Reference Services, and Nadia Kousari, Visual Reference Librarian, Indiana Historical Society; Allison DeArcangelis, Special Collections Librarian, Newberry Library; Justin Davis, Librarian, and Laura Eliason, Rare Books and Manuscripts Librarian, Indiana State Library; Cinda Nofziger, Archivist, and Diana Bachman, Reference Staff, Bentley Historical Library; Lynn Houghton, Special Collections Librarian, Western Michigan State University; Ashley Steenson, historian, University of Mississippi; Charles Scott, Library Resource Technician, Iowa State Historical Library & Archives; Austin Setter, historian, Western Michigan State University; Kathleen Feduccia, Librarian, Nashville Public Library; Benna Vaughan, Special Collections and Manuscripts Archivist, Baylor University; John C. Varner, Special Collections & Archives Librarian, Auburn University Libraries; Lynn Niedermeier, Manuscripts & Folklife Archives Librarian, Western Kentucky State University; Becky Denes, Librarian, Center for Archival Collections, Jerome Library, Bowling Green State University; Kathy Shoemaker, Reference Coordinator, Stuart A. Rose Manuscript, Archives, & Rare Book Library, Emory University; Kayla Barrett, Archivist, Georgia Archives; Jennifer McGillan, Coordinator of Manuscripts, Mississippi State University; Peter McCarthy, Librarian, and Heather Richmond, Archivist, State Historical Society of Missouri; Ed Busch, Archivist, Michigan State University; Brittney Falter, Research Services Coordinator, Special Collections Research Center, George Mason University; Stephanie Pezzella, Museum Curator, Arlington Heights Historical Museum; Kendall Newton, Reference Services,

Dolph Briscoe Center for American History; Sean Eisele, Special Collections Librarian, Vigo County Public Library; Christina Lucas, Curator of Collections and Exhibitions, Pearce Museum at Navarro College; Christine Schmid Engels, Archives Manager, Cincinnati Museum Center; Becki Plunkett, Special Collections Archivist, State Historical Society of Iowa; Barbara A. McClurkin, Archivist, Western History Collections, University of Oklahoma Libraries; Randall J. Smith, Assistant Curator, Howard County Historical Society; Matthew Turi, Manuscripts Research and Instruction Librarian, Wilson Library; Jenny McElroy, Reference Librarian, Gale Family Library, Minnesota Historical Society; John Versluis, Dean of the Texas Heritage Museum, Hill College; Amy Lucadamo, College Archivist, Gettysburg College, Musselman Library; Allison Dillard, Research Center, Georgia Historical Society; Nancy Dupree, Research Archivist, and Meredith McDonough, Digital Assets Coordinator, Alabama Department of Archives and History; Patty Stringfellow, Director, Jasper County Public Library; Geoffery Stark and Misha Gardner, University of Arkansas Special Collections; Marc Brodsky, Public Services and Reference Archivist, Virginia Tech; Tal Nadan, Reference Archivist, New York Public Library; Carla Carlson, Assistant Curator, Historical Manuscripts, The University of Southern Mississippi; the Midwest Genealogy Center Reference Staff; and finally, Melody Klaas, Librarian, Missouri River Regional Library. They all have been instrumental in the collection of the materials used in this book.

I want thank Abigail Hastings for sharing the "Autobiography of James Polk Brownlow, Jr." and William Griffing for sharing "J.V. Hinchman's Pocket Journal," both of which offered important firsthand accounts of the actions during the Nashville Campaign.

I want to express my gratitude to Andy Papen, Jim Lewis, and James D. Kay who read various sections of the manuscript prior to its completion. In particular, Andy Papen read the entire manuscript and his efforts were very valuable in the completion of this project. The effort and expertise of these readers are greatly appreciated. James Kay has a unique and extensive expertise regarding the Battle of Nashville. He spent much of his valuable time to show me the areas where much of the cavalry action took place in the battle of December 15–16, 1864. He unselfishly shared his knowledge of the battlefield which enabled me to have a greater understanding of how the cavalry actions occurred. Without his assistance, I would have missed some of the most valuable aspects of the Battle of Nashville.

Lastly, I would like to thank George Skoch who produced the maps for this book. George is an expert in map production, and I could not have completed this book without his assistance and expertise.

Foreword
by James D. Kay, Jr.

It was August 1966. I was six years old. The war in Vietnam was escalating; riots were beginning across the United States and the world. These were times of great change. I was oblivious to all of this when my father moved us from Mt. Juliet, Tennessee, to Oak Hill, just south of Nashville. In our backyard on Oak Valley Lane was an old stacked stone wall that ran for miles. The wall fascinated me. When was it built? Why was it built? Why was it located where it was? Why was the trail along the wall named Kirkman Lane? I walked this bridle path almost every day to school at Robertson Academy. Others rode horses on the well-worn path. I would walk to the battlefield marker showing Stewart's Line which noted fighting at this wall. One day I found an arrowhead and a few weeks later a Minié ball. In looking at old maps I discovered that our home was in the center of the second day of fighting of a great Civil War battlefield. In that month, I discovered my passion in life—the Battle of Nashville.

There have been numerous books since Thomas Hay first published his essay in 1928 on the battle. Stanley Horn's *The Decisive Battle of Nashville* was the first in 1954 and many have followed. I have read and studied every publication since. I most enjoyed the writings of Wiley Sword and my Auburn friend James McDonough, who, like me, was fascinated by the Nashville battlefield at an early age. Unfortunately, none of the authors, other than McDonough, ever lived on the battlefield, to my knowledge, and many authors spent little time traversing the hills and valleys to precisely pinpoint where the lines and batteries were located on December 16, 1864.

The Nashville battlefield has virtually been obliterated. The Battle of Nashville Preservation Society, Inc., has preserved Redoubt 1 on Benham Avenue and the Shy's Hill site on Benton Smith Road. Other than Ft. Negley, Travelers Rest, Granbury's Lunette and Kelley's Point, there is really no place to go to visit any of the original sites. All have succumbed to the bulldozer and "progress." This is even more startling when we consider that Nashville was one of the largest battlefields of the war, encompassing more than 20 square miles. I still live in Oak Hill, approximately 600 yards from where we moved in 1966. I walk the battlefield daily. I know where each brigade was formed and where the charges were made, where the men died and where those that did not die surrendered or retreated. I know where the hidden remnants of the trenches still run in my neighbors' back yards. On my land is a part of the old earthworks from Dent's Alabama battery where 13 live shells were discovered in one deep hole in the seventies. There are only a handful of us left that know these little gems of the Nashville battlefield. Hank Williams, Jr., Mark Swann and Thomas Cartwright traversed these places in the 1960s and early 1970s as teenagers with their metal detectors. My old friend Paul Clements stood on Redbud Hill in the early eighties and wept as he watched the development of Burton Hills and the tear down of the Compton mansion where Lieutenant Colonel William Shy was taken after his death. A few other good men also know where the treasures still lie but there are only a handful left. Soon we will all be gone. Unless others step up now, this history will be forever lost.

I am so pleased that Dennis Belcher asked me to write this foreword and assist him with some technical aspects and troop positions. The author has taken the time to walk and drive with me the sites pertinent to the cavalry action during the Battle of Nashville. Unless you live in the area and walk the terrain, it is impossible to determine from the official reports which hill was occupied, fortified or attacked during the battle. There are so many tall hills in Oak Hill and Forrest Hills that, unless you are on site, you simply cannot envision what positions some of the eyewitnesses were really discussing more than 150 years ago. The author took the critical time needed to learn this information firsthand and I thoroughly enjoyed our time together standing on the ridges and in the driveways of some of my friends who allowed us access where I could point out precisely where the troops moved, fought and died.

This work gives details that most of the prior authors either missed or did not include. Specifically, the retreat by Cheatham's corps through the "gap in the hills," which is present-day Lakeview Drive, and through the Radnor Lake State Park, and the work of Colonel David Coleman with Ector's Brigade in protecting this retreat are finally noted. Furthermore, the author's work on the Battle of the Barricade, which sprawled over the present-day Richland Country Club and south to present-day Maryland Way, have really not received the depth from other authors that was necessary. I am so pleased that the author took the time to describe these encounters in detail and provide the finest Nashville action maps ever published.

Just like the 1960s, we live in a changing time and a changing world. Political discussion in virtual reality is beyond aggressive and the American Civil War and its 620,000 American casualties are a thing of the past. Fortunately, a very few remain to protect the record for history the blood that was spilled into the Nashville dirt. The author is one of these men. I know that you will enjoy this fine work.

James D. Kay, Jr., is president of the Battle of Nashville Preservation Society, Inc.

Preface

The Nashville Campaign is one the most compelling and controversial campaigns of the Civil War. In regard to the cavalry operations, the campaign would pit the young and energetic James Harrison Wilson and his Union cavalry against the cunning and experienced Nathan Bedford Forrest with his Confederate cavalry. This campaign would mark the ability of Forrest to use his finite resources of men, equipment, and supplies to support Hood's overall objectives. On the Union side, the campaign would test Wilson's ability to organize, equip and hastily prepare his cavalry forces to meet the aggressive Forrest. Overall, the cavalry operations were conducted by experienced troops with four years of preparation for this type of campaign. The importance of this campaign cannot be overstated because the Army of Tennessee was one of the last two large armies of the Confederacy. If the campaign proved successful, Hood could push into Kentucky or Virginia, thus relieving pressure on Lee besieged in Virginia.

By today's standards, many would question whether the outcome of the campaign was ever in doubt; however, this campaign was anything but a forgone conclusion. John Bell Hood, a master of maneuver, aggressively stalked his Northern adversaries, and George Thomas' forces were assembled in a short period of time in some of the most adverse circumstances. Sherman took, in his opinion, the elite infantry corps, along with many cavalry mounts when he began his march to the sea, leaving Thomas in a difficult situation. Like Wilson, the outcome of the Nashville Campaign depended on Thomas' ability to cobble together enough troops to stop the Southern advance. As the two armies converged, the outcome of the Battle of Nashville did not occur until an hour before dark on the second day of the battle. Applying the words of the Duke of Wellington, the Nashville Campaign was "the nearest run thing you ever saw in your life."

One of the problems of relating the history of the cavalry actions during this campaign is the temptation of being drawn in the large, ongoing controversies which did not directly relate to the cavalry. It was tempting to delve into these infantry- and army-level issues, but these shoals, for the most part, have been avoided in this work. Those controversies include such issues as Hood's overall command ability, Hood's decision to wait three weeks in northern Alabama before starting the campaign, the whole issue of the Spring Hill affair, Hood's attack at Franklin, and Hood's decision to besiege Nashville for two weeks. The controversies from the Union point of view include Schofield's performance in the campaign, the speed of Thomas' actions at Nashville, and who was responsible for the success at Franklin. Historians have addressed, and are still addressing, these issues after 150 years.

Instead, the cavalry had issues of their own. These are numerous and some overflow directly into these infantry-based discussions. Among these are Wilson's performance on November 29, Forrest's action during the Union evacuation at Spring Hill, Forrest's proposed attack on the Federal rear on November 30, Forrest's absence from the battle on December 16, Wilson's interactions with Schofield and Wilson's less than aggressive pursuit on December 16, to name a few. Despite these issues, the actions of the cavalry forces of both armies proved to be important and directly impacted how the campaign developed and concluded.

In regard to this book, there are just a few items that need to be clarified. For example, A.J. Smith commanded a wing of XVI Corps prior to the Battle of Nashville. When he arrived, this command was renamed Detachment, Army of the Tennessee. Because this is such an unwieldy term, the designation of XVI Corps was retained to identify Smith's command. There are a couple of names that may be confusing, and as a point of clarification, this work will utilize Waynesborough, instead of the currently-used Waynesboro. In addition, the term Hillsboro Pike was used instead of Hillsborough Pike, names used interchangeably in various reports. On the second day of the Battle of Nashville, there is often some confusion regarding two geographic positions—Compton's Hill and Orchard Hill. These locations are called Shy's Hill and Overton Hill today and maps often show these names; however, in 1864, these locations were called Compton's Hill and Orchard Hill, so those terms are used in this book. In regard to the maps in this book, these were designed to show the cavalry actions and the infantry units are shown only in generalities. Also, the Confederate cavalry reports are scarce and often incomplete while the Union cavalry have more extensive reports. This is not an attempt to slight the Southern forces, but it is just an unfortunate state of affairs. Many of the Confederates records were lost or destroyed at the end of the war. Finally, personal accounts are used and quoted often in this work. There is nothing so real as the descriptions given in the voice of those who participated in the event.

In this campaign, Nathan Bedford Forrest, based on his prior actions during the war, occupied the attention of the Federal commanders. Sherman long believed that Forrest was his greatest threat and Thomas, at Nashville, decided to wait until his cavalry force was sufficient to deal with Forrest before attacking Hood. Forrest's part in the campaign would prove to be increasingly difficult as Hood got closer to Nashville. He had three veteran cavalry divisions moving in concert with the Confederate infantry, but he had little hope of adding reinforcements. He needed to utilize his forces wisely, screening Hood's infantry and pushing aside resistance during the advance to Nashville. Forrest relied on the command abilities of his experienced division commanders and the performance of his veteran cavalry troops in this campaign.

On the Union side, James H. Wilson was young and inexperienced at this level of command in the Federal cavalry. He assumed command of a cavalry corps sorely neglected and disregarded by Sherman. He was initially outmanned by Forrest and he turned his attention to the rapid mounting, equipping and organizing of enough troops to face his adversaries. In this campaign, his chief of staff, E.B. Beaumont, should be recognized for much of the ultimate success, because he had the responsibility of handling the inglorious administrative duty of locating and equipping new troops while Wilson served at the front. Wilson would be successful if he could organize a new cavalry force while battling a foe marching toward Nashville.

The personalities and command abilities of the top cavalry commanders were of great importance in this campaign. Forrest was the supreme independent cavalry commander, but during this campaign he was once again attached to a large army. His ability to cooperate with the other Confederate commanders would be tested in the Nashville Campaign. When Forrest was present with the Confederate infantry, morale immediately increased and his reputation of winning battles bolstered the confidence of the soldiers of the Army of Tennessee. In regard to Wilson, his memoirs left the impression of a commander who was arrogant, self-assured, and a stranger to humility; however, it is important to remember that the person who writes their memoirs in their senior years is not the person who participated in the events. This seems to be the case with Wilson. His actions during the campaign, with notable exceptions, seem to be more collegial and cooperative than his memoirs suggest. He made an immediate friend with Thomas, who, in return, made decisions which cemented Wilson's reputation as an exemplary cavalry commander.

This campaign also highlighted important changes in cavalry tactics. While mounted cavalry fights occurred in this campaign, dismounted cavalry was probably never used to this scale and with such success. Also, cavalry commanders no longer just commanded cavalry, as demonstrated in the fights at Murfreesboro and during the withdrawal of the Confederate army, where cavalry officers commanded both infantry and cavalry. In addition, never in the Civil War was there closer support by the cavalry for infantry actions than in the Battle of Nashville for the Union forces, a marked contrast to Hood's utilization of his cavalry forces during this battle. Overall, the opposing cavalries made direct contributions to the outcome of this campaign and the results set the stage for how the cavalry operations would play out in 1865. The Nashville Campaign reflected the stark realities of the war across the country in December 1864 and would mark an important part of the death knell for the Confederacy.

Part One
Prelude

Chapter One

The Situation on September 4, 1864

> It was at Nashville that Hood, wisely or not, risked all on one cast of the dice...
> —Stanley Horn

The Battle of Nashville, fought in December 1864, would be called *the* decisive battle of the Civil War by some historians. This remarkable campaign revealed as much about the situation of the Southern armies in the fall of 1864 as it did about the Union armies. The pendulum swung in favor of the Federal forces at this point in the war, but the aggressively minded John Bell Hood, who succeeded Joseph Johnston as the commander of the Army of Tennessee in July 1864, decided to again advance northward at the end of the Atlanta Campaign. He took a smaller army on the offensive to the limits of Nashville, the second most heavily defended city in the United States. Much about Hood's character was seen in this decision as he faced the "Rock of Chickamauga," George Thomas, and his generals. Thomas, seen as slow and plodding by some, had accomplished much for the Union armies in the war. The story of the Nashville Campaign also shows two of the most intriguing cavalry commanders in the war—the legendary Confederate cavalry commander Nathan Bedford Forrest and the rising star for the Union, James H. Wilson. The cavalries of these two commanders would be pitted against each other and the stakes could not have been higher. The cavalry operations would pit the experience and cunning of Forrest against the confidence and energy of Wilson. Cavalries on both sides made important contributions in the campaign and while the battles fought in this campaign did not end the war, they set the stage for the final events of 1865 in the west. The cavalries of the North and South would fight to the bitter end and the honor and the glory of men in the saddle would play out on the fields and hills south of Nashville.[1]

The Union Situation at Atlanta—September 1864

The Atlanta Campaign, perhaps better named the campaign to destroy the Army of Tennessee, extended for four months, culminating in the Battle of Jonesborough, fought 20 miles south of the Atlanta on August 31 and September 1. Jonesborough, a village, which happened to be on the Macon & Western Railroad, held no particular strategic value to the Union armies, but the railroad did. This battle forced Hood to evacuate Atlanta. This campaign began in early May 1864 and Sherman's three armies

Chapter One. The Situation on September 4, 1864

constantly battled the Southern troops for four hot months while maneuvering in the countryside. By mid–July, the Confederate army retreated behind the fortifications of Atlanta and on July 18, the 33-year-old Hood replaced Johnston as commander of the Army of Tennessee.[2]

Hood, referred to as "Sam" by his friends, ranks among the most controversial leaders of the Civil War. Hood, born in Owingsville, Kentucky, was the son of a prosperous physician and grew up headstrong. He achieved his appointment to the United States Military Academy due to the influence of his uncle, a U.S. representative. Hood graduated in 1853, finishing 44th in a class of 52. Upon his graduation, he became part of the 4th U.S. Infantry and served in Missouri and California. In 1855, he transferred to the 2nd U.S. Cavalry in Texas. He served on the frontier (as did many other officers destined to participate in the Civil War) until 1861 when he offered his services to the Confederacy. Hood was appointed colonel of the 4th Texas Infantry in 1861 and in March 1862 he was promoted to the rank of brigadier general and given command of the Texas Brigade in the Army of Northern Virginia. Hood served in many battles in the east including the Battle of Gaines Mill in which he received notable recognition for his bravery and leadership. In October 1862, he was again promoted, this time to the rank of major general, and he subsequently led his division in the Second Battle of Bull Run, Antietam, Fredericksburg, and Gettysburg. At the latter battle, he received a wound which permanently incapacitated his left arm. After he recuperated, he moved his division to reinforce Bragg's army in September 1863 and participated in the Battle of Chickamauga. During this battle, he received another wound, which resulted in the amputation of his right leg. The wounds left him with one useless arm, which he carried in a sling, and with the need to move about with crutches. In February 1864, he received a promotion to the rank of lieutenant general and was permanently assigned to the Army of Tennessee. Hood commanded his corps in the Atlanta Campaign until July, when he was named to command the Confederate forces in that campaign.[3]

General John Bell Hood ordered his cavalry to "break the line of communication on the two [rail]roads running from Nashville to the army" (Library of Congress).

Hood assumed command because of the successes of Sherman's three armies, but also through the machinations of Braxton Bragg, the unsuccessful, previous commander of the Army of Tennessee. Bragg traveled to Atlanta on July 13 and stayed for four days during which time he assembled the information he would need to recommend replacing Joseph Johnston. Hood's aggressiveness and his close relationship with Jefferson Davis secured his place as commander of the Army of Tennessee, but this aggressiveness had a price. In the five infantry battles in the Atlanta Campaign after Hood gained command, four resulted in Union victories and these four also resulted in fewer Federal casualties than those of Hood's Confederates. Despite the losses, Hood proudly exclaimed that these battles allowed him to hold Atlanta for 46 days. Remarkably, Hood would explain some of his defeats and failure to hold Atlanta resulted from the "timid defense" policies that had been part of Johnston's strategy.[4]

At the end of the Atlanta Campaign, praises from important figures swiftly acknowledged Sherman's success at Atlanta. With Grant's armies bogged down at Petersburg and Richmond, the victory was important particularly because of the upcoming presidential election. On September 3, Lincoln wrote, "The national thanks are tendered by the President to Maj. Gen. W.T. Sherman and the gallant officers and soldiers of his command before Atlanta, for the distinguished ability, courage, and perseverance displayed in the campaign in Georgia, which, under Divine favor, has resulted in the capture of the city of Atlanta." Grant also wrote a personal note of congratulations to Sherman the next morning.[5]

The citizens in the North would cast their votes in the presidential election in November and because Grant remained stalemated by Lee in Virginia, the President needed this victory at Atlanta. Sherman would write in his memoirs that the capture of Atlanta made the election a certainty for Lincoln, who had had a tough political campaign against George McClellan. There can be no doubt that the capture of Atlanta provided a dramatic victory needed by those who supported the Northern cause; however, Sherman would be criticized for allowing Hood's army to escape. When the campaign began, Sherman's objective was the destruction of the Army of Tennessee, but as the summer advanced, the capture of Atlanta became his primary objective and when Hood evacuated the city, Sherman embraced the victory as Hood marched away. Historian Albert Castel observed that Sherman outnumbered the Confederate army and that Sherman was poised to strike a decisive blow to the retreating army but "did not close his fist." Because Sherman did not destroy the Confederate forces at Atlanta, the adage that campaigns without decisive battles will result in battles being fought somewhere else in the future proved providential.[6]

The Union and Confederate cavalries were relatively equal during the Atlanta Campaign. Sherman had five cavalry divisions at his disposal, four from the Army of the Cumberland—Edward McCook's First Division, Kenner Garrard's Second Division, Hugh Judson Kilpatrick's Third Division, and Alvan Gillem's Fourth Division. In addition, Major General George Stoneman's cavalry division of the Army of the Ohio completed Sherman's cavalry forces. Facing Sherman during the Atlanta Campaign were four divisions of Wheeler's cavalry commanded by William T. Martin, William Y.C. Humes, John H. Kelly, and William "Red" Hicks Jackson.[7]

The cavalry attached to Sherman's armies went through four tough months on various levels. One in three cavalrymen would be lost in this campaign, a very high percentage for cavalry. In addition, at the end of the campaign many of the regiments were dismounted due to the loss of the all-important mounts. Sherman's urgings not to spare the horseflesh resulted in the loss of many good horses through starvation and overuse, particularly early in the campaign. Sherman showed similar disregard of some of the top cavalry commanders as he did for the horses. Washington L. Elliott, chief of cavalry of four of the five cavalry divisions, was virtually ignored throughout the campaign to such an extent that he merely served as an additional staff officer for George Thomas. Sherman chose to personally direct the actions of the cavalry divisions. Only Edward McCook and H. Judson Kilpatrick appeared to find favor from army headquarters. Sherman saw Alvan Gillem's Tennessee division as a mere political command while he totally disregarded Kenner Garrard as too timid throughout the campaign despite George Thomas' counsel that Garrard was, in fact, Sherman's best cavalry commander. Sherman also had severe reservations about Stoneman, who ultimately destroyed his division in an attempt to liberate Andersonville and another Union prisoner of war camp during a poorly planned dash for glory. The puzzling aspect of Sherman's relationship with Stoneman occurred after Stoneman's expedition when Sherman, rather than chastising him, rewarded him with a new command.[8]

Wheeler's Raid, August 10—September 17, 1864

Joseph Wheeler's Confederate cavalry corps also had four months of grueling duty during the Atlanta Campaign. By the end of August, Wheeler commanded a large cavalry corps that amounted to greater than 13,000 men. Wheeler, brave to a fault, had had varying degrees of success while commanding the cavalry corps. So far in his career Wheeler had commanded two notable cavalry raids with mixed results. He had shown sparks of greatness while demonstrating a remarkable inability to deal with the enemy on other occasions. Wheeler was defeated by David Stanley's Union cavalry during the Tullahoma Campaign, and at Chickamauga he was severely criticized for his poor performance. In contrast, during the Atlanta Campaign in perhaps his greatest effort of the entire war, he led his cavalry in repulsing three simultaneous Union cavalry raids in late July, which resulted in the destruction of Stoneman's division, a serious defeat for Edward McCook, and stalling Kenner Garrard's division, which had served primarily as a diversion.[9]

A couple of weeks after Wheeler's commendable actions of dealing with the three Union cavalry divisions, he began his third notable cavalry raid, which would extend from August 10 to September 9. Hood ordered Wheeler to "break the line of communication on the two [rail]roads running from Nashville to the army" and return to his position with the Army of Tennessee. Wheeler took more than 4,000 men and moved north on August 10. He took three of his four division commanders on the raid, Will Martin, John H. Kelly and William Y.C. Humes, and at the end, only Humes remained. Kelly was mortally wounded on September 2 near Franklin and died two days later, and Will Martin was relieved of command for his late arrival at Dalton on August 14–15. Hood hoped that Wheeler would sever Sherman's supply lines and relieve the pressure mounting on his troops in Atlanta, but the raid did not achieve the desired results. Wheeler took a path through northern Georgia, into east Tennessee. Then, Wheeler turned west and rode into Middle Tennessee where the Federal pursuit intensified. He finally halted his cavalry at Tuscumbia on September 17. Wheeler embellished his accomplishments during the raid, but his biographer wrote that Hood dismissed these as "so much window dressing." Sherman's campaign report also echoed the unsuccessful results of Wheeler raid: "Our roads and telegraph are all repaired, and the cars run with regularity and speed." But Wheeler continued to overstate his successes and he boasted that he had destroyed 50 miles of railroad. "Every fight thus far with the enemy successful, capturing and damaging large numbers." During the raid, William Hicks Jackson's division remained with Hood's army.[10]

Both Wheeler and Hood would be severely criticized for the raid. The Federal cavalry near Atlanta was significantly weakened after its own disastrous raids south of Atlanta and only two divisions remained intact. The movement of Wheeler to the rear allowed Sherman's horsemen a respite and his infantry more room to maneuver. The destruction that Wheeler accomplished was quickly repaired and Sherman paid virtually no attention to Wheeler's activities. Wheeler certainly did not cause Sherman to lose his new focus of capturing Atlanta while the raid was completed. Nathan Bedford Forrest, commanding a Confederate corps in Mississippi, met with Wheeler 10 days after his raid and reported, "His command is in a demoralized condition. He claims to have about 2,000 men with him; his adjutant general says, however, that he will not be able to raise and carry back with him exceeding 1,000, and in all probability not over 500." Forrest lamented that his old brigade, attached to Wheeler's cavalry in November 1863, had only 60 men remaining of the 2,300 men transferred to him. Hood would argue that his decision to send Wheeler on a raid on the rear of the Union force was a good one, but, in the final tally, the war of attrition took a heavy toll on the Southern cavalry. For the average Union soldier at the front, the lack of impact on the Union rear, wrote Illinois infantryman Joseph Franklin Culver, was "most gratifying." In the end, Hood's army still had cavalry along its flanks, but fewer than before, and the trains still traveled from Nashville to Atlanta to supply Sherman's armies.[11]

After the Atlanta Campaign, the cavalries on both sides were worn down. While much of Wheeler's raiding column was in poor condition, the remainder of the Confederate cavalry still provided effective duty near Atlanta. If the Confederate reports were correct, Hood still had about 8,000 mounted forces near Atlanta. After the Atlanta Campaign and the raid through Georgia and Tennessee, Wheeler again retained overall command of cavalry near Atlanta. In contrast, dramatic command assignments would be made in the Federal cavalry a few months after the conclusion of the Atlanta Campaign. In the meantime, three Union cavalry divisions remained mounted and ready for service, Garrard's, Gillem's and Kilpatrick's. The remainder of McCook's division hastened to remount, but in the meantime, it was scattered in the rear on guard duty at various locations. George Stoneman temporarily remained in a Confederate prison and Colonel Israel Garrard commanded the fragment of the cavalry division of the Army of the Ohio. The cavalries on both sides of the line were battered and still in the saddle, but they needed time to recuperate after such a strenuous campaign.[12]

The Situation Further to the West—Summer 1864

To the west, Nathan Bedford Forrest, referred to as Bedford by his friends, like Hood in many ways was one of the most aggressive and controversial commanders in the war. Forrest excelled at independent cavalry operations and had a string of accomplishments to prove it. On the other hand, when assigned typical cavalry support duty while attached to a large army, he had yet to demonstrate an exceptional ability to accomplish these tasks. Historian David Powell, in his analysis of the Confederate cavalry at Chickamauga, recorded Forrest's limitations as a new corps commander attached to a large army. However, Powell acknowledged that, at Chickamauga, Forrest was just beginning to evolve into his new role. Afterward, Forrest, while still operating independently, continued to improve his skills. Forrest angrily left Bragg's army in October 1863 and spent the next year in Mississippi and Tennessee improving those skills as a corps commander. So effective was Forrest, Sherman believed he could have been the most important impediment to the Union armies' advance in the Atlanta Campaign.[13]

In early 1864, Forrest received a promotion to the rank of major general after leaving the Army of Tennessee and moved to Oxford, Mississippi, to command Forrest's Cavalry Department in west Tennessee and northern Mississippi. Forrest charged his men to "drive the enemy from our soil." The First and Second Brigades would be combined into a full division under the command of James R. Chalmers. In March, Abraham Buford arrived to assume command of the Second Division (Third and Fourth Brigades). Stephen D. Lee had overall command of the cavalry within this department, but Lee also directly handled the cavalry south of Forrest's command. General Leonidas Polk had command of the Department of Mississippi and East Louisiana.[14]

While Sherman's three armies advanced on Atlanta, important actions, though much smaller in scope, occurred to the west. In 1864, Sherman had attempted to deal with Forrest on several occasions. During the Atlanta Campaign, Sherman was concerned about the supply line of three armies which stretched from Nashville toward Atlanta, and he wanted Forrest contained. In February, Sherman was partially successful in the Meridian Campaign, but Forrest handily defeated the Union cavalry under the command of William Sooy Smith.[15]

After the Meridian Campaign, an 8,000-man strong Union column commanded by Brigadier General Samuel Sturgis marched toward Corinth on June 1, with the objectives of minimizing Forrest's presence in Mississippi by defeating him in the field and then destroying the Mobile and Ohio Railroad, which was used to supply the Confederate forces in northern Mississippi. Sturgis' column, including over 3,000 cavalry troops under the command of Benjamin Grierson, moved toward Brice's Crossroads on June 10. Forrest aggressively attacked the flanks of Sturgis' column and his artillery riddled the Union lines. The battle was desperately fought by both sides and certainly, for the U.S. Colored Infantry, the incentives to fight were life and freedom. Only two months before, the incident at Fort Pillow occurred and in March 1864, a raid into Kentucky resulted in a demand for the surrender of a Union garrison where Abraham Bu-

Nathan Bedford Forrest urged his men to "drive the enemy from our soil" (Library of Congress).

ford promised that the African American soldiers would be returned to their masters if they surrendered. If they did not surrender, no quarter would be given. Ultimately, Forrest threatened to cut off the Federal forces at Brice's Crossroads which resulted in a panicked retreat. Union losses totaled about 2,500 men, including 300 cavalry troops, and Forrest, remarkably, defeated a force twice his size.[16]

The third expedition directed at keeping Forrest bottlenecked in Mississippi resulted in the Battle of Tupelo on July 14–15. This time Major General A.J. Smith and Brigadier General Joseph Mower led this expedition of 14,000 men and squared off against Stephen Lee's infantry and Forrest's cavalry near Tupelo. The campaign was marked by excessively hot weather. Union soldier, Charles Treadway, wrote that he anticipated no movement of his regiment until "the weather gets a little cooler. It is so hot here that it appears as though the earth will burn." Despite the temperatures, Smith moved toward Forrest and Lee. This XVI Corps column reached Mississippi and turned east toward Tupelo. Confederate generals Lee and Forrest decided a battle with Smith could be successful based on past victories, and so "decided to fight Smith where he showed an inclination to fight or attack at the first sign of retreat." A few days later, the Confederate forces of about 8,000 men were defeated just west of Tupelo and Forrest received a wound to his foot which kept him out of service for three weeks. The Union column contained two brigades of Grierson's cavalry division, Edward Winslow's and Datus Coon's Second and Third Brigades, which reported fewer than 100 casualties for the expedition.[17]

Next, A.J. Smith led another expedition to Oxford, Mississippi, in mid–August and skirmished with James Chalmers' Confederate cavalry division; however, while Smith marched to Oxford, Forrest focused his attention on Memphis. While Smith was in Oxford, Forrest struck Memphis on August 21. Forrest, realizing that he couldn't contend with Smith's large force, attacked the Union garrison at Memphis and at the same time, hoped to draw Smith away from Mississippi. Forrest attacked Memphis and after some skirmishing, he withdrew as Smith hastened his column back to the north. Meanwhile, back at Memphis, Major General Cadwallader C. Washburn, commander of the District of West Tennessee, barely escaped capture by slipping out of a basement window at Union headquarters and down an alley. Forrest and Washburn had exchanged contentious communications after the fight at Brice's Crossroad about the treatment of prisoners, and his capture would have been particularly pleasing for Forrest. The attack caused quite a stir at Memphis while capturing 600 people (some civilians) along with horses and mules. The greatest reward for Forrest was the return of Smith's column north and an increase in morale for many Southerners. Forrest also lost some support of the locals in Memphis as his men pillaged during the raid, carried away invalids from hospitals, and shot hospital guards and citizens, particularly African Americans. Upon hearing of the raid, Sherman wrote, "If you get a chance send word to Forrest I admire his dash but not his judgement. The oftener he runs his head against Memphis the better."[18]

Clearly, the major Union cavalry efforts in Mississippi and western Tennessee in 1864 focused on Forrest's cavalry, and so far, Forrest had had the greater successes, despite the setback at Tupelo. Forrest's biographer wrote that Forrest had fared well in these campaigns and he accomplished his objective of protecting Mississippi which provided grain and sustenance for his cavalry. In contrast, Sherman also had achieved his goal of keeping Forrest out of Tennessee and Georgia. At the beginning of September, Forrest had established his headquarters at Grenada, Mississippi, and Sherman and the bulk of his cavalry were outside Atlanta and extending to Nashville. Benjamin Grierson's cavalry division had the primary duty in northern Mississippi.[19]

Organization of the Cavalries

In October 1863, Ulysses S. Grant was given command of the Military Division of the Mississippi which included commands of the departments of the Ohio, the Cumberland and the Tennessee. This appointment gave Grant the ability to coordinate most of the military efforts in the west, including the cavalry. Before the establishment of this division, the cavalry commands reported to the department commanders. Now, Grant had the ability to unite his commands and direct the various units where they were most needed. A good example of this was assigning Edward McCook's First Cavalry Division of the Army of the Cumberland to work in conjunction with the Army of the Ohio in eastern Tennessee in the winter of 1863–1864. Grant initially appointed Brigadier General William Sooy Smith as chief of cavalry for the Military Division of the Mississippi, but he left much of the actual day-to-day functions of the cavalry divisions unchanged. Smith would only directly command the various cavalry units when there were cross-departmental actions or "when practicable." Grant told Smith his duties: "You will endeavor to supply all deficiencies in arms, equipments, and horses at the earliest moment and hold the cavalry always ready for active service.... When the appearance of the enemy is in such numbers and in such directions as to bring cavalry of two or more armies in the pursuit, the military division chief of cavalry should, when practicable, take command in person." In addition, Smith could issue general orders about the functioning of the cavalry: foraging, discipline and general activities. Of paramount importance, Smith needed to ensure that cavalry had the equipment, weapons and mounts needed to operate in the field. While Smith had the authority to directly command the cavalry in the field, much of his responsibilities remained administrative.[20]

General William Sooy Smith (pictured here ca. 1870) was appointed chief of cavalry for the Military Division of the Mississippi in 1863 (Library of Congress).

Smith found a large number of cavalry in the division when he assumed command. The Army of the Ohio had some 8,000 cavalrymen and the cavalry of the Army of the Cumberland had swelled to three divisions amounting to over 10,000 troopers and officers. Finally, Brigadier General Benjamin Grierson commanded the cavalry for the Army of the Tennessee amounting to 6,500 men in late 1863. In January, Sherman told Smith to directly command the cavalry division of the Army of the Tennessee in the Meridian Campaign. Smith also utilized his new authority and drew some of the regiments of the Army of the Cumberland to join Grierson's cavalry division during the expedition. The campaign aimed at the destruction of three railroads near Meridian while offensively challenging the Confederate forces in Mississippi. While Sherman's infantry successfully reached Meridian and destroyed the railroads, the cavalry suffered a stunning defeat. Despite outnumbering Confederate defenders by more than 3 to 1, Forrest attacked the larger Union column, sent it retreating northward, and defeated Sherman's entire left flank. The performance of Smith jaded Sherman's outlook on the cavalry. Sherman wrote his wife, "I am down on William Sooy Smith.... He could have come to me, and I know it." Sherman, a very important person to the cavalry in the west, walked away with distrust and disregard for the mounted forces, a distrust clearly demonstrated when Sherman took control of the Atlanta Campaign. Smith resigned in July 1864 due to rheumatoid arthritis, and Brigadier General Richard W. Johnson was temporarily appointed chief of cavalry for the Military Division of the Mississippi on August 21, 1864. Johnson commanded an infantry division at the beginning of the Atlanta Campaign, but in May he had been struck just above his liver with a fragment of an artillery shell. His wound kept him from service until July 18 when he returned to his division, but only for a short time. Johnson explained that he "was really unfitted for active service, and General Sherman assigned me to duty as chief of cavalry, and ordered me to take post at Nashville and superintend the equipping and forwarding of all cavalry reaching that city."[21]

On the other side of the field, the cavalries in the Confederacy were also army centric, and tracking the various military departments and districts was often confusing to all involved. Jefferson Davis and his War Department tried over 35 configurations for the various military departments and 85 command structures. In northern Mississippi, northern Alabama, Georgia and Tennessee, two large cavalry corps operated under the command of Joseph Wheeler and Nathan Bedford Forrest. In the case of Wheeler, he had commanded the cavalry corps attached to the Army of Tennessee since November 1862 in the important Stones River, Tullahoma, Chickamauga, and Atlanta Campaigns. During the Tullahoma Campaign, both Forrest, commanding a division, and Wheeler, commanding a corps, participated. Next, during the Chickamauga Campaign, Forrest and Wheeler each commanded cavalry corps. Once the campaign concluded, Forrest was dispatched to Mississippi to organize his own command and Wheeler assumed full command of the cavalry, some of it being Forrest's corps, attached to the Army of Tennessee. As the Atlanta Campaign came to an end, the importance of Wheeler's raid into Tennessee in August 1864 set the stage for the forces that would participate in the Nashville Campaign. By the end of the raid, Wheeler's raiding force was exhausted and devastated after a month in the saddle. The remainder of Wheeler's command remained with Hood's army, which has just evacuated Atlanta.[22]

In 1864, Forrest had participated in various actions, including a raid on Paducah, the Meridian Campaign, the Brice's Crossroads battle, the Tupelo expedition, and finally the Oxford/Memphis affair. Overall, he had greater success than Wheeler, although his cavalry suffered sorely from the inability of the Confederate government to supply, equip, and arm his troopers. His ability to offensively take the battle to the Federal troops proved a constant source of irritation and concern for both Washburn in Memphis and Sherman near Atlanta. As the campaign for Nashville developed, it would be Forrest who would lead the cavalry in the campaign. Wheeler's losses and his need to move eastward left the cavalry duties in Middle Tennessee to Nathan Bedford Forrest, commanding about 7,000 cavalry.[23]

Chapter Two

Hood Prepares to March to Tennessee

>Our cavalry and our people will harass and destroy his army....
>—Jefferson Davis

Military actions extended across the combatants' lines in August and September 1864. Certainly, the conclusion of the Atlanta Campaign marked a successful campaign for the Federal forces, but more actions unfolded. In the west, Sterling Price began his Missouri raid on August 28 as he swept a 12,000-man Confederate column, supplemented by local pro–Southern forces through the state. Price crossed his forces into Missouri on September 19 and then proceeded to raid across the state. The last battle during the raid did not occur until the end of October. In the east, Jubal Early was active in the Shenandoah Valley in August and the Union siege of Richmond and Petersburg extended into the autumn. Along the Gulf of Mexico coast, the Union army and navy had just concluded a campaign against Mobile on August 23, successfully capturing Fort Gaines and Fort Morgan. The Federal navy forced the Confederate navy to surrender and effectively closed one of the Confederacy's last two open ports.[1]

The full force of the Union armies, now with twice the number of soldiers as the Confederate States, stretched the ability of the Southern forces to defend what remained of the Confederacy. Outside of Virginia, the greatest concentration of Union and Confederate forces remained in the vicinity of Atlanta. At the conclusion of the Atlanta Campaign, the all too common policy of casting blame continued in the command ranks of the Confederate forces. Hood, who had about 40,000 men present and available for duty, put the blame on the loss of the campaign on Joseph Johnston for his defensive strategy and he felt he had gained an army "enfeebled in number and in spirit by long retreat and by severe and apparently fruitless losses." He proudly stated that when he took command, and through his offensive efforts, the "tone constantly improved and hope returned," but not all in the Southern army agreed with Hood's assessment. General Lawrence "Sul" Ross of the Confederate cavalry wrote to his wife on September 14: "They all call loudly for the Old hero Genl. Johnston.... When Johnston left this army, I think it was the finest and best army I ever heard of to the number, but now it is hacked and the men will not charge Breastworks, and it is 20,000 men weaker now than when he left." In regard to the recent loss of Jonesborough, Hood blamed that loss on another top-ranking Confederate officer, William Hardee, who made a "disgraceful effort" even though Hardee faced six Union corps compared to only two for the Confederate forces. There is little doubt that Hood faced a situation where the odds were stacked against him, but he had striven for this position. Now, he sought to blame the losses on others who had also faced the same disparate odds. After reading Hood's campaign report, Johnston informed Hood that he planned to prefer charges against him for his comments, but the state of the war declined so much that no court was ever convened. In the meantime, Hood was given command of the new Department of Tennessee and Georgia.[2]

Sherman, at conclusion of the Atlanta Campaign, withdrew his army to Atlanta and gave his troops a month's rest. Sherman gave no immediate tally of men present for duty at the end of the campaign, but he was proud of his army and personally proud of his accomplishments. Like Hood, he had issues of his own with his subordinates in the recent campaign. He called Joseph Hooker, who had recently resigned because he was not given command of the Army of the Tennessee, a fool and declared that John Schofield was slow and left much of the fighting for others. Of George Thomas, he told General Henry Halleck, Grant's chief of staff, that he was slow, but "true as steel." Halleck agreed and called Thomas a war horse and "always sure." In regard to the war, Sherman was already contemplating his next move on September 4—a winter campaign pushing further south and east. In regard to Atlanta, he planned to make it a transportation hub and no more. He wanted to send the pro–Union citizens to the rear and the pro–Southern citizens through the enemy lines. He intended that nothing remain of Atlanta except for the railroad. Sherman told Henry Halleck his philosophy for the next phase of the war. "If the people raise a howl against my barbarity and cruelty I will answer that war is war, and not popularity-seeking. If they want peace they and their relatives must stop war."[3]

What Next?

Both Sherman and Hood were faced with a similar question from dissimilar points of view. Sherman had slightly more than 80,000 Union troops in the vicinity of Atlanta and Hood had about 40,000 in the neighboring countryside. Both generals pondered their next steps. Hood felt that only offensive actions and victories would restore the fighting spirit to the Army of Tennessee. He knew that Sherman would not be content to remain stationary and he faced the two choices—prepare to resist Sherman's further movement south or take the war to the Union forces. He had just criticized Johnston for a weak campaign of defensive actions.

General William T. Sherman exclaimed, "I will answer that war is war" (Library of Congress).

Clearly, he could not take the same strategy. Besides, Jefferson Davis desired an offensive war with the Confederate forces striking into Tennessee and Kentucky.[4]

Hood chose to advance northward and he explained, "Something was absolutely demanded, and I rightly judged that an advance, at all promising success, would go far to restore its fighting spirit." Perhaps, Hood had no other choice. The momentum of the war had shifted in favor of the Northern forces. Hood was outnumbered by a fresher and better equipped army, and by driving northward he could cut Sherman's supply lines and threaten the rear of the Union armies, forcing them to retreat to deal with this new Confederate offensive. Initially, Hood envisioned marching northward, moving into Kentucky and possibly even relieving some of the pressure on Lee's army in Virginia. When Hood sent Wheeler on the raid in the rear of Sherman's army in August, he hoped the cavalry would sever the railroad forcing Sherman to withdraw. Next, Hood hoped that Forrest could join in the same effort, but by mid–September, he realized the cavalry could not permanently accomplish the destruction of the railroad. This left only one option and this meant offensive actions for the infantry. He concluded that he needed to march his forces around Sherman's right flank in a northern advance while destroying the railroad leading to Atlanta. This bold move by a smaller force would accomplish Hood's desire for offensive action by striking where Sherman was most vulnerable.[5]

So Hood began to move the bulk of his forces on September 18 and his troops pulled up the rails from other railroads, reestablishing rail service to West Point. Hood's army moved until its left flank touched the Chattahoochee River and he established his headquarters at Palmetto, a few miles south of the river, and remained there while the army was resupplied. Hood sent orders for Wheeler's cavalry to return to the main body of the army, but in the meantime, William H. Jackson's and Alfred Iverson's cavalry had the duty of providing security for his army. On September 25 while Hood remained at Palmetto, he received a visit from Jefferson Davis, a friend and supporter, for two days during which time they reviewed the troops and made speeches. Hood discussed his strategy with Davis. He planned to attack Sherman's supply line north of Atlanta and he hoped that a mobile Confederate army could avert a major battle while pulling the bulk of the Federal army from Atlanta. Most importantly, Hood hoped that Sherman would split his army, making the odds more even, and then Hood could defeat a wing of the Federal army on his chosen ground.[6]

On his way to visit Hood, Davis made a speech in Macon on September 23 and addressed the local citizens. He compared Sherman's situation with that of Napoleon in the 1812 Russia campaign. "What, though misfortune has befallen our arms from Decatur to Jonesboro, our cause is not lost. Sherman cannot keep up his long line of communication, and retreat sooner or later, he must. And when that day comes, the fate that befell the army of the French Empire and its retreat from Moscow will be reacted. Our cavalry and our people will harass and destroy his army as did the Cossacks that of Napoleon, and the Yankee General, like him will escape with only a body guard." When Davis reviewed the troops with Hood, he told the soldiers the strategy of swinging around Sherman's rear, destroying his supply line and then the Union forces would have to retreat northward. The refugee situation, the large number of civilians moving south to escape Sherman's blue coated soldiers, also inspired the soldiers to increase their resolve to repel the northern invaders. There remained two factions within the ranks of the Southern forces at Atlanta—those who wanted Hood to command and those who remained loyal to Johnston. While reviewing the troops, the president and Hood heard various calls for Johnston, and when asked for three cheers for Davis some Tennessee soldiers refused. Many still liked Johnston and remained wary of Hood. All was not well in the Southern army.[7]

As Hood planned to swing to the north, Sherman made plans of his own. Sherman received a message from Grant on September 20 asking his opinion regarding the next actions for his army. With the closure of Mobile to outside commerce and trade, only one other port remained open—Wilmington, North Carolina. Sherman suggested that Grant march south toward Wilmington, that Major General Edward Canby should hold the Mississippi River, and Sherman would march his army across Georgia, in a bold "march to the sea." While this was a very risky move by Sherman, he explained: "I would not hesitate to cross the State of Georgia with 60,000 men.... Where a million of people live my army won't starve..."[8]

Hood Prepares to March and the Federal Defense Begins

When Hood moved to Palmetto, Sherman soon discovered the shift of the Confederate forces and anticipated Hood's next move. When Hood began his move northward, Sherman decided to focus on Hood's infantry and cavalry which were threatening the railroad. Sherman told Grant that Hood appeared to be planning on marching to the Alabama state line and he felt he needed to "secure what I have." Grant agreed with Sherman and pondered what Hood would be able to accomplish because his subsistence would be so difficult as he moved further north. Importantly, the Union forces had spies in the area where Jefferson Davis gave his speeches and as a result, Sherman knew that Forrest had launched a raid on the railroads in Tennessee and that Hood would "soon be there," so the Union generals were in a conundrum—they wanted to march toward the sea but Forrest and Hood appeared to be targeting Alabama or Tennessee. To address this threat, Sherman and Grant decided to deal with Hood and Forrest from Nashville and they began ordering reinforcements to meet this Confederate threat. The call went out to Kentucky, Missouri and other locations for troops, including Major General A.J. Smith's XVI Corps (Right Wing) which was in pursuit of Sterling Price in Missouri.[9]

In regard to the cavalry and Hood's overall plan of disrupting communications and supplies to Sherman's armies at Atlanta, Hood could not have done more. Much of the Southern cavalry went to work attacking the Union forces and infrastructure all along the line in the west. Brigadier General James R. Chalmers' cavalry division in Mississippi began destroying the Memphis & Charleston Railroad east of Memphis. Sterling Price had surged out of Arkansas and rode across the state of Missouri. Hood had Wheeler's cavalry concluding a raid on the railroads extending through Tennessee and Alabama. Philip Roddey's cavalry command was instructed to begin attacking the supply lines in northern Alabama. In addition, the northward march by the Army of Tennessee would destroy the railroad directly north of Atlanta and, finally, he gained agreement from Richard Taylor to send Forrest's cavalry into Alabama and Tennessee to strike the railroad in yet another raid. The overall understanding of the Southern mounted forces included cooperation between Forrest and Wheeler, but Wheeler's command was in such poor condition after his recent raid, Forrest knew he had little hope of support from Wheeler. Hood again called for Wheeler to rejoin his army, but Wheeler dragged his feet in an apparent desire to operate away from the Army of Tennessee as his command recuperated.[10]

Then, Sherman also made decisions while still setting his sights on the march across Georgia. He decided to send George Thomas, whom he thought was a slow but reliable commander, to Nashville to deal with the new threat there. He planned to send two infantry corps, IV Corps and XXIII Corps, under command of David Stanley and John Schofield to assist in the defense of Tennessee. He also temporarily assigned Major General James D. Morgan's infantry division to assist in the defense of Tennessee. Sherman detailed his plans in a message to Henry Halleck and explained his intent to march across Georgia. He felt that Thomas could deal with Hood's infantry and he gave Forrest a great compliment. "His cavalry will travel a hundred miles in less time than ours will ten." Sherman concluded that if Forrest was in the rear, he took it for granted that the railroad would be cut, but he felt enough troops remained in the rear to prevent Forrest from permanently severing the railroad.[11]

While Hood and Sherman contemplated their next moves, the Union cavalry was reorganizing. Richard Johnson, the temporary chief of cavalry for the Military Division of the Mississippi, began his new job in Nashville and ran into immediate problems. He found a cavalry command which desperately needed an improved command structure and better organization. "There are several regiments of Tennessee cavalry claiming to be independent of General Sherman or any one else save Andy Johnson. These regiments violate safeguards, rob, and murder in open daylight, and refuse to report the facts to any one except the Governor." Johnson took immediate steps to deal with the issue by refusing to supply and equip these regiments. Johnson explained that if they wanted to be outside the control of the Military Division of the Mississippi, then he had no obligation to supply or even deal with them. He knew this would cause immediate political issues, but he saw no other way to bring these troops under control. While Johnson accepted this posting, Sherman began looking for a more permanent chief of cavalry and Grant offered recently promoted Major General Romeyn B. Ayres from the Army of the Potomac for the position. Sherman balked at this suggestion and asked that either James H. Wilson or David Gregg be given the job.[12]

Forrest's Raid

While Hood marched his army around Sherman at Atlanta, to the west, Forrest mounted his cavalry to assist the effort. Lieutenant General Richard Taylor arrived at Meridian, Mississippi, and assumed command of the Department of Mississippi, Alabama, and Georgia on September 6. The Confederate government had gone through several changes in the past months and rearranged officers and departments to meet the changing situation in the field. Taylor, son of former president Zachary Taylor, had commanded troops in the District of Western Louisiana and earlier in the year successfully defeated Nathaniel Banks in the ill-fated Red River Campaign. Taylor was subsequently rewarded with a promotion to the rank of lieutenant general and now the command of the department. Five minutes after he arrived to take command of the new department, he received a telegram from Jefferson Davis informing him that Forrest was ready to make a raid on the Federal infrastructure in Tennessee.

Taylor acknowledged the telegram and cut Forrest's orders to begin the raid with the objective of conducting "operations on the enemy's lines of communication, as well as to interfere with the transportation of supplies and re-enforcements to General Sherman's army."[13]

Total Cavalry Under Forrest's Command September 30, 1864

	Officers	*Men*
Cavalry	376	4,259
Artillery	18	268
Total	394	4,527

The force he took on his expedition totaled 2,960 cavalry, 88 artillerymen, and 159 dismounted cavalry (effective numbers) troops.[14]

Forrest's Cavalry—Maj. Gen. Nathan B. Forrest

Chalmers' Division	
First Brigade	*Second Brigade**
Col. Edmund W. Rucker	Col. Robert McCulloch
7th Tennessee, Lt. Col. William F. Taylor	7th Mississippi
12th Tennessee, Col. John U. Green	8th Mississippi
14th Tennessee, Lt. Col. Raleigh R. White	18th Mississippi Battalion
15th Tennessee, Col. Francis M. Stewart	2nd Missouri
26th Tenn. Battalion, Lt. Col. David Kelley	Willis' (Texas) battalion
	Hudson's (Mississippi) battery (one section)

*On detached service to the gulf and the commanding officers were not recorded.

Buford's Division	
Third Brigade	*Fourth Brigade*
Brig. Gen. Hylan B. Lyon	Col. Tyree H. Bell
3rd Kent. Mounted Inftry, Col. Gustavus Holt	2nd Tennessee, Col. Clark R. Barteau
7th Kent. Mounted Infantry, Col. Edward Crossland	16th Tenn., Col. Andrew Wilson
8th Kent. Mounted Inftry, Lt. Col. Absal. Shacklett	18th Tenn., Col. John F. Newsom
12th Kentucky Cavalry, Col. W.W. Faulkner	20th Tenn., Col. Robert M. Russell

Artillery
Hudson's (Mississippi) battery, Lt. Edwin S. Walton
Morton's (Tennessee) battery, Lt. T. Sanders Sale
Rice's (Tennessee) battery, Capt. T.W. Rice
Thrall's (Arkansas) battery, Capt. James C. Thrall[15]

With Forrest on the raid, the regular cavalry duties in Mississippi fell to James Chalmers' division which relocated to Grenada. Forrest began this expedition on September 16 when he left his headquarters at Verona, Mississippi (just south of Tupelo). Then, he moved north to the Memphis and Charleston Railroad at Cherokee Station in northwest Alabama and completed the preparations for the raid. With 10 days' rations, Forrest set out on September 21 and crossed the Tennessee River at Newport. As soon as he crossed, Edward Hatch's Union cavalry reported the movement. Then, Forrest marched to within five miles of Florence, Alabama. The next day, Forrest rode toward Athens, Alabama, and was reinforced by Roddey's northern Alabama cavalry brigade. With Roddey's cavalry, about 1,000 men under the command of Colonel William A. Johnson (4th Alabama Cavalry and veteran of the Brice's Crossroads battle), Forrest's force totaled about 4,500 men of which 400 were dismounted until they could obtain horses captured from the Federal army. Later that night, Forrest did just that. His troopers captured a corral between Athens and Decatur, and then set about destroying the telegraph and railroad track.[16]

Roddey's cavalry had moved behind Union lines before joining Forrest and had alerted the Union commanders to the possibility of a new enemy raid. Colonel Jacob Biffle's 9th Tennessee Cavalry (CSA) dealt with some immediate needs by raiding the mills in northern Alabama, gathering up what grain he could find. Biffle, with about 400 troopers, crossed the Tennessee River near Henryville on September 18. A second column of Roddey's cavalry also crossed the river with similar instructions and Brigadier General Robert Granger sent three Union cavalry regiments (3rd, 10th, and 12th Tennessee Cavalry) to deal with this Confederate cavalry force. Meanwhile, Brigadier General John Starkweather, commanding the Union forces at Pulaski, mobilized his troops and sought out Biffle, only to find him gone as he closed in on him. Without an adequate number of cavalry, Starkweather's infantry had little hope of catching Biffle. The Union troops were equally concerned that Wheeler might again move back into Tennessee in another attempt to disrupt supply lines. It was no great surprise when word reached the various Union headquarters that Southern cavalry was observed near Athens. The problem was how to concentrate the Union forces to reach the elusive Confederate cavalry. Sherman had pulled many of the veteran infantry and cavalry regiments to Atlanta and he left many new or inexperienced troops dispersed throughout the state to guard the railroad lines. Sherman felt his troops in the rear could use the telegraph to rapidly communicate any concerns about an enemy attack and then use the railroad to concentrate reinforcements to deal with any threats.[17]

The primary Union military districts involved in the upcoming actions were the District of Tennessee commanded by Major General Lovell Rousseau and the District of Northern Alabama commanded by General Robert Granger. In addition, James Steedman commanded troops at Chattanooga. Colonel George Spalding, commanding the Fourth Cavalry Division of the Army of the Cumberland, had Lieutenant Colonel Jacob Thornburgh's cavalry brigade (2nd, 3rd and 4th Tennessee) assigned to the district in northern Alabama. Within the District of Tennessee, Rousseau's command stretched across a wide geography, including Bridgeport, Nashville, defenses of the Nashville and Chattanooga Railroad, Springfield, Fort Donelson, Clarksville, Gallatin, troops on the Nashville and Northwestern Railroad, Tullahoma, and Columbia.[18]

Union Cavalry in the District of Tennessee—
Major General Lovell Rousseau[19]

Defenses of the Nashville & Chattanooga RR.	
12th Indiana Cavalry, Col. Edward Anderson	
Troops on the Nashville & Northwestern Railroad	
Columbia, Tennessee—Col. William B. Sipes	
Detachments of First, Second, and Third Brigades, Second Cavalry Division	
District of Northern Alabama—Brig General R.S. Granger	
Decatur, Alabama	*Huntsville, Alabama*
Col. Charles C. Doolittle	Col. Gilbert M.L. Johnson
10th Indiana Cav. (detach.), Maj. G.R. Swallow	13th Indiana Cav, Lt. Col. W.T. Pepper
First Brigade, Fourth Cavalry Division	*Pulaski, Tennessee*
Lt. Col. Jacob M. Thornburgh	Brig. Gen. John C. Starkweather
2nd Tennessee Cavalry, Lt. Col. Wm F. Prosser	9th Indiana Cav., Col. George W. Jackson
3rd Tennessee Cavalry, Lt. George W. Wester	10th Indiana Cavalry, Col. Thomas N. Pace
4th Tennessee Cavalry, Maj. Meshack Stephens	5th Tennessee Cav., Maj. John F. Armstrong
	10th Tennessee Cav., Capt. D.W. Baker
	2th Tennessee Cav., Maj. John S. Kirwan

Forrest Strikes into Alabama and Tennessee

During Forrest's raid, September 16–October 6, the Southern cavalry proved a formidable opponent for the Union troops along the railroad running from Pulaski, Tennessee, to Decatur, Alabama. Forrest caused long term damage to this rail line. Along the way, he captured the Union garrison at Athens; destroyed the 300-foot-long, 72-foot-high Sulfur Creek railroad trestle; and advanced to the outskirts of Pulaski. By the time Forrest reached Pulaski, the Union reinforcements had arrived and repulsed the Confederate attack on the town. Afterwards, Forrest caused little additional real damage, but he threatened Fayetteville and Huntsville and tried to re-capture Athens after Union troops re-claimed the garrison. The Federal troops repulsed the Confederate attacks, including Abraham Buford's investment at Athens. Then, Forrest moved west, threatening Columbia and Spring Hill before moving back over the Tennessee River.[20]

As the raid unfolded, the Union forces hurried to meet the threat. Brigadier General John Croxton's cavalry brigade arrived to pit mounted cavalry against mounted cavalry because, although Federal cavalry regiments guarded the railroads from Nashville, many of these were dismounted. As Forrest moved west, Brigadier General Edward Hatch's 3,000 cavalry troops were dispatched from western Tennessee to join in the pursuit, or more properly, the containment of the raiding Confederates. By October 4, Hatch joined Croxton and the two commands set out in earnest to find Forrest with orders to "press Forrest to the death." By the time Rousseau adequately mounted enough troops and by the time Hatch began his pursuit from the west, the raid was over. The news excited those local citizens who heard of Forrest's success and Hood's movement northward.[21]

The Results of the Raid

Lovell Rousseau also began to advance the Union infantry forces on Forrest as the raid ended. On October 3, Forrest was at Lawrenceburg, Tennessee, and then the moved toward Florence the next day. Forrest reached Florence on October 5 and found the river swollen due to recent rains. As the Union cavalry closed in on him, he called on Lieutenant Colonel Frances M. Windes, 4th Alabama Cavalry, to provide security as the Southern cavalry moved across the Tennessee River near Florence. The river was so high the Confederate cavalry had to be ferried across the river in overloaded boats during a high wind. Forrest was in a precarious position as the Union troops converged to his location but he had to wait for the ferry boats. Forrest, rightly concerned about getting trapped on the north side of the river, ordered those still on the north bank to swim 70 yards to a large island out of the line of fire from the trailing Union pursuers. Forrest recognized Colonel Andrew Wilson, 16th Tennessee, for his efforts in skirmishing with Union troops which allowed Forrest's cavalry to reach the island. The Union troops did not dare to attempt to swim to the island and the Southern cavalry simply waited to be ferried to the south bank of the river. Forrest wrote: "Every man reached the island in safety. Colonel Wilson is entitled to the commendation of his Government and the lasting gratitude for the faithful [manner] in which he performed this important and hazardous trust."[22]

Forrest reached Cherokee Station on October 6, the starting point of his raid. While the raid was officially over at this point, one final event set the stage for more serious actions the next month. Because Forrest worried about the Union forces moving across the Tennessee River in pursuit, he dispatched David Kelley's battalion and artillery to Eastport to ensure the enemy did not attempt to cross the river. George Thomas had enlisted the assistance of gunboats to prevent the crossing of the river by the Confederates. The next day Kelley found two gunboats and three transports on the river and he ambushed them. Kelley concealed his troops and artillery until a Union infantry brigade disembarked. Then, Kelley opened on the Federal transports and gunboats. Colonel George Hoge, commanding the infantry brigade, reported: "The first fire from the artillery caused the boats to push off from shore. Many in attempting to reach the boat were drowned, 12 were killed on the bank, and a large number killed and wounded on the boat; about 30 prisoners captured, with 3 James rifled guns, 60 small-arms, 20 horses, 4 boat cables, with some artillery harness. It was evident that a preconcerted plan had been arranged to capture my command."[23]

Hoge commanded a brigade of infantry (113th Illinois Infantry; Company G, 2nd Missouri Artillery; 61st USCT; and 120th Illinois Infantry) being sent to Eastport to provide security against a river crossing. His brigade was being transported on three boats, the *City of Pekin, Kenton,* and *Aurora,* accompanied by armed boats, the USS *Undine,* a tinclad gunboat, and USS *Key West,* a wooden, stern-wheel driven gunboat. As the boats approached Eastport, there was no sign of the enemy and Hoge ordered his men to disembark. He sent two lieutenants of his staff on a mounted reconnaissance immediately upon landing and the officers rode about 500 yards when they were fired upon by Kelley's troopers waiting in ambush. Ten minutes later, the Confederate artillery on the bluffs opened fire on the gunboats and the Union infantry. One battery was located on the heights at Eastport (estimated to contain six guns) and the three rifled cannon also fired from the bluffs at Chickasaw. Hoge hurriedly positioned his troops in battle line. The Confederate artillery focused on the gunboats and had their ranges. Hoge reported "every shot doing more or less execution." The USS *Undine* was one of the first casualties, receiving two hits from the rifled cannons, and receiving enough damage to cause the boat to list. The USS *Key West* also received two hits and Lieutenant Edward M. King wanted to get the boats away from the shelling, but Hoge's men were still on shore. Hoge contemplated his predicament—"a superior force of the enemy in my front and a deep river directly in my rear." Hoge told King to hold on until the infantry could be re-boarded. Hoge described: "Just at this time a shell from the enemy struck a caisson of the battery on board the *Kenton*, exploding it and setting fire to the boat. Immediately after this a caisson exploded on the *Aurora*, setting fire to her, and also cutting her steampipe. A scene of confusion then began. The boats, in spite of all I could do, backed out, parting their lines, leaving about two-thirds of the command on the shore. Fortunately, after great exertion the flames on board of the *Aurora* and *Kenton* were extinguished." All three transports were disabled, and the two gunboats, while damaged, remained afloat. Hoge's men moved out of range of the artillery and were taken back aboard the vessels. Hoge abandoned a section of artillery in making his escape and, in the end, returned to Johnsonville. He reported that he had a total of 74 casualties.[24]

Forrest claimed during the entire raid that he captured 86 officers, 67 non-military employees, 1,274 soldiers, and 933 black soldiers (which he disregarded as actual soldiers). He also reported inflicting over 1,000 casualties on the Union forces while capturing 800 horses, seven field guns, and a large amount of booty. He concluded: "The greatest damage, however, done to the enemy was in the complete destruction of the railroad from Decatur to Spring Hill, with the exception of the Duck River bridge. It will require months to repair the injury done to the road, and may possibly be the means of forcing the evacuation of Pulaski and Columbia, and thus relieve the people from further oppression." In addition, the Southern cavalry became fully mounted after capturing the Union horses and claimed enough supplies from the Union garrisons to fully cloth the command. In return, Forrest had some casualties of his own: 47 killed, 293 wounded. Two notable casualties were Lieutenant Colonel Jesse A. Forrest, Forrest's brother, and Colonel William Johnson. Overall, Forrest had nothing but praise for his commanders. Forrest initially stopped at Cherokee, Alabama, and began pulling his cavalry to Corinth.[25]

The tally of the damage to the railroads was compiled by Union Brigadier General D.C. McCallum, Director, General and Manager Military Railroads. McCallum summarized:

1. One engine and twelve cars were burned on a bridge at Decatur Junction and another three cars were destroyed between Huntsville and Stevenson;
2. The greatest damage occurred between Pulaski and Athens where Forrest destroyed thirty miles of track and all the bridges, including the bridge over the Elk River, the 1,100 feet-long bridge on the Stevenson-Decatur stretch along with two and a half miles of track;

3. Near Columbia, three bridges were burnt and three miles of track;
4. The Nashville to Chattanooga line was virtually undamaged; and
5. The railroad service would be back to normal by October 20.

George Kryder, a member of the 3rd Ohio Cavalry, complimented Forrest: "Old Forrest has gone back across the Tennessee River without much loss and he damaged the Rail Road considerable."[26]

Lovell Rousseau summarized the overall situation, one which had haunted the Union forces in Tennessee since the beginning of the war. "Forrest is here to stay unless driven back and routed by a superior cavalry force. Infantry can cause him to change camp but cannot drive him out of the State. Forrest's movements are much more cautious.... Cavalry is wanted. I have here about 3,000, not enough to fight him without support." It was impossible to cover the state of Tennessee and anticipate where Forrest, Wheeler or Roddey would strike next, but Rousseau was angry and wanted to pursue Forrest south of the Tennessee River. Rousseau wanted to take the war to the Confederates: "I beg to be allowed to pay back the enemy for all the trouble they have given and damage they have done us." By October 20, the Union scouts discovered Forrest located near Eastport and Corinth and Major General Cadwallader C. Washburn contemplated advancing against him, but with only 2,700 cavalry troops, he felt he did not have enough men to successfully challenge him.[27]

In regard to the Union armies at Atlanta, neither Wheeler's Raid in August and September, nor Forrest's Raid in September and October, accomplished the objective of forcing Sherman to return to Tennessee. Sherman received word on October 1 that the railroads were intact between Nashville and Chattanooga, but the Nashville-Decatur line was disrupted. This convinced Sherman that he could not keep the railroads running and, ironically, Hood's efforts to disrupt the railroad unleashed Sherman to make one of the most famous marches of the war. "No army can keep an enemy off my long line...," wrote Sherman to Halleck. In a bold decision, Sherman decided to abandon his communication and supply line due to the difficulty in maintaining its defense. He would march across Georgia and live off the land. However, Sherman took many of the battle-hardened troops with him and he left Thomas with Stanley, Schofield, and A.J. Smith, if he ever arrived, to face Forrest and Hood, but before he could begin, Hood began his march northward.[28]

Hood Begins His March North

Hood left his camps at Palmetto on September 29 to begin his march northward while Forrest struck the railroad in Tennessee. A few days later, Jefferson Davis appointed Pierre G.T. Beauregard overall command of both Richard Taylor and Hood, but Davis gave the new commanding general little authority. William H. Jackson's cavalry division screened the advance of the infantry column and Hood left Alfred Iverson's cavalry to keep an eye on the large concentration of Union forces at Atlanta. Hood began marching over the same steps which had been recently trod in the Atlanta Campaign when he reached Lost Mountain, west of Marietta, on October 3. Jackson's cavalry had light action while skirmishing with some Union cavalry forces, but the overall movement went unopposed. The Confederate infantry went to work the next day when

Chapter Two. Hood Prepares to March to Tennessee

A.P. Stewart's infantry destroyed the railroad at Acworth and Big Shanty, gathering up about 400 prisoners assigned to protect the railroad. Next, Hood, in need of supplies of his own, marched toward Allatoona to capture the supply depot and destroy the bridge over the Etowah River, making a Federal pursuit a longer and more difficult process. Major General Samuel French's division attacked the Federal garrison at Allatoona on October 5 but despite some initial success, French received information from Frank Armstrong's cavalry brigade that a large Federal force advanced on his position. The information, while probably premature, caused French to withdraw before he could capture the supply depot or burn the bridge. In these initial moves, Hood destroyed about 10 miles of track between Atlanta and Marietta, but on October 6, Hood, believing the Union forces were moving toward him, moved in a westward direction. Then, he turned northward across the Coosa River and moved up the west bank of Oostanaula until he reached the railroad between Resaca, the site of a bloody battle in May, and Mill Creek Gap on October 13. When Hood crossed the Coosa, Wheeler's cavalry finally rejoined his army. Hood again began destroying the tracks and then captured about a thousand Union troops at Tilton, Dalton and Mill Creek Gap. By this time, Washington L. Elliott's Federal cavalry arrived and pursued the Confederate army as the opposing cavalries skirmished daily. Elliott's cavalry successfully clashed with the 8th Texas Cavalry near Rome in mid–October claiming the Texans' colors as a prize. Then, Hood turned southwest and headed for Gadsden, Alabama, while the Federal cavalry and infantry followed on the heels of the column.[29]

Sherman had been unsuccessful in establishing any spies in Hood's army while it remained at Palmetto. As result, Sherman did not know that Hood started his march until October 1. Of the 81,000 effective troops Sherman reported at the end of the Atlanta Campaign, about 9,400 of those were cavalrymen, an official reduction of about 3,000 men from the start of the campaign. Sherman acknowledged that he had only two cavalry divisions to utilize in tracking Hood's army, Kenner Garrard's Second Division and H. Judson Kilpatrick's Third Division. Sherman wanted Kilpatrick in good condition to join him in the march to the sea, so he used Garrard's division to pursue Hood.[30]

Sherman expected Hood would march west into Alabama but when he decided to strike the railroad leading directly to Atlanta, Sherman, while postponing his march to the sea, set his troops in motion. Slocum's XX Corps was ordered to remain in Atlanta and protect the bridge over the Chattahoochee and then he ordered the XIV, XV, XVII, IV and XXIII corps to head for Smyrna on October 4 and the next day advanced to Kennesaw Mountain. When Sherman reached Kennesaw Mountain, he could hear the fighting as French's Confederates tried to capture the Union supply depot at Allatoona, where a million rations were stored.[31]

While action took place in Georgia and Alabama, George Thomas prepared his defenses in Tennessee. He called on Major General Cadwallader C. Washburn, headquartered at Memphis, to assist in the defensive and offensive efforts in Tennessee. Thomas primarily wanted Washburn to track Forrest who had slipped back into Mississippi. With Hood's destination being unknown, Thomas still worried about another cavalry raid into Tennessee. He knew that Forrest had stopped in the Corinth and Iuka area of Mississippi. While in Iuka, Forrest discussed his immediate plans with Richard Taylor on October 12. After his initial success against the five boats carrying Hoge's infantry brigade a few days earlier at Eastport, Forrest wanted to stop the flow of supplies on the rivers. "It is highly important that this line be interrupted if not entirely destroyed, as I learned during my recent operations in Middle Tennessee that it was by this route that the enemy received most of his supplies at Atlanta." Forrest also reported that his cavalry was in poor condition after the recent raid. Forrest recorded about 400 casualties and he still had 500 men on the north side of the Tennessee River, now isolated from his command. Even with 500 of Chalmers' cavalry troops joining his command, he estimated he might have 3,400 men. Forrest also noted a problem which plagued the Confederate cavalry—lack of discipline. Forrest noted that Roddey's cavalry had many stragglers during the previous campaign. "Such a state of affairs is disreputable and humiliating to my feelings. It is a burlesque upon military discipline." Discipline problems plagued both armies and would continue to be an issue throughout the campaign.[32]

On October 20 Hood's army reached Gadsden, Alabama, and he was joined there by Beauregard, commanding the Military Division of the West. In regard to Hood, Beauregard would be nothing more than an adviser. He could only command troops when he was physically present with the army and he could only interfere with Hood in the event of a crisis. When Beauregard arrived, Hood announced his new plan which was made without the approval of his superiors in Richmond or Beauregard. Hood later wrote that had he sought approval, the plan would not have been approved. Hood wanted Sherman to divide his forces so that he might destroy them in detail, but he perceived that the bulk of the Federal armies was in pursuit. He was not ready for pitched battle and, on the Union side of the line, Sherman concluded that Hood wanted to draw the Federal armies northward, so both generals were initially thwarted. Sherman wanted to march further south and Hood wanted to defeat parts of the Federal forces. Neither plan was working well. At Gadsden, Hood re-supplied his armies and discussed his next moves with Beauregard. He planned to turn his march northward again and take Bridgeport, a town that had been in Union hands since July 1863. He believed this movement would sever the railroad leading to Atlanta and, at the same time, regain all the territory that had been lost during the past year. However, Hood's plans called for Forrest to be raiding throughout Tennessee. Forrest had just completed his raid into Tennessee only a couple of weeks earlier and now Forrest focused on activity west of Nashville along the Tennessee River. Forrest, whose headquarters were in Jackson, Tennessee, on October 21, assessed his command and found he had about 3,000 effective men for duty, 400 fewer than he reported a few days before. He observed: "[M]y troops are in a much worse condition than I expected. Since crossing the river a large number of my horses have died, and many of my men are sick. I have been compelled to allow a large number of my men [to] go home to get new horses, and consequently I find my command greatly diminished in numbers."[33]

The Federal Army Pursues Hood

Meanwhile, Sherman had the unenviable task of chasing Hood who did not want to offer battle and who had a variety of potential targets. Garrard's Second Cavalry Division remained on the trail of the Confederate column, and by October 11, Garrard moved west of Rome with Sherman again threatening the flank of Hood's army with XXIII Corps. Garrard successfully closed on some of Jackson's cavalry screening for Hood, claiming two artillery pieces and some prisoners in the skirmish. Sherman was still unsure where Hood intended to go—east or west. Brigadier General Green B. Raum's brigade moved to reinforce the garrison at Resaca just before Hood arrived and aided in the defense of the town. Hood withdrew but he succeeded in destroying about 10 miles of track around Dalton. The war had certainly taken a turn for the worse as the Southern commanders continued to threaten to kill all the defenders if they did not surrender. Just as Forrest and Buford had demanded surrenders by threatening dire consequents if the garrisons refused to capitulate, so Hood carried those same threats. At Dalton and Resaca, Hood threatened "surrendered white officers and men would be paroled in a few days; but that if the post was carried by assault no prisoners would be taken." True to his words about black soldiers, a few days later John Crittenden, an Alabama soldier, wrote in his diary: "I saw 400 negro troops taken at Dalton Gen. Hood is letting the owners take them home." When Sherman arrived at Resaca on October 14, he felt he could mount an attack and catch Hood in a flanking movement. Sherman spread his pursuing columns to attack but Hood successfully slipped the noose. "Hood, however, was little encumbered with trains, and marched with great rapidity.... He evidently wanted to avoid a fight."[34]

By mid–October, George Thomas continued aligning his troops in preparation to meet Hood's advance into Alabama or Tennessee. Succeeding in expelling the Confederate cavalry after the recent raids, he now faced 35,000 infantry accompanied by the same cavalry which he fought a few weeks before. He pulled two cavalry commands into service—Croxton's First Cavalry Brigade of Edward McCook's First Division and Hatch's division of the District of Western Tennessee. Thomas also called for the cavalry in Kentucky to move to Nashville. Meanwhile, Sherman's armies (accompanied by Watkins' brigade and Garrard's division) still trailed Hood's Southern army.[35]

Hatch's 3,000 cavalry, many armed with multi-shot Spencer carbines, joined in the defenses in middle Tennessee reducing the advantages of Forrest's mobility and this caused Forrest more concern as the Union cavalry forces concentrated. Forrest hoped to delay Hatch's cavalry movement eastward, but he was unsuccessful. He decided that as long as the Union cavalry remained on the north side of the Tennessee River, no immediate action would be taken. As Hood moved ever westward and away from Sherman forces, the situation became more critical for the Union forces in Tennessee. Thomas employed what cavalry he had to keep watch for potential river crossings. Robert S. Granger, commanding the Federal Military District of Northern Alabama, placed the 2nd Tennessee Cavalry (U.S.) as pickets along the Tennessee River. In the meantime, Thomas began to mount his dismounted cavalry which had served as guards along the railroad, including the 9th and 10th Indiana regiments.[36]

On October 21, Thomas optimistically wrote to Henry Halleck: "I feel confident that I can defend the line of Tennessee with the force General Sherman proposes to leave with me, and shall proceed at once to organize the troops and be ready as soon as possible after the arrival of the Fourth Corps to operate against Forrest in West Tennessee, and drive the enemy out of that portion of the State also." At this point, Thomas did not know that Hood planned to push directly northward and he appeared to believe that he had sufficient forces to deal with Forrest. Thomas was mounting as much of his cavalry for which he could find mounts and as quickly as possible. As a result, he told Sherman that with IV Corps and strong contingents of cavalry he would be able to deal the threats he faced. In addition, Hatch's division was located at Clifton, Tennessee, about 40 miles east of Jackson, Forrest's new headquarters. Forrest had moved back northward into Tennessee and he wanted to fulfill his objective of dealing with the boats on the Tennessee River.[37]

Back in Alabama, Hood complained that he couldn't make his move on Bridgeport, but this was exactly what Sherman hoped he would do. Sherman planned to swing his forces and cut Hood off from the south, but as Hood remained in Gadsden on October 20, he had the option of just moving further west if Sherman continued his pursuit. Sherman chose to stop and consider his next action while his men repaired the railroad. While paused, he communicated with Henry Slocum at Atlanta about the disruption in rail service. Slocum replied that he had plenty of supplies but he still needed to collect forage for his animals until the tracks were repaired. Near Atlanta, Robert Winn, 3rd Kentucky Cavalry, wrote that despite being cut off from the north for several weeks, "our rations had not been cut down in the least." While Garrard's cavalry remained on duty trailing Hood's army, Sherman correctly summarized the situation: "Hood's movements and strategy had demonstrated that he had an army capable of endangering at all times my communications, but unable to meet me in open fight. To follow him would simply amount to being decoyed away from Georgia, with little prospect of overtaking and overwhelming him. To remain on the defensive would have been bad policy for an army of so great value as the one I then commanded, and I was forced to adopt a course more fruitful in results than the naked one of following him to the southwest." Sherman wanted to be marching for the sea and he could chase Hood all winter. When Hood pulled out of Gadsden, heading west, Sherman decided he had had enough. On October 22, Hood reached Guntersville along the Tennessee River, with Wheeler's cavalry on the flanks and rear of the Army of Tennessee. Four days later, Sherman sent David Stanley's IV Corps to Chattanooga under the authority of George Thomas, now in Nashville. Four days after that, he ordered John Schofield's XXIII Corps in the same direction, also under Thomas' command.[38]

On October 22, Beauregard informed Richard Taylor that he was going to assign Forrest's cavalry to Hood's Army of Tennessee. William Hicks Jackson's division, which had remained in Atlanta during Wheeler's raid, was sent for duty along the railroads in north Alabama. On the same day, Chalmers' cavalry division was ordered forward to join Forrest's cavalry near McLemoresville (a few miles north of Jackson, Tennessee). Roddey's cavalry division was also assigned duty to assist Hood's army as it marched through northern Alabama, including repairing the railroad which could carry much needed supplies from Corinth. On October 25, Hood marched toward Decatur and he tested a crossing of the Tennessee River, but he met enough resistance to abort the crossing which included fire from the gunboat *General Thomas* and Robert Granger's infantry and cavalry. The stiff resistance by Granger's command, which included the 2nd, 3rd, and 4th Tennessee Cavalry and part of the 10th Indiana Cavalry, caused Hood to move further west in his effort to cross the Tennessee River. Meanwhile, Stanley's IV Corps advanced to Pulaski from Chattanooga via train on October 27.[39]

In regard to the Federal cavalry, James Wilson, the newly arrived permanent chief of cavalry of the Military Division of the Mississippi, ordered Benjamin Grierson to prepare Hatch's cavalry for movement to Georgia, orders which would be rescinded a few days later because of Hood's and Forrest's actions. On October 27, Croxton's cavalry brigade moved to Florence as Federal infantry reinforcements reached Robert Granger on the north side of Tennessee River opposite Decatur. Both commanders reported no unusual activity from the enemy. While Croxton waited alone, Granger received

Chapter Two. Hood Prepares to March to Tennessee

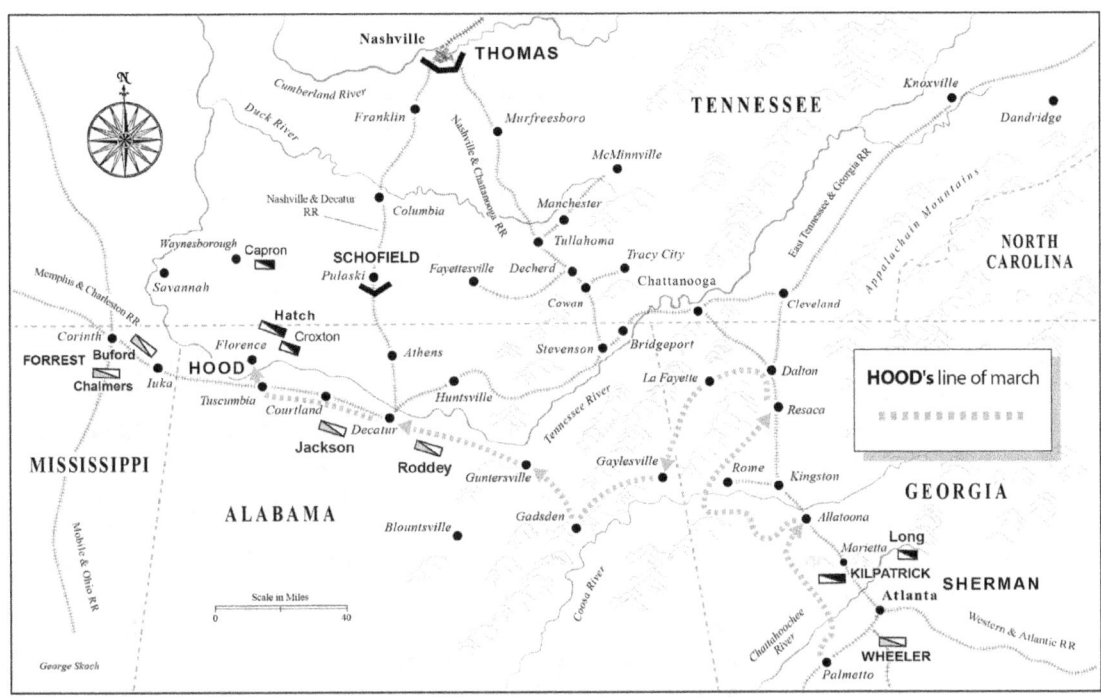

General location of cavalry forces, mid–November 1864.

five new regiments which gave him a better chance of repulsing a crossing. James O. Walton, 10th Indiana Cavalry, attached to Granger's command wrote in a letter: "We was attacked by Hood's army on 26th and fight continued until yesterday [October 30] ... they are aiming to cross the river..." Another Union cavalryman, George Clark, who passed his 22nd birthday in the trail of Hood's army, wrote: "I am growing old fast."[40]

Captain J.C. Van Duzer, superintendent of the telegraph service, reported the situation at the end of the day on October 27: "It seems that Sherman has lost Hood and does not know where to look for him. Rebels were at Blue Mountain, but not there now, while attack on Decatur induces belief that they are in Tennessee near Guntersville. In case it proves they are there Sherman intends a grand raid through Middle Georgia, leaving Thomas to look out for Tennessee by himself." Sherman had been planning to march across Georgia for some time and now decided to begin.[41]

The next day, Croxton located the crossing point for Hood's army after Granger's stubborn defense at Decatur. Hood began laying a pontoon bridge at Bainbridge Crossing at Florence on October 29. Superseding the orders from O.O. Howard and James H. Wilson for Hatch to go to Georgia, Thomas ordered Hatch forward by railroad to reinforce Croxton. Stanley's IV Corps also continued westward by rail on October 30 to Pulaski to meet the threat of Hood's advancing army. At 9:00 p.m. on October 29, Croxton reported to Thomas, "It is reported that Hood's entire army ... expects to cross the river at Bainbridge tonight.... I will do what I can to prevent their crossing, keeping you fully advised." Hood, observing the buildup of Union infantry at Decatur, simply marched further west to make his crossing and at the same time moved closer to the Confederate supply depot at Corinth. On October 31, Hood wrote to J.A. Seddon, Secretary of War: "Florence is in our possession and the pontoon bridge is being laid down. I hope to be able to advance across the river so soon as supplies can be obtained." Croxton moved his brigade to the point of the crossing and tried to repulse the enemy infantry, but there were just too many Confederates. Croxton, commanding slightly over 1,000 men, wrote: "I will send my transportation to Pulaski, and do what I can to stay their progress."[42]

Sherman now focused on the march to the sea and left Hood to George Thomas. Sherman reorganized his army and dismantled the very large Army of the Cumberland. Sherman sent IV and XXIII Corps to work directly for Thomas at Nashville, while most of the remainder of the Army of the Cumberland was reorganized as the Army of Georgia. Thomas was also promised A.J. Smith's Right Wing of the XVI Corps upon the completion of Price's Raid; however, Smith remained in pursuit of Price's cavalry in Missouri. In addition, Thomas had control of all the garrisons in Tennessee and the entire cavalry corps west of Atlanta and east of Memphis, which would be reorganized soon under the command of Wilson. Sherman concluded, "These forces I judged would enable General Thomas to defend the railroad from Chattanooga back, including Nashville and Decatur, and give him an army with which he could successfully cope with Hood should the latter cross the Tennessee northward." With this decision, Sherman essentially shuttled the "Hood problem" off to Thomas while he prepared to make his march to the sea. Thomas in the meantime scrambled to cobble together enough troops to deal with 40,000 Confederates marching west into Federal controlled territory. Sherman wrote to Thomas, "If you can defend the line of the Tennessee in my absence of three months, it is all I ask." When Sherman left, he took along H. Judson Kilpatrick's cavalry division to accompany his army.[43]

On October 30, Hood's army reached Florence, Alabama, and the next day Hood established his headquarters in Tuscumbia. Hood reasoned to follow Sherman back toward Atlanta would be to abandon the territory that he had regained, somewhat of a boast just because his army had marched through it. Both Hood and Sherman had achieved their stated objectives. Hood wanted Sherman's armies divided and Sherman wanted to be marching to the sea. Now, Hood set his eyes on Thomas and any other isolated Union forces along the way. Hood would make a statement that would haunt him after the campaign: "If beaten I should leave the army in better condition than it would be if I attempted a retrograde movement against Sherman." Hood had moved his army ever westward without consulting Beauregard and Beauregard knew he needed to meet with Hood. He had considered traveling to Hood's headquarters on two occasions only to hear he was no longer where he expected him to be. Finally, Hood and Beauregard met on November 3 and discussed the options for the army. Until this time, neither general had finalized plans for the next movement of the Army of Tennessee and from this meeting came the plan to march into Tennessee. Beauregard gave Hood a compromise option of dividing his army with part advancing on Thomas and the other resisting Sherman's campaign. Hood, believing that his army was too small to divide, chose to continue his advance on Thomas' forces. Just as Sherman chose Kilpatrick to accompany his army, Beauregard chose Forrest to accompany Hood's army. William H. Jackson's cavalry, which had previously been attached to the Army of Mississippi, and which had not participated in Wheeler's raid, remained with Forrest. Wheeler and his cavalry were dispatched back to Georgia to resist Sherman's new campaign.[44]

The stage was set. Hood's Army of Tennessee would begin the campaign in November 1864 accompanied by Forrest's cavalry corps supplemented by Jackson's division. This force would face George Thomas with two infantry corps and variously assembled cavalry forces. A.J. Smith's XVI Corps, still fighting in Missouri, would join Thomas as soon as possible, and Thomas would draw in the forces of Rousseau's District of Tennessee and Steedman's District of the Etowah. In addition, Thomas had the garrison of Nashville to add to his strength.

Major General George Thomas

George Thomas, despite Sherman's allegations that he was slow, was one of the best generals in the Union army. Thomas, smart, deliberate, reliable, always seemed to be where he was needed. By 1864, Thomas had the full war behind him. Thomas, a Virginian by birth, was 48 years old as the Nashville Campaign began. He attended the United States Military Academy and graduated in 1840, 12th in his class of 42, and his roommate was William Sherman. Because of his vast experience, Thomas personally knew many of the commanders on both sides during the war. He even served in the Mexican War alongside Braxton Bragg. In 1851, Thomas became an instructor of artillery at West Point under the command of Robert E. Lee and he soon had additional duties teaching cavalry tactics where he earned the nickname "Old Slow Trot." Thomas stopped the cadets from galloping the older mounts without reason, saving the horses from potential injury. Among the cadets that Thomas instructed were J.E.B. Stuart, Fitzhugh Lee, John Schofield, Alexander McCook, David Stanley, James McPherson, Oliver Howard and John Bell Hood. When the Civil War began, Thomas committed his talents to the Union much to the displeasure of friends, family, and other pro–Southern members of the military. They felt because he was Virginian that his place was in the Confederate Army, but Thomas disagreed. This choice to remain with the Union Army resulted in great pain for Thomas because, not only did he receive the resentment from those in the South, he was also looked upon with distrust from many in the North. Even Lincoln had concerns about placing a native Southerner in a high position in the army.[45]

General George Thomas bravely told Sherman, "With Schofield and Stanley I feel confident I can drive Hood back" (Library of Congress).

Thomas stubbornly continued on his path of letting his actions speak for themselves. This began at the Battle of Mill Springs, continued at Shiloh, Perryville, Stones River, Chickamauga, Chattanooga, and the Atlanta Campaign. Despite Thomas' steady and resolute ability to the fight the enemy, he was passed over in favor of others for promotion, often paying the price for making decisions for the benefit of the army at the cost of advancement. After the Perryville Campaign, Thomas refused command of the Army of the Ohio because he thought the action would be detrimental to the army, only to be passed over with William Rosecrans. Only after the Battle of Chickamauga was Thomas recognized for his solid contribution of saving the Union forces and earned him a new nickname, "the Rock of Chickamauga." Still, when Grant assumed command of the Union forces at Chattanooga a few months later, he decided to let Thomas' Army of the Cumberland take a secondary role in the battle at Missionary Ridge. However, the men under Thomas' command, and without orders, assailed Missionary Ridge winning the battle there. Then, Thomas led the Army of Cumberland, which was Sherman's largest force, during the Atlanta Campaign with good results, but Thomas differed in many ways from Sherman. While Sherman embraced taking the war to the citizens of Georgia, Thomas warned against the barbarous acts of war or "we will find that in destroying the rebels we have destroyed the Union." Thomas opposed Sherman's tactics which appeared impetuous and ill-planned at times—the Battle of Kennesaw Mountain, Stanley's attack at Lovejoy's Station, and McCook's and Stoneman's cavalry raids. While aggressiveness and dash yielded good results at times, at other times, the price was dear. Finally, Thomas and Sherman disagreed about cavalry commanders. Sherman was disappointed in Kenner Garrard as commander of the Second Cavalry Division throughout the Atlanta Campaign, but Thomas cautioned Sherman that upon some thoughtful consideration he would find that Garrard was his best division commander. Thomas was right, although Sherman chose the boastful H. Judson Kilpatrick to accompany his next campaign. In the meantime, the Second Cavalry Division, which had been commanded by Garrard, had successfully led Sherman's pursuit over the past two months.[46]

Thomas did not want to command the troops in Tennessee while Sherman marched to the sea. Thomas wrote to Sherman on October 18: "There is one thing, however, I don't wish to be left in command of the defenses of Tennessee unless you and the authorities in Washington deem it absolutely necessary." One of the top objectives set forth by the Union military commanders six months before was the destruction of the Army of Tennessee. Thomas objected to Sherman's new plan because it abandoned this goal. Sherman replied the march was not just for military reasons, but because it would prove the "vulnerability of the South." Sherman's plan to march to the sea reflected his strategy—"I will make the interior of Georgia feel the weight of war. It is folly for me to be moving our armies on the reports of scouts and citizens. We must maintain the offensive." Thomas wanted to join in this new campaign, but he accepted his new task of defending Tennessee as he had throughout his career by faithfully following his orders.[47]

On the last day of October, Thomas summarized the situation that he faced in a message to Henry Halleck. Hood had crossed the Tennessee River at Florence and it was apparent that Tennessee was the next target for the Southern army. Croxton would soon be reinforced by Hatch's Division. Stanley's IV Corps marched for Pulaski and even though Schofield was still in Resaca, he had orders to move to Tennessee with all haste. Thomas bravely wrote, "With Schofield and Stanley I feel confident I can drive Hood back." Thomas had received 12 new regiments over the past couple of weeks and they had been distributed to the various garrisons across the state and re-filling brigades which needed men. That meant that Thomas had no great reserve of troops to call on to meet Hood's advance. Still, the decisions were made—George Thomas would pull together his forces to meet Hood's advance northward. The details of the campaign would be determined when Hood decided exactly where he would attack, a location still unclear to all.[48]

Chapter Three

The Union Cavalry in the Nashville Campaign

Cavalry is useless for defense; its only power is in a vigorous offensive.
—James H. Wilson

On October 4, Ulysses Grant's message to Sherman introduced a new figure to the Union cavalry in the Division of the Mississippi—James H. Wilson. "I have asked that he be brevetted a major-general, and assigned with that rank. I believe Wilson will add 50 per cent to the effectiveness of your cavalry," wrote Grant. Wilson promptly replied: "Am on my way to command Sherman's cavalry, and as the generals with it are all my seniors, I want ample and complete authority. I think it should be reorganized as a corps, with efficient brigade and division commanders, as in the East."[1]

In regard to the Union cavalry, it is fortunate that Wilson was assigned to command. Wilson had the approval of Grant and, more tentatively, of Sherman. Sherman remained disappointed in the cavalry during the recent Atlanta Campaign, except for Edward McCook and H. Judson Kilpatrick. Sherman continued his disparaging comments about the cavalry even into the pursuit of Hood in September and October. Finally, Washington L. Elliott, who had nothing to lose, wrote his objection to Sherman's comments, just as Kenner Garrard had done earlier in the summer. "My cavalry has never avoided the cavalry of the enemy in any force; it has too often contended with it and with success.... The orders of the major-general commanding have been complied with, and to enable me to do so I held my command in readiness, picketing only the roads, and sending out scouts until I could learn what disposition he wished made. I do not regard the remarks derogatory to my command, when made by those unacquainted with the orders given me, but desiring to do my duty and obey orders, as does my command, I confess that it is not only discouraging but mortifying to hear of the major-general commanding censuring the cavalry publicly in the hearing of officers and enlisted men." Sherman merely replied, "Our cavalry is wanting in enterprise." Likewise, Sherman had few supporters in the cavalry, but for the effective use of the cavalry in the west, it needed to operate as Sherman desired, even in light of Sherman's poor management of this arm of his command. With Wilson hand-picked by Grant and approved by Sherman, there was reason to hope that the cavalry would be able to function at a higher level under Wilson's command.[2]

When Wilson gained command of the cavalry in the Military Division of Mississippi, he gained good, experienced cavalrymen and commanders. On October 31, he reported the makeup of his new command:

Cavalry Corps, Military Division of the Mississippi, October 31, 1864[3]

Department of the Cumberland— Brig. Gen. Washington Lafayette Elliott			
	Present for Duty	Aggregate Present and Absent	
First Division (McCook)	3,319	7,403	Calhoun, GA
Second Division (K. Garrard)	2,973	8,751	Rome, GA
Third Division (Kilpatrick)	3,928	7,479	Stilesborough, GA
First Brigade, Fourth Division (Thornburgh)	1,229	1,853	Decatur, AL
Second Brigade, Fourth Division (Clift)	1,235	2,513	Pulaski, TN
Cavalry Corps District of West Tennessee— Brig. Gen. Benjamin Grierson			
First Division (Hatch)	2,897	5,934	Pulaski, TN
Second Division (Winslow)	4,608	8,302	Missouri
Army of the Ohio—Col. Israel Garrard			
First Brigade (Capron)	963	1,978	Pulaski, TN
District of Tennessee			
9th Indiana	319	901	Pulaski, TN
10th Indiana	238	360	Pulaski, TN
11th Indiana	742	1,115	Larkinsville, AL
12th Indiana	190	878	Tullahoma, TN
13th Indiana	661	1,034	—
Unassigned			
15th Pennsylvania	287	576	Wauhatchie, TN
4th United States	371	688	Gaylesville, AL
Total	23,965*	49,770	
*Corps headquarters staff included five officers.			

The new chief of cavalry made an appraisal of his command and wrote to Grant regarding the condition of his men. His first intention was to organize cavalry that could be mounted and moved against the enemy, while leaving a sufficient "police force" of cavalry to guard the railroads in middle Tennessee. The most recent tabulation of cavalry coming under Wilson's command showed an impressive aggregate total of 50,000 men; however, the reality revealed something decidedly different. The effective mounted troops amounted to a mere 14,000 men, including those cavalry units assigned to railroad security. The three active divisions that had been previously assigned to the Army of the Cumberland during the Atlanta Campaign had mounted only 4,500 troopers—about 1,500 each for the divisions under Garrard, Kilpatrick and McCook. About the same number of men from these divisions were dismounted and relegated to garrison and security duty which testified to poor management of the mounts during the recent campaign. Next, Israel Garrard commanded the remnants of the division assigned to the Army of Ohio, essentially just Colonel Horace Capron's brigade, which had been shattered during an ill-conceived raid to liberate prisoners of war at Andersonville. Garrard had regiments in Louisville awaiting remounts and only parts of two regiments remained in the field at Atlanta. Under Wilson's plans, Benjamin Grierson who had commanded the cavalry corps in western Tennessee and Mississippi would be reassigned to command a division previously commanded by Edward Winslow, and Hatch's division in western Tennessee remained unchanged except for picking up a few regiments of Winslow's division. Winslow's division had been absent over the past few months because it had been assigned to the Department of Missouri in response to Price's Missouri Raid. Wilson received some good news, because he had five new Indiana cavalry regiments awaiting assignment. However, the new regiments had never been mounted due to the shortage of mounts. Finally, Wilson had two divisions of Tennessee cavalry and he planned to allow these men to remain in Tennessee on security duty. In all, Wilson had six effective divisions, excluding Winslow's and the two Tennessee divisions.[4]

Six divisions of cavalry, totaling 20,000–30,000 men by Wilson's estimate, which could offer offensive action against the enemy's cavalry, should have been good news to all; however, Wilson reported the bad news: "But what are the facts now? We cannot raise 6,000 and because horses, arms, and equipments have not been furnished." The neglect of the cavalry under Sherman's command was now reflected in Wilson's and Richard Johnson's reports. At best, the condition of the Union cavalry was neglected and mismanaged. Troopers were dismounted and equipment was non-uniform, even totally absent in some instances. Reports from the various divisions were sporadic in some cases, non-existent in others. No district-level reports from the four divisions of the Army of

James Harrison Wilson boldly declared, "[W]e shall soon destroy their cavalry and establish the invincibility of our own" (Library of Congress).

the Cumberland had been filed since May and, likewise, none had ever been received from the Army of the Ohio. The cavalry on paper remained impressive but the facts revealed that care and re-supply was necessary to get the cavalry in the west back up to full fighting potential.[5]

Grant and Sherman chose Wilson because of his ability to offensively use the cavalry, and Wilson wanted to do just that, but he needed mounted cavalry. Richard Johnson had already started a plan to remount and re-equip the cavalry when Wilson assumed command. The initial request to the ordnance department included, 10,000 Spencer carbines, and Sharps carbines if the Spencer carbines were unavailable. Next, he wanted the same amount of horse equipment and sabers. Wilson appealed to the Cavalry Bureau in Washington to concentrate on arming and mounting his cavalry, and he needed Sherman's support for an "inexorable policy of concentration." Wilson wanted his cavalry out of Tennessee and in the saddle in Georgia, the Carolinas, and Alabama, deep in the territory remaining under Confederate control. He wrote: "[W]e shall soon destroy their cavalry and establish the invincibility of our own." To Wilson's advantage, he had the support of Grant, but Sherman's apathy regarding the cavalry was reflected by Wilson who told Grant that Sherman didn't expect any important action by the cavalry. Wilson correctly surmised Sherman's attitude and worried that he faced a policy which would diminish the impact of his mounted troops. Wilson summarized: "[B]ut if General Thomas is left in Tennessee the infantry forces must necessarily be more or less divided between him and General Sherman; if the cavalry force is divided equally between them, we shall effect nothing. Cavalry is useless for defense; its only power is in a vigorous offensive; therefore I urge its concentration south of the Tennessee and hurling it into the bowels of the South in masses." Wilson's bravado did not contemplate Hood and Forrest marching on Nashville.[6]

Wilson directed his immediate attention on remounting the cavalry divisions. While that was being accomplished, Hatch's division, which was in good condition, had been ordered to join Croxton's brigade to face the threat of Hood's and Forrest's immediate march. Wilson also wanted Grierson to assemble the remnants of Winslow's division and the cavalry in Mississippi in preparation for action in that state and Alabama, but Grierson only reluctantly accepted Wilson's command. Grierson wrote, "Thus my command is scattered, leaving me less than 2,000 mounted men." Grierson was frustrated. "I have worked hard for the past six months to place my command in condition for the field, and, in spite of several unsuccessful expeditions made by General Sturgis and others who were sent here to command my troops, I had at length succeeded in organizing, mounting, and arming my entire force, and at the time my command was scattered I had the finest and most effective cavalry command in the West."[7]

Wilson announced his plans to reorganize his new cavalry corps: First Division, Edward McCook; Second Division, Eli Long (to replace Kenner Garrard); Third Division, Judson Kilpatrick; Fourth Division, Benjamin Grierson; Fifth Division, Edward Hatch; Sixth Division, Emory Upton (cavalry of Army of the Ohio supplemented with the new Indiana regiments); Seventh Division, Edward Winslow's (Wilson intended to split this current command between Grierson and Hatch); and, finally, Eighth and Ninth Divisions, the two Tennessee divisions.[8]

In addition, Kenner Garrard, Washington L. Elliott, and Joseph Knipe (most recently assigned as chief of cavalry of the Army of the Tennessee in October) were going to be reassigned to infantry. Garrard was reassigned due to his running conflict with Sherman, and Knipe and Elliott lost their positions because Wilson abolished the position of chief of cavalry for individual armies. Wilson wanted personal control of the cavalry divisions without having to negotiate orders through army-level cavalry chiefs. He initially placed Richard Johnson in charge of much of the administration and organization of the cavalry in the west. The success of Wilson's plan depended upon the ability to operate offensively and to do that Wilson felt he needed to get out of Tennessee.[9]

As Wilson assumed command of the cavalry, he wisely chose to keep Richard Johnson. Johnson was an experienced, collegial and well-liked commander. He knew how to get things done and he worked well with others commanders. Wilson asked Johnson to continue to "remount, arm, and equip all the cavalry" in preparation for further action in the war. For the upcoming campaign, Wilson would not have time to implement all his proposed changes and, initially, he was definitely not on the offensive. The units which would be important in the upcoming campaign included: Croxton's First Brigade of Edward McCook's division, Hatch's Division, Richard Johnson's division, and Joseph Knipe's division. The cavalry troops of these commanders, now under the command of their new chief of cavalry would need to work together to battle the formidable Nathan Bedford Forrest and his cavalry.[10]

General Benjamin Grierson spoke proudly of his command as the "most effective cavalry command in the West" (Library of Congress).

Edward McCook's First Division

Croxton's Brigade

On October 31, John Croxton commanded an experienced cavalry brigade of four regiments supported by Edward McCook, a cool, dependable cavalry commander, but McCook was trying to rebuild his division after Sherman sent it on an unsuccessful mission in July to Lovejoy's Station. Now in November, McCook's Second and Third Brigades, under the command of Oscar La Grange and Louis Watkins, were in the process of being re-mounted and reorganized in Louisville, and only Croxton's brigade was mounted and in the field.

Chapter Three. The Union Cavalry in the Nashville Campaign

First Cavalry Division—Brig. Gen. Edward McCook

November–December 1864 Campaign
First Brigade—Brig. Gen. John T. Croxton[11]
8th Iowa, Col. Joseph B. Dorr
4th Kentucky Mounted Infantry, Lt. Col Robert M. Kelly
2nd Michigan, Lt. Col. Benjamin Smith
1st Tennessee, Lt. Col. Calvin M. Dyer
18th Indiana Battery, Capt. Moses M. Beck

Croxton is most commonly known for his exploits in 1865, but prior to that time he had a remarkable experience in the Civil War. Croxton was a rising star for the Union cavalry. He was a native Kentuckian, born on November 20, 1837, a mere 27 years old in September 1864. Croxton was born and raised in Bourbon County near Paris, Kentucky, the oldest of 12 children. He strongly opposed slavery and equally supported the Union. Ironically, Croxton was the son of a prosperous Kentucky farmer, originally from Virginia, who had slaves of his own. When Croxton was still a boy, he saved his money to buy Sharps rifles for those in "Bleeding Kansas" who fought to make that state free.

One of his classmates and life-long friend at Paris was Robert M. Kelly, a man who would serve with him in the same regiment, 4th Kentucky Mounted Infantry, during the Civil War. Croxton began attending Yale University in 1854 as a sophomore and graduated in 1857 and he taught school in Georgetown, Kentucky, after graduation. In 1858, he was admitted to the bar in Kentucky after studying under Judge James F. Robinson and he began practicing law the next year. When the war began, he rushed to enlist in the Union Army and rode throughout Bourbon and the surrounding counties recruiting men. He was initially appointed lieutenant colonel in the 4th Kentucky Infantry which was commanded by Colonel Speed Fry.[12]

Too little is known of his pre-war life, but much of what is known about him comes from a single letter written in 1855 from Yale. Croxton wrote to his father and declared that he was not an abolitionist in the "Kentucky

General John Croxton, a smart, energetic and efficient brigade commander (Library of Congress).

acceptance of the term," that is, "a negro stealer," and did not support this as an effective method of abolishing slavery. Instead, he said he was, and had always been, an "Emancipationist." He thought the solution to the slavery problem was gradually emancipating slaves and returning them to Africa, and he thought labor should be done by white laborers. He worked out a financial model in which the exchange of black laborers for white ones would increase the number of citizens in Kentucky by slowing the westward movement of industrious families in search of a good living. He concluded his letter by saying that his "appeal goes to the heart by way of the purse." He felt any solution to the slavery problem needed to be based on good financial arguments. Croxton's position was not well accepted in his hometown and his was only one of two votes cast in Paris for Lincoln in the 1860 election. So unpopular was his political position, that he went to vote armed because he expected to be attacked by those opposed to his views.[13]

Croxton, a smart, energetic, efficient officer, was active throughout the war, beginning with the Battle of Mill Springs. Colonel Speed Fry was promoted to brigade command in March 1862, and Croxton subsequently received a promotion to the rank of colonel and given full command of the 4th Kentucky Infantry. The 4th Kentucky missed active participation in the Battle of Perryville and the Battle of Stones River. Croxton's regiment marched through the muddy roads during the Tullahoma Campaign and afterward, he was promoted to brigade command prior to the Battle of Chickamauga. During that battle, Croxton's brigade saw extensive action, being the first brigade entering the fight on September 19, while initially clashing with Forrest's cavalry. Croxton's brigade fought throughout the first day and, on the morning of the second day of the battle, he had the misfortune of being only one brigade away from the Confederate breakthrough near Brotherton farm. Croxton's brigade was folded back on itself as the battle intensified and Croxton was wounded severely in his thigh as he rallied his brigade. Though not fully recovered from his wound, he led the regiment in the Battle of Missionary Ridge. As the Union lines moved up Missionary Ridge, a shell burst near him. He was buried under the debris of a hut and dirt which pinned him to the ground, reopening his wounded leg. After the battle, he needed a more extensive recuperative period. In spring 1864, the 4th Kentucky reenlisted as veterans and became a mounted infantry regiment. George Thomas wrote a commendation for Croxton for his service at Chickamauga and Croxton was rewarded with a promotion to the rank of brigadier general in July 1864. Upon his promotion, Croxton gained command of the First Brigade in Edward McCook's division during the Atlanta Campaign.[14]

Croxton always seemed to be in the center of the action. About a week later, he led the First Brigade in McCook's Raid to Lovejoy's Station. The Confederate cavalry caught McCook's division as it was making its escape and Croxton commanded the rearguard until McCook was cut off near Brown's Mill. Croxton put much of the heavy rearguard fighting on his beloved 4th Kentucky which suffered severe losses in the action. Just south of Newnan on July 30, the Federal cavalry had to cut its way out. Croxton became separated from his command during the fight and did not reach the Union lines until almost two weeks later. Although no accurate casualties were reported for McCook's Raid (reports vary from 20 to 66 percent losses), Croxton's brigade suffered greatly. Since that defeat, Croxton's brigade had been sent to the rear on security duty while being re-mounted. Most recently, his experienced cavalry brigade tried to fend off Wheeler in August and Forrest in September during their Tennessee raids.[15]

Edward Hatch's Fifth Division

Edward Hatch is a well-known, but often overlooked, Union cavalry commander in the western theater of the Civil War. Hatch had an exemplary war record and this record would extend after the war. Hatch, son of an attorney, was born in Bangor, Maine, on April 22, 1831. He attended Norwich Military Academy which produced such notable officers as Grenville M. Dodge, Joseph A. Mower, Thomas E.G. Ransom, William "Bull" Nelson, and Hatch (class of 1850). Hatch began to earn his living by investing in a manufacturing facility in Norfolk, Virginia. Then, he traveled west looking for new business opportunities including spending some time in a logging camp in Wisconsin. He continued in the logging business long enough acquire some capital and then he returned to the east. He moved his family to Muscatine, Iowa, in 1855 where he continued in the lumber business. When the war started, Hatch traveled to Norfolk to try to salvage part of the business which had been confiscated by the Confederacy, but he was arrested as a spy. Fortunately, he was able to escape and he returned to Muscatine where he helped organize a company in the 2nd Iowa Cavalry in July 1861. Hatch was initially elected to the rank of captain, but he soon received promotions to major and lieutenant colonel and he commanded the regiment at that rank until June 1862 when he was promoted to the rank of colonel. Hatch commanded cavalry in many engagements, including the Siege of New Madrid and Island No. 10; Battle at Farmington, Mississippi; fights at Boonville, Mississippi, in May and July 1862; Battle of Iuka; Battle of Corinth; Grant's advance along the Mississippi Central Railroad, December 1862; Grierson's Raid in April 1863 with fights at Coffeeville, Palo Alto and Birmingham; Battle of Jackson in July 1863; and the fight at Collierville, Tennessee, in November 1863. More recently he commanded the Union cavalry in the expedition to Oxford, Mississippi, in August 1864. Quartermaster Sergeant Richard Surby described him: "In stature he is about five feet ten inches, well proportioned, of a florid complexion, dark hair slightly tinged with grey, a high forehead, a full blue eye, beaming with intelligence, and when in battle or excited they shine like meteors, a Roman nose, a well shaped mouth and chin, thin lips, denoting firmness; his upper lip displays a heavy dark mustache; his dress is neat and very plain—no gaudy display. He

General Edward Hatch, described by one of his men as "a strict disciplinarian, loved and respected by his troops" (Library of Congress).

possesses a cool, collected mind, that sees things at a glance, is a splendid horseman.... He is a strict disciplinarian, loved and respected by his troops, and requires no more of his officers and men than he performs himself." Despite his excellent record of service, Hatch did not escape Sherman's almost universal dislike of cavalry. In October 1863, Sherman wrote: "[A]dmit I am not satisfied with Hatch's management. I hear of no collision, of no killed. He seems to hover round when he should dash in with the saber and pistol."[16]

Fifth Cavalry Division—Brig. Gen. Edward Hatch

November–December 1864 Campaign	
*First Brigade**—Col. Robert R. Stewart	*Second Brigade*—Col. Datus E. Coon
3rd Illinois, Lt. Col. Robert H. Carnahan	6th Illinois, Lt. Col. John Lynch
11th Indiana, Lt. Col. Abram Sharra	7th Illinois, Maj. John M. Graham
12th Missouri, Col. Oliver Wells	9th Illinois, Capt. Joseph W. Harper
10th Tennessee: Maj. William P. Story, Maj. James T. Abernathy	2nd Iowa, Maj. Charles C. Horton
	12th Tennessee, Col. George Spalding
	1st Illinois Light Artillery, Battery I, Lt. Joseph A. McCarthey
*Colonel Oliver Wells, 12th Missouri Cavalry, commanded the brigade until November 28, 1864.	

Robert "Bob" R. Stewart was an experienced colonel who had served in the war since 1861. Stewart grew up in Terra Haute, Indiana, the son of a landlord and tavern owner. Before the Civil War, he joined Philip Kearney's company of dragoons and participated in the Mexican War. Then, he joined the California Gold Rush and returned to Terre Haute in 1858. When the war began, he helped organize Company I of the 1st Indiana Cavalry in June 1861 and was elected captain. In November, he was promoted to the rank of lieutenant colonel of the 2nd Indiana Cavalry, commanded by Edward McCook. Stewart was captured by John Hunt Morgan's cavalry during the Battle of Hartsville, Tennessee, in December 1862. He was subsequently exchanged and back in command of the 2nd Indiana prior to the Tullahoma Campaign. His brother James Stewart would ultimately be commissioned colonel of the 2nd Indiana and Robert Stewart would be named colonel of the

Colonel Robert Stewart, late colonel of 11th Indiana Cavalry, commanded a veteran cavalry brigade (Indiana Historical Society, M0822).

11th Indiana Cavalry upon its organization in February 1864. The 11th Indiana, initially dismounted, had its first duty guarding the railroads near Larkinsville in northern Alabama. Stewart would leave Nashville on November 24 and assume brigade command on November 28; in the meantime, Oliver Wells, 12th Missouri Cavalry, would have nominal command of the brigade.[17]

Datus Ensign Coon commanded Hatch's Second Brigade. Coon, born on February 20, 1831, in Madison County, New York, was a newspaperman living in Iowa before the war. In 1856, he started the *Democrat* in Mitchell County, Iowa, and two years later he started the *Cerro Gordo Press* in Mason City. In 1860, he established yet another newspaper in Ellington. When the war began, he assisted in organizing Company I of the 2nd Iowa Cavalry. He served initially under the command of Washington L. Elliott and then under Hatch. He became a major in the regiment in September 1861 and he was promoted to the rank of colonel in 1864, the third colonel of the regiment. Coon was an experienced commander and comfortable in the saddle. He had been through many battles with the 2nd Iowa, including the Siege of New Madrid and Island No. 10; battle at Farmington; Siege of Corinth; Battles of Iuka and Corinth; the Meridian Campaign; the Yazoo River Campaign; and the subsequent battles in Mississippi and western Tennessee. Once Hatch was promoted to brigade command in the fall of 1862, Coon gained command of the regiment, and in the summer of 1864, Coon was promoted to brigade command. The historian of the 2nd Iowa described Coon as "a zealous worker and brave fighter."[18]

Colonel Datus E. Coon, "a zealous worker and brave fighter" (Mollus Mass Civil War Collection, United States Army Heritage and Education Center, Carlisle, Pennsylvania).

Richard Johnson's Sixth Division

Richard Johnson was born a few miles east of Paducah in Livingston County, Kentucky, in the village of Smithland on February 27, 1827. Johnson was the son of a country doctor and both of his parents died when he was just 10 years old. He lived with his half-brother, Dr. John Milton Johnson, who helped gain an appointment for Richard to the United States Military Academy. Johnson began his studies in 1844 and he initially struggled academically, particularly with mathematics. Johnson soon overcame these initial issues and he graduated in 1849, 30th in a class of 43. Prior to attending West Point, he was called Richard, but his classmates began referring to him as "R. W." which remained his nicknamed throughout the war. Upon graduation, he initially served in Minnesota before being transferred to Texas in the 1st U.S. Infantry until 1855 when he was assigned to Jefferson Barracks in St. Louis as part of the 2nd U.S. Cavalry. He soon returned to the frontier, primarily in Texas, as part of the cavalry. When the war began, Johnson remained in the Union army and initially served in the defense of Washington, D.C. Johnson was promoted to the rank of lieutenant colonel in the 3rd Kentucky Cavalry until he was promoted to the rank of brigadier general, in command of a brigade of Ohio and Indiana infantry. In August 1862, Johnson's infantry and cavalry troops were defeated by John Hunt Morgan's cavalry near Gallatin, Tennessee, and Johnson was captured. He was subsequently exchanged and returned to command a division of infantry during the Stones River Campaign. His division was routed on the morning of December 31, 1862, as Alexander McCook's corps was propelled rearward by a furious Confederate attack. He continued to command an infantry division in the Tullahoma, Chickamauga, Chattanooga, and Atlanta campaigns. Johnson was severely wounded at the Battle of New Hope Church during the Atlanta Campaign and afterward had been given temporary command of the cavalry in the west prior to Wilson's arrival. He demonstrated an unselfish willingness to work to get the cavalry into fighting condition. While Wilson gave initial indications that Johnson would be returned to Thomas for assignment, conditions unfolded so fast that Johnson gained command of the Sixth Cavalry Division which Wilson intended for Emory Upton. Instead, by mid–December Upton arrived to command the Fourth Cavalry Division.[19]

General Richard Johnson, veteran commander of the Sixth Cavalry Division (Library of Congress).

Sixth Division—Brig. Gen. Richard W. Johnson

November–December 1864 Campaign	
First Brigade—Col. Thomas Harrison*	*Second Brigade*—Col. James Biddle
16th Illinois, Maj. Charles H. Beeres	14th Illinois, Maj. Haviland Tompkins
5th Iowa, Lt. Col. Harlon Baird	6th Indiana, Maj. Jacob S. Stephens
7th Ohio, Col. Israel Garrard	8th Michigan, Col. Elisha Mix 3rd Tennessee, Maj. Benjamin Cunningham 4th U.S., Battery I, Lt. Frank G. Smith
*Horace Capron commanded the brigade until December 1, 1864.	

Chapter Three. The Union Cavalry in the Nashville Campaign

As Hood continued to march toward Alabama and Tennessee, George Thomas, after expelling Forrest and Wheeler south of the Tennessee River, began to call in reinforcements. On October 15, John Schofield, commanding the Army of the Ohio which amounted to XXIII Corps, consented to send 1,500 cavalry troops (8th Michigan, 14th and 16th Illinois) under command of Horace Capron from Lexington, Kentucky.[20]

Prior to the Nashville Campaign, a single cavalry brigade, Capron's, remained of the cavalry division of the Army of the Ohio under overall command of Israel Garrard. As previously mentioned, George Stoneman's division had been shattered in the Atlanta Campaign. During Stoneman's raid, the division, after reaching Macon, had been cut-off and Stoneman ordered his brigades to try to cut their way back to the Union lines near Atlanta. Just as Capron's brigade reached the Union lines, it was attacked and decimated. Capron and some of his staff made it to the Union lines while most of the brigade was captured. In October 1864, Capron was 60 years old and certainly one of the oldest cavalry brigade commanders in the war. He was born in Attleboro, Massachusetts, and his parents subsequently moved to Whitesboro, New York. He had an active life. He worked as a superintendent of the Printing Cloth Works in Maryland and other clothing mills while in his twenties. Because of his success in manufacturing, the governor of Maryland even called on him to deal with some unlawful laborers who were responsible for a "reign of terror" along the Baltimore & Washington Railroad in 1834. He remained active in the clothing, water power, and agriculture businesses through the end of the 1840s. In 1852, he participated in an expedition through Indian Territory to the Pacific Ocean. After the expedition, he moved to Illinois and immersed himself in agricultural production from 1854 until the beginning of the Civil War. He became the first colonel of the 14th Illinois Cavalry which was mustered into service in January 1863. Capron led the regiment in the pursuit of John Hunt Morgan during his raid into the north in the summer of 1863. Then, the regiment accompanied Ambrose Burnside's advance on Knoxville and subsequently participated in the East Tennessee Campaign in the winter of 1863–1864. He commanded a brigade during the Atlanta Campaign until Stoneman's Raid in late July and early August, and he com-

Colonel Horace Capron, one of the oldest Union cavalry commanders, directed a brigade until the end of November (Library of Congress).

manded the remnants of the brigade after the campaign. He would lead his brigade until December 1 when Colonel Thomas Harrison assumed command.[21]

Colonel Thomas J. Harrison was a man of "large and command presence" and he was greatly liked by his men as an effective and efficient commander. Harrison, a native of Shelby County, Kentucky, moved to Crawfordsville, Indiana, when he was six years old. He attended Wabash College, but did not complete his program of study. He left college in 1849, moved to Kokomo, and began teaching school. While teaching, he studied law under the supervision of Judge Nathaniel Linsday, his future father-in-law. He completed his studies and joined a partnership with Judge Linsday. In 1858, he was elected to the state legislature and was one of the first to enlist when the war began. After serving in a three-month regiment, he aided in raising the 39th Indiana Infantry and was commissioned colonel. He led the regiment at the Battle of Stones Rivers. Harrison succeeded in mounting the regiment in the spring 1863, and the regiment subsequently became the 8th Indiana Cavalry in October. Harrison's command made significant contributions during the Battle of Chickamauga operating on the southern flank before the battle and his men aided in the defense of a cavalry supply train on the way to the battle. On the last day of the Battle of Chickamauga, Harrison's Spencer rifles joined those of John Wilder's brigade in an attack on the left flank of the Confederate infantry. Harrison commanded a brigade during Rousseau's Raid (July 10–22) and commanded the provisional cavalry division during McCook's Raid (July 27–30), in which he was captured and later exchanged. Harrison was an experienced commander at home at the head of the column.[22]

James Biddle, born in Philadelphia on December 11, 1832, had a strong connection with the military and northern politics. His grandfather was the deputy quartermaster-general of the Continental Army during the Revolution and his grandmother was the daughter of the governor of Rhode Island. He enlisted when the Civil War began and received a commission as first lieutenant and quartermaster of the 10th New York Volunteers on May 2, 1861. He soon received a promotion and a commission as captain in the U.S. infantry. Biddle worked with the Union forces in Kentucky in 1862 and received recognition for his contributions during the Battle of Richmond (Kentucky) on November 11, 1862, earning him command of a regiment and a promotion to the rank of colonel. Most

Colonel James Biddle (Mollus Mass Civil War Collection, United States Army Heritage and Education Center, Carlisle, Pennsylvania).

of the 71st Indiana Infantry was captured during the Union defeat in this battle and the remainder of the regiment was reorganized as the 6th Indiana Cavalry which Biddle would command. The 6th Indiana Cavalry spent most of the next year in Indiana as part of the District of Indiana and Michigan and joined in the pursuit of John Hunt Morgan during his raid into Indiana and Ohio the following summer of 1863. In October 1863, Biddle and the 6th Indiana Cavalry (four companies) were attached to headquarters of IX Corps and joined in the Knoxville Campaign. He commanded a provisional brigade during the Battle of Campbell's Station. Subsequently, his regiment participated in several actions in the East Tennessee Campaign including the siege of Knoxville and the fighting at Bull's Gap. He returned his regiment to Mount Sterling, Kentucky, to be remounted and in April 1864, Biddle was given brigade command in the Army of the Ohio. During the Atlanta Campaign, Biddle commanded the Second Brigade in Stoneman's cavalry (16th Illinois, 5th Indiana, 6th Indiana, 12th Kentucky). He was captured on July 31, 1864, and imprisoned for two months after Stoneman's ill-fated raid to Macon, Georgia, with most of Stoneman's cavalry. Biddle and his command had been subsequently returned to Middle Tennessee but these troopers had no mounts.[23]

Joseph F. Knipe's Division

Joseph Farmer Knipe was born on March 20, 1823, at Mount Joy, Pennsylvania, the son of a blacksmith. Knipe apprenticed as a cobbler in Philadelphia, but seeking a different life, he enlisted in the 2nd U.S. Artillery in 1842. Knipe advanced in rank to sergeant at the beginning of the Mexican War, but in 1847 he left the army and began an occupation in the railroad industry. After a while, he moved to the mercantile business. As the Civil War approached, he enlisted in the Pennsylvania militia and served as aide-de-camp to General Edward Williams, a personal friend of Knipe's. When the war began, Knipe, promoted to the rank of major, remained with General Williams who worked to organize and train new volunteers. In September 1861, Knipe was selected colonel of the 46th Pennsylvania Infantry and the regiment was sent to man the garrison at Harper's Ferry.[24]

Knipe commanded his regiment in the campaign against Stonewall Jackson's forces in the Shenandoah Campaign in 1862. He was wounded in the First Battle of Winchester and again wounded at the Battle of Cedar

General Joseph Knipe (Library of Congress).

Mountain. During the Battle of Antietam, Knipe gained brigade command after the death of General Joseph Mansfield. He was promoted to the rank of brigadier general on April 13, 1863, and two weeks later he faced Stonewall Jackson's surprise flank attack in northern Virginia. At Chancellorsville, Knipe commanded the Second Brigade in Alpheus Williams' division in XII Corps and reported 452 casualties as his brigade worked at stopping the Confederate attack which had been so successful on XI Corps. Knipe was away from the army during the Gettysburg Campaign recuperating from his wounds and malaria. After the Battle of Gettysburg, Knipe and his corps moved to Chattanooga to support Rosecrans' besieged Army of the Cumberland. Here, Knipe's brigade had security duty protecting the railroad connection from Nashville to Chattanooga. Next, he commanded the First Brigade of William's division in XX Corps (occasionally commanding the division) during the Atlanta Campaign and provided leadership in the major battles during the campaign.[25]

In an interesting twist in his career, Knipe requested duty commanding cavalry after the Atlanta Campaign. On September 18, Knipe was given command as chief of cavalry for the Army of the Tennessee much to the displeasure of Benjamin Grierson, but this was to be a short assignment due to Wilson's decision a month later to do away with all the chiefs of cavalry. Instead, Knipe assumed the command of the Seventh Cavalry Division on November 16, but Wilson intended to send Knipe back to infantry command for which he might have been more ably suited. There can be no doubt that Knipe had proved his worth in the numerous battles during the war and probably deserved a promotion to a rank such as chief of cavalry. Although Wilson worried about an infantry commander leading one of his divisions, Knipe again proved himself and remained as a cavalry division commander until the end of the war.[26]

Brigadier General John Henry Hammond was born June 30, 1833, in New York City. His father died when he was still a young boy and his family moved to Campbell County, Kentucky. Hammond was educated in Bethany, Virginia. From approximately 1847 to 1851, he attended Jesuit College in Cincinnati and completed a course of study in civil engineering. Afterwards, he worked in New York for a couple of years before returning to the family farm for a year. Next, Hammond went to Clinton, Iowa, from October of 1854 to 1857. He traveled to Spain and Switzerland where he learned about grape and wine production. In 1857, he traveled to California to begin experimenting with grape production there. When the war began, Hammond returned to Kentucky and received an appointment as assistant adjutant general on Sherman's staff with the rank of major. On December 12, 1863, Major General John Logan recommended Hammond for promotion due to his "energy and industry of office…. He has enterprise, zeal for the cause, and personal bravery, and great perseverance."[27]

Hammond gained recognition during the Battle of Shiloh where he was noted as having offered important service in rallying and directing the troops. By May, Hammond was acknowledged as Sherman's chief of staff. By December 1862, Hammond had been promoted to the rank of lieutenant colonel and he remained at that rank and position until the mid-winter (1863–1864) when Hammond was released from adjutant general duties and served solely as Sherman's chief of staff. A few months later Hammond was assigned duty dealing with new recruits for Sherman's armies. Logan's recommendation for promotion received endorsement from Ulysses Grant, and upon Wilson's arrival to command the cavalry in the west, Hammond was given command of a brigade in Knipe's division at the rank of brigadier general. Certainly, the recommendations of such high-ranking officers as Logan, Grant and Sherman influenced Wilson's decision. While Wilson worked to ensure that cavalry officers had previous experience commanding cavalry, his decision to put Hammond in charge of a cavalry brigade remains somewhat puzzling. Hammond quickly proved his worth as the Nashville Campaign began and he proved a solid, aggressive commander in Wilson's cavalry.[28]

Seventh Cavalry Division—Brig. Gen. Joseph F. Knipe

November–December 1864 Campaign	
First Brigade— Brig Gen. John H. Hammond	*Second Brigade—* Col. Gilbert M.L. Johnson
9th Indiana, Col. George W. Jackson	12th Indiana, Col. Edward Anderson
10th Indiana, Lt. Col. Benjamin Gresham	13th Indiana, Lt. Col. William T. Pepper
19th Pennsylvania, Lt. Col. Joseph C. Hess	6th Tennessee, Col. Fielding Hurst
2nd Tennessee, Lt. Col. William R. Cook	Ohio Light, 14th Battery, Lt. Wm. Myers
4th Tennessee, Lt. Col. Jacob M. Thornburgh	

Gilbert Marquis Lafayette Johnson was born in Warren County, Ohio, on November 4, 1837. Before the war he was a "commission merchant." When the war began he was elected first lieutenant in the 2nd Indiana Cavalry and in April 1862 he was promoted to the rank of captain. When the 11th Indiana Cavalry was organized in March 1864, he took over as lieutenant colonel of the regiment. The next month he was given command of the newly organized 13th Indiana Cavalry. The 13th Indiana Cavalry, the last cavalry regiment to be organized in Indiana during the war, was organized in Kokomo and New Albany, Indiana. Johnson was appointed colonel on April 19, 1864, and was assigned duty in Nashville and Huntsville guarding the railroad. While participating in the defense of the railroad during Forrest's raid in September and October, Johnson had his first significant action with the defense of Huntsville from Abraham Buford's attack. Soon afterwards, the regiment was shipped to Paducah in anticipation of a Confederate attack. Then, it was moved to Louisville to be mounted, and it returned to La Vergne, Tennessee, on December 1.[29]

Chief of Cavalry—James H. Wilson

James Harrison Wilson was born near Shawneetown, Illinois, in 1837, near the Ohio River. Wilson's family emigrated from Virginia to Kentucky and then on to Illinois. His grandfather served in the first Illinois legislature and the Wilson family became financially and politically influential in Illinois. His father was a ferryman, sheriff, stockraiser, and county treasurer at Shawneetown, and he served in the militia in the Black Hawk War. During the conflict, Wilson's father met such notable regular army figures as Winfield Scott, Zachary Taylor, Jefferson Davis, Albert Sidney Johnston, and Joseph E. Johnston. James Wilson showed himself to be smart and efficient early in his life. He attended local schools until he was 15 years old. He enrolled in McKendree College in the winter of 1854–1855 in preparation for his introduction into West Point.[30]

Wilson received his appointment to West Point through the endorsement of Major Samuel K. Casey, Captain John M. Cunningham, Samuel S. Marshall and U.S. Representative Willis Allen, "my warm personal friends." He entered West Point on July 5, 1855, as the only class to be enrolled as a five-year class. One hundred and twenty students arrived to begin their education as the Class of 1860. Wilson finished sixth in a class of 41 at the United States Military Academy in 1860 that included fellow cavalryman, Wesley Merritt. He was referred to as one of the "boy wonders" by historian James Jones.[31]

Wilson opposed slavery but he believed that the law allowed it. He also supported Stephen Douglas over Lincoln in the 1860 election. Upon graduation, Wilson was commissioned second lieutenant of Topographical Engineers at Fort Vancouver in Washington. Wilson served as topographical engineer early in the war and he joined in one of the first amphibious expeditions of the war in the Port Royal Expedition. While this action was successful, Wilson thought the land forces had been underutilized and that they should have been pushed overland. Next, he participated in the Battle of Fort Pulaski on the Savannah River in Georgia. The fort surrendered in April 1862 in the successful Union operation and Wilson received a promotion to the rank of major for his actions. Wilson remained on duty near Hilton Head while the Peninsula Campaign was fought to the north, but in August he received orders to report to Washington for assignment. In Wilson's memoirs, he did not speak highly of his commanders and showed a clear lack of humility; "I had done my best to encourage my commanding officers and to embolden them to push forward against the enemy, and while I had failed, it is pleasant to reflect that I had not made myself a nuisance nor lost their friendship." Upon his arrival in Washington, he learned that Grant needed engineering officers and he decided to request assignment with him. Until he received an appointment to Grant's command, he offered his services to the army in the east. He felt he might provide some service as aide-de-camp to George McClellan during the Maryland Campaign. Wilson disliked Halleck and soon became disillusioned by McClellan during and after the Battle of Antietam, which strengthened his resolve to join Grant's army. Wilson transferred to the war in the west as part of Grant's staff in November 1862, and in 1863 he served as inspector general and Chief of Topographical Engineers of the Army of the Tennessee where he had risen to the rank of lieutenant colonel in January 1863. Wilson accompanied Grant's armies through the Vicksburg Campaign, to Chattanooga, and East Tennessee. He made powerful allies of Grant and his chief of staff, John Rawlins. "My relations with both Rawlins and our common chief grew more and more intimate, and as long as we served together we were as three men with but a single purpose," wrote Wilson. As Grant rose in his career, Wilson cultivated this increasingly powerful ally. He became adept as operating in the political, as well as the military, environment within Grant's army. Major General William Rosecrans offered him a position commanding three engineer regiments, but Wilson discovered that Grant planned to promote him to the rank of brigadier general. He chose to defer commanding the engineers with a rank of colonel for the new position with a rank of general, approved early in 1864.[32]

In early 1864, Grant also began looking for an appropriate cavalry officer to replace George Crook who had been transferred to the war in West Virginia. In an interesting set of communications, it was a request from Assistant Secretary of War Charles Dana that decided Crook's replacement; however, the decision was apparently made without consultation with George Thomas or Washington L. Elliott. Dana requested

James H. Wilson, who served as inspector general for Grant, to be chief of the U.S. Cavalry Bureau. "It is a question of saving millions of money and rendering the cavalry arm everywhere efficient," remarked Dana. The result was essentially a swap, Wilson for Kenner Garrard. Garrard had been running the Cavalry Bureau, and when Wilson went to Washington, Garrard was assigned command of the Second Cavalry Division in the Army of the Cumberland. Wilson would state in his memoirs that he improved the acquisition of mounts and arms for the cavalry in his short stay in the Cavalry Bureau. He also opposed the organization of Tennessee cavalry regiments until proper arms and mounts could be obtained. Ironically, when Wilson assumed command of the cavalry in Tennessee in 1864, he found that Andrew Johnson had organized several regiments which had been rejected in Washington. The Tennessee cavalry regiments were stationed in relative proximity to their homes and therefore many of the soldiers were often absent. Wilson explained: "It was a great disappointment to find these regiments under my command, but it was my plain duty to do the best I could to make them effective. Under the ample authority allowed me I scattered them among the Northern troops where they would have closer supervision and better discipline, but many of the officers were untrained and inefficient." Discipline became an immediate and troubling issue, just as Richard Johnson had found with some of the Tennessee regiments. "A number were drunken rowdies who used their authority to terrorize the people among whom they were stationed. Several field officers were court-martialed and dismissed for absence without leave, and this made it necessary to fill the vacancies with better men, not always the next in rank." To make these necessary changes in rank by the most effective commanders rather than the commanders next in line required the agreement of Governor Andrew Johnson. When Wilson visited Johnson, he described his experience: "He received me with coldness and reserve, and, when I stated my business, which I did frankly and fully, he became angry and burst out with the declaration that he would not permit me to asperse the Tennessee cavalry or its officers, alleging that they were as good as any in the service. As this was far from the fact and we were from the start widely at variance on the subject, I rose to take my leave, remarking: 'I am sorry I called upon you, Governor. I hoped to obtain your friendly cooperation, but I have made a mistake and will try to get on without your help.' Whereupon he said: 'Why are you sorry?' To which I replied: 'Because I am disillusioned. I came here thinking that you were a statesman and patriot, but I am sorry to find that you are merely a politician of the common sort. I read your speech in the Senate against secession and I said to myself, here is a man worthy to be President, but this interview convinces me that I am wrong.'" Wilson observed that after this direct confrontation Johnson became conciliatory, but he never trusted him afterward.[33]

By May 1864, Wilson was released from his duties with the Cavalry Bureau and sent directly to command the 3rd Division in Phil Sheridan's cavalry corps in Virginia. Wilson was often out-spoken and did not suffer from a lack of confidence. He often told others, including his superiors, why the operations, personnel, and organization of the army were defective. He did this as part of a group of officers in whom Grant placed his confidence. Recently arriving at Grant's armies in the east, he declared: "The simple fact was that the army organization itself was bad throughout. The staff arrangements were sadly defective and orders for movements were frequently lacking in detail and coherence, and were, therefore, executed poorly and ineffectually."[34]

Wilson's appraisal for his appointment was outlined in his memoirs. "Obviously,

Wilson (center, slightly reclining, with right arm on the step and scabbard visible by his left leg) with his staff in the eastern theater, summer 1864 (Library of Congress).

I owed the opportunity which the new detail brought me largely to General Grant's impressions while serving with him in the close and intimate relations of the two great campaigns of Vicksburg and Chattanooga. Those good impressions had doubtless been strengthened by my administration of the Cavalry Bureau as well as by my experience with the Third Cavalry Division in the Virginia campaigns. It was perhaps known to him that a prejudice existed against me on the part of those who had been overslaughed by my assignment to that command, but this strengthened rather than weakened me with him for the simple reason that he was not only responsible for it, but subject to a similar criticism from those he had superseded in still higher command." Wilson reasoned that Grant's recommendation had to be approved by the secretary of war and president and so his appointment was by the approval of his superiors, not just Grant.[35]

Wilson arrived at Sherman's headquarters at Gaylesville, Alabama, on October 22 and he discussed the situation in Tennessee, Alabama, and Georgia with him. After a formal meeting, Sherman and Wilson talked over a campfire on a "clear, fresh, and crisp" night in front of Sherman's tent. Sherman had all but given up hope of drawing Hood into a decisive battle and he concluded to begin his march to the sea "content to leave him to the care of General Thomas, although he did not seem to have any clear idea of the troops Thomas would be able to gather, how long it would take, or when they would be able to confront the enemy. He had selected the flower of his three armies, amounting to about sixty thousand infantry and five thousand cavalry, with plenty of artillery, all under his favorite leaders, for his own column..." Wilson discussed the situation regarding other cavalry officers who were his seniors in experience—W.L. Elliott, Kenner Garrard, George Stoneman and Benjamin Grierson. Wilson wrote: "They were all my seniors and, although my brevet and my assignment there under gave me an indisputable right to command them, I thought it best for all concerned that they should be disposed of as Garrard had been, and, as Sherman fully concurred, they were also relieved in turn from further service with the cavalry." Wilson also decided to gather all the scattered cavalry regiments and escorts and drew them back in the cavalry corps. Sherman directed Wilson to go to Nashville to assist Thomas, while H. Judson Kilpatrick's division was fully remounted and armed to join Sherman's march across Georgia.[36]

The reorganization of the cavalry did not come without its share of controversy. One of the warhorses for the Union cavalry in the west was Benjamin Grierson. Grierson had command of two divisions of cavalry in the west—Hatch's and Winslow's divisions. Grierson was flabbergasted in October, before Wilson's appointment, when he discovered Knipe had assumed command of the cavalry, as chief of cavalry, in Mississippi and western Tennessee instead of Grierson. Grierson appealed directly to Sherman to reverse this decision which had been made by O.O. Howard. Sherman and Howard tried to calm Grierson while reassuring him that Knipe would not directly command cavalry but instead, he would be the chief of cavalry, in a more staff-like position. Howard wrote to Grierson: "Surely you do not wish to leave the field and go upon staff duty." When Wilson took command, he finalized Howard's decision to give Grierson command of a single division. He ordered Grierson to assume command of Winslow's division. Grierson's and Wilson's subsequent interaction would be so contentious that it would result in Wilson's removal of Grierson from command of the division in December.[37]

In summary, the Union cavalry was now commanded by the politically and militarily connected James H. Wilson, whose biographer characterized him as "ambitious, impatient, outspoken, a stranger to humility and self-doubt." While Wilson added the much-needed energy to the cavalry in the west, he had spent only about six months in the saddle and appeared, at least in his memoirs, to have the unique insight in correcting most of the problems in the military organization and operations in the Civil War as he gained the upper hand in his encounters with the politicians he met. His memoirs and his insights might have been clearly different had he entered in the war in 1862 at Nashville where he would have faced six Confederate cavalry brigades with only two of his own. His callousness of dispatching Garrard, Elliott and Grierson would have been more palatable had Wilson offered a good reason for the dismissal rather than simply they were senior to him.[38]

Chapter Four

The Confederate Cavalry in the Nashville Campaign

"War means fighting and fighting means killing."
—attributed to Nathan Bedford Forrest

On November 14, 1863, Nathan Bedford Forrest moved to a new cavalry command into West Tennessee and Mississippi, and by the end of the month, he established his headquarters at Holly Springs, Mississippi. His assigned territory included the northern part of the Department of East Louisiana and Mississippi. When Forrest arrived at his new assignment, the cavalry of this Confederate department fell under the command of Major General Stephen Dill Lee. Although Forrest would not be active for some months, the term "Forrest's Command," also known as Forrest's Cavalry, first appeared in the *Official Records* after March 1, 1864, and, at that time, he reported directly to Lee. Both James Chalmers' and Abraham Buford's divisions had also been organized at this point. Wirt Adams' cavalry division also served in Mississippi under Lee's command, separately from Forrest's cavalry corps. The other cavalry division reporting directly to Lee was that of William Hicks Jackson's command of five brigades. Lee was not altogether pleased with Forrest's arrival in Mississippi, because initially, it appeared that the War Department wanted Forrest and Lee to have equal commands. This did not sit well with Lee. Leonidas Polk intervened on the behalf of Lee, and Lee gained overall command of the cavalry in Mississippi and Louisiana. The situation quickly advanced past these initial concerns, because both Lee, who would be promoted to command of the Department of Alabama, Mississippi, and East Louisiana in May 1864, and part of Jackson's division would join the Army of Tennessee during the Atlanta Campaign. In August, Lee moved to Atlanta and Dabney Maury assumed command of the military department upon Lee's departure. Upon Maury's arrival in August, he found about 7,000 cavalry troops in Mississippi, western Tennessee, and eastern Louisiana. In regard to this cavalry force, Wirt Adams was assigned to the area from Natchez to Grenada along the Mississippi river. Forrest maintained his position in northern Mississippi with the largest cavalry force of about 6,000 men. Brigadier General Philip Roddey was ordered to support Forrest from his territory in northern Alabama. Roddey had the additional responsibility of harassing the rear of Sherman's armies whenever practical.[1]

Nathan Bedford Forrest had a war's worth of experience behind him and he had an impressive string of victories. A Tennessee native, Forrest proved to be one of the most talented Confederate cavalry officers in the war. Forrest was born in 1821 near Chapel Hill, Tennessee, and he grew up in modest means. Due to the death of his father, he became the provider for his family by the time he was in his teens. He married Mary Montgomery in 1845 and became rich in financial dealings with livestock, real estate and slave trading. When the war began he enlisted as a private and raised a cavalry battalion at his own expense. Forrest gained national attention when he refused to surrender his command at Fort Donelson and he led his troops through Union lines rather than surrender. He participated in the Battle of Shiloh and caused havoc to the Union army in Tennessee and Mississippi afterward.[2]

Forrest was recognized as one of the most the efficient and effective cavalry commanders in the Civil War. He was a master at offensive actions, and historian John R. Sanders remarked that Forrest's leadership skill in the areas of "maneuver, firepower, deception, offense and leadership fairly leap off the page." Much has been written about this Confederate cavalry commander who like Sherman was not always likeable, but who thought war was not something to be liked. Forrest, with almost no formal training, rose to one of the highest ranks in the Confederate Army and he gained the respect of his comrades and enemies alike. Many historians have analyzed Forrest's command abilities; a commander with a complex personality who fought to win. He earned the respect of his men while demanding discipline. His approaches to fighting were always practical and often unorthodox. Among the quotes attributed to Forrest is "war means fighting and fighting means killing."[3]

Chalmers' Division

In the Nashville Campaign, Forrest would operate with three divisions. Just as in the Union cavalry, the Southern cavalry in the Nashville Campaign was commanded by experienced officers who had been through some of the most significant fighting in the western theater. Brigadier General James Ronald Chalmers, commander of Forrest's First Division, was born in Halifax County, Virginia, on January 11, 1831. His family relocated to Holly Springs, Mississippi, while Chalmers was still young. He continued his educational training at South Carolina College and then returned home to Holly Springs to prepare for a career as an attorney. He was admitted to the Mississippi Bar in 1853. Chalmers had a promising career before him and he served as district attorney before the war, but the fires of secession blazed in Mississippi in 1860 and 1861. He served as a delegate in the secession convention in Mississippi, and on January 9, 1861, the state voted to leave the Union. As the war began, Chalmers became the colonel of the 9th Mississippi Infantry and the regiment was sent to Pensacola where Chalmers served under Braxton Bragg. Chalmers became a brigade commander in the fall of 1861 and brigadier general early in 1862.[4]

Chalmers' contribution to the Confederacy was immediate and his command abilities were recognized by his commanding officers. In February 1862, he was given command of the Confederate troops between Memphis and the Tennessee River. At the Battle of Shiloh, Chalmers' Second Brigade served in Brigadier General Jones M. Withers' Second Division of Bragg's Corps, and Chalmers suffered about 450 casualties during the battle. Bragg wrote of Chalmers' actions: "Brig. Gen. James R. Chalmers, at the head of his gallant Mississippians filled—he could not have exceeded—the measure of my expectations. Never were troops and commander more worthy of each other and of their State." After the Battle of Shiloh, Chalmers commanded a cavalry brigade, but his health began to deteriorate. He gave up his command to Joseph Wheeler who happened to be the right person at the right time. After his recuperation, Chalmers commanded an infantry brigade during the Stones River Campaign in Wither's division and he was wounded by an exploding shell during the battle. The losses to Chalmers' brigade were again high, totaling almost 550 casualties during the battle.[5]

By April 1863, Chalmers had command of the Confederate troops in northern Mississippi, and his attentions were focused on organizing mounted troops. In the months after the Stones River battle, Chalmers, still recovering from his wound, had been given command of the Fifth Military District of the Department of Mississippi and East Louisiana under overall command of Lieutenant General John C. Pemberton. The Union armies firmly held Memphis and easily moved out of Memphis and LaGrange on expeditions into Mississippi. In addition, the Union armies were determined to capture Vicksburg and, as a result, large concentrations of enemy infantry and cavalry were constantly present. Chalmers maintained what presence he could in northern Mississippi throughout the Vicksburg Campaign and during its aftermath. In October 1863, he initiated a raid in northern Mississippi and into western Tennessee. Afterward, Chalmers' efforts were directed at harassing Union forces and destroying the railroads. Chalmers next significant actions were at Collierville, Moscow, and La Fayette; he was often pitted against Edward Hatch's cavalry, armed with repeating rifles, which proved to be a formidable adversary. Chalmers' raids could not have been expected to be great military successes, but rather served as diversions, joint actions with S.D. Lee's cavalry and nuisance actions against a superior enemy. Help was on the way for Chalmers when Forrest arrived after the Chickamauga Campaign.[6]

However, things were not going well for Chalmers who typically commanded 700–2,000 troops, when in November, General Samuel Ferguson assumed command of the troops of northern Mississippi. Chalmers' command reverted back to those troops he had previously commanded in northern Mississippi, essentially the command of a small division of cavalry (Slemon's and McCulloch's brigades) and sometimes just a single brigade. In addition, Chalmers had issues with Joseph Johnston and he wrote to Johnston's chief of staff Benjamin Ewell, "I have received more reprimands lately from General Johnston than in all my military career previously, which I think were evidences of great dissatisfaction, and I feel that I am not fully trusted, because I am the senior brigadier in the cavalry of Mississippi, and am kept in command of a brigade, while my junior commands a division." Chalmers' actions in Mississippi also caused some controversy with the local citizens as he carried out orders to destroy cotton

General James R. Chalmers, a cool, level-headed commander who fought to the end (Library of Congress).

rather allow it to fall into Union hands. In addition, Forrest's arrival began a struggle for command of the troops in Mississippi, Alabama, Louisiana, and western Tennessee. Chalmers watched as he initially received orders from Lee and "requests" from Forrest regarding his brigade. In February, Chalmers participated in the repulse of William Sooy Smith's cavalry expedition during the Meridian Campaign. In March and April, Chalmers' division participated in Forrest's raid into western Kentucky and Tennessee, including the incident at Fort Pillow where Forrest proudly described, "The river was dyed with the blood of the slaughtered for 200 yards." On March 10, 1864, Forrest became disenchanted with Chalmers and decided to have him relieved of command. "I am satisfied that I have not and shall not receive the co-operation of Brigadier-General Chalmers, and that matters of the smallest moment will continue, as they have heretofore done, to be a source of annoyance to myself and detrimental to the service, and, holding myself responsible to the proper authority for all orders I have or may hereafter issue, I deem it both necessary and beneficial that we should separate." However, Chalmers was not removed and initially the two often operated apart geographically. The command issue calmed somewhat as time passed and Chalmers participated in the subsequent cavalry actions under Forrest's command in 1864.[7]

Chalmer's Division: Brig. Gen. James R. Chalmers

Rucker's Brigade: Col. Edmund W. Rucker		**Biffle's Brigade:** Col. Jacob B. Biffle
7th Alabama	5th Mississippi	4th Tennessee Cavalry
7th Tennessee	12th Tennessee	9th Tennessee Cavalry
14th Tennessee	15th Tennessee	10th Tennessee Cavalry
26th Tennessee Battalion (Forrest's Regiment Tennessee Cavalry) Young's (Croft's Georgia) battery		

Tennessean Edmund Winchester Rucker was born on July 22, 1835, in Rutherford County. Rucker received his early education in the country schools of Wilson County, Tennessee. His father was a country doctor and a farmer and his mother was the daughter of a general who served in the war of 1812. Rucker spent much of his youth on the family farms in Wilson and DeKalb Counties and while receiving no further formal education, he left home at the age of 18 to join a surveying crew working on the Nashville & Decatur Railroad. Through these experiences, he moved to Memphis and set up a business as an engineer. In 1858, he was named city engineer for Memphis. Just before Tennessee seceded, he enlisted in a company of sappers and miners and was assigned duty at Columbus, Kentucky, and at Fort Pillow on the Mississippi River. Although Rucker enlisted as a private, his experience proved valuable to this company and he was promoted to the rank of lieutenant of engineers in the summer of 1861. Soon thereafter, he was promoted to the rank of captain of artillery and he commanded a company of Illinois men who manned Battery No. 1 during the Siege of New Madrid and Island No. 10. Rucker was praised by Brigadier General John P. McCown as performing his duty with "obstinate courage worthy of praise."[8]

In the summer of 1862, he again transferred, assumed command of the 16th ("Rucker's") Tennessee Cavalry Battalion, and was sent to eastern Tennessee. He commanded garrisons at Cleveland and Kingston where he had the unpleasant task of rounding up conscripts. In 1863, his battalion was united with the 12th Tennessee Battalion to form Rucker's Legion attached to Forrest's cavalry corps. At this point in the war, Rucker had little combat experience but he led this command in the Chickamauga Campaign. Rucker's regiment served in Brigadier General Henry B. Davidson's brigade in Pegram's cavalry division during the battle. After Chickamauga, Rucker became part of John Kelly's division and Warren Grigsby's brigade in Wheeler's corps. When Forrest transferred to Mississippi, Rucker and his command also moved west. When he arrived in Mississippi in May 1864, he was given brigade command in Chalmers' division. His initial command consisted of the 8th Mississippi Regiment, 18th Mississippi Battalion, and 7th Tennessee Regiment. Rucker's brigade fought at Brice's Crossroads and at Tupelo where Rucker was severely wounded and his brigade was noted for gallantry during the battle. After the battle at Tupelo, Rucker's brigade was dissolved.[9]

Rucker recuperated from his wounds and he received a strong endorsement from Forrest to return to duty at the end of August. He was assigned command of "Rucker's Brigade" which included the 7th Tennessee Cavalry, Neely's Tennessee cavalry regiment, 12th Tennessee Cavalry, Stewart's Tennessee cavalry regiment, and the 26th Tennessee Battalion Cavalry (Forrest's old regiment). Chalmers again served as his division commander.[10]

Jacob Barnett Biffle commanded the Second Brigade in Chalmers' division. He was born on May 31, 1830, in Wayne County, Tennessee. The military was in his blood, his father having served in the War of 1812, and he would prove to be an effective cavalry commander for the Confederacy. Before the war, Biffle was a "well-to-do Wayne County" farmer with personal property amounting to greater than $40,000. At the onset of the war, Biffle assisted in the formation of Biffle's 2nd Tennessee Battalion that would be consolidated to form the 6th (1st) Tennessee Cavalry under the command of Colonel James T. Wheeler in the summer of 1862. When Wheeler was appointed colonel of the regiment, Biffle decided to raise a new regiment in October 1862. The regiment would be organized as the 19th Tennessee Cavalry, but it would be mustered out as the 9th Tennessee Cavalry at the end of the war. Biffle's

Colonel Edmund Rucker, a Tennessean of "obstinate courage worthy of praise" (Alabama Department of Archives and History, Montgomery, Alabama).

regiment joined Forrest's raid into western Tennessee in December 1862 and saw action at Jackson and Parker's Crossroads. Next, Biffle had the unpleasant duty of rounding up stragglers, conscripts, and deserters early in 1863, but in March he joined the cavalry action in the Union defeats at Thompson's Station and Brentwood. Biffle's cavalry also saw action at Chapel Hill and Savannah later in the spring. He remained active in Nicholas N. Cox's/George Dibrell's brigade of Forrest's cavalry division and the regiment provided good service throughout the spring and summer in several skirmishes in Tennessee and Mississippi. At Chickamauga, Biffle's regiment (now known at the 9th Tennessee) was part of Dibrell's brigade of Armstrong's cavalry division.[11]

When Forrest transferred to Mississippi, Biffle remained with Wheeler's newly reorganized cavalry near Chattanooga and participated in Wheeler's October 1863 raid and the East Tennessee Campaign in the winter of 1863–1864 in Brigadier General William Y.C. Humes' brigade in Armstrong's division. Then, in late 1863, Biffle became the brigade commander in Longstreet's cavalry in eastern Tennessee. He returned to Joseph Wheeler's command as the east Tennessee campaign fizzled and when the Atlanta Campaign began, he returned to command his old regiment in George Dibrell's brigade in Will Martin's division. Biffle joined Wheeler on his August–September raid through Tennessee. He was re-assigned to Forrest's command after the Atlanta Campaign leading a brigade of Tennessee cavalry, a part of Dibrell's old brigade, about 2,000 men strong, and joined in Forrest's raid into northern Alabama and Tennessee in September–October 1864.[12]

Biffle's brigade would operate as a demi-brigade (9th, 10th, and half of the 4th Tennessee regiments) in the upcoming campaign. The rest of the brigade, Shaw's Battalion and 13th Tennessee regiment along with part of the 4th Tennessee, would remain in Georgia under the command of Joseph Wheeler.[13]

Buford's Division

Abraham Buford, born on January 18, 1820, came from a prosperous family in Woodford County, Kentucky. Buford had two cousins who also became generals in the Civil War, Napoleon and John. All three of the Bufords attended West Point. Abraham, "Abe," Buford initially attended Centre College in Danville, Kentucky, before attending West Point where he graduated in 1841. His initial military service began along the western frontier. Like many military men of the time, Buford participated in the Mexican War and received a promotion to the rank of captain for bravery at Buena Vista. In 1854, he resigned from the army and moved back to Versailles where he spent his time raising and training race horses. While his cousins joined the Union Army, Abraham did not commit his services and experience to either side, preferring to remain neutral. When Bragg entered Kentucky during the Perryville Campaign, Buford decided to offer his services to the Confederacy and was appointed brigadier general on September 2, 1862, and given brigade command of the 3rd, 5th, and 6th Kentucky cavalries. Buford was a giant of a man, reportedly weighing 320 pounds, and he had a red beard and hair. Buford was a strong advocate of states' rights but opposed secession. He was described as the "son of Mars in temperament as physique, he was a born fighter, and … rigid a disciplinarian."[14]

First, Abraham Buford's brigade was ordered somewhat belatedly to join in the actions in Middle Tennessee in the fall of 1862 and thereafter, it was assigned primarily to support Wheeler's brigade in the Battle of Stones River. While Buford made the deepest penetration into the Union western flank on December 31, his troopers saw light action during the battle. He was not always cooperative in his interactions with other officers. Buford had only been in the war a few short months and by January 1863, he had had two clashes with other officers, first E. Kirby Smith and then after the Battle of Stones River with his subordinate, Colonel R.J. Butler of the 3rd Kentucky Cavalry. Bragg sent Buford, who had a "contentious personality," to Mississippi presumably to remove Buford from the charges and counter charges made by Butler.[15]

Buford arrived in Mississippi and was assigned brigade command of infantry in Major General William W. Loring's division. His first notable action occurred at Champion Hill where his brigade saw relatively light action. He commanded eight infantry regiments and eight artillery pieces during the battle. After the Union successes in the battle, Buford and the rest of Loring's division did not retreat to Vicksburg but remained at large and joined Joseph Johnston's troops. Buford remained in Loring's division generally throughout 1863 and into 1864. Buford participated in the Meridian Campaign, and in March 1864, he gained command of a cavalry division, supervising Colonel A.P. Thompson's (later Crossland's) and Colonel Tyree H. Bell's brigades in Forrest's cavalry. This cavalry division moved with Forrest into western Tennessee and Kentucky in March–April 1864 but did not directly participate in the fight at Fort Pillow. At the Battle of Tupelo, his division saw extensive action and Buford recorded about 1,000 casualties of the 3,200 men he commanded. Afterward, his division resisted A.J. Smith's Oxford Expedition and participated in Forrest's raid into northern Alabama and Tennessee in September–October 1864.[16]

General Abraham Buford, a native of Kentucky and a combative leader with a "contentious personality" (Alabama Department of Archives and History, Montgomery, Alabama).

Buford's Cavalry Division

Bell's Brigade: Col. Tyree H. Bell	**Crossland's Brigade:** Col. Edward Crossland
2nd Tennessee Cavalry	3rd Kentucky Cavalry
19th Tennessee Cavalry	7th Kentucky Cavalry
20th Tennessee Cavalry	8th Kentucky Cavalry
21st Tennessee Cavalry	12th Kentucky Cavalry
Nixon's Tennessee Cavalry Regiment	Huey's Kentucky Battalion

Chapter Four. The Confederate Cavalry in the Nashville Campaign

Tyree Harris Bell, a native Kentuckian, commanded Bell's Brigade of Buford's division. Bell, born on September 15, 1815, grew up on the family plantation at Gallatin, Tennessee, where the family had moved while Bell was still a boy. Bell was educated in country schools, most notably, the one-room, Thomas English School, and as he matured he eventually managed his own plantation. He was married in 1841 and his influential father-in-law, Josiah Walton, proved a worthy mentor for Bell. Walton was a strong Methodist with experience in politics and the military. In the winter of 1857, Bell moved his family to Dyer County where he bought 350 acres of land and began planting. Bell had nine children by the time the Civil War began.[17]

Bell supported Tennessee's decision to secede and assisted in the organization of a company of the "Newbern Blues" which became the 12th Tennessee Volunteer Infantry. Bell met with General Gideon Pillow to discuss the organization of the regiment and when the regimental elections were held, Bell was elected lieutenant colonel and Robert Milton Russell, an 1848 West Point graduate and former professional soldier, was elected colonel. The 12th Tennessee, made up mostly of men from Gibson County, spent the summer of 1861 near Union City and Jackson, and in early September the regiment moved to Columbus, Kentucky.

Bell, not a young man, commanded the 12th Tennessee when Russell assumed command of the brigade and he led the regiment at the Battle of Belmont in November 1861. Bell commanded the regiment at the Battle of Shiloh where he had two horses killed under him and he was shot in the chest, although this, fortunately, was only a "slight wound." After the Battle of Shiloh, new regimental elections placed Bell as colonel of the regiment and Russell returned to Gibson County to raise another regiment, but he was captured along the way. Bell, the new regimental commander, returned home for six weeks to recuperate from his wounds. Next, he led his regiment in the overwhelming Confederate victory at the Battle of Richmond; however, there exists few details of the extent of its participation in the fight. In the summer of 1863, Bell became interested in the activities of partisan mounted forces in Tennessee. He believed he could effectively recruit men for the Confederate cavalry to expel the Northern troops operating in Tennessee. In the meantime, he was elected as a delegate to the state political convention. Soon thereafter, Bell gave up command of the infantry regiment and

Colonel Tyree Harris Bell (*Life of Lieutenant General, Nathan Bedford Forrest*, **John Allan Wyeth, 1899**).

went to work as part of Gideon Pillow's Conscript Bureau, and he had charge of organizing small partisan bands and other local units into more cohesive fighting forces. Bell's brigade of irregulars arrived outside Chattanooga about the time Forrest was ordered to western Tennessee and Mississippi. Forrest met with Bell and he decided to add Bell to his command. Forrest initially appointed him to recruiting and conscription duty in the Trenton, Tennessee, area, but in early 1864, Bell was rewarded with command of a cavalry brigade consisting of five Tennessee regiments after Forrest observed Bell's participation in actions near Bolivar, the Hatchie River, and Collierville on December 23–27, 1863. Bell's brigade saw additional action during the Meridian Campaign, but Bell was sick and away from his command. Subsequently, Bell joined a raid to Paducah, Kentucky, in March 1864 and later, his brigade had notable service at Fort Pillow, Brice's Crossroads, Tupelo, and Johnsonville. Certainly, the action at Fort Pillow remains a painful event in the war and an unjustified atrocity in Tennessee in 1864. Bell filed no after-action report but acknowledged after the war that "promiscuous shooting" took place on both white and black soldiers and he stated this was "contrary to the commands of the commanding officer." Throughout the Confederate cavalry actions in 1864, Bell operated with the confidence of Forrest and he, in return, supported Forrest's actions. At Brice's Crossroads, Bell's brigade arrived in the nick of time to ensure Forrest's victory. His arrival earned him the nickname of "Blucher of Brice's Crossroad," but his arrival cost his brigade 40 percent of the Confederate casualties, a high price by any standard. At Connewah Crossroads in the Tupelo Campaign, Bell's brigade attacked Major General A.J. Smith's Union column only to be repulsed. He participated in the subsequent battle and recorded severe losses of about 400 of 1,300 men engaged in the battle. In addition, five of his regimental commanders were wounded. Bell liked Buford and enjoyed serving under his command. Bell's brigade recuperated after the Tupelo Campaign and joined Forrest's raid into Middle Tennessee at the end of September.[18]

Commanding Buford's Second Brigade was Colonel Edward Crossland, late colonel of the 7th Kentucky Mounted Infantry. He was born in Hickman County, Kentucky, on June 30, 1827. Prior to the war, he served as sheriff, later he became an attorney, and subsequently served in the Kentucky legislature. Crossland began the war as a captain in the 1st Kentucky Infantry and served the first year of the

Colonel Edward Crossland, commander of the Kentucky Brigade, "[b]rave, enterprising, kind, and considerate" (*Confederate Veteran*, 1911, Vol. 19).

war in this one-year regiment. Next, Crossland attained the rank of lieutenant colonel of the 7th Kentucky Infantry and after the Battle of Shiloh, when the colonel of the regiment had been killed, the 7th Kentucky reorganized and Crossland was elected colonel. In early 1864, the 7th Kentucky was mounted and Crossland was given brigade command in Forrest's cavalry. Crossland was wounded three times during the war, one time at Paducah in March 1864, the next time at Tupelo in July 1864, and once in the Nashville Campaign. He was described as "[b]rave, enterprising, kind, and considerate."[19]

Jackson's Cavalry Division

William "Red" Hicks Jackson, born October 1, 1835, in Paris, Tennessee, was the son of a physician. Although Jackson appears to have many nicknames, the family correspondence referred to him as "Billy" and he signed many of his letters as "Bill." The family moved to Jackson, Tennessee, in 1840. His brother would also become notable in his own right—Howell Edmunds Jackson, a future justice of the United States Supreme Court. William H. Jackson attended college in west Tennessee for a short time before accepting an appointment to the United States Military Academy in 1852. In 1856, he graduated 38th in a class of 49 graduates which included Lunsford Lomax and Fitzhugh Lee. Upon graduation, Jackson received a commission as second lieutenant in the Mounted Rifles, a cavalry-like regiment in the United States Army. The Mounted Rifles, originally referred to as mounted infantry, had very vague duties and ultimately was re-designated as the 3rd U.S. Cavalry. Jackson spent the years before the war at various locations on the western frontier, including Fort Bliss, Texas, and Fort Craig, New Mexico Territory. His duties resulted in interactions with the indigenous populations, including the Navajo tribe, and he participated in actions against the Kiowa and Comanche tribes.[20]

About a month after the firing on Fort Sumter and a month before Tennessee seceded from the Union, Jackson resigned his commission in the U.S. Army and soon thereafter accepted a commission in the Confederate Army. Jackson did not advocate secession, but he followed his state to the Confederacy. He initially served on the staff of Gideon Pillow and on November 7, 1861, he was severely wounded during the Battle of Belmont (Missouri). He was shot in the side and the ball remained in his body throughout the war. The battle was inconclusive and Jackson's father, a physician, traveled to the site of the battle and retrieved him. He was moved by ambulance to Jackson, Tennessee, where his father treated him until he could return to duty early in 1862. In April 1862, Jackson, an "avid horseman," was appointed colonel of the 7th Tennessee Cavalry and month later he rode with his regiment to Paducah, Kentucky, in an unsuccessful attempt to destroy the Federal store houses. Subsequently, he participated in many actions, including the Battle of Shiloh, where he almost captured Ulysses Grant, and an expedition to La Fayette Station, Medon, Britton Lane, and the Battle of Corinth. At Britton Lane, he lost 179 men killed-in-action, according to Federal reports. During the Battle of Corinth, Jackson commanded a small brigade of cavalry. In December 1862, he was promoted to the rank of brigadier general as a result of his actions in Van Dorn's December 1862 raid on Holly Springs and afterward he continued to command cavalry in the Vicksburg and Meridian campaigns.[21]

Jackson had the reputation for "cool, calculated courage" and he demonstrated this when he assumed command of a division of cavalry in Van Dorn's corps in April 1863. He participated in the successful action at Thompson's Station and later in the year he joined Joseph Johnston's attempted relief of Pemberton at Vicksburg. Jackson also commanded a cavalry division during the siege of Jackson in July. In August, he continued to serve under S.D. Lee's command and had about 3,000–3,500 cavalrymen present for duty. He continued his service during the Meridian Campaign with good results. In the Atlanta Campaign, he commanded his division through the entire campaign.[22]

Jackson's Cavalry Division

Armstrong's Brigade: Brig. Gen. Frank C. Armstrong	Ross's Brigade: Brig. Gen. Lawrence S. Ross
1st Mississippi Cavalry	3rd Texas Cavalry
2nd Mississippi Cavalry	6th Texas Cavalry
28th Mississippi Cavalry	9th Texas Cavalry
Ballentine's Miss Regiment	1st Texas Legion
Artillery: Morton's Tennessee Battery, Slocumb's Louisiana Battery	

Frank C. Armstrong, an experienced cavalry officer before the war, shared much of Forrest's ability to act decisively and independently. While Armstrong was still very young, being born in November 1835, he gained experience in the First Dragoons in the U.S. Army and this made him an ideal commander in Forrest's cavalry. Armstrong was born in the Indian Territory, the son of an army officer, and upon the death of his father, his mother married General Persifor Smith. He completed his education at Holy Cross Academy in Massachusetts. Armstrong accompanied his stepfather on an expedition to New Mexico where he demonstrated his natural abilities which subsequently gained him a commission as lieutenant in the First Dragoons. He remained in the U.S. Army and even fought for the North during First Bull Run, but he subsequently resigned his commission and offered his talents to the Confederacy.[23]

Armstrong initially served on the staffs of General Ben McCulloch, Colonel James McIntosh and General Earl Van Dorn in Missouri and Ar-

General William "Red" Hicks Jackson, 1856 West Point graduate, was known for his "cool, calculated courage" (*Life of Lieutenant General, Nathan Bedford Forrest*, John Allan Wyeth, 1899).

Chapter Four. The Confederate Cavalry in the Nashville Campaign 69

kansas. The Confederacy needed experienced officers and Armstrong soon gained command of the 3rd Louisiana Infantry. Next, he put his mounted experience to work as he gained command of a cavalry brigade in Sterling Price's army. His cavalry saw active service during the Iuka and Corinth battles and his actions demonstrated an ability to fight and act independently. However, when ordered to carry out a reconnaissance expedition into Tennessee, Armstrong decided to conduct a raid rather than a reconnaissance which resulted in his repulse at Britton's Lane. His successes far outweighed this lapse, including a successful rearguard action after the Battle of Corinth. He received a promotion to the rank of brigadier general in 1862 and served as a brigade commander in Forrest's division while providing commendable service in the winter and spring of 1862–1863, most notably at the Union defeats at Thompson's Station and Brentwood.[24]

Armstrong's brigade was part of Forrest's division through the Tullahoma Campaign and when William Rosecrans began his advance on Chattanooga in August 1863, Armstrong commanded a division in Forrest's newly organized cavalry corps during the Chickamauga Campaign. His division ably provided security and offensive action during the battle, but when the battle concluded Armstrong fell under Wheeler's command. He continued to command a division in William T. Martin's Corps in the East Tennessee Campaign in the winter of 1864. A member of the 1st Mississippi Cavalry referred to Armstrong as "stern & rigid & requires every man to 'come up to scratch.'" Armstrong requested a transfer to Stephen Lee's cavalry in Mississippi in February, and in March he was released from his duty with the Army of Tennessee and sent there. Forrest was happy to learn "that Brigadier-General Armstrong will report to me." Forrest presumably wanted Armstrong to replace James Chalmers whom he expected to relieve of command. As it happened, Chalmers was not relieved of command and Armstrong, instead, was assigned to duty with Stephen D. Lee's cavalry, south of Forrest's location. Ultimately, Armstrong's brigade fell under William H. Jackson's authority and Armstrong commanded a brigade during the Atlanta Campaign.[25]

Lawrence Sullivan "Sul" Ross commanded the Second Brigade of Jackson's division. Ross, an Iowa Territory native, was born on September 27, 1838, at Bentonsport. The next year, his family moved to Milam County, Texas, in hope of improving their economic situation. The family moved to Austin, and then to Waco in 1849. His father was a settler and landowner in Waco and Lawrence attended schools at the different locations. "Sul," whose father greatly valued education, initially enrolled at Baylor University and then he completed his education at Wesleyan University in

General Frank Armstrong, "stern & rigid & requires every man to 'come up to scratch'" (Alabama Department of Archives and History, Montgomery, Alabama).

Florence, Alabama, in 1859. Ross saw the value of his university degree and used it as a platform to launch his military career. His interest in the military began during his junior year at college and when he returned home for the summer, he worked for the U.S. Army under Major Earl Van Dorn on the Brazos Indian Reservation. Ross participated in a campaign against the Comanche Indians in September and October 1858. He received a commendation for his actions during the battle at Wichita Village which almost cost him his life when he suffered from two serious wounds, an arrow in the shoulder and a bullet wound to the body. He recovered from his wounds and returned to Florence to complete his college degree.[26]

After completing his degree, Ross joined the Texas Rangers, obtained the rank of first lieutenant and then captain, and joined in an unsuccessful campaign against the Comanche Indians. Ross gained more recognition for his leadership abilities during the campaign and Governor Sam Houston authorized Ross to raise his own company of rangers in the Young County area. His subsequent actions resulted in frequent interactions with U.S. Army troops and other militia-like units. He participated in the raid on Native Americans at Pease River in December 1860 which made him even more notable to his fellow Texans. In February 1861, Texas seceded from the Union and a month later, the state joined the Confederate States of America. As the Civil War began, he enlisted as part of a company raised by his brother, Peter, which was organized as the 6th Texas Cavalry.[27]

Ross was promoted to the rank of major and first served under command of Colonel Barton Stone. The 6th Texas initially served under General Ben McCullough in Arkansas, and soon thereafter, as part of Earl Van Dorn's troops in northwest Arkansas and Missouri. In late February 1862, Ross participated in his first cavalry raid behind Federal lines. Ross' regiment also saw action in the Confederate loss at Pea Ridge and suffered only light casualties. Ross blamed the loss on the command abilities of Van Dorn, and to damage his ego even more, due to a poor ability to supply the troops, Ross' cavalry was dismounted and had to fight on foot afterward. In May 1862, the men of the 6th Texas elected Ross as their colonel. He led the regiment during the siege of Corinth and later in the Battle of Corinth in which his command played a significant role. At the Battle of Corinth, he was thrown from his horse during the fight and his regiment was "deci-

General Lawrence "Sul" Ross commanded a brigade of Texas cavalry (Mollus Mass Civil War Collection, United States Army Heritage and Education Center, Carlisle, Pennsylvania).

mated" during the assault on Battery Robinett. During the Confederate withdrawal, he assumed temporary command of Phifer's Brigade at the Battle at Davis Bridge.[28]

After the Battle of Corinth, the 6th Texas was remounted and became part of Jackson's cavalry brigade. Ross was granted detached duty in Texas for a couple of months and returned to the regiment in January 1863. After his return, Ross served as part of Van Dorn's corps which moved into Tennessee in support of Bragg's Army of Tennessee. Ross saw action at Thompson's Station and the skirmish at Franklin, but in May, Van Dorn was shot by a jealous husband. Then, Ross' cavalry returned to Mississippi and served in the Vicksburg Campaign where Ross gained command of the Texas Cavalry Brigade. He received a promotion to the rank of brigadier general in early 1864 and he led his brigade during the Meridian Campaign in February. Ross' brigade served under Forrest in 1864 until the beginning of the Atlanta Campaign when Jackson's division was initially moved to Rome, Georgia. Ross recorded that during his three months in the Atlanta Campaign, his brigade had 86 encounters with the enemy. Perhaps, the most notable cavalry action during the campaign for Ross included the successful repulse of McCook's cavalry division during his raid to Lovejoy's Station which netted several Union prisoners. Ross and his men wanted to be in the Trans-Mississippi department, or at least, along the Mississippi River and Ross appealed to the former governor of Texas to intercede on behalf of the Texas brigade for a transfer west. In the fall of 1864, Ross remained part of Jackson's division when it was moved to northern Alabama.[29]

Lyon's and Roddey's Cavalry

There were two additional Confederate cavalry commands which would prove to be important in the Nashville Campaign. The first was Brigadier General Hylan B. Lyon's brigade. Lyon was born on February 22, 1836, on a farm in Caldwell County, Kentucky, near Eddyville. Lyon's father died in 1839 and his mother died a few years later; at the age of eight, he moved into the household of F.H. Skinner in the town of Eddyville. When he was 14, he attended the Masonic University of Kentucky in LaGrange for 18 months. Then, he had a short stay at a college in Princeton, Kentucky, before he was offered an opportunity to attend the United States Military Academy at West Point in 1852. He graduated 19th in a class of 49 in 1856 and graduated with William H. Jackson and Fitzhugh Lee. Upon his graduation, he was assigned to the 2nd U.S. Artillery in Fort Myers and, while there, his command had the duty of removing the Seminole Indians to the Indian Territory. In 1857, he transferred to the 3rd U.S. Artillery at Fort Yuma, California, and subsequently participated in several military actions against the Indians in the west and with various engineering projects. Lyon took a leave of absence in September 1860 to return to Kentucky and he resigned in April 1861 to join the Confederate Army.[30]

Lyon was initially elected captain in the 3rd Kentucky Infantry (CSA) under the command of Colonel Lloyd Tilghman. The regiment marched to Bowling Green, Kentucky, and Lyon's company was detached to an artillery unit, designated as Lyon's Battery. Lyon was offered promotion to the rank of major in the 45th Virginia Infantry, but he declined, choosing to stay in Kentucky. His artillery company became known as Cobb's Kentucky Battery after Lyon's departure. When Lyon declined his promotion, Brigadier General Simon B. Buckner appointed Lyon chief of artillery for his division, but he soon thereafter received a promotion to the rank of lieutenant colonel in the 8th Kentucky Infantry. Lyon's regiment fought at the Battle of Fort Donelson where he was captured. He was exchanged and rejoined his regiment at Vicksburg. One of his initial actions after his exchange was to join Earl Van Dorn's successful raid on Grant's supply depot at Holly Springs in December 1862. Lyon saw several actions during the Vicksburg Campaign and participated in the Battle of Jackson in July 1863. Next, Lyon gained command of the Kentucky cavalry brigade under Forrest's command. After the Battle of Chickamauga, Lyon's brigade (two regiments) joined the Confederate troops in the East Tennessee Campaign under Wheeler's command. Lyon then accepted several positions in the winter of 1863–1864, including some responsibility for artillery at Dalton, Georgia, and recruiting duties in Alabama, before returning in March 1864 to Forrest's corps as colonel of the Kentucky Cavalry Brigade (3rd, 7th, 8th Kentucky cavalries). He led this brigade at the Battle of Brice's Crossroads, Battle of Tupelo, Forrest's Raid into Tennessee, including the fights at Sulfur Trestle and Pulaski. He was promoted to brigadier general after the Battle of Brice's Crossroads. At the end of August, Lyon's brigade consisted of the 3rd Kentucky, 7th Kentucky, 8th Kentucky, and 12th Kentucky cavalries. On October 27, 1864, Lyon assumed command of the Department of Western Kentucky and he established his new headquarters at Paris, Tennessee. While away from the direct command of Forrest, he would assist Forrest in the upcoming actions in the Nashville Campaign.[31]

Brigadier General Philip Dale Roddey was born in Moulton, Alabama, in 1820. Roddey had various trades before the war including tailor and sheriff, and he finally settled on the occupation of a steam boatman on the Tennessee River. When the Civil War began, Roddey organized a company of mounted men and entered the war. Roddey's men initially performed scouting duty and received Bragg's praise for their actions at Shiloh. After that battle, Roddey acted as detached cavalry in a partisan role with orders to strike the enemy whenever possible. By the close of 1862, Roddey maintained his position at Tuscumbia with his cavalry regiment. His cavalry saw action at Tuscumbia in February and Columbia, Tennessee, in March 1863. He also found a strong force under the command of Brigadier General Grenville Dodge, which participated in the failed Abel Streight raid, and fought it stubbornly during its advance to Courtland.

General Philip Dale Roddey, greatly loved by the pro–Confederate citizens of northern Alabama (Library of Congress).

Soon afterward, he was promoted to the rank of brigadier general and gained command of three cavalry regiments, one unorganized regiment, and Ferrell's Georgia Battery. While Roddey's brigade remained in northern Alabama, it provided additional manpower and protected the far west flank of Bragg's army in the Chickamauga Campaign, but he was available to join in cavalry operations near Chattanooga. Roddey attempted to support Joseph Wheeler in his October 1863 raid, but he was unsuccessful in reaching Wheeler before the Confederate defeat at Farmington, Tennessee. Roddey remained a valuable component of the Southern strategy in Alabama and the local citizens highly praised his efforts in the northern part of the state. The citizens credited Roddey with successfully keeping the Northerners away from them.[32]

Roddey remained very active in northern Alabama throughout 1864. His brigade started skirmishing with Union cavalry in early January at Shoal Creek and he pressed northward into Union territory to Athens. In February, Roddey's brigade moved to Dalton, Georgia, only to be active again in Alabama early in March. The Union commanders reported Roddey skirmishing at various locations in April. In April 1864, Roddey's cavalry, about 2,000 men strong, became part of the Department of Alabama, Mississippi, and East Louisiana. Roddey skirmished with the Federal troops in various engagements throughout the summer in connection with the Atlanta Campaign. He initiated the cavalry actions in Forrest's raid in September 1864 and directly participated in the expedition.[33]

Cavalry in the District of Northern Alabama

Roddey's Brigade—Brig. Gen. P.D. Roddey
5th Alabama Cavalry: Col. Josiah Patterson
53rd Alabama Cavalry: Col. M.W. Harmon
Roddey's Cavalry Regiment: Lt. Col. W.A. Johnson
Unorganized troops: Capt. W.R. Julian
Georgia Battery: Capt. C.B. Ferrell

In the upcoming campaign, the fighting would heavily fall on Chalmers', Buford's, and Jackson's divisions, but all the other cavalry units would play a part. The actual number of cavalry which directly participated in the Nashville Campaign remains somewhat unclear, but Forrest would state that he had 5,000 troops, excluding Lyon and Roddey. Other sources would report 5,500 men in Forrest's command. Many historians, and certainly the Union commanders, would estimate Forrest's force exceeded these numbers. Forrest's cavalry corps was negatively impacted by its inability to gain more reinforcements as the campaign continued. Forrest's numbers would initially exceed those of the Union cavalry, but as the campaign advanced, Wilson's ability to supplement his forces would result in a much greater number of Federal horsemen.

Part Two
The Advance on Nashville

Chapter Five

Forrest Attacks Johnsonville and Hood Prepares to Advance into Tennessee

"The great predominating, absorbing desire is to cut Sherman's line of communication."

—Nathan Bedford Forrest

November would be busy for the Union and Confederate cavalry forces in the west, and the first few days of the month resulted in a remarkable attack by the Confederate cavalry on the Union supply line west of Nashville. With Hood's army on the north side of the Tennessee River, the situation became serious for the Union forces in Tennessee. To complicate matters for the Federal forces being assembled in Nashville, two units which had been designated for Thomas' defense were unavailable. Colonel Edward Winslow's cavalry division was exhausted after recently traveling through Arkansas into Missouri and subsequently ending up in the Indian Territory after chasing Sterling Price during his Missouri Raid. Abraham Lot wrote in his diary from the Indian Territory that Winslow's column "made slow time with our poor Starved Horses, many of them died." More importantly, A.J. Smith's XVI Corps infantry had just shared in the pursuit of Price and was still a long distance from Nashville. This left Croxton and Hatch in the saddle facing Forrest's cavalry with whatever infantry, in addition to Schofield's and Stanley's corps, that Thomas could assemble.[1]

In late October, Wheeler's cavalry was given more responsibility for the area around Atlanta and two brigades of William H. Jackson's cavalry division were shifted west to northern Alabama to protect the Mobile and Ohio Railroad and the Memphis and Charleston Railroad. Jackson would strengthen Hood's cavalry when Forrest arrived in northern Alabama. In the meantime, Hood ordered Forrest "as soon as practicable" to report to army headquarters, but Forrest would not arrive until mid–November. Despite this summons, Forrest had already moved his forces into Tennessee after his successes in October against Union gunboats and transports near Eastport. Now, he directed his attention to the Union supply line on the Tennessee River and the supply depot at Johnsonville, Tennessee, where he felt he could best delay the supply of Union troops in Middle Tennessee and Georgia.[2]

In early October, Forrest planned to direct his cavalry to capture Fort Heiman just north of the Union supply depot at Johnsonville and then prevent any further supply of Johnsonville by riverboats. Forrest believed that his artillery was sufficient to deal with the tinclad gunboats on the Tennessee River. After two failed efforts to stop the supplies from reaching Sherman with raids on the railroads, Forrest thought he could achieve greater success by attacking the supply line near Johnsonville. He discovered during his latest raid into Middle Tennessee that much of the supplies traveled by river transport to Johnsonville, to Nashville via railroad, and then by rail further south. Forrest wrote that a "great predominating, absorbing desire is to cut Sherman's line of communication." In addition, Forrest hoped to gain new recruits and food supplies from the countryside.[3]

On October 16, Forrest began a 23-day raid that would culminate with an attack on the supply depot at Johnsonville, located on the east bank of the Tennessee River, on the newly constructed 78-mile Nashville & Northwestern Military Railroad which connected the Tennessee River to Nashville. Early in the war three fortifications, Fort Donelson, Fort Henry and Fort Heiman, were constructed along the Tennessee and Cumberland rivers by the Confederacy to control the movement on both rivers. All three forts were captured by mid–February 1862 and the Union navy controlled of the rivers since. While Thomas concentrated on Hood, Forrest turned his attention to the Federal supply line and the riverboats on the Tennessee River.[4]

Confederate Blockade Near Fort Heiman and Paris Landing

Forrest put his plan into motion on October 16 when he sent Tyree Bell's brigade riding from Corinth to Lavinia about 10 miles northeast of Jackson, Tennessee. Two days later, he ordered Buford and his Kentucky brigade to Lexington, Tennessee, to keep an eye on Hatch's Federal cavalry. Then, Forrest and Rucker's brigade moved to Jackson where James Chalmers joined him with McCulloch's and Mabry's brigades. Forrest moved north of Johnsonville and there he would remain for about 10 days blockading the river and utilizing land-based artillery to attack any boats moving along the river. Occupying the area near Fort Heiman, Forrest captured the *Mazeppa* on October 29. The next day the riverboat *Anna* was damaged, although it escaped, while being escorted by the tinclad gunboat *Undine*. The transport, *Venus*, a stern wheel boat, and *J.W. Cheesman*, a side wheel boat which was towing a barge, were forced to surrender along with the *Undine*. The *J.W. Cheesman* was unloaded and burned.[5]

On November 2, Lieutenant Edward King, commanding the Federal gunboats to the south, found both the captured boats, full of Confederate troops. King ordered the Union gunboats to open fire which disabled the *Venus*, forcing it ashore where the Confederate troops made a hasty departure. The *Undine* withdrew under the protection of the Confederate artillery.[6]

Forrest kept the Union commanders focused on the blockade north of Johnsonville and attempted to deceive his opponents into further losses. At noon on November 3, Forrest ordered the *Undine* to steam to within a mile of Johnsonville, enticing the Federal gunboats to engage the captured boats. As the Union gunboats moved toward the *Undine*, it inched northward, hoping to draw the pursuers into the muzzles of the waiting land-based artillery. The Union gunboats refused to fall for the ploy, even though Forrest made two efforts to draw the Federal boats into a trap. Only Forrest's sharpshooters succeeded in firing into the gunboats. In the meantime, Abraham Buford sent Colonel Hinchie P. Mabry's Brigade, (4th, 6th and 38th Mississippi cavalries) and the 7th Tennessee Cavalry accompanied by Captain J.C. Thrall's Battery to set up a position opposite the Federal supply depot at Johnsonville.[7]

Chapter Five. Forrest Attacks and Hood Prepares to Advance 77

Despite the setback of losing the *Venus* and ultimate destruction of the *Undine*, which was burned by the Confederates rather than allowing the boat to fall back into Union hands, Forrest kept a close eye on the supply depot at Johnsonville and noticed a lot of activity at the wharfs. Several boats were being unloaded and others were waiting their turn. Forrest wrote: "The landing and banks (several acres in extent) are piled with freight for Sherman's army; all the houses are full, and trains are running incessantly night and day in removing them." While blockading the river was one method of stopping the flow of supplies to Johnsonville, the supply depot itself provided a tempting target for the Confederate cavalry. On November 3, Forrest implemented the next phase of his plan when he moved into position to attack the transports and the depot at Johnsonville. While on this expedition, he received orders to join Hood in north Alabama. The past few days yielded good results, but he decided to break off his attack and move to Hood after the action on November 4. Forrest told Richard Taylor that he would obey his orders, but he felt he was far more successful where he was. In anticipation of the movement to join Hood's army, Forrest sent some of his cavalry to secure a crossing at the Tennessee River at Perryville, about 20 miles south of his position. But first, he wanted a shot at the supply depot at Johnsonville.[8]

The Attack on Johnsonville

November 4 was another rainy morning and despite having moved through the mud caused by three days of rain, all of Forrest's troops had arrived and prepared for the attack on the supply depot. Chalmers received Thrall's veteran battery, alternately nicknamed the "Arkansas Rats" or "Arkansas Braves," the previous day and Buford's Kentucky cavalry also arrived from Paducah. Forrest observed numerous targets as the day began—eight transports, three gunboats, and 11 barges docked at the wharfs as well as the normal activity at the numerous warehouses and sawmills. The 100-acre facility promised a wealth of supplies desperately needed by the Union troops. A formidable redoubt on the eminence beyond the depot served as a reminder that destroying the depot would not be an easy task. Forrest positioned his troops with the purpose of bombarding the facility and the boats in the water. On the west side of the river, the ground formed a small bluff about 25 feet above the waterline, but the none of the timber had been cut near the river which would have allowed the Federal troops to easily observe the activity directly across the river from the depot. Forrest positioned his artillery overnight behind hastily prepared works and camouflaged so the enemy would not discover his plan. Thrall's battery, four 12-pounder howitzers, was positioned above Johnsonville, and Morton's and Hudson's batteries were placed opposite the depot. All the Confederates cannons were placed in dug out positions where the soil protected the guns on four sides, making them barely visible when unmasked.[9]

Forrest's artillery, supported by his cavalrymen on the west side of the river, opened fire on the boats and the depot in the early afternoon. When the firing was completed, Forrest had secured a major victory on the Union depot, destroying (or forcing the scuttling) all the boats, and producing a fire storm which swept through much of the depot. The largest warehouse and six barges escaped the carnage but just about everything else was destroyed in the attack. Forrest claimed for the entire raid: "I captured and destroyed 4 gun-boats, 14 transports, 20 barges, 26 pieces of artillery, $6,700,000

Union supply depot at Johnsonville, target of Forrest's attack on November 4, 1864 (Library of Congress).

worth of property, and 150 prisoners.... My loss during the entire trip was 2 killed and 9 wounded; that of the enemy will probably reach 500 killed, wounded, and prisoners." Forrest praised his commanders, in particular, Chalmers' and Buford's "skill, coolness, and undaunted courage."[10]

Despite the Confederate victory, George Thomas told Colonel Charles R. Thompson, commander of the garrison at Johnsonville, "not think of abandoning place" and remained confident in the safety of the remaining troops. There was no direct threat to the troops if Forrest remained on the west side of the river. The Federal assessment of the loss was great. "The total money value of the property destroyed and captured during the operations of the rebels on the Tennessee River, including steam-boats and barges, is about $2,200,000."[11]

It remains remarkable that Acting Lieutenant Edward King (commander of the river bound forces), Captain Henry Howland (assistant quartermaster) and Thompson all had clear warnings that the depot would likely be attacked and failed to either detect or adequately prepare for that event, other than preparing the transports to be burned. Cooler heads reasoned that with Forrest's troopers on the west side of the river there was no immediate threat of capturing the transports which were intentionally burned by the Federal commanders. The Federal boats were outmatched, but was their burning necessary in light of no immediate threat of capture? In addition, it remains unclear whether the firing of the transports actually led to the subsequent firestorm on the depot, but it appears likely. Forrest, obviously, accomplished a legendary feat by moving his artillery directly across from a depot which was expecting an attack, including digging dugouts for his guns, without being detected. For this to have occurred, the Federal troops (land and water) demonstrated a clear lack of vigilance especially in light of an expectation of attack. In the end, Forrest claimed a major victory at Johnsonville with destruction of gunboats, transports and barges over the past week. In addition, the destruction of the millions of dollars of supplies amounted to a severe blow to the Union troops in the war. The attack increased the morale within Hood's army and the soldiers anticipated 50,000 pairs of shoes (in fact, 9,000) which rumor held that Forrest had captured. However, the next day after Forrest's withdrawal, the depot was back in business, albeit in a modified manner. Not all the warehouses were destroyed and the railroad was still operational. There were only minor losses in personnel at the depot, the Union navy still controlled the Tennessee River, and the temporary blockade failed to stop the flow of supplies. Still, Forrest was needed elsewhere. Reinforcements from XXIII Corps arrived within a week to provide more protection for the warehouses and railroad. However, by the end of November the supply depot at Johnsonville was ordered to be closed and within three days the facility was evacuated. It was again opened in 1865 after the Battle of Nashville had concluded. All the top Union commanding officers, Howland, Thompson, and King, faced some fashion of inquiry regarding their actions at Johnsonville and all were exonerated.[12]

Hood Prepares to Make the Next Move

After crossing part of his army over the Tennessee River, Hood remained stationary at Florence for three weeks. The weather and the poor condition of Hood's supply line made it slow and difficult to move the much-needed supplies to the army at Florence. Hood wrote in his report the reason for the delay: "On the 21st of November, after a delay of three weeks, caused by the bad condition of the railroad from Okolona to Cherokee, and of the dirt road from the latter point to Florence, and also by the absence of Major-General Forrest's command..." Others would read Hood's delay as desperate hope that the elections in the north, held on November 8, 1864, would yield good results for the Confederacy. The father of Confederate cavalry general William H. Jackson wrote to him that if McClellan won, the war would be over by March and the Confederacy would be recognized. If Lincoln won the election, the war would go on as usual, but if George McClellan won, then peace negotiations, part of the Democratic party's platform, would likely begin. While Hood delayed, some in the South worked behind the scenes to encourage those in the Confederate government to initiate peace talks of their own while the South was still strong enough to have a bargaining position.

Ultimately, Lincoln decidedly won the election and many in the South saw the victory as the end of any hope for peace. "The North demands an unconditional surrender ... of all our rights and privileges as a free and enlightened people," wrote a Southern newspaper, but not everyone in the Confederate army wanted McClellan to win. Major John N. Coleman, 3rd Texas Cavalry, wrote to his fiancé that he wanted Lincoln to be elected and despite the outcome: "The yanks need not think we will submit because old Abe has been reelected."[13]

Trooper Henry Kratzer McVey, 8th Iowa Cavalry, related a conversation with a Confederate cavalryman across the lines on Shoal Creek, north of Florence. McVey's regiment was seriously depleted as a result of a raid during the Atlanta Campaign in which more than 300 of the troopers were captured and still remained in a prisoner of war camp. The Confederate trooper yelled: "Say Yank, who youalls going to vote for president?" The Union trooper replied, "Lincoln.... Who are you going to vote for?" After a short silence the Confederate replied, "Oh, Lincoln, of course." Sid Champion, 28th Mississippi Cavalry, described in a letter to his wife that he frequently talked to the Union cavalrymen and described them as sociable and talkative.[14]

Historian Thomas Robson Hay believed Hood delayed at Tuscumbia due to the "anxiety concerning what Sherman would do." Hay argued that there really was no practical reason to delay at Tuscumbia at all. Hood made his own decisions as he directed the Army of Tennessee's day-to-day operations, and he left his commanding officer, Beauregard, without any direct knowledge of his plan at all. After meeting with Hood in October, Beauregard expected Hood to cross the Tennessee River at Gunter's Landing only to learn "casually and to my surprise" that Hood decided to advance further west before making a crossing at Florence. The relationship between Hood and Beauregard spiraled downward. Historian David Rey Moody wrote of Hood: "This campaign would be run his way, without interference from anyone." The effective force under Hood's command was officially reported as 27,285 including three infantry corps of 25,085 men and an additional 2,200 artillerymen. Beauregard noted that Hood made no account of his mounted forces which included: "Jackson's division consisted of three brigades, estimated at 2,000 men; General Forrest's command estimated at 3,500 men, and General Roddey's at 2,000; making an aggregate of 34,785." Roddey's cavalry while properly reported as part of Hood's army had the responsibility of protecting the supply and communication lines from Tuscumbia to Corinth to Meridian.[15]

Strength of the Army of Tennessee on the 6th of November, 1864[16]

	Present		
	Effective	**Total**	**Aggregate**
November 6, 1864:			
Infantry	25,889	34,559	38,119
Cavalry*	2,306	3,258	3,532
Artillery	2,405	2,913	3,068
Total	30,600	40,730	44,719

*This does not include about 2,000 cavalry of Jackson's division and the same number of Roddey's cavalry.

Chapter Five. Forrest Attacks and Hood Prepares to Advance

The delay in moving against Thomas after crossing the river at Florence gave Hood's scouts an opportunity to observe the enemy forces at Pulaski which was secured by Stanley's IV Corps and John Schofield's XXIII Corps, totaling greater than 20,000 men. The Confederates concluded to make a quick strike north into Middle Tennessee before all the Union forces could concentrate there, but the three-week delay gave the Union forces an opportunity to prepare for this attack. Once the advance began, Hood decided to move directly north to Lawrenceburg, and then to either Pulaski or Columbia as opportunities presented themselves. Forrest was ordered to join Hood's army either at Lawrenceburg or Waynesborough, after first making a demonstration on Columbia to divert the attention of the Union commanders. Forrest sent his cavalry to Florence over three routes—Rucker's brigade via Mount Pleasant, the remainder of Chalmers' division by way of Iuka, and Buford traveled to Corinth. Hood's advance was supposed to begin on November 9, and later delayed until November 15, only to be delayed yet again. Hood settled for Armstrong's cavalry brigade crossing over a pontoon bridge on November 7. Beauregard advised Hood to watch his rear and flanks as he marched into Tennessee but he also told Hood he needed to inform his commanding officer about his plan. "General Taylor and myself will always be anxious to aid you in your present campaign with all the means at our control; but these being limited, ample previous notice for what may be required should be given, to enable us to make all necessary preparations."[17]

One of Hood's main objectives depended upon Sherman dividing his forces by mid–November. On November 14, this objective was met when Joseph Wheeler wrote to Hood that Sherman's armies would immediately depart Atlanta for Augusta and Savannah. Beauregard and Hood both realized this meant only Thomas remained in Middle Tennessee. Wheeler was dispatched to Georgia and Forrest's and Jackson's cavalry remained with Hood, except for a single brigade of Jackson's cavalry which became part of Wheeler's forces. As Sherman initiated his march toward the coast, Beauregard prompted Hood on November 17 to "take the offensive at the earliest practicable moment and deal the enemy rapid and vigorous blows, striking him while thus dispersed, and by this means distract Sherman's advance into Georgia." Beauregard felt he had given Hood all the troops that could be reasonably spared including a large cavalry force. Beauregard wrote that as the campaign began, Hood "confronted in Middle Tennessee by General Thomas with only two corps (about 20,000 infantry and artillery) and about 6,000 cavalry, General Sherman being in Georgia with four corps (about 40,000 infantry and artillery) and about 4,000 cavalry, at a long distance from us, with muddy roads, burned bridges, and broad devastated districts between the two armies." For the plan to be successful, noted Beauregard, Hood needed to swiftly move forward before Thomas received reinforcements, but Hood remained stalled in northern Alabama.[18]

When Forrest began his movement to Florence, he found the Tennessee River too high to cross and moved the bulk of his command to Florence by longer routes. He was able to send part of Rucker's brigade across the river and Rucker attempted to fulfill Hood's orders to make a demonstration near Waynesborough. Forrest finally arrived at Florence on November 14 and a group of Tennessee soldiers greeted him with a serenade. In response, Forrest offered a speech encouraging the men to continue the fight. Just a few days earlier Forrest sent a message to Richard Taylor: "[I] will never weary in defending our cause, which must ultimately triumph. Faith is the duty of the hour. We will succeed." Upon his arrival, Forrest assumed command of the cavalry attached to

Hood's army which included his present command (3,000–3,500), two brigades of William Jackson's division, and Biffle's small brigade, in all, amounting to about 5,500 men. Forrest would state that he had about 5,000 cavalry troops for the campaign, although various numbers have been estimated for his force. The Union reports often greatly overestimated the true number while the Southern reports appear to have underestimated the number of men in Forrest's force.[19]

Stephen Dill Lee's corps moved across the river on October 31 at Florence, but from November 1 to 12, Hood remained near his headquarters on the southern bank of the Tennessee River at Tuscumbia. Armstrong's Mississippi cavalry brigade formed a screen across the front of Lee's troops for the weeks Hood remained stationary. Cheatham's infantry corps was ordered across the river on November 10 to join Lee's men, but the pontoon bridge was damaged due to the heavy rains which occurred on November 9. Cheatham's men made the crossing on November 13 and Hood moved his headquarters to the north side of the river the same day. A.P. Stewart's corps remained on the south side of the river because of poor weather and the swollen river.[20]

Any reluctance to Hood's plan to march into Tennessee was gone on November 17 when Beauregard urged Hood to boldly advance northward. Beauregard gave authority to issue whatever orders Hood needed even when he moved into another Confederate military department *vis a vis* Richard Taylor's. Beauregard also ordered Hood to send Jackson's cavalry division to join Wheeler as he prepared to slow Sherman's march in Georgia, a request at which Hood would balk. Hood wanted to keep all his cavalry unless Beauregard insisted; however, Beauregard did insist, but only if the loss of the division would not threaten the success of the expedition. Hood simply replied the loss of Jackson "would materially endanger the success of the operations of this army," and Hood pointed out that Wheeler already had 13 cavalry brigades in his command which should be enough. Hood strengthened his argument to keep Jackson's cavalry: "General Forrest thinks his force of cavalry entirely insufficient without Jackson's division." Ultimately, Jackson would operate with two brigades and Samuel Ferguson's brigade would become part of Wheeler's cavalry opposing Sherman. One additional item worried Beauregard as Hood planned his advance. He received ominous reports of a Federal buildup of troops under Major General Edward Canby and Major General C.C. Wash-

The Tennessee River, deep, wide, and swollen by the recent rains (Library of Congress).

Chapter Five. Forrest Attacks and Hood Prepares to Advance

burn at Memphis along the Mississippi River and the movement of A.J. Smith's XVI Corps moving from Missouri into Tennessee. Beauregard's first concern was the Confederate supply depot in Corinth and the railroads which carried the supplies to Hood; the success of the expedition required the Confederate army to move swiftly before the Union army could concentrate its forces.[21]

It is remarkable that the Army of Tennessee had accomplished what it had so far, because it was so poorly supplied and equipped. Hood also knew many of his troops had not been paid in nine months and he told his troops the money would soon arrive. To highlight the poor conditions within the Southern army, Hood was short of bread for his troops. He told his troops: "The commanding general announces to the army that on the march we are about commencing there may be a scarcity of the bread ration. He confidently appeals to the officers and men to meet this privation, should it come, in a cheerful, manly spirit with which they have heretofore encountered similar and greater hardships. The privation, at most, will be of short duration, and while it lasts the meat ration can be proportionately increased." Hood promised his troops that their bellies would be filled from the abundance in the countryside of Tennessee. All they needed to do was to march north and take it. One Alabama soldier wrote to his wife: "[W]e are going to take a tramp to Tennessee & perhaps we may return & perhaps we may not." A member of Chalmers' cavalry division, Captain W.O. Dodd, would write: "[W]e were going to redeem Tennessee and Kentucky, and the morale of the army was excellent."[22]

Chapter Six

Florence to Columbia

[H]old the enemy, "If it sacrifices every man of your command."
—W.L. Sanford

Forrest's Cavalry Prepares for the Advance into Tennessee

Forrest ordered Chalmers' division on November 17 to join Jackson's division already on the north side of the Tennessee River and Buford's division crossed the next day. On November 20, Hood sent orders to Forrest to start cutting the communications and supply lines in the rear of the Union forces at Pulaski. Hood told Forrest through his adjutant general to pick some "bold, reliable men" and cut the telegraph between Pulaski and Nashville. Jackson prepared his division for battle by sending a stirring message to his men: "We are about entering upon an active and important campaign, one that will require the utmost promptness and precision in the execution of all orders and stubborn fighting on the part of all of us. Associated as we are now with a new and gallant command, I appeal to you to do your whole duty as soldiers; behave as gentlemen on the march and in action; endure hardships without a murmur; show proper respect to citizens and private property; have no straggling, and let every man be in his place at all times." Jackson followed with a second set of orders designed to alleviate the bread shortage. Once the Confederates moved north, they were ordered to capture the mills to start grinding grain for bread and to collect all the cattle to be used for rations. In addition to rations, the Confederate army was in dire need of clothing and just about everything else. This would be a difficult, wet, cold campaign particularly for the Southern soldiers.[1]

It is worthy to note that both the Union and Confederate forces had significant numbers of cavalry, even though, these units were dispersed across a broad geography. Some units were dismounted and others poorly armed. The problem remained—how to cover all the territory and still concentrate enough cavalry to offer an effective offense or defense. On November 20, Richard Taylor commanding the Department of Alabama, Mississippi, and East Louisiana reported his cavalry forces (exclusive of Jackson's division) assigned to Hood's army.

District of North Alabama[2]

Brig. Gen. Philip D. Roddey
4th Alabama Cavalry, Lt. Col. F.M. Windes
5th Alabama Cavalry, Lt. Col. James M. Warren
10th Alabama Cavalry, Col. Richard O. Pickett
Burtwell's (Alabama) cavalry, Col. John R.B. Burtwell
Moreland's (Alabama) cavalry, Lt. Col. M.D. Moreland
Stuart's battalion (Alabama) cavalry, Maj. James H. Stuart
Ferrell's (Georgia) battery, Capt. Coleman B. Ferrell

Cavalry Corps*

Maj. Gen. Nathan B. Forrest	
Buford's Division	
Lyon's (Crossland's) Brigade	*Bell's Brigade*
3rd Kentucky Mted Infantry, Col. Gustavus Holt	7th Alabama Cav., Col. Joseph Hodgson
7th Kentucky Mted Infantry, Col. Edward Crossland	2nd Tennessee Cav., Col. Clark Barteau
8th Kentucky Mted Infantry, Lt. Col. A.R. Shacklett	15th Tenn. Cav, Col. Robert Russell
12th Kentucky Cavalry, Col. W.W. Faulkner	16th Tenn. Cav., Col. Andrew Wilson
	19th Tenn. Cav., Lt Col. Wm. Walker Newsom's (Tenn.) cavalry, Col. John F. Newsom
	Duff's (Mississippi) cavalry, Col. William L. Duff
Chalmers' Division	
Rucker's Brigade	*McCulloch's Brigade* (Reported in District of the Gulf)
7th Tennessee Cavalry, Lt. Col. William F. Taylor	
12th Tennessee Cavalry, ----- -----	
14th Tennessee Cavalry, Lt. Col. Raleigh R. White.	
15th Tennessee Cavalry, ----- -----	
Forrest's (Tennessee) cavalry, Lt. Col. David C. Kelley	
Artillery	
Morton's (Tennessee) battery, Lt. T. Sanders Sale	
Hudson (Mississippi) Battery, Lt. Edwin S. Walton	
Rice's (Tennessee) battery, Capt. T.W. Rice	
Thrall's (Arkansas) battery, Capt. James C. Thrall	
*Missing from this list are Biffle's brigade and William Hicks Jackson's division—Ross' and Armstrong's brigades.	

While McCulloch's brigade was detached from Chalmers' division, Chalmers would gain Biffle's brigade, the remnants of George Dibrell's old brigade, which varied from one to three regiments at different times in the campaign.

George Thomas Prepares to Meet the Enemy

Hood correctly assessed that the Union forces were not fully in place as he contemplated his advance into Middle Tennessee. Essentially, George Thomas had Stanley's IV Corps and Schofield's XXIII Corps facing Hood's army in the field, but he also had some freshly recruited regiments filtering into Nashville. Even with these troops, this was a far cry from the Union armies which pursued the Army of Tennessee during the Atlanta Campaign. The tables were turned—now Hood was the aggressor and the Union troops were the defenders.[3]

Thomas's Forces on November 20[4]

(O = Officers, M = Men)

	Present for Duty, Equipped							
	Infantry		*Cavalry*		*Artillery*		*Total*	
Command	O	M	O	M	O	M	O	M
General headquarters	....	....	....	....	....	....	....	....
Fourth Army Corps	714	12,405	....	....	23	765	737	13,170
Twenty-Third Army Corps	443	9,380	....	....	12	523	455	9,903
District of Tennessee	716	17,018	....	....	56	2,266	772	19,284
District of the Etowah	163	5,332	....	....	47	1,494	210	6,826
Reserve Brigade	29	891	....	....	....	....	29	891
Unassigned infantry	28	1,047	....	....	....	....	....	....
Unassigned artillery	....	....	....	....	7	228	7	228
Total	2,093	46,073	....	....	145	5,276	2,238	51,349

Cavalry Forces

(O = Officers, M = Men)

	Present for Duty, Equipped							
	Infantry		*Cavalry*		*Artillery*		*Total*	
Command	O	M	O	M	O	M	O	M
Cavalry Corps (Wilson):	....	....	....	....	....	....	....	....
General headquarters	....	....	9	137	....	....	9	137
First Division (McCook)	....	....	89	1,666	4	80	93	1,746
Second Division (Long)	....	....	47	507	2	101	49	608
Fifth Division (Hatch)	....	....	113	2,749	....	....	113	2,749
Sixth Division (Johnson)	....	....	43	885	....	....	43	885

	Present for Duty, Equipped							
	Infantry		Cavalry		Artillery		Total	
Command	O	M	O	M	O	M	O	M
Seventh Division (Knipe)	....	....	**107**	**2,174**	**5**	**144**	**112**	**2,318**
Unattached	....	....	139	2,913	....	....	139	2,913
Total	....	....	547	11,031	11	325	558	11,356

The units in bolded font represent the Federal cavalry in the field facing Hood's advance on November 20; only Croxton's brigade in McCook's division was present in the field.

This summary of forces showed that Hood had about 34,000 men facing a total of 62,000 Federal troops at Thomas's disposal on November 20. However, the Union forces were scattered throughout the area and had yet to be concentrated. The locations of the various units reflected a defensive arrangement which attempted to protect critical Federal transportation and communications centers while focusing on the concentration of Hood's army. The principal locations of Union forces were located at the following:

Unit	Location
General Headquarters	Nashville
IV Corps	Pulaski
XXIII (2nd and 3rd Divisions)	Pulaski
District of Etowah	Bridgeport and Chattanooga
Reserve Brigade	Nashville
Unassigned Infantry	Chattanooga
Unassigned Artillery	On steamer *Stones River* and Chattanooga
District of Tennessee	Various locations, including Nashville, Springfield, Fort Donelson, Clarksville, Gallatin, Columbia, N. Alabama, Decatur and others[5]

On November 20, Wilson established his Union cavalry headquarters at Nashville. Edward McCook had two dismounted cavalry brigades at Louisville along with Eli Long's dismounted cavalry division. Only Croxton's First Brigade of McCook's division was fully mounted and in the field at Taylor's Springs, Alabama. Hatch's division was also fully mounted, and in the field, providing reconnaissance and security in Middle Tennessee. Richard Johnson's new division consisted initially only of Capron's brigade, from the Army of the Ohio, and it was already in the field as other regiments arrived for duty. Other unattached cavalry included the 15th Pennsylvania and 9th, 10th, 11th, 12th and 13th Indiana cavalries at various locations. As the campaign began, Wilson would state that he began the campaign with about 4,300 men—Hatch with 2,500, Croxton with 1,000 and Capron with 800 men.[6]

The Issue of Command of the Federal Infantry Corps

The IV Corps and XXIII Corps at Pulaski, which would provide the initial resistance to the Confederate advance, fell under the overall command of John Schofield in a somewhat awkward situation. David Stanley technically outranked Schofield by date of commission to the rank of major general and, by normal army rules, should have been given overall command simply based on seniority. This whole issue of command began at the end of August when Schofield commanding the Army of the Ohio and Stanley commanding IV Corps worked together during the advance on Jonesborough, Georgia. The awkwardness arose from the question of whether a corps commander held rank over a commander of an army. The issue was essentially side-stepped and both Schofield and Stanley easily worked past this incident.[7]

Now, in November the same situation arose and this time both generals were corps commanders under the command of Thomas and ultimately Sherman. At Pulaski, Stanley commanded 12,000 men in IV Corps and Schofield commanded 10,000 in XXIII Corps. As Schofield moved his troops toward Pulaski, Thomas gave command to Union forces in the field to Schofield. The order cited Schofield's departmental command (commander of the Army of the Ohio) as the reason for granting overall command to him. The whole issue of who was in command was never brought up by Stanley and Schofield recorded Stanley told him he never desired to claim command. However, Stanley was the most experienced commander with numerous battles under his belt compared to Schofield who had relatively light combat experience.[8]

Wilson's Command Issues

While Schofield and Stanley worked out the command situation at Pulaski, James Wilson had problems of his own. He had cavalry in Louisville waiting to move to Nashville, but on November 16 he found they were delayed due to a lack of blankets. Even though there were plenty of blankets, the transportation department failed to ship them. In addition, Wilson was still missing Winslow's division of cavalry, much to Wilson's displeasure, and Benjamin Grierson was not helping. Wilson sent two withering messages regarding the wayward cavalry. The first came on November 19 when E.B. Beaumont wrote to Captain S.L. Woodward, Grierson's assistant adjutant general. "I am informed by Major Brackett, of the Cavalry Bureau, that you contemplate ordering the men of Grierson's division now at Saint Louis to Memphis. If General Grierson has given you any such orders as this it is a violation of instructions from General Thomas, and if you take any steps toward obeying it you will be dismissed from the service in all probability." Beaumont told Woodward to have Winslow's cavalry arriving in St. Louis remounted as soon as possible and then sent to Nashville. To ensure Grierson knew Wilson's orders, Beaumont told Woodward to show a copy of the letter personally to Grierson, and in his absence, to his staff. Then, revealing more concerns, Beaumont asked: "Where is General Grierson? Answer." Thomas sent a following message with the same information which added the weight of his authority by directing Winslow to Nashville.[9]

Beaumont was a highly effective chief of staff. His full name was Eugene Beauharnais Beaumont and he was born in Pennsylvania on August 2, 1837. He graduated from the U.S. Military Academy in 1861. He became Ambrose Burnside's aide-de-camp and participated in the Battle of Bull Run. After the battle he was assigned duty in the 1st U.S. Cavalry, but by the fall of 1861, he served as aide-de-camp to General John Sedgwick. He served in the Shenandoah Valley and he subsequently contracted typhoid fever and was relieved of duty to recuperate. Next, he served as aide-de-camp to Henry Halleck until he fully recovered his health. Then, he rejoined Sedgwick's staff in the field in May 1863 during the Gettysburg, Rappahannock and Wilderness Campaigns. Beaumont joined Wilson's staff in June 1864 and had become an important member of the cavalry command since that time. Beaumont, though a staff officer, would receive the Medal of Honor for his actions during the Nashville Campaign on December 17 and for actions during the subsequent Selma campaign.[10]

Grierson was reluctant to accept the new organization and he appeared to be sulking after the loss of his role as chief of cavalry and, now, to be serving under Wilson. Wilson wanted there to be no mistake that he commanded the cavalry in the west and he wanted his cavalry at Nashville. To make matters worse in Wilson's eyes, Grierson was not at Memphis or at St. Louis and had made no effort to tell Wilson that he would be away from his posting. "In spite of instructions sent you by Captain Woodward, of your staff, it seems that you misunderstood the instructions of General Thomas, now vested with ample authority over all the troops left in the Military Division of the Mississippi.... My letter of instructions to you was clear and unmistakable, and neither yourself nor your adjutant-general could reasonably affect to construe them into a warrant for ordering them to Memphis.... I am also informed that instead of being at Saint Louis attending to the orders sent you through Captain Woodward, you are now, or have been, at Chicago, Ill. There being no record at army headquarters of a leave of absence to you, you will report without delay by what authority you are absent from Saint Louis or Memphis, your original post." It was clear from these messages that Wilson perceived that Grierson worked in opposition to Wilson's orders.[11]

Wilson's Cavalry and the Federal Infantry at Pulaski

Stanley's IV Corps began its movement toward Pulaski during the first few days of November and most of the infantry soon reached the town although some of the troops were detailed to secure the supply train which did not reach Pulaski until November 12. Then, Stanley began enhancing the defenses and entrenchments in preparation for Hood's advance. In a more convoluted path, Schofield's XXIII Corps arrived in Johnsonville on November 5, and then returned to Nashville two days later after finding that Forrest no longer threatened the supply depot. After leaving some troops to guard Johnsonville, XXIII Corps remained in Nashville until November 13 when it marched to join Stanley at Pulaski. Both corps remained behind defenses awaiting Hood's next moves. In the meantime, Thomas hurriedly assembled the remainder of his infantry and Wilson's cavalry.[12]

As the drama at Johnsonville played out, Wilson tried to pull together a stronger force of cavalry to join in Thomas' defenses, but Sherman also wanted to begin his march to the sea. As a result, Sherman ordered all the mounts he needed to be drawn from the other cavalry units, and in particular, McCook's First Cavalry Division, excepting John Croxton's brigade, and Eli Long's Second Cavalry Division. The resulting dismounted cavalry had been sent to Louisville until they could be remounted and equipped. After meeting with Sherman in the field, Wilson traveled to Nashville to complete the reorganization of the cavalry. He reported to Thomas on November 6 and began his official duties as chief of cavalry for the Military Division of the Mississippi.[13]

Initially, Hatch's cavalry division was mounted because it had been intended to join in the Sherman campaign, but George Thomas halted its movement and ordered it to remain in Middle Tennessee. In addition, Croxton's and Capron's brigades joined in the defense of Middle Tennessee, a part of the state where the war had taken a terrible toll. Many of the homes in the countryside had either been abandoned or burned after three and half years of war. Capron's brigade reached Pulaski in early November. Croxton's cavalry brigade had seen most of the action over the past 30 days, first moving to ensure that Forrest had been dispatched over the Tennessee River in early October, and most recently, in the tracking of Hood's army at Florence. Croxton had about 1,000 troopers as he settled into position close to Hood at the Shoal Creek bridge just north of Florence, but Croxton's men felt they had too much territory to defend, too many enemies and too few Union cavalrymen. George Monlux, 8th Iowa Cavalry, wrote, "We burnt all the bridges and went along the creek and chopped trees into the fords and otherwise obstructed them as much as possible." Croxton gained some detachments of the 10th and 12th Tennessee Cavalry to assist in forming a defensive line, and he had also been promised the dismounted 9th and 10th Indiana cavalries. The Federal cavalry held its position until November 5, when a Confederate infantry force pushed northward and forced the cavalry rearward to Sugar Creek. Meanwhile on November 5, Hatch, acting on a request from David Stanley, moved from his position at Pulaski toward Florence to join Croxton in front of Hood's army. Hatch arrived just in time to stabilize Croxton's position and the two Federal commands extended a line of pickets from Shoal Creek to the confluence of Elk River and the Tennessee River. George Monlux welcomed the veterans in Hatch's division which he described as "well clothed," compared to Croxton's men who wore ragged uniforms. The Union cavalry skirmished daily with Confederate forces for the next five days. On November 9, Hatch made a general attack on the Jackson's cavalry which had been sparring with his troops and Datus Coon's brigade captured some unfinished enemy works. Hatch observed that part of Hood's army had crossed the Tennessee River while more infantry waited on the south bank. After forming a stronger cavalry line, Hatch distributed axes to his men who began felling trees across the roads the Union cavalry anticipated to be Hood's line of march.[14]

General David S. Stanley, the battle-hardened veteran, commanded IV Corps (Library of Congress).

Acting on Thomas' orders, Hatch and Croxton continued to watch the main body of the army from their position at Taylor's Springs. On November 14, the activity of the enemy near this position increased and Hatch ordered Croxton to attack the enemy pickets along the Huntsville Road in case Hood marched to the east. Croxton captured a trooper of the 28th Mississippi Cavalry who told the Union officers that Stephen Lee's corps was on the north side of the Tennessee River and more troops had planned to cross the river on November 12, but the pontoon bridge "gave way" due to high water and again the following day. In regard to the enemy cavalry, the prisoner confirmed that Armstrong's brigade had already crossed to the north side of the river and Jackson's other brigade, Ross,' was in position at Tuscumbia. The remainder of Forrest's cavalry had not reached Florence at this point but was expected at any time. The prisoner revealed, "Forrest is to take them on a great raid as far as the Ohio. Hood, he thinks, is to go to Nashville." The prisoner overestimated the size of Forrest's cavalry due to arrive which supposedly totaled 12,000 to 15,000 men. The prisoner proved to be a wealth of information and he said the Confederate soldiers had not been paid for 14 months and the cavalry horses were in "low condition." Supporting this new intelligence, Hatch observed an increasing number of campfires in front of his position. Hatch and Croxton skirmished routinely with Confederate troops over three weeks, and Hatch's division succeeded in cutting the enemy pontoon bridge three times during this period.[15]

Federal Troops Prepare to Meet the Confederate Advance

On Union side of the line, Schofield, Stanley and Thomas did not know where Hood intended to march. On November 14, Thomas kept his cavalry on constant watch for Hood's movements and he told Hatch to prepare to move northward with the advance of Hood's army. The initial movements by Hood caused Hatch to extend his right flank in anticipation of a general movement to Columbia, but the reports were premature as Hood lingered along the Tennessee River at Florence for another week. Both Croxton and Hatch were pushed back by strong advances by the Confederate cavalry starting on November 15. In the meantime, Capron's brigade rode to Mount Pleasant on November 16 and scouted toward Waynesborough where he found that Edmund Rucker's Confederate cavalry brigade had just passed through the town a few days before. Rucker, who was following Forrest's orders to make a demonstration in the area, appeared to have no serious intent to engage the enemy. Capron correctly surmised that Rucker's brigade was just falling back after the action at Johnsonville, but he noted the seriousness of Forrest operating on the north side of the Tennessee River. Capron sent a large number of scouts to cover the territory south of Mount Pleasant to observe any movements by the Confederate cavalry toward Columbia or Pulaski. Hatch also skirmished with Rucker's cavalry as it rode to Florence on November 16. Hatch drove in Rucker's pickets in some light skirmishing and picked up two prisoners from the 7th Tennessee Cavalry. Hatch discovered Rucker's brigade was composed of the 7th, 12th, 15th and 26th Tennessee cavalries, and wrote, "Forrest is marching up the river; his main column was thirty miles yesterday from Tuscumbia, on the way to Florence." Forrest had already arrived in Florence at this point and would lead the advance before Hood's infantry in a few days. Extending his line westward, Hatch wanted to be able to fully screen the area around Florence to ensure no enemy forces slipped past the Federal lines. Capron, at Waynesborough, extended the Union flank farther west making sure that flank was secure.[16]

Hatch wrote to Wilson on November 16 that the horses in his division were in good condition despite the wet, cold weather. His division had been in the field now for 48 days and his men had no tents and little communications from commanding officers. Hatch told Wilson: "We shall try to cut their pontoons again tonight. The last attempt nearly succeeded; many of the anchor ropes were cut, when our boats capsized against the bridge. It was so weakened, however, it broke as a part of Stewart's corps attempted crossing. The enemy have 4,000 cavalry, with their infantry, on this side of the Tennessee.... If I had another brigade of cavalry the enemy should not have an ear of corn outside of their infantry lines."[17]

On November 17, Hatch continued to hold his line and observed the Confederate divisions near the Tennessee River as conditions permitted. He wrote to Wilson: "It is with great difficulty I can get light rations to my command. My old division is now three days without rations, and the country has been so thoroughly devastated [that] parched corn is the only resource." Hatch expected a supply train with five days' rations that evening and he knew the importance of holding his position. Forage for the mounts seemed to be his greatest concern. He hoped to be able to hold his position until Hood revealed his plan to attack or moved further west. Hatch wrote, "I know of no way of watching him so effectual as pressing his picket-line constantly."[18]

General John Schofield, commander of XXIII Corps, was appointed to overall command of the Union forces at Pulaski (Library of Congress).

Hatch's cavalry again clashed with the Confederate infantry and cavalry on November 17 while the enemy attempted to forage in the countryside. Hatch took every opportunity to find the enemy and drive them back to their lines. In one engagement, his men killed two and mortally wounded another three before driving them back. He exclaimed: "The skirmish was a sharp one." Alonzo Aulsbro, 2nd Michigan, also reported skirmishing with the enemy and lamented the wet and soggy conditions. He wrote on November 18 that he expected another fight with the enemy but he hoped the enemy would wait until the rain was over.[19]

On November 18, Capron's brigade reached Waynesborough and began scouting the area around the town. He clashed with Confederate cavalry scouts during the rain-filled day's movement and he had one man killed, one mortally wounded and another severely wounded during the fighting. Capron questioned the citizens in his area who told him that some of Hood's army occupied the north bank of the river and that Forrest had scouts pressing as far north as Lawrenceburg. Major Charles Beeres, 16th Illinois Cavalry, sent a 100-man patrol from Mount Pleasant to Lawrenceburg looking for the enemy and found nothing but small parties of irregulars near Campbellsville. Capron had lost contact with Hatch, but he planned to heavily scout the territory south and east of his headquarters the next day. Capron, who was operating without specific orders, was nervous and he sent a message to Schofield that he felt isolated in his position, "our right and rear being entirely exposed. The nearest and only communication with Lawrenceburg is eighteen miles to our rear upon the Mount Pleasant road, and it is fourteen miles from that point to said town, making by the nearest route thirty-two miles from Waynesborough to Lawrenceburg, there being no direct road east from this point, as indicated by the maps." Capron, like Hatch, had problems with rations and forage for the mounts, but the veterans planned to continue their screen as long as they could. Capron's troopers were already showing signs of fatigue. Trooper Garrison Wright, 8th Michigan, wrote to his sister that he had been in the saddle for the past 10 days, some days traveling as much as 40 miles, and had not the time to write. Capron also received some unreliable reports from the local population that he faced not only Forrest's main cavalry force moving northward from Florence, Biffle's brigade was spotted at Clifton about 15 miles west of his position, and another Confederate cavalry force at Linden, 28 miles north. The weather made scouting and movement difficult for Capron's men. "The roads are fast becoming impassable."[20]

Hood still remained relatively stationary, but Hatch spotted increased activity among Hood's troops on November 18. Forrest began moving the remainder of his cavalry to the north side of the river that morning. Hatch believed that Hood would begin marching the next day, but A.P. Stewart's corps had yet to cross the river. Based on the positions of Forrest's cavalry, he predicted Forrest would move northward on the Waynesborough Road, but he expected Hood's main column to march directly toward Lawrenceburg. Hatch thought Hood had 35,000 infantry, but his estimate of Forrest's command was too high—10,000 troopers. Forrest's cavalry moved into position in front of the Confederate infantry and Hatch believed that Forrest planned to destroy the railroad between Nashville and Pulaski, or perhaps at Murfreesboro.[21]

Thomas, in return, increased his preparation for a fight and he wrote to Schofield: "If the enemy advances in force, as General Hatch believes, have everything in readiness either to fight him at Pulaski, if he advances on that place, or cover the railroad and concentrate at Columbia, should he attempt to turn your right flank.... Report to me at once, should you be compelled to leave Pulaski.... I can hardly think, however, that the enemy will attempt to advance in such weather as we now have." Both Thomas and Schofield underestimated Hood's ability to rapidly march in the poor weather conditions. Optimistically, the Union generals expected Hood to be bogged down in his march, and Thomas hoped to be able to move Smith's XVI Corps to Pulaski before Hood became a threat.[22]

The Nashville Campaign Begins—Hood Marches for Columbia

The heavy rains on November 13 and 14 stalled any movements by Hood's army after crossing the river. On November 16, Jefferson Davis called for a day of fasting and prayer and duties were limited that day. Two days later, Sul Ross moved his cavalry brigade to the north side of the river to join Armstrong's brigade. The colonel of the 9th Texas Cavalry, Dudley Jones, in Ross' brigade wanted so much to be part of the movement that he rode at the head of his regiment despite the fact he was still on medical leave. Hood remained in place until November 19 as he concentrated troops on the north side of the Tennessee River, and he wrote, "The cavalry is moving now." A.P. Stewart's infantry corps prepared to cross the river behind Lee's corps which had been ordered to begin marching northward the next morning at 5 a.m., but the weather continued to be unsuitable for rapid marching and the supply trains sank in the muddy roads. Lee moved his corps about 10 miles during the day and Stewart's corps finally made its crossing. Hood sent a rousing letter of encouragement to the men of the Army of Tennessee in which he promised the campaign was "full of auspicious fruit to your country and lasting renown to yourselves." On November 21, Cheatham's corps began marching early along the Waynesborough Road and stopped for the night about 12 miles north of Florence. Lee's corps moved up the Chisolm Road, and Stewart moved northward on the Lawrenceburg Road. Both of these latter corps moved east of Cheatham on parallel roads and Forrest concentrated his cavalry to screen the movement on the eastern flank with Jackson's and Buford's divisions while Chalmers' division preceded the western and center columns. The next morning (November 22) the Southern army continued its march and Cheatham marched 18 miles during the day. Hood's line of march effectively placed his army to the west of the two Union corps at Pulaski and threatened to either by-pass the defenders or turn to cut them off from the north. To be successful, Hood wrote: "I hoped to be able to place the army between these forces of the enemy and Nashville." Hood's initial objective was Columbia where he would be able to effectively isolate the two Union corps at Pulaski from reinforcements to the north. The race was on for Columbia.[23]

General Benjamin Cheatham led his corps on the western flank on the Waynesborough Road (Library of Congress).

Cavalry: Buford and Jackson Vs. Hatch and Croxton

November 19–20: The First Cavalry Action— Skirmish at Butler Creek

In the field near Pulaski, Schofield tried to develop a defensive position along a line of march of which he was still unsure. Schofield told Hatch to leave a small cavalry force to watch Hood's infantry movements, but he wanted most of Hatch's division to resist Forrest's advance northward. Schofield still believed Forrest intended to cut the railroad between Pulaski and Nashville and he wanted to keep the Federal cavalry in front of Forrest to prevent this. If Forrest continued to move toward Columbia, Hatch needed to stop him at the river crossings. In the meantime, Schofield decided to move some of his infantry to Lynnville and Columbia to extend the Union defensive line further west.

As the armies of both sides moved into position at the initial phase of the campaign, the mounted forces would be immediately put to the test. Four Union cavalry brigades had the task of observing and delaying Hood's march. The brigades of Capron, Coon, Croxton and Colonel Oliver Wells would face three divisions of Forrest's cavalry—Buford's, Chalmers', and Jackson's. The skill, speed, and fighting ability of these cavalry forces would be tested over the next two weeks and the result greatly impacted the overcome of the overall campaign.

On another rainy day (November 19), Hatch faced the first movements of the Forrest's cavalry in a heated skirmish at Butler Creek. The skirmish began at noon when Coon's brigade on Butler Creek Road (parallel to the Waynesborough and Florence road on the west side of Shoal Creek) was surprised by the Buford's and Jackson's cavalry divisions advancing in the direction of Lawrenceburg. Coon had orders to establish his bivouac on Butler Creek after skirmishing with Confederate cavalry the day before. He crossed his brigade over Shoal Creek, a rock bottomed creek about 100 yards wide, at Cowpen's Ford early in the morning. He moved with his supply train (a pack train) on the expedition, but he soon encountered some of Buford's cavalry. The initial clash went in favor of Coon's cavalry which had been sent out to determine the location and strength of the Confederate forces. At noon, a party of Crossland's Kentucky brigade from Buford's division was foraging when the Union cavalry surprised them, but the day did not follow the Union cavalry's plan. A battalion of the 9th Illinois Cavalry, patrolling the Waynesborough Road, came on the Kentuckians and the Union officer told his men to observe only; however, one of the troopers saw an opportunity and took a shot at one of the Confederate cavalrymen. Then, the Kentuckians attacked, only to be repulsed by the 9th Illinois. The counterfire by the Illinois cavalry was so fierce the Kentuckians hastily withdrew leaving two of Buford's headquarters wagons in the hands of Coon's troopers. At this point, the 2nd Iowa was positioned at Big Butler Creek and the remainder of Coon's brigade held a position at the crossroads with the road leading to Florence.[24]

After hearing the gunfire in the initial skirmish, Armstrong's Mississippi brigade arrived from the south and engaged Coon's troopers. Hatch had already observed Armstrong's brigade as it moved along the road with four regiments of cavalry, designated as "mounted infantry" by the Federals. More of Buford's Confederate troopers also arrived at the gallop and struck Coon's right flank and pushed it back toward Shoal Creek. During the battle, Colonel Edward Crossland commanding the Kentucky brigade was severely wounded for the third time in 1864.[25]

Hatch said that Coon's brigade whipped Buford in the opening action but Coon hardly "whipped" Buford and Jackson in the later Confederate attack. Coon provided the most detailed Union account of Hatch's cavalry actions during the entire Confederate movement to Columbia. In the second engagement of the day, Coon's brigade patrolled Chisolm Road near Butler Creek along the Tennessee-Alabama state line. He had split his command with the 9th Illinois watching two roads—the Waynesborough Road (Capt. Anthony E. Mock, commanding one battalion) and the road leading to Florence (Capt. J.W. Harper, commanding the remainder of the regiment) while the 6th Illinois Cavalry guarded the supply train. In a steady rain, the 2nd Iowa Cavalry soon encountered Buford's cavalry division at Big Butler Creek. While observing the large body of Confederate cavalry, Coon knew his ability to maneuver was restricted because of his brigade supply train, and he ordered the 6th Illinois Cavalry to escort the train across Shoal Creek by the most expedient route, overland down the valley of the Little Butler Creek, even though the troopers had to cut a trail to an abandoned crossing to even gain access to the creek during the skirmish. Coon found Confederates approaching from the northwest and south. After sorting his supply train and hearing an increasing amount of gunfire, Coon rode to see how the two regiments were faring and when Coon arrived, he found both the 2nd Iowa and 9th Illinois in trouble. The 2nd Iowa was holding back a larger force of Confederate cavalry, edging to the north of the Iowans. Sergeant Lyman Pierce, 2nd Iowa, described the Union regiments falling back in "considerable disorder." Meanwhile, Harper's 9th Illinois faced the same situation from a large force of Confederate cavalry (having the "appearance of being infantry," i.e., dismounted) advancing from the south. Harper held the key to Coon's hope of slipping away from the enemy. Harper needed to hold the enemy long enough for the 2nd Iowa to withdraw down the Little Butler Valley. Coon had not forgotten about Mock's battalion, on the northern part of his line, and he sent a message to him telling him to withdraw as quickly as possible to prevent being cut off.[26]

Coon stabilized the 2nd Iowa and sent orders to the 9th Illinois to withdraw to the right and rear under the cover of the 2nd Iowa's Spencer carbines. The 9th Illinois obeyed the order and fell back down the Little Butler valley to a narrow choke point between two bluffs at the confluence of the Little Butler and Big Butler rivers. The 9th Illinois fell into line and prepared to cover the withdrawal of the 2nd Iowa which by this time was heavily pressed by Armstrong's brigade moving on its flank. Coon described the 2nd Iowa's situation as "truly critical." The Iowans withdrew while nearly being flanked by the rebel cavalry and then fell in line in the rear of the 9th Illinois. Coon had hoped to hold his position until Mock's battalion reached the withdrawing Federal line, but he was unable due to increasing pressure from the enemy. Coon continued these leap frog movements for two miles, effectively holding back the enemy cavalry, but the Confederate pressure was too much for Coon. Coon's regiments finally reached Shoal Creek and the troopers gave a sigh of relief when they saw the supply train, artillery and ambulances safely on the other side of the creek. Importantly, Coon saw troopers of the 6th Illinois Cavalry dismounted and ready to cover the retreating regiments as they crossed Shoal Creek. Coon described: "A lively skirmish was kept up by the rear guard while the command passed down the steep miry bank by file obliquely 150 feet. The mortification and apparent chagrin of the rebels when they found their prey had unexpectedly escaped was made known by those hideous yells, such as only rebels can make." Mock's battalion of the 9th Illinois, cut off during the fight, reached the Union camp after dark. Coon, who narrowly escaped a disaster, held the east side of Shoal Creek but he sent scouts to watch all the crossings and roads in the area that night. Coon wrote: "I had left in the morning, with the firm conclusion, as previously reported, that Butler's Creek was by no means a desirable location to encamp."[27]

Subsequently, prisoners told their captors that all of Forrest's cavalry was moving north in advance of the infantry. Hatch concluded that the initial clash indicated that Hood's infantry would probably march to Waynesborough while the cavalry would strike the railroad. Hatch, like Schofield and Thomas, doubted the Confederates could make much of the march because "the roads are in the very worst condition." Hatch asked Schofield if the Confederate infantry and cavalry moved in separate columns what should the cavalry do. Schofield responded: "[Y]ou will have to do the best you can to accomplish two objects, viz: to observe the movements of his infantry, and oppose his cavalry. If his infantry and cavalry take different directions quite a small force will be sufficient to watch the movements of the infantry, and you will be able to use the main body of your troops to operate against the enemy's cavalry."[28]

The next day (November 20) Hatch observed Forrest on the move and based on the initial movements, Hatch decided to concentrate his forces at Lexington, Alabama. Croxton moved with Hatch's division but left a small force to watch for enemy movement on the Huntsville Road. Hatch was still unsure of which line of march Hood would take, but he still believed Hood would move his infantry north and then send the cavalry to cut the railroad between Pulaski and Nashville.[29]

Hatch captured a courier belonging to Rucker's brigade during the day and the message gave advance warning of Forrest's movements. Rucker's message stated: "General Forrest has issued orders that the command be in readiness to move Monday morning, with four days' cooked rations; he further remarked that General Forrest is coming out on this road to-day, and looking for him now.... I would beg to remain where I now am till morning, being yet unsupplied with ammunition; but will be obliged to move then somewhere on account of forage." Not only did Hatch determine when Forrest planned to begin his movement, he also found that the Confederate cavalry was seriously undersupplied.[30]

To meet the enemy threat, Schofield placed Hatch on Forrest's right flank, in position to screen an attack intended for the railroad. These orders left Capron on the west flank further separated from the remainder of the Union forces; however, Capron still had the option of falling back to Columbia upon Silas Strickland's infantry brigade. Schofield planned to move an infantry division to Lynnville, about half way between Pulaski and Columbia, to support Hatch's cavalry while extending his right flank. Next, he wrote to Thomas: "It may be that Forrest is only moving out to encamp on the waters of Buffalo River, where, I understand, forage is abundant. It seems hardly probable that he will attempt aggressive operations while the roads are so bad." After considering Thomas' suggestion, Schofield decided to move two divisions (Jacob Cox's and George Wagner's) 10 miles north of Pulaski on November 20 while leaving two divisions under Stanley's command at Pulaski. He explained to Thomas that Hood needed to move to Lawrenceburg whether he intended to march to Columbia or Pulaski. A large force at Lynnville offered a good position to cover the railroad and served as a good starting point to cover either Columbia or Pulaski once Hood made his move. In response, Thomas ordered one of Thomas Ruger's brigades (Colonel O.H. Moore's which had been protecting Johnsonville) to Columbia.[31]

The Cavalry on the Move

Hatch had his entire force (three brigades) concentrated near Lexington in preparation of withdrawing to Pulaski after clashing with Buford and Jackson the prior day. Starting at 3:00 a.m., Coon moved back to the Alabama-Tennessee state line near Bluewater Camp. Coon sent a battalion of the 9th Illinois, under command of Captain A.E. Mock, to the Waynesborough Road to observe the Confederates along that road and again found serious trouble. As the Illinois troopers rode back to the east, they found they had ridden into the middle of Chalmers' advancing cavalry division and had to ride across the countryside to prevent from captured. While trying to avoid capture, Mock happened upon Chalmers' division supply train and overwhelmed the unsuspecting guards "capturing several wagons and prisoners and fifty mules, besides much plunder which he could not bring away," wrote Coon. While the 9th Illinois was destroying the Confederate supply train, Chalmers' division counterattacked the Illinois cavalry which made a hasty withdrawal. Rucker's brigade led the Confederate advance toward Henryville, and Chalmers and his staff train moved about an hour later. James Dinkins of Chalmers' cavalry rode forward and soon found that the 9th Illinois had attacked the supply train scattering the supplies over the countryside. Upon discovering the empty wagons, the Confederate cavalry set off in pursuit. The trailing Confederate column soon found the 9th Illinois retreating, still in possession of the captured mules, captured drivers, and ex-slaves. Dinkins recalled that the 9th Illinois appeared to be lost and were retreating along the same trail that had just used. The attack on the supply train angered Chalmers and seeing the Federals retreating, he yelled: "Charge them! Charge them!" The Southern troopers spurred their horses and charged forward. The Union troopers scattered in all directions, abandoning the mules and prisoners.[32]

Mock, commanding the battalion, found some loyal citizens who served as guides and led the regiment back to Coon's headquarters. One attempt to obtain help from the citizens went badly. One of the 9th Illinois approached a woman who was immediately suspicious. She said, "I believe you un's are Yankees," but the Union cavalrymen assured her they were Confederate. She was too smart and replied, "You un's don't talk like we un's and your hair is shorter than our boys." The sight of Confederate cavalry approaching in the distance ended the discussion and the Union cavalrymen rode away. Coon sent a rider asking for reinforcements, but the Confederate cavalry scooped him up before he could reach the Union lines. Mock had a hard day and lost 30 men, mostly captured, but he had attacked Chalmers train and captured some important papers which outlined Hood's line of march. At sunset, the Confederate cavalry found Coon's main body of pickets on both roads leading north and drove them to the rear.[33]

Forrest had encamped his Confederate cavalry along Shoal Creek as Hood moved his infantry in preparation for the movement north. Lieutenant R.J. Black, 7th Tennessee Cavalry, found that starting the advance that "we all came near freezing." Forrest threw his cavalry in front of the infantry columns on November 21, and he ordered Chalmers to move by way of West Point, Kelly's Forge, Henryville, and Mount Pleasant. Buford and Jackson had orders to move on the road to Lawrenceburg then swing to the southeast to screen the Federal troops from the advancing infantry. Forrest wrote: "Both these divisions had several engagements with the enemy, and were almost constantly skirmishing with him, but drove him in every encounter." Despite Hatch's belief that Forrest wanted to destroy the railroad, Forrest intended to push Hatch and

Croxton back to the east, clearing the way for Hood's infantry to march unimpeded to Columbia.[34]

Frank Armstrong's brigade led the advance of Jackson's division on November 21. Following Armstrong's Mississippi brigade was Ross's small brigade of 686 men—3rd Texas Cavalry, 218; 6th Regiment Texas Cavalry, 218; 9th Regiment Texas Cavalry, 110; and 27th Texas Cavalry, 140. Ross proudly exclaimed, "With this small force we joined the advance into Tennessee, strong in heart and resolved to make up in zeal and courage what was wanting in numbers."[35]

November 21–22: Hood's Army Moves into Tennessee; Action at Lawrenceburg

The next morning, November 21, was cold and snow fell in the afternoon. Coon's reconnaissance found Hood's entire army moving northward. Upon observing Hood's initial line of march, the Union commanders worried Forrest might slip between Hatch and Capron, around Schofield's right flank; in response, Hatch shifted Croxton's brigade closer to Capron and north of Lexington. Schofield also alerted Silas Strickland at Columbia to prepare to meet 10,000 Confederate cavalry moving in that direction. Elsewhere, Hatch, about 12 miles south of Lawrenceburg, had his scouts along the roads to the south and discovered Lee's corps 20 miles from Florence on the Butler Creek road. Cheatham's corps marched on the Waynesborough and Florence road about 15 miles from Florence. A.P. Stewart's corps brought up the rear about six miles from Florence at Wilson's Crossroads. The Confederate cavalry rode on different roads, screening the infantry, while avoiding congestion. Hatch continued to slow the Confederate cavalry whenever possible through quick skirmishes. After observing the line of march that day, Hatch determined that Hood was heading for Columbia, not toward Pulaski. Hatch estimated Hood's strength to be "infantry, from 30,000 to 35,000, 60 pieces of artillery, and 10,000 cavalry. There is no doubt of their advance."[36]

Corporal J.A. Bigger, 2nd Mississippi Cavalry, recorded in his diary that Armstrong's brigade advanced about six miles in the direction of Lawrenceburg. Bigger seemed as intent on foraging as fighting with the enemy, and he discovered that danger lurked and not all of it was caused by the Union cavalry. Bigger's comrade, James Albritten, described as a "good boy," was killed in the day's activities. Albritten remounted his horse after some foraging and as he attempted to replace his carbine on the saddle in the cold weather, the gun discharged mortally wounding the Southern trooper. His comrades took him to a private home to tend to his wound but he died later that night.[37]

Based on Hatch's observations and knowing Hood outnumbered his infantry and cavalry, Thomas suggested that Schofield pull back to Columbia. Meanwhile, Wilson hurriedly found additional cavalry regiments to move to Middle Tennessee, but with Forrest and Hood advancing, it appeared he could not accomplish this in time. Thomas felt once A.J. Smith arrived from Missouri, he would pull in some of his other infantry from across the state to effectively meet Hood's army, but it was the cavalry that worried him because Forrest had such a propensity of striking vital areas quickly and effectively. Thomas wrote to Henry Halleck in Washington: "[B]ut his cavalry will greatly outnumber mine until I can get General Wilson's force back from Louisville." In regard to Hatch's cavalry, Schofield recorded that evening: "He moves toward Lawrenceburg today to meet Forrest's advance."[38]

In the early morning hours of November 22, Hatch sent a message to Capron: "Hold on where you are until pressed back, scout well your right flank, endeavor to learn if the enemy are moving round your right toward Nashville. I will keep your left well scouted." This was a promise Hatch would not be able to keep.[39]

As Hood moved northward, Thomas decided to pull his forces back toward a line centered on Columbia and assemble as many troops as he could, including R.S. Granger's troops near Huntsville and Tuscumbia which he ordered to Shelbyville and Murfreesboro. After re-positioning his divisions, Schofield reasoned, "This will be the best disposition we can make to meet Forrest if he attempts a raid. Then, if Hood advances with his entire army, Stanley can join me at Lynnville, where we can fight Hood, or retire to Columbia, according to circumstances. I do not believe Hood can get this far, if he attempts it, while the roads are so bad." Hood's ability to march in the adverse conditions continued to surprise the Federal commanders. Schofield initially planned to hold Stanley at Pulaski but when he realized that Hood appeared to be marching directly for Columbia, he ordered him to march north on the morning of November 23. Schofield told Jacob Cox that after reaching Lynnville on November 22 that he should continue his march to Columbia. This order was fortuitous for the Union forces because Hood's march achieved more than Schofield expected. Thomas agreed with Schofield's plan to start moving northward and he also told Schofield that Wilson was on his way to take command of the cavalry in the field.[40]

General Stephen Dill Lee led his corps in the center of Army of Tennessee (Library of Congress).

General A.P. Stewart led his corps on the eastern flank of the Confederate Army (*Battles and Leaders of the Civil War, Vol. III* [1887], p. 338).

Jackson, Buford and Hatch:
Action at Lawrenceburg, November 22

Hatch moved to meet the enemy at Lawrenceburg, and at sunrise, Jackson's and Buford's divisions attacked the Federal cavalry pickets south of the town. Lawrenceburg had been a prosperous town of about 600 people prior to the war, but it was vastly different now. Much of the town had been abandoned when the Federals claimed Nashville in 1862. Now, in 1864, the county had a Unionist government and some of the people were returning to the town. Still, most of the town was abandoned as the Federal cavalry moved through the streets which had turned to mud in the wet weather. "[M]orning cold and the ground frozen hard," wrote Datus Coon, whose brigade would be active on November 22. At noon, the Confederate cavalry reached Coon's position and began firing on the Federal pickets. Coon ordered a battalion of the 2nd Iowa to probe ahead to find the size and location of the advancing Confederate cavalry. The Iowans rode south and found a strong force of the enemy about three miles south in some bluffs along the road. The battalion skirmished with the enemy for about an hour before being pushed back toward the town. At 2:00 p.m., there was little doubt about the size of the enemy force as lines of gray-coated soldiers approached the town.[41]

Ross's brigade was involved with much of the fighting during the day. His brigade led the Confederate advance and about 12 miles from Lawrenceville, he encountered the Federal pickets. Attacking the Federal pickets, Ross dismounted the 3rd Texas and two squadrons of the 1st Texas Legion and made a steady advance pushing the enemy from one position to another until they reached the town. Lieutenant George Griscom noted in his diary that the 9th Texas advanced through a severe snow storm and relied on Young's battery to help drive the Union cavalry rearward.[42]

Approaching Lawrenceburg, the Confederate cavalry formed a broad arc encompassing the front of the town. Lieutenant Robert Morris, 21st Tennessee Cavalry, recalled the attack on the defending Union cavalry began by driving the Federals into Lawrenceburg. Two Confederate regiments approached from the north, Bell's entire brigade moved from the southwest, and Crossland's brigade moved directly toward the town in the center. As the Southern cavalry approached, Hatch ordered Coon to withdraw to the north side of the town and into battle line. Then, the Union and Confederate artillery opened on one another for about an hour. The artillery duel had little effect on either side but Hatch, again, ordered Coon to fall back—this time along the Pulaski Road. After the exchange of artillery fire, the Confederate cavalry gained possession of the town. Morris noted: "So swiftly and hardly were the enemy pressed that their camp was taken and a good deal of valuable material and much-needed rations captured." Coon continued his withdrawal about seven miles into position behind Croxton's brigade. The Federal rearguard fought throughout the day, and from 10:00 a.m. until dark, holding the Confederate columns at bay.[43]

At 11:00 p.m. on November 22, Hatch, east of Lawrenceburg on the Pulaski Road, wrote to Schofield: "There is no question about the advance of General Hood's army being in Lawrenceburg tonight; infantry with some cavalry. I shall pass within ten miles of Pulaski on my way to Campbellsville, and any orders you may have would reach me there. I shall reach that point about daylight." Hatch also sent orders which attempted to keep the cavalry units in some sort of a unified line while withdrawing northward overnight. Hatch also wrote to Thomas at 8:15 p.m. about the events of the day, including

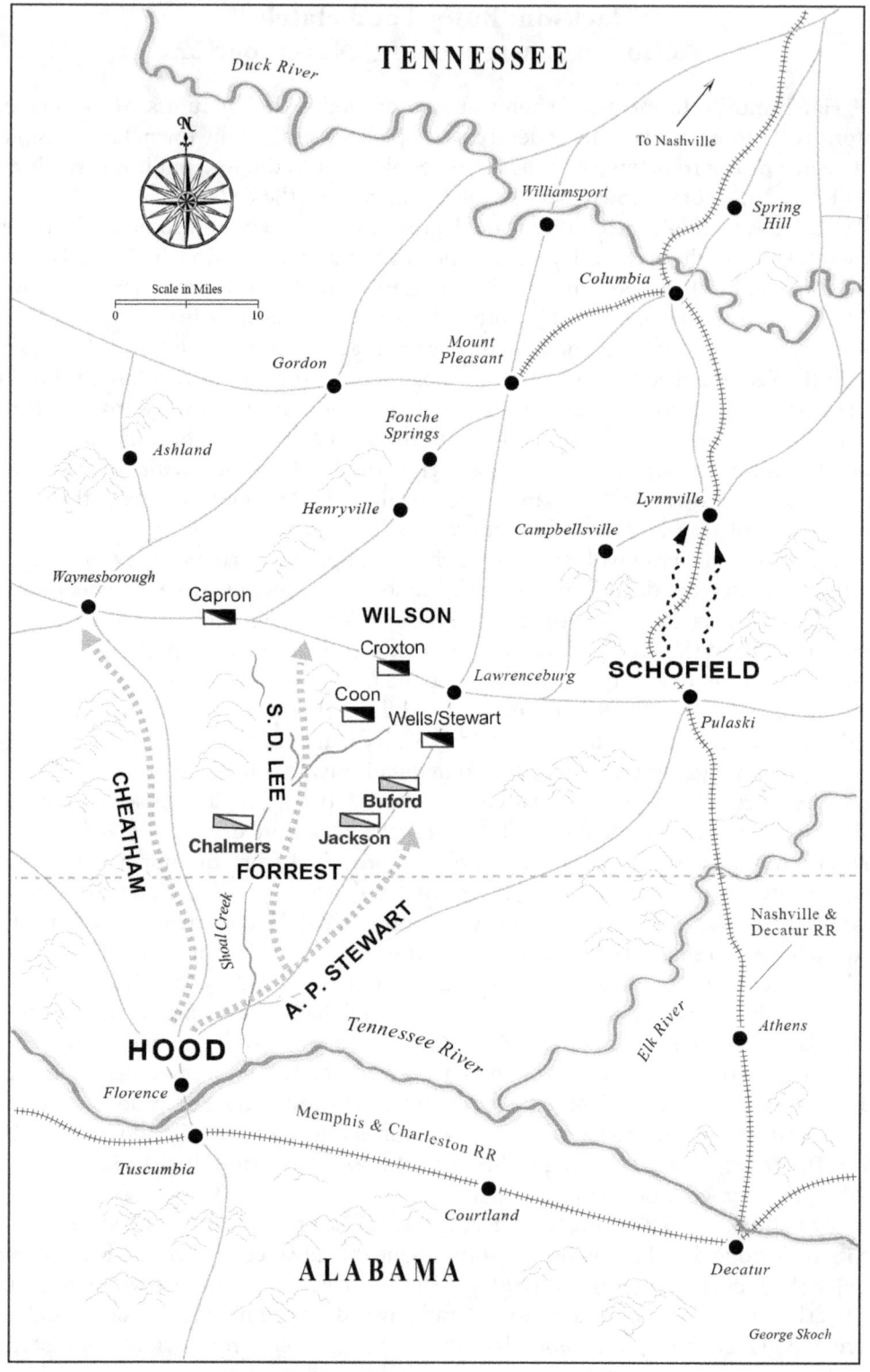

Hood's line of march from Florence.

the shelling of Coon's brigade and its being forced away from Lawrenceburg, turning his right flank in the process. Hatch also told Thomas about the threat the enemy posed and that he would move toward Campbellsville the next day.[44]

The night was long for the cavalry on both sides of the line. Henry Mortimer Hempstead, 2nd Michigan, wrote in his journal: "The intensely cold weather did not prevent the Jonnies from being active." Hempstead's regiment had picket duty that night and late into the evening, the Confederate cavalry finally settled into camp. The enemy cavalry gathered what wood they could find and started fires to stay warm. Hempstead and another officer stealthily approached the enemy camp and stopped about a "half rifle shot" away. Hempstead observed one of the enemy troopers "cheered loudly for McClellan winding up with an oath." The two men eased away from the enemy and fortified the pickets, believing they would be attacked very early the next morning.[45]

On the Confederate side of the line, Armstrong who was described as a demanding commander who often joined his men around a campfire. He would remove his saber and become "one of the most pleasant, chatty agreeable men," wrote a member of the 1st Mississippi Cavalry.[46]

November 23: Hatch Skirmishes East of Lawrenceburg and Schofield Begins to March to Columbia

Schofield hurriedly realigned his infantry as Hood's line of march was revealed. Schofield rode to Lynnville on the morning of November 23 and ordered Stanley to withdraw the final two Union divisions to that location that afternoon. With Stanley's withdrawal, the railroad from Lynnville to Decatur fell in the hands of Hood's army. Lynnville, a village of about 30 homes, had been mostly burned two weeks earlier by the 10th Tennessee Cavalry (U.S.) after being fired upon by Southern sympathizers. Wilson arrived at Campbellsville and moved to assume direct command of the cavalry forces in the field for the first time. Schofield wrote: "General Wilson is here, and will start for Campbellsville, [about two miles due west of Lynnville] to join Hatch, in a few moments. Stanley will be here tonight, and Cox ten miles above."[47]

Early in the morning Croxton's brigade moved forward to face the Confederate cavalry on the Lawrenceburg and Pulaski road, relieving Hatch's other two brigades (Wells' and Coon's) which held the forward position the day before. A couple of troopers from Croxton's brigade approached a farmhouse that morning and met a pleasant lady who told them her husband was a colonel in Forrest's cavalry. She shared a corn pone with them and told them they needed just to move along. She said if they stayed there too long Forrest could give them plenty provisions. The men mounted and withdrew with the rest of the 2nd Michigan Cavalry.[48]

While Hatch was being pushed back along his front, Capron also found himself facing a large number of enemy cavalry that evening and Colonel Strickland at Columbia reported that Capron had been forced back from Henryville to Fouche Springs, eight miles south of Mount Pleasant during the day. Meanwhile, Hood's infantry movement resulted in Schofield shifting west to keep the Confederates from swinging around his flank. Schofield wrote to Jacob Cox: "General Hatch has moved his force in front of Lynnville to the vicinity of Campbellsville. I will join you at Lynnville about noon today.... If you have information that he is moving in that direction, move at once to check him, leaving Wagner until I arrive. I only want to hold the railroad until I can get all the stores from here, when I will withdraw to Columbia."[49]

November 24: Cavalry Fights at Campbellsville and Lynnville

On November 23, Hood continued marching to Columbia. Cheatham's corps and Hood's headquarters marched another 18 miles during the day and ended the day about four miles north of Waynesborough on the Mount Pleasant–Waynesborough Road. The accounts of the day's fighting are virtually impossible to reconcile between the Union and Confederate reports; however, the overall result showed the Union cavalry on the eastern flank withdrawing under heavy pressure from the Confederate cavalry while the Federal infantry shifted northward.

The next day (November 24), the fighting continued in earnest as Hatch's cavalry fell back another five miles to Campbellsville while skirmishing with Jackson's and Buford's divisions. After skirmishing with Croxton the previous day, Jackson's division was joined by Buford's division late in the afternoon and the two Confederate commands continued north on November 24. Oliver Wells moved his First Brigade a mile west of Campbellsville on Big Creek. Soon, the Confederate dismounted cavalry attacked Hatch's right flank, causing Hatch to mistake them for infantry troops. In the initial clash, Buford's division arrived on the scene first, after swinging nearly around the rear of Hatch's division and during this first action against the Confederate cavalry, Wells' brigade successfully handled the enemy. At 9:00 a.m., the 3rd Illinois, 12th Missouri, and 7th Illinois counterattacked Buford's cavalry, "turning his left and driving the division two miles in confusion onto infantry supports," wrote Hatch. Buford initially attacked with Bell's brigade and Huey's Kentucky battalion. Sergeant Lyman Pierce, 2nd Iowa, recalled that the Confederate cavalry tried to entice the Federal cavalry into a trap by pushing ahead and then allowing their center to appear to be withdrawing, but to no avail.[50]

Wells commanded the First Brigade of Hatch's division for a few more days until Colonel Robert Stewart arrived, and Lieutenant William Shaver of the 12th Missouri found the brigade in a difficult position. After the initial skirmish, Buford advanced his division from the west in another attack on Wells' brigade. Shaver, a pre-war physician from Steelville, Missouri, recalled that his brigade had been driven north for the past two days. He wrote: "Buford ... pitched into us at Campbellsville." Shaver also noted that the initial cavalry fight went in favor of the Union cavalry, but the "Confederate infantry came up and drove us toward Columbia." The infantry referred to this report was dismounted Confederate cavalry, in particular, the 19th Tennessee Cavalry which was recognized for its efforts in the fight. The losses in Wells' brigade amounted to eight killed, 15 wounded and 100 taken prisoner, a heavy loss. The Union officers probably over estimated the number of prisoners because several of these men filtered into the Union camps a few days later after being cut off by the Southern advance.[51]

Wells led Hatch's re-positioning that morning. Coon had also moved rearward again on November 24 and reached Campbellsville at 9:00 a.m. and then moved about a mile and a half north of the town to encamp. Coon's stay would be a short one, because patrols found that the enemy was moving on the town with "vedettes standing on every high bluff in sight." Scouts soon discovered Jackson's cavalry advancing from the

Chapter Six. Florence to Columbia 105

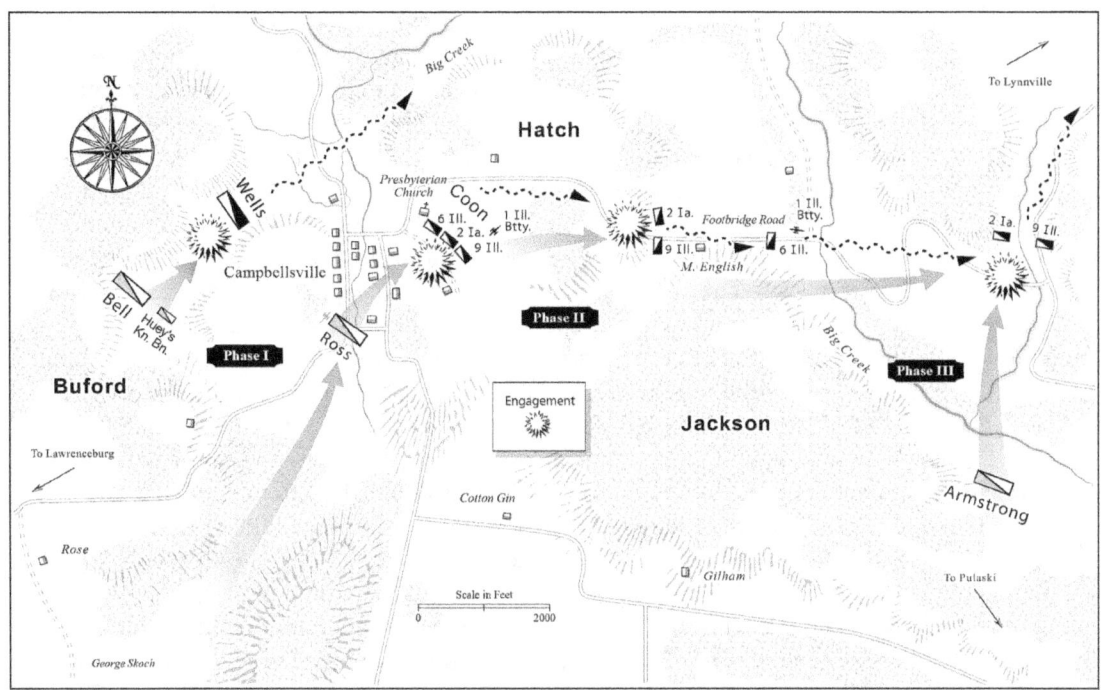

Cavalry fight at Campbellsville, November 24, 1864.

south. Hatch ordered increased security and, then, the First Brigade was attacked about a half mile from town by Buford's division, riding from the southwest. Coon ordered his regiments into line at Campbellsville while throwing down the fences, but this wasn't completed before Jackson's columns emerged on the horizon. Buford ordered the 19th Tennessee Cavalry to attack Wells just as Ross' cavalry brigade arrived on the scene. Jackson moved Ross' brigade forward and then attacked from the southwest with Armstrong's brigade, while Young's battery hammered away at the Federal position. Coon's brigade fell into line at Campbellsville attempting to secure Wells' flank and route of escape. Coon, observing the long lines of gray-clad cavalry, withdrew to the east side of Campbellsville holding open the road to Lynnville, anticipating that Wells, "reported in a critical situation," would need to withdraw in that direction. Coon's brigade would have four heated engagements with the enemy cavalry—Campbellsville, ¾ mile east of town, two miles east of town, and finally at Lynnville.[52]

Wells' initial success was reversing as Coon's Second Brigade prepared to the meet the enemy on the east side of the town near a church. Coon placed the 2nd Iowa in the middle of his battle line with the 6th Illinois on the right and the 9th Illinois on the left. Around noon, his troopers were barely out their saddles when Ross' Confederates arrived "in heavy force on the south and west side of the town," wrote Coon. Hatch's artillery opened up on the enemy as soon as they came within range (about a mile and a half away). Coon recorded: "The effect of the cannonading was excellent, causing the whole rebel column to halt for at least one hour and deploy in heavy force." In the meantime, a second Confederate column (Armstrong's brigade) moved to the east of the Union cavalry making for the Lynnville Road, Coon's best route of retreat. Deciding to withdraw, Coon sent the 2nd Iowa about three quarters of a mile east of the town to check this advance but the Iowans found the column too strong to hold for long. Coon still needed to hold the road for Wells' withdrawing cavalry. Coon sent the 9th Illinois to bolster the 2nd Iowa resulting in both regiments fighting a heated skirmish, still outnumbered by the advancing Confederate troops. Coon continued: "[T]heir position soon became intolerable, as the enemy was undoubtedly moving their main column by the right flank, to get possession of the road in their rear." Sergeant Lyman Pierce, 2nd Iowa, described the fire on his position as a "ceaseless sheet of murderous lead." Coon asked Hatch for help and he ordered Coon to fall back and despite the situation with the First Brigade. As the Federals moved to the rear, the Confederate artillery, a thousand yards away, opened up on this position and Coon dismounted his men until the led-horses, 6th Illinois, and artillery passed to the rear. Despite the volleys being fired by the approaching enemy troopers, Coon had no casualties with the exception of two horses, but he could no longer hold his position. Coon fell back further east along Footbridge Road.[53]

Earlier that morning, Jackson received a message from Forrest warning him about protecting his flanks, but Jackson had little concerns about that. Ross's brigade had another active day on November 24 as his cavalry again led the advance northward. As the Union cavalry withdrew that morning, Ross followed, reaching Campbellsville at noon, and observed Hatch's division preparing to meet the Confederate advance. Ross dismounted the 3rd Texas and gave orders for the regiment to lead the attack. Ross unlimbered Young's battery which opened fire on Coon's brigade. The 6th Texas Cavalry moved into position to support the battery and the 9th Texas Cavalry and the Texas Legion were moved into battle line on the right of the brigade to be thrown into the fight. Ross wrote: "I ordered everything forward. The Ninth Texas and Legion, led by their respective commanders, Colonel Jones and Lieutenant-Colonel Whitfield, rushed forward at a gallop, and passing through the village fell upon the enemy's moving squadrons with such irresistible force as to scatter them in every direction, pursuing and capturing numbers of prisoners, horses, equipments, small-arms, accouterments, and four stand of colors ... but, while endeavoring to withdraw his broken and discomfitted squadrons, was attacked vigorously in flank by a portion of General Armstrong's brigade and his rout made complete." The fight began in the village and second skirmish resulted just east of the town as the Federal artillery withdrew.[54]

Lieutenant George Griscom, adjutant of the 9th Texas Cavalry, described that the Federals began pulling back and Ross rode among his brigade ordering the regiments to charge them during this withdrawal. Colonel Dudley Jones, 9th Texas, spurred his horse and ordered "charge!" The 9th Texas, supported by the 1st Texas Legion, gave the Rebel Yell and attacked Coon's brigade two miles east of Campbellsville. The Texans cut Coon's column in half while charging directly into the Federals. So heated was the fight, that Jones participated in the hand-to-hand fighting, firing his revolver until he ran out of bullets and "threw it away & sabering a fellow & grappling for his gun," described Griscom. Jones looked up in time to see another Union trooper approaching and avoided injury by throwing himself out of his saddle, escaping only with a hole through his hat, losing a plug of hair in the process.[55]

Ross surged ahead with Armstrong's brigade attacking the eastern flank of Coon's brigade. During the fight, Hatch, himself, was nearly captured by a surprise attack. Coon's men continued fighting the advancing enemy as Hatch oversaw the efforts of his two brigades. Two miles east of Campbellsville, the site of third Federal position, Coon's men were falling back toward a "narrow gorge" just as a group of Armstrong's troops

Chapter Six. Florence to Columbia 107

pushed into the Federal left flank. Hatch's escort company, Company M, 6th Illinois, saw the enemy attacking and spurred their horses into a melee of sabers and revolvers, holding the enemy at bay until the enemy withdrew from the skirmish. The 9th Illinois had been withdrawing into the gorge when the attack came but turned and fell into line at the mouth of the gap. The 9th Illinois had just dismounted "when they received a heavy fire from a brigade of the enemy. Not a particle daunted, the captain ordered his men forward until it became a hand to hand fight," explained Coon. Coon, supervising the withdrawal a quarter mile west of this unfolding situation, was unaware of the threat of being cut off. The 9th Illinois was in a perilous situation themselves. The troopers began the day with 60 rounds of ammunition and during their fight, they found their ammunition was nearly exhausted.[56]

The 9th Illinois fell into position along a ridge and found themselves facing a line of Confederate cavalry charging from a farmstead through an orchard. The first volley from the Illinois cavalry stopped the attack and the Southerners reformed at the farm buildings and prepared for another charge. The charge reached a fence and the price of continuing to run across an open field into the muzzles of the waiting Union cavalry caused the Confederates to seek shelter behind the fence. Soon, more Southern reinforcements joined the line of soldiers behind the fence and the Illinois commander knew he couldn't hold his position. He sent messengers asking for reinforcements. A third line of Confederate cavalry arrived and Captain Anthony Mock ordered the desperate Union cavalry "to take good aim, shoot low, and make every shot count." Then, the sound of "charge" echoed and all the Confederates surged forward at the run, crashing into the 9th Illinois, resulting in hand-to-hand fighting. The 9th Illinois held its ground, repeatedly repulsing the enemy from this position and during the last charge the regiment had no ammunition but met the attack "with the butts of his carbines, and the enemy repulsed, though the company in the center, of twenty-five men, had 14 men killed while fighting in line." Seeing the weight of the battle in favor of the cavalry in gray, Mock ordered his men to "fall back." The Union regiment ran back to their horses, leapt into the saddles, and made a hasty retreat before the onrushing Confederates.[57]

Coon quickly ordered the 2nd Iowa to take position in the gap until the 9th Illinois could withdraw. The placement of the Iowans in this natural choke-point proved a dangerous place to be. Coon described: "No sooner had the Ninth Illinois passed through the line of the Second Iowa than the rebel brigade came at double-quick up the hollow, colors in front, and in another instant was in line of battle. Three hundred Spencers from the Second Iowa drove them back in confusion; but a moment, however, intervened when the rebels rallied." The Iowa regiment recorded 30 casualties in as many minutes. Coon had to leave six men wounded on the field and the 2nd Iowa formed the rear guard as the brigade rode three miles to Lynnville, arriving there at 4:00 p.m. There, Hatch's division held the enemy until dark and then the division received orders to ride to Columbia.[58]

In Hatch's report, he did not indicate any details regarding Wells' or Croxton's brigades. In regard to Wells' brigade, its initial successes soon turned into a hasty withdrawal and the loss of 100 troopers presumed prisoners of the Confederate cavalry. Wells' regiments reunited with Coon's brigade as both brigades headed for Lynnville after the fight. In regard to Hatch's claims of repulsing the enemy, Henry Mortimer Hempstead, 2nd Michigan, recorded: "I am not fully prepared to believe that the enemy got the worst of it." In the day's action, Forrest declared he had engaged Hatch's division and fought him in a vigorous engagement. Forrest claimed 100 prisoners and several others killed and wounded in the fighting in which he "routed" Hatch. Others in the Confederate cavalry also claimed victory as Hatch's cavalry was driven back to the infantry lines. The combination of Buford and Jackson, a mixture of Tennesseans, Mississippians, Kentuckians and Texans, carried the day and the "fierce attack was, indeed, irresistible," wrote J.G. Deupree, 1st Mississippi Cavalry.[59]

In all, Coon's brigade had four fighting positions during the day's battles, Croxton was unengaged, and Wells been pushed precipitately eastward. Hatch had had a difficult day at Campbellsville. Schofield reported: "I have just heard from Hatch. At 4 o'clock he was at Lynnville; had been fighting one division and a brigade of rebel cavalry during the day; will move this way to-night; he has [had] pretty hard work, but has done well." Schofield misread the attack on Hatch as an indication that Hood intended to attack Pulaski instead of Columbia, a mistake which would soon become evident.[60]

While the heated cavalry fights continued, the Federal infantry thought the cavalry was doing well. First Lieutenant Francis Stewart, 49th Ohio Infantry, wrote about the positive efforts of the cavalry: "All went off nicely in the forenoon. the cavalry which was covering our rear coming from Pulaski came up this morning and found the enemies cavalry in force at Linnville where they had a sharp fight with them last evening. Rebel cavalry under gen Forest made their appearance in front at 2 PM and immediately commenced skirmishing with us, which has been kept up for more or less all afternoon. However, without doing us any harm."[61]

Ross described: "The last of his forces, in full flight, disappeared in the direction of Lynnville about sunset, and we saw nothing more of them south of Duck River. Our loss in the fight at Campbellsville was only 5 men wounded, while our captures, I found upon investigation, summed up to be 84 prisoners and all their horses, equipments, and small arms, 4 stand of colors, and 65 beef-cattle." The day belonged to Jackson and Buford.[62]

Chalmers' Division and Capron's Cavalry Brigade

November 19–20: Cavalry Actions on the West Flank

While Hatch covered the front and east flank of the bulk of Hood's army, Horace Capron's Federal cavalry brigade was in the most precarious position as Hood and Forrest swung to the west of Pulaski and moved toward Columbia. Initially, Schofield told Hatch, rather dismissively, that Capron had "wandered off to Waynesborough. I am trying to get him back," but Capron was right where he needed to be, preparing to meet Chalmers' cavalry division, screening Cheatham's and Lee's corps. Schofield wanted the cavalry closer and he ordered Capron, while still watching for Forrest, to move back to "unite with General Hatch, who will move between Forrest and the railroad." In a blunt message, Schofield told Capron on November 20: "You seem to have entirely misunderstood your instructions, and I expect to hear of the capture of your command. Move back at once toward Mount Pleasant as far as the intersection of the Lawrenceburg road, and from that point scout toward Lawrenceburg and Waynesborough and on the lateral roads.... Possibly you may get this in time." In Schofield's message, he had presumed that the bulk of Hood's infantry marched toward to Lawrenceburg, but Cheatham's full infantry corps was marching directly for Capron's brigade.[63]

Schofield also alerted Captain James Strong, 8th Michigan Cavalry, who was in charge of the courier line, via Strickland commanding an infantry brigade at Columbia, to tell Capron about the risks from the Confederate cavalry in the field. "Look out sharply for Forrest, and inform me and Colonel Capron of any movement you may discover.... Colonel Capron is ordered to move back toward Mount Pleasant as far as the intersection of the Lawrenceburg road." From Waynesborough, Capron replied to Schofield that his scouts had found no concentration of enemies west of his position or in his rear. He explained that he temporarily held his cavalry at Waynesborough due to the availability of feed for his mounts and rations for his men. Despite his position, he had a strong scout in the direction of Florence the day before and found enemy cavalry four miles south of his position. His men drove the enemy 12 miles before finding a larger concentration of Chalmers' cavalry. Capron explained the roads wet and soggy, forage scarce, and rations almost non-existent. He still had not been able to open communications with Hatch, but he promised to push his scouts further east the next day to try to find him. While Capron could find no evidence of Hood marching in his direction, this would soon change.[64]

The men of Capron's command would ultimately be angered by Schofield's off-handed remarks that the brigade had wandered off to the right. After the Atlanta Campaign, the brigade had been transported to Louisville to be remounted and re-armed, not with carbines, but with bulky infantry-style Springfield muskets. Then, the brigade was ordered to watch the western flank of Schofield's two corps without adequate arms, feed for their mounts, rations for the men, or communications with just about anyone. Capron wrote to Wilson, as he assumed command, from his position at Waynesborough: "We are in an isolated position, being about fifty-five miles from supplies in any direction. The country around for twenty miles is completely swept of everything by troops who have lately passed through here, and the roads are next to impassable." Capron had scouts patrolling 20 miles in each direction. He told Wilson that he had been ordered to take an advance position on the western flank of Schofield's troops and to begin communicating with Hatch who was supposed to have been moving toward Capron. He discounted the misunderstanding of Schofield's orders, but he complained that he has received no replies to his messages. Capron had regularly sent messages to Schofield but none of his couriers had returned. "I am at a loss to know what to do in the absence of any further instructions from any source.... I shall be able to eke out our subsistence for a day or two longer by gathering in for twenty miles around everything eatable for man or beast. What with the impassable roads, incessant rain, heavy scouting, and the necessity for their bringing in their forage, our horses are fast being made unserviceable and useless." Capron wrote to Schofield: "The country in every direction is destitute of everything for man or beast. The roads impassable for teams. It is impossible to advance my main force. I can obtain forage a few days longer at this place, but no rations of consequence. I can hear nothing of General Hatch."[65]

Strickland, commanding the Union garrison at Columbia, relayed instructions from Schofield for Capron to watch for the Confederate cavalry and move east toward Hatch's division. Some of the men of Capron's brigade would bitterly recall their duty, and particularly how they were portrayed. Hatch had previously told Capron he expected him to unite with Hatch's cavalry line, while still extending westward to the river. Instead, columns of infantry and three divisions of cavalry threatened to cut Capron off from the remainder of the Union force to the east. As Hatch's cavalry had been pushed back to the east from Lawrenceburg, Capron became more isolated.[66]

Once the Confederate advance began, the Union cavalry on the western flank had important duty in preventing Hood from marching past Schofield's infantry. W.L. Sanford, 14th Illinois, observed: "The incessant rains had rendered all the roads so nearly impassable, as to cause both General Thomas and General Schofield to believe that Hood could not possibly advance." Hood would prove to the Union commanders that he could march in the existing conditions. In regard to the Federal cavalry, Croxton and Hatch faced a large amount of enemy cavalry followed by Lee's and Stewart's corps. Capron's small brigade of about 800 men was situated in the correct location to resist Cheatham, Lee, and Chalmers as much as possible.[67]

Capron's brigade remained on watch at daybreak on November 21. With the approaching cavalry and columns of Confederate infantry on the Waynesborough Road, Capron prepared to fall back from Waynesborough that afternoon as instructed. Capron, still in the dark about most of the movements of the Federal and Confederate troops, sent scouts to ascertain that the enemy had not already moved past the right flank or the rear of his brigade. During a cold and sleeting dusk, Capron began moving his cavalry toward Henryville (northwest of Lawrenceburg and in the direction of Mount Pleasant) over roads covered with "a glare of ice." In an unfortunate incident, some of the buildings in Waynesborough were set afire as Capron pulled out of the village. Waynesborough, the county seat, was a small village in 1864 and had been largely abandoned due to the constant movement of troops in the area during the war. Wayne County had voted to remain in the Union, but it also had a strong pro–Confederate contingent.[68]

November 22: Capron's Cavalry Prepares to Resist the Advance

At 9 p.m., Captain James Strong, commanding couriers, wrote to Schofield and reported that Capron had reached the Lawrenceburg Road after leaving Waynesborough at 2:00 p.m. Even before he received Schofield's latest orders, Capron had already decided to move back to the east. This placed Capron east of Waynesborough and west of Lawrenceville in the direction of Mount Pleasant on November 22. Jacob Biffle's Confederate troopers rode into Waynesborough only to find Capron recently withdrawn from the town. The Southern troopers also noticed the weather had taken a decided turn colder and they tarried only a short time as they moved onto Capron's trail. Meanwhile, Strickland observed 75 Confederate cavalry troopers at Mount Pleasant on November 21, but he confidently said he had "made ample preparations for Forrest or any other force coming this way."[69]

Capron had scouts out, still only observing small detachments of Confederate cavalry on scouting missions. The Union scouts discovered an enemy courier line extending to Columbia which Capron intended to destroy the next day. The roads remained in deplorable condition due to the recent wet, cold weather. Communications remained poor and Capron wrote to Schofield: "I have not been able to obtain any intelligence of General Hatch, nor have I heard from you, and am in doubts as to what is best to be done." Capron told Schofield about the terrible condition of the roads and that the road had "sunk several feet in mud" at various locations. Moving in these conditions had taken a heavy toll on his mounts but he had not found any enemy within 15 miles of his position. Further, the overall condition of Capron's brigade was not good. Capron explained: "My force present is 1,000 men, temporarily armed with Springfield muskets, an arm that we have had no experience with.... I have sent back to Columbia for rations, clothing, and horseshoes."[70]

Capron Fights Chalmers at Henryville and Fouche Springs—November 23

Capron received his first communications late on November 22 from Hatch, ordering him to stay in his current position and to put his cavalry between Forrest and the railroad. Hatch's division was more than 20 miles away, far away from his promise to secure Capron's left flank. Hatch did not know what Capron faced and his cavalry had been pushed back toward Pulaski the day before by Buford and Jackson. Capron moved his brigade just north of Henryville, a mile north of the road leading directly from Lawrenceburg on the evening of November 22. Capron sent a detachment with a message for Hatch, but immediately the Union troopers came hurriedly back with Rucker's Confederate horsemen in pursuit. Rucker's cavalrymen effectively dealt with Capron's detachment with many in the party being captured or killed. The Confederate cavalry closed in on Capron's position where two heated skirmishes would result the next day—the first just north of Henryville and the second at Fouche Springs.[71]

On November 23, Capron sent patrols to the west to ensure the area was clear, but Chalmers' cavalry harassed the isolated groups of Union cavalry. Chalmers' scouts were initially surprised when they found Union cavalry in line behind a glade at Henryville where they found a "vast aggregation, about a million, of Yankees," wrote a Southern cavalryman. As Chalmers screened the advance of the Confederate infantry corps, Rucker's lone brigade moved northward toward Mount Pleasant while Jacob Biffle's small brigade secured Waynesborough and the roads to the west. Capron had selected his position well, but he had been unable to gain reinforcements overnight. Lieutenant Colonel Raleigh White, 14th Tennessee Cavalry (CSA), leading the advance of Rucker's brigade, found Capron's position. The Federal cavalry had prepared for battle by building barricades, and Rucker's brigade attacked the Federal pickets at Henryville at 2 p.m.[72]

With the increased number and boldness of the clashes with Chalmers' cavalry, Capron knew he faced a general movement directed at his location. "Our situation was critical; the emergency demanded prompt action to secure my command from being captured," wrote Capron. He drew his scouting parties back to the main body of the brigade and as they returned, they brought news that Rucker's cavalry was approaching. Capron immediately sent scouts to determine that his rear was clear of enemy cavalry as he prepared to meet the enemy.[73]

As he prepared to fight, Capron established two defensive lines—the forward position, just north of Henryville, to meet the first enemy attack and the second position, a few miles to the rear at Fouche Springs, where he placed the main concentration of his brigade to cover the withdrawal of forces in the front. Capron had little time to choose these defensive sites and he discounted a road leading directly from the south which intersected the road which led from Henryville to Fouche Springs. Capron left what he referred to as a light force of cavalry—two squadrons of the 14th Illinois, part of the 8th Michigan and a portion of the 16th Illinois in the forward position behind barricades under the command of Captain H.C. Connelly, and the remainder of the brigade two miles to the rear.[74]

At the second defensive position, Capron dismounted his troopers and set his men to preparing barricades, while also strengthening his flanks. The clash between Capron's rearguard and Chalmers' cavalry should have been a pretty straight forward affair. The Union troopers north of Henryville were posted behind a barricade and were awaiting an attack by Rucker's brigade which they planned to delay and then slowly withdraw to the main body at Fouche Springs. They had not counted on Forrest's arrival with his escort. As Chalmers approached Henryville at sundown, Forrest arrived and took control of the situation. He ordered Rucker to push directly ahead into the Federal rearguard at Henryville, David Kelley's regiment would swing around the left flank, and Forrest's escort would insert itself from the Confederate right flank, effectively encircling the rearguard. Forrest and his escort edged up the Lawrenceburg Road as darkness approached and instead of immediately attacking Capron's main concentration of cavalry, Forrest interposed his cavalry between the Federal rearguard and Capron's primary cavalry force. Working in Forrest's favor was the fact that his escort carried Spencer carbines and many wore rubber slickers which concealed their gray uniforms. Connelly, unaware of the situation in the rear, sent a detachment of one officer and 10 men to open communications with Capron. As the detail moved to the rear, the troopers saw a body of men but in the dim light could not tell whether they were Union or Confederate, seeing that some wore blue overcoats, while others wore gray blankets around their shoulders. A Federal officer rode ahead and disappeared in the midst of the body of soldiers. The rest of the detail approached only to be greeted with a volley from the waiting group of soldiers. In the meantime, the rearguard, behind the barricades, consisting of about a regiment, was attacked in force by Rucker.[75]

Captain Connelly wrote, "Forrest by this time had gotten between our command (the rear guard) and the main command, and was quietly picking up our men; moving between our forces." The 10-man detachment was the first to be gobbled up by Forrest. Next, W.L. Sanford, 14th Illinois, silently moved from the rearguard barricades with a handful of his regiment to try to establish communications with Capron's main body of cavalry. They had ridden a short distance when they found a body of cavalry in the darkness, but Sanford could not tell if they were Union or Confederate. He spoke to the men and the commanding officer "replied with one shot at short range with his revolver, and to this day I can see the flash of that shot in my face, but the bullet missed me, and struck a little fellow on my right, Joseph Murry of my company. The bullet struck him two or three inches above the right ear. He dropped forward on his horse's neck. I reached down and caught him by the cape of his overcoat, and kept him from falling off, until he came to. I finally got him straightened up, all covered with blood. This was the only shot fired by them, and we came out with the loss of two guns. We found out afterward that it was General Forrest and his escort, who were quietly picking up our men and horses." H.C. Connelly declared that the ball which wounded Murry was definitely fired by Forrest himself. The shot began the fight of Capron's rearguard to reach the safety with the main concentration of Union forces at Fouche Springs. Tragically, Horace Capron's eldest son was killed in the fighting.[76]

A member of the Tennessee cavalry recalled the series of fights as Capron's rearguard fought its way back to the main body of cavalry. Isaac N. Rainey, 7th Tennessee Cavalry, posed the question: "[W]hat army in the world today has a Lieutenant

General who would lead 90 men in a charge like that?" A Confederate officer noticed Forrest's countenance as he prepared the ambush and described him as "care worn, but carries the bold defiant expression he had of old." Forrest and his escort initially ran into Capron's line which Rainey described as being behind barricades, and then withdrew. Then, he turned his attention to a detachment coming from the rearguard and moved to intercept these men. After the initial clash with Connelly's rearguard, Forrest charged ahead only to find the enemy had withdrawn—"not a Yankee was to be seen." Forrest dismounted and ambushed another group of withdrawing Union cavalry. Rainey joined in the ambush and "poured a volley into them; then all was still death." Forrest remounted his men and found another body of Union cavalry trotting to the rear. "Another volley and they divided again," wrote Rainey. Yet another group of Union cavalry approached, this time hurrying to the rear at a gallop and they fired directly into Forrest's escort. "Balls came pretty thick, but none of us was hurt." As Federal rearguard fought its way to the rear, no stragglers were found, only 16 dead horses.[77]

Connelly had been in a tight situation. He had Rucker's brigade moving in his front as the explosion of gunfire echoed in the rear. He sent Captain John Hattery, 16th Illinois, with 25 men to determine what was happening in the rear of his position. Hattery only rode a couple of hundred yards when Forrest's escort opened a volley on the small Federal detachment. Hearing the gunfire in the rear, Connelly made a precipitous withdrawal from the barricades. The Confederate cavalry was reloading just as the retreating Union column reached their position and the Confederates unleashed another volley. The officers cut their way through along the road, but the trailing column scattered and moved "pell mell" across the countryside. Connelly's 16th Illinois followed the portion of the 8th Michigan which had just scattered. Connelly followed and explained: "I saw the importance of promptly charging out and calling upon comrades to follow, the whole column followed. The men set up a terrific yell, and, dashing on to the rebel lines, fired their Springfield guns. The Confederate line broke and ran like sheep, and we brought out safely every man we had with us."[78]

James Chalmers ordered Rucker to press Capron's brigade on the Waynesborough–Mt. Pleasant Road after the first skirmish near Henryville. Rucker then found the second line of Union cavalry near Fouche Springs (about five miles south of Mt. Pleasant) and "a sharp skirmish ensured." At Henryville, Chalmers captured 45 prisoners and another 20 prisoners in the withdrawal to Fouche Springs. "Our loss in this affair was slight," wrote Chalmers. J.P. Young, 7th Tennessee (CSA), remarked that a near disaster was averted as Rucker's cavalry advanced and unknowingly ran into Forrest and his escort. Rucker's men heard the loud yells of Forrest's men and recognized them before they fired into their ranks.[79]

Likewise, during the fighting in the increasingly dark evening, Forrest was nearly killed. A Federal cavalryman approached him and placed his revolver near Forrest's chest and demanded that he surrender. Forrest was saved by the quick thinking of Major John P. Strange, adjutant general, who knocked the revolver away just as it fired, the bullet careening harmlessly into the night. James Dinkins recalled that Forrest struck the Federal rearguard just as it was getting dark while the enemy was moving through a wooded area. "They did not think we were mean enough to continue the fight after night. General Forrest dashed through their ranks, and scattered them in great confusion. The force which General Chalmers was fighting, hearing the firing in their rear, retreated.... In the meantime, Chalmers and Rucker, hearing the firing, and noting the panic, charged in column, the men yelling like Indians, driving or capturing every thing before them."[80]

In Forrest's after-action report, he stated that he had gained the rear of Capron's cavalry at Henryville and that he made a charge on the enemy with his escort alone, routing the enemy and capturing "50 prisoners, 20 horses and 1 ambulance." W.L. Sanford, 14th Illinois, agreed that Forrest interposed his escort behind the rearguard but he disputed the claim that Forrest had moved to the rear of Capron's brigade. Capron's move to his second position successfully prevented Forrest from threatening the entire brigade. The judicious placement of Federal detachments on the flanks prevented Lt. Colonel David C. Kelley approaching the other flank (west) from joining Forrest in his attack. Kelley commanded the 26th Tennessee Battalion Cavalry (Forrest's old regiment) but he met a solid line of Union cavalry in his attempt to gain the rear of the defenders. Once consolidated the 26th Tennessee Battalion and other components were referred to as the 3rd Tennessee Cavalry Regiment. Kelley had just received a nominal promotion to colonel and his command was granted full regimental status the day before.[81]

Forrest's ambush caused a great surprise to the retreating Union cavalry. While this is true, the men of Capron's brigade bitterly recalled Forrest's success resulted from Confederates wearing Union overcoats. Sanford wrote: "Relative to his placing his men in ambush, if there was anything more in this line than the shameful violation of the recognized rules of modern warfare, by concealing the identity of his men in the uniform of union men, it will be found in the truthful account of Captain Connelly, of the heroic charge made by our rear guard through the lines of Forrest's veterans." Capron explained that after the rearguard reached the line at Fouche Springs, a line of Confederate cavalry attacked Capron's main position and the Confederate cavalry was so close they opened fired "directly in the faces of our men." This Confederate force swung past the rearguard, only to be surprised by the resolve of the Union cavalry in the rear. "Their fire was promptly returned, and a rapid interchange followed. In the midst of the noise and confusion of the battle a shout and firing were heard in the rear of this attacking force, and in the next moment their line was rent asunder, and our men from the front dashed into our lines." Capron had some serious losses in the engagements, including some key officers in the brigade.[82]

The 16th Illinois lost some men of the initial detachment heading for the rear but Sanford's detachment of the 14th Illinois Cavalry returned without loss. Sanford concluded: "General Forrest's claim that at Henryville they captured 45 prisoners, and that he captured at Fouche's springs 50 prisoners, may be correct, nor is it a wonderful result, when we remember that scouting parties were liable to be cut off while coming in, and we know that detachments on our flanks fighting on foot, had their horses captured, and in moving on foot portions of these detachments were cut off and captured."[83]

Darkness prevented the combatants from capitalizing on the situation as each ran into ambushes. Many in Capron's brigade felt they had had the hardest duty during this period of the campaign and had successfully blocked the westward route of Hood's march at a critical time with a single small brigade while being cut off the rest of the Federal forces. In regard to what Schofield commented about Capron's wandering off to the right, W.L. Sanford would write that Capron "should undoubtedly be pardoned for misunderstanding the orders of his superior; if indeed, he did misunderstand them. It was surely a very fortunate mistake." In the end, the Confederate cavalry successfully dealt with the Federal blocking force resulting in the beginning of a fighting withdrawal by Capron's brigade. From Capron's point of view, his small brigade had held the enemy for six to eight hours, a significant and an important time period for the Federal forces.[84]

November 24: Capron's Withdrawal from Mt. Pleasant to Columbia

While the Union generals pondered whether Hood would move toward Pulaski, a fortuitous encounter by Hatch's cavalry resulted in the capture of a Confederate dispatch which revealed Hood's intention of moving directly on Columbia. Hood chose not to attack the defenses that the Union force had been constructing for the past two weeks at Pulaski. Stanley moved his corps to Lynnville on the evening of November 23 where George Wagner's Second Division had moved the previous day. Stanley, evacuating Pulaski on the afternoon of November 23, wrote, "The roads, however, off the pikes were very bad, it having rained very heavily for some days, and then frozen, but not hard enough to bear wagons." Stanley did not remain at Lynnville long after one of Capron's trooper arrived at Schofield's headquarters and reported that Hood threatened to move past the western flank of the Union infantry. Despite the bad roads, Stanley knew the risk this posed and he began marching northward at 1:00 a.m. Jacob Cox's division was closer to Columbia and he began moving at the same time. Stanley would write that Cox's arrival at Columbia the next morning saved "Capron's brigade of cavalry from annihilation and perhaps the town of Columbia from capture."[85]

On November 24, a day described as comfortably warm and bright, Capron seemed in relatively good shape after his recent clash with Forrest's cavalry, but his brigade was being whittled down. From 12 miles southwest of Mount Pleasant on November 23, he wrote to Hatch acknowledging his orders to maintain a strong reconnaissance effort, but he had found the enemy that evening. Capron had withdrawn closer to Mount Pleasant overnight, reaching the town in the early hours, after the recent fight at Fouche Springs.[86]

While Capron fought at Fouche Springs and Henryville, the news of Confederate cavalry's success against Hatch reached Capron and this greatly impacted the morale of the brigade. "This only added to the before almost hopelessness of our situation. An order now came to Capron that he must check Hood's advance, if it sacrificed his whole command," wrote W.L. Sanford. As Capron's brigade began the next day, slowly retreating to the rear, it moved away from the trees and hills into open ground which was not advantageous for delaying the Confederate advance. Capron, still attempting to follow his orders of delaying Hood's march, prepared his defenses to gain whatever advantage he could from the terrain. Capron built barricades while placing detachments of cavalry on the flanks to keep Forrest out of the rear. Sanford wrote: "Ours was a task such as was seldom expected of so small a force, and therefore Schofield, realizing this, accompanied his orders to hold the enemy with, 'If it sacrifices every man of your command.'" The troopers set about a fighting withdrawal, intent on holding out as long as possible, slowing Hood's and Forrest's march, and therefore preventing the enemy from reaching Columbia.[87]

Forrest was the master of the territory around Capron's brigade to such an extent, that one of the Confederate couriers riding over the countryside with orders for William H. Jackson was captured twice by his own comrades. Hoping to find reinforcements,

Capron was again disappointed when he reached Mount Pleasant and found the garrison infantry gone. He had no hope of holding Mount Pleasant because the terrain was so open, the Confederate forces easily flanked the Union cavalry's position. As a result, Capron withdrew a few miles to the north and again fell into a line of battle, but he found Forrest's cavalry moving past his flanks. Upon Capron's withdrawal, Forrest's cavalry descended on the abandoned Union garrison at Mt. Pleasant securing thousands of rounds of ammunition. Capron withdrew about six miles south of Columbia and then he refused to retreat any farther. He understood his orders—Hood and Forrest could not reach Columbia. Capron prepared to carry out the orders to the very end of his brigade. Soon, cavalry scouts returned with important news. The Confederate columns were seen "marching on a parallel road, until the head of a long column was in advance of our position." Still, Capron gave no orders to withdraw even though he received five similar messages from his scouts. He would stay and fight Forrest as long as his command would last.[88]

Captain Connelly, 16th Illinois, explained the situation: "Our situation was critical, our left was entirely unprotected. We received no communication from General Hatch, who seemed to have all he could do to take care of himself. On the morning of the 24th I was with the rearguard under Major Beers. We were strongly pressed, but fell back with deliberation. Colonel Capron had his little army in line of battle when I came up. I rode up to him and asked him if he intended to make a stand there. He replied that Generals Schofield and Wilson were raining dispatches on him, insisting that he must resist the enemy's advance if it destroyed his command. That the infantry had not yet reached Columbia, and that the 5th Iowa cavalry would be with us soon. I called his attention to the Confederate lines moving on both our flanks, evidently intending to form a junction, and capture us. I said to Colonel Capron: 'If we remain here we will be surrounded by an overwhelming force in a few minutes and captured.'" Connelly looked over the size of the Federal force and barely 600 men remained in the saddle.[89]

Capron rode to the top of an eminence and observed the advance Forrest's cavalry and artillery. He knew that Forrest was pushing along his flanks and that if the artillery opened on his position, he had little hope of surviving. Finally, Capron reasoned that time had run out and sacrificing his command without materially delaying the Confederate advance did no good. Then, Capron went into action and tried to deceive Forrest into believing he would stay and fight. He left a skeleton force at the barricade and began withdrawing the bulk of his force out of sight of the enemy. Capron moved most of his command behind a wooded hill and this allowed him to withdraw without being seen. He left a rearguard in place "to deceive the enemy as far as possible in regard to our intentions, and to mislead them in regard to our strength.... I had congratulated myself on a successful movement, when suddenly my rear guard was overwhelmed, and driven in upon us, with Forrest's command sabering them at their discretion."[90]

W.L. Sanford explained: "As our men below the rank of orderly sergeants possessed no cavalry arms of any kind, it was utterly impossible to resist an impetuous cavalry charge. With their muskets empty and no time to reload, they were as really disarmed as if holding in their hands only clubs. To have attempted to fight on foot, would not only result in being surrounded by an overwhelming force and captured, but would have permitted the flanking columns of the enemy to have pressed on into Columbia unopposed. Nothing could be done by the rear guard unarmed but to mount and get out of the way.... To maintain an orderly rapid retreat under the circumstances was beyond the power of any officers." The retreating Union cavalry began a "wild ride" as it withdrew with Chalmers' cavalry hot on its heels. Sanford described that part of the cavalry rode down a country lane which narrowed resulting in "a perfect jam of running horses.... Disorderly as was this hasty retreat, we sincerely believe, that under the same circumstances, General Sheridan himself could have done no better."[91]

Capron rode among his men trying to rally them, and during the skirmish and retreat, he galloped along a road toward Columbia when a six-team mule wagon exploded onto the road at full speed. The lead mule tripped, went down, and the other mules tumbled across the road overturning the wagon in the process. Capron was riding at full speed when this happened right in front of him, and he was unable to stop. He rode into the conflagration of wagon, teamsters, and mules, and, while being thrown with his horse, suffered a severe pelvis injury. After the accident, he was unable to ride again. He was forced to ride in an ambulance to Columbia and within a few days, he would be relieved of duty due to the injury.[92]

When Capron started his withdrawal the day before, he dispatched a rider to Columbia seeking assistance in holding back the Confederate column. When the courier reached Columbia, he found no hope for assistance and then, he mounted a fresh horse and headed down the Pulaski Road. The rider found Schofield and explained the situation. This resulted in orders for Cox to hurry to Columbia. Schofield told Cox that Hood was steadily flanking the Federals and the race was on to see who could reach Columbia first. Schofield rode with Stanley's two divisions marching in the same direction.[93]

All looked hopeless as Capron's brigade retreated toward Columbia and when all seemed lost, solid lines of blue-coated infantry came running into position in a field south of the town. The infantry arriving at Columbia was Cox's troops hurrying forward just in time to check the Confederate advance. Cox's infantry fell into line about a mile and a half south of Columbia which encouraged the cavalry to rally and take position on the right of the infantry. Cox and Capron held the Confederates for three hours along a creek until Stanley's IV Corps arrived on the scene. Sanford declared: "[T]hus was Columbia and Schofield's army saved, by the most heroic efforts of Capron's brigade.... Though some critics, who know nothing of such service, have criticised this movement of Capron's brigade as a 'disorderly panic,' yet not one of our commanders speak of it in other than respectful terms." While the Union forces saw the actions of the opposing forces as a race to Columbia, Hood steadily continued his infantry march toward Columbia.[94]

Chalmers explained that Rucker's brigade struck Capron's cavalry seven miles south of Columbia and routed them, following them to the edge of the town, capturing about 30 prisoners. Lieutenant Colonel William Azariah Dawson, 15th Tennessee Cavalry, attacked a Union color guard with his revolver blazing but he quickly fired all his bullets. Still, he did not relent but tried to physically claim the flag, and he was shot and killed in the process. The arrival of Cox's and Stanley's infantry stopped Chalmers' pursuit although they exchanged shots with the enemy throughout the afternoon. Chalmers' division remained in front of Columbia through November 27 sniping at the enemy.[95]

The evidence of the hard-fought cavalry fights between Capron and Chalmers greeted the Confederate infantry steadily marching north. Colonel James Cooper, 20th Tennessee Infantry, observed dead horses and dead men still lying beside the roads as the infantry trudged along the muddy roads to Columbia.[96]

November 24—The Armies Converge on Columbia

The possibility of the Confederates slipping past the Union right flank resonated with Thomas at Nashville who ordered Ruger to send his best two regiments (91st Indiana and 123rd Indiana) to cover the crossings on the Duck River west of Columbia at Williamsport and Centerville. The roads and the line of march also drew the three Southern corps together as they converged on Mount Pleasant the next day. Lee camped about nine miles south of Mount Pleasant with Cheatham to his rear, and Stewart behind Cheatham. Importantly, Schofield had successfully shifted his infantry to Columbia, and the swift marches of Cox and Stanley had dashed any hopes of separating the two Union corps from Nashville.[97]

In the afternoon of November 24, Schofield contemplated his defensive positions as he faced a larger enemy force. He wrote to Thomas and asked some important questions. "Do you think it important to hold Columbia? My force is not large enough to cover the town and railroad bridge." Schofield grasped the situation and realized the success of his defense depended on choosing the right defensive position and preventing his forces from being outmaneuvered. Thomas replied to Schofield that if he could not hold Columbia, then to withdraw to the north side of the river and to try to prevent Hood from crossing.[98]

James Wilson in Command in the Field

With Capron, Hatch, and Croxton approaching Columbia, James Wilson continued to organize the cavalry into an effective fighting corps and he concentrated his forces as Hood approached. On November 24 Wilson's command at Columbia consisted of 4,800 men, bolstered with some reinforcements (notably the 5th Iowa) being received: Hatch's division—2,000 men; Croxton brigade—1,300 men; and Capron's brigade—1,500 men. Wilson gave orders for his forces to take up position on the north side of the Duck River, watching the crossing between Columbia and the Lewisburg Pike.[99]

Wilson's optimistic plans for the cavalry of the west were put on hold as he assembled regiments and brigades in a piecemeal fashion. Certainly, the history of the Union cavalry during this campaign centers on the efforts to draw together an effective cavalry force. On November 17, Wilson formally organized the Sixth Cavalry division under command of Richard Johnson, although Johnson did not assume command until November 24. Johnson had little time to assemble and get to know his new command. Johnson had been given temporary command of the post at Pulaski as the Union infantry pulled out and he had moved to Columbia as it appeared the concentration of both armies centered on that town. Johnson found the Sixth Division had only one brigade—Capron's, consisting of the 14th Illinois, 16th Illinois and 8th Michigan cavalries. The 5th Indiana, also part of the brigade, had been detached and away from the area. The three regiments consisted of only 800 men after the previous skirmishes with Chalmers' division. Johnson found the brigade was "poorly armed and equipped, and I regret to say considerably demoralized by an unsuccessful campaign of some duration against an enemy superior to them in numbers, mount, and equipment." Fortunately, the 5th Iowa arrived on November 24 under the command of, Major J. Morris Young,

Chapter Six. Florence to Columbia

and added 500 men, armed with Spencer carbines, to Johnson's division. Croxton's "fine brigade," technically part of McCook's First Division, was temporary assigned to Johnson' division until more regiments could be located.[100]

Wilson's chief of staff wrote (to Wilson) a long letter about the situation with the cavalry on November 23. George Thomas ordered all the cavalry previously assigned to Robert Granger to be moved to Nashville to join Wilson's main body of cavalry. The 11th Indiana Cavalry consisted of 621 mounted troopers armed with Maynard carbines and was on the way to Columbia. E.B. Beaumont informed Wilson that the 3rd Tennessee, 4th Tennessee, 10th Tennessee, 12th Tennessee, and part of the 9th Indiana cavalries were present at Nashville and that he was working as quickly as possible to get the regiments into the field. Additional good news greeted Wilson—the 7th Ohio Cavalry under command of the veteran, Israel Garrard, was ready to move forward. Beaumont, a highly regarded staff officer, told Wilson: "I hope you will give Forrest a small whirl on the Winchester style."[101] Wilson ordered Beaumont to put J.H. Hammond in charge of new cavalry regiments and to assemble Granger's cavalry and "fit them up and get the regiments together. Tell Captain Green to fix up the Tenth and Twelfth Tennessee; work night and day until it is done; order them to report to Hatch, via Columbia. I want the Fourth [U.S.] Cavalry as soon as possible, with all its men." Thomas urged the cavalry inspector at Louisville to get McCook's and Long's cavalry equipped and mounted as soon as possible. Beaumont added that some of Hatch's division from Memphis was due to arrive, but Winslow's cavalry would never reach Nashville in time. However, Washburn, in Memphis, sent special orders on November 24 to the 6th Tennessee Cavalry and the 19th Pennsylvania Cavalry to join Wilson's cavalry at Nashville.[102]

Beaumont and Wilson had cobbled together 1,000 cavalry troopers and they were being dispatched to Columbia and expected to arrive there on November 25. This cavalry was "well mounted and fully equipped" and was being transported directly to Columbia to Wilson headquarters. Beaumont told Wilson that he would be able to get as many as three regiments moving to Columbia under command of Israel Garrard. The 4th Tennessee Cavalry would soon be ready to advance also and the 10th Indiana Cavalry was moving north to Nashville from Huntsville. All the forces converged on Columbia.[103]

Chapter Seven

The Armies Move into Position at Columbia

> It grieves me to have to feel that so many splendid men are going to be sacrificed.
> —Douglas Cater

Hood Reaches Columbia

On November 25, Hood's concerns eased in regard to his supplies as he set up his headquarters at Mt. Pleasant. The bounty of Tennessee had removed the hunger pangs of his soldiers, and Hood proudly wrote to Beauregard, "The enemy have abandoned Pulaski, and are moving toward Nashville.... Plenty of mills now in our possession. I think I will have no difficulty about supplies." Hood's trailing infantry plodded along the wet and muddy roads toward Columbia with the bulk of the army arriving there on November 26–27. Hood turned his attention to the geography through which he had just marched and ordered Roddey's cavalry to start destroying the railroads in northern Alabama in the wake of the Union withdrawal.[1]

Meanwhile on the Union side of the line, Thomas wrote to Grant about the confusion of orders from Memphis which delayed the arrival of additional cavalry. Much of this letter focused on the importance of the Union cavalry and Thomas made a point of explaining that his current problems resulted from Sherman stripping his cavalry for the sake of Sherman's own army. In addition, the endless communications with Washburn in Memphis had failed to deliver Winslow's all-important cavalry division. Price's Raid ended on October 28 and a month later, Winslow's division was still far away. "The transportation of Generals Hatch's and Grierson's cavalry was ordered by General Washburn, I am told, to be turned in at Memphis, which has crippled the only cavalry I have at this time. All of my cavalry was dismounted to furnish horses to Kilpatrick's division, which went with General Sherman. My dismounted cavalry is now detained at Louisville awaiting arms and horses—horses are arriving slowly and arms have been detained somewhere *en route* for more than a month.... The moment I can get my cavalry I will march against Hood, and if Forrest can be reached he will be punished." Thomas, a straight-forward and trusty commander, overestimated Forrest's cavalry in his reports for the next two weeks.[2]

Also on November 25, Thomas sent Schofield instructions to abandon Columbia and move to the north side of the river if necessary, but Thomas felt the cavalry should be the first line of defense if Hood marched to the east to destroy the railroad to Chattanooga. Five Federal cavalry regiments from northern Alabama were due to arrive in Murfreesboro that day to assist in guarding the railroad, and Robert Milroy's infantry in Tullahoma had also been ordered to Murfreesboro. Thomas told Schofield that the cavalry needed to cover a broad front, extending as far east as Shelbyville. More cavalry from Hatch's division from western Tennessee was due to arrive soon, although they were dismounted. Thomas explained that Smith's XVI Corps would be sent either to Murfreesboro or to Schofield as the campaign developed over the next few days.[3]

As the Federal troops filled in the defenses at Columbia, they had the option of two lines of fortifications—an outer line and an inner line. The infantry began constructing and improving the defenses as they waited for Hood's army to arrive. The fortifications improved the Union troops' positions, but Thomas Wood, Third Division of IV Corps, stated that he could hold out against anything except a determined infantry attack, because there was a half mile gap between his line and Cox's. Wood humorously observed that he was "stretched out like an India rubber string." The pressure of Hood's approaching infantry resulted in Schofield's decision to contract his lines and move IV Corps and XXIII Corps to the north side of the river. He sent orders to David Stanley to move his corps into the inner lines that evening after dark and sent orders to Jacob Cox to start moving troops to the north side of the river over a pontoon bridge.[4]

The Cavalry Moves to Columbia

Wilson sent a message to E.B. Beaumont telling him not to wait for a full brigade to be organized but to send regiments forward individually as soon as possible, and that he would reassign regiments as they arrived. In addition, Wilson was brooking no dissent or resistance within the ranks of the cavalry. He insisted on discipline of the regiments as they moved through the country and he told Beaumont to arrest Lieutenant Colonel G.W. Bridges, 10th Tennessee, for neglecting his duty and disobeying orders resulting from excessive alcohol consumption. Beaumont replied: "Tonight I placed him under arrest." He also put some of Richard Johnson's troops on provost duty to deal with some of the wayward troops causing problems in the countryside. Wilson acted quickly and decisively, and he told his officers the details of their actions would be worked out after the campaign. He also instructed Beaumont to get Grierson's new division (Winslow's) in St. Louis mounted and on its way to Middle Tennessee. Alluding to Grierson's absence, he told Beaumont, "[H]e must not leave the command till he is thoroughly satisfied it is coming as well as the men at Memphis." Meanwhile, the 9th and 10th Indiana and 11th and 12th Tennessee cavalry regiments were in transit to Nashville that day to be mounted and equipped. Wilson wanted the Indiana cavalry mounted first and he implored: "Continue your exertions." He also ordered Colonel Thomas Harrison, late colonel of 8th Indiana Cavalry, forward to Columbia and he wrote to Hatch: "Colonel Harrison ... is a very valuable officer, and I desire to give him one of your brigades." Hatch readily accepted Harrison, who had yet to arrive at Columbia, to replace Oliver Wells, but upon his arrival he assumed command of Capron's brigade in Johnson's division due to Capron's injury. J.H. Hammond had just arrived in Tennessee and was greeted with his orders to assume command of 1,200 troopers of the 4th Tennessee and 9th Indiana cavalries mounted on horses in "fair condition." Hammond quickly assessed his regiments and decided they would be ready to move on Sunday evening (November 27) or Monday morning. He was gratified that the regiments were equipped with Maynard and Burnside carbines and well clothed.[5]

Johnson's Sixth Cavalry Division was busy on November 25 at Columbia, because Schofield wanted to know where Hood and his cavalry were located. Johnson sent Capron's brigade to scout the eastern flank of the Federal forces at Columbia. Wilson wanted to keep a close watch on the Duck River to ensure that Forrest did not cross and swing around the rear of Schofield's infantry. Some of the Union cavalry guarded the fords to the west, joining with Union infantry which had arrived at Centerville and Williamsport. Croxton joined Capron by scouting along the Duck River as far east as Shelbyville. Johnson also had scouts on the Pulaski and Campbellsville roads leading to Columbia, but Forrest's cavalry provided such an effective screen that the Federals found little information about the position of the enemy forces. Johnson's men finally found some enemy troops but it was so dark by the time they located the enemy force, they couldn't determine if they were cavalry or infantry.[6]

General John H. Hammond believed the "strength of our cavalry acting, as it always should, on the offensive" (Mollus Mass Civil War Collection, United States Army Heritage and Education Center, Carlisle, Pennsylvania).

Pulling Together Reinforcements

R.S. Granger's troops began arriving later on November 25 at Murfreesboro and took up position near the town, and this allowed the Union forces which had concentrated there to move back to railroad security in the area around Murfreesboro. Thomas also began to contemplate the Union troops at Chattanooga as part of his strategy. He asked James Steedman if he had enough troops to guard Chattanooga and still threaten the rear of Hood's army. Thomas considered Hood's advance on Nashville and knew this left Hood's rear vulnerable to attack from Steedman, who could move his troops by rail somewhere east and south of Hood. Steedman replied that he had 5,000 troops which could join in the fight. This was good news for Thomas who replied: "There is no indication at present that the enemy will get on the railroad, but I simply wish you to be prepared to act should they do so." As the Union troops withdrew from north Alabama, Philip Roddey attacked Decatur setting fire to a large Federal supply building and claiming abandoned saddles and 15 pontoon boats.[7]

Chapter Seven. The Armies Move into Position at Columbia

November 26—Patrolling the Duck River

At Nashville, the first of Smith's XVI Corps infantry arrived, promising enough troops to meet Hood's advancing army. Thomas called on the U.S. Navy to proceed up the Tennessee River on reconnaissance missions to try to find out anything new regarding the Confederate advance, but after the recent exchanges with Forrest's cavalry, Thomas cautioned that the gunboats should be iron-clads which could withstand artillery fire. To the south, the telegraph operators at Franklin reported heavy cannonading at Columbia throughout the day suggesting the arrival of Hood's infantry at Columbia. So far, Schofield mainly faced dismounted cavalry demonstrating against his lines, but he discovered the long columns of infantry marching from Mt. Pleasant. In preparation for a major fight at Columbia, Schofield sent orders to Stanley to abandon Columbia by moving IV Corps to the north side of the river that night.[8]

Wilson saw the greatest risk as being the crossing of the Duck River east of Columbia, and he contemplated how to use his cavalry troops to meet the movements of 5,000 men of Forrest's cavalry. Johnson's division continued patrolling various crossings 10 miles in either direction, and later in the day, Wilson established his headquarters about four miles east of Columbia at Leftwich's House, a few miles west of Rally Hill. Capron's brigade also held the crossing on Lewisburg–Franklin Pike near Hardison's Mill, the most direct route to Franklin on the eastern flank of the army. Moving on the soggy and muddy roads continued to be difficult for the cavalry. Due to the recent rains, the condition of the roads was deplorable. Jacob Cox noted: "The road, or path, between the turnpike and railroad proves, on examination, to be of the very worst description; might serve to pass a train in an emergency, but would be a slow and difficult route..."[9]

Johnson wrote to Wilson that although everything was quiet along his front, the river would not keep Forrest's cavalry from crossing at any number of locations. Captain W.B. Smith, 8th Michigan Cavalry, scouted south of the

General A. J. Smith, a highly regarded commander, hurried his infantry to Nashville (Library of Congress).

river and confirmed the poor conditions of the roads, in particular the Lewisburg Pike: "found the road very bad all the way, and thinks it impassable for wagons and artillery." Smith found no large concentrations of the enemy, but he determined that Huey's Mill, four miles west of the Lewisburg Pike, as a likely place for the enemy to cross. After receiving this report, Johnson, who had gained command of Croxton's brigade, ordered some men to guard the crossing.[10]

While W.B. Smith found no enemy cavalry, Lieutenant L.H. Patten, 8th Michigan, did find a large number of enemy cavalry during his scout that day. Patten commanded a patrol of 15 men from Capron's brigade which scouted toward Berlin that evening directly south of the Duck River on the Lewisburg Pike. Patten found the enemy "cavalry in force; saw their camp-fires, apparently a heavy force, about half a mile, as nearly as he could judge, to right of road; thinks the enemy were just forming their lines on this road, as he heard them moving on pike before he reached them; drew their fire, and returned it." The 8th Michigan withdrew, trailed by the Confederates for a short distance.[11]

Croxton's men secured Huey's Ford as ordered, and found that it could, indeed, be forded by swimming. A few miles further east Croxton found other fords between Huey's Mill and Hardison's Mill which could also be forded. Croxton left only a few men at Huey's Mill because the campaign was taking such a heavy toll on his men through the constant reconnaissance and skirmishing. Croxton had been sparring with the enemy since late September. In addition, Wilson directed Croxton to move to cavalry headquarters in order to concentrate the cavalry. Croxton left a small detachment at Huey's Mill and had the bulk of his brigade in the saddle the next morning, riding for headquarters. Wilson wrote to Johnson at 8:20 p.m.: "General Schofield is very solicitous about the crossings of Duck River. Be good enough to have them well watched from the Lewisburg pike to Williamsport." Wilson also told Johnson that Croxton had reinforcements (350 men and 250 additional mounts) awaiting his arrival the next day.[12]

Croxton intended to have his brigade fully moving the next morning as did J.H. Hammond. Hammond planned to move from Nashville to join Wilson at Columbia: "[T]he troops under my command will move at daybreak tomorrow morning, the Fourth Tennessee first, and Ninth Indiana following at 10 a.m." In regard to Johnson's division, he sent Capron a series of orders about scouting the area but he told Capron that the bulk of the cavalry would concentrate south of Rally Hill. Facing Forrest's cavalry, Wilson knew it would virtually impossible to fully prevent a crossing of the Duck River by such a mobile force as Forrest's. More importantly, Wilson needed the timely information of where and when Forrest crossed. Johnson urged Capron to report often to headquarters: "Do not spare any pains to inform yourself thoroughly of the condition of all the fords on your beat, and, so far as possible, of the movements and designs of the enemy." Meanwhile, Johnson sent all of the division supply trains toward Rally Hill, about 10 miles northeast of Columbia. Only ambulances and ammunition wagons remained with the cavalry units.[13]

Wilson's new regiments rode toward the front, with more on the way. Thomas requisitioned the 13th Indiana Cavalry from R.S. Granger and had it sent to Nashville, then assigned to Wilson. Colonel Alvin Matzdorff, commanding the garrison at Franklin, also reported to Thomas that the 11th Indiana, which had been mounted for just over a month, arrived there on November 25 and that 258 men of the 12th Tennessee Cavalry arrived that evening (November 26). In addition, Colonel Israel Garrard moved his 7th Ohio Cavalry toward Columbia during the day, fulfilling his orders to try to clear bands of guerrillas "infesting the country" between Franklin and Columbia along the way. The remainder of the 12th Tennessee was fully mounted and the 10th Tennessee partially mounted, and these regiments were also moving to the front. Beaumont wrote to Wilson: "All is well here now, but we have had to work hard."[14]

The Confederates had been active during the day and prepared for heavy skirmishing the next day. As the Confederate infantry marched northward, they were rewarded with scenes of Confederate cavalry escorting captured Union troopers. E.H. Rennolds, 5th Tennessee Infantry, recorded in his diary: "Met 48 Yankees captured by Forrest." Rennolds noted that the infantry marched through the fields of the various cavalry duels over the past few days. William H. Jackson sent orders to his brigade commanders: "Brigade commanders will have their commands in readiness to move to-morrow morning at 7 o'clock, with four days' cooked rations ... and sixty rounds of ammunition to the man. The move tomorrow will be short, and rations can be prepared for the day as they are required, without interfering with the four days' already cooked." Jackson told his men to leave spare horses behind and he wanted the horses shod that evening in preparation for an extended fight.[15]

Some of Hood's soldiers had a chance to relax and despite the orders against pillaging the local farms, some of men returned to camp with some fresh pork after foraging the area. Douglas Cater, a native Texan, only reluctantly acknowledged a hearty pork breakfast. His friend, noticing his depressed attitude, inquired, "Hey man, you are not whipped are you?" Cater replied that he wasn't, "but it grieves me to have to feel that so many splendid men are going to be sacrificed on this trip to Nashville which we cannot hold even if we take it."[16]

November 27—Guarding the Fords

Just after noon on November 27, Schofield wrote to Thomas that he planned to hold his position on the north side of the river until Hood made his next move. Schofield told Cox, who was already on the north side of the river, that he thought Hood would probably cross the Duck River east of Columbia and that Wilson was guarding the fords. Indeed, Wilson had most of his available units on the east flank, although the forces at each of the fords were small and could not have repelled a determined attempt to cross. Wilson did not expect his cavalry to hold the fords but it was of paramount importance to know when Forrest made a crossing so that he could block further movements by the Confederates. Wilson still had not been able to determine Hood's line of march. He worried that Forrest would move past his flank and he planned to send a strong reconnaissance force 40 miles to the east. Capron's scouts had discovered a group of 300 enemy cavalry moving in the direction of Shelbyville that morning. In addition, Capron planned to scout south on the Lewisburg Pike in hopes of finding the main body of the enemy.[17]

In the meantime, some of Wilson's cavalry were fighting near Columbia, and Schofield told Wilson: "[Y]our cavalry at the next ford below here has been driven back; it reports itself driven by infantry." A regiment of infantry was dispatched to meet the threat and to determine the seriousness of the movement. Schofield asked for a brigade of cavalry to return to the right flank of his army to watch for enemy movements and Wilson ordered Oliver Wells' brigade to take up position there. Hood's army was large and impressive as it reached Columbia and everyone speculated about the next move. Rumors of the "grand offensive" of Hood's army which intended to march into Kentucky reached the men of the 7th Ohio as they rode toward Wilson's position. Captain Theodore Allen of that regiment simply wrote in his diary, "Can't see it."[18]

Croxton's brigade watched the Duck River near Columbia on November 27 and reported more rumors of Confederate infantry on the south side of the river. Croxton, whose headquarters were initially established at Crawford's House, had the responsibility of guarding the fords east of Columbia to Capron's position. Croxton felt Hardison's Mill on the Lewisburg Pike near the Duck River was the most likely crossing for the enemy troops, but Huey's Mill also provided an excellent point for a crossing. As a result, Richard Johnson followed up with a message to burn Huey's Mill and to send a battalion to protect the ford. Johnson aware of the strategic value of the crossing at Hardison's Mill optimistically wrote: "The ford at the Lewisburg pike is understood, from the report of citizens, not to be passable at this stage of water." Croxton's men captured a member of Cheatham's corps who confirmed that the Confederate infantry intended to move east of Columbia and perhaps cross the river near Huey's Mill. The prisoner also told Croxton that Forrest had ordered his men to cook several days' rations in anticipation of active campaigning.[19]

Wilson initially held the concentration of his cavalry about four miles east of Columbia but as reports of increased activity on the south side of the river increased, he distributed his men all along the northern bank of the Duck River east of town. Horace Capron's headquarters remained near Hardison's Mill. Capron had cavalry riding to the east and south but he reported finding nothing of any significance. At 3:30 p.m., Capron sent his third message to Johnson and reported that he found only Sam Hardison's small band of guerrillas near Shelbyville. He passed on a series of rumors to Johnson, but little direct observations. At 4:00 p.m. Johnson told Capron to send a strong force of troopers down the Lewisburg Pike toward Lewisburg and Cornersville to scout the enemy. This was a precarious task because it sent men into an area known to be filled with Confederate cavalry. While this was dangerous duty, Capron's troopers were successful in their reconnaissance. His scouts discovered from local citizens that the 11th Tennessee Cavalry (CSA) had been observed near Chapel Hill on the Nolensville Pike. A scout also reached Lewisburg and found only an abandoned Confederate cavalry camp. A local citizen told the troopers that the Confederates had been very active that day and a body of Confederate cavalry, about 150 men strong, had just moved away an hour before their arrival.[20]

Meanwhile, Israel Garrard's 7th Ohio was only a few miles away. He reported from Spring Hill at 1:30 p.m., and that following George Thomas' orders, he established a courier line utilizing the 12th Tennessee Cavalry between Franklin and Columbia. In addition, he ordered this regiment to take care of any guerrilla activity in the area and finally, to escort the supply trains of XXIII Corps. Then, Garrard promised to ride to Rally Hill with the 10th Tennessee and 7th Ohio cavalries. The 7th Ohio had moved from Atlanta a few weeks earlier and Captain Theodore Allen of the regiment was happy to leave. He had seen enough of General H. Judson Kilpatrick of whom he described in his diary as a "humbug." The 7th Ohio went into camp around midnight at Rally Hill, tired and sore.[21]

Milroy Moves from Tullahoma to Murfreesboro

From Tullahoma, Major General Robert H. Milroy, in charge of railroad security, began to feel the pressure of the advancing Confederate army. Milroy would soon engage the enemy firsthand, but on November 27 the small number of cavalry, 4th Tennessee Cavalry, he had available supported the reconnaissance that Capron had just reported to Johnson and Wilson. His troopers discovered that Confederates were foraging at Shelbyville, claiming all the livestock they could find. Milroy concluded, with the withdrawal from Pulaski and northern Alabama, the railroad would be destroyed by the advancing enemy. Milroy told his troops, that if the enemy pushed northward, to burn bridges to slow their advance.[22]

The presence of an increased number of Confederate troops deeply concerned Milroy who chided Major John F. Armstrong, commanding 5th Tennessee Cavalry, by saying, "Had he known that you had such a mere handful of men he would not have permitted" them to move into area known to be infested with the enemy. Milroy sent the remainder of the 5th Tennessee to Armstrong to assist in his reconnaissance. Milroy warned: "Forrest may come over to this railroad through Lincoln County. The general commanding directs that you send out scouts on the roads west and northwest, and to keep yourself well posted as to the movements of the enemy.... Skirmish their advance and fall back this way, being careful not to be gobbled." All along the line, Hood was pushing northward.[23]

Chapter Eight

Columbia: Forrest Pushes Across the Duck River

"Hood is going to flank us on one side or other."
—James H. Wilson

The Multiple Actions in November

Hood's movements in Middle Tennessee were just a piece, albeit a very large piece, of the numerous actions by the Confederate armies in November and December, but the Confederacy was being overwhelmed. George Thomas scrambled to pull together a defense to meet Hood's army, and the Southern forces seemed to have the upper hand, at least, temporarily. Elsewhere, other Confederate forces faced threats of their own. Of course, Grant had Robert E. Lee's forces besieged in Virginia, and Sherman's march to the sea was under way. In addition to these threats to the Confederate states, Brigadier General Albert Lee led a raid on the Confederates operating in the area near Baton Rouge by striking into southern Mississippi. Lee moved his cavalry to Port Hudson on November 14 and then began an 80-mile expedition capturing Camp Beauregard, striking the Confederate positions at Liberty, and then moving on to Brookhaven, Mississippi, in this successful raid, which ended on November 21. This raid was followed by another raid beginning on November 23 under Major General Edward Canby's orders which supported Sherman's actions in Georgia by distracting the Confederates in Mississippi. This raid, commanded by Colonel Embury D. Osband, 3rd U.S. Colored Cavalry, lasted until December 4 and successfully targeted the rail system running north out of Jackson. The primary objective was the destruction of the Mississippi Central Railroad's Black River Bridge which could have cut supplies to Hood for months to come. Osband's actions were quite successful as Dabney Maury repositioned his Confederate forces to meet the threats of the raids; however, the claim that the railroad bridge had been destroyed ran contrary to the Confederate reports which described the bridge as receiving only slight damage. In addition to these raids, Beauregard correctly observed the build-up of Federal troops at Memphis which would result in another Federal raid beginning on December 21. In the meantime, Beauregard and Maury had to deal with yet another Federal threat, this time from Pensacola, which prompted Beauregard to order Wirt Adams' Confederate troops to secure Selma and Montgomery.[1]

While Beauregard watched these expeditions, he urged Hood to push toward Nashville. Beauregard correctly perceived that Sherman wanted to march to the coast and then move north to join Grant to complete the destruction of Lee's army. Beauregard wrote to Jefferson Davis on November 24, "Have ordered General Hood to take active-offensive in Middle Tennessee to relieve General Lee." He wrote to Hood: "Sherman's movement is progressing rapidly toward Atlantic coast, doubtless to re-enforce Grant." Beauregard told Hood that it was imperative to march into Tennessee as a way of relieving pressure on other Confederate positions, but the march needed to be initiated quickly. To assist in distracting the Union forces as much as he could, Hood ordered Brigadier General Hyland Lyon to begin a raid of his own. Hood wanted Lyon to destroy the Louisville and Nashville Railroad between Bowling Green and Nashville and the railroad connection between Nashville and Clarksville.[2]

Hood Plans His Next Step

Near Columbia on the evening of November 27, Hood met with his generals and in the subsequent discussion, he told Forrest to send his cavalry across the Duck River early the next morning in preparation for the construction of pontoon bridges to be used by the infantry. Hood needed Forrest's cavalry to screen his infantry which would either fight Schofield or outmarch him. He told his commanders at this council of war held in the Warfield mansion on Pulaski Pike that, if all went well, most of Stewart's corps would hold Schofield in place north of the river at Columbia while the rest of the army would cross on pontoon bridges at Davis' Ford, three miles east of town. Afterwards, Forrest ordered Buford's division to cross Duck River 10 miles east of Columbia on the Lewisburg—Franklin Pike at Hardison's Mill, three miles west (seven miles east of Columbia) Chalmers' division would cross at Holland's Ford, and finally Jackson's division would cross at Huey's Mill (four miles east of Columbia). Biffle's "demi-brigade" (9th and 10th Tennessee cavalries) and Forrest would cross near Davis' Ford, another mile or so east of Huey's Mill. The locations of the crossing are more accurately described as Chalmers crossing at Holland's Mill, Jackson crossing at Wallace's Mill, and Buford crossing at Hardison's Mill, and, finally, Forrest and Biffle crossing just east of Davis Ford. It is important to note that there have been various other locations of crossings (including Hall's Mill and Lillard's Mill) described by different participants and historians.[3]

These orders, when executed, would not come as a surprise to the Union cavalry, because Wilson had the river picketed for miles in each direction from Columbia. The problem was how to set up a screen, miles long, and then concentrate enough cavalry to stop a strong advance over the river. Wilson received good news when Schofield moved his infantry to the north side of the river which offered him more flexibility and security. The bad news according to historian Thomas Robson Hay was that Schofield, rather than continuing to retreat, stopped and delayed for an entire day as Hood crossed his cavalry and began crossing his infantry, and "nearly lost his army in doing so."[4]

November 28—Forrest Forces a Crossing on the Duck River

The Confederate actions in Tennessee included Hood's advance towards Nashville, but another significant campaign was going on in eastern Tennessee. The Confederate forces in East Tennessee had occupied a considerable amount of the attention by the Union commanders, including Thomas, for weeks. John C. Breckinridge's Confederate forces fought Union forces near Bull Gap since late October and the campaign carried into November. Breckinridge successfully attacked Alvan Gillem's Union column on November 14, driving it to Strawberry Plains. In late November, the Union forces responded. General George Stoneman and General Stephen Burbridge led columns from Knoxville to retake Bull's Gap.[5]

Meanwhile at Columbia, all of Schofield's infantry moved to the north side of the Duck River overnight. Cox's division held a position near the bridge at Columbia and Stanley moved his corps to the rear of Cox. Thomas Ruger's troops held the railroad bridge west of the town. Schofield over-confidently told Thomas: "I think I can now stop Hood's advance by any line near this, and meet in time any distant movement to turn my position. I regret extremely the necessity of withdrawing from Columbia.... I have all the fords above and below this place well watched and guarded as far as possible." Schofield conceded to Thomas that he could not stop Forrest from crossing the river, due to the numerous fords along the river.[6]

Schofield's movement was initially misread by Hood who thought that the Union infantry had withdrawn in the direction of Nashville instead of just to the north side of the river. While the Union divisions were realigned, Hood prepared to put his army in motion. He optimistically wrote to Secretary of War James A. Seddon: "Our army is moving forward." Hood's men entered Columbia and promptly began plundering the town. Hood's adjutant general wrote to the corps commanders to keep their men in check. "The commanding general is pained to learn that officers and men from this army entered the town of Columbia this morning and wantonly and disgracefully plundered private and public property. He earnestly calls upon all well-disposed officers and men to check this un-soldier-like and ruinous conduct. If it cannot be done by example and moral persuasion, harsher means will be used."[7]

Thomas received an ominous report from Schofield on November 28: "The enemy was crossing in force a short distance this side of the Lewisburg pike at noon today, and had driven our cavalry back across the river and the pike at the same time. The force is reported to be infantry, but I do not regard it as very probable. Wilson has gone with his main force to learn the facts, and drive the enemy back, if practicable." Schofield told Thomas he had doubts about the report, but he wisely asked, if Hood was crossing the Duck River, where Thomas wanted to fight. Smith's XVI Corps troops, when they fully arrived, would have to be moved to that location and Schofield had to get his troops there also.[8]

At 6:00 p.m., Schofield reported that the crossing of the Confederate cavalry was definite. Two hours later Thomas replied that if Schofield felt he could hold the line along the Duck River to do so and then he would march Smith's corps to reinforce Schofield. Then, Smith and Schofield could begin their movement against Hood, and if that wasn't practical, he would wait for Wilson to fully get his cavalry in the field. Thomas advised Schofield to guard well the crossings to the west to prevent a surprise movement by the Confederates around his western flank also. He told Schofield that if the infantry could obstruct the main roads with felled trees, then Wilson's cavalry "will be able to retard, if not prevent, Hood from crossing, after the roads are thoroughly obstructed." Upon receiving further communications, Thomas told Schofield if Hood was threatening his flank to consider falling back to Franklin. Importantly, Schofield had

Thomas' approval to retreat to Franklin and he knew that Wilson was fighting Forrest on the Lewisburg-Franklin Pike, some 10 miles east of his position.[9]

A Busy Day for the Cavalry

As a reminder, Wilson operated with about two divisions. Hatch commanded a two-brigade (Datus Coon's and Robert Stewart's brigades) division (about 2,800 men). Stewart officially assumed command of the First Brigade on November 28. The second division was Johnson's hastily organized command and initially consisted of Horace Capron's brigade of about 920 men supplemented by the newly arrived 5th Iowa, plus the newly re-assigned brigade commanded by John Croxton's (about 1,000 men). Hammond's brigade of Knipe's division was hastily moving forward but would not arrive until the next day. This left Wilson with only four brigades of cavalry (4,700 men) to face Forrest's three divisions—Chalmers', Buford's, and Jackson's, consisting of six brigades and according to Forrest, totaling 5,000 men.[10]

Forrest carried out the previous evening's orders and sent his cavalry to cross over the Duck River east of Columbia. Wilson's cavalry observed the increased Confederate activity and the first rumors of overnight activity permeated the Federal reports. Croxton's brigade occupied the north bank of the Duck River from Huey's Mill and connected with Capron's pickets east of Cedar Creek, another four to five miles east. The first messages came from Croxton's cavalry posted near Huey's Mill that reported "rebel infantry are moving on the opposite side of the river toward the mouth of Cedar Creek, and that they intend crossing them where the Lewisburg pike crosses Duck River." Capron had scouts on the Shelbyville Pike and discovered 30 enemy cavalry moving in their direction and the 11th Tennessee Cavalry (CSA) rode six miles past Chapel Hill (about 10 miles north of Lewisburg) in the direction of the Chattanooga railroad at 8 p.m. the night before. Capron's scouts heard what they thought were infantry and cavalry moving during the night and he expected both to be in Lewisburg on November 28; Capron contemplated Hood crossing the bulk of his infantry over the river, continuing on to Nashville. Wilson calmly reported that most of this information amounted to just rumors and he had no proof of these movements.[11]

Wilson positioned Capron (near Hardison Mill), Croxton (near Huey's Mill, extending eastward) and Coon (in reserve on the Shelbyville Road) east of Columbia and he intended to concentrate the Federal cavalry south of Rally Hill when Forrest made his advance. Stewart's brigade patrolled the west side of Columbia. In addition, Croxton had, at least, a battalion of the 8th Iowa detached, patrolling the far western flank of the Federal line at Williamsport. At 9:40 a.m., Richard Johnson sent Wilson (received at 12:15 p.m.) Capron's scouting report. Capron confirmed a brigade of enemy cavalry approached the river from the south on Lewisburg Pike and he placed the bulk of his brigade into position to resist a crossing at three primary locations. Capron cautioned that there were numerous crossings along the river that Forrest could use. He concluded his message: "I have my force in readiness to concentrate at either of them should the enemy attempt a crossing."[12]

The men of both armies suffered through the rain until about noon. Then, Croxton reported that Hood's infantry, really Forrest's cavalry troopers, were crossing "in force" at Huey's Mill and he responded by sending reinforcements to the small cavalry battalion already at that location. At 1:00 p.m., Wilson forwarded this message to Schofield with the comment, "I can scarcely credit this, though will find out at once." Wilson's disbelief quickly became reality when Croxton sent another message, "Major Thornburgh, commanding battalion at Huey's Mill, reports that the enemy are crossing in three [columns?] above that point, and appear to be striking across to the left of him." Croxton was correct about the crossings as Chalmers and Jackson crossed the river east of Croxton's position, threatening the left flank of his troops near Huey's Mill. At 1:50 p.m., Wilson forwarded the message to Schofield without the skepticism of the previous message and promised to obtain more information. Ten minutes later Wilson sent another message to Schofield explaining that the fords being used by Forrest's cavalry offered good access to the Shelbyville Road, a good road, leading to the Lewisburg Pike at Orr's Crossroads, the location of Capron's headquarters. Chalmers' division crossed east of Huey's Mill and Jackson crossed west of Hardison's Mill and both Southern cavalry divisions easily moved past the flanks of Croxton and Capron's cavalry forces.[13]

Croxton sent a company toward the river accompanied by a staff officer and by the time the detachment reached the river, it was enveloped by two columns of enemy cavalry, Chalmers' and Jackson's divisions—one crossing to the west and the other to the east of the Federal detachment. The company hid in some trees and finally made its escape that night under the cover of darkness. Chalmers' and Jackson's divisions surged across the river with little difficulty while Buford's division met a stubborn defense by Capron's brigade at Hardison's Mill. A trooper of Chalmers' brigade explained the Duck River was swollen by the rain and the taller horses were able to swim fairly easily across the stream, but the smaller horses "were almost washed away by the swift stream." Corporal J.A. Bigger, 2nd Mississippi Cavalry, recorded that his regiment had little difficulty crossing the river which was 100 yards wide, "rocky and shoaly—some places 1 foot deep and other places 4 feet." At 2:10 p.m., Capron's cavalry had been driven to the north side of the Duck River by Buford's division, described as a "heavy force of the enemy; he is now fighting them across river." Realizing the seriousness of this situation, Wilson told Schofield to send Stewart's brigade which was on the west side of Columbia to join the rest of the cavalry at Rally Hill. Wilson advised Stewart to ride a circuitous route to Spring Hill to avoid unexpectedly running into the Confederate cavalry which already had possession of parts of the north side of the Duck River. Wilson realized that his three brigades faced a movement in force along his flank.[14]

Edward Hatch's Fifth Division Repositions

Hatch's day began early on November 28. As Hatch prepared for action, he had time to organize his Fifth Cavalry division "on the fly" into two brigades.

Fifth Cavalry Division—Brigadier General Edward Hatch

First Brigade—Col. Robert R. Stewart	*Second Brigade*—Col. Datus E. Coon
11th Indiana Cavalry	2nd Iowa Cavalry
12th Missouri Cavalry	12th Tennessee Cavalry
3rd Illinois Cavalry	6th Illinois Cavalry
10th Tennessee Cavalry	9th Illinois Cavalry[15]

Wilson sent him orders just after midnight the evening before to move Stewart's brigade to Knob Grass Creek, a few miles west of Columbia. Stewart's brigade was scattered on various duties. Stewart had orders to throw a line of pickets from west of Columbia to Williamsport, about 10 to 15 miles further west to guard the fords along the river, and his brigade would also scout on the southern side of the river toward Mount Pleasant. Wilson ordered the 10th Tennessee Cavalry to Rally Hill early in the day to support the defenses along that flank and the 12th Tennessee remained on duty escorting the supply trains of XXIII Corps moving toward the rear. With these orders, Stewart started his duties south and west of Columbia and Coon's brigade patrolled the north side of the river just east of Columbia.[16]

Just after noon, Wilson, still unsure of the advance of Forrest's cavalry, wrote to Hatch to hurry the 12th Tennessee to his position and he told Hatch to order Stewart to guard the telegraph lines from Columbia to Thompson's Station. Wilson wrote, "The commanding officer of the Twelfth Missouri complains that his command is badly broken down; I observed, however, that his horses were able to trot through deep mud.... The practice of trotting and galloping horses must be discontinued." Soon, Stewart received orders to move to Spring Hill and then to Rally Hill to join the rest of the cavalry. The 12th Missouri would just have to encourage their horses for one more ride.[17]

Datus Coon remained in position east of Columbia until 2:00 p.m. when he received orders to move east on the Shelbyville Road. On November 26 and 27, Coon bivouacked eight miles east of Columbia, but he had moved closer to the east side of Columbia on the morning of November 28, and was positioned on the Shelbyville Road northeast of Davis' Ford. Coon, who would not be involved in the heavy skirmishing during the day, ordered "boots and saddles" when his scouts found the enemy crossing the river east of his position. At this point, the enemy opened fire on the pickets on the Shelbyville road and Coon discovered that Chalmers' cavalry had moved past his eastern flank. "By aid of a glass the enemy could be seen in heavy force through the thin fog, about two miles distant. I ordered a battalion of the Second Iowa ... to support the pickets, while the command made preparations to move." Hatch ordered Coon to send his artillery and supply train to the rear to Hurt's Crossroads where Wilson chose to concentrate his cavalry that evening. Coon's brigade saw relatively light action during the day and, based on his report, Wilson recognized that Forrest had simply maneuvered past Coon's brigade while scarcely firing a shot. At Hurt's Crossroads, Coon set up barricades and prepared for fighting the next day.[18]

Buford's Division Fights Johnson's Sixth Division

Richard Johnson's division would have the hardest, yet most productive, action of the Union cavalry during the day. Croxton and the ailing Capron commanded Johnson's brigades, also just reorganized. In addition, the 7th Ohio Cavalry and 5th Iowa Cavalry had just arrived for duty on November 28. The 7th Ohio was commanded by Colonel Israel Garrard who had previously commanded the remnants of the cavalry of the Army of the Ohio after its raid during the Atlanta Campaign in August. When Garrard arrived for duty, he technically outranked Capron, but he graciously refused command and allowed Capron to continue to direct the actions of the brigade. In the meantime, Colonel Thomas Harrison approached the concentrating cavalry corps expecting to assume

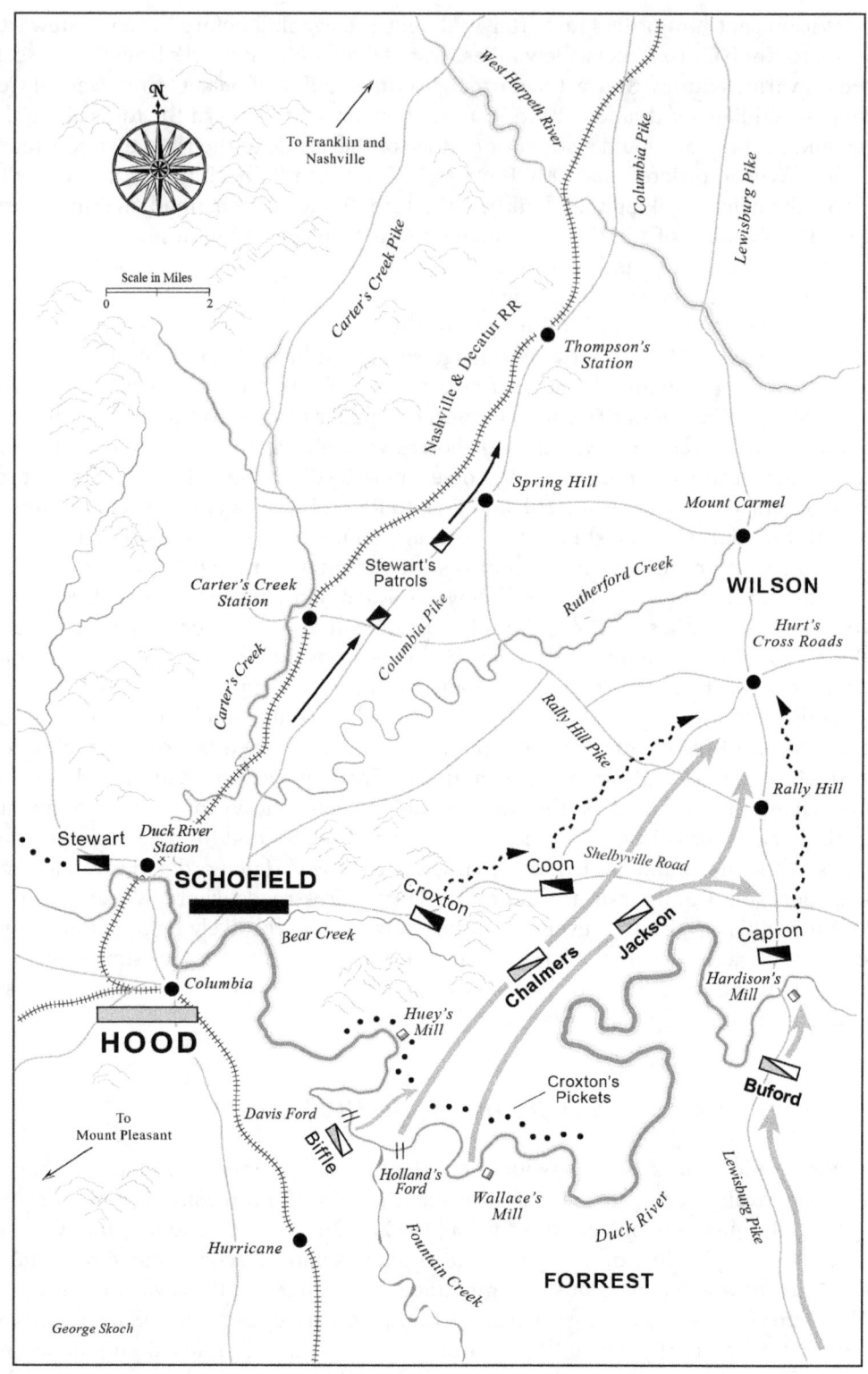

Forrest crosses the Duck River, November 28, 1864.

command of Stewart's brigade of Hatch's division, but Wilson directed him to take to command of Capron's brigade due to his injury. After the Atlanta Campaign, the 5th Iowa Cavalry operated as a consolidation of the original 5th Iowa Cavalry and the newly mounted 5th Iowa Infantry, which bolstered the regimental numbers.[19]

Croxton knew the enemy was preparing to attack based on the noises and movements heard overnight. Croxton's battalion held Huey's Mill with pickets extending eastward toward Capron's position on Lewisburg Pike. The details of Croxton's action are sketchy; however, the movement of Chalmers' division over Holland's Ford and Jackson's division crossing at Wallace's Ford precluded a determined defense by Croxton. With Chalmers and Jackson in his rear and on his flank, his position was untenable. Russell Thornburg (1st Tennessee Cavalry) of John Croxton's brigade reported the enemy crossing the Duck River three miles east (above) of Huey's Mill. Croxton received orders from Johnson to extract his brigade and fall back to Hurt's Crossroads on the Lewisburg Pike after 2:00 p.m. At the same time, Johnson sent similar orders to Thomas Harrison who had just officially assumed command of Capron's brigade; however, Harrison had not yet reached his brigade which led to a difficult day for the troops at Hardison's Mill.[20]

Capron, again, seemed to be the center of attention on November 28. Capron, still suffering from the injury he sustained in a fall a few days earlier, established his headquarters at the junction of Shelbyville Road and Lewisburg Pike. He retained some of the newly arrived 7th Ohio for headquarters security while dispersing the rest of the regiment and the remainder of his brigade to guard the various crossings and roads. The 16th Illinois Cavalry and part of the 8th Michigan Cavalry moved to guard the Lewisburg–Franklin Pike. Major J. Morris Young, commanding the newly arrived 5th Iowa along with part of the 14th Illinois Cavalry, moved into position at a crossing (Morris' Ford) a half mile west of Lewisburg Pike. The rest of the 14th Illinois was divided into smaller units and sent to the other various crossings to the east. Finally, Capron sent a small group of 25 men to set up a post on Shelbyville Road in the most eastern part

Federal cavalry skirmish with the advancing Confederates (*Battles and Leaders of the Civil War*, Vol. III [1887], p. 255).

of the Union line. Almost immediately L.H. Patten, 8th Michigan Cavalry, reported to Capron that he did not have enough men to watch the numerous fords on the Duck River and this, in a single message, summarized Wilson's situation.[21]

Capron's brigade had been hard pressed during the advance on Columbia and now faced Buford's initial advance in the morning. At 10:25 a.m., Richard Johnson reported that a reconnaissance force had discovered enemy pickets at Morris Ford and that "Major Young, Fifth Iowa ... says ... a brigade of rebel cavalry encamped within two miles, and that Wheeler and Forrest are moving in that direction (eastward); this is common report of citizens." Capron ordered reconnaissance detachments to find the enemy and push them hard enough to determine the strength and location of the enemy forces. Capron's brigade was in a difficult position but the ailing Capron was determined to hold his position. Between Huey's Mill and Lewisburg Pike, there were six fords which could be used by Forrest's cavalry. At 1:10 p.m., Wilson told Johnson to hold his positions as long as possible and reinforce those troops being attacked. "Direct Colonel Harrison (or Capron) to hold the crossing of Duck River in his front as long as possible, and be ready to support him promptly with Croxton's and Garrard's brigades. You had better move Croxton at once, who will assume command till you arrive." Johnson received these orders at 2:00 p.m. but by that time Croxton had been ordered to the rear with no mention of supporting of Capron.[22]

Capron, to the east of Croxton, began the day at Hardison's Mill, but on edge. Hardison's Mill was a small community centered around a mill on the Duck River along Lewisburg Pike. The original mill was built around 1820 by Charles Hardison and the mill was later operated by his son Calvin Hardison for some 50 years. A saw mill and a wool factory were later added to the operation, in addition to the grist mill, in the 1840s. A store and post office were also established in 1844 by Calvin Hardison. The community would be the center of most of the cavalry actions during the day. Capron's scouting party south of the Duck River ran into Confederate cavalry pickets and drove them to the rear, discovering a large force of mounted troops close behind. The Union troopers got close enough to find a brigade of

Thomas J. Harrison, a man of "large and command presence," assumed command of Capron's brigade (courtesy Howard County Historical Society, Kokomo, Indiana).

Chapter Eight. Columbia: Forrest Pushes Across the Duck River 137

enemy cavalry (believed to be Jackson's) near Bethlehem Church. The large body of cavalry caused immediate concerns for the Union commanders on the north side of the river, even though at this point the enemy was not pressing northward. Soon everything changed. At 11:20 a.m. Capron reported the aggressive movement of Confederates on the south side of the river. "My force sent across the Duck River has been driven back to this side by a heavy force, and I am now engaging him across the river." At 2:40 p.m., Capron's cavalry stubbornly refused to give up the crossing and Capron again reported to Johnson: "[T]he enemy are now engaging me from across the river at Hardison's Mill Ford and Morris' Ford (half a mile below Hardison's), with at least a brigade. He also shows a column moving up the river to my left." At 4:30 p.m., Capron, still at Hardison's Mill, reported a large column of infantry across the river and "Heavy skirmishing still continues in my front." Then, he explained: "There is a heavy force of infantry, cavalry, and artillery pressing us; too strong for us; they are moving up on our left. I will hold them, if possible. The Seventh Ohio is here."[23]

At 3:30 p.m., new orders were sent for Capron to proceed to Hurt's Crossroads to unite with Croxton and Hatch. The orders cautioned: "Have a care for your right flank, and fall back slowly. The enemy now confronts Hatch in considerable force." It is unlikely the orders to withdraw ever reached Capron or Harrison. As a result, Capron remained in a dangerous position and he would write later that he was unaware of any order to withdraw until 7:00 p.m. when the conditions on the field had already forced his retreat. W.L. Sanford bitterly wrote: "As to any explanations of the inefficient management of the cavalry forces under Generals Wilson and Johnson, on the 28th day of November, 1864, when the cavalry were under such explicit orders to oppose the crossing of the river by any portion of Hood's army, and when the safety of our army so much depended upon the heroic resistance by our cavalry, I am thankful that I am not appointed to defend the course of our cavalry commanders...."[24]

Capron battled Buford successfully across the Duck River until 4:00 p.m. While focusing on keeping Buford's division on the south side of the river, Ross' brigade surprised him. Capron discovered Ross was on the north side of the river when a squadron his cavalry came riding hard from the west with 40 enemy cavalry galloping behind them. "This was the first positive information that we had that any of Forrest's cavalry were on our side of the river," wrote Sanford, 14th Illinois Cavalry. Capron dispatched 50 men of the 7th Ohio to drive off the enemy troopers. Sanford and another officer followed the 7th Ohio troopers and found two enemy soldiers riding along a lane. They followed the two Rebels and then had a big surprise. As they emerged in a clearing, "we were fired upon from seemingly every tree and rock, until we neared our picket post. How many shots were fired at us we could only imagine, as we did not stop to count noses, having just then more important business on hand. We then supposed that we had run the gauntlet of a rebel battalion, and deemed ourselves fortunate that with singing bullets before us and behind us as we swiftly passed them, that neither ourselves nor our horses had received a scratch, and no injury except a slight retarding of the flow of blood to our faces, which our comrades declared were as pale as our mother's dish cloths…. A ready and well aimed volley from the boys at the post killed their leader, a Captain Wharton, of the 3d Texas Cavalry, as papers in his pockets showed. There is no doubt but many of their number were wounded, for they were driven back in disorder, and there were a number of our command who were crack marksmen." Ross' brigade followed up the attack and moved swiftly to Capron's headquarters which was unprepared to resist the attack. With Ross arriving at Capron's headquarters, this left much of his brigade in a precarious situation in their original position, opposing Buford to the south.[25]

When Croxton withdrew earlier in the day, Jackson's cavalry division surged across the Duck River with Armstrong's brigade leading the advance. Ross's brigade, which crossed the river at Fountain Creek, followed Armstrong's brigade and then moved east on Shelbyville Road in the afternoon. Ross did not encounter any significant number of Union cavalry until he neared the Lewisburg Pike—Shelbyville Road intersection (Orr's Crossroads). Then, a "spirited engagement ensued, begun by the Third Texas, which being dispatched to attack a train of wagons moving in direction of Franklin," explained Ross. The 3rd Texas reaching Lewisburg Pike, was driven back by the Federal cavalry. The Texas Legion (27th Texas Regiment) spurred their horses and rode to assist the 3rd Texas. As they approached, Colonel Edwin Hawkins ordered "charge, which was made in gallant style, and resulted in forcing the Yankees from the field in confusion, and with the loss of several prisoners and the colors of the Seventh Ohio Cavalry." While the 3rd Texas and the Texas Legion were engaged in their fight, the 6th Texas slammed into the Union cavalry to the right of the other Texas regiments "capturing an entire company of the Seventh Ohio Cavalry, three stand of colors, several wagons loaded with ordnance, and a considerable number of horses with their equipments." The only regiment in Ross' brigade not engaged, at this point, was the 9th Texas which had been assigned to provide security on a road leading to Hardison's Mill.[26]

Captain Richard C. Rankin, 7th Ohio Cavalry, explained the Federal account of Ross' attack. The 7th Ohio had just arrived at Capron's headquarters and the Ohioans were placed in various positions in company-sized units to support Capron's brigade—Company A sent toward Croxton down river, Company B and C on the Shelbyville Road scouting toward Columbia, Company E and the remainder of the regiment in columns of squadrons north of Capron's position at Hardison's Mill. Late in the afternoon, Capron ordered the brigade train to move to Hurt's Crossroads guarded by a company of 7th Ohio (presumably Co. A). At that point, Ross' cavalry came riding from the west and Companies B and C met the Confederate cavalry, and Company E was cut off by the advancing Confederate line. Ross's men attacked the head of the supply train hoping to stop its northward progress, forcing the supply train behind the line of the 7th Ohio. Rankin recalled: "A volley was poured into the enemy by the two companies already in position and a saber charge was immediately made, the remainder of the regiment coming into position in time, thereby driving the enemy from the road and held them in check…." The initial counter attack stymied the 3rd Texas Cavalry as described by Ross.[27]

Capron, who was near the river, was cut off from communications with Johnson and Wilson. A rider arrived with erroneous information that Hood had already crossed the river and that Schofield's infantry was streaming northward toward Franklin. In addition, the rider declared that Hatch and Croxton had been driven to the rear and Wilson could not be found. Capron and Garrard conferred and decided to attempt to hold their position until dark. Immediately after this decision, another rider arrived reporting the advance of Ross' brigade on Shelbyville Road from the direction of Columbia. Capron returned to his headquarters and found the 7th Ohio already battling Ross' cavalry at Orr's Crossroads near his headquarters. Capron recalled the intensity of the battle: "It was then in the dusk of the evening, and the flash of the weapons of the contending forces seemed to encircle the camp." The sun began to sink below the horizon and Capron sent a rider to tell Young to withdraw because the enemy was in his rear. At that point, the Federal supply train came streaming back toward headquarters after having been attacked. Then, Garrard saw an opportunity and he led an attack by the 7th Ohio which opened another trail and the wagons slipped away into the night. Again, Ross' cavalry attacked, overwhelming some of the Union troopers who tried to make their escape. "Immediately upon this a confused mass of our pickets ... were driven in upon us. Not one drew rein, but charged past us, overthrowing everything in their way, and with them out went every man with the exception of myself, staff officers, and a few orderlies," exclaimed Capron. Finally, Capron and his staff escaped in the confusion. Captain Theodore Allen, commanding Company D, moving from Hardison's Mill arrived on the scene observing about 300 enemy cavalry moving through the fields. Before the enemy cavalry, Allen saw a stampede of trains and stragglers. From Allen's account, his company fell back a few miles north toward Franklin—Lewisburg Pike being joined there by Capron, his staff, and most of the rest of the 7th Ohio closely followed by Ross' cavalry. Next, the newly formed Union line received some unexpected support when some of Coon's brigade arrived from their position near Rally Hill to stabilize the situation. Allen felt his regiment had been isolated and without support in the fight and reported a loss of 90 men, plus one officer captured, and one man wounded. He wrote, "The regiment fought hard & suffered severely."[28]

Richard Rankin, 7th Ohio, described the loss of the regimental colors. When Capron made the decision to retreat to the north, the color sergeant agreed to ride to Rankin's position to inform him to prepare his company for the withdrawal. Ross' Confederates and Rankin's Union lines were only 30 yards apart and the sergeant "rode directly into the rebel lines and was captured." The Union cavalry withdrew about six miles to Flat Creek abandoning their dead and wounded still on the field.[29]

Much of the other actions by Wilson, Hatch and Croxton were unknown to Capron as his brigade battled Buford's division. Unknown to Capron were the movements of Schofield's infantry to the north side of the river and Forrest across the river. Due to the poor communication systems of the times, many in the brigade would later find that Wilson had ordered Johnson to move Croxton to support Capron, an order which was never carried out. W.L. Sanford bitterly recalled: "So far from supporting Capron in any manner, though both Generals Johnson and Wilson knew that the enemy crossed the river below us [west] in strong force soon after noon, neither one of them ever notified Colonel Capron of this movement of the enemy, but left his command to be annihilated, and hurriedly retreated with their own commands, without making any resistance of consequence."[30]

Young's Charge at Orr's Crossroads

While Ross was fighting at Orr's Crossroads, at 4:30 p.m., J. Morris Young (adjutant for Capron's brigade) and most of Capron's brigade remained engaged with Buford on Lewisburg Pike at two fords on the Duck River. The Federal cavalry had effectively held Buford in position throughout the afternoon. Although still unknown to Young, Ross' brigade put the cavalry facing Buford in a dangerous position. While Capron stated he sent orders for Young to withdraw, Young's account differed: "At 5 p.m. my patrols and pickets reported the enemy in force in my rear and Colonel Capron, commanding the brigade, gone."[31]

At this point, Young thought the 5th Iowa was alone facing a deteriorating situation. Young moved the 5th Iowa to Lewisburg Pike in column of fours and prepared to attempt to his cut way northward. He was soon surprised when the 8th Michigan, 14th Illinois and 16th Illinois regiments arrived on the pike, in total greater than 1,000 Union cavalrymen. With the enemy converging from all directions, these regiments were formed: "Eighth Michigan in line dismounted, to the left of and perpendicular to the head of the Fifth Iowa column; the Sixteenth Illinois disposed in like manner on the right; the led horses of both regiments to follow up at a safe distance in their respective rears; the Fourteenth Illinois was placed in column of fours, to the left and rear of the Eighth Michigan and parallel to the Fifth Iowa, which was in column on the turnpike." The Union troops on the west side of this column were the most vulnerable to an attack by the enemy because Ross' cavalry was still concentrated on that side of the pike. The 5th Iowa led the advance northward and as soon as Ross' men opened fire, the dismounted troopers quickly mounted and followed the 5th Iowa which led the column in a saber charge. It took 15 minutes to get into position and another 15 minutes to reach Ross' cavalry which had moved behind barricades. "We received their fire and instantly sounded the 'charge,' riding them down and scattering them in all directions." Young explained, "Permit me to add in closing the fact of the growing confidence amongst our troops that good cavalry never can be captured." Colonel Elisha Mix, 8th Michigan Cavalry, wrote to his wife, that this action "saved the army." Trooper George Garrison wrote to his sister a few days later that 8th Michigan had hard duty: "I have seen all the fighting I want to see. Our regiment has been cut up pretty bad." Ross' report of the second fight confirmed Young's account. Ross wrote that after he drove off Capron and the 7th Ohio he knew there were still Federal troops near Hardison's Mill. "Colonel Hawkins [Texas Legion] was therefore ordered up the pike with his regiment to reconnoiter, and had proceeded but a short distance before he was met by a brigade of Federal cavalry. An exciting fight ensued, lasting about half an hour, when the enemy, having much the larger force, succeeded in passing by us, receiving as he did so a severe fire into his flanks." The Texas Legion took the brunt of the charge from Young's column.[32]

Reconciling the various accounts of this fight between Capron's brigade and Buford's and Ross's troops is difficult at best. Ross's success appeared to be the attack primarily against the 7th Ohio Cavalry. The claims of the numbers of colors and booty taken in the fight are dissimilar in the various accounts. Capron's personal separation from the remainder of the brigade at Hardison's Mill resulted due to the situation which unexpectedly exploded at his headquarters. The Union regiments at Hardison's Mill rightly gained the credit of stalling Buford's division throughout the day. Young's success at cutting his way out, while exciting, does not include the actions of the 7th Ohio and parts of the 14th Illinois in their fights with Ross. Finally, in regard to Johnson's and Wilson's orders not reaching Capron, this occurred due to the poor communication methods of the time and confusion of who commanded the brigade at this point—Harrison or Capron. Croxton did not mention receiving any orders to support Capron. Probably, Johnson expected Capron's orders to withdraw to be carried out and there was no need to send Croxton to support a position which was being evacuated.

In regard to the fighting at Hardison's Mill on the Confederate side, Abraham Buford faced a rain swollen river and the Union cavalry had a small fort or redoubt built on the north bank. The Federals held a solid line and Confederate officers initially concluded that trying to force a crossing in such conditions would result in serious losses.

Chapter Eight. Columbia: Forrest Pushes Across the Duck River

There were no dramatic attempts to force the crossing and the combatants simply exchanged shots across the stream. Buford finally decided to send Colonel John Newsom's 18th Tennessee Cavalry upstream to find a crossing and then apply pressure to the Federal eastern flank. In the meantime, Colonel Clark Barteau's 22nd (2nd) Tennessee Cavalry built a raft large enough to move a dozen troopers across the torrent to support Newsom. The raft came apart during the crossing, but the effort so encouraged the regiment that the entire unit plunged their horses into the river. This put two regiments on the north shore with the rest firing across the river. Buford also got some much-needed help from Ross' Confederate cavalry already on the north side of the river, but Buford was already making progress in removing the Federal forces at the crossings.[33]

By 4:30 p.m., the Confederate cavalry had overall good positions on the north side of the Duck River and only Buford's division remained bogged on Lewisburg Pike. Forrest's success came from his ability to concentrate his entire corps on the dispersed Federal units covering 10 miles of the river. Wilson withdrew Croxton and Coon from their vulnerable positions back toward Rally Hill. And, he sent important and ominous information—if the cavalry had been pushed backed to Rally Hill, this opened up the roads leading to Spring Hill, in the rear of Schofield's infantry, to Forrest's cavalry should Forrest choose to ride in that direction. Wilson wrote to Schofield: "You had better look out for that place. I am doing all I can to carry out your instructions; shall get my force together first. The enemy may turn in your rear between us." Wilson told Schofield that he was preparing to meet Forrest the next day and told him to send Stewart's and Hammond's brigades to Spring Hill. "I'll get everything on the Lewisburg road tonight. All quiet at Hardin's [Hardison'] Mill last account. Enemy seem to be massing and moving in that direction. I'll try for Hurt's [Crossroads] tonight." Schofield confirmed Wilson's report about an hour later. "Rebel cavalry is crossing the river very near the left of our infantry. I fear this indicates that your cavalry pickets have all been withdrawn from the river. Please see to it. The river in our immediate vicinity should not be left without cavalry pickets." There is no record that Wilson acted on re-establishing pickets after Forrest pushed his cavalry to the north, but the situation was long past picketing. Wilson was trying to concentrate his cavalry to prevent Forrest from turning the entire left flank.[34]

Chalmers' and Jackson's divisions moved across the river with relative ease. At 11:00 p.m., Buford sent a message to Forrest informing him that he would not reach the rest of the cavalry until the next day. By that time, Chalmers had advanced four miles north of the river, and Jackson's division had pressed toward Hurt's Crossroads with Armstrong's brigade leading the pursuit, but Forrest told Armstrong not to press the Federals until all of Chalmers' division arrived.[35]

The Infantry's Uneasiness

Later in the afternoon, Schofield's infantry commanders knew that Forrest had crossed the river. Thomas Wood worried about his position, on the left of Franklin Pike, and told David Stanley that the cavalry along his flank had been withdrawn. This concerned Wood because "two regiments of rebel cavalry have crossed the river," probably Jacob Biffle's Confederate brigade. Wood's concern resulted from the cavalry withdrawal which left a gaping hole through which the "whole rebel army may be over on our left flank without hindrance." Upon further contemplation and because the Union cavalry had been driven back, Wood decided to extend his flank. Wood, a stickler for detail, even questioned Schofield's entire plan of remaining in such a non-defensible position. Wood, a veteran campaigner, knew that his flank was threatened. "It seems to me a little strange that General Schofield does not intimate what measures he proposes to adopt to protect ourselves and guard our trains, and still more strange that he does not initiate such measures at once, as the enemy, according to his own statement, has crossed the river in force. It is perfectly patent to my mind, if the enemy has crossed in force, that General Wilson will not be able to check him. It requires no oracle to predict the effect of the enemy's reaching the Franklin pike in our rear." Wood was correct and it would have benefited Schofield to listen to Wood's concerns. If Wilson had been driven back to Hurt's Crossroads, Schofield's rear was already threatened.[36]

Jacob Cox was also feeling uneasy. Cox noticed that the position of his command seemed to be encircled based on a large bend in the river. This gave the enemy the opportunity to fire on him from three sides and, more importantly, left him vulnerable to capture if the enemy surged across the river. In addition, he did not have enough men to form a solid defensive line with IV Corps. He informed Schofield that he was covering a four-mile front. "I am glad to know that you propose visiting this part of the line this morning. The enemy pushed down to the river at dawn and commenced a lively skirmish, which continues." As the day passed, Schofield became increasingly uneasy himself. While Cox and Wood worried about their flanks, Schofield sent word to Thomas Ruger to hold his position near the railroad bridge and he ordered Ruger to be sure to burn the railroad bridge that night to keep it out of enemy hands. He ordered the 800-wagon supply train to move to Franklin the next day.[37]

Wilson's Decisions on November 28

As Hammond's brigade hurried forward, Wilson sent orders to get this brigade to the main body of cavalry. "[S]trike off to the eastward and try and get on the Lewisburg and Franklin pike. The general commanding will concentrate the cavalry about Hurt's Cross-Roads tonight." Wilson sent regular updates to Schofield throughout the day as events unfolded and at 1 a.m. Wilson told Schofield, again, that Forrest had successfully crossed and threatened Schofield's flank. He advised Schofield to withdraw to Franklin "at once." At 3:00 a.m. the next morning, Wilson, at Hurt's Crossroads on Franklin and Lewisburg Pike, summarized the actions in a report to George Thomas. The bulk of Forrest's cavalry had crossed the Duck River and moved north on the road where Wilson had his headquarters. The Confederates had crossed on Franklin–Lewisburg Pike, and at several fords along a seven mile stretch of the Duck River extending to Columbia. A Confederate train had been moved to the Duck River with enough pontoons to construct three bridges and Wilson expected the bridges to be in place by midnight. Fortunately, Wilson had drawn all of his cavalry to his headquarters, except Hammond's command (whose location was still unknown to Wilson) and Stewart's brigade. Wilson told Thomas, "I shall delay the enemy all in my power, if he presses me, and follow him wherever he goes." Wilson explained that he had scouts as far east as Shelbyville, and that prisoners said that Hood intended on reaching Nashville by way of Franklin. Based on these reports and the cavalry observations, he felt the next line of defense would be

Chapter Eight. Columbia: Forrest Pushes Across the Duck River

along the Harpeth River while keeping a close watch on Nolensville. Wilson cautioned, "Everything should be got off the Chattanooga road today. Hurry forward all the cavalry via Nolensville. I think everything should be concentrated at Nashville."[38]

Pushing the Union cavalry away from the river and further to the rear was a key part of the strategy by Forrest to keep Schofield's flank open to attack by Hood's infantry. As long as Forrest drove Wilson further northward, Hood had the chance of outmarching Schofield who merely extended the lines of his infantry during the day. Hood was on verge of cutting Schofield off from Nashville and the reinforcements waiting there. Forrest's cavalry had done good duty during the day and yet Schofield lingered at Columbia. This poses the question as to the proper action of Wilson's cavalry.

Wilson had two additional brigades moving to unite with the bulk of the Union cavalry—Stewart's and Hammond's. Both Wilson and Schofield knew a pontoon bridge had been installed by Hood during the night of November 28. This gave Hood the step he needed to march past Schofield's flank and Wilson told Schofield of this threat. Schofield needed to withdraw "at once." Wilson would write: "Schofield lost at least twelve hours in getting out of Columbia after he knew that Hood had crossed Duck River above and was marching on Spring Hill." There were two primary routes to Franklin and Schofield's infantry held one while Wilson's cavalry held the other at Hurt's Crossroads. With all of his cavalry at this location, except for the brigades still en route, he felt he had done all that he could with the three brigades engaged during the day. It was Schofield who needed to start marching to Franklin, but Schofield hesitated. While Wilson was critical of Schofield, some historians were, in return, critical of Wilson. Historian Thomas Robson Hay felt that Wilson erred by staying at Hurt's Crossroads and should have moved to Spring Hill to be in place to block Hood's advance. Similarly, Jacob Cox would later write that Wilson erred by remaining in his position on Lewisburg Pike because this allowed Forrest direct access to Spring Hill. In return, Wilson felt he had explained to Schofield not only Hood's potential plan, but Wilson's own plan for the next day, which Schofield seemed to accept. Wilson wrote to Thomas that he believed Forrest and Hood still intended to march northward to Nashville. Wilson reasoned: "This being true, I shall probably cross the Harpeth midway between Triune and Franklin and aim for Nolensville." Hay would argue that had Wilson moved toward Spring Hill, Forrest would not have continued toward Nashville, but followed Wilson toward Spring Hill.[39]

Wilson was open to criticism whichever decision he made. If he had contracted on Schofield's flank, Forrest had an open road to perhaps Spring Hill or Thompson's Station, but definitely to Franklin. If he held a position on the Lewisburg Pike, Schofield's flank was vulnerable. Only two things could have produced a positive outcome—Schofield needed to retreat at the pace of Wilson or Wilson needed to fight Forrest to a standstill on the Lewisburg Pike. In regard to the second choice, with only three brigades Wilson just did not have enough cavalry to do that, and in regard to the first choice, Schofield dallied too long at Columbia. While Wilson would misread some of the Confederate intentions over the next two days, he "had learned enough of Hood's movement to divine its purpose," wrote Ohio infantry officer John Shellenberger.[40]

Wilson and his cavalry fell back to Hurt's Crossroads, an intersection of the roads about five miles north of the Duck River, during the evening under the pressure of Forrest's cavalry, and the Confederate cavalry continued past Rally Hill to face Wilson. Armstrong's brigade pressed the Union cavalry to the crossroads as the trailing columns moved to support his action. Ross's brigade of Jackson's cavalry had removed the resistance blocking Buford's division from crossing the river. At 8:30 p.m. Wilson wrote to Schofield about the situation at his location regarding Capron's and Young's fighting on Lewisburg Pike. He added: "The force of the enemy is believed to be all of Forrest's command moving in this direction. The orderly who left your headquarters late this evening with the dispatch in regard to Colonel Stewart's brigade saw nothing of the enemy moving toward the Franklin pike. He is evidently aiming for this road or Murfreesborough.... I have ... also sent a party to Spring Hill for Colonel Stewart's brigade and Hammond. I'll communicate from here again as soon as the movements of the enemy can be determined in the morning. Prisoners say that Hood is going to flank us on one side or other." Wilson's messages, which had started out as confident early in the day, now echoed deep concern about his position. Importantly, Wilson told Schofield that Forrest's actions had opened Schofield's flank to an attack.[41]

On the evening of November 28, the initiative fell to Hood who considered his next moves. As he turned in for the night, Hood said good-bye to a chaplain in Confederate army, Charles Todd Quintard, and he told the cleric: "The enemy must give me fight or I will be in Nashville before tomorrow night." Hood still had no definite plan to deal with Schofield and seemed content to let the events unfold. The next day would be fateful for both armies and set the stage for the remainder of the campaign.[42]

Part Three
The Battle for Nashville

Chapter Nine

Spring Hill and Franklin

Hatch and Croxton made a beautiful fight.
—James H. Wilson

November 29—Schofield Considers Evacuation

At 3:30 a.m. on November 29, Thomas wrote to Schofield: "I desire you to fall back from Columbia and to take up your position at Franklin, leaving a sufficient force at Spring Hill to contest the enemy's progress until you are securely posted at Franklin." To coincide with Schofield's movements, Thomas withdrew the other troops west of Columbia, northward. At 8:20 a.m., Schofield replied to Thomas that Wilson's reconnaissance revealed the Confederate infantry and cavalry were already on the north side of the river; however, Schofield calmly explained that he had an infantry force moving five miles to the point of the crossing to verify the information. The telegraphs remained quiet until Schofield sent a one-line message to Thomas at 1:00 p.m. to have pontoons placed across the Harpeth River at Franklin "at once" in anticipation of withdrawal by the Union troops toward Nashville. Things had changed significantly over the intervening hours.[1]

At 8:00 a.m., David Stanley had two divisions underway marching to Spring Hill in what might have been the beginning of Stanley's most important duty during the Civil War. Stanley initially planned to have both divisions move to Spring Hill, but Schofield stopped Nathan Kimball's First Division at Rutherford's Creek about five miles north of Columbia while Schofield decided when he would withdraw the rest of his infantry. Meanwhile, the 800-wagon supply train and several artillery batteries plodded northward along a muddy road accompanied by Brigadier General George Wagner's Second Division. Wood's Third Division remained with Schofield's infantry at Columbia. The process of withdrawal would not be easy over the soggy ground. At 10:30 a.m., William Sinclair, Stanley's chief of staff, explained the plan of withdrawal to the quartermasters: "As soon as the Second Division and artillery pass, see that all trains are shoved ahead for Spring Hill. The First Division is to remain at Rutherford's Creek until all wagons pass."[2]

Union Cavalry Actions—November 29

From his temporary headquarters at Hurt's Crossroads, Wilson diligently sent information to Schofield at 1:00 a.m. about the enemy's movements. The day before, Forrest

Chapter Nine. Spring Hill and Franklin

left Columbia at 4:30 p.m. and joined the cavalry south of Rally Hill. In the meantime, the Confederate infantry was expected to cross the river over three pontoon bridges due to be completed overnight. All of the Confederate cavalry had concentrated near Widow Shannon's on the Columbia-Shelbyville Road, except Buford's division, near Rally Hill, with Wilson's main concentration of Federal cavalry just to the north. In the 1:00 a.m. message, Wilson told Schofield that it seemed the Confederate cavalry intended to march to Franklin. He then advised Schofield that to prevent from being flanked he needed to march the infantry to Spring Hill arriving there by 10:00 a.m. on a gray, overcast November 29. Wilson explained his situation: "I'll keep on this road and hold the enemy all I can. If I had Hammond and Stewart here, I think they could not make anything until their infantry caught up. Communicate with me by Thompson's Station or Spring Hill, and thence eastward." Wilson told Schofield he hoped to hold Forrest at the Ridge Meeting House, a few miles due east from Thompson's Station. Then, still expecting Forrest to swing to the east, Wilson planned to move toward Nolensville to again block the Confederate cavalry. Wilson continued, "There may be no strong advance of the enemy's cavalry till the infantry have crossed, which will be between now and daylight. Get back to Franklin without delay, leaving a small force to detain the enemy. The rebels will move by this road toward that point." Wilson could not have given a better reconnaissance report. Schofield replied to Wilson at 8:15 a.m. that he had received the message and directed him to try to delay the enemy as long as possible and to communicate in the future with him via Spring Hill through Stanley. Based on this response, Wilson concluded that Schofield had accepted the plan and that Wilson's responsibility centered on keeping Forrest from striking north of the Harpeth River, while securing the Lewisburg Pike. Wilson believed Schofield would withdraw to Franklin during the day.[3]

At 10:45 a.m. Schofield, still at Columbia, knew he was in for a hard day as he waited on the north side of the Duck River. Despite Wilson's and Schofield's agreement, Schofield had calmly disregarded the urgency in Wilson's overnight communications and waited until P. Sidney Post's brigade scouted east along the river. Finally confirming a large force of Hood's infantry had already crossed the river, he sent a message to Stanley to hold the road open at Spring Hill and to try to gain Wilson's cooperation in halting the Confederate advance. "I will try to hold the enemy until dark, and then draw back. Select a good position at Spring Hill, covering the approaches, and send out parties to reconnoiter on all roads leading east and southeast." Remarkably, Schofield, knowing that Wilson was withdrawing to a position east of Thompson's Station, told Stanley to tell Wilson not to let the enemy "get between us." However, this message was too late and Wilson could do little in regard to preventing the Confederate cavalry from reaching Spring Hill, because his understanding was that a slow withdrawal to the Harpeth River had been agreed upon. Schofield had misinterpreted Hood's intent. He believed that Hood planned to move against the Federal forces at Columbia.[4]

In the subsequent hours, Forrest's cavalry vigorously attacked Wilson's mounted forces and followed them farther north. Forrest had the advantage of concentrating his troops and of knowing Hood's plan. Hood intended to march Cheatham's corps, Stewart's corps, and one division of Lee's corps around Schofield's eastern flank to Spring Hill while the rest of his infantry held Schofield's infantry at Columbia. Meanwhile, Wilson believed the Federal forces would stay ahead of Hood by jointly marching north on parallel roads. By 10:00 a.m., Wilson had withdrawn five miles north of Hurt's Crossroads to Mount Carmel, another crossroads on Lewisburg–Franklin Pike which intersected with the Murfreesboro Road. Wilson sent a message to Schofield from Mount Carmel, five miles directly east of Spring Hill, that doomed any cooperation with Stanley's division at Spring Hill when he wrote that Forrest's cavalry was pushing his cavalry northward. Two hours later, another message was dispatched to Schofield detailing a steady withdrawal, to just east of Thompson's Station; at this location, Wilson had discovered part of Forrest's cavalry had moved in another direction. "Some of the officers of the command think that Forrest has divided his forces, sending some up on the Davis Ford road, but in the opinion of the general there is no doubt he has gone to Nashville with his whole force. The general will endeavor to cover Franklin as much as possible until you get there.... Please let him know what time General Schofield will get through with the infantry." Wilson incorrectly interpreted where Forrest moved the bulk of the cavalry. He thought the missing Southern cavalry had gone toward Franklin or Nolensville but instead, it was moving to Spring Hill to meet Wagner's division. The messages clearly showed that Wilson expected Schofield to be in full retreat, revealing a serious lack of agreement between Wilson and Schofield. At 4:10 p.m., Wilson, who had just received Schofield's 8:15 a.m. message, reported from four miles east of Franklin: "The enemy, after having pressed my command back this side of Ridge Meeting-House, has disappeared; I think, moving, via Peytonsville [east of the Lewisburg–Franklin Pike], toward Nashville." Wilson dispatched Johnson's division north of the Harpeth River, making sure Forrest didn't swing around the eastern flank which would threaten the Nashville & Chattanooga Railroad or the city of Nashville to attack. Next, he held his position with Hammond's newly arrived brigade and Hatch's division east of Franklin. Wilson fretted that he had held on too long at Hurt's Crossroads which allowed Forrest time to gain a step on the eastern flank. He was still under the impression that Schofield had withdrawn as agreed upon because he heard noise of fighting near Spring Hill. Wilson wrote: "I have heard heavy firing in your direction all day, and feel very solicitous for you. I hope that you will pass the Harpeth tonight." Wilson had executed a slow withdrawal of cavalry during the day, but he missed Forrest's movements and he was very mistaken that Schofield had withdrawn at daylight from Columbia.[5]

The Cavalry Fights Along the Lewisburg Pike

The day held significant actions for the cavalry on both sides of the line. Wilson's cavalry moved early on November 29, planning a fighting withdrawal. The Federal cavalrymen slept fitfully overnight, with their horses saddled, behind hastily prepared, rough barricades. At 4:00 a.m. John Croxton's brigade assumed the cavalry rearguard duty while Coon's and Harrison's brigades withdrew to Mount Carmel. Croxton asked Wilson, upon receiving his orders, if Wilson intended to fight, and Wilson replied, "Only when necessary to delay the enemy." The veteran Croxton gave Wilson his thoughts about the day's assignment. "I think I understand you, and all I have to say is, if you don't intend to fight for all you are worth, please get your horse cavalry out of the way and give me a clear road!" This statement offered insight in the statement that Wilson was being "driven" north. There is little doubt that Forrest had the upper hand, but by placing a single brigade to hold Forrest, Wilson implemented a fighting withdrawal.[6]

Coon moved his brigade to Mount Carmel directly east of Spring Hill while Crox-

Chapter Nine. Spring Hill and Franklin

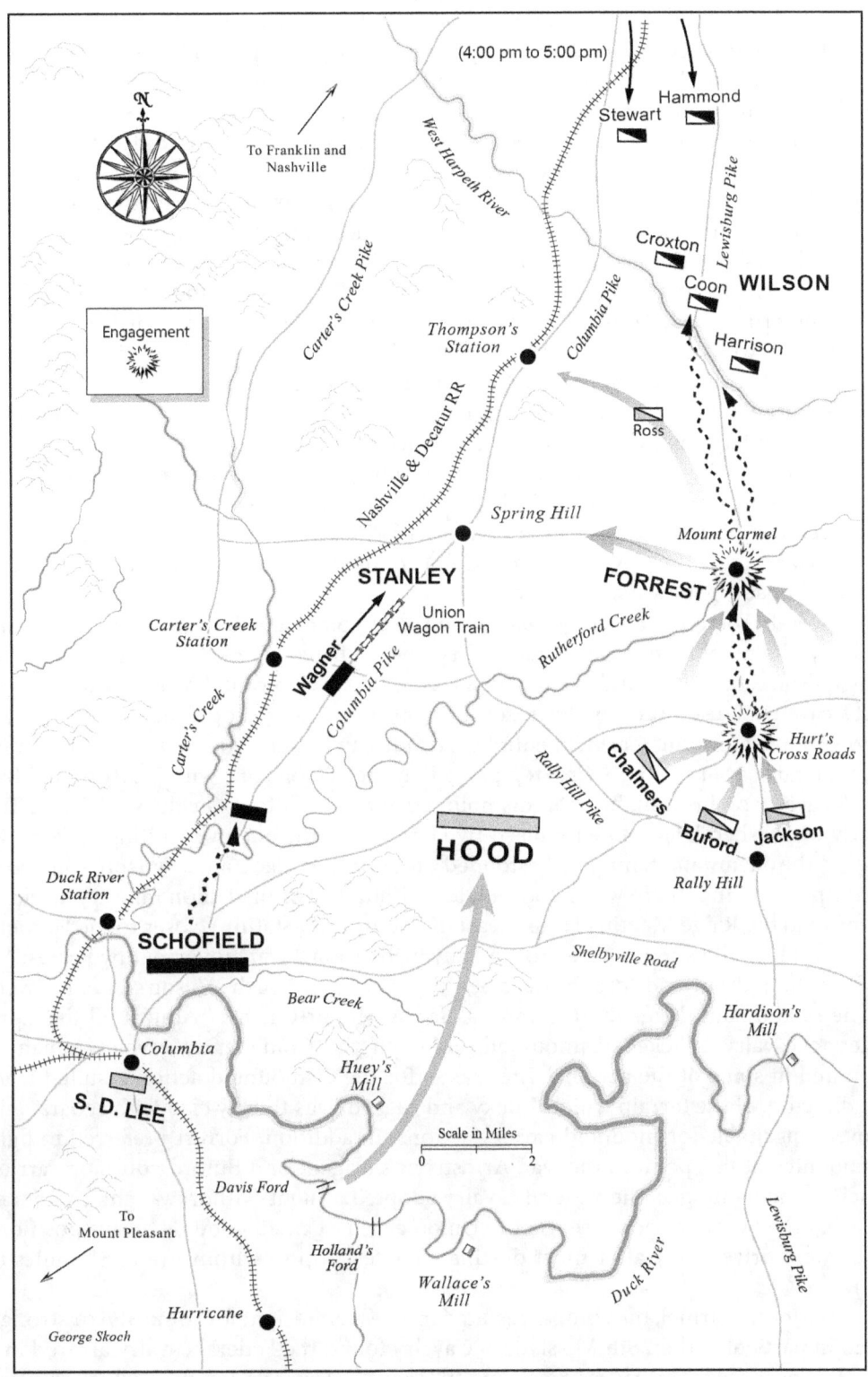

Forrest pushes northward, November 29, 1864.

ton held a steady line withdrawing north of Hurt's Crossroads until about nine o'clock when the pressure from Forrest's cavalry forced Croxton to make a hasty retreat. Croxton initially placed the 1st Tennessee and 2nd Michigan behind rough barricades of rails and logs on the road leading north. The first attack was repulsed by Croxton's brigade which "opened such a rapid fire upon his troops that they broke and fled to the rear, leaving several dead and wounded in our front," wrote W.R. Carter, 1st Tennessee Cavalry. Croxton's troopers first met Jackson's cavalry division with Armstrong's brigade leading the advance, but Forrest told Armstrong not to push too aggressively until he had Chalmers' and Buford's divisions in place to join in the fight. Corporal J.A. Bigger, in his diary, wrote that the initial clash resulted in a "hard little fight—28th Miss. of our Bridg. suffering most." With the arrival of the additional Confederate divisions, Croxton couldn't withstand the attack and retreated toward Coon's and Harrison's waiting brigades in the direction of Mount Carmel. Harrison fell into line between Coon and Croxton. (Stewart's brigade, in the process of reaching Wilson, would not arrive until 4:00 in the afternoon.) Croxton's forces stopped at locations favorable to a temporary defense before withdrawing again. As Forrest advanced, he soon found Croxton withdrew to Coon's and Harrison's brigades in line behind barricades. Harrison joined in the defense in his first formal assignment under Wilson's command. A veteran of many battles Harrison, only a few days after taking command, wrote to his wife telling her of the fine brigade he now commanded.[7]

Overall, Forrest dealt fairly easily with the Union defenses during the day. Unlike infantry, the mobility of cavalry allowed Forrest to flank any of the fortified positions that Wilson established, and when it appeared that Croxton would be overtaken by Forrest's cavalry, Wilson ordered his reserve troops into line to stop Confederate attacks. Coon, in line at Mount Carmel behind barricades, unleashed volleys into the pursuing Confederate cavalrymen. As Croxton passed through Coon's line with Jackson's and Buford's cavalry on his trail, his men dismounted and moved to cover the west flank. The newly established Union line repulsed two charges by the enemy resulting in "a heavy loss" to the enemy and temporarily stopped the attack. At 10:00 a.m., Wilson, still under the impression that there was a coordinated withdrawal of the Union infantry, decided to move to the Ridge Meeting House (east of Thompson's Station) closer to the Harpeth River and Franklin and prepared to stop any further northern movement by Forrest.[8]

Authors Pryor and Jordan described the attacks in which Wilson's cavalry "were borne steadily but doggedly rearward, as far as Mount Carmel." Almost all the Confederate cavalry attacked dismounted, although the Confederate cavalry remained mounted in some of the actions. The reason for the dismounted action resulted from the difficulty of the terrain which "rocky and rugged, was thickly clad with cedars" and proved unsuitable for mounted cavalry actions. In addition, Forrest preferred to fight dismounted at this point in the war. Armstrong's brigade and Buford's division carried much of the fighting as the Federal cavalry adopted a "fight-withdraw-fight" system of delaying the Southern advance. As the Union cavalry gained good defensive positions "they were driven only after most obstinate contests up to within five or six miles of Franklin."[9]

At Mount Carmel, the combat resulted in a desperate fight for some of Armstrong's men. In particular, the 28th Mississippi Cavalry found the Federal cavalry arrayed in a long line near the crossroads. Armstrong attacked the Federals' left flank which resulted in a bloody fight that took a severe toll on the color bearers of the 28th Mississippi. The regimental colors were given to the regiment by the ladies of Columbus and had accompanied the regiment throughout 1863 and 1864. At Mount Carmel, the color bearer was shot and as he fell another soldier caught the flag before it hit the ground. This solder was immediately shot and fell, and the flag was grabbed by another soldier. The battle continued with the flag held high through the remainder for the fight.[10]

Datus Coon explained that at two miles north of Mount Carmel: "I ordered the brigade mounted. I then withdrew by brigade in line of regiments, each regiment in line of squadrons in column of fours. The enemy, discovering this formation, charged down the pike, in column of fours, on a small company of the Ninth Illinois Cavalry, which was acting as rear guard. In accordance with previous instructions from me the company did not halt, but continued to fall back, leading the enemy between the flanking columns right and left, who opened upon them a raking fire, throwing them into confusion, and ending the pursuit for the day."[11]

As Wilson's fighting ended, Forrest focused on Spring Hill and the rear of Schofield's infantry. From Mount Carmel, Forrest sent the bulk of his cavalry toward Spring Hill and Ross' brigade trailed Wilson's forces northward. Near the Ridge Meeting House, Forrest sent Ross to Thompson's Station as Wilson paused and then withdrew toward Franklin. Forrest wrote: "After waiting a short time for my troops to close up, I moved rapidly toward Spring Hill with my entire command." As Forrest rode west to Spring Hill, he ran into small groups of Federal infantry and cavalry at 11:00 a.m. Forrest and the small group of Union infantry and cavalry skirmished until about noon as Forrest tried to reach the pike at Spring Hill.[12]

The 12th Tennessee Cavalry (U.S.) Clashes with Buford's Cavalry

When the Southern cavalry stopped battling Wilson, he had a chance to reorganize his cavalry in the field, but after a short time, he ominously heard "heavy artillery firing" from the direction of Spring Hill. Wilson's communications had been cut off from Schofield for much of the day but he expected Schofield to be moving his troops to Franklin, as agreed upon. Instead what he heard was, first the 12th Tennessee Cavalry and hastily assembled small Federal units fighting Forrest's cavalry, and then Stanley's and Wagner's infantry battling Hood's cavalry and infantry throughout the afternoon. Still, it is somewhat remarkable that Wilson could not discover the nature of fighting at Spring Hill. Historian Thomas Robson Hay correctly observed: "He made no attempt to join Schofield nor did Schofield appear to expect him to make any effort to do so, or even communicate with him." Wilson stuck with his plan to impede Forrest or any other force on the Lewisburg Pike while Schofield dealt with the enemy on the Columbia—Franklin Pike. Wilson slowly moved northward until he reached Douglass Church about four miles southeast of Franklin.[13]

Perhaps, the most important cavalry report of the day came from Lieutenant Colonel Charles C. Hoefling, 12th Tennessee Cavalry, from Spring Hill. In a message to Schofield, Hoefling reported the disposition of the 12th Tennessee. "Three companies been left on picket between Huly [Hurts] CrossRoads and Rolough [Rally] Hill; were attacked, and they retreated to this place, reporting Buford's division of cavalry marching on this place to attack the wagon trains between here and Columbia. I [have] only a small force, 200 of regiment; all the rest is on courier-line.... Communication between here and cavalry headquarters is cut off." Fortunately for the Federals, Hoefling was an experienced cavalryman with prior service in the 4th U.S. Cavalry; he hastily gathered troops to resist the advance of the Confederate cavalry.[14]

Sometimes, minutes are important. Hoefling's small contingent of Federal cavalry provided the first line of defense against Forrest's cavalry riding hard for Spring Hill. Hoefling assembled a reasonably good defense with the 12th Tennessee, parts of the 3rd Illinois, three companies of the 11th Tennessee and one company of the 2nd Michigan cavalries. With the main body of Wilson's cavalry moving back along Lewisburg Turnpike, there was little to hold the Confederate cavalry from gaining the important position at Spring Hill, except this small body of Federal cavalry. While Hoefling's force stubbornly tried to hold back the Confederate cavalry, he knew he had to communicate what was happening, which he did by sending riders to hurry Stanley along. Wagner's division was still two and a half miles away from Spring Hill when he was informed at 11:30 a.m. that Forrest's cavalry approached Spring Hill. Soon thereafter, Armstrong's brigade, supported with the 14th Tennessee Cavalry, arrived to join in the fight about two miles east of Spring Hill. Hoefling's defenders held the advancing Confederate cavalry about an hour, slowly being pushed to the outskirts of Spring Hill. Hoefling's defense was no match for the number of Confederate cavalry arriving at Spring Hill, but the Federal cavalry force received some much-needed assistance as four companies of the 73rd Illinois Infantry, which had been on straggler duty, prepared barricades in Spring Hill as the Confederate cavalry emerged on the horizon. Hearing the gunfire off to the east, the small number of Federal infantrymen prepared to fight. Upon the arrival of Chalmers' cavalry, Hoefling's men retreated grudgingly to the town, but fortunately for the Federals, Wagner's infantry came streaming into position. Meanwhile, Stanley had not been slow and he hurried his men to the small village. He arrived at 12:30 p.m. "just in time" to drive the advance elements of Forrest's cavalry back from Spring Hill. This was a dramatic bit of military skill marked by the command ability of Hoefling, resolve by the small number of cavalry and infantry, and the sense of urgency demonstrated by Stanley and Wagner.[15]

Forrest won the day against Wilson's cavalry, but now he faced Wagner's infantry division marching northward. When Forrest arrived at Spring Hill, he positioned his cavalry just east of the town with Armstrong's brigade on the north end of the line, Buford's division in the center and Chalmers' division on the south end of the line facing west. Just as it appeared that Forrest's cavalry would claim the town, Emerson Opdycke's infantry brigade hurriedly trotted through Spring Hill and faced northeast, while Colonel John Q. Lane's brigade followed behind. Lane's men pressed to the east toward the 2nd Mississippi Cavalry which held a position atop a ridge. Pushing the Mississippians from their position, Lane moved back toward the town and fell into line east of the pike. Wagner ordered Luther Bradley's trailing brigade south and east of the town. Now in position, the Southern cavalry and Federal infantry would fight throughout the afternoon.[16]

"They was in there sure enough, wasn't they, Chalmers?"

Wagner's infantry secured the village, but Forrest still focused on the supply train plodding along the pike and, initially, he mistakenly believed that only Union cavalry held the front line. The Confederate cavalry had fallen into a line on the ridge east of Spring Hill and the arriving Federal infantry moved onto a lower ridge closer to town, but much of Luther Bradley's infantry was screened by some woods in front of his position. Accordingly, Forrest ordered Chalmers to charge the defenders in front of him and strike the supply train. Forrest had observed the supply train moving northward toward Spring Hill and he thought he could successfully attack the column just south of the town in the vicinity of a tollgate on Rally Hill Pike. Forrest, being a volatile individual at times, had trained his subordinates to follow orders and Chalmers did just that. This time Forrest was wrong and Bradley's concentrated volleys into Chalmers' men proved the point. James Dinkins of Chalmers' cavalry offered a slightly different twist to the same episode. According to Dinkins, Rucker and Chalmers scouted ahead after driving Hoefling's men into Spring Hill and found that Stanley's infantry had arrived. In the meantime, supported by the infantry, Hoefling's men returned to their position just east of the pike. At this point, Forrest rode up to Chalmers and demanded: "Why don't you drive those fellows off?" Chalmers replied: "Why, there are three divisions of infantry in breast-works behind the cavalry, and, further, my men are out of ammunition and broken down." Forrest disagreed and said, "I think you are mistaken; that is only a small cavalry force. I will lend you Wilson's regiment, which, together with your escort company, will drive them away." Chalmers, who knew better than to argue, merely replied: "All right; let me have Wilson; I will try it." As the Confederate cavalry cleared a grove of trees with Chalmers leading the charge, the entire Union line opened on the attacking line with effect.[17]

Chalmers' force approached the town dismounted. Forrest described: "I ordered my command to push the enemy's right flank with all possible vigor. At the same time I ordered Brigadier-General Buford to send me a regiment mounted. He sent the Twenty-first Tennessee, Colonel [Andrew] Wilson commanding, which I ordered to charge upon the enemy. Colonel Wilson at the head of his splendid regiment made a gallant charge through an open field. He received three wounds, but refused to leave his command." Tyree Bell, the stout, ruddy-faced, 5'10" tall Confederate commander, left the command of his brigade to a subordinate and rode forward to join in the fight with Wilson's regiment. Wilson understood the orders from Forrest to mean that he needed to charge a column of infantry with Bell leading the charge. Before this attack took place, Forrest told Bell he did not mean for Bell to join in such an attack but Bell, his deep blue eyes ablaze, replied that he wanted to lead the attack. Bell's attack sent Stanley's infantry skirmishers scattering back to the main infantry line and Bell recalled that the attack was made under some of the heaviest gunfire of the war. Chalmers had no choice but to call off the attack and he returned to Forrest who had observed the fight. Realizing his mistake, Forrest looked at Chalmers and said, "They was in there sure enough, wasn't they, Chalmers?" Chalmers replied: "Yes ... that is the second time I found them there."[18]

After the repulse, Buford's division charged the Union position and had a similar experience. Buford first encountered the pickets of the small contingent of Federal cavalry about two miles from Spring Hill. This force which stalled the arrival of the Confederate cavalry was driven back to the town and then, Colonel William Faulkner's Kentucky brigade unexpectedly ran into Wagner's infantry in line along a crest of a hill. In the afternoon, Buford reorganized his division and again tried to push ahead only to be repulsed as his men used their last ammunition. John Johnston of Rucker's brigade (14th Tennessee Cavalry) watched Buford's attacks. During one of the attacks, Johnston

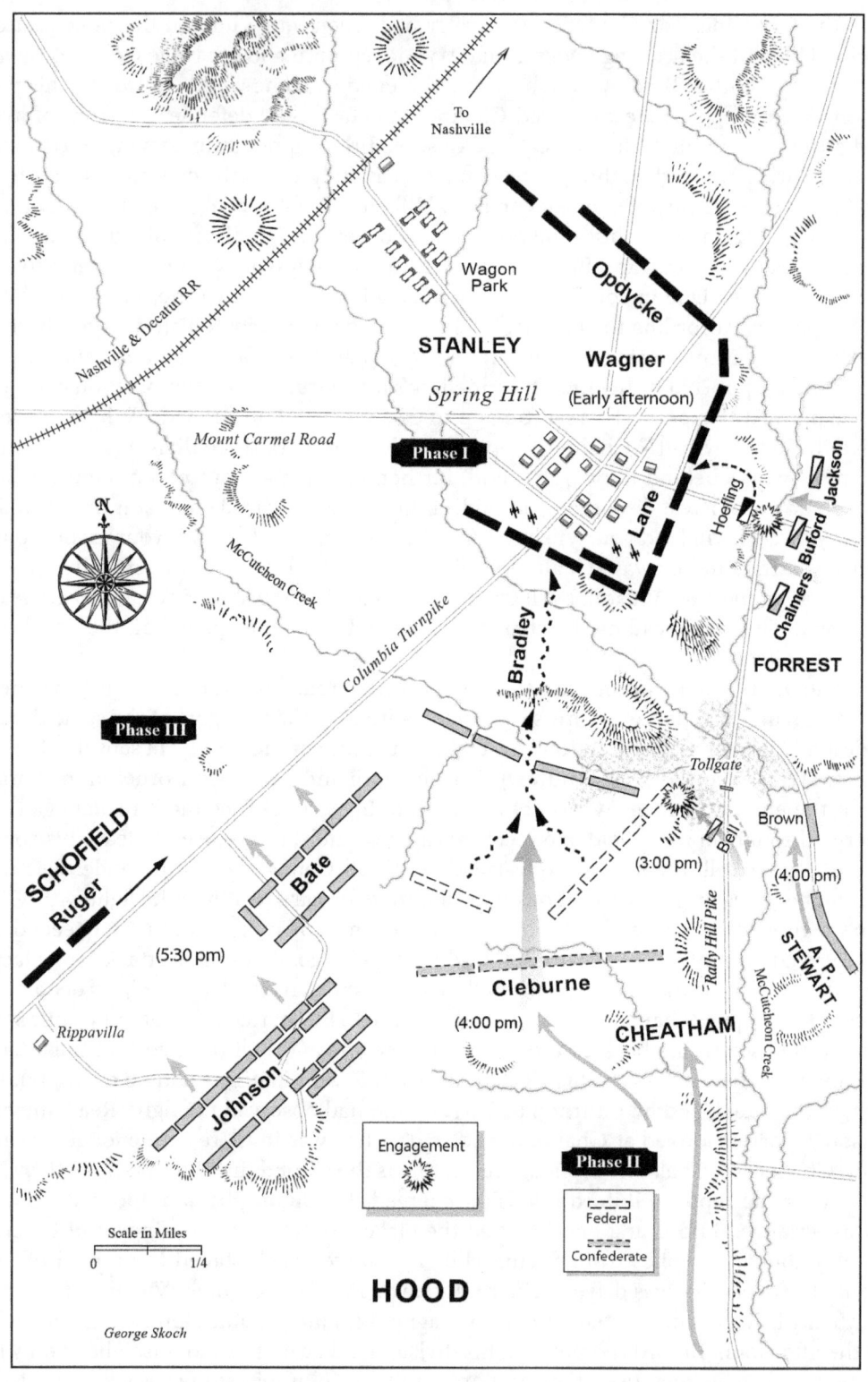

Cavalry actions at Spring Hill, November 29, 1864.

saw Buford's cavalry thunder down the Union line in a mounted attack in which the "old general himself galloped at the head of his men." When Buford moved to the right of Chalmers' division, he came under a terrific fire of the Union artillery and this put an end to the mounted charge. H.A. Tyler, Buford's inspector general, explained that the addition of the Federal infantry to the picture compelled Forrest to fall back about 400 yards east of the pike. Forrest's cavalry battled for several hours before Patrick Cleburne moved into position to make an infantry attack on Wagner's division.[19]

Battle of Spring Hill and Union Movement to Franklin

As with many battles in the Civil War, the unplanned convergence of troops on a particular location resulted in some of the most important battles. The events around Spring Hill remain some of the most argued and controversial of the war. In hindsight, it appeared that Hood intentionally planned to cut Schofield off at Spring Hill in a rapid march around his flank, but this may not have been his plan for the day. Historian Thomas Connelly argued that Hood planned to gain the Franklin Pike at Spring Hill and then outmarch Schofield to Nashville rather than battling the Union forces at the small village. This encounter at Spring Hill and Hood's focus on Nashville might be one reason why Hood seemed so unprepared for the action which unfolded on November 29.[20]

Forrest explained, "About this time I received orders from General Hood to hold my position at all hazards, as the advance of his infantry column was only two miles distant and rapidly advancing. I ordered up my command, already dismounted. Colonel Bell's brigade was the first to reach me, when I immediately ordered it to the attack." Bell reached his brigade from his prior duty and prepared them to attack and at that moment the long lines of gray-clad infantry could be seen in the distance. Patrick Cleburne's division had just arrived. Bell shifted his men to the flank of the Confederate infantry, hastily falling into line. Bell assessed the situation of his brigade and found his troopers had about four rounds per man. Then at 3:00 p.m., Forrest ordered his line to attack. Short on ammunition, but long on the "Rebel Yell," Bell's men raced toward the Union line. Bell's men ran across an open field while the line of blue clad soldiers remained behind a barricade of rails. Seeing that the charge would not be successful, Bell halted his men in a clump of trees. He looked around for help and sent to the rear for reinforcements. Nixon's 22nd/20th Tennessee hurried to the front to join Bell. Bell proudly claimed his success in pushing a group of Luther Bradley's Union soldiers rearward. Lieutenant Colonel Robert C. Brown, 64th Ohio Infantry, had moved his infantry as far east as the Peters house when he found Confederate cavalry moving around both of his flanks. Having moved too far east, Brown's regiment was nearly surrounded by the enemy cavalry before it rejoined the main Union line. In the meantime, Major General John Brown's Confederate infantry arrived and fell into line just to the rear of Bell's cavalry.[21]

Ross' Brigade at Thompson's Station

While Hoefling, wounded during the fighting, was initially holding Buford's cavalry back at Spring Hill, Ross' brigade had moved by a more northern route and struck the Union forces a few miles north at Thompson's Station. Ross drove off the small number of Union cavalry guarding some supply wagons on Franklin Pike and 9th Texas and the Texas Legion scooped up some prisoners. Meanwhile, the 6th Texas and 3rd Texas, on their way to burn the depot at Thompson's Station, captured a single supply wagon. In addition, these two regiments came upon a train and attacked. The engineer unhitched the locomotive from the cars and the cars rolled down an incline until they came under the protection of a Union blockhouse and despite the efforts of the Texans, they could not stop the cars or overcome the defenses of the blockhouse. The cars found temporary safety at Thompson's Station by rolling northward and the locomotive made its escape heading south. However, the Confederate advance would result in all the rail equipment being destroyed or captured the next day.[22]

F.M. Postgate, 175th Ohio, was part of a wagon train during Ross' actions near Thompson's Station. Despite being warned to move either to Spring Hill or Franklin the day before, the Ohioans guarding the wagon train found themselves threatened by Ross' brigade. The commander of the wagon train placed the train unseen behind a hill and worked in conjunction with the railroad engineer. The locomotive drove directly through part of Ross' cavalry which were "utterly dumbfounded" by the maneuver and at the same time, the teamsters whipped their teams emerging "from behind the hill as though shot from the muzzle of a cannon," making their escape.[23]

Cleburne Attacks Wagner

Meanwhile, Wagner's division was battling the Confederates for possession of Spring Hill when Stanley received the message from Schofield telling him to keep the pike open. He realized he had a long afternoon ahead if he was to prevent the approaching Confederates from gaining the Union rear, with only a single division. At Columbia, Schofield turned his remaining infantry to face Hood's infantry to the east. Schofield seemed to think that Hood would attack his infantry remaining there. The bulk of Schofield's troops re-positioned near Columbia until about 3:00 p.m. when Schofield issued orders to withdraw to Franklin at 5:00 p.m. Except for an incredible stroke of good fortune, Schofield had waited too long. Hood did not plan to attack at Columbia. Instead, he had marched the bulk of his infantry northward and now had the opportunity to cut Schofield off at Spring Hill.[24]

The stakes could not have been higher for IV Corps and XXIII Corps on November 29. Stanley wrote later in life that November 29 "was the biggest day's work I ever accomplished for the United States." What occurred on November 29 directly impacted how the battles would play out the next day and subsequently, the Battle of Nashville in mid–December. Hood had declared that he wanted to face smaller parts of the Union army and defeat them in detail. He could now do just that if he could block Schofield's retreat from Columbia. He had that chance as the Confederate cavalry and infantry hurried to Spring Hill while Schofield remained at Columbia trying to determine his next movement. Opdycke's and Lane's brigades protected as much space about the village which served as a park for the supply trains and artillery. Bradley's brigade was positioned on a wooded knoll about three-quarters of a mile southeast of the village. Stanley needed to hold the road open for the rest of Schofield's infantry while protecting an 800-wagon supply train and 50 artillery pieces.[25]

Stanley who initially thought his Second Division was just facing Forrest's cavalry soon found he faced the recently arriving Confederate infantry. At 4:00 p.m., Cleburne's Confederate infantry attacked Bradley's brigade. Stanley dared not move more troops to fight the enemy due to the risk of losing the supply train to the enemy cavalry. He noted, "Thus we were threatened and attacked from every direction, and it was impossible to send any re-enforcements to Bradley's brigade, which had become quite severely engaged, lest in so doing we should expose the train and artillery park to destruction." But Stanley was a veteran campaigner, and more importantly, he was lucky on the battlefield. Cleburne's infantry initially had good success with Bradley's brigade, and it appeared that all would lost for the Federals—Schofield's path of retreat, the supply train and Wagner's division. As Bradley's lines crumbled, Stanley ordered his artillery to open fire on the advancing Confederate lines. Stanley had been hard pressed, at least twice in the war, at Corinth in May 1862 and again at Resaca in 1864. Both times, it appeared Stanley's command would be devastated. Then just as now, he relied on his artillery to save the day. As the Confederate infantry pursued Bradley's crumbling lines, Stanley ordered the artillery to open fire. "[T]he fire of six batteries appalled them. The ground was planted in corn and was very muddy, and if the Johnnies in gray were not hit with artillery missiles, they were covered with mud ... our cannonade was simply magnificent." As the cannons fired, Stanley repositioned Lane's brigade to support the infantry receiving the attack. Then, the attack was over. Facing 50 pieces of artillery with fresh Union infantry re-positioning, the Confederate attack ceased.[26]

While the fight at Spring Hill was a remarkable victory for the Union army, the miracle was yet to come. At the sun went down, Stanley stoutly defended the Franklin–Columbia Turnpike, but the full might of Hood's army extended in his front two and half miles long. The controversy of what occurred next at Spring Hill still rages today. Why did the Confederate army which had outmarched Schofield not continue the attack on Stanley and Wagner? Historian J.P. Young, 7th Tennessee Cavalry, offered the comments of James Chalmers in a personal communication after the war. General John Brown, whose division first reached the flank of Bell's cavalry brigade, explained that he could not advance on Wagner's division because, just as he prepared to advance, the cavalry had been withdrawn from his flank without any communication to him. He found he had no cavalry or artillery support, and more importantly, he had a fully uncovered right flank. Brown found he "was left in a position where I must meet with inevitable disaster if I advanced on Spring Hill." He chose to pause and get clarification from his commanders before advancing further. In this affair, there would be opinions about various orders given and received by several commanders, not just Brown.[27]

Chalmers rode to Brown's headquarters and asked him why he was not advancing, but Brown replied, "I have no orders." Chalmers, who was on excellent terms with Brown, realized the pressure Brown felt about his situation because Brown had replied "very curtly." Chalmers, taken aback by the response, replied in the same manner, "General, when I was circumstanced as you are at Shiloh, I attacked without orders." Brown merely said, "I would prefer to wait for orders." Then, Chalmers spurred his horse and rode away. Brown was but one of several commanders who would be questioned about their actions in this affair.[28]

The Federal Night Actions

The next important task for the Federal commanders required moving the rest of Schofield's infantry, which arrived from Columbia, past Hood's army. Stanley reported, "General Schofield arrived from Columbia at 7 o'clock in the evening with Ruger's division. He found the enemy on the pike, and had quite a skirmish in driving them off. My pickets had reported seeing rebel columns passing east of our position as if to get possession of the hills at Thompson's Station, and the anxious question arose whether we could force our way through to Franklin."[29]

The battle during the afternoon in which Stanley had stopped the Confederate attack and actions in the evening would be among the most remarkable events in this campaign. In an unlikely decision, Schofield, with Stanley firmly in place, decided to try to march the Union forces past Hood's army, that stretched to the east of Spring Hill, in full view of the enemy campfires. This was accomplished with scarcely a hitch as the Union divisions began marching northward to Franklin. Jacob Cox's division marched out of Spring Hill by 1:00 a.m., and then came the slow exit of the supply train, 800 wagons long. The supply train included not only ammunition and other supplies but ambulances and the ever so important artillery. Stanley knew only a miracle would save the train. The movement began with each wagon passing single file over a small bridge, and all 800 wagons had to be out of Spring Hill by daylight. Stanley recorded: "So close were the enemy on our flank that, when a column was not passing, it was difficult for a staff officer or an orderly to get through on the road.... Unless this could be done, and the corps put in motion, we were sure of being attacked at daylight and of being compelled to fight under every disadvantage. I was strongly advised to burn the train, and move on with the troops and such wagons as could be saved, but I determined to make an effort to save the train." Stanley put his staff officers to work hurrying the wagons northward and just when things appeared to being going well, a messenger arrived and told Stanley that the column had been attacked north of Thompson's Station. The disaster Stanley had feared occurred when Jackson's Confederate cavalry attacked the Union column north of Spring Hill. Stanley feared the entire Union train would be lost.[30]

The attack on the Union wagon train by Jackson's cavalry division was noted in Union reports stating that several wagons were burned. Schofield placed Ruger's division with the task of removing the cavalry resistance on the way to Thompson's Station. Stanley's headquarters escort also played an important part in repulsing the night attack. Stanley's escort came riding from the dark, and the Confederate cavalry withdrew unable to determine the number of men who were attacking. Afterwards, Jackson's division remained some distance from the train and "Stanley had wisely ordered two infantry divisions, Kimball's and Wood's, to escort the main segments of the wagon train, and they were soon observed marching protectively alongside the slow-moving wagons," explained historian Wiley Sword. From 1 a.m. until daybreak, the Union artillery and wagon train quietly moved out of Spring Hill and along the Franklin Turnpike toward Franklin. Stanley noted it was a starlit night as the wagon train inched toward Franklin. Miraculously, Schofield and Stanley extracted all the infantry, an 800-wagon supply train, and artillery batteries with only a few wagons being lost.[31]

The Confederate Cavalry's Role in Schofield's Evacuation

Earlier that evening A.P. Stewart and Forrest went to Hood's headquarters to discuss their orders. During this meeting Hood turned to Forrest and asked: "[I]f he could not throw his cavalry upon the turnpike in time to check the Federal retreat?" Forrest replied that two of his divisions were without ammunition and only Jackson's division had enough ammunition to conduct an attack. Hood told Forrest that he would supply ammunition from the infantry stores, because the cavalry wagons had not yet reached the main column. Forrest promised Hood that he would do his best about carrying out this request. Then, he ordered Jackson's division to Thompson's Station to secure the pike leading to Franklin.[32]

General William Bate met with Hood between 10 o'clock and midnight and told him about an earlier brush with Schofield's column. According to Bate, Hood replied, "'It makes no difference now,' or 'It is all right anyhow, for General Forrest as you see had just left and informed me that he holds the turnpike with a portion of his force at Spring Hill and will stop the enemy if he tries to pass.'" This was quite a different version of the account that Forrest only had one division with adequate ammunition and that he would attempt to hold the pike with the force on hand.[33]

Chalmers' and Buford's divisions were not supplied with ammunition that evening as Hood had promised and historians Pryor and Jordan stated that Forrest sent a message to Hood reporting this along with the details of placing only Jackson's cavalry north of the town. As a result, Jackson's division moved north of Spring Hill to stop any movements to or from Franklin. Ross moved his brigade under the direction of one of Forrest's staff officers who was familiar with the area. Along Franklin Pike, Ross dismounted three of his regiments (leaving the 9th Texas in the saddle) in preparation of attacking the supply train. Ross drew his men to within 100 yards of the Pike and at 2:00 a.m., the Texas Legion opened the fight by firing a volley into the train. Ross noted the carbine fire resulted in "killing several Yankees and mules, and rushed forward with a yell, producing among the teamsters and wagon guards a perfect stampede. The Yankees lost thirty-nine wagons, some of which were destroyed and others abandoned for the want of the teams, which we brought off. We captured also several prisoners." Ross held the pike for about a half an hour before the Federal infantry arrived and drove the Texans away. P.B. Simmons, 6th Texas Cavalry, recalled that couriers were sent to hurry the Texas Legion and the 9th Texas to assist in attack on the train, but the "Yanks made it too hot for us." With the train now protected by infantry, Ross had no choice but to watch the slow movement north of entire train. Private Benjamin Smith, 72nd Illinois Infantry, wrote in his journal that he knew the Confederate cavalry "were on our flanks all night long, but did no serious damage, to our wagon trains; we kept a good force of infantry with them." As a result, Buford and Chalmers, still without ammunition, offered little support to the efforts of Jackson to hold the pike north of Spring Hill.[34]

Corporal J.A. Bigger, 2nd Mississippi Cavalry, recorded in his diary that Armstrong also formed his brigade across the Columbia Pike north of Spring Hill and marched southward toward Spring Hill until they ran into lines of infantry. "We got in front of the whole federal army," wrote Bigger. Then, the brigade moved a mile away from the pike and settled in for the night. At 10:00 p.m., Armstrong ordered his brigade to quietly move forward until they found the Union army marching steadily northward. Bigger wrote: "Our whole Division of Cavalry lined up and down the Pike, counted off and every 3rd man was ordered to the front a few paces and deployed five paces apart and ordered to go towards the Pike until we were fired on." The Southern cavalry reached about 100 yards from the pike when the Union soldiers opened fire. Armstrong's men found cover and returned fire. It was too dark to see their targets and Bigger explained that he could only fire at sounds. Armstrong remained in place until the next morning when the last wagons moved out of sight.[35]

From a cavalry perspective, there remains the question of how the entire Union force could have marched past Hood's army and, at least, Jackson's division, without a general alarm being sounded. Confederate general Samuel French wrote in his autobiography, "Occasionally we heard some picket firing toward the north. It was Gen. Ross's men on the road to Franklin.... Ye gods! will no geese give them warning as they did in ancient Rome?" Thomas John Brown rhetorically asked the question in his graduate research into the command abilities of Hood, why the Confederate cavalry did not properly notify army headquarters of the withdrawal of Schofield's troops. Perhaps, more importantly, Brown asked why Forrest was not criticized after the war for this lapse. He wrote: "The mystery is why Forrest failed to send word to the commanding general. Taken at face value, this represents a terrible and irresponsible blunder, but perhaps no one bothered to inform Forrest, and he assumed that things had been taken care of. Here again, fatigue may have played a role. Hood, Forrest, Cheatham, and the mass of private soldiers experienced the numbing effects of exhaustion. Whatever the reason, and no definitive evidence has yet emerged to reveal what it was, Bedford Forrest has never been significantly criticized for his failure to close the pike and for not reporting it to Hood. Why? Perhaps, because in the post-war years dominated by the Lost Cause mythologists, Forrest joined Robert E. Lee as an unassailable Confederate icon." Indeed, Forrest's actions have received little scrutiny over the years. A member of Chalmers' cavalry division, Captain W.O. Dodd, would write after the war: "Who was to blame for the blunder? No one accuses either General Stewart or Forrest of being in any way responsible." William Bate related the conversation with Hood between 10:00 p.m. and midnight. Hood told Bate that Forrest had just left and had control of the pike. Hood concluded: "We can sleep quietly tonight." In other accounts, Forrest told Hood he would do his best. Brown's question was echoed in historian David Rey Moody's doctoral research in 1993. G. Campbell Brown, a staff officer in Ewell's Corps, recorded a conversation he had with Governor Isham Harris in 1868 and simply drew the conclusion that Forrest had let the Federal infantry march northward because they were too strong for Ross. Historian Stanley Horn also described the Confederate explanation of events as merely a situation where Jackson's division was not strong enough to stop the entire Federal column. Neither account addressed the importance of sounding an alarm at army headquarters. In contrast, Brown summarized that Forrest's action was "an inexplicable movement in light of his previous career."[36]

Forrest and Jackson were not alone in observing the Federal army march into the night. States Rights Gist and Otho Strahl, Confederate brigade commanders, and Colonel Ellison Capers, 24th South Carolina Infantry, observed the Federals moving north. Capers wrote: "Later on in the night we could hear the rolling of wheels over the pike, as the enemy's artillery and wagons moved on to Franklin." In a unique but confusing account, Tyree Bell recalled that the developing situation north of Spring Hill was formally reported to the cavalry headquarters and the situation was next reported to army headquarters, albeit in the wee hours of the morning. An officer on Bell's staff had been directed by Forrest to take a message to William H. Jackson sending his cavalry to Carter's Creek Pike but the retreating lines of Union infantry precluded this. At 3:00 a.m., the staff officer returned to Forrest's headquarters and Forrest got out of bed and went to Hood's headquarters to report the situation. Bell did not go to Hood's tent and could offer no further details.[37]

By the next morning, Hood awoke to find that Ruger's, Cox's, Wood's, Kimball's and Wagner's divisions had simply and quietly walked past the sleeping soldiers of his army and even more unbelievable, the entire 800 wagons and artillery were gone. The opportunity to isolate the Union forces and destroy them in turn was lost; now IV Corps and XXIII Corps were united and marching toward Franklin. When Hood became aware of what had happened he unleashed his anger, and much of it fell on Pat Cleburne and Benjamin Cheatham. Historians, still today, argue the fault of the affair at Spring Hill, and importantly, historians still argue whether Hood's anger at the outcome at Spring Hill set the table for the Battle of Franklin which occurred on November 30. There is little doubt that the inability of Hood to move his various forces into position while capitalizing on a successful march, in conjunction with a series of incomplete and confusing orders, prevented an opportunity to inflict severe damage on Schofield's infantry. Schofield, who had made a critical error of his own by delaying so long at Colum-

A supply train, 800 wagons long, creeped northward overnight away from Spring Hill. It would have resembled this supply train photographed in Virginia (Library of Congress).

bia, had just received a reprieve. Following the decision to delay three weeks at Florence, this action marked Hood's second critical error in the campaign.[38]

One final item that is often included in the story of the affair at Spring Hill was Forrest's visit to Mrs. Jessie Peters for a short conversation. Mrs. Peters allegedly had a strong attraction to General Earl Van Dorn, Forrest's commanding officer in 1863, to such an extent that Mrs. Peters' husband shot and killed Van Dorn. The particulars of the encounter in November 1864 were not recorded, only that Forrest paid his respects. Earlier in the day, Abraham Buford promptly drove some of his subordinates away from the Peters house. Some of the men stopped to speak to Mrs. Peters and Buford rapidly sent them on their way "cursing us and abusing us in his peculiar style," wrote Confederate cavalryman John Johnston.[39]

Wilson Assembles His Cavalry Near the Harpeth River

Wilson had been cut off from Spring Hill from about 10 o'clock, but he had open lines of communications to Nashville. Despite the communication issues, Wilson sent messages at regular intervals throughout the day about the situation with his cavalry. At 2:00 p.m., Wilson wrote to Thomas that the enemy "pressed the rear of my column" until he reached the Ridge Meeting House, east of Thompson's Station on Lewisburg Pike. Forrest's greatest pressure came on Wilson's left flank (east) and based on this, Wilson believed that Forrest intended to turn that flank in his movement towards Nashville. However, Wilson observed some of Forrest's cavalry turning toward Spring Hill but Wilson missed this major movement by the enemy as most of the enemy cavalry moved in that direction. So sure was Wilson that Forrest was moving around the eastern flank, he wrote to George Thomas: "You had better look out for Forrest at Nashville tomorrow noon; I'll be there before or very soon after he makes his appearance."[40]

On the other hand, Wilson's efforts to gather to new troops were paying off. Hammond's small brigade reached Franklin after opening communications with Schofield and Wilson. Schofield had initially ordered Hammond to Spring Hill if he could not find Wilson, but Hammond received updated orders directing his command to Lewisburg Pike to Wilson's headquarters. This was an unfortunate turn of events, because Hammond could have provided important duty had he remained at Spring Hill; however, Hammond had problems. He had 1,000 cavalry troops which he described as "Men very green, but in good heart," but he couldn't fully arm his men. He had only 600 carbines, 300 pistols and 300 sabers for all 1,000 men, and to make matters worse, he had no percussion caps for the ammunition he did have. He had his men stripping infantry musket ammunition for use in the cavalry carbines, before he could join Wilson. He eventually gained enough caps for 45 rounds for each carbine. He also had some Maynard carbines which had no ammunition. Undaunted, he pledged to join Wilson near Mount Carmel.[41]

Fortunately for Wilson, he had finally gotten all of his brigades together. Stewart's brigade also hustled forward to reach Wilson's main concentration of cavalry. At 4:30 p.m., Wilson ordered Stewart's cavalry, which had just arrived, to continue across the Harpeth River at Franklin and to ride to the Triune–Nolensville Road to serve as a blocking force for the enemy cavalry believed heading toward Nashville. Part of Stewart's cavalry, 10th Tennessee Cavalry, had been escorting a provision train, but with the advance of the Confederates, the train was halted and returned to Nashville. After leaving escort duty, the 10th Tennessee was also dispatched to Nolensville to watch for enemy movements at that location.[42]

At 10:00 p.m., Wilson again reported to Schofield, this time from Matthews' House, two and half miles east of Franklin. Wilson had just arrived at this new headquarters with Hammond's brigade and Hatch's division after guarding the Franklin–Lewisburg Pike. Wilson kept the pike posted but decided to move his cavalry into camp just north of the Harpeth River. Hatch's scouts ranged far to the west and discovered Jackson's cavalry near Thompson's Station. Wilson had the Harpeth River picketed for miles to the east. He also wanted to know what Schofield planned for the next day and wrote to him: "I am very anxious to know your position and the result of the day's operations. I think it probable that a part of the enemy's cavalry this afternoon aimed to strike your rear or flank at Thompson's Station."[43]

Importantly for Wilson, he had just assembled enough cavalry to face Forrest on more favorable terms. Hammond's brigade reached Wilson's main body and had duty overnight guarding the line on the Harpeth River back to Franklin and as far east as Triune. Early on November 30, Wilson sent Hammond's brigade to Triune, Hatch remained at Matthews' House, Croxton's brigade held the Lewisburg Pike at Douglass Church (about a mile and a half south of the river), and finally, Harrison's brigade was held in reserve near Matthews' house.[44]

Summary of the Cavalry Actions During the Spring Hill Affair

The fighting at Spring Hill was minor in terms of the Civil War, but the affair at Spring Hill held momentous implications for the entire Nashville Campaign.

At the close of the day, Forrest achieved his objective of maneuvering Wilson away from Schofield's vulnerable flank. Once Forrest moved Wilson far enough away from the Union infantry, he turned to his real objective—cutting the line of retreat of the Federal infantry column. While being cut off from Schofield, Wilson believed he had accomplished what he had intended, withdrawing along Lewisburg Pike while keeping Forrest away from the rear. Others would agree with Wilson's decision—historian Thomas Van Horne would summarize that Schofield had received orders from George Thomas to withdraw from Columbia 15 hours before he did so. He wrote: "[E]ven without these orders Schofield had ample information and advice from Wilson to justify the movement at early dawn."[45]

In a critical assessment, Wilson's modern-day biographer, Edward Longacre, called the decisions made by Wilson to be "the most serious tactical error of his military career." Forrest moved his cavalry across the Duck River with relative ease and then pursued the Union cavalry north on Lewisburg Pike. In addition, he successfully confused Wilson as to his true intent. In the process, Forrest successfully opened Schofield to a vulnerable flank attack, possibly even cutting off the line of retreat of the Union forces to Franklin. Forrest, a veteran with his established command, accomplished his duties and worked well overall with Hood. In regard to the actions of the Confederate cavalry, the major concern related to the evacuation of the Union forces to the north of Spring Hill. That evening, Jackson's division had been ordered to Fitzgerald's and Thompson's Station and had, in fact, attacked the column; however, it remains remarkable that the passage of the entire Union force did not result in the alarms bells sounding and a greater response of some sort from the Confederate cavalry, if only in waking up those at army headquarters. Most historians focus their attention on the complex question of Hood's infantry action during this affair but the response by the Confederate cavalry generally receives little scrutiny. Brigadier General Daniel Harris Reynolds wrote in his diary: "We should have by all means thrown some of our forces across the Pike early in the night—then the only escape of the enemy would have been by the Carter's Creek Pike."[46]

The Federal cavalry is a more complex discussion. Did Wilson really make a major tactical error during this part of the campaign? The Federal cavalry had a relatively new commander who was desperately pulling as many cavalry regiments as could be mounted into the fight. Coon's, Capron's/Harrison's, and Croxton's brigades were really the only available forces ready to fight. Richard Johnson, an experienced and veteran campaigner, was also assembling regiments as quickly as possible, and Capron's brigade perhaps provided the greatest contribution by holding Buford's command in place along the Duck River. Overall, the outcome of the actions on November 28–29 was not surprising.

Perhaps a greater issue, the thing not working well, was the cooperation between Schofield and Wilson. The problem centered on communications and perhaps ego. Schofield nearly lost his two corps in this part of the Nashville Campaign due to his lethargy in ordering the retreat from Columbia. Wilson told him that he needed to withdraw but Schofield chose not to do that. During the actions on November 29, Wilson's command became separated from Schofield's main force, and he had been unable to keep communications open to army headquarters. Wilson could have remained in communication most of the day assuming Schofield had followed "his" direction by retreating to Franklin, and Schofield should have. Wilson, with three brigades, certainly had his hands full with Forrest on the morning of November 29, but he needed to know, not assume, what Schofield was doing. With Wilson withdrawing throughout the day, Schofield directed him to communicate through Spring Hill. If Wilson had been able to stay on the flank of Schofield that morning, then Schofield would have known definitively about Hood's march toward Spring Hill. Finally, Wilson misread Forrest's intent. He expected Forrest to be moving toward Nashville, by a more eastern route, and Wilson gave Forrest the opportunity to clear Schofield's left flank, opening it to an attack by Hood's rapidly marching infantry. Forrest's biographer, John Allan Wyeth, described Wilson's dilemma when he wrote that Wilson was fully occupied keeping Forrest south of the Harpeth River and away from Franklin while the Confederate forces, cavalry and infantry, descended on Spring Hill. Despite these issues, Wilson doggedly followed the agreed upon plan with Schofield that he would slowly withdraw to the Harpeth River throughout the day. There was no expectation, on either Schofield's or Wilson's part, that the cavalry would protect Schofield's flank during the day. In examining the communications between these two generals, it is difficult to place blame on Wilson for his actions.[47]

With the advantage of hindsight, this would be the last day in this campaign that the Confederate cavalry would have the advantage. So far, Forrest had operated well with a force of cavalry intended for the entire campaign, while Wilson had one division and two brigades in place during this phase of the campaign. However, the numerous resources by Union forces provided more and fresh cavalry regiments, in particular the arrival of J.H. Hammond's brigade, 7th Ohio, and the 5th Iowa, which gave Wilson a numerical advantage for the first time in the campaign, as Schofield's infantry moved closer to infantry reinforcements at Nashville. As the days passed, more and more Union cavalry regiments appeared, and these were ill omens for Forrest and the Confederate cavalry.

November 30—Battle of Franklin

Schofield's weary troops reached Franklin on the morning of November 30 and he quickly distributed his men with orders to begin improving the defenses around the town should Hood continue his pursuit. The trailing IV Corps reached Franklin about noon and, soon, Hood's army followed in the trail of the Union infantry. Schofield faced a serious situation after he arrived at Franklin. He found the swollen Harpeth River, which ran through Franklin, but he had no expedient way of moving his troops and wagons across the river. The river had some fords which still allowed troops to cross, but the pontoon bridges which he had requested from Thomas the previous day had not arrived and the bridge across the river had been destroyed. If Schofield wanted to save his supply train, he needed hold Hood away from the town until a wagon bridge could be constructed. In the meantime, he positioned his troops to meet an attack and ordered Wood's division to the north side of the river for security. The wagon bridge was finished by noon, but the slow process of getting 800 wagons across the bridge meant it would be nightfall before Schofield could again proceed northward.[48]

Thomas still desired to hold Hood away from Nashville if this was practical, but he didn't want Schofield to engage in any major battles. Thomas wired Schofield that if he could hold Hood at Franklin, then Smith's XVI Corps could probably reach him within three days. Schofield replied, "I do not believe I can. I can doubtless hold him one day, but will hazard something in doing that. He now has a large force, probably two corps, in my front, and seems prepared to cross the river above and below. I think he can effect a crossing tomorrow, in spite of all my efforts, and probably tonight, if he attempts it. A worse position than this for an inferior force could hardly be found." Hood had just demonstrated his ability to move around Schofield's positions at Columbia and Schofield faced a similar situation at Franklin.[49]

As the Union position at Franklin was being sorted, confidence increased within the Union ranks. Schofield and Stanley consulted in the afternoon at Schofield's headquarters on the north side of the Harpeth River. The two generals worked through the final details of the defense and planned their steady retreat over the last 20 miles to Nashville. While the two commanding generals were meeting, Jacob Cox had command of the rest of infantry at the defenses in Franklin. As the Union defenses were being prepared, George Wagner's division which fought so stoutly the day before was ordered to defend Winstead Hill, about two miles south of Franklin, until dark, as a rear guard.[50]

Wagner noticed lines of Confederate infantry marching toward his position and being so exposed, he ordered his division to march toward Franklin. Due to a confused series of orders and chain of command, Wagner marched and countermarched until he finally tried to resist a superior enemy force. Past Wagner's men, the Confederates faced three lines of defenses; despite the formidable defenses at Franklin, Hood remained determined to the attack the Union line. On the Union side of the line, and despite the warning given by Wagner, the Union officers were surprised when the mass of gray clad soldiers appeared outside Franklin. Stanley asked the controversial question of many Union and Confederate officers and historians for years afterward, "Why try this desperate assault?"[51]

Lane and Conrad, brigade commanders, appealed to Wagner to retire to the Union defenses, but Wagner refused, sending messages to both commanders to "fight like hell." It was impossible for Lane and Conrad to withstand the Confederate attack and the brigades inevitably ran for the defenses at Franklin with the Confederates on their heels. In some cases, the Confederates were intermixed with the running Union soldiers and entered the Union works together, confusing the defenders at the main Union line. All along the remaining Union line, it was a different story. The Union infantry looking across the fields and firmly behind excellent defenses released a terrible volley into the approaching Confederate lines. It was the Union center, encumbered by Wagner's routed brigades that threatened the collapse of the Union line.[52]

As Wagner's troops ran to the Union lines, their disorganization unnerved the Union soldiers manning the defenses and some of these soldiers turned and joined the rout. The Confederate attack began in earnest at 4 p.m. and when the attack began, the Confederate army flung itself at the Union line. Hood's infantry paid a terrible price in the frontal assault at Franklin, but it appeared it would break the Union center. Union reinforcements made a determined counterattack and stopped the Southern momentum. David Stanley, who left Schofield to reach the battle, was the only Union general to be wounded during the battle. He was shot in the neck while rallying the Federal troops during the counterattack. The Union counterattack included several regiments, but Emerson Opdycke's brigade made a notable effort in stopping Hood's breakthrough on the Union center. Afterward, several additional attempts were made to penetrate the Union line, but without success. At sundown, the Confederates held some of the outer defenses. The last Confederate attack took place at 9:00 p.m., but again the attack failed. Schofield decided to continue northward to unite his forces with Thomas but he had to extricate the troops and march 20 miles to Nashville. He still feared another flanking movement by Hood, so at midnight the Union troops began their march to Nashville with the Union flanks withdrawing first, followed by the pickets which retreated after the army was across the Harpeth River.[53]

The next morning Schofield's infantry and cavalry had withdrawn and marched for Nashville. As it turned out, the Battle of Franklin was a decisive Union victory, but the battle was saved by quick thinking by key Union officers. For Hood, the Battle of Franklin was a bloody affair with an estimated 2,300 Union casualties compared to more than 6,000 casualties for the Confederate army. In addition to the massive losses of Hood's army at Franklin were the great command losses which included, 14 Confederate generals (six killed or mortally wounded, seven wounded, and one captured) and 53 regimental commanders. The loss of these officers, particularly Major General Patrick Cleburne, was incalculable. The losses had been so severe, "In Cleburne's division the highest ranking officer left in Granbury's brigade was a captain...."[54]

Cavalry Actions

The Battle of Franklin was principally an infantry battle, but the cavalry forces on both sides were active throughout the day. At 5:30 a.m. on November 30, the threat of

Forrest's cavalry remained a major concern for Schofield after what he perceived to be Wilson's inability to deal with Forrest the prior day. Schofield wrote to Thomas: "I shall try and get Wilson on my flank this morning. Forrest was all around us yesterday, but we brushed him away during the evening, and came through. Hood attacked in front and flank, but did not hurt us." Schofield's description of Wilson's efforts on November 29 was unfair and suggested that Schofield intended Wilson to be closely posted on his flanks. Wilson, while missing some of Forrest's intended actions the previous day, remained just where he told Schofield he would be. It was Schofield's lethargic movement from Columbia, and underestimation of his opponent which had nearly doomed his command, not the cavalry. Never had such a set of events worked in the favor of the Union forces as had unfolded at Spring Hill and Schofield safely marched toward Franklin through luck more than skill. On November 30, Schofield faced the same situation as he had two days before when Forrest crossed the river and pushed his cavalry to the rear. By 10:00 a.m., the conditions regarding the cavalry situation had not improved in Schofield's mind. The large supply train inched closer to Franklin and about half of the infantry arrived. Schofield reported: "Wilson is here, and has his cavalry on my flank. I do not know where Forrest is; he may have gone east, but, no doubt, will strike our flank and rear again soon. Wilson is entirely unable to cope with him. Of course I cannot prevent Hood from crossing the Harpeth whenever he may attempt it." By 11:00 a.m., the remaining infantry and trains arrived at Franklin and the Confederate infantry continued its advance.[55]

In fairness, Schofield admitted he could not hold Hood's army and prepared Thomas for a withdrawal northward. In the meantime, Thomas hoped to reorganize the cavalry which with some notable exceptions had been quickly cobbled together. Thomas, showing more confidence in Wilson than Schofield, wrote: "I should like to know what Wilson thinks he can do to aid you in holding Hood." In the afternoon, Schofield replied: "I will refer your question to General Wilson this evening; I think he can do very little. I have no doubt Forrest will be in my rear tomorrow, or doing some greater mischief.... I have just learned that the enemy's cavalry is already crossing three miles below. I will have lively times with my trains again." Thomas got the message from Schofield and approved the withdrawal. Thomas had no desire that Schofield and Stanley be destroyed while trying to hold a superior force.[56]

Schofield's regard for the cavalry got no better during the day. At almost 1:00 p.m., David Stanley received a message: "The commanding general directs me to inform you that the enemy is pushing General Croxton's cavalry, either up the river on this side or across the river. The general desires General Wood to look out for the trains." However, the assessment of Union cavalry was about to change. Despite the opinion of Schofield, Wilson's men, reinforced with Stewart's and Hammond's brigades, were confidently in place and would give a good accounting on November 30.[57]

As the day began, Wilson reassembled his cavalry after the prior day's actions. The evening before he sent Hammond's cavalry brigade to Triune and Nolensville, but there was no enemy cavalry in the area. The 10th Tennessee Cavalry (U.S.) reported only small squads of enemy cavalry had been observed and the total number of enemy amounted to only about 25 men. At 7:00 a.m., Wilson ordered Hammond to return to a position about four miles northeast of cavalry headquarters. He sent Croxton's brigade to scout and screen the southern side of the river while the remainder of the cavalry prepared to meet any advance over the river. While the scouting missions were taking place, the 1st Tennessee, part of Croxton's brigade, moved into position on Lewisburg Pike and the rest of the brigade fell into line in the rear.[58]

Wilson positioned the majority of his men two and half miles east of Franklin at Matthews' House (at a crossroads of the Murfreesboro Road and the road to Hughes' Ford) until he received new orders from Schofield or until he located Forrest's cavalry. Despite the previous action with the Confederate cavalry and now bolstered by Hammond's 1,000 men and Stewart's arrival, the Federal cavalry was ready to fight. Wilson sent strong reconnaissance forces in the direction of Peytonsville (about eight miles southeast of Franklin) and to the Ridge Meeting House in search of the enemy. Wilson had a short wait. Schofield sent a message to him at 5:35 a.m. telling him: "I want you to cover my immediate flank and rear, today at least, with a portion of your troops. I will be near this place, and I hope on the north bank of the Harpeth." Wilson had good reason to worry about Forrest's cavalry because Forrest wanted to again cross the river east of Franklin and attack the Federal's flank or rear as Schofield feared. Hood met with Forrest at the Harrison house to discuss the plan of battle where he disregarded Forrest's suggestion and told him to hold the cavalry in readiness to complete the victory which his infantry would achieve that day. As a result, Forrest placed Chalmers' division on Hood's western flank while Buford's and Jackson's divisions followed the Union troops toward Winstead Hill and later moved to the eastern flank of the Confederate army.[59]

Many in the Southern army had no knowledge of the previous day's controversies. South Carolina soldier, James A. Tillman, recorded in his journal that Cleburne and Forrest "drove them yesterday," but the withdrawal of the Federal army from Spring Hill frustrated many Confederate commanders. A chaplain of the 49th Tennessee Infantry encountered Forrest on the Franklin Pike after the withdrawal of the Union army and overheard Forrest speaking to another Confederate officer. "General, O General, if they had given me just one of your brigades, just one of 'em to fling across the pike, I'd ha' tuck the whole d___ shebang!" Another Confederate soldier, John M. Copley, reported that when Forrest found the Union army had withdrawn in the night he was so "enraged that his face turned almost to a chalky whiteness, and his lips quivered."[60]

Cavalry on the Western Flank

With the evacuation of the Union column from Spring Hill, Forrest obtained ammunition from the infantry stores for Chalmers' and Buford's divisions while he waited for his supply trains to be brought forward from Columbia. Once the ammunition was distributed, Forrest ordered Chalmers to ride to Carter's Creek Pike to attack the Federal supply train which Forrest understood had been unable to move forward. The Confederate cavalry found the Union supply train had moved away toward Franklin during the night. Then, Forrest sent Buford and Jackson hurriedly to find Schofield's column and the cavalry harassed Opdycke's rearguard until George Wagner set up his defenses at Winstead Hill. Gus Smith, an Ohio infantryman, recalled the Confederate cavalry attempted to attack the rear of the supply train. "Forrest came swooping down on us like a 'Kansas cyclone,' whooping and shouting at the top of their voices," but to no avail, as the Federal infantry held a firm line near the supply train and withdrew after allowing it to advance northward, only to stop and repeat the exercise again. Then, Forrest stopped and became the first principal Confederate officer to see the panorama of the Federal lines at Franklin. The Confederate infantry arrived later and took up the duty of pushing Wagner back toward Franklin. Forrest ordered Buford's and Jackson's divisions toward the Harpeth River on the extreme eastern flank of the army and Chalmers' division remained on the left flank. Chalmers was the first Confederate force to reach the Union lines on the western flank. At 2:30 p.m., the 7th Tennessee Cavalry (CSA) dismounted and advanced, pushing the Union pickets back to the main line. Because Forrest was with the other two divisions on the right flank, Hood directly commanded Chalmers. James Dinkins of Chalmers' division recalled observing the Union infantry: "From our position we could see three lines of breast-works encircling the town, and each line was full of infantry and artillery." Chalmers knew this would be a difficult fight and he sent a messenger to Hood telling him what lay ahead. Hood replied that Chalmers needed to charge at once. Chalmers could not believe that Hood understood the situation and sent a second message explaining in more detail the strength and position of the enemy. Again, the message returned—charge at once. Then, the entire Confederate line surged forward.[61]

At 4:30 p.m., Chalmers' division joined in the attack which had erupted into an explosion of artillery and musket fire. Chalmers dismounted his men and moved along the left flank of Bate's infantry during the battle. Bate clashed with Ruger's and Kimball's infantry lines. Chalmers described: "My line was pressed forward until the skirmishers were within sixty yards of the fortifications, but my force was too small to justify an attempt to storm them, and I could only hold my position." He ordered his men to move along the flank of the advancing infantry and charged across an open cornfield supporting the infantry which reached the first line of works. Chalmers' attack, described

The Confederate soldiers overlooked the plain in front of Franklin (*Battles and Leaders of the Civil War*, Vol. IV [1888], p. 447).

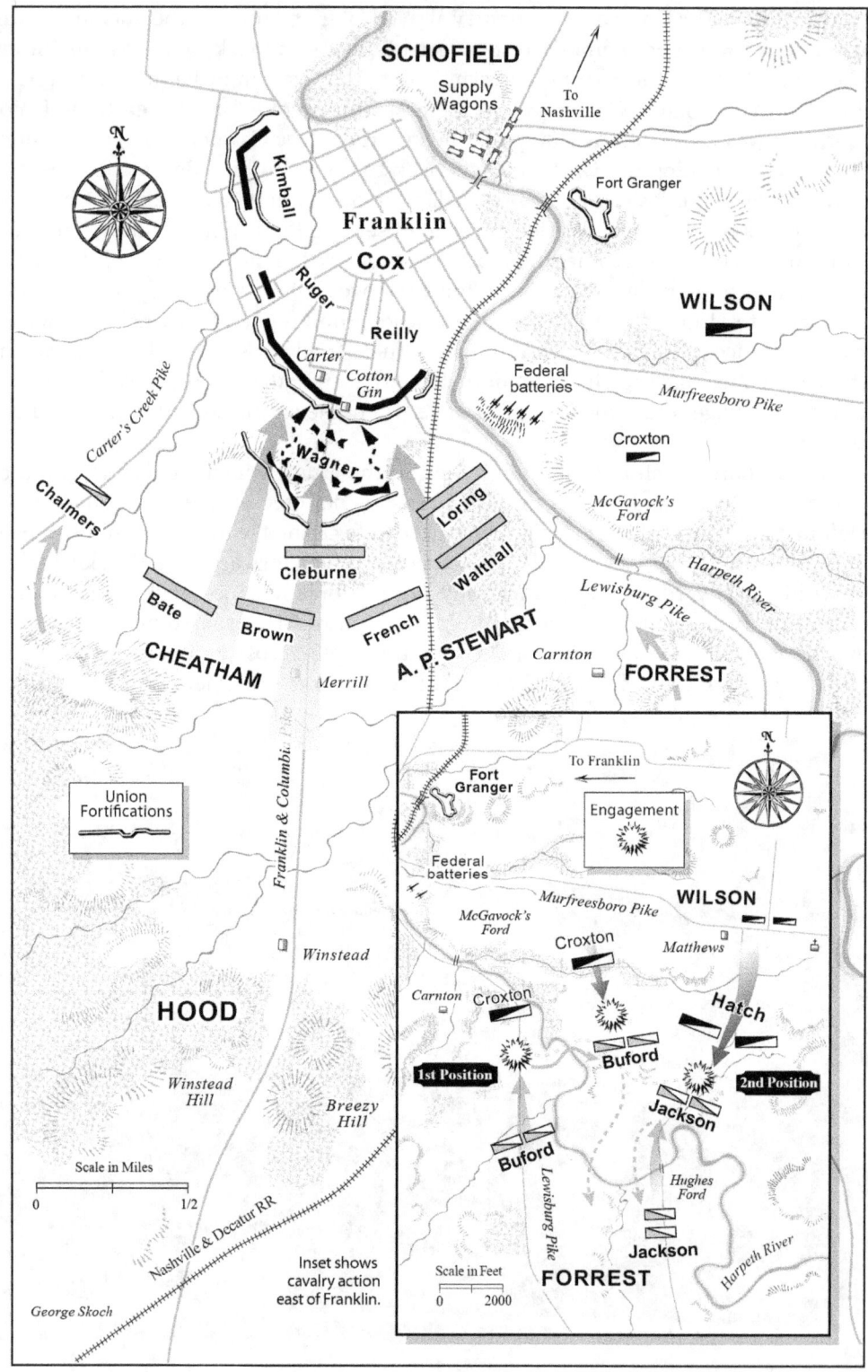

Cavalry actions at the Battle of Franklin, November 30, 1864.

by Jacob Cox from the Union position, was boldly made and easily repulsed. Chalmers failed to add much to the Confederate attack, partly, because he struggled to keep up with Bate's infantry. The right flank of Bate's men pushed over the outer defenses but the left flank (supported by Chalmers) "was driven back" resulting in an arched line. Chalmers stopped, secured the flank, and remained in place until 1:00 a.m. In the meantime, the battle had raged. James Dinkins wrote: "If hell be more terrifying than the scenes of the six or seven hours which followed ... then I abjure mankind to halt and consider."[62]

Lieutenant James Brownlow, Jr., 9th Tennessee Cavalry of Biffle's brigade, recalled that being on the extreme left flank his regiment did not engage the Union infantry in front, but he observed the hard fighting by the infantry on the right. "I knew they were being kiled by the holesale. I think that was the greatest mistake that was made during the ware. I never felt mutch like fighting after that." Chalmers advanced no farther but held his position "which we did during the night and until an early hour in the morning, when the skirmish line was pushed forward and was the first to enter the town, capturing some 20 prisoners."[63]

Cavalry on the Eastern Flank

On the right flank, much of Buford's cavalry marched along the right flank of General William Loring's infantry division as Hood prepared for his attack and Jackson's cavalry moved along the south bank of the Harpeth River. Essentially, Hood gave Forrest orders to secure the flanks and upon the victory by his infantry to prepare to "complete the ruin" of the enemy as it retreated to Nashville later in the day by dashing the cavalry on the routed Union troops. Later in the afternoon, Forrest ordered Jackson to move across the Harpeth River while Buford's cavalry marched on the flank of the infantry in an oblique route. Jackson, upon receiving his orders for the day, told his commanders, "Do your duty, behave like gentlemen, respect citizens and their property, and endure hardships without a murmur." Then, the cavalry troops on the east swung into their saddles and prepared for the battle.[64]

Croxton's Defense on Lewisburg Pike

Croxton began the day at the Matthews' House on Franklin–Murfreesboro Pike. He immediately moved south of the Harpeth River to the vicinity of Douglass Church, about a mile south of the Harpeth River, on Lewisburg Pike. Wilson told Croxton to screen the enemy cavalry and, if pressed, to withdraw and re-cross the Harpeth River at McGavock's Ford, about a mile and a half east of Franklin. The Kentucky Confederate brigade arrived in front of Croxton at 10:00 a.m. but the situation remained quiet until 11:00 a.m. when the enemy skirmishers moved into position to sweep along the river while threatening Schofield's left flank. The Confederate infantry troops remained on the south side of the river and a trooper of the 2nd Michigan mused that the river could have been forded with success in any number of places. As the enemy approached, the 1st Tennessee, which had held a forward position, fell back to the main line of Croxton's cavalry, and the first line of Confederates met a volley from the Federal cavalry. Marshall Thatcher, 2nd Michigan Cavalry, recalled his regiment, armed with Spencer repeating rifles, first encountered Forrest's cavalry about three miles southeast of Franklin.

"They were not disposed to give way so easily, but came again with something like their Thompson's station vigor." The Union troopers again fired into the ranks of the Confederate cavalry and the enemy continued to move "steadily up to charging distance, burst forth, a perfect avalanche of horses and men, and in a moment more would surely sweep back across the Harpeth our little band of rifles. But there was the creek to cross down and up and the range was close. Again that row of rifles gleamed in strong, vigorous arms; along those barrels quick eyes caught the sights; the finger, true to the eye, fondles the trigger for an instant only and, one! two! three! Times 500 bullets sped true to the mark, and not a soul crossed the stream." Much of the ground in front of Croxton was wooded and became hillier the further north one traveled toward Franklin and the terrain gave both the Confederates and Union troops some protection. The 1st Tennessee and 2nd Michigan cavalries held the advanced positions of Croxton's line. While the Union troopers fired at their adversaries, the veteran Lieutenant Colonel Benjamin Smith (2nd Michigan) sat on a log with his bridle over his arm, smoking his pipe.[65]

Some of the first fighting between Croxton and Buford's cavalry was observed by the citizens in the area. Lucy Henderson Horton recalled that her father, a physician, and the children stood near a carriage house and watched the opposing cavalries begin the fighting on the eastern flank. "We heard the Rebel yell as the men advanced across a field to a skirt of woods near Douglass Church." After successfully stymying the initial attack, nothing further occurred until 1:00 p.m. as Croxton pulled the brigade back a mile closer to McGavock's Ford. Here, barricades were built in preparation for a desperate fight to prevent a crossing of the Harpeth River. Croxton arrived to supervise the positioning of his Michigan cavalry and all appeared quiet. Then, a shot rang out, revealing the enemy just ahead. Obviously, the sight of a Union cavalry general proved too valuable a target to pass up, but the shot missed and Croxton did not react. He calmly told the commanders of the 2nd Michigan to hold their position as long as possible and to keep a clear path of retreat across the river. At one point in the fighting, the 2nd Michigan remained in line too long and sought a way to retreat. Just as the enemy approached, an explosion of carbine fire from the flank revealed the position of Joseph Dorr's 8th Iowa which allowed the 2nd Michigan to escape.[66]

Croxton, slowly falling back, skirmished with the increasing number of enemy but no further fighting resulted and an hour later, Croxton fell back to another wooded area with his left on Harpeth River, extending across Lewisburg Pike. At 2:00 p.m. "their cavalry made a dash, and, being repulsed, moved up the river toward Hughes' Ford…" Croxton probably saw the movement of Jackson's cavalry division toward Hughes' Ford where Hatch's division was positioned, but he still faced Buford's division pressing forward. Then, Croxton faced a more serious threat as columns of A.P. Stewart's infantry corps joined Buford's cavalry and marched toward Franklin, and ultimately, past Croxton's position. While Croxton contemplated his situation, the surgeon of the 22nd Mississippi Infantry worried about what awaited the infantry at Franklin. Dr. G.C. Phillips remarked, "I do not like this quietness. It is ominous, and I fear the men are going to be annihilated." With the Confederate cavalry moving east of his position and now facing infantry, Croxton followed his orders and prepared to cross the river at McGavock's Ford.[67]

At 3:00 p.m., a Union scout advanced just a few yards before he found the position of the enemy and then hurried back to Croxton reporting lines of Confederates advancing. At the same time, Croxton found Confederate infantry marching past his flank on its way to Franklin. A rider from Croxton dashed to the regiments with new orders. "If you are whipping the rebels, go in!" Taking this as an order to attack, the 2nd Michigan moved forward into a line of the enemy about 300 yards in front. The Michigan cavalry "moved forward without hesitation; first a walk, then a trot, and struck the enemy at a run. But the advance of the enemy was only a small force compared with their solid lines under cover of the woods and brush, and when these were reached, up rose two lines of infantry and poured a rattling fire into our regiment." The 2nd Michigan so surprised the enemy, they did not deliver a full volley. Marshall Thatcher knew his regiment would pay for the impetuous advance into Loring's infantry division and Buford's cavalry division. "We had stirred them up and were prepared to take the consequences, and a very stubborn fall back fight continued past our former position our reserve being also swept back with the others the last to cross the river, some of the men being dragged across, clinging to a comrade's horse, and some of them captured; no time for mounting, the woods swarming with Confederates, and the air thick with bullets; but for some reason their firing was wild and comparatively few were hit. Our friends were ready to receive us and check the enemy, which they did at the banks of the Harpeth, and the left flank of our army was held firmly." Henry Mortimer Hempstead recorded in his journal that much of the success of the 2nd Michigan resulted from holding a good position. The regiment was concealed in a wooded area that limited the Confederate cavalry's ability to maneuver. The 2nd Michigan had just charged a division of Confederate infantry and cavalry and had retreated with minor losses. Croxton arrived on the scene and told the men: "You have made the best cavalry fight I have seen during the war." He said the brigade would hold the ford "if Schofield could only take care of himself." He decided to leave the 2nd Michigan on the southern bank of the river to harass the enemy infantry and cavalry, while withdrawing the rest of the brigade. The 2nd Michigan would maintain its position until Buford's cavalry decided to move northward across the river and then the regiment re-joined Croxton's brigade.[68]

Tyree Bell's account agreed with Croxton's. Bell recalled that some of the Union cavalry moved back to the north side of the Harpeth River but not all the cavalry directly in front of his division withdrew, presumably referring to the 2nd Michigan Cavalry, armed with repeating carbines. At 4:00 p.m., Bell sent a courier to Forrest telling him that it was impossible to advance further. The Union cavalry, supported by artillery in place further downstream, fought "with a fury." When Forrest received the message, he said, "Well, Bell can get in the hottest places in the quickest time of any man I ever saw." Unable to move ahead, Forrest ordered Buford to cross the river, joining Jackson's division. Bell recalled that his brigade crossed at Ewing's Branch near the Lewisburg Pike and immediately ran into an even hotter fight than he had just left. "Yankee field artillery joined in," noted Bell. Wilson's men were prepared and held their ground. Henry George, Kentucky, cavalryman, agreed with the other reports noting that as the Confederate infantry marched closer to Franklin, Buford ordered his dismounted men back into the saddle. George noted a "hot contest" between Buford's and Croxton's cavalry, but Croxton's cavalry was driven across the river.[69]

Buford and Jackson Advance Across the River

Wilson remained at his headquarters and at 1:45 p.m., he relayed information to Schofield that the enemy infantry was approaching Hughes' Ford intending to cross at that location. Wilson sent scouts to determine the reliability of this information and he ordered Richard Johnson to position his division to resist this advance. An hour later, Wilson reported that the enemy infantry had just moved past Hughes' Ford directly for Franklin, and he still had been unable to determine if the enemy intended a flanking movement over the river or to advance on Franklin. However, the Harpeth River appeared to offer little impediment to crossing of the enemy cavalry or infantry. Wilson reported, "Citizens say they can cross anywhere." Also, Hammond, on the eastern flank, had already reported that the river offered little difficulty for an enemy crossing. At 3:00 p.m., Wilson found his answer and dispatched a message to Schofield about Jackson's cavalry: "[T]he enemy charged the picket at Hughes' Ford and ... crossed." Wilson's message did not indicate the efforts of the cavalry to resist the crossing at this location, if any, even though it was being watched by the Union cavalry. Schofield replied that he would send a brigade of infantry from Thomas Wood's division as reinforcements to meet the enemy near the ford. At 3:45 p.m., Wilson merely reported, "There is sharp skirmishing in my front."[70]

Richard Johnson reported that the enemy crossed at Hughes' Ford (Jackson's division) and another large body of the enemy (Buford's division) moved westward along the south side of the river. Wilson endorsed his message 20 minutes later. "There is no doubt of this. It has come in all along the line—cavalry." George Monlux, 8th Iowa Cavalry, described that for a while Croxton's cavalry stared across the river at Forrest's cavalry, both forces just slightly out of range—"watching each other." The Confederate infantry marched toward Franklin as the Iowa cavalry watched from the north bank of the river. The Iowans fired into the marching infantry which scarcely noticed them, except for an occasional returned shot, one of which killed Iowan, Joseph Nixon. Johnson's other brigade Harrison's, held in reserve, was not engaged in the fight; however, at least, some of the reports from the 7th Ohio describe that this regiment had provided pickets which were driven in about 3:00 p.m. near Hughes' Ford.[71]

Once Buford's division joined Jackson's across the Harpeth River, Wilson moved Hatch's division and Croxton's brigade to resist the advance. Croxton prepared to attack the Confederate cavalry in the flank after it crossed the river when a rider from Colonel Joseph Dorr's 8th Iowa Cavalry arrived with alarming news. The Confederate infantry was crossing the river between McGavock's Ford and Franklin. The rider exclaimed that a column of infantry moved past their position and the Iowans opened on the infantry from across the river. The infantry continued its march to the west and Dorr perceived that once past his position, the infantry would cross the river. This was important and disturbing news. Croxton acted quickly and decisively by sending the 8th Iowa Cavalry and the 4th Kentucky Mounted Infantry to resist the infantry crossing. Croxton soon found Dorr's report to "be unfounded," and in the meantime, he moved the 2nd Michigan and 1st Tennessee forming a line with Hatch's men on his left flank and engaged Buford's division. Croxton, then, ordered Dorr's regiment and the 4th Kentucky to join the remainder of the brigade attacking Buford's division on the north side of the river.[72]

Croxton's brigade had fallen into line at McGavock's Ford with the 1st Tennessee facing Buford's cavalry and Hatch's division advanced from the north. The 2nd Michigan initially supported the 1st Tennessee which fought the enemy and retired to resupply with ammunition. The 2nd Michigan moved to replace the Tennesseans, quietly advanced under hail of fire, not firing a shot until "at close range, the brigade supporting on the flanks, a volley was given and only twice repeated, when the enemy broke and fled across the Harpeth, closely pursued by the Second," explained Marshall Thatcher. The 2nd Michigan was so close on the heels of the retreating cavalry, they claimed "their ambulances, filled with wounded, in the middle of the river."[73]

Hatch's Attack Near Hughes Ford

While Croxton had a busy day, Hatch's division remained unengaged near Matthews' House. Hatch held a strong position on a second set of hills overlooking open fields on the road leading to Hughes' Ford. Hatch held an important crossroads with his division which gave him an excellent field of fire. At 3:00 p.m., he found Jackson's division moving over the wooded bluffs immediately on the north side of the Harpeth River. Wilson told Hatch to push the enemy to the south side of the river. Some of the regiments of Stewart's brigade had been detached on escort duty, but the remaining regiments joined Coon in attacking Jackson's cavalry. This left Hatch with 6th, 7th, 9th Illinois, 2nd Iowa, and 12th Tennessee, accompanied by part of the 3rd Illinois and three companies of the 11th Indiana cavalry to deal with the Southern cavalry. Coon's brigade remained in camp until noon when some of the pickets at Hughes' Ford were driven in by Armstrong's cavalry. Coon dispatched the 6th Illinois to strengthen the position at Hughes' Ford and he also sent the 2nd Iowa to the east on the Nolensville Road to protect the eastern flank. At three o'clock, Coon advanced about a half a mile with his brigade and saw the Confederate cavalry arrive on a high bluff in his front.[74]

"The enemy was posted on a strong hill on the opposite side of Harpeth River, from which position he was firing upon our troops on the Lewisburg pike," wrote Forrest. Forrest initially sent Jackson's division across the Harpeth River to neutralize the Federals on the hill while taking "position in line of battle on the right of Stewart's corps, covering the ground from the Lewisburg pike to Harpeth River. Skirmishing at once commenced, and Buford's division rapidly advancing drove the enemy across Harpeth River, where he joined the cavalry. Brigadier-General Jackson engaged the united forces of both infantry and cavalry, and held him in check until night, when he threw forward his pickets and retired across Harpeth for the purpose of replenishing his ammunition. The enemy held strong position commanding all the fords." Although, Wood planned to send a brigade of infantry to bolster the Union line, the fighting was over before the infantry was dispatched. Forrest only faced Wilson's cavalry in this fight. In addition, there are various interpretations of which hill Forrest directed Jackson to capture—did Forrest intend Jackson to press on the north side of the river to Fort Granger which would threaten the rear of the Federal position or to just move the Federal cavalry away from the hills at Hughes' Ford or McGavock's Ford?[75]

Also, the exact locations of the crossings of Jackson and Buford seem to be less than certain. Most accounts give Jackson's crossing point as Hughes' Ford while Buford followed Croxton's cavalry by crossing near McGavock's Ford. Based on Croxton's report, it seems likely that Buford crossed in the vicinity of McGavock's Ford, but probably slightly east so that it could join Jackson's cavalry, now in the bluffs on the north side of the river. Tyree Bell recorded that his brigade crossed at Ewing's Branch near the Lewisburg Pike, slightly east of McGavock's Ford. Unfortunately, Buford left no formal report and Forrest did not address the crossing locations.[76]

Hatch described: "The hills were very abrupt, and the enemy had possession of all but one, and were then well round on my left flank. The men of my command dismounted, the line moved forward to the foot of the hills, when the order was given to charge, the men going over them in great spirit. Giving the command a moment to breathe, we again charged, when the enemy broke in confusion, and at 7 o'clock in the evening we had driven them over Harpeth River, from two to three miles distant from our first line of battle."[77]

Lieutenant George Griscom, 9th Texas, a native of Pennsylvania, lived in Weatherford, Texas, before the war. Griscom was a veteran and he became adjutant upon the appointment of Dudley Jones to command the regiment. Griscom explained that Ross' brigade drove the Federal pickets over the river at Hughes Ford. Once across the river, Ross ordered his brigade to mount and it remained in line until 3:00 p.m. As Coon advanced, Colonel Dudley Jones ordered the 9th Texas, supported by the 3rd Texas, to charge the Union cavalry in their front. The Texans drove back Hatch's forward line, now "two stampeded regiments," until they ran into the main body of the Hatch's cavalry troops. Hatch ordered his line to charge and after a heated melee, Jones ordered—retreat. In an interesting indictment, Griscom alleged a Union regiment was drunk when it charged the retreating Texans. The 3rd Texas led a counter charge and the 9th Texas, rallying, drove the Federal cavalry rearward. During the fight, Colonel Jones drove his saber into a Federal trooper with such force the blade broke from the hilt. Griscom also noted in his diary that the counter charge stabilized the Texas line which held on until Armstrong's cavalry on the right was driven back across the river. Ross, now having an untenable position, withdrew across the river also.[78]

Ross explained that when he crossed Hughes' Ford he routed a Union cavalry regiment, the 2nd Iowa Cavalry, but the Union regiment was supported by another cavalry regiment, the 6th Illinois, which, in turn, drove Ross rearward. According to R.W. Surby, 7th Illinois Cavalry, Hatch had formed a line with his cavalry facing a high bluff in front of the Confederate cavalry. Facing Jackson's cavalry was a portion of the 10th Tennessee, the 3rd, 6th, 9th and 7th Illinois cavalries in line in order from left to right, all dismounted. The 2nd Iowa Cavalry held an advanced position, as skirmishers. The 6th Illinois used up its ammunition after moving to support the 2nd Iowa and was withdrawing back to the main line when Ross decided to take advantage of the withdrawing Union regiments. The enemy attacked into the remaining Federal regiments, only to be repulsed. A countercharge by the 3rd Texas stalled the Union advance which again advanced on Ross' brigade. Ross rallied his troops and stood in his stirrups: "Boys, if you don't run, they will!" The men of Ross' cavalry proudly declared that Ross never taught his bugler how to sound "retreat." Ross claimed: "By the charge of the Third Texas we gained possession of an eminence overlooking the enemy's position, and held it until late in the evening, when, discovering an intention on the part of [the] Yankee commander to advance his entire force, and being without any support, I withdrew to the south side of the river again."[79]

Sergeant Birney McClean explained what was probably the best Union version of this fight: "Co. K, 2d Iowa, was placed on picket in front of Coon's Brigade, and was soon attacked, falling back, fighting, and were then relieved by the 6th Ill. They were forced back until protected by the guns of the brigade, the rebels now making a charge, which was quickly repulsed, the 6th, 7th, and 9th Ill. in turn charging the foe in our front, and the fight of an hour was over; not alone in our front, but all along the line about Franklin." Trooper D.B. Spencer, 7th Illinois, recorded: "We did charge up a long hill, driving back the enemy's skirmish line, when we came on to a heavy line with their colors, and with a hurrah went for them, firing as we went and without a moment's halt."[80]

A.W. "Tuck" Sparks, 9th Texas Cavalry, described Sul Ross' Texas cavalry clashed with a Tennessee cavalry regiment. Sparks recalled that only the 3rd Texas, 6th Texas, and one battalion of the Texas Legion moved over the Harpeth River, while the rest of brigade remained on the south side of the river as security. Ross' brigade was initially driven back by Hatch's division and then rallied; then, the Federal cavalry and Ross' horsemen charged each other. As the two forces met, the "two opposing lines absolutely passed through each other." Ross ordered his men into line and prepared to meet the next charge and then, standing in his stirrups, Ross ordered his men to charge the Union cavalry. The charge resulted in a furious fight between the two lines. At dark, the Southern cavalry had been driven to the south bank of the Harpeth River.[81]

William Mason Worthington, 1st Mississippi Cavalry and staff officer in Armstrong's brigade, wrote to his younger brother that Armstrong's men expected to drive into the rear of Union position at Franklin and, despite Ross' description of the battle, the men of the 1st Mississippi saw Ross' brigade roughly pushed south of the Harpeth River. "We were driving them in fine style as had been our custom for a week previously when all at once we encountered an overwhelming force—the concentrated Cavalry of the whole Yankee Army. Ross' brigade was driven back across the River 'in less than no time,' and it was only by the most stubborn fighting that we were able to come off creditably."[82]

The scanty Confederate cavalry reports agree, generally, with Federal ones. At 6:30 p.m., Forrest communicated with William H. Jackson through his assistant adjutant general. "The major-general directs that if you cannot hold your position you will fall back on this side of the river, leaving a guard at the ford, and report in person at these headquarters, at the bridge on the Lewisburg pike, near the residence of General De Graffenried."[83]

So used to success by Forrest's cavalry, the common soldier again expected success for Buford and Jackson. Hood had easily marched to Columbia and gained the march to Spring Hill; now, the Union troops were fleeing north. The presence of Forrest on the heels on the fleeing Union soldiers only increased the confidence of many common soldiers. Sam Watkins, 1st Tennessee Infantry, wrote: "Everything betokened a rout, and a stampede of the Yankee army. Double quick! Forrest is in the rear," but today, Wilson's line held and drove the Confederates back across the river.[84]

The Battle Ends

Wilson repulsed both Jackson and Buford without utilizing his entire force. Richard Johnson was on the battlefield with Croxton, but Harrison's brigade was held in reserve. Some of the troopers picketed several other fords along the Harpeth River, including Davis' and Henderson's, and Johnson assigned the 5th Iowa Cavalry to the western flank of the Union forces at Franklin. Johnson ordered Harrison's brigade to cover the eastern flank of Hatch's division where it remained unengaged during the battle. In addition, Hammond's newly arrived brigade maintained its position as a reserve force, four miles away. James Goodwin, 4th Tennessee Cavalry (U.S.), confirmed that Hammond's brigade was not involved in the fighting, but he did hear the fighting. Goodwin wrote that it was an "awfully grand sound."[85]

Wilson proudly reported a more successful day for his cavalry after successfully repulsing the Confederate cavalry at Hughes' Ford. Wilson wrote: "[T]he orders were promptly executed, and by night the rebels were driven across the river at every point. The conduct of the troops, and particularly of Generals Hatch and Croxton, was most admirable." At 5:30 p.m., Wilson received the positive news regarding the infantry battle at Franklin from Schofield. "We have whipped them here at every point. The general ... desires you to remain with your command till daylight and watch the river closely, then fall back on the flanks of the rear guard." Despite the Union success at Franklin, Schofield intended to continue his withdrawal to Nashville.[86]

In an interesting note, Tyree Bell gave some important insight in the lack of a more aggressive attack on Wilson near Hughes' and McGavock's fords. Bell recalled after the repulse of Forrest's cavalry along the Harpeth River, that Forrest issued orders to scout the north side of the river and to prepare to move on the rear of Schofield troops, just as he had done at Columbia. However, the news of the massive defeat took away the hopes of encircling Schofield and Forrest decided to disengage from Wilson's cavalry. The dominance of the Southern cavalry in this campaign came to an end along the Harpeth River. At 9 p.m., Wilson issued his orders for the withdrawal of the cavalry toward Brentwood. Hatch's division and Harrison's brigade would march between the Brentwood and Franklin pikes keeping the roads free for the infantry to use. Each of the cavalry commands had orders to delay any pursuit by Forrest's cavalry.[87]

Summary of Cavalry Actions

Historian Thomas R. Hay summarized the cavalry actions near Hughes' Ford as being a "fierce fight ... which only ended about 5 p.m." He concluded that the Federal cavalry totaled about 5,000 men and without Chalmers' division, Jackson and Buford would only had about 3,000 men, but only Hatch's division and Croxton's brigade were involved in the repulse. Neither Harrison's or Hammond's brigades played an important part in the fight. While Stewart's brigade had been in the fight, some of the regiments had been detached. It is more likely that the opposing commands had relatively equal numbers rather equal than lop-sided in favor of the Union cavalry. Importantly, Hay pointed out the increasing disregard that Schofield showed to his cavalry. Hay wrote: "Schofield, who had no faith in the effectiveness of the cavalry, prior to the battle of Franklin ... was offensively gratuitous in acknowledging the importance of Wilson's work ... it is hardly too much to say that Wilson's work saved Schofield from being cut off and defeated. On the march from Pulaski it was always at the front securing information and giving timely warning of Hood's movements. At Franklin Schofield's line of retreat was kept open and the army's sage withdrawal insured." Overall, the Federal cavalry withdrawing steadily in front of the Confederate cavalry had handled itself commendably and had performed, certainly, no worse than Schofield's infantry.[88]

However, Wilson would be open to criticism and Schofield blasted the cavalry in his report:

> On my arrival at Franklin I gained the first information from General Wilson since the enemy commenced his advance from Duck River. I learned that he had been driven back and had crossed the Harpeth above Franklin on the preceding day, leaving my left and rear entirely open to the enemy's cavalry. By my direction he sent General Hatch's division forward again, on the Lewisburg

pike, to hold Forrest in check until my trains and troops could reach Franklin. This was successfully done, and General Hatch then retired before a superior force, and recrossed the river, connecting with my infantry pickets on the north bank, early in the afternoon. A short time before the infantry attack commenced the enemy's cavalry forced a crossing about three miles above Franklin, and drove back our cavalry, for a time seriously threatening our trains, which were accumulating on the north bank, and moving toward Nashville. I sent General Wilson orders, which he had, however, anticipated, to drive the enemy back at all hazards, and moved a brigade of General Wood's division to support him, if necessary. At the moment of the first decisive repulse of the enemy's infantry I received the most gratifying intelligence that General Wilson had driven the rebel cavalry back across the river. This rendered my immediate left and rear secure for the time being.... The enemy having nearly double my force of infantry and quite double my cavalry, could easily turn any position I might take and seriously endanger my rear.

Only one division of the enemy's cavalry had been engaged with General Wilson during the 30th. The remaining three divisions were free to strike my line of communications, which they could easily do about Brentwood by daylight the next morning. My experience on the 29th had shown how utterly inferior in force my cavalry was to that of the enemy, and that even my immediate flank and rear were insecure, while my communication with Nashville was entirely without protection. I could not even rely upon getting up the ammunition necessary for another battle.[89]

Wilson, rightly incensed by this report, would write later that he never received the orders Schofield referred to in his reports and this report contained many errors. After the Battle of Franklin, Wilson would no longer be under Schofield's command, which obviously pleased him. Wilson wrote, "The simple fact is, that from the time I assumed active command in the field south of Columbia on November 22, 1864, until our imperiled army, with its trains intact, was safely within our fortified lines at Nashville, I was left almost entirely to my own resources. To whatever cause Schofield's contemptuous estimate of my command was due, whether to my comparative youth, or to a doubt of my capacity, or to the obvious inferiority of my force, it is certain that, thereafter, and especially at Nashville, he took a far kinder view of the fighting ability of the cavalry." In contrast to Schofield, Wilson had a much better relationship with Thomas and these two generals mutually supported one another, resulting in a stronger and better army.[90]

In regard to Forrest's cavalry, Chalmers worked along the left flank in spite of the demonstrated effectiveness of concentrating the cavalry in the crossing of the Duck River two days before. In the final analysis, Chalmers would have been more effective working with the rest of the cavalry. This was especially true in light of the fact that Chalmers' division failed to offer much support to Bate's infantry. After the war, Wilson pondered the question of the outcome of the fights near Hughes' Ford and McGavock's Ford had Chalmers also been involved and he conceded: "[I]t is possible it [the attack] would have succeeded in driving us back." The addition of Chalmers to Jackson and Buford would have offered a greater opportunity for Forrest's underutilized cavalry to drive Wilson away from Schofield's eastern flank.[91]

The decision of how to utilize Forrest's cavalry resonates to today. In his biography of Forrest, ex-Confederate soldier and historian, John Allan Wyeth, wrote that Forrest told Hood before the battle at Franklin: "[I]f you will give me one strong division of infantry and with my cavalry, I will agree to flank the Federals from their works within two hours' time." Some accounts of this plan specified that Forrest wanted to reach Hollow Tree Gap, some 15 miles north if he hoped to swing past Wilson. The final council of war that Hood held with his generals took place at 2:30 p.m. and it would have been difficult, if not impossible, for Forrest to have reached this location until well after sunset, particularly accompanied by an infantry division. In addition, the cavalry Forrest faced on November 30 had been supplemented by two brigades overnight. Actually, Buford and Jackson were repulsed during the day with only three Union cavalry brigades while two fresh brigades were held in reserve. Wood's IV Division was also posted on the north side of the river to deal with any attempt to directly attack the flank and rear of the Union forces at Franklin. What Forrest had planned is not known, and he was very familiar with the territory. He had shown a propensity to strike unexpectedly and effectively throughout his career, and he could have yielded interesting results. Certainly, Forrest would have had greater flexibility for maneuver and this might have resulted in a more effective use of his mobile force, rather than marching straight ahead into the waiting guns of the Federal army.[92]

The Battle of Franklin represented the third critical event in the campaign and resulted in the loss of so many men and commanders which Hood could ill afford to lose. Hood lost three men to every one that Schofield lost. The Union commanders would make this kind of trade every day until the Army of Tennessee was gone. Lieutenant O.A. Abbott, 9th Illinois Cavalry, would write: "If Franklin was a victory for Hood, another such would destroy him." The question remains today—should Hood have stopped the advance on Nashville on November 30? Historian Hay concluded: "Hood's force was poorly clothed and poorly fed and suffered greatly from the cold and inclement weather, while its adversary, well fed, well clothed, daily growing stronger, more resolute, and more confident in itself and its leadership, was vigorously making ready to deliver a blow that would be irresistible."[93]

Final Actions of the Day November 30

At the close of the day, Schofield reported the results of the Confederate attacks at Franklin. Indeed, the Union forces had won the battle, inflicting severe losses on Hood's army in one of the most fiercely fought battles of the war. Schofield wrote to Thomas: "The enemy made a heavy and persistent attack with about two corps, commencing at 4 p.m. and lasting until after dark. He was repulsed at all points, with very heavy loss, probably 5,000 or 6,000 men. Our loss is probably not more than one-tenth that number. We have captured about 1,000 men, including one brigadier-general."[94]

Schofield withdrew northward to Nashville overnight and Hood seemed intent on following him. At Nashville, Thomas received A.J. Smith's reinforcements during the last 24 hours and felt increasingly confident of his position. He also ordered James Steedman's 5,000 troops from the District of the Etowah to Nashville, abandoning the plan to threaten Hood's rear. Despite the welcome news of having a strong defensive position, the perceived superiority of the Confederate cavalry plagued the Union commander. Thomas wrote to Henry Halleck about his plans and his hopes that he would "be able to manage Hood, notwithstanding his great superiority in the number of his cavalry." Both Thomas and Schofield worried about Forrest's cavalry and Thomas admitted that the retreat to Nashville was prompted by Forrest. "Hood, at present, has a cavalry force so much larger than mine that I have been compelled to fall back and concentrate on Nashville; but as soon as I can get my cavalry back from Louisville I feel confident I can drive him back." In reality, Forrest no longer had a superior number of cavalry troops, but Forrest's persona was so great that it forced Thomas into a more defensive strategy, a strategy in which he felt more secure.⁹⁵

Despite the bloody battle and the heavy Confederate casualties, Hood sent congratulations to his troops. "The commanding general congratulates the army upon the success achieved yesterday over our enemy by their heroic and determined courage. The enemy have been sent in disorder and confusion to Nashville, and while we lament the fall of many gallant officers and brave men, we have shown to our countrymen that we can carry any position occupied by our enemy." Hood would state in his memoirs that the battle actually increased the morale of his troops. In an interesting note, the *Chicago Tribune* published a rumor that Forrest had been killed during the fight. At the conclusion of the battle, the Federal army continued to retreat and many Southern soldiers believed they won the fight, but among the Confederate troops there was little doubt of the price paid at Franklin. E.H. Rennolds, 5th Tennessee Infantry (CSA) wrote in his diary: "The slaughter of rebels has been great." Robert Lewis Bliss of Forrest's cavalry would write his mother the next day and say: "Again the work of slaughter has been going on...." Another Confederate wrote: "We went up to Nashville barefooted, worried and disheartened." The battle, in which the Federals used over 100 wagonloads of ammunition, was so intense that some of the local citizens at Franklin had to rake the spent balls out of their yards.⁹⁶

Thomas Pulls Rousseau's Command into the Defense

Major General Robert H. Milroy's duty protecting the railroad from his headquarters at Tullahoma had been unpleasant to him because he wanted to be in the action. Milroy had been soundly defeated in the Second Battle of Winchester and had since been shelved by the Federal high command. As early as mid–September, he appealed to George Thomas for greater responsibility. "[Y]ou will soon reorganize to some extent the army of the Cumberland. If such should be the case I would respectfully ask that I may not be overlooked. I think I have done penance long enough in the year of your glorious fighting to atone for sins past & prospective." Milroy commanded a group of raw recruits and many troops that had only a few days left in their enlistment. His troops were scattered along the railroad with little incentive for discipline or interest in their tasks. Milroy felt he was still a good officer and wrote: "I am not needed here." In addition, he had the unpleasant duty of trying to maintain order in an area of divided loyalties and the treatment of citizens of both sides was often violent. He told Thomas that surely some of the division commanders needed a rest after so much fighting and he felt he could offer good service in the war. Unknown to Milroy, he would become embroiled again in the fighting in just over a week when Forrest moved north in September and again in December, he would meet a greater threat.⁹⁷

Thomas still could not know the full intent of Hood's advance, but he wanted to take no chances that Hood would swing to the east and destroy the railroads to Chattanooga. He ordered Milroy to pack up his troops and move to Murfreesboro to supplement the garrison already there. Rousseau, who had just moved his headquarters from Nashville to Murfreesboro, reported on November 29 that all was quiet. To the south, Robert Granger had pulled out of Huntsville and Rousseau prepared to move his forces to Nashville, if needed. "The troops here are mostly raw, but would be of use to you in an emergency." There was a human aspect to the Federal withdrawal from Huntsville which related to the ex-slaves. They did not want to remain and be claimed as property. A local resident of Huntsville, Mary Jane Chadick, wrote: "Many families in town are left tonight without a single servant, all gone to the Yankees. The country all around the depot is perfectly black with them."[98]

Chapter Ten

Hood Marches to Nashville

"Give him no peace."—Ulysses Grant

December 1: The Movement to Nashville

On December 1, George Thomas felt much more confident than the day before. The Union soldiers, from Thomas to the privates in the ranks, knew that Hood had been severely repulsed at Franklin, but the threat was not over as Schofield marched further northward. The Confederate cavalry which had the ability to move quickly and attack vulnerable positions now remained the biggest immediate threat. Overall for the Union forces, Steedman was en route to Nashville and A.J. Smith's corps had arrived in the city within the past 24 hours. Once IV Corps and XXIII Corps reached Nashville, the threat of a defeat of Federal forces in detail was largely gone. The concentrated Union forces in Nashville would be more than strong enough to meet Hood's army. Thomas explained to Halleck that after the battle at Franklin he planned to assemble the Union forces at Nashville until Wilson's cavalry could be concentrated and equipped to meet Forrest. While the need to pause and improve the number of Union cavalry was important, Thomas erroneously estimated that Forrest outnumbered his cavalry by four to one and he used this excuse as the basis for remaining on the defensive. "I therefore think it best to wait here until Wilson can equip all his cavalry. If Hood attacks me here, he will be more seriously damaged than he was yesterday; if he remains until Wilson gets equipped, I can whip him and will move against him at once." Otherwise, Thomas had his troops where he wanted them—Murfreesboro, Chattanooga, Bridgeport, Stevenson, and the Elk River bridge were secure. Now, the Federal troops were ready to fight Hood and letters sent to the North echoed this sentiment. Benjamin Nourse, Chicago Board of Trade Horse Artillery, wrote of Hood's advance: "Let him come only so they don't put us in the works." Nourse, part of the cavalry, only wanted an open field in which to fight.[1]

On the Confederate side of the field, the commanders claimed victory at Franklin because Schofield continued his retreat, but no one could erase images of the empty ranks of soldiers and officers after the battle. Hood paused at Franklin, but soon sent orders to his commanders to begin marching again. His columns of infantry marched northward with A.P. Stewart following Lee's corps up the Nashville-Brentwood Pike. Hood wrote: "General Forrest reports the enemy in full retreat from Brentwood, and he pressing them." Hood's communications to Seddon and Beauregard regarding the battle were less than complete. He claimed the positive aspects of the battle—Schofield's withdrawal, the capture of Federal colors, prisoners, and the Union dead and wounded left at Franklin. He listed the losses of his generals, but he did not report the full extent of his losses. Even a few days later, Hood tried to diminish his losses in the eyes of his superiors: "Our loss of officers in the battle of Franklin, on the 30th, was excessively large in proportion to the loss of men. The medical director reports a very large proportion of slightly wounded men."[2]

Hood continued to focus on his successes. With the Union forces concentrating at Nashville, Philip Roddey's cavalry gathered up the spoils from the vacated territory including a couple of locomotives and some railcars in north Alabama. Hood insisted that the railroad be repaired to Decatur, Alabama, and, envisioning his ultimate success, he optimistically wrote, "The permanent occupation of this country absolutely requires that this road be repaired." Then, Hood ordered Roddey to destroy the railroad in the territory the Union forces had vacated and he ordered him to join the main concentration of Hood's army. Trooper James Walton, 10th Indiana Cavalry and part of the Union troops evacuating Decatur, observed Roddey's troopers moving into town just as the Federal troops were withdrawing. Walton explained that the Federal troops left little behind: "We burned everything we could not take. I think they were badly disappointed because the town before them was all burning."[3]

Cavalry Actions

The day began early at cavalry headquarters on December 1. At 2:00 a.m., Wilson ordered his commanders to keep a close eye out for the enemy attempting to swing past the cavalry screen. Stewart's brigade had just returned from an expedition to Nolensville, and Hammond's brigade held a position near Triune. Neither commander found any concentrations of enemy cavalry in those areas, nor did other cavalry scouts find anything to the west or north of the Harpeth River. Schofield's aide-de-camp told Wilson to cover the rear of the infantry columns: "If the enemy press heavily he [Schofield] wishes you to act stubbornly on the defensive." At 9:00 a.m., Wilson had his screen in place with Hatch, Hammond, and Johnson moving north on different roads and still observed no enemy cavalry, but that did not last long. By noon, Wilson found himself pushed by Forrest's cavalry. "Since my last the enemy has begun skirmishing with my rear near Wilson's Mill.... A prisoner from the rebel infantry, just brought in, says the rebels crossed Harpeth early this morning and are marching on."[4]

Forrest had his cavalry in the saddle in the morning in pursuit of the Union column. As Chalmers' division moved across the battlefield, one cavalryman, James Dinkins, wrote: "[T]he scene was indescribable.... Notwithstanding General Schofield retreated about two A.M., leaving his dead and wounded in our hands, our army was badly whipped. The men knew that no earthly good had been accomplished, and that the flower of the army had fallen. They had hoped for brilliant results in Tennessee, but met disaster."[5]

Forrest crossed the Harpeth River at dawn and advanced north on Wilson Pike. He found the Federal cavalry rearguard at Wilson's Crossroads and he ordered Morton's battery to open fire. The Federals, holding the crossroads, attempted to stop a flanking movement by Buford's division, but Buford led his cavalry in a charge and successfully captured several prisoners in the skirmish. The action at this location was scarcely mentioned in the Union records, but Hammond's and Stewart's brigades

Chapter Ten. Hood Marches to Nashville

carried most of the fight. As Wilson's cavalry screened the withdrawal to Nashville, the 13th Indiana Cavalry scouted to the east and found no significant numbers of enemy cavalry near Nolensville. However, Colonel Gilbert M.L. Johnson, commanding the 13th Indiana operating in the Murfreesboro area, reported the aftermath of the fight at Wilson's Crossroads when he found some stragglers of the 11th Indiana Cavalry who reported "they have been severely dealt with and routed" in a fight eight miles east of Nolensville. These troopers reported the effective use of Morton's artillery to dislodge the Union defenders. Johnson gathered two companies of Major Jehu Hannum's, 11th Indiana Cavalry of Stewart's brigade, which had been routed, organized them, and sent them toward Nashville. Johnson's regiment was three miles east of the skirmish and did not participate in the fight, but he was clearly concerned about these events, writing after Hannum continued northward, "whether he reached Nashville or not I cannot state..."[6]

The extent of the participation of Stewart's brigade in the fight at Wilson's Crossroad is unknown, but there are a few accounts of Hammond's fight with Buford. The only mention of the affair from the Union commanders came from Wilson, who wrote this was a "pretty sharp skirmish at Brentwood." Hammond's brigade had moved to Wilson's Mill or Crossroads, and trailed Stewart's brigade of the Fifth Division, which had halted to feed the mounts. Hammond, on rearguard, delayed too long because of Stewart's decision and Buford caught the Federal cavalry. Wilson recorded Hammond was able to extract his command "without material difficulty"; however, the 9th Indiana Cavalry made the first contact with Forrest's cavalry and after a "hotly contested fight" Hammond's brigade withdrew in the direction of Murfreesboro.[7]

Captain R.H. Crowder, 11th Indiana Cavalry, gave a firsthand account of his reg-

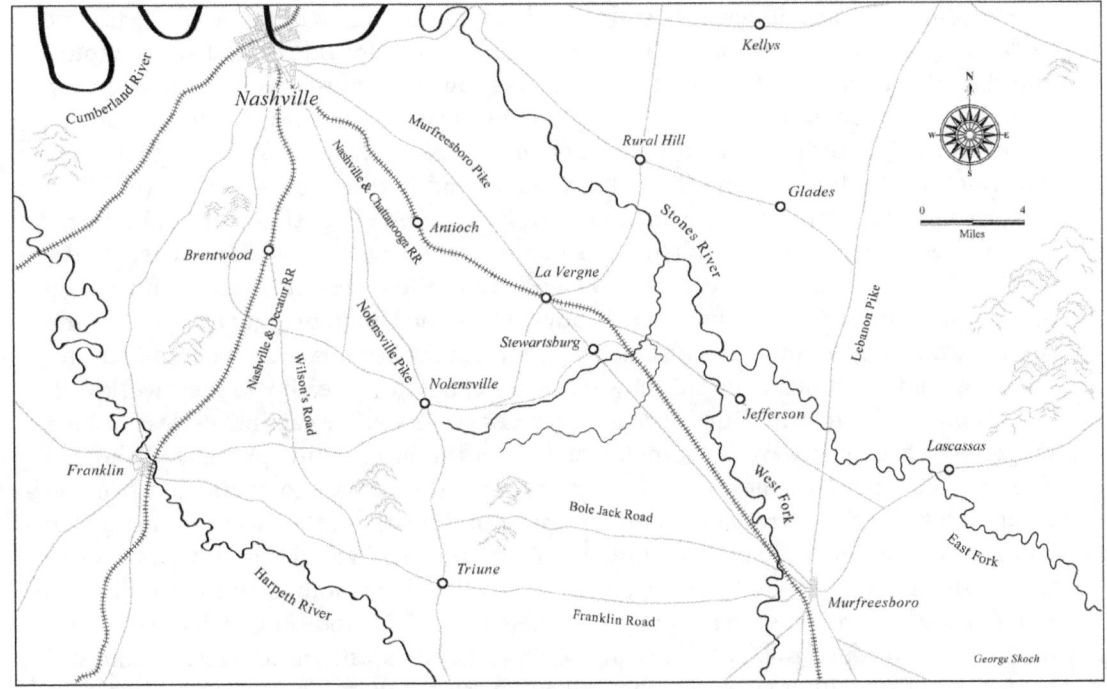

Middle Tennessee, 1864.

iment at Wilson's Crossroads. The Indiana cavalry sent some companies out as skirmishers to meet Buford's approaching horsemen. "We ... drove the Reb skirmishers, killing one man, and advancing our line when the Rebs brought forward a piece of artillery. Well, so far we were concerned. I wasn't as fearful of the artillery as of the small guns and I never thought of it driving our horses back.... But as soon as the artillery opened fire our cavalry began to fall back and the cavalry skirmishers left in a hurry but I thought the men holding our horses would remain and the cavalry skirmishers were doing no good. And so I still fired away.... I told them to let them go to thunder with their cannons. They couldn't hurt us. But when the Rebs saw our cavalry falling back they came forward yelling. A whole Regt. came charging down a lane toward us. And we wisely concluded that he who fights and runs away might live to fight another day. So we started but we did not run. We stopped at every house and fence and gave the Rebs a shot. I told the boys our horses were behind a little hill not far from where we left them and I thought they were but when we got there they were half a mile from us and still coming.... I came to a horse soon, all saddled. I mounted but the horse wouldn't go and the boys got ahead of me." Once in saddle and getting his horse to finally move, Captain Crowder ordered a volley into the swiftest of the advancing Confederates and then "skedaddled."[8]

The 9th Indiana Cavalry, which had yet to experience a direct fight with the enemy, also experienced a difficult time under the Confederate guns at Wilson's Crossroads. Sergeant Major Daniel W. Comstock wrote: "To those of us who had not yet seen a rebel under arms the suspense, the constant expectation of battle, was more trying than actual fighting afterwards proved. On this day when the sound of musketry drew nearer and nearer, we were drawn up in line, and with drawn sabres awaited the appearance of the enemy and an order to 'charge.'" The Indiana cavalrymen had not long to wait. The 9th Indiana was still having breakfast when a picket came riding to the main line exclaiming, "the enemy was upon us." The orders rang out for the 9th Indiana to mount and then it was moved at a walk down the pike toward Buford's approaching cavalry. Soon, the regiment came under an irregular fire from the enemy positioned on the ridge. "At the first discharge a horse went down; directly a man was shot; another horse fell. Thicker and thicker came the bullets; fiercer and fiercer grew the rebel yell." This was the introduction of the 9th Indiana Cavalry to serious fighting and the regiment was ordered to dismount and fall into line behind a stone wall. This offered safety to the troopers but their mounts were being killed behind them. Major Virgil Lyon rode up and down the line yelling, "Give 'em hell, boys." Once the Union regiment moved behind the wall, the Confederate attack stalled and the enemy artillery was ordered forward. "The boys did not flinch from this new experience, but kept steadily to their work with the coolness of veterans. Our Maynard carbines were weak weapons, useless at long range—our fire must have been ineffectual..." As the 9th Indiana exchanged shots, a rider arrived from Hammond ordering the retreat. This proved to be difficult because it exposed the Indiana troopers to direct fire from the enemy, they were almost out of ammunition, and now there were more men than horses. In addition, Buford's cavalry was closing in. Finally, the Indianans made a dash for their mounts and several had to ride double; Buford's cavalrymen were on their heels. "On and on through wood and field, rushing through rail fences, tearing down stone walls with bleeding hands and still behind, and from either side, the rebel yell and hissing bullets." A sigh of relief went up as the 9th Indiana reached the main concentration of Hammond's brigade, only to be dismayed as they dismounted. Immediately, the other regiment they had just reached, mounted and spurred their horses to the rear. "The abandoned, dismounted men took to a cornfield and many of them escaped." The fight went in favor of the Southern cavalry, but it also paid a heavy price. Stephen Jordan, 9th Tennessee Cavalry (CSA) wrote: "[O]ur loss considerable. Yankees driven."[9]

After the successful actions at Wilson's Crossroads, Forrest sent Jackson's and Buford's divisions to Brentwood. Chalmers, who began the day still on the left flank, saw light action during the advance toward Nashville. Chalmers moved his division northward on Hillsboro Pike, forded the Harpeth River west of Franklin, and continued to Brentwood. Next, he moved his division east to Franklin Pike, hoping to catch the retreating Federal army or rearguard, but they had already passed. Chalmers joined Buford and Jackson at Brentwood and then Forrest, still hoping to catch the retreating Union column, discovered the Union infantry had passed up Franklin Pike several hours earlier. Once Forrest arrived at the hills outside of Nashville, he knew his quarry had reached the defenses of the town. He set his blacksmiths and farriers the task of caring for the mounts. He ordered his farriers to recondition the mounts from new shoes, to feeding and watering the horses. Forrest told his men to work day and night until the mounts were fully ready for the next battle. While the horses were groomed and cared for, the local pro–Confederate residents heartily welcomed the cavalry in gray.[10]

Wilson, on the other hand, moved the bulk of his cavalry to within five miles of Nashville on Nolensville Pike while the infantry moved on the western roads. He wrote to Thomas that he found a good defensive position. "If you can protect my right flank by infantry we can beat Forrest's whole force.... No enemy in my front yet." Wilson was running low on ammunition and he requested that Beaumont forward the 4th U.S. Cavalry along with the cavalry troops which had been newly equipped in Nashville, plus any stragglers they found, to Thompson's Chapel, Wilson's new headquarters. To enhance his position, he also asked Beaumont to send three artillery batteries to this position.[11]

Beaumont replied that the cavalry at Nashville had been armed, equipped, and in line stretching from the Cumberland River to the Murfreesboro Pike under command of Brigadier General Louis Watkins of Edward McCook's First Division. Watkins had been assigned command of the cavalry at Nashville while Wilson remained in the field and Watkins' own mounted cavalry brigade was expected to arrive later in the day. Beaumont planned to send reinforcements to Wilson; however, these orders were countermanded before they were implemented. At 7:30 p.m., Wilson ordered the withdrawal of the cavalry to the friendly confines of Nashville beginning at 6:00 a.m. the next morning. Just after moving into the fortifications, Forrest arrived with two divisions, again too late.[12]

December 2: Trouble for Thomas

Over the past three weeks, George Thomas scrambled to pull together the forces that Sherman assigned to him, but those in Washington immediately disapproved of his actions despite the impressive victory at Franklin. Thomas prepared IV Corps, XXIII Corps, Steedman's District of the Etowah, and A.J. Smith's XVI Corps to meet the enemy, but this force had just been concentrated the day before. Edwin Stanton wrote to Grant: "The President feels solicitous about the disposition of General Thomas to lay in fortifications for an indefinite period 'until Wilson gets equipments.' This looks like the McClellan and Rosecrans strategy of do nothing and let the rebels raid the country." Granted, Thomas complained that his cavalry did not equal Forrest's, but he was known to be a slow and deliberate commander while also being one of the most reliable and efficient in the Union Army. The next two weeks would mark one of the most unfortunate sets of communications and decisions made toward one of the Union's best generals as Grant and Stanton contemplated Thomas' removal.[13]

Grant's initial response to Stanton seemed to support Thomas and he suggested that Stanton give Thomas the authority to seize any mounts, even from loyal citizens, that he needed to mount his cavalry, a request Stanton granted later that day. He cautioned: "It looks as if Forrest will flank around Thomas until Thomas is equal to him in cavalry." Grant wrote to Thomas on December 2, "If Hood is permitted to remain quietly about Nashville, you will lose all the road back to Chattanooga, and possibly have to abandon the line of the Tennessee…. [Y]ou should attack him before he fortifies." Grant followed with another message a few hours later. "After the repulse of Hood at Franklin, it looks to me that instead of falling back to Nashville, we should have taken the offensive against the enemy where he was … give him no peace." These communications would mark the beginning of many messages over the next week urging Thomas to advance against Hood.[14]

Thomas replied to Grant with an explanation of his plan. Until just the day before, he had fewer than 5,000 men to defend Nashville and Schofield had been pursued by a superior number of enemy infantry. The arrival of Smith, Steedman and Schofield made his position a strong one. Still, Thomas felt a deficiency of cavalry: "I now have enough infantry to assume the offensive, if I had more cavalry, and will take the field anyhow as soon as the remainder of General McCook's division of cavalry reaches here, which I hope it will do in two or three days." Then, Thomas reminded his superiors that his position had been dictated by Sherman's desire to march to the sea. Sherman had left Thomas with the "two weakest corps of General Sherman's army and all the dismounted cavalry except one brigade, and the task of reorganizing and equipping has met with many delays, which have enabled Hood to take advantage of my crippled condition." Thomas promised to fight in a few days, and he followed with a similar message to Henry Halleck stressing his efforts to get his command concentrated. "I have labored under many disadvantages since assuming the direction of affairs here, not the least of which was the reorganizing, remounting, and equipping of a cavalry force sufficient to contend with Forrest."[15]

As Hood approached Nashville, he placed his army on the heights south of the city. Stephen Lee's corps formed the center of the Confederate line on Franklin Pike. Stewart's corps moved to his left and Cheatham's corps moved to the right. Hood ordered: "The entire line of the army will curve forward…. Each position will be strengthened as soon as taken, and extended as fast as strengthened. Artillery will be placed in all favorable positions…. Not a cartridge of any kind will be burned until further orders, unless the enemy should advance on us." Forrest also made some important decisions during the day including transferring his cavalry troops without arms to the infantry.[16]

After arriving at Nashville, Forrest shifted his focus to the Nashville–Chattanooga Railroad which ran through Murfreesboro to Chattanooga. On December 2, he sent Chalmers to the western flank of the army to guard the Hillsboro and Hardin pikes. With the capitol of Tennessee clearly in sight, he sent Buford's and Jackson's divisions

View of Nashville. Hood advanced his troops to the heights south of the city (Library of Congress).

to the eastern flank. He posted Buford's division at Asylum Hill, the place where Buford previously fought during the Stones River Campaign almost two years ago. Jackson was assigned duty protecting Nashville and Mill Creek Pike. Soon, the infantry arrived and this allowed Forrest opportunities for more offensive action; he ordered Buford's division to begin destroying the railroad and attacking blockhouses from Nashville to Murfreesboro. As Forrest moved toward Murfreesboro, Chalmers initially assigned Rucker's brigade to hold Franklin Pike and moved Biffle's small brigade to cover Hillsboro and Hardin pikes.[17]

While focusing on the railroads near Murfreesboro, Forrest intended his cavalry to do what they did best—raid the rear of the Federal forces at Nashville. Tyree Bell wanted to make a raid on Gallatin and destroy the Louisville & Nashville Railroad while picking off any Federal garrisons that were vulnerable. Forrest also considered sending the remainder of Buford's and Jackson's cavalry on similar missions. Just prior to Bell leaving for Gallatin, Hood's orders arrived for Forrest to move on Murfreesboro.[18]

As Forrest moved his cavalry south of Nashville, Wilson settled into position on the north side of the Cumberland River at Edgefield, while he attempted to re-fit and organize his cavalry. He still had problems with his division commander in Memphis. Benjamin Grierson continued his litany of reasons for delaying the movement of cavalry from Memphis and this time it was because the troopers had not been paid in six months. In contrast, John Croxton whose cavalry had been such a reliable part of the defense against Hood's army wrote to Wilson that evening requesting just 48 hours respite. He noted: "I desire also to have two regiments paid that have drawn no pay for twelve months. For more than three months my command has been upon the most arduous service, separated from its transportation and baggage, and needs rest, and must have it."[19]

Chalmers Blockades the Cumberland River— Naval Skirmish at Bell's Mill

Over the past few months, Forrest had taken aim at the riverboats on the Tennessee and Cumberland Rivers, including actions in October and November at Eastport and Johnsonville, and now Chalmers directed Lieutenant Colonel David Kelley to blockade the Cumberland River west of Nashville. On December 3, Kelley with 300 men and two pieces of field artillery moved into position to enforce a blockade about 12 miles west of Nashville at a point called Bell's Mill. With this small force, he captured two transports on their way to Nashville loaded with horses and mules on the first day of his blockade. Kelley, an ordained Methodist minister and referred to as one of Forrest's "right hand men," had served in the Confederate cavalry since 1861 and had experience dealing with riverboats through his actions at Eastport and Johnsonville. He commanded the newly consolidated 3rd Tennessee Cavalry (CSA) and his first barrage from two 10-pounder Parrott guns of T.H. Rice's battery resulted in the capture of the *Prima Donna* and the *Prairie State* while the third disabled transport, *Magnet*, evaded capture by drifting down stream.[20]

Colonel Israel Garrard, 7th Ohio Cavalry, had his command guarding the ferries (north and west) of Nashville on December 3 and at 8:00 p.m. reported the attack on Federal riverboats. The captain and crew of the boat went ashore and then sought assistance from a proper gunboat to retrieve the craft. An hour later, Lieutenant Commander Le Roy Fitch, commanding the

Colonel David Kelley commanded the Confederate cavalry which blockaded the Cumberland River west of Nashville (*Life of Lieutenant General, Nathan Bedford Forrest*, John Allan Wyeth, 1899).

Chapter Ten. Hood Marches to Nashville

9th and 10th Districts, Mississippi Squadron, ordered a fleet of boats to assist the captain when he received the information that Kelley had artillery planted on the south side of the river firing on transports. Fitch decided that he needed to recapture the transports or force the Confederates to burn them, therefore depriving them of the booty on the boats. It was a dark and cloudy night when Fitch moved the *Carondelet, Fairplay, Moose, Reindeer,* and *Silver Lake* in the direction of the two captured boats. Upon arriving at Bell's Mill, Fitch ordered the *Carondelet* to run the battery, firing on Kelley's position with grape and canister in the process. Then, the four other boats ran the shore battery, turned, and fired as they moved past the artillery. When *Carondelet,* leading the way, opened fire, Kelley's cavalrymen and artillery, positioned in an upper and lower battery, returned fire. Fitch believed the smoke from his guns and the smokestacks obscured the view of those on the boats while Kelley had better visibility. Fitch had to wait for the smoke to disperse because he feared the boats might collide, but Fitch's gunners kept firing in the meantime. The Federal boats' barrages finally silenced the musket fire, but the Confederate artillery continued to hammer away, with most of the shells passing overhead. Fitch's boat, *Carondelet,* was hit twice in the fight, receiving only minor damage. There was just too much firepower on the river and Kelley's guns were finally silenced. The Federal river forces towed the two captured transports along with most of the recaptured prisoners and supplies, but the horses and mules had already been moved ashore. By 6:00 a.m. on December 4, the Federal gunboats, plus the damaged boat *Magnet,* "moved eastward past Kelley's position without firing a shot and returned to Nashville."[21]

The gunboats silenced the artillery on shore, but the Confederate cavalrymen still had plenty of fight in them. Trooper A.C. McLeary, 12th Tennessee (CSA), noted that some of his regiment had sampled the alcohol on the captured boats. Emboldened by the alcohol, every time the Union gunboats fired, they stood and yelled as loud as they could. Their courage from the bottle extended to their building a fire so that the gunboats had a better target during the barrage.[22]

Fitch wrote to Thomas that he had silenced Kelley's artillery for a time, but he

USS *Neosho* (watercolor by Dr. Oscar Parkes, courtesy Dr. Oscar Parkes, London, England, 1936. U.S. Naval History and Heritage Command Photograph).

cautioned that it was temporary. He silenced them but there was no assurance that the Confederate artillery would not just be rolled back into place the next day. Fitch planned to return with an iron-clad that morning to observe the situation, but he urged Thomas to stop the river traffic until the position was secured. Richard Johnson's cavalry scouted the area around Bell's Mill on the north bank, finding no evidence of the Confederate cavalry attempting to cross the river, but Kelley's pickets were observed across the river.²³

Hood liked what Kelley had accomplished and sent a message to keep up the good work along the river. Kelley received a more direct order from Hood on December 4: "[Y]ou will continue to stop all the transports you can, and if an infantry brigade will assist it can be ordered to you from General Stewart." Elsewhere, Chalmers' cavalry remained unengaged on December 5, but on December 6, he gained some greater flexibility in regard to blockading the river again. The bulk of Forrest's cavalry had been moved to Murfreesboro and the infantry relieved Rucker's brigade from duty on the Hillsboro Pike. Chalmers ordered most the brigade, plus two 12-pounder howitzers toward Kelley's position on the Cumberland River.²⁴

Fitch again decided to attempt to move some of the transports, which had been

Sketch of gunboats on the Cumberland River near Nashville (Library of Congress).

held at Nashville, past the enemy positions at Bell's Mill. This time Fitch was aboard the iron-clad monitor, the USS *Neosho*. Fitch kept the rest of his convoy a few miles behind him as he approached Kelley's position. He soon "discovered a large rebel force and were at once opened upon by a very heavy volley of musketry and some fourteen pieces of artillery above, abreast of, and below us. I at once directed the pilots to run slow, and returned the fire." In contrast to Fitch's report about the large number of Confederate artillery, Chalmers just mentioned Kelley being reinforced with two additional guns. The USS *Neosho* fired grape and canister and silenced much of the musket fire. Based on the Confederate positions on the bluffs of the river, Kelley had difficulty in lowering the muzzles of the cannons and his artillery did little damage to the iron-clad.[25]

Fitch sent the convoy of transports back to Nashville and the *Neosho* and *Carondelet* returned fire on the Confederate position in an artillery duel. The *Neosho* ran the batteries and the two iron-clads fired on the Confederate guns, ultimately silencing them at dusk. "We passed up again just after dark, but were only saluted with two guns as we passed and then could get no more responses." The *Neosho* received 100 hits during the day, "but received no injury whatever," wrote Fitch. Not included in Fitch's report was a shell which penetrated the magazine, but failed to explode.[26]

Chalmers felt he had greater success. "[A] monitor appeared in front of our batteries and attempted to force the passage of the river, but was badly damaged and driven back, and on several subsequent occasions fleets of gun-boats repeated the attempt without success." Fitch reported no such Confederate successes on that day: "The 7th instant we were employed coaling and mending one of the *Neosho*'s steam pipes, which was leaking badly, and also repairing one of the *Carondelet*'s boilers, which was also leaking badly." The situation at Bell's Mill would remain unchanged until the Battle of Nashville began on December 15. In the meantime, Chalmers had enough cavalry in position and enough guns to blockade the Federal river fleet.[27]

December 3–4

On December 3, Wilson's cavalry at Nashville had guard duty and some itchy trigger fingers nearly resulted in firing on unsuspecting Federal infantry. Luckily, no one was wounded. Wilson ordered his men to start collecting mounts and he assigned the various geographic areas to different divisions to ensure there were no conflicts or overlap. For the rest of the cavalry, he sent out several scouting missions to keep an eye on the Confederate forces.[28]

Hammond established his headquarters near the Cumberland River on the Gallatin Road and guarded the eastern flank. Hammond had an interesting day on December 2 as he attempted to send out smaller scouting parties, but they were attacked by Confederate forces. A battalion scouting south of Nashville was chased back to within three miles of Nashville by a significant body of Confederate cavalry. Hammond found, wherever he sent his scouting parties, Confederate cavalry in bands of 75 to 100 men were waiting. "I will try to disperse some of them. I find that I cannot send less than fifty men three miles from camp." Hammond also discovered that horses and cattle were being stolen or furnished to the enemy by Southern sympathizing citizens. Hammond lamented: "A crying evil exists in the fact that almost every citizen, without reference to politics, has protection from some general or other for his horses, mules, forage, stock, etc.; without trespassing on these, it will puzzle any one to subsist his command." Hammond even reverted to dressing small groups of cavalrymen in civilian clothes to scout the south side of the Cumberland River to avoid attracting the attention of the Southern mounted forces. As Hammond moved his command, he found the Louisville and Nashville Railroad at Gallatin only lightly defended, a location Tyree Bell planned to attack. Should Forrest attack that location, he would be able to easily close the railroad for several months, just as John Hunt Morgan had done in 1862.[29]

While the Union army focused on concentrating its forces and strengthening the cavalry, Hood assessed his situation and began to call for reinforcements. The various expeditions by Union forces paralyzed much of the effort to reinforce Hood. Kirby Smith in the Trans-Mississippi was urged to make some action to stymie the Federal reinforcements from Missouri and Arkansas. Hood even called for Breckinridge's forces, already engaged in eastern Tennessee, to join his army. He resorted to drawing men from the valuable Confederate depot at Corinth which supplied Hood's own army. All the while, the Confederate commanders tried to keep the Union forces at bay at other locations. The Confederate commanders appealed to governors in various states to provide militia to replace troops which could be moved to the front. To make matters worse for the Hood's army, some of his soldiers had not been paid in a year, resulting in lower morale. In addition, the soldiers lacked some of basic needs and Beauregard wrote: "Our armies in this military division are sadly in need of every description of military supplies—horses and mules for artillery and other transportation, blankets, clothing, bacon, etc., are needed." This would prove a cold, wet campaign for the Confederate soldiers.[30]

Meanwhile, the Confederates strengthened their position overlooking Nashville and the weather continued to plague the poorly clad soldiers. Newspaper reporters converged on the Southern commanders and asked their plans. Cheatham curtly responded to one reporter that "Hood had orders to go to Nashville or go to hell." In an ironic situation, The Rev. Charles Quintard, future Episcopal bishop of Tennessee, bunked with Forrest due to the lack of adequate shelter. The irony of this was not lost on the soldiers who commented: "It was the lion and lamb lying down together."[31]

December 5—Telegrams from Washington

Henry Halleck was not insensitive to the situation that Thomas faced in Nashville and as the telegraph wires hummed, Halleck reminded Grant that Thomas worked very hard to pull his forces together. Halleck also stressed to Grant that it had taken A.J. Smith 31 days to reach Nashville after Rosecrans received his orders. Thomas optimistically told Halleck that his position was a good one and "hope to be able to report 10,000 cavalry mounted and equipped in less than a week, when I shall feel able to march against Hood." At Nashville, Thomas and Wilson struggled to find enough mounts for the cavalry despite claims from Washington that more than enough horses had been sent to the cavalry. Halleck sent a message to Grant that if Wilson did not have enough horses "it may be safely assumed that the cavalry of that army will never be mounted." Thomas wanted to avoid the inevitable argument of whose numbers were correct. Thomas merely stated: "I have seen General Wilson tonight, who encourages me to hope that he will be able to mount 6,000 or 7,000 in three days from this time."

Meanwhile, Grant pushed Thomas to take the offensive against Hood. "Time strengthens him, in all probability, as much as it does you."[32]

Thomas replied later that night, asking patience on the part of those in Washington. He calmly told Halleck that Hood's advance had stopped south of Nashville, implying that immediate action was unnecessary. Thomas' soldiers agreed with his assessment. A Missouri soldier wrote, "what Hood is doing we dont know, nor care a great deal, if he fights us here we can whip him." Hood was giving Thomas the time he needed to prepare for his attack. Thomas told Halleck that he would move against Hood on December 7, two days hence. Thomas knew that Hood's supply line was stretched and the delay stressed Hood's army while benefiting his own. From the west, Thomas received an apology from Rosecrans about the delay of Winslow's cavalry and he explained the delay resulted from a lack of horses, but Rosecrans' days were numbered and a couple of days later Grenville Dodge superseded Rosecrans in Missouri. It remains somewhat a mystery why Rosecrans was removed, but Grant held a long dislike for Rosecrans.[33]

Meanwhile, the apparent never-ending excuses for the delay of moving cavalry from Memphis to Nashville continued. Despite the various promises and urgings, Winslow's cavalry would not reach Nashville in time to assist in the upcoming battle and the problem was not with Winslow. Washburn and ultimately Major General Napoleon Dana, who gained command of the Department of Mississippi on December 8, did not want to give up the cavalry regardless of the communications which were exchanged the weeks leading up to the battle. Newly promoted Lieutenant Colonel Henry E. Noyes, cavalry assistant inspector general, met with Washburn in Memphis about releasing Winslow and gained his agreement to release part of the command. Noyes wrote of Winslow, who had been recently wounded: "I judge him to be a very efficient officer.... He was perfectly informed on the most minute points ... of his command, and seemed to take great pride in it. I think his opinion worthy of more than ordinary consideration.... In Memphis I learned that General Grierson was at his home in Jacksonville, Ill. He had been absent several weeks..."[34]

The Third Battle of Murfreesboro (December 4–7): "The Battle of the Cedars"

Murfreesboro was the second important location where the Union forces concentrated in Middle Tennessee and about 8,000 Union soldiers defended Fortress Rosecrans, the fort just north of the town. General Lovell Rousseau, whose headquarters had been in Nashville, moved to Murfreesboro on November 28 and was joined by General Robert Milroy two days later. Rousseau and Milroy had orders from Thomas to hold Murfreesboro if attacked. Faced with a large, concentrated Union army at Nashville, Hood was faced with a dilemma—how to defeat a larger entrenched enemy force. Hood had planned to defeat the Union forces in detail whenever possible and now, he considered the Union forces at Murfreesboro. First, the troops at that location proved to be a problem, because having 8,000 enemy troops in his rear, was a constant threat. Secondly, Hood needed to get Thomas away from his entrenchments at Nashville. Hood decided to seize the initiative to defeat part of the Unions forces. Hood wrote: "Should this force attempt to leave Murfreesborough, or should the enemy attempt to re-enforce it, I hope to be able to defeat them." William Bate's infantry division, which marched toward Nashville after the Battle of Franklin, was re-directed to Murfreesboro to begin destroying the railroad there. Hood assigned Forrest to command an expedition to Murfreesboro, including authority over Bate's infantry. Forrest left Chalmers' division at Nashville and pulled Jackson's and Buford's divisions to Murfreesboro.[35]

The Confederate cavalry began a series of attacks on the blockhouses along the railroad running from Nashville to Murfreesboro on December 2. Blockhouse No. 2 was attacked that day and the unexpected arrival of a train loaded with the 14th and 44th U.S. Colored Infantry from the District of the Etowah allowed the Federal defenders to hold out under a barrage of seven guns which fired 460 shells on the blockhouse from 10:00 a.m. until dark. A staff officer of Armstrong's brigade wrote, "Our guns made shingles & sand fly out of the block house, until darkness came on." Then, the Union troops evacuated the blockhouse with only minor casualties. Forrest began picking off other blockhouses which protected the railroad and bridges south of Nashville. Blockhouse No. 1, four miles south of Nashville, surrendered on December 3, but

Blockhouse on the Nashville and Chattanooga Railroad (Library of Congress).

the capture of the blockhouses was no easy task as Abraham Buford soon discovered. While considering how to dislodge the defenders in Blockhouse No. 1, Forrest rode up to him and demanded that he capture the blockhouse. Buford, known to be testy himself, snapped: "How do you expect me to take it, General?" Forrest answered, "Stop the port-holes with rails and burn it." After this exchange, Buford called on Morton's battery to force the surrender. Next, Buford's division surrounded Blockhouse No. 3, near Antioch, and 32 defenders surrendered after a 36-hour attack. In total, the initial operations netted 150 prisoners, the destruction of a blockhouse and two stockades. Forrest received orders on December 4 to proceed to Murfreesboro and in conjunction with Bate, "to see if it was practicable to take the place." Then, Forrest moved the two cavalry divisions to Murfreesboro while leaving Colonel George H. Nixon's 20th Tennessee Cavalry (CSA) of Bell's Brigade with 250 men to watch Nashville–Murfreesboro Pike northward to the Cumberland River.[36]

Bate Attacks Blockhouse No. 7

The change in orders to include the destruction of the Union forces at Murfreesboro did not sit well with Bate. He questioned how such a small force would compel 8,000 Federal forces to give up Fortress Rosecrans. Bate moved his division via Wilkinson Turnpike which crossed Overall Creek about five miles northeast of Murfreesboro. Bate wanted to reach Overall Creek by the end of the day and as he approached the creek and found Blockhouse No. 7, he advanced three regiments of Florida Infantry (1st–3rd Florida, 7th Florida, 1st–4th Florida regiments of Finley's brigade) on the west bank of the creek supported by Washington's battery (three 12-pound Napoleons). Once in place, Bate ordered the artillery to fire on the blockhouse across the creek which guarded the railroad bridge. Brigadier General Thomas. B. Smith commanding Tyler's Georgia and Tennessee brigade served as the reserve in the attack on the blockhouse while Brigadier General Henry Jackson's Georgia brigade started tearing up the railroad tracks. Earlier that morning, Rousseau had ordered the 13th Indiana Cavalry to reconnoiter the area from Murfreesboro north to La Vergne. At noon, Colonel Gilbert Marquis LaFayette Johnson's 13th Indiana Cavalry encountered a detachment of 5th Tennessee Cavalry (U.S.) and discovered that the enemy was attacking Blockhouse No. 7. Johnson was an experienced officer who began his service in October 1861 as a lieutenant in the 2nd Indiana Cavalry and he had most recently served as a staff officer for Thomas. As Johnson scouted toward the blockhouse, the Confederate artillery opened on the Union troopers and Johnson sent some couriers riding back to Murfreesboro as the cavalrymen fell into battle line. Johnson had expected his command to ride to La Vergne and camp there for the night, but now he found himself in a heated fight along Overall Creek. As he advanced, he pushed the enemy skirmishers to the north side of the creek. Johnson wrote: "A brisk skirmish was kept up, the creek intervening, the enemy at the same time opening on us with three pieces of artillery." Johnson's regiment had been assigned duty at Huntsville since the end of May and had seen relatively light action. In October, six companies had been moved to defend Paducah and had returned to the area near La Vergne only a couple of days before.[37]

After receiving the report from the 13th Indiana, Milroy, who wanted desperately to get back into the war, got his chance. He marched ahead with 8th Minnesota, 61st

Illinois, 174th Ohio Infantries, and Lieutenant John McGurrin's section of the 13th New York Artillery. Milroy hurried toward the sound of gunfire between Johnson's cavalry and Bate's artillery and infantry. The Federal infantry reached the blockhouse in the evening, and Milroy moved a skirmish line to the creek while McGurrin unlimbered his guns on a rise about 900 yards from the Confederate position. From Bate's vantage, he observed Milroy's arrival and his movement on Bate's left flank attempted to prevent the Confederate infantry from crossing over the creek. Milroy ordered the 61st Illinois to form as skirmishers and the sent the 8th Minnesota to the vicinity of the blockhouse which rested near the railroad crossing on Overall Creek, one half mile north of Nashville Pike. Milroy told the commander of the 8th Minnesota that once he reached his location to flank the enemy battery if practical. Milroy advanced his skirmishers across the creek with most of them crossing over the bridge on Nashville Pike "under a galling fire, and drove back the rebel sharpshooters." Once the skirmishers crossed the bridge, the 174th Ohio Infantry followed while receiving fire from infantry and artillery, and then fell into battle line. Milroy misread the forces he faced, supposing them to be only Forrest's dismounted cavalry. When Bate saw the Union troops falling into line in front of his position, he ordered Tyler's brigade, which had been serving as a reserve, forward.[38]

Milroy reasoned, with his infantry in place on the north side of the creek, that a good cavalry charge would cause the enemy "cavalry" to break off the fight. Milroy found Johnson more than ready to take on the task on the flat ground north of Overall Creek. "Colonel Johnson with his gallant regiment ... were anxious to try the experiment," wrote Milroy. It was approaching dusk, and Johnson moved his cavalry across the bridge and passed through a gap in the line of the 174th Ohio Infantry. The 13th Indiana Cavalry fell into line and at the shout, "Charge!" the troopers spurred their horses and thundered forward. "The colonel moved forward on the enemy in the most splendid and impetuous style," wrote Milroy.[39]

Bate felt that the arrival of Tyler's infantry helped defeat Johnson's cavalry attack and he gave credit to his artillery which blasted the 13th Indiana Cavalry with double canister. Bate explained that his Florida brigade was outnumbered and the Union volleys ripped into his line driving Lash's men (Finley's Brigade) back from the creek. Then, Bate ordered Jackson's brigade into the position held by the Floridians and Tyler sent a full volley into the Milroy's infantry sending it back over the creek. According to Bate, this gave him possession of the field.[40]

General William Bate (Alabama Department of Archives and History, Montgomery, Alabama).

Bate's claims of forcing Milroy

back after the cavalry charge were disputed by not only Milroy but by his own artillery commander. So close was the cavalry charge on the Confederate artillery, Joseph A. Charlaron, commanding the battery, recalled his own expected demise. "[T]he enemy's line of horses, madly coming at us, unchecked by Leverich's canister. There was no time to halt, to come into battery, to do anything but meet the clash, which I saw, from the impetus the cavalry line had gathered, was but an instant off. Turning to Johnson, I said: 'Leverich has failed to check them! They're on us! Have you a weapon?' 'Not a penknife,' he replied; and, as I raised my sword arm to guard my head from an expected saber stroke, as a few more strides would bring the foe and us together, I realized that the horses alone of that line of battle were charging us. The riders had been swept off by Leverich's canister. On they came, however, at unabated speed, some thirty or forty horses, riderless, but aligned, sweeping like a whirlwind past us through the intervals of the seconds that followed, over guns and men and disorganized infantry, and far to our rear,

Gilbert M. L. Johnson led a cavalry charge on the Confederate position along Overall Creek (Mollus Mass Civil War Collection, United States Army Heritage and Education Center, Carlisle, Pennsylvania).

adding to the confusion that prevailed. This line gone, the second or other squadron could be dimly descried in confusion—its riders wheeling about and around to retrace their steps as fast as possible—their regiment cured of further aggressiveness on that flank." Then, looking for his supporting infantry, he exclaimed: "Our infantry that had been around me, with but few exceptions, had disappeared."[41]

The charge of the 13th Indiana Cavalry caused much excitement on both sides of the line as it rode directly for Chalaron's artillery. Johnson's troopers were plagued with the infantry-style Enfield muskets which allowed only one shot and could only be reloaded on horseback with the greatest difficulty. Just as the charge began, the Confederate artillerymen, realizing their peril, shifted its fire to Johnson's cavalry, checking the Federal horsemen no more than 50 yards away. However, this charge and the advance of the Union infantry had unnerved the Confederate infantry which withdrew. In return, the Confederate guns continued to shell the 13th Indiana as it returned to the Union lines. Then, the cannoneers turned their attentions to the advancing infantry, shelling them; however, without infantry support, the battery could not maintain its position, and it limbered and moved to the rear.[42]

Johnson ordered his troopers back across the creek under the cover of the creek bank, but not before he received some shots from some skittish Union soldiers in the blockhouse. The light was failing but Johnson, after reorganizing his regiment, rode forward again around the hill in front of his position only to find Bate had retired.[43]

Milroy saw that Johnson could not reach the artillery as the cavalry angled away from the Confederate line. Then, he sent the 174th Ohio forward "which advanced with a terrific rolling fire upon the enemy, capturing a number of prisoners who dared not to arise from the ground to run away amid a sheet of lead." Colonel Minor T. Thomas, 8th Minnesota Infantry, also saw the vulnerable Confederate battery and just as he moved his men into position to attack the battery, he was surprised to see the Johnson's cavalry surge across the field. When the Federal cavalry left the field, Thomas held his position and fired to support the cavalry withdrawal.[44]

The sun had set as the fighting ended and Milroy had driven the enemy, which had ceased firing, over a quarter mile. The 8th Minnesota had not found a crossing over the creek and Milroy withdrew the 174th Ohio leisurely back across the creek along with the skirmishers of the 61st Illinois. Milroy noted that these regiments "withdrew in the most perfect order, bringing off their dead, wounded, and prisoners," as did the 13th Indiana Cavalry which crossed unimpeded over the bridge. Milroy did not take up the pursuit, because it was too dark and stumbling around in the dark would have been a poor decision. Milroy ordered the withdrawal and reached Murfreesboro at 1:00 a.m.[45]

Bate received no assistance from the Confederate cavalry during this fight and only a single of squadron of cavalry arrived that night after the fight had concluded. Bate wrote: "I certainly did not suppose this was all the support I was to get from General Forrest." The cavalry relieved the infantry pickets and Bate pulled back to the rear of Stewarts Creek. Bate recorded his losses as 15 killed, 59 wounded (including Colonel Robert Bullock, commander of the Florida brigade) and 13 missing. Bate thought that Milroy's losses were greater than his and he noted that he buried some of Milroy's dead. Bate showed some petulance in his after-action report, probably unfairly, directed at the cavalry which had yet to unite with Bate's infantry; however, this would not be the last report from Bate suggesting an expectation of greater assistance from Forrest's cavalry in the fights around Murfreesboro.[46]

General Henry Jackson of Bate's division sent a personal and confidential report to Cheatham on December 10 with an explanation for the performance of his troops during the battle. He explained that his men moved forward against the blockhouse and Milroy, but was ordered to withdraw to a point on Murfreesboro-Nashville Pike because of the approach of Federal cavalry. Confusion resulted when a messenger arrived stating that the cavalry was actually Confederate troops and would assume Jackson's position. Jackson received orders that "I should withdraw my command and place it in camp a mile to the rear." As Jackson started to the rear, this latest order was countermanded and he was ordered to the front, but by the time Jackson reached the battle line it was dark. The situation at this point was sheer confusion and retreating Confederate troops surged through his forming lines, taking his left with them. Jackson's right held its position and returned fire, but it was too late to save the day.[47]

Rousseau reported that Blockhouse No. 7 was attacked by Bate's division which unleashed a barrage of 74 shells on the blockhouse without causing any significant damage. Milroy remained in possession of the field, losing four men killed-in-action and another 49 wounded by Rousseau's count. The Federals captured about 30 prisoners and Milroy reported seeing eight to 10 enemy dead on the field.[48]

Once the fight was over, the Union forces returned to Fortress Rosecrans, the largest fort built during the Civil War. The fortress covered 225 acres and stretched about a mile in width. The fortress, built from January to June 1863, sat astride Stones River and the Nashville and Chattanooga Railroad, just north of Murfreesboro on Nashville Pike. Since its completion the fortress served as a supply center for Union operations as the Federal forces moved further into the South. The fortress had earthen walls supported by lunettes and four redoubts. The engineers proudly claimed that the fortress could not be taken by any attack, if it was properly manned.[49]

The garrison at Murfreesboro observed increased attention from the Confederates over the next few days. Thomas acknowledged that the telegraph had been cut to Murfreesboro and the railroad broken. The Union troops considered the repair of both, but the environment was too dangerous. Rousseau found that the Confederates remained in force in the area and cancelled an attempt to complete repairs. While Hood's intentions remained unclear, he still had some flexibility of remaining outside Nashville or marching further east.[50]

Forrest Moves Toward Murfreesboro

On the morning of December 5, Forrest moved his cavalry force toward Murfreesboro and along the way, Buford's division captured Blockhouse No. 4 at La Vergne while Jackson's division surrounded a fort on the hill nearby, claiming 80 prisoners, two cannon, and large amounts of stores in the process. Then, Forrest moved further south and united with Bate's infantry about four miles south of La Vergne. The Confederate forces marched over the same ground the Union army had marched only two years before during the Stones River Campaign. When Forrest arrived, he brought two additional infantry brigades (Brigadier General Claudius Sears' and Colonel Joseph Palmer's). Forrest sent Jackson's cavalry division along Wilkinson Pike and Murfreesboro-Nashville Pike in front of the main Confederate force. Jackson's division screened westward to Salem Pike. Jackson drove the Federal pickets into the defensive works at Murfreesboro, and Forrest placed Buford's division on the Confederate east flank screening from Murfreesboro-Nashville Pike eastward to Lebanon Pike.[51]

Before Forrest's arrival, Bate also spent the day capturing the blockhouses on Stewarts Creek, Read's Branch and at Smyrna, but the Union defenders evacuated and escaped before any fighting occurred. Bate sent his men to burn the empty blockhouses and the bridges they protected. He soon found he had new orders upon Forrest's arrival and he wrote: "The order to keep in view the object of my mission, viz, 'to destroy the railroad,' seemed to be revoked, and offensive operations against Murfreesborough assumed, which did not accord with my judgment, as I was satisfied there were 8,000 or 10,000 Federals within, strongly fortified and with a large amount of artillery in position. Not deeming it prudent to attack such works manned with twice our numbers, I, however, readily gave cheerful co-operation." Bate, unhappy about the unfolding events, realized the chain of command and that Hood had added new elements to the plans since he received his initial orders. Later, Bate received a message directly from Hood which clearly stated "that the defeat of that portion of the enemy at Murfreesborough is of the first importance." Bate stopped the destruction of the railroad and moved with Forrest to invest the impressive Union fortifications at Murfreesboro.

With the infantry and cavalry united, they camped for the night and considered their next move.[52]

The Union forces remained contentedly behind their walls at Murfreesboro for the next two days while Forrest demonstrated and skirmished with the Union defenders in an "impudent" manner explained Rousseau. Gilbert Johnson had his cavalry out the next two days on various details, scouting enemy positions. In two particularly notable actions, two blockhouses (Blockhouse No. 7, four miles north of Murfreesboro, and Blockhouse No. 9, at Bell Buckle) successfully resisted all the Confederate attacks. The men in Blockhouse No. 7 continued to be besieged for 13 days and fired over 8,000 rounds of ammunition before being successfully relieved later in the month.[53]

On December 6, Forrest ordered the infantry to advance on the Union fortress in an attempt to entice the Federals to move outside the walls of the fort, but the plan was unsuccessful. Forrest wrote: "After skirmishing for two hours the enemy ceased firing, and showed no disposition to give battle." Rousseau and Milroy were in no rush. Forrest sent Armstrong's brigade to scout the enemy defenses to find some weaknesses, but he found no opportunities for a Confederate attack. Forrest moved his cavalry to reinforce Sears' and Palmer's infantry brigades that night, and Bate sent his skirmishers around the perimeter of the Union defenses and began building defenses in front of his position.[54]

The 22nd (2nd) Tennessee Cavalry (CSA) lost their colonel, Clark Barteau, during the skirmishes on December 6. At dusk, some of the Confederate scouts reported that enemy was approaching through a wooded area; Barteau became impatient awaiting further information and rode ahead to observe the movement. As he moved through the undergrowth, his horse snorted and this attracted the attention of a nearby Federal picket. As soon as the horse snorted, a shot rang out and Barteau felt the impact of the ball strike his body. He remained in his saddle, but dropping his revolver, spurred his horse to the rear and reached camp, badly wounded. This ended Barteau's time in the Civil War and Lieutenant Colonel George Morton assumed command of the regiment. Union general Milroy only recorded that a brigade of Confederate cavalry attacked the Union pickets and that a few infantry regiments were sent to disperse them.[55]

December 7—Battle of the Cedars

Rousseau was not one to remain inactive for long. The Union forces were ready to take action on December 7 and Milroy marched due west out of the fort onto Salem Pike. From General Joseph Palmer's position on an elevation outside of Fortress Rosecrans, the Confederate officers observed infantry, cavalry and artillery emerge from the fort. Then, Forrest withdrew his forces to Wilkinson Pike, to a position favorable for his defense, and prepared to fight. Sam Dunlap, 1st Missouri Artillery, explained that Forrest's strategy relied on drawing the Union troops outside the fort and then defeating them in an open field. Now, Forrest had his chance. Milroy's expedition was not designed to be a full battle against Forrest and Bate. Instead, he followed Lovell Rousseau's orders to make a reconnaissance and to "feel the enemy in the vicinity of this post." Milroy's column included six infantry regiments and one section each of 13th New York Artillery and 12th Ohio Artillery. In addition, he had a small detachment of the 5th Tennessee Cavalry plus the dismounted 12th Indiana Cavalry.[56]

Milroy's expedition included temporary brigades formed just for this action:

First Brigade—Colonel Minor Thomas—(1,973 men)

174th Ohio Infantry	61st Illinois Infantry	8th Minnesota Infantry
13th New York Arty. (one section—Bundy)	12th Ohio Arty. (one section—Billings)	

Second Brigade—Colonel Edward Anderson (1,326 men)

177th Ohio Infantry	178th Ohio Infantry	181st Ohio Infantry
12th Indiana Cavalry (dismounted)		

At 10:00 a.m., the 5th Tennessee Cavalry led Milroy's westward march on Salem Pike and ran into Confederate cavalry pickets about a half mile outside the fort. Forrest's cavalry fell back as Milroy pushed ahead behind the 5th Tennessee's screen and the skirmishers of the 61st Illinois Infantry. Milroy found his first serious resistance at the crossing of Stones River where about 300 Confederate cavalrymen held the west bank. Milroy put the Federal artillery to work and the Southern cavalry withdrew under the fire of the guns. A local citizen, Mrs. Spence, told Milroy that Jackson's cavalry division was positioned another mile to the west, but that the main body of the Confederate forces (Forrest and Bate) had moved to Wilkinson Pike, three miles northwest of Fortress Rosecrans. Milroy decided to march in that direction. Perhaps Mrs. Spence was just protecting her investment, because Milroy's troops assisted in driving 60 of her "fine, fat hogs" to safety and protecting them from the clutches of the hungry Confederates. Milroy marched north to Franklin Pike and then continued up Gresham Lane to within a half mile of Forrest's infantry waiting in line on Wilkinson Pike and as he approached, he came under fire from six-guns of Confederate artillery.[57]

Bate had moved his division to Wilkinson Pike where Forrest decided to resist the Federal attack. When Milroy marched out of the fort, Forrest initially told Bate to prepare to attack the fortress; however,

General Robert Milroy, a general who wanted desperately to get back into action (Library of Congress).

Forrest changed this order and abdicated direct command of the infantry in favor of Bate, although he still had overall command of the cavalry and infantry. With the infantry now under Bate's command, Forrest told him to move the infantry to a position on the pike near the Gresham farm. Bate complied with the order "under the personal direction of General Forrest" and he placed the brigades in line with Sears' to the west, Palmer's in the center, and Finley's on the east, and Jackson's and Tyler's brigades were held in reserve. Once in line, the Confederate infantrymen hastily prepared some rough defensive works of rails and logs. Bate did not specify the placement of his artillery only that it was in the most advantageous position. Soon, Milroy's force arrived presenting a front to the Confederate position and the Southern artillery opened up. Then, Forrest told Bate to forget about the reserve and move all the infantry brigades into line. Bate obeyed and moved Jackson's brigade to the left of Finley's brigade. Sears moved from the right flank to the left refusing the flank in a parallel line to the Nashville Pike. (Bate did not mention the location of Tyler's brigade.)[58]

Maj. Gen. Nathan B. Forrest

Cavalry Corps	
Buford's Division—Abraham Buford	***Jackson's Division***—William Hicks Jackson
Bell's Brigade—Col. Tyree Bell	Armstrong's Brigade—Brig. Gen. Frank C. Armstrong
Crossland's Brigade—Col. Edward Crossland	Ross's Brigade—Brig. Gen. Lawrence S. Ross
Infantry Units	
Bate's Division—Maj. Gen. William B. Bate	***Stevenson's Division***
Tyler's Brigade—Brig. Gen. Thomas B. Smith	Brown's & Reynolds's Brigade—Brig. Gen. Joseph B. Palmer
Finley's Brigade—Major Jacob A. Lash	***French's Division***
Jackson's Brigade—Brig. Gen. Henry R. Jackson	Sears's Brigade—Brig. Gen. Claudius W. Sears

The 13th New York Battery, having advanced without caissons, unlimbered and returned fire "in an equally spirited style," but it took only 30 minutes to deplete the New Yorkers' ammunition. Both sides deemed it unwise to attack across the flat, open ground between the two lines. Observing that this line of attack might put the Confederates between his forces and the fortress, Milroy withdrew, moved east, and then approached the Southern line through a wooded area. His repositioning put the fortress directly to his rear. When the Union attack resumed, it came in two battle lines, with Thomas' brigade leading the attack and Anderson's Second Brigade following. Just as the soldiers discovered in December 1862 during the Battle of Stones River, the movements in this area were difficult.[59]

Milroy advanced on the Confederate position, by marching in a diagonal line and turning the Confederate left flank. Then, Forrest ordered the Confederate line to shift to the left as the Federal lines emerged from a wooded area. Sears initiated the shift with

Jackson following, but the two brigades moved too far left. Bate hurriedly filled the gap which was forming between Jackson and Palmer with Tyler's (Smith's) brigade. Palmer and Sears moved into position into the defensive works that had been previously constructed. Smith's troops now faced the "full front of the enemy, which was within 200 yards, driving in our skirmishers, the cavalry on the left having fallen back with but slight resistance," wrote Bate. The decision by Milroy to shift his attack was a good one and he utilized the woods to move his troops for the attack and emerged a short distance from the Confederate infantry line. Bate bitterly recalled the Confederates thought Milroy had retired to Murfreesboro: "[N]o information being received by me from the cavalry in my front), did not admit of sufficient time to adjust the line before he was upon us, hence there was a space of perhaps 75 or 100 yards between Smith's right and Finley's left. Jackson and Sears were immediately ordered to move, under the conduct of a staff officer, Major Shaaff, by the right flank and align on Smith's left, who was now engaged with the main line of the enemy. The enemy's line came diagonally from the left and struck Finley's and Palmer's brigades, crumbling and driving them from the temporary works. Meanwhile Smith's (Tyler's) and the right of Jackson's brigade, which was getting in position, drove back in gallant style the right of the enemy's line which confronted them." Forrest rode among the infantry as the battle intensified, telling them, "Men, all I ask of you is to hold the enemy back for fifteen minutes, which will give me sufficient time to gain their rear with my cavalry." Instead, much of the Confederate infantry merely crumbled. Bate did not see the Finley's, Palmer's, or Sears' brigades until that night, because Forrest exercised direct command over these troops as they rallied in the rear. Bate remained near the battle line with only two brigades still in line—Smith's and Jackson's. Fortunately for the Confederates, Milroy did not press his advantage and this allowed Bate time to organize these two brigades. Forrest subsequently ordered Bate to pull back several miles to the rear to Stewarts Creek. Bate recorded that he "leisurely" pulled the two brigades to the rear to join Forrest, the cavalry, the artillery, and Sears,' Palmer's and Finley's brigades. Bate quietly placed some of the blame on the lack of observations and participation by the cavalry and he noted: "If the cavalry on either flank was seriously engaged, I was not aware of it. In this day's fight there were 19 killed, 73 wounded, and 122 missing.... In addition, two guns of that gallant battery, Slocomb's, commanded by Lieutenant Chalaron were lost in the fighting."[60]

Forrest was dismayed as the infantry broke for the rear and he personally tried to rally the crumbling Confederate line. He wrote: "The enemy moved boldly forward, driving in my pickets, when the infantry, with the exception of Smith's brigade, from some cause which I cannot explain, made a shameful retreat, losing two pieces of artillery." Forrest grabbed the colors and began yelling and waving the flag in a futile attempt to stop the rout. Forrest glumly declared: "[T]hey could not be moved by any entreaty or appeal to their patriotism. Major-General Bate did the same thing, but was equally as unsuccessful as myself." Then, Forrest ordered Armstrong's and Ross' cavalry brigades to hold back the enemy pursuit and Forrest reported they performed their duty well, "thereby checking his farther advance." While the fighting took place on Wilkinson Pike, Buford moved into Murfreesboro with artillery and began shelling the town. Forrest sent orders to Buford to join in the fighting northwest of town, but Buford "did not receive these orders in time."[61]

One of the "shoeless Confederates" of Forrest's command remarked that "we lost the day by some of our infantry giving way, and narrowly escaped capture." Despite

Bate's comments about the Confederate cavalry, Sam Dunlap, the Missouri artilleryman, gave Armstrong's cavalry credit for preventing his capture when the infantry broke. "Had it not been for a detachment of Forrest's cavalry coming to our rescue, capture would have been inevitable." Dunlap observed the loss of the two Louisiana guns as his battery headed for the rear. Dunlap also saw Forrest standing in his stirrups waving the infantry colors endeavoring to rally his troops. "Men for God's sake, rally! Don't run off the field & leave the artillery to do all the fighting." Forrest was furious. There was also an account which claimed that Forrest actually shot one of the retreating soldiers in an effort to stop the stampede.[62]

Richard Hancock, 2nd Tennessee Cavalry (CSA), also documented the efforts of Jackson's cavalry during the fight which stopped the battle from being an uncontrolled route. Hancock noted that Ross' brigade moved to the front and helped delay the Union pursuit, as the cavalry supported the eastern flank and threatened the Federal right flank and rear. William Worthington, Armstrong's staff officer, wrote, "Forrest thought we had them sure, but in the end we had to make a demonstration on their rear to keep them from running Bates out of the country."[63]

Milroy had no easy task and described: "I advanced upon the enemy, through the brush, cedars, rocks, and logs, under a heavy fire of artillery." When the attack began, Milroy was devoid of artillery, because he had sent the 13th New York to the fort to replenish its ammunition. Forrest's cannons roared as the Union soldiers emerged from the trees. Nevertheless, Milroy's troops surged ahead. His skirmishers pushed the enemy's skirmishers back according to Milroy until they reached an open cotton field where the Confederate troops waited behind defenses. "I ordered an advance, and the front line moved forward into the edge of the wood, where for a few minutes the roar and fire

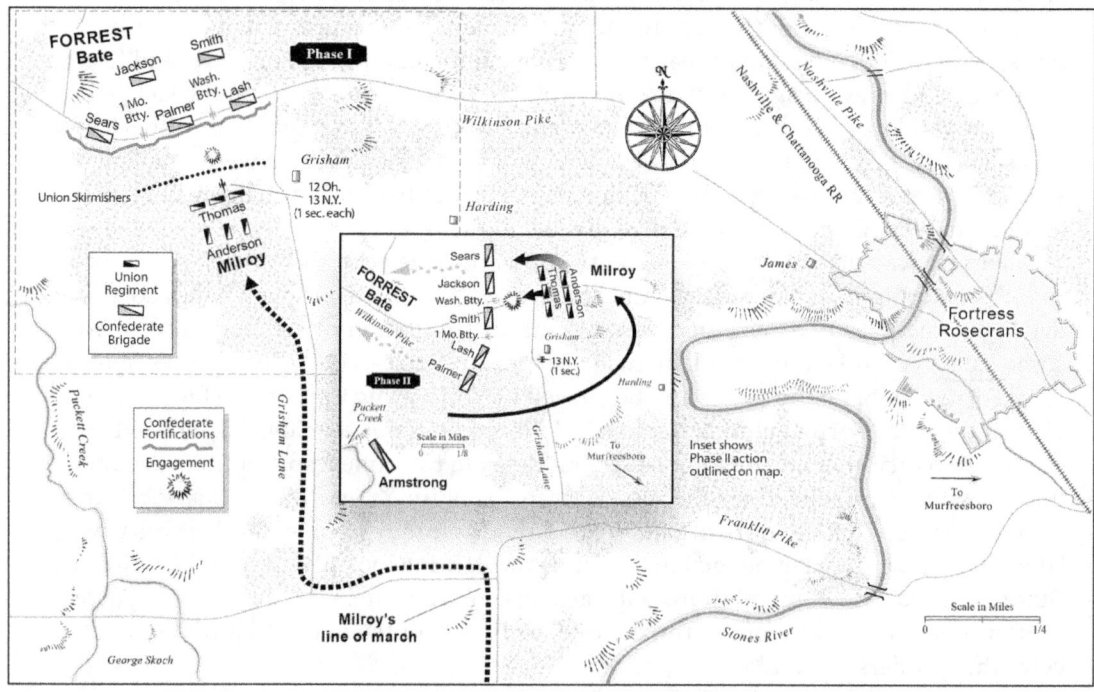

Battle of the Cedars, December 7, 1864.

of musketry was like the thunder of a volcano, and the line wavered as if moving against a hurricane." Milroy, facing five brigades with only two of his own, worried that the center of his line would falter and he ordered the 174th Ohio Infantry to run from the left flank to the center. The troops already in the center saw the Ohioans moving to their support, continued their attack and "advanced with a yell and darted over the enemy's works, capturing many prisoners and putting the enemy to a hasty flight." This broke the Confederate infantry line and resulted in the capture of several enemy soldiers, one battle flag and two 12-pound Napoleon guns. After the attack, Milroy returned to the fortress, but prior to the withdrawal, the 13th New York Artillery arrived just in time to observe a large body of Confederate cavalry, Armstrong's brigade, moving from its position on Salem Pike. The battery opened fire on the horsemen who withdrew soon thereafter.[64]

Colonel Edward Anderson, 12th Indiana Cavalry, commanding Second Brigade led these troops into position during the artillery barrage and discovered the 178th Ohio Infantry had never been under fire. Anderson understood the importance of easing this regiment into battle and he ordered the men to lie down until the artillery fire concluded. Then, he marched his entire brigade to the right, extending Milroy's front. Anderson ordered the 12th Indiana Cavalry to the eastern end of the line, and Milroy arrived, taking personal command of the 178th Ohio. The 177th Ohio Infantry formed on the left of the cavalry. As the attack began, the 12th Indiana and 177th Ohio immediately ran into enemy musket fire. "Sharp firing along the line showed that the general had not been mistaken in supposing it necessary to protect the right flank," wrote Anderson. Milroy proved himself worthy by leading the 178th Ohio into battle and Anderson described: "[M]arching it left in front, led it to the extreme left and conducted it personally into battle. Of the action of this regiment I am unable to speak thereafter, but have no question as to its gallantry, as the almost reckless daring of the general cannot be other than infectious." The 12th Indiana Cavalry moved ahead on the right over Wilkinson Pike and fell into battle line in a cotton field, pouring volley after volley into the defenders where they "had extemporized earth-works and planted his batteries." The Indianans moved to support the Federal skirmishers which were taking heavy fire. Lieutenant Colonel Alfred Reed, commanding the 12th Indiana, pushed forward as the Confederates retreated. When the enemy withdrew, Anderson received orders to hold his position and subsequently, he was ordered to return to the fortress with the 12th Indiana Cavalry providing rearguard duties.[65]

The 12th Indiana Cavalry reported the greatest Union casualties during the fight— one man killed and 11 men wounded. Anderson's brigade losses amounted to one killed and 23 men wounded, and he complimented Milroy on his actions. "No one, however, would be surprised that troops would stand gallantly under fire, as they could all the time see the general they loved in the fore front of battle, where the bullets were flying most thickly. These troops would follow General Milroy wherever he might lead..." A Tennessee cavalryman wrote a description of the actions at Murfreesboro. Trooper William Carson wrote: "Milroy got tired of him and he walked his men out of the fortifications and went to him like killer snakes."[66]

While the battle raged on the north side of town, Buford's division supported by a section of Morton's Battery arrived in Murfreesboro and began shelling the courthouse. Lovell Rousseau sent one of the batteries from Fortress Rosecrans to deal with Morton's guns. One of Federal shells fell amid Morton's section, killing three horses and putting a gun out of action. Morton declared: "I will take off my gun or die in the attempt." Tyree Bell's men pitched in to assist Morton, manually lifting the gun and carrying it away while a group of Union soldiers watched. This ended the attack on Murfreesboro, but some Federal cavalry followed up Buford's retreat. After moving some distance away from town, Buford reformed his men and repulsed the pursuit. Richard Hancock, 22nd (2nd) Tennessee Cavalry, recorded that two lady rebels, Miss Joe Eaton, of Murfreesboro, and Miss Tennie Bethel, of Woodbury, also joined in the fighting at Murfreesboro.[67]

The next day Bate returned to the original duty of destroying the railroad, but he wrote: "[B]ut little progress was made, in consequence of the extreme bad weather; the snow fell rapidly and the ground was freezing." Bate's infantry had worn out their shoes which they received at the beginning of the campaign and as the snow began to fly, the men were almost bare-footed. If the men did not have shoes, they did have a "superabundance of rations" from the mills the Southern army had put into use. Bate and Forrest had little hope of capturing the fortress and the Union forces were not unwise enough to allow themselves to be defeated in detail. In the meantime, Bate received his formal orders to march to Nashville and join Cheatham's corps on the east flank of the Confederate army. Bate marched through sleet, snow and rain which "made the surface of the earth a sheet of ice. Nearly one-fourth of the men were still barefooted, yet plodded 'their weary way' under these adverse circumstance (many with bleeding feet)..."[68]

Two days after the battle, Hood ordered Smith's brigade (commanded by Colonel Charles H. Olmstead) of Georgia infantry to replace Bate. Of note, Forrest dispatched Buford's division to picket the Cumberland River, east of Nashville, near the Hermitage on December 11. The next day Jackson's cavalry began destroying the railroad from La Vergne to Murfreesboro. Two days later, Jackson captured a train with 17 cars, carrying 200 men of the 61st Illinois Infantry and 60,000–200,000 rations, depending upon the account. On December 15, Forrest received word from Hood to prepare for action because of the battle at Nashville and the next day Forrest moved his entire command to Wilkinson's Crossroads in order to assist Hood's army. Essentially, little other action occurred after December 7 as two-thirds of the Confederate cavalry remained in the Murfreesboro area until after the Battle of Nashville. Importantly, this meant that only Chalmers' division would face the increasingly strong Union cavalry which was concentrating at Nashville.[69]

While obviously facing morale problems, Hood ordered that the early successes of Forrest at Murfreesboro be read to the troops outside Nashville on December 5 and 6. "Major-General Forrest captured, this morning, the block-house and fort at La Vergne, with some commissary stores, 100 prisoners, two pieces of artillery, 100 small-arms and ammunition, with about 20 wagons and some teams. General Bate has burned three block-houses." Hood did not read the results of the fighting on December 7 to the troops.[70]

Lyon's Raid: December 6—January 15

On the day Hood began his march from Florence, Brigadier General Hylan Lyon received orders at his headquarters in Corinth to move north across the Tennessee and Cumberland Rivers to attack and capture Clarksville. Then, if possible, Hood wanted Lyon to destroy the railroad and telegraph systems north of Nashville, and to get grain from the mills for bread for his army. When Lyon, commander of the Department of Western Kentucky, received his orders, he had his two brigades at Corinth for rearmament.[71]

With Kentucky in the hands of Union forces, Lyon had a difficult task and his entire force totaled about 800 men—"undisciplined and but poorly organized, and two pieces of artillery (12-pounder howitzers)," wrote Lyon. All of this force consisted of green troops who had seen no more than four months service. Lyon formed two brigades— First Brigade, commanded by Colonel James J. Turner, 30th Tennessee Infantry, and Second Brigade, commanded by Colonel James Q. Chenoweth, Chenoweth's regiment. Lyon's brigades were mounted, except for about 100 men, but the men had almost no equipment to face the winter. Many were without shoes, uniforms, blankets or overcoats; however, they did have arms with which to fight.[72]

Lyon returned to his headquarters at Paris, Tennessee, and he began his raid on December 6. Lyon had not been idle after receiving his orders as he pondered how to cross the Tennessee River. Prior to starting his raid, he ordered boats to be constructed that could carry his men across the river and, now, he put these boats to good use. He moved his two brigades from Paris to Danville about 10 miles due east and on December 8, he successfully completed the crossing of the river. The next day he rode another 10 miles east and captured Cumberland City. At Cumberland City, Lyon was still about 30 miles downstream from Clarksville and about 10 miles east (upstream) from Fort Donelson. Lyon captured a large steamboat loaded with supplies, converted the boat into a ferry, and moved his men across the Cumberland River. On the evening of December 9, he captured two additional steamers and four barges. He claimed 50 prisoners and then burned the boats and barges which, along with the provisions, Lyon estimated to be worth a million dollars.[73]

The rumors of Lyon's column crossing the Cumberland River were confirmed on December 10 when Colonel William Forbes, 42nd Missouri Infantry, discovered that Lyon captured the transport *Thomas E. Tutt* at Cumberland City and then completed his crossing during the day with about 4,000 men, a greatly exaggerated number. Forbes, with no mounted forces, had little chance of catching Lyon. Edward McCook, leading two brigades of the First Cavalry Division, moved his newly mounted cavalry to meet Lyon. Union scouts reported on December 11 that Lyon was north of the Cumberland River near LaFayette, about 12 miles south of Hopkinsville.[74]

Lyon moved to Clarksville, but he found the garrison too large to attack. Sergeant Eugene Read, 3rd Illinois Cavalry, described the fortifications which "stands on a very high mound below the town, it has the appearance of being strong, extensive, it commands the river." Lyon settled for tearing up the railroad and telegraph lines in the area. While one regiment was destroying the tracks, Lyon moved on to Hopkinsville where he found the 400-man garrison had evacuated and moved to Russellville. These early successes by the Confederate cavalry did little to reduce the impact of the cold weather which descended on the Confederate troopers, but the capture of Hopkinsville allowed Lyon to find shoes and clothing for half his men. Then, Lyon left half of his command at Hopkinsville and rode with the remainder to Cadiz, Princeton, and Eddyville, each town guarded with about 200 U.S.C.T. When Lyon's cavalry arrived, the garrisons had evacuated and then Lyon ordered the courthouses to be burned because they served as barracks for Union soldiers. Lieutenant Colonel Samuel F. Johnson, 52nd Kentucky Infantry, also discovered that Lyon was "conscripting every able-bodied man."[75]

McCook had received orders to move Watkins' Third Brigade and Oscar H. La Grange's Second Brigade (3rd Indiana, 4th Indiana, and 1st Wisconsin) to Bowling Green on December 11. McCook, a mainstay of the Union cavalry, was showing the effects of the war. He had recently been suffering from an inflammation of the lungs and had been on medical leave. Now, he led his cavalry in the cold winter weather after Lyon's cavalry. He moved his command northward from Nashville and reached Franklin on December 13. The initial reports indicated that Lyon had about 1,500 men at Hopkinsville, another overestimate of the actual number of Confederate cavalry. McCook rode with La Grange's brigade and met Watkins' brigade at Franklin, about 40 miles east of Hopkinsville on December 14. Watkins' brigade consisted of the 4th, 6th and 7th Kentucky Cavalry regiments, supported by the 18th Indiana Artillery. Watkins, a veteran cavalry commander, complained of the condition of the roads which were so slippery, "most of the men dismounted and led their horses to save themselves from being crippled by their falling." When McCook's column reached Russellville, Watkins gained command of the Samuel Johnson's mounted regiment.[76]

On the morning of December 15, the Union cavalry rode toward Hopkinsville and reached Fairview, nine miles east of Hopkinsville, that night. Watkins led the advance and ran into the advance scouts of Chenoweth's cavalry. The Federals killed one man, wounded another, and captured one lieutenant and eight others in the initial skirmishes. After resting for four hours, at 1:00 a.m., McCook had his men back in the saddle and riding for Hopkinsville, arriving there at daylight. He divided his column three miles east of town and sent Watkins to the right, with orders to swing around the rear of the Confederates and block the roads leading out of town. As McCook expected, the enemy occupied the heights east of town and when he approached with La Grange's brigade, one cannon fired and a heavy volley of musket fire followed. McCook's veterans continued to advance and the "rebels ran away, abandoning their artillery, caisson, and ammunition, nearly all of them throwing away their guns." Most of the retreating Confederates moved northeast on the Greenville Road, but McCook felt he had planned for this contingency by placing Watkins' brigade on the roads leading out of town, hoping to bag all of Lyon's cavalry. Even the best plans go awry; the Greenville Road was not covered and Confederates made their escape.

General Edward McCook, the war-horse of Union cavalry in the west, commanded the First Cavalry Division (Library of Congress).

McCook questioned Louis Watkins after the fight and Watkins replied that Colonel John Faulkner, 7th Kentucky Cavalry, while in place, mistook the Confederate cavalry for Union troops and allowed them to ride past. Instead of bagging the entire force, McCook settled for capturing 57 men and four officers, along with a few others killed and wounded. Among the mortally wounded was Colonel Reuben Ross, a West Point graduate in 1853, who was clubbed by a Union cavalryman during the skirmish and died a few days later. McCook discovered he faced only one brigade of about 500 enemy soldiers and that Lyon had departed for Princeton with his other brigade.[77]

Lyon soon discovered Chenoweth had been driven from Hopkinsville and that one artillery piece had been captured. Lyon met Chenoweth's pursuers about 12 miles from town and successfully stopped them, but Lyon knew he was outmanned and withdrew about 20 miles from Hopkinsville for the night. As the Confederate cavalry rode away, Lyon began a raid with a 16-hour head start over McCook's cavalry. The veteran McCook understood how these raids unfolded. Unless one knew the route of the raid, it was a frustrating ride on the trail of the enemy, so, on December 18, he sent Watkins back to Hopkinsville to guard the area and advanced with La Grange's Second Brigade.[78]

Lyon unified his command again when Chenoweth arrived and then rode through Charlestown and Madisonville (burning the courthouse here) and crossed the Green River at Ashbysburg. La Grange's brigade trailed Lyon and struggled to find ways to continue the pursuit in a trail of burned bridges. La Grange caught Lyon's rearguard on December 18 near Ashbysburg. La Grange sent a 100-man battalion to force a fight while the main column caught up. They fired on the retreating Confederates about three miles from the Green River killing one and wounding three. The battalion advanced and found that Lyon had selected his position well. A narrow neck of land, bordered by impassable swamps on either side, led to the main body of dismounted Confederate cavalry behind old earthen works. While the main column moved forward, La Grange, as a ruse and delaying for time, sent a demand for surrender under a flag of truce. La Grange chuckled: "General Lyon, understanding the real situation, declined compliance." Lyon

Colonel Oscar La Grange, commander of the 1st Wisconsin Cavalry, "enjoyed nothing more than a headlong cavalry charge" (Mollus Mass Civil War Collection, United States Army Heritage and Education Center, Military History Institute, Carlisle, Pennsylvania).

placed a rearguard in the woods to hold La Grange's men on the narrow neck of land while he ferried his troopers across the river. Once across, he burned the ferry boats. La Grange was able to drive some of Lyon's rearguard into the river, killing one and capturing seven. A few of the rearguard actually drowned while trying to swim across the river, but Lyon evaded his pursuers. Lyon discarded four wagons, an ambulance, medical supplies, other baggage and most of his conscripted recruits during this escape. Now, La Grange remained on the south back of the Green River and with the help of the steamer *D.B. Campbell*, he was able to cross his brigade on December 21–22.[79]

While Lyon justified the burning of the courthouses because they housed enemy soldiers, the local citizens saw the raid as very destructive to their daily lives. "General Lyon & his men had done us in Madisonville. They have not only taken goods from our merchants and taken every horse that would answer there purpose & burnt the courthouse," wrote a local citizen, Joseph Fuquay. Lyon continued to Hartford where he burned another courthouse and captured about 50 prisoners. Then, he moved to Leitchfield, while dispatching 50 men to Elizabethtown who captured prisoners and intended to burn the depot, courthouse, stockades, and trestle. In the meantime, he moved his main body to Nolin Station (south of Elizabethtown) on the Louisville and Nashville Railroad, where Lyon captured a train with Union soldiers on board. Then, disaster hit. Lyon found out the outcome of the Battle of Nashville. He wrote that this "had a very demoralizing effect upon my command (which were all new recruits), and within two days after it was ascertained that the Confederate army had left Tennessee 500 of my men deserted and returned to their homes."[80]

At 1 a.m. on December 22, La Grange continued his pursuit to Hartford where he found another three burned bridges. La Grange forded his command in the icy December water and he made a hard ride of 115 miles directly for Elizabethtown, arriving there on December 24, successfully forcing the enemy away from the destruction of the bridge and trestle. He was less successful at the trestles and depots at Nolin and Glendale. The depot at Elizabethtown was still burning as the Union cavalry rode into town. La Grange rested his mounts, but the Federal scouts determined Lyon was heading for Greensburg. La Grange continued his pursuit at sunrise on December 25. He finally broke off the pursuit at Greensburg and he was able to capture "29 of the enemy, including 2 majors and 2 lieutenants, 1 of each grade belonging to General Lyon's staff." Homer Carpenter, 4th Indiana Cavalry, gave a good summary of the advantages that Lyon had over of the trailing Federals. "Every serviceable horse in the country through which they passed was taken to keep their men freshly mounted. Every bridge in their rear destroyed."[81]

Lyon knew it was time to return to the friendly confines of the south. He rode though Hodgenville (birthplace of Abraham Lincoln), Campbellsville, Columbia, Burkesville, Livingston, Sparta, McMinnville, Winchester and then crossed the Tennessee River again at Gunter's Landing, Alabama. When possible, he destroyed army stores and bridges along the way. Lyon kept up his ride, all the while knowing the Union cavalry was on his trail. He was successful until he reached the Tennessee River; there, he found Federal gunboats patrolling the flooded river. He was able to cross most of his troops, but his rearguard was trapped and captured by the Union troops. Lyon would claim that 50 men were captured due to their straggling, while Union reports reported twice that number. Finally, Lyon was attacked near Red Hill which resulted in another 95 men being captured. What was left of his command ultimately arrived in Tuscaloosa "in a very jaded condition."[82]

The final cavalry regiment Lyon encountered was the 15th Pennsylvania Cavalry of Johnson's Sixth Cavalry Division. Colonel William Palmer found the remnants of Lyon's division at Red Hill and he dispatched a battalion to encircle the Confederate cavalry. With one of his two remaining battalions he quietly moved past the sleeping enemy cavalry, amounting to about 150 men, intending to capture Lyon who was quartered in the house of Tom Noble with his staff and escort, about a half a mile past the enlisted men's camp. Palmer's battalion captured many of Lyon's troopers and Palmer wrote: "This was done; nearly all the horses and arms and most of the men being captured, the remainder of the men making their escape on foot in the dark. In the meantime my advance guard had reached General Lyon's headquarters, and captured him at the door of Noble's house, in his night clothes. The general surrendered to Sergt. Arthur P. Lyon, while the advance guard was charging the escort.... The general begged permission to put on his pantaloons, coat, and boots, which Sergeant Lyon unfortunately granted, and went into the bedroom with him for that purpose. At that moment the escort fired a volley at the advance guard, when the sergeant said, 'Come, general, I can't allow you much more time.' The general then suddenly seized a pistol and shot the sergeant, killing him instantly, and made his escape through the back door in the dark, it being a half hour before daybreak." Lyon's escort fled also, leaving everything they had at the house. Palmer had detected another set of campfires which turned out to be an artillery camp and captured Lyon's final 12-pounder artillery piece which had been left behind. There could not have been many in Lyon's force who reached Tuscaloosa at the end of the raid. Palmer's regiment consisted of a mere 180 men.[83]

While riding through Kentucky, Lyon enforced the Confederate conscript law and impressed into service 400 men, but he succeeded in getting only about 100 back to Paris, Tennessee. Lyon also robbed the bank in Hopkinsville of "a small sum of Federal money, which I have turned over to the quartermaster, to be used in defraying the expenses of the expedition, and for which he will render a proper account." Rumors of robbery plagued the Southerners after the raid. James Wiswell, 4th U.S. Cavalry, wrote that some of his friends who intended to spend the holidays in the north had been captured and robbed by Lyon's men.[84]

Lyon declared his raid a success, because he had accomplished so much with a group of green troops. He captured three steamboats and burned eight courthouses and numerous other structures, including bridges, depots and stockades, along with capturing 250 prisoners. Lyon also claimed he had kept two brigades of McCook's cavalry tied up in Kentucky, instead of being at Nashville. William Palmer gave an accounting of the price to Lyon's division, which had indeed accomplished all that Lyon stated. Palmer pointed out that Lyon moved into Kentucky with 800–1,000 men, two field pieces and picked up another 400 conscripts. When he reached the Tennessee River, he had about 250 men remaining in his command and he left about 100 of those on the north side of the river as he made in his escape. When Palmer attacked him at Red Hill, he took another 95 prisoners and 120 horses. Palmer summarized: "I do not think Lyon's command will give much more trouble as an organization." Oscar LaGrange added that his pursuit never allowed his men to demonstrate their fighting potential. He added: "[B]ut the discipline they observed was in pleasing contrast with the conduct of the stragglers of the enemy, who burned houses and forage, ravished women, and plundered indiscriminately on their line of march."[85]

McCook commented that his efforts did not accomplish all he had hoped, but he knew the type of force he pursued could not have been caught unless he had more cavalry with which to cut him off. "I am satisfied that everything was done that could be done.... The Second Brigade marched 416 miles and the Third Brigade 325 miles over the worst roads I ever saw. During part of the time the weather was extremely cold and both men and animals suffered much. On the night of the 23d 100 men of the Second Brigade had their feet frozen."[86]

December 6–7: Grant Orders Thomas to Attack Hood

Grant's patience was gone by late afternoon on December 6 when he told Thomas: "Attack Hood at once, and wait no longer for a remount of your cavalry. There is great danger of delay resulting in a campaign back to the Ohio River." Many in the Federal army agreed with Grant and believed that Hood would not attack such a strong Federal position as Nashville. Franklin J. Hammond, Iowa, cavalryman, wrote his sister in December and told her he thought Hood intended to cross the river and march into Kentucky. Grant's was a peremptory order and needed to be carried out. Prior to receiving this communication, Thomas wrote to Grant and explained that his updated plan included a re-organized cavalry corps which would include 6,000–8,000 troopers. He urged patience as Wilson collected enough horses to mount this force over the next three days. Thomas, again overestimating Forrest's cavalry, told Grant that Forrest had 12,000 horsemen and that he needed all the cavalry he could mount to oppose him. Thomas replied an hour after receiving Grant's peremptory order to attack. "I will make the necessary dispositions and attack Hood at once, agreeably to your order, though I believe it will be hazardous with the small force of cavalry now at my service."[87]

After Rosecrans' removal in Missouri, Grant contemplated removing Thomas in Tennessee. He wrote to Edwin Stanton on December 7: "You probably saw my order to Thomas to attack. If he does not do it promptly, I would recommend superseding him by Schofield, leav-

General Ulysses Grant, commander of all the Union armies, was frustrated by the delays in attacking Hood (Library of Congress).

ing Thomas subordinate." Meanwhile Thomas continued on his course to deal with Hood.[88]

While Thomas defended his preparations at Nashville, Beauregard found himself defending his decisions to Jefferson Davis in regard to Hood's expedition. As Hood remained stationary in position outside Nashville, Beauregard explained that he did not stop Hood's campaign into Tennessee based on five reasons: (1) the roads back into Georgia from Tennessee were virtually impassable to the artillery and supply due to the heavy rain; (2) Hood was out of position and 275 miles away from the head of Sherman's armies with little hope of catching Sherman; (3) the impact of moving Hood back into Georgia would have destroyed morale and depleted the Southern army due to increased desertions; (4) moving Hood to Georgia would have resulted in the sacrifice of Montgomery, Selma, and Mobile because Thomas would be unopposed by Confederate troops; and (5) Beauregard had been promised local troops to supplement the defenses against Sherman's march. Beauregard concluded that "by defeating Thomas' army, and such other forces as might hastily be sent against him, he would compel Sherman, should he reach the coast of Georgia or South Carolina, to repair at once to the defense of Kentucky, and perhaps Ohio, and thus prevent him from re-enforcing Grant." Despite this defense, Beauregard had not been pleased with how this campaign had been conducted.[89]

At Nashville, even some of Hood's highest-ranking officers did not know what Hood planned to do next. Hood had the option of moving further east, striking Murfreesboro on his way to Knoxville or Chattanooga, or going into winter quarters and taking up the war in better weather. Some Confederate officers confidently reasoned that they had driven Thomas permanently inside the defenses of Nashville, that Chalmers had blockaded the river, and that soon Forrest and Lyon would destroy the Louisville and Nashville Railroad; however, the impressive lines of blue clad soldiers, the fortifications, and the Union artillery all caused the Confederates to pause in their offensive thinking. Until Hood made his decision, the Southern soldiers huddled on the barren hills, stripped of timber, observing the spires of Nashville firmly behind the Union army.[90]

December 8–9: An Ice Storm Hits Nashville

In preparation for the offensive against Hood, a pontoon bridge was ordered to be constructed across the Cumberland River for use by the cavalry and Wilson even obtained a ferryboat, the *Metamora*, for that same purpose. In addition, Wilson called all of his divisions to concentrate at his headquarters at Edgefield, except La Grange's and Watkins' brigades dealing with Lyon's raid into Kentucky. Wilson ordered Eli Long's Second Division to Nashville and to bring as many mounts as possible; however, the inability to fully equip the cavalry in Louisville meant that Long would not reach Nashville in time for the upcoming battle. Overall, Wilson still felt he needed 4,000 horses.[91]

Edward Hatch, Richard Johnson and Thomas Harrison were also individually ordered to bring their commands to Nashville by Friday, December 9; a day was filled with snow, rain, and sleet. Joining the other brigade commanders at Edgefield was Colonel Gilbert Johnson, who was named commander of the Second Brigade in Knipe's division on December 6. Johnson had been active in the area near Fortress Rosecrans with the 13th Indiana Cavalry, and he gained the 6th Tennessee and 12th Indiana regiments, along with the 13th Indiana, for his new brigade. At Edgefield, Wilson continued to add men and artillery to his cavalry. Wilson obtained the 6th Indiana Cavalry from Steedman's District of the Etowah, and the regiment was attached to Johnson's division. Next, Wilson turned his attention to his artillery. He sought reassurance that the Chicago Board of Trade Horse Artillery was equipped and ready to go. He also gained control of the 4th U.S. Artillery, Battery I which he assigned to Johnson's Sixth Cavalry Division.[92]

After Wilson concluded the conference with his division commanders, he told Thomas his cavalry would not be ready to start campaigning until Sunday December 11. "There are 3,000 well-mounted men absent, some of whom cannot get back [before] tomorrow night, and when they do arrive will be necessarily considerably jaded. The horses they bring will require shoeing, and some time to issue." As Wilson organized the cavalry, he again rearranged regiments and brigades. He formally announced the reorganization of the Sixth Division.[93]

Sixth Cavalry Division[94]

Brigadier General Richard Johnson		
First Brigade	*Second Brigade*	*Third Brigade*
Col. Thomas J. Harrison	Col. James Biddle	—
8th Michigan	5th Indiana	15th Pennsylvania
14th Illinois	6th Indiana	5th Tennessee
16th Illinois	5th Iowa	
7th Ohio	3rd Tennessee	

J.H. Hammond made his daily report for the first time to Brigadier General Joseph F. Knipe, Seventh Division commander, on December 9. Hammond, who had been reporting directly to Wilson, upon his arrival in Middle Tennessee was officially assigned to Knipe's division the next day. Knipe had been in Memphis while Hammond had been scouting in the area around Gallatin and Lebanon, and discovered that the rumors of Confederate action in the area had evaporated. Biffle's Confederate cavalry had been reported at Lebanon, but the local citizens suggested that he had returned to the Confederate army near Nashville.[95]

By December 8, Grant sent a message to Halleck which signaled more trouble for Thomas. "If Thomas has not struck yet, he ought to be ordered to hand over his command to Schofield. There is no better man to repel an attack than Thomas, but I fear he is too cautious to ever take the initiative." Halleck responded that if Grant gave the order to relieve Thomas of command, he would carry it out, but he cautioned, "The responsibility, however, will be yours, as no one here, so far as I am informed, wishes General Thomas' removal." Halleck's advice temporarily calmed Grant and Grant replied not to relieve him, but to remind him of the importance of "immediate action." In the meantime, Thomas wrote to Halleck about his situation at Nashville and the message carried an implied promise to begin offensive actions once Wilson got squared away on Sunday, December 11.[96]

Unfortunately, an ice storm struck Nashville and prevented Thomas from starting his offensive. He wrote to Halleck: "I regret that General Grant should feel dissatisfaction at my delay in attacking the enemy. I feel conscious that I have done everything in my power to prepare, and that the troops could not have been gotten ready before this, and if he should order me to be relieved I will submit without a murmur. A terrible storm of freezing rain has come on since daylight, which will render an attack impossible until it breaks." Thomas also sent the same message about the storm to Grant and he explained that he could not attack as planned. At 7:30 p.m., Grant accepted Thomas' explanation for the new delay and withdrew the orders removing Thomas from command. Grant concluded: "I hope most sincerely that there will be no necessity of repeating the orders, and that the facts will show that you have been right all the time."⁹⁷

General Henry Halleck cautioned Grant, "no one here, so far as I am informed, wishes General Thomas' removal" (Library of Congress).

Throughout the day, Thomas communicated with his corps commanders and told them to prepare to attack once the weather improved and in return, all the commanders reported that Hood remained stationary. After the Confederate defeat at Murfreesboro on December 7, Hood ordered Forrest to remain outside Murfreesboro even though there was little hope causing damage to Rousseau and Milroy. Hood felt he could not leave the large force of infantry at Murfreesboro unattended with the developing situation at Nashville. Hood needed Bate's division back at Nashville and he initially planned to replace Bate and Sears with additional infantry but he was unable to do so while facing so many Union troops. Hood suggested to Forrest that he open a gap in the Confederate lines to entice a Federal withdrawal and then Forrest would be able to strike the Federals on his own terms. In the meantime, Forrest could do little and settled for just observing the enemy forces. Hood still hoped to ambush any reinforcements moving away from Nashville to aid Rousseau and cautioned A.P. Stewart to be ready to attack any forces trying to abandon Murfreesboro and reach Nashville.⁹⁸

December 10–11: Wilson's Cavalry Moves into Postion

As Thomas usually did, he asked his corps commanders daily about the status of their commands and the enemies. Hood's position remained relatively unchanged but the weather was still so bad there was no hope of offensive action. Thomas Wood provided the answer Thomas needed. "The ground between the enemy's lines and my own is covered with a heavy sleet, which would make the handling of troops very difficult, if not impracticable. I am confident troops cannot move with facility. From the condition of the ground an offensive movement would necessarily be feeble, and feebleness of movement would almost certainly result in failure." A Southern soldier agreed with the assessment about the weather, writing in his diary that on the treeless ridge, it felt like the wind was blowing 60 miles per hour. He lamented that it was impossible to get warm.[99]

Grant and Thomas exchanged familiar messages on December 11 with Grant pushing Thomas to begin his offensive and Thomas agreeing to do so as soon as the weather permitted. Grant urged: "If you delay attack longer the mortifying spectacle will be witnessed of a rebel army moving for the Ohio River, and you will be forced to act, accepting such weather as you find. Let there be no further delay.... Delay no longer for weather or re-enforcements." The situation between Grant and Thomas falls outside the scope to this study, but James Steedman would write that Schofield was fueling Grant's animosity against Thomas. Steedman alleged that Schofield wrote to Grant: "It is the opinion of all our officers with whom I have conversed that General Thomas is too tardy in moving against the enemy." Schofield would deny these assertions in his memoirs, but James Wilson recorded that when Thomas asked his commanders if anyone objected to his plans, all agreed except Schofield who remained silent. Again, Schofield would state that he had already given his approval to Thomas personally, despite his silence during this meeting. The role Schofield played during the campaign remains controversial and his dilatory actions would continue into the battle a few days later.[100]

In a meeting of his top Union commanders, Wilson was present and when Thomas asked for comments from his commanders, Wilson spoke boldly that Thomas was making the right decision by delaying the attack. He told the group that attacking on ice covered hills would be detrimental to any mounted action. Then, he spoke about an attack in general and said he could successfully man Hood's line with his dismounted cavalry all "armed with a basket of brickbats, he would undertake the repulse of the whole of Thomas's infantry." The remark was greeted with a sly smile from Thomas and some of his generals, and the young, brash Wilson had just made some friends.[101]

As the armies remained stationary, the local citizens often had contentious interactions and criticisms of the Union cavalry at Nashville. Miss Margaret "Maggie" Lindsley, a pro–Union resident of Nashville, recorded in her journal that one of Louis Watkins' staff officers called on her family. Miss Lindsley was enraged by the officer's denunciation of Lincoln and she referred to such Union officers as "poppinjays." She expressed disappointment in the Union troops, including Wilson. "Even the poor negroes are being turned out of their homes everywhere by private soldiers. Such is General Wilson's *discipline!*"[102]

The Continuing Saga of the Fourth Cavalry Division

Off to the west, Winslow's cavalry division remained at Cairo, awaiting new orders. Winslow wrote to Wilson: "I shall go to Memphis to-night, to make every effort to have the detachments there ordered and forwarded to Nashville. I had got orders once for this from Major-General Washburn, but Major-General Dana has thus far delayed movements, thinking it not unlikely that the portions in Missouri might join him at Memphis. Major-General Halleck has, however, definitely settled that matter. I have left Colonel Benteen full instructions to push for Nashville from Clarksville." Benteen's orders directed him to disembark the cavalry at Clarksville and then proceed overland to Nashville, clearing out any enemies along the way. Halleck cleared the obstacles with Dana by telling him the cavalry and mounts would go to Nashville and after Hood was taken care of there, then he could have the return of the cavalry he wanted along the Mississippi River. However, this story was not yet complete.[103]

Afterward, Wilson relieved Benjamin Grierson of command of the Fourth Cavalry Division and appointed Emory Upton to this position. There was a decided reluctance in cooperation from the cavalry forces in Memphis to such an extent that Winslow felt compelled write to Wilson a few days later: "Major-General Dana will not allow them to leave until after the return of an expedition to the Mobile and Ohio Railroad, in which we are to take part. I do not know by what authority we are kept, but do know that my whole command is suffering very much by this long-continued separation. I sincerely hope Major-General Wilson will cause this portion to be brought to Nashville at once. I am powerless here, or anywhere, in this matter; but had my efforts here been properly seconded by Brigadier-General Grierson, I am perfectly confident that we should now be in Nashville. I am not complaining of General Grierson, or of any one, but I do not hesitate to say that if the affairs and condition of my command could be seen by others as by myself, there would have been a different result." Winslow's message clearly demonstrated that Grierson resisted Wilson's authority and had since he had been superseded by Knipe as chief of cavalry for the Army of the Tennessee. Historian Steven Starr concluded that Wilson's decision to replace Grierson, "one of the outstandingly fine officers," was "fully justified." Grierson had petulantly and passively resisted Wilson's efforts to extend his command over him.[104]

The Cavalry Moves into Position

At Nashville, Wilson prepared his cavalry for action and he told the division commanders to fully mount regiments by taking horses from partially mounted regiments. His plan of obtaining mounts from the countryside proved inadequate and this forced him to fully mount specific regiments while leaving several regiments only partially mounted or totally dismounted. Meanwhile, Lieutenant Colonel Harlon Baird and the 5th Iowa arrived at Edgefield on December 10 after a seven-day expedition which took his regiment to Hopkinsville and Russellville, Kentucky, looking for the enemy and trying to obtain mounts for the cavalry. He was able to collect about 300 horses. The collection of horses, or rather the confiscation of mounts, did not suit many of the civilians in Kentucky. Two high ranking legal representatives in Kentucky (J.F. Speed and Bland Ballard) complained to the secretary of war: "The general impressment of horses by the military is so oppressive here that we cannot think it meets your approbation. All horses are taken without regard to the occupation of the owner or his loyalty." No one was exempt from the collection of horses, including railroads, stage lines, livery stables, farmers, and even circuses. The confiscation of horses was despised by the troopers. Colonel Elisha Mix, 8th Michigan Cavalry, wrote to his wife that the shortage of mounts and finding more was "worse than fighting the Rebels."[105]

Looking westward across Nashville with capitol and the river in view (Library of Congress).

Despite the shortage of mounts, Wilson's success in concentrating his cavalry at Edgefield was public knowledge because the citizens near Nashville saw thousands of cavalrymen in the area. Wilson quickly gathered 7,000 mounts for his cavalry corps and this fact was reported to the Confederates. Hood thought that such a large cavalry force was preparing to make a raid on the Confederate communications and supply lines and he warned Forrest that his cavalry might be needed to neutralize the Federal cavalry. "Should they cross up the river, General Hood thinks it would be best for you to meet them and drive them back with your main force of cavalry," wrote A. P Mason, Hood's acting adjutant general.[106]

The Federal cavalry prepared for the upcoming fight. Henry Kratzer McVey, an Iowa cavalryman, recalled being awakened at 1:00 a.m. to a loud clang of noise and his first thought was that the battle had begun. He soon found it was nothing other than blacksmiths re-shoeing the mounts. McVey recalled the scene: "The blacksmith shops were long barrack like buildings. The forges on each side of a pace in the center. The smiths were mostly negros, two at a forge. It was night. The negros were hallowing and singing and swearing. The fires were shining and altogether it made a grewsome picture and scared our poor horses out of their wits." Confidence was high among the Federal cavalry and increased daily. Joseph Rabb, 6th Indiana Cavalry, newly arrived at Nashville and part of James Biddle's brigade wrote to sister: "I don't see what old Hood means. He doesn't try to take the place, but then it would do him no good to try for we would just murder his men." Thomas ordered Wilson to begin crossing the Cumberland River on December 12 and Wilson was as ready as he ever would be. The pontoons, ferries and bridges would be put to good use. Wilson made a final addition of artillery (14th Ohio Battery) to Knipe's Seventh Division. Wilson issued his marching orders for the next day which called for every man in the cavalry corps to cross the river supplied with three days' rations.[107]

Of McCook's division, only Croxton's brigade would participate in the further actions at Nashville. Croxton had been able to re-mount his brigade, except for the 4th Kentucky Mounted Infantry, Croxton's old regiment. This regiment still needed about 300 horses. In regard to Hatch's division, Hatch was in the saddle and riding over the ground he intended to advance the next day. Hatch expected his entire division to be mounted and ready to advance with only the 6th Illinois Cavalry still trying to obtain more mounts. The artillery was fully mounted and ready for action. Johnson's Sixth Cavalry Division was not so lucky. Johnson took the horses of the 8th Michigan and 14th Illinois and mounted the rest of the 7th Ohio and 16th Illinois in his First Brigade (Harrison's). In the Second Brigade (Biddle's), only one regiment was mounted, the 5th Iowa Cavalry of 590 men. Johnson reported the 8th Michigan, 6th Illinois and 14th Illinois all dismounted at Edgefield, and 5th Indiana dismounted at Louisville. Johnson also received a small influx of unassigned cavalrymen awaiting transport to their regiments. Fifteenth Pennsylvania cavalryman Eben Ellison and few of his comrades were assigned to Biddle's dismounted brigade because they could not reach their regiment in northern Alabama.[108]

December 12–13 Cavalry Actions

Although the weather had improved, conditions were still too adverse to begin the attack. Benjamin Nourse, Chicago Board of Trade Horse Artillery, noted in his diary: "6° above and this is Nashville, Tenn., good sleighing." Thomas wrote to Halleck and explained the situation. "I have the troops ready to make the attack on the enemy as soon as the sleet which now covers the ground has melted sufficiently to enable the men to march.... It has taken the entire day to place my cavalry in position, and it has only been finally effected with imminent risk and many serious accidents, resulting from the number of horses falling with their riders on the roads. Under these circumstances I believe an attack at this time would only result in a useless sacrifice of life." The weather continued to improve on December 13 and Hood's position remained unchanged. However, Grant's patience had worn out and he ordered General John Logan to Nashville to replace Thomas.[109]

On the Confederate side of the line, Hood received further bad news. Hood struggled with morale, particularly after the Battle of Franklin, and the long stay on the cold hills south of Nashville did little to improve the spirits of his men. If he hoped to receive a surge of recruits to his army, he was again to be disappointed. His provost marshal told him on December 13 that after entering Tennessee only a handful of men had enlisted: "Cheatham's corps, 85; Stewart's corps, 36; Lee's corps, 31; post duty, 7; cavalry, 4; artillery, 1; total, 164. Johnson's division has had assigned to it 296 dismounted cavalry, of whom all have deserted except 42." Numerous reports of "lawless conduct and frequent depredations" rippled through the Confederate army with reports blaming bands of Confederate troops for stealing and worse.[110]

There appeared to be some re-positioning by Hood's troops, but no significant movement was detected on December 12 and 13. Hood ordered Biffle's brigade from Chalmers' division to the right of the army. Lieutenant James Brownlow, 9th Tennessee Cavalry, wrote of the condition of the move to the eastern flank: "We were ordered to go to the exstream right of the army on Sones river. The ground was literaly covered with ice. It was verry cold."[111]

To make matters worse for Hood, Wilson's cavalry surged across the Cumberland River the day before. The Federal cavalry was clearly on Hood's mind, to such an extent that he wrote to J.A. Seddon, Secretary of War, a one line message that once Sherman completed his "raid" all the available cavalry needed to be sent to him. Once the Federal cavalry moved into position, they awaited the first orders to actively engage the enemy on December 14. This signaled that finally Thomas would move and the action

After Hood's army waited, the Confederate soldiers suffered the cold, freezing weather on the hills south of Nashville (Library of Congress).

that Hood seemed to have desired would finally take place. Hood wrote to A.P. Stewart that the Union cavalry was moving into position in preparation for an attack. Hood told Stewart to move a brigade of infantry (Ector's) to Hardin Pike to bolster the single regiment holding that position. "Should the enemy commence operating with their cavalry on Chalmers' side, you must give Chalmers such assistance as you think necessary, keeping in communication with Chalmers." Hood sent a similar message to alert James Chalmers of impending action. Chalmers' line was stretched very thin, but he had the 7th Alabama Cavalry guarding the flank of Ector's infantry brigade, commanded by Colonel David Coleman, in the area between the Hardin and Hillsboro pikes. Rucker's headquarters was on Charlotte Pike and Kelley's regiment was still at Bell's Mill.[112]

December 14

The messages from Washington continued to arrive in Nashville, and this time Halleck wrote that it was imperative for Thomas to attack. On December 14, Thomas issued his orders for the attack the next day and he directed Wilson's cavalry to move along the right flank of A.J. Smith's infantry. Wilson sent his own orders to begin the attack the next morning:

"**SPECIAL FIELD ORDERS No. 3**
HEADQUARTERS CAVALRY CORPS,
Nashville, Tenn., December 14, 1864.
The Cavalry Corps will be prepared to move on the enemy tomorrow at 6 a.m., in the following order:
I. The Fifth Division, Brigadier-General Hatch commanding, will debouch from the fortifications at or near the Hardin pike, and move with its right flank on the Hardin pike and its left flank connecting with the infantry of Major-General Smith. As soon as the rebel advance position is carried by General Smith, and its own front cleared of the enemy, it will swing to the left, endeavoring to envelope and take in reverse the enemy's left flank.
II. Croxton's brigade, of the First Division, will debouch near the Hardin pike by the dirt road between that and the Charlotte pike, and will move with his left flank connecting with Fifth Division and his right following the line of ridge between the Charlotte and Hardin pikes. After clearing the Hardin pike of any enemy that may be upon it, and crossing Richland Creek, it will conform in its movements to that of the Fifth Division.
III. The Sixth Division, Brigadier-General Johnson commanding, will move by the Charlotte pike, and clear that road of the enemy, pushing as far as Davidson's house, covering the right and rear of the entire movement from the enemy's left, communication being kept up with General Croxton by patrols or skirmishers, as may be found most convenient. The guns of the enemy on the river at Bell's Landing and the forces with them should be captured.
IV. The Seventh Division, Brigadier-General Knipe commanding, will be held in reserve between the Charlotte and Hardin pikes, ready to move in any direction that the exigencies of the action may demand. It will not debouch from the fortifications till they have been cleared and the success of the general movement determined.
V. The object of the entire operations of the cavalry is to clear the enemy from its immediate front, cover the right of the infantry, envelope the enemy's left flank, and, if possible, reach the Franklin pike somewhere in the vicinity of Brentwood. The greatest celerity of movement is therefore necessary. No wheels will accompany the troops except the artillery. As much forage should be carried on the horses as practicable and three days' rations for the men."[113]

Wilson also called his high-ranking commanders to his headquarters to discuss the final plans for the next day's actions. After this meeting, Hatch issued orders for his divi-

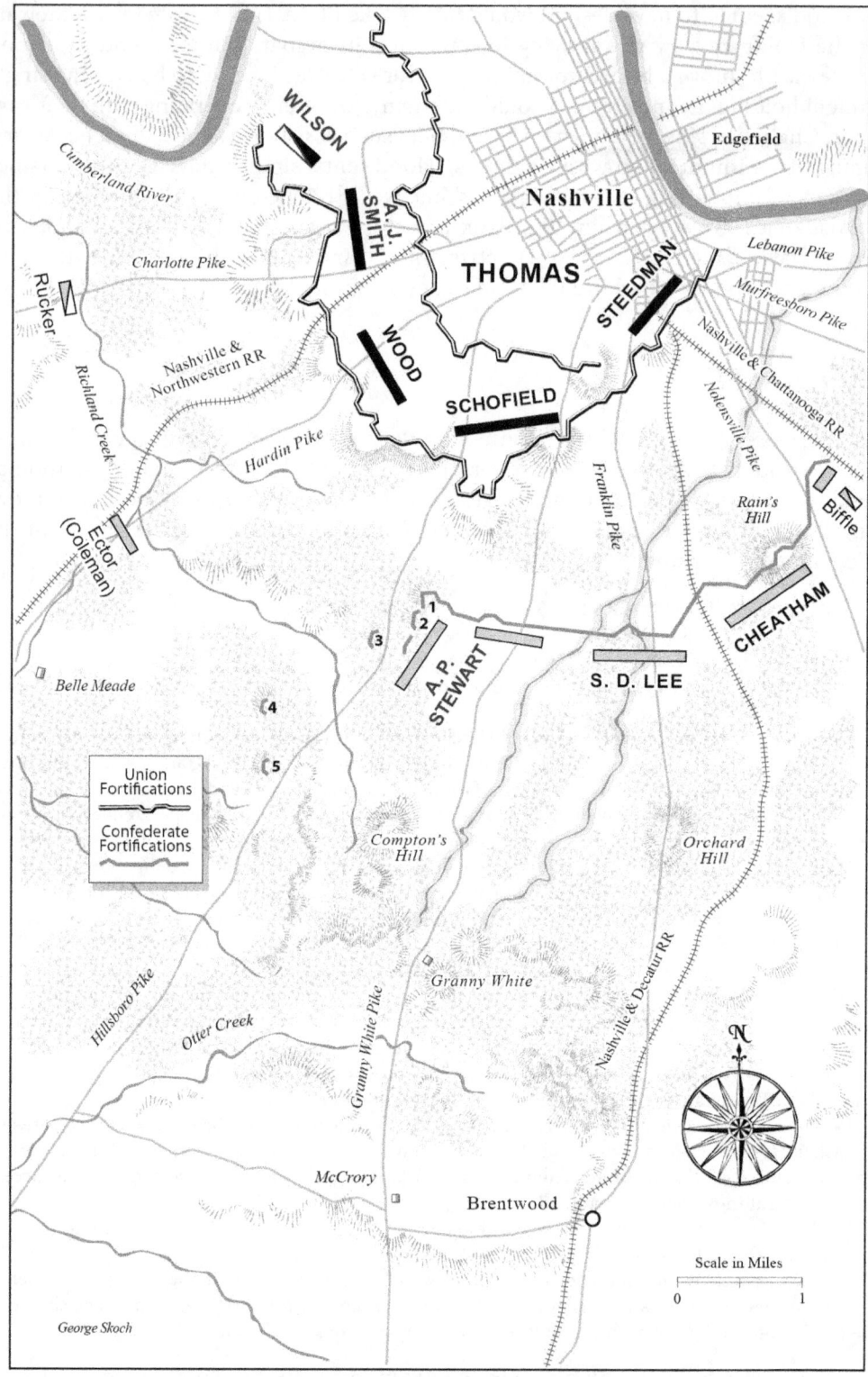

The opposing forces, December 14, 1864.

sion the next day. He told Coon that the left flank of his brigade would move in concert with Smith's infantry "conforming to the movements of the infantry line" and he told Robert Stewart that his brigade would move to the right of Coon's. Hatch told his men to act "vigorously" and to seize any opportunity to attack the enemy. The Confederate cavalry (Rucker's brigade) still had artillery at Bell's Mill and Wilson ordered Johnson to join with the navy in neutralizing the enemy at this location on December 15. The Federal navy planned to move gunboats and start shelling the Confederates the next morning. "This battery is opposite and near Davidson's house, as was supposed, and the general commanding thinks by moving with rapidity you can capture it."[114]

Despite the delay in attacking Hood, Thomas and Wilson accomplished what they intended and that boded well for the Federal cavalry, not only at Nashville, but for the upcoming year. Captain Francis Stewart, 49th Ohio Infantry, observed the impressive sight as Wilson wheeled his cavalry into position on December 14: "The large cavalry force under Gen. Wilson which has been collecting for last two weeks on the opposite side of the river and taking up positions on the right of the infantry. It is the largest and best cavalry force that has ever been had in this dept numbering about 15,000 strong. Under the leadership of Gen. Wilson will do good work." General Henry Boynton would summarize, perhaps, Wilson's greatest contribution to the upcoming battle when wrote that many generals had organized effective cavalry forces, but few had accomplished this in the winter and pursued by an enemy army. The methodical George Thomas saw the value in developing such a strong body of cavalry and made sure Wilson accomplished this plan.[115]

The general movement by Thomas' infantry and Wilson's cavalry would be directed at the western flank of the Confederate Army which was covered by Chalmers' cavalry. With Forrest still at Murfreesboro, Chalmers had a nearly impossible mission and he knew it. Chalmers explained: "I wrote to General Hood, showing the strength of my command and the length of the line which I was expected to hold, and that it would be impossible for me to maintain my position if attacked unless supported." Ector's infantry brigade re-positioned during the day, relieving Chalmers of duty on the Hardin Pike, but Chalmers still covered four miles from the flank of Hood's infantry to Bell's Mill. Historian Stanley Horn would call the use of the small bodies of cavalry to extend Hood's infantry lines on both flanks a "masterpiece of military ineptitude." Nevertheless, Chalmers would be in position to meet the full movement of the Union army the next morning.[116]

Trooper William Black (11th Indiana Cavalry) of Stewart's brigade recorded his thoughts in a letter on the evening before the battle. The pickets were about a thousand yards apart. "We are having hard times only half rations to eat mud half knee deep and very foggy." George Monlux, 8th Iowa Cavalry, noted that the men of Wilson's command felt they had been on the defensive since Hood started his advance from Florence. According to Monlux, the Union cavalrymen were anxious for the offensive actions to begin. In the meantime, the troopers prepared for the battle and tried to stay warm.[117]

Chapter Eleven

The Battle of Nashville—
December 15, 1864

The Confederates "fite like devils."—Eli Russell

It was quite a unique scenario that developed at Nashville in December 1864—a much smaller force besieging a force twice its size. "Yet, the military practicality of the matter was in serious doubt, as Hood knew all too well," wrote historian Wiley Sword. Hood's objective was the destruction of Thomas' army, not the capture of Nashville. Hood had been unsuccessful in defeating the Union forces at Spring Hill and Franklin, and he had little hope of pushing into Kentucky with the large Union army in his rear at Nashville. He received no significant numbers of reinforcements and to return south would be to admit defeat, something he would not do. His only hope was to defensively defeat Thomas, so he waited and, as he waited, his army suffered from adverse weather conditions and poor supplies on the heights south of Nashville while Thomas steadily grew stronger. The Confederate soldiers were aware of the situation they faced. They knew they had lost much of the momentum of the campaign after the Battle of Franklin, but the common soldier tried to make the best of the situation he had been given. A member of the 35th Alabama Infantry reasoned his course was to stick "close to our colors." Hood had no large influx of reinforcements to bolster his army to improve the chance of success of besieging Thomas and he knew the Union army would ultimately attack him. Selecting an excellent defensive position, he planned to draw the Union army away from their strong defenses and crush them as they attacked his lines of infantry.[1]

In some ways, the weather conditions continued to improve as the ice melted on December 15, but as the temperatures increased, a dense fog covered the countryside. In the resulting poor visibility, Thomas deliberately prepared the attack on the enemy. Thomas intended to place the greatest pressure on Hood's western flank while the remainder of the army pushed ahead in demonstrations which would hold the other Confederate forces in place. Over the past few days, Hood had extended his forces eastward to improve his defensive position and presumably to be closer to Forrest's command still at Murfreesboro. A.J. Smith's XVI Corps, Thomas Wood's IV Corps, and Wilson's reinvigorated cavalry corps (now 12,000 men strong) would make the main attack in a large wheeling movement on the western flank. Steedman's District of the Etowah would attack the eastern portion of Hood's line and Schofield's XXIII Corps would be held in reserve and thrown into the battle where there was an opportunity. The remainder of the Union forces would secure the lines at Nashville and the vacated positions of the attacking forces.[2]

Facing Thomas, Hood placed Cheatham's infantry corps on the eastern flank, ex-

Chapter Eleven. The Battle of Nashville—December 15, 1864

tending to the Nolensville Road with his left near Franklin Pike. Stephen D. Lee held the Confederate center—uniting with Cheatham on his right and extending to Granny White Pike on the left. A.P. Stewart's corps held the position with Lee on his right and his left aligned along Hillsboro Pike. This left Rucker's cavalry brigade to hold a position west of Stewart's line and Chalmers' other brigade, Biffle's, on the eastern flank. Meanwhile, Forrest and the bulk of the Confederate cavalry remained unengaged outside Murfreesboro. Chalmers initially placed his headquarters three miles away from Stewart's position and extended his line so that it made a connection with the Cumberland River which Rucker had blockaded for two weeks. The 7th Alabama Cavalry had the major responsibility of picketing the area from Stewart's flank to the main body of Rucker's cavalry on Charlotte Pike.[3]

Hood had not been idle over the past two weeks and had enhanced the Confederate defenses, including digging rifle pits and building five redoubts on his western flank. These redoubts could hold about 100 men and the structures, logs behind earthen walls, also served to protect artillery in these forts but, Redoubt 4 and Redoubt 5 had not been completed. A trench three feet deep was dug outside of the walls for the supporting infantry and the inside walls were eight feet high. Also, these last two redoubts were built outside the Confederate line and were vulnerable to capture by advancing Union troops if they could reach them. On the western flank, rifle pits had also been placed along a 1,000-yard long stone wall. Hood's shortage of men (only 23,000 strong) challenged his ability to man the various defensive positions and this made the redoubts on the extreme left vulnerable targets for the attacking Union soldiers (over 55,000 strong).[4]

Though outnumbered, Hood had the advantage of holding the high ground and to defeat Hood, the Union army needed to march up hills devoid of cover and into the sights of the Confederate guns. This was not going to be an easy battle and the Union soldiers respected their adversaries in gray. Trooper Eli Russell, 2nd Michigan Cavalry, wrote to his wife in December that the Confederates "fite like devils."[5]

Wilson had spent all his time since gaining command of the cavalry in the west assembling, organizing, equipping and mounting his forces. During the initial part of the campaign, Forrest had the upper hand—three veteran divisions pushing four Union brigades steadily to the rear. At Franklin, Wilson gained parity with his Confederate opponents and now the might of the Union forces finally resulted in the assemblage of an impressive cavalry corps. "The effective force was 12,500 men, 9,000 horses, 2,000 of which were scarcely fit for service," wrote Wilson. Wilson's cavalry, which would mostly operate dismounted during the battle, marched south of the Cumberland River near Charlotte Pike and prepared to attack Hood's lines in conjunction with the infantry on the morning of December 15.[6]

Wilson ordered his commanders to prepare for operations at 6 a.m., but it was so foggy that A.J. Smith's XVI Corps could not advance until 10:00 a.m. Leading Smith's infantry attack on the western flank was Kenner Garrard's division on the left, John McArthur's division on the right, and Jonathan Moore's division moving in the center and rear as the reserve of Smith's corps. Most of Wilson's cavalry started the day up to six miles away from the enemy flank and they needed to march through a large valley which circled the southern margin of Nashville. Meanwhile, Steedman on the eastern flank had two assignments—to guard Nashville and to make a demonstration on the eastern flank. He began his attack at 8:00 a.m. and later in the morning made another push on the Confederate positions which resulted in a bloody repulse. Steedman's at-

The outer Union defenses at Nashville, where the cavalry awaited their orders to attack (Library of Congress).

tacking brigades merely served as a diversion, but Hood recognized it as such and this gave him the flexibility of shifting troops to the western flank as the battle developed.[7]

One of the most interesting aspects of the cavalry actions during this battle was Wilson's and Thomas' decision to utilize most of the cavalry as dismounted troops, despite the exhaustive efforts to mount as many men as possible. There was no definitive explanation for this decision. Colonel Lucius Hubbard, brigade commander in Smith's XVI Corps, explained that a large number of horses were injured trying to get the cavalry into position. Historian Jerry Keenan concluded the terrain was unsuitable for mounted actions and Wilson, while not addressing this issue, merely stated that the dismounted cavalry needed to move in conjunction with the infantry units. Regardless of the reason, this represented one of the most remarkable uses of cavalry in a major battle in the Civil War.[8]

The Attack on the West Flank

Finally, the fog lifted and the attacking Union forces on the western flank pushed toward the waiting lines of gray clad soldiers. On the western flank, the forward Confederate defensive positions were supported by a four-gun battery, about a half mile southeast of the Hardin Pike. The attack pushed toward this initial obstacle and the Union artillery moved forward and began an intense barrage at one o'clock. Colonel David Coleman's brigade of French's division, still named Ector's Brigade, had the duty around Redoubt No. 4 and No. 5, two primary targets on the western flank for the Union troops. A.P. Stewart had placed Coleman's men along Hardin Pike to present a solid front from the main Confederate line to Chalmers' cavalry on Charlotte Pike. As the Union barrage slowly ended, Smith's infantry and Hatch's cavalry surged toward the Confederate line. Private William H. Gilliard, 11th Missouri Infantry, would claim that he fired the first shot in the attack as the Battle of Nashville began on the western flank.[9]

Johnson's Sixth Cavalry Division and Croxton's Brigade

Brig. Gen. Richard W. Johnson	
First Brigade—Col. Thomas J. Harrison	*Second Brigade*—Col. James Biddle
16th Illinois, Maj. Charles H. Beeres	14th Illinois, Maj. Haviland Tompkins
5th Iowa, Lt. Col. Harlon Baird	6th Indiana, Maj. Jacob S. Stephens
7th Ohio, Col. Israel Garrard	8th Michigan, Col. Elisha Mix
	3rd Tennessee, Maj. Benjamin Cunningham
Artillery	
4th United States, Battery I, Lt. Frank G. Smith	

Chalmers received a courier from Hood at his headquarters on Charlotte Pike at 2:00 a.m. alerting him to a potential attack on the morning of December 15. Both Chalmers and Coleman would be in desperate situations as the mass of Union troops began their attack. Rucker's brigade, stretched thin from the Cumberland River to Coleman's infantry, would receive the thrust of Richard Johnson's cavalry division. One of Rucker's troopers, John Johnston (14th Tennessee Cavalry), recalled that Rucker's command was some three miles away from the nearest Confederate infantry unit. Initially, linking the large space between Chalmers' main cavalry force and Coleman was a single cavalry regiment, 7th Alabama Cavalry, of about 300 troopers commanded by Colonel Joseph Hodgson. After receiving Hood's communication, Chalmers shifted more regiments closer to the infantry.[10]

At 4 o'clock a.m., Richard Johnson moved his cavalry division onto Charlotte Pike past the interior fortification to the outer fortifications where he encountered Smith's infantry corps. Johnson had been ordered to move forward while protecting Thomas' flank and rear, but the plans changed when he had to wait until Smith moved his infantry. Specifically, Johnson had been told to move his cavalry in conjunction with Smith's infantry while driving the Confederate cavalry away from its blockade at Bell's Mill but, as a result of the fog, the entire movement on the western flank stalled for several hours. One Federal trooper described the fog as so dense he could not see a horse or man 10 feet away. While Johnson prepared to begin his advance, many on the battlefield heard the Federal gunboats firing on Rucker's position at Bell's Mill. Unknown to the Federal commanders, Kelley had evacuated his position the evening before. At 11:00 a.m., Johnson received instructions from Wilson that Smith was ready to attack and to prepare his cavalry to move at the same time. As the attack began, a section of Confederate artillery, in place on a ridge beyond Richland Creek, opened fire on Johnson's advancing lines and Johnson ordered his guns of Battery I, 4th U.S. Artillery, to return the fire from the Douglass House. Johnson ordered James Biddle to send a strong line of skirmishers to lead the Federal advance on Chalmers' cavalry. Biddle placed his dismounted regiments across Charlotte Pike and, behind his skirmishers, he advanced on the enemy position. Chalmers' cavalry formed a defensive line on a ridge behind Richland Creek which extended from the Cumberland River to Hardin Pike. Thomas Harrison's mounted brigade moved behind Biddle's, but Biddle, whose troopers plodded through the deep mud, moved too slowly to suit Johnson. Johnson concluded several factors caused Biddle's men to move so slowly: "[O]wing, I suppose, partly to their being unused to maneuver as infantry, partly to the difficulty in crossing the creek [Richland Creek], and partly to their sabers, which the commanding officer of the Fourteenth Illinois Cavalry had, with a singular shortsightedness, permitted his men to bring with them." It is unclear who ordered the dismounted cavalry to march with sabers, but Biddle's men would not be the only brigade shackled with these weapons. W.L. Sanford, 14th Illinois, recalled that many of the dismounted cavalry threw their sabers in piles as they marched by, but many others questioned this: "What right have we, without orders, to disarm ourselves in time of battle?" The frustrated Johnson sent Harrison's brigade, riding past Biddle's dismounted cavalry, to attack "with all possible energy. My order was executed with commendable celerity."[11]

To make matters worse, Biddle's brigade while being dismounted was also poorly armed. Some of the regiments amounted to small numbers of men, being depleted after years of war. Some of Biddle's regiments still carried the infantry-style Springfield muskets and, in the case of the 8th Michigan, they apparently carried no long guns at all. Colonel Elisha Mix stated that his regiment was designated as "light cavalry" and was the only regiment to carry that title. His men were armed with sabers and revolvers only. Biddle had been ordered "with a strong skirmish line covering his front to cross the creek, drive in the enemy's skirmishers, and assault the enemy's barricades on the crest of the ridge beyond." Now, this task fell to Harrison's mounted brigade.[12]

The boom of artillery signaled the beginning of the Union attack. From the ridge, the Confederate cavalrymen saw the panorama of the advancing bluecoats. "Look! Look! Just look at the Yankees!" exclaimed one of the troopers. Despite the difficulty of getting the Union attack under way, J.P. Young, 7th Tennessee (CSA) watched the mass of Federal skirmishers emerge "pouring over the hills and through the valleys." Hearing the explosion of the guns, the reserves of Rucker's cavalry near Charlotte Pike swung into their saddles and rode in the direction of Nashville to move into the prepared defenses. The long lines of blue-coated soldiers steadily marched ahead. John Johnston, 14th Tennessee, explained the "day was cloudless and balmy, the ground still covered with patches of the rapidly melting snow." The Confederate troopers prepared themselves for the fight they knew would come. They moved onto the ridge, behind barricades of rails, and awaited the arrival of the Union troops. As the Confederate cavalry fell into line, Chalmers rode among the men encouraging them to hold the line and aligning the defenses.[13]

The Confederates watched the unfolding display in front of them. Tennessee cavalryman, John Johnston, observed the Federal infantry and cavalry lines begin their

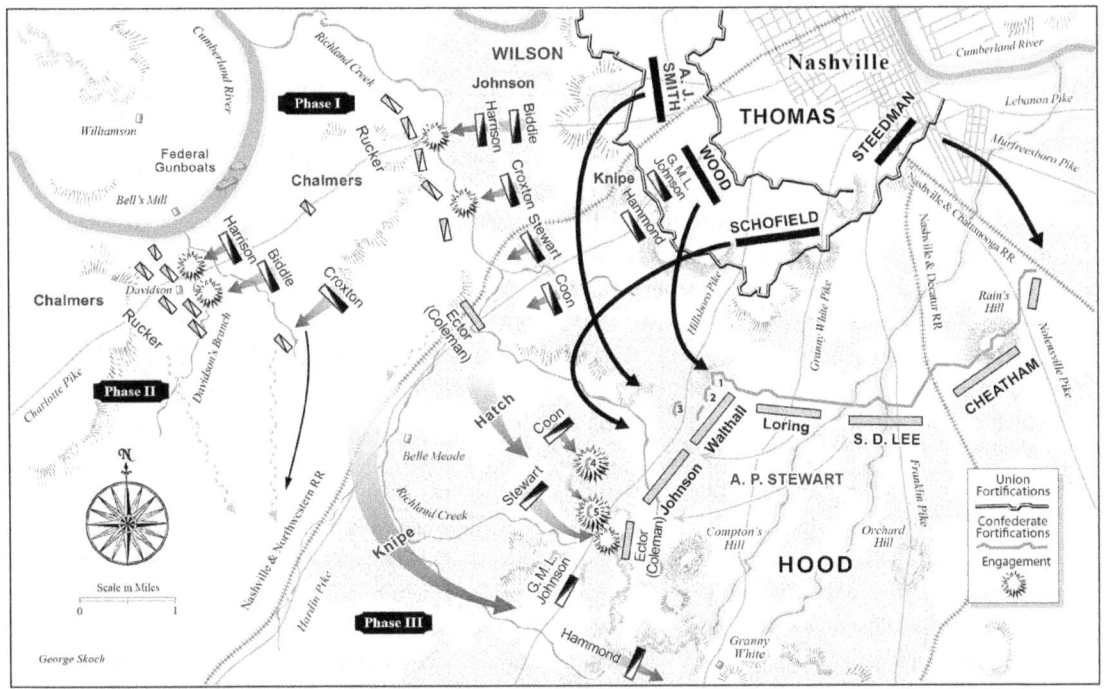

Cavalry actions, December 15, 1864. *Phase I*: Attack along Richland Creek; *Phase II*: Johnson battles Rucker at Davidson House; *Phase III*: Hatch and Knipe attack the western flank of the Confederate line.

attack "in beautiful form and as steady as on dress parade." The fighting began with some light skirmishing as the long lines of blue-coated soldiers marched forward. It was unnerving for Rucker's men as a full infantry division began marching in their direction, but almost immediately, the infantry made large wheeling turn and moved off toward the main battle line. Johnston remarked that the size of the attack gave the Southern defenders a "feeling of helplessness." In their wake came Johnson's Federal cavalry moving directly for Rucker's position. As Johnson's division advanced, the artillery batteries hammered away and the Union gunboats on the river joined in the battle by firing on the Confederate positions near the river. "This artillery duel lasted an hour or more. Our dismounted cavalry patiently taking their fire without power to return it," wrote W.L. Sanford. The 14th Illinois and 6th Indiana supported the Union batteries while the other regiments pressed the enemy. The echo of the large guns on the gunboats encouraged the Union cavalrymen on the field.[14]

Harrison surged past Biddle's brigade and he ordered the 5th Iowa to dismount. The Iowans engaged Rucker's skirmishers along Charlotte Pike and pushed the skirmishers across Richland Creek, about four miles from Nashville and a mile or so outside the outer fortifications. At the same time, the 16th Illinois Cavalry thundered forward on the left flank over the creek and then "charged mounted up the long slope to the ridge upon which the enemy's battery and dismounted men in barricades were posted." The Illinoisans intended to capture the battery either by forcing the supporting troops away or killing the artillery horses before they could withdraw the guns. Johnson wrote, "I never saw a charge more gallantly made or more persistently pressed than this. It failed only by a few moments." Major Charles Beeres, in command of the 16th Illinois, had the misfortune to encounter a stone wall which his horses could not clear while advancing up the hill. The Confederate soldiers felt they were outnumbered and put up a "bold front and dallied with them," noted John Johnston. Theodore Allen, 7th Ohio, described in his diary: "The enemy resists our advance stubbornly."[15]

The Federal attack stalled and the troopers pondered how to get past the wall, but in the meantime, the Confederate artillery, Walton's Battery, and cavalry seeing their predicament hastily limbered and rode away. Croxton's Union cavalry brigade moved along the left of Johnson and succeeded in turning Rucker's flank, forcing his right back toward Charlotte Pike and the Cumberland River. Rucker planned to hold the Federal attack as long as possible, hoping to maintain the cohesiveness of Hood's left flank, but there were just too many Union troopers to hold the position. Upon observing the Confederate withdrawal, Richard Johnson urged his division forward. J.P. Young, 7th Tennessee Cavalry (CSA), watched the attack begin from his position on Charlotte Pike and saw the enemy skirmishers advancing "in clouds" toward his position. As Johnson advanced, the infantry and cavalry battle to the east resulted in Coleman's infantry brigade, which had secured Chalmers' right flank, being pushed back further east to the main Confederate line. Some of Rucker's regiment extended into the area between Charlotte Pike and Harding Pike and faced Croxton's advance which proceeded faster than Johnson now that Coleman's brigade withdrew. The cavalry trying to hold the area vacated by the infantry were driven back by Croxton. On Charlotte Pike, Young's men fought a line of cavalry in the front when they discovered Croxton's Union cavalry edging around the flank. Lieutenant Colonel William F. Taylor, commanding the 7th Tennessee, moved to block the flanking movement. He placed a stack of squadrons which fired and then retreated to the rear of the stack, while the next squadron fired. Young wrote: "This saved the regiment." The retreating squadrons held on as long as possible, sometimes facing the enemy only yards away.[16]

Chalmers' cavalry fell back and made a second attempt to halt the Federal cavalry at Cochran's House with little success. "Harrison hustled them with amusing celerity, and drove him rapidly to Davidson's house," wrote Johnson. At Davidson's house (about five miles from the outer fortifications), Chalmers' defense stiffened, as he gained some of his men who had been forced westward by Croxton's advance. John Johnston recalled that his regiment arrived at the gallop and joined in the defense at this location. Again, posting his troops extending from the river to a knoll at Davidson's house, Chalmers prepared a good defense to meet Johnson's attack by placing his artillery near the house which covered the pike and the bridge over Davidson's Branch. Johnson's division had good success as long as it operated along the Charlotte Pike but at 2:15 p.m. Johnson observed the enemy had moved east over the pike. Johnson then followed the enemy, now over six miles from Nashville. Chalmers' cavalry was firmly behind barricades at all the crossings over the creek. Johnson explained: "Harrison's men, in the energy of his pursuit not observing, or at least not appreciating, the advantages of the enemy's position, attempted to follow the enemy's rear directly into his works, and in this too gallant effort, one company of the Seventh Ohio was roughly handled, losing one man seriously wounded, and several captured, including Lieutenant Little, the commanding officer. Our advance being stayed by this repulse, the enemy opened a sharp fire from his battery, doing us, however, no damage." A participant in this attack, R.C. Rankin, 7th Ohio, recalled some reluctance and concern about making the charge. The Federals saw four

Chapter Eleven. The Battle of Nashville—December 15, 1864

pieces of artillery stuck in the mud in a cornfield and this enticed them to make a bold attempt to capture the guns. Israel Garrard ordered Captain Andrew Hall to take three companies over a bridge, with the promise of support by another two companies closely following behind. The 5th Iowa Cavalry had yet to arrive on the scene and Rankin asked, "Isn't that a little premature? Would not be well to wait for till 5th Iowa comes up...?" Garrard replied, "Captain, I want you to make the charge." The Confederate artillery added firepower to the Confederate position, and Johnson ordered Battery I, 4th U.S. Artillery, commanded by Lieutenant Frank G. Smith, forward to engage the Confederate guns. Rankin recalled the five attacking companies were aligned in columns of four and the order was given to attack in the midst of "shot and shell coming thick and fast." The attack proceeded over a ridge, down the hill, over a fence, across a creek and a narrow bridge, and across another small stream. At 30 yards from the enemy line, Rankin looked over his shoulder and to his dismay, he saw half the attacking force failed to make it past the bridge. Rankin's company had been reduced to 16–18 men during the attack so far, and he halted the attack, realizing it had failed. Meanwhile, the dismounted cavalry of Biddle's brigade arrived and began filing into the Federal line. Between the Federals and the Confederates lay an open field and the Union cavalry had to move down a gradual slope in full view of the enemy guns. Chalmers had the additional advantage of having a steep approach to his lines. Chalmers' position was a strong one, and Johnson made no further progress.[17]

A member of Chalmers' division described the repulse of Johnson's division which included a counterattack on the 7th Ohio by the Southern cavalrymen. "General Chalmers quickly got a battery of smooth-bore guns in position, and, when the column of cavalry crossed the branch and started up the hill, grape shot were used with fearful effect. It was a terrible scene. Men and horses were killed, and others stumbled and fell over

The old Davidson homeplace, where Chalmers and Johnson fought on the afternoon of December 15 (undated photograph, courtesy Tennessee State Library & Archives)

them. Our guns continued to fire, and the enemy on the right, shocked by the result, began to retreat. Rucker saw the opportunity, and, grasping a flag, raised it above his head and ordered a charge. He dashed along in front of his line, urging his men to push on. At the same time, General Chalmers with his escort charged them on the left, and within three minutes the enemy was on the run." After this clash, the two lines halted and remained facing each other across Davidson Branch.[18]

As the Confederate troopers fired from behind their barricades, the advancing Union cavalry fell into line and returned fire. John Johnston fired and then heard a solid "thump" as a ball struck the man at his side. Johnston tore open the shirt of the wounded man and only found a dark pink indentation on the man's chest. He had been struck with a "spent ball" much to the relief of the wounded soldier, who reloaded and continued firing.[19]

With a couple of hours of daylight remaining, Harrison and Johnson assessed their situation, as Biddle's men reached Harrison's position. The Union officers concluded they could not push past the barricades and deal with the Confederate artillery without substantial losses. Johnson sent a message to Wilson explaining that his right flank extended to the Cumberland River and that the 7th Ohio had attacked with no success. Croxton's brigade was some distance away on Johnson's left flank and Johnson appealed to him for assistance. Johnson hoped that Croxton could throw his brigade into the fight and together they could dislodge Chalmers. Johnson wrote: "I accordingly maneuvered my troops so as to attract the attention of the enemy to me, while Croxton, who was now a long distance to my left and rear, should comply with a request which I sent him to close up on my left and swing around so as to envelop the enemy's right and cut him off from the Charlotte pike." The plan was a good one, if Croxton could reach the position in time. In the meantime, Johnson sent couriers to the gunboats urging the continued firing on the Confederate line, and the navy readily complied. "[T]he tremendous discharges of his heavy guns contributed largely, I doubt not, to the already serious demoralization of the enemy." Trooper Theodore Allen, 7th Ohio, noted that the gunboats assisted in the attack and "made the woods roar, with their 100 pounders." Southern cavalryman John Johnston agreed and said the gunboats made the "air and the earth quiver." While the gunboats did their part, Wilson gave orders to Croxton to move toward Hillsboro Pike which prevented him from assisting Johnson. Johnson marched his men down the slope in preparation for an assault on Chalmers' line while he waited for Croxton's arrival but did not give the order to attack. By the time Johnson learned Croxton could not assist him, the day was over and he camped for the night. Despite being stymied by the Confederates, Johnson felt he had accomplished his orders and had moved Chalmers about 8 miles from Nashville. He knew the fight was not over and he sent orders to be ready to attack again at 4:00 a.m. on December 16.[20]

In regard to Chalmers' efforts, he had performed remarkable service and successfully stopped Johnson's advance with about 1,200 men, but he had little joy. A major battle was occurring to his right and the Union army was winning the day. He needed to find his way back to Hood's flank and later in the evening, Chalmers ordered his cavalry to retire toward the main Confederate line. He left the 7th Alabama Cavalry to hold the line in front of Harrison's and Biddle's brigades while moving the rest of his command across Hardin Pike and then to Hillsboro Pike. As Chalmers moved north, he rode to Belle Meade, his headquarters, only to find it in possession of the Union cavalry and his supply train captured. Chalmers charged the small enemy force in possession of

Belle Meade, scattering them and then continued northward; he soon encountered the more substantial force of Croxton's brigade just north of the plantation ready to fight. James Dinkins recalled: "As they rode back, Bleecker saw Miss Seline Harding standing on the stone arm of the front steps waving her handkerchief. The bullets were falling thick and fast about her, but she had no fear in her heart. She looked like a goddess. She was the gamest little human being in all the crowd. Bleecker passed and caught the handkerchief, and urged her to go into the house, but she would not, until the boys had disappeared behind the barn." Chalmers had no doubt about the difficult position of his division after the fighting during the day. John Johnston wrote: "How short the day seemed, and how soon the night came."[21]

Johnson made little comment regarding Biddle's brigade after the first part of the battle. Biddle merely reported that his brigade served in a support role for most of the fight and when Chalmers made his last stand at Davidson's house, his regiments filled in the gaps in Harrison's line. "Here the Sixth Indiana Cavalry supported the artillery, the Fourteenth Illinois Cavalry filling a gap between the mounted portion of the Sixth Division and the First Division, General Croxton." Theodore Allen, 7th Ohio, would conclude his diary entry: "Hard work all day.... The gunboats aids us very materially with their big guns..."[22]

Croxton's First Cavalry Brigade, First Cavalry Division

Brig. Gen. John T. Croxton
8th Iowa, Col. Joseph B. Dorr
4th Kentucky (mounted infantry), Col. Robert M. Kelly
2nd Michigan, Lt. Col. Benjamin Smith
1st Tennessee, Lt. Col. Calvin M. Dyer
Artillery
Illinois Light Artillery, Board of Trade Battery, Capt. George I. Robinson

As the battle unfolded, the citizens at Nashville moved to the housetops and along some of the hills to watch the Union attack. Lieutenant Colonel Isaac R. Sherwood, 111th Ohio Infantry, recalled that the hills were "black with human beings" as they stood in awe of the unfolding battle. Croxton's mounted brigade advanced, to the left of Johnson's division, between Hardin and Charlotte pikes. Croxton had served under Hatch and Johnson at various times during the past month, but now he operated independently. After getting his troopers ready to advance at 4:00 a.m. Croxton's initial movements, like Johnson's, did not go smoothly and he became entangled with two brigades of McArthur's infantry. He began the day outside the fortifications near the Nashville & Northwestern Railroad to the right of Hatch's division and the left of Johnson's. He waited until the infantry began the attack and then he rode forward, initially riding between the railroad and Charlotte Pike. He sent out skirmishers in advance of his main force and then began to hurry ahead. A sharp skirmish resulted just before noon and Croxton paused along a ridge "overlooking a valley and remained there for some time, enemy on the ridge ahead." When McArthur's infantry began its wheeling movement, Croxton continued ahead and crossed Richland Creek, threatening Rucker's right flank. With Johnson pushing ahead and Croxton along his flank and rear, Rucker had little choice but to withdraw.[23]

The acting quartermaster for the 2nd Michigan, Henry Hempstead, watched the battle unfold from his position in the rear and wrote: "I could see the flash and hear the roar of the cavalry carbines ... and the muskets of Smith's corps high up among the hills in our front as they steadily doubled up and drove back the left of Hood's Army."[24]

With Rucker's first withdrawal, Croxton continued his advance trying to hold a line between the advancing forces. He found a Confederate artillery battery in place on Charlotte Pike "which I could not pass." George Monlux, 8th Iowa, watched as the Confederate battery fired on the Union troops and then, the Chicago Board of Trade Horse Artillery, attached to Croxton's brigade "came quietly marching along the pike." The veteran Federal battery moved forward and when they came in range of the Confederate battery it increased to a gallop, stopping about 500 yards away from the enemy guns. In the meantime, Croxton ordered his regiments into line with the 2nd Michigan on the right and the 8th Iowa in support. The two batteries were within plan sight of each other and Monlux described it "as no grander sight" in the war. The Federal cavalrymen were temporarily mesmerized by the workings of the two batteries. Then, Croxton observed a line of Confederate cavalry on the hills to his front and he ordered two regiments to dismount and charge up the hill; despite having to push through some dense cane brakes, the enemy was "driven at the first dash." This action widened the void in the Confederate left flank between Coleman and Chalmers. An officer in Coleman's brigade, Lieutenant J.T. Tunnel observed a "vast body of cavalry maneuvering to our left front" followed by infantry. Coleman held out as long as he could and ordered his men to run the two miles back to the main Confederate line. Afterward, Croxton planned to join Hatch, but he was ordered by Colonel A.J. Alexander, Wilson's chief of staff—"arriving directed me to remain, supporting General Johnson, which I did until sundown, when I proceeded, by order of the general commanding, to rejoin the corps on the Hillsborough pike." As Croxton prepared to move toward Hillsboro Pike, Chalmers' cavalry was withdrawing and ran directly in front of Croxton's brigade. "[W]e encountered them on the Hardin pike, and I accordingly left the Fourth Kentucky Mounted Infantry at Williams' house to cover that road."[25]

The Confederates Croxton encountered near the Hardin Pike resulted in the last fight of the day for this brigade. The clash between Croxton and Chalmers was a serendipitous encounter. Chalmers realizing the difficult situation he faced on Charlotte Pike stealthily moved most of Rucker's brigade north. The Confederate cavalrymen were ordered to move quietly and not to speak over a whisper. Just at dark, Croxton sent the 1st Tennessee to the left of the brigade and the regiment received fire from Confederates behind a stone wall. Croxton told Lieutenant Colonel Calvin Dyer to lead his Tennesseans in an attack and with a yell, the troopers surged forward. Seeing the enemy only by the flash of their carbines, the 1st Tennessee rushed toward the wall under a steady fire and leapt among the defenders, 5th Mississippi Cavalry, who headed for the rear, but not before sending some near misses in the direction of Croxton who was mounted and moving with his troops. The colonel of the 8th Iowa Cavalry also had a narrow escape as the darkness made it impossible to see. The 8th Iowa came upon some men in a cane brake near to the action of the 1st Tennessee and the colonel yelled, "Who are you out there? If you are rebels we can whip the devil out of you." This was greeted with an explosion of carbine fire. The colonel, chastised but unharmed, hurried back behind his lines. After running into Croxton, Rucker's men disengaged and moved farther away to Hillsboro Pike where they set up a barricade and established a picket line some distance away from Croxton's men. At dusk, Croxton crossed Hardin Pike and moved to his assigned position on Hillsboro Pike, camping about five and a half miles from Nashville.[26]

Hatch's Fifth Cavalry Division

Brig. Gen. Edward Hatch	
First Brigade—Col. Robert R. Stewart	*Second Brigade*—Col. Datus E. Coon
3rd Illinois, Lt. Col. Robert H. Carnahan	6th Illinois, Lt. Col. John Lynch
11th Indiana, Lt. Col. Abram Sharra	7th Illinois, Maj. John M. Graham
12th Missouri, Col. Oliver Wells	9th Illinois, Captain Joseph W. Harper
10th Tennessee: Maj. William Story (mw), Maj. James T. Abernathy	2nd Iowa, Maj. Charles C. Horton
	12th Tennessee Cav., Col. George Spalding (w)
Artillery	
Battery I, 1st Illinois Light Artillery, Lt. Joseph A. McCarthey	

Meanwhile, Hatch's Fifth Division started the day's action on the left of Croxton and the right of Smith's infantry. Wood's IV Corps advanced southward with Smith on his right. At 12:30 p.m., Smith and Hatch moved into line with Wood as the main attack on the west flank began. McArthur's division (William L. McMillen's, Lucius F. Hubbard's and Sylvester G. Hill's brigades) of Smith's corps connected with Hatch's division. Hatch ran into the line of David Coleman's infantry and some of Chalmers' cavalry "well intrenched on both sides of Richland Creek" near Hardin Pike. After a quick and "sharp fight," the Confederate troops, outnumbered, headed for the rear and Hatch moved his cavalry past Hardin's house. Coleman had little hope of holding his position, because Hatch's cavalry slipped around the flank and nearly enveloped the Southern brigade. Hatch's division advancing along the right flank was dismounted, except for one regiment in each brigade (12th Tennessee in Coon's brigade and the 12th Missouri in Stewart's brigade) which remained in the saddle. The led horses for the other regiments moved in the rear of their respective regiments. Hatch's division ran into a line of rifle pits and barricades, and he ordered Stewart's dismounted cavalry to charge the defenders. Stewart's brigade travelled due south, charging ahead and driving the enemy "down the Hardin Road." Lieutenant Preston Sharp, 12th Missouri, noted in his diary that his regiment attacked the enemy making two "desperate" charges during this action, both successful. Coon's brigade remained connected to the attacking infantry and this gave Stewart's brigade the opportunity and obligation to clear the enemy off the flank. After Stewart's men drove Coleman's infantry back to the main Confederate line, they redirected their efforts to securing Coon's right flank by swinging in an easterly direction. While moving toward the enemy lines, Hatch marched over "stumpy" ground, found the end of Hood's line and moved past it with Stewart's brigade.[27]

Around 2:15 p.m. the attack on the extreme left of the Confederate line continued in earnest as the dismounted cavalrymen and the First Brigade of Brigadier General John McArthur's Division, commanded by Colonel William McMillen (114th Illinois, 93rd Indiana, 10th Minnesota, 72nd Ohio, 95th Ohio, and Cogswell's Light Artillery), supported by Hubbard's Second Brigade, attacked the Confederate line. The attack focused on driving Coleman's infantry away from the flank and, then, on two redoubts. Redoubt No. 4, containing four 12-pounder cannons, was the first fort in front of the regiments of McMillen's, Hubbard's and Coon's brigades. These redoubts were defended by Major General Edward Walthall's Division. Specifically, Redoubt 4, containing about 150 infantry defenders in addition to the gun crews, was commanded by Captain John Lumsden. Lumsden, a graduate of the Virginia Military Institute, had no delusions about his situation and had already told A.P. Stewart that under a concentrated attack the redoubt would not hold. Located about 600 yards southeast was Redoubt No. 5, containing two 12-pound Napoleon cannons, and this fort, defended with about 100 men, had been under construction the morning of the battle.[28]

Just before the attack began, Coon spent an hour just aligning his troops in preparation for the advance in conjunction with the infantry which presented "a most magnificent spectacle." Just as Croxton had found an immediate opportunity to strike the enemy, when Coon crossed the Hardin Pike and as Coleman's infantry headed for the rear, he also found one—a Confederate wagon train moving south, and he ordered Colonel George Spalding's 12th Tennessee to seize it. By mid-day, Spalding led his 12th Tennessee (mounted) ahead and captured Chalmers headquarters train of 14 to 20 wagons (depending on the account) with Chalmers's divisional records, clothing, and a safe. The Scottish-born Spalding, commanding the regiment which had offered such important service during the fight at Spring Hill, captured 40 men during the attack. Chalmers had established his headquarters at Belle Meade Plantation and the large wheeling maneuver of the Federal troops, which drove Coleman's infantry rearward, gave the 12th Tennessee the opportunity to claim the train. Next, Hatch marched from Williams' house toward Hillsboro Pike and then reconnected with the infantry after these preliminary fights with the enemy cavalry and infantry. Ahead, the two redoubts were clearly seen. Hatch wheeled Battery I, First Illinois Light Artillery, into place and ordered a barrage on the nearest redoubt, Redoubt No. 4, still unfinished positioned on a hill in full view of the advancing Federal army. Coon's brigade lined up to attack the redoubt and then, moved forward.[29]

Coon's brigade advanced in the great half wheel movement and being on the outside of the wheel, the cavalry had moved a greater distance. This, no doubt, drew a few smiles from the foot-weary infantrymen. Coon's men, armed with 100 rounds of ammunition at daybreak, marched about three miles at "double-quick" and he moved his men into position on the enemy west flank about a mile and a quarter from Hardin Pike. After moving his artillery into place, he initially positioned the 7th Illinois and 2nd Iowa in support of the battery. Then, the Union artillery opened fire and also immediately the guns in the redoubt returned fire. The two batteries continued to fire at each other for about an hour as the Union cavalry inched closer. The redoubt had already been under fire for hours by several batteries of Union artillery. When about 500 yards from the redoubt, Hatch ordered Coon to charge. Coon ordered the 7th

Chapter Eleven. The Battle of Nashville—December 15, 1864

The Union lines surged ahead toward the waiting Confederates on the hills (A.R. Waud sketch showing the charge at Fredericksburg, Library of Congress).

Illinois, 2nd Iowa, 9th Illinois, and 6th Illinois (positioned from right to left) to attack. The two regiments on the right of the line charged across an open field (except two stone fences), but the left two regiments had to move through a dense thicket. Coon remained in the saddle and rode among his troops in preparation for the attack. "At the word 'Forward!' stone [fences and] thickets were very slight impediments in the way of this veteran brigade," wrote Coon. The enemy artillerymen were using shells as the attack began, but they quickly changed to canister. Lieutenant A.O. Abbott, 9th Illinois Cavalry, waited with the regiment as the artillery continued firing until a large explosion racked the redoubt as a caisson erupted in fire, followed closely by a second explosion. Then, without orders the Illinois cavalry, in line, raced toward the redoubt. The Union cavalrymen soon felt the heavy fire from the infantry in support of the redoubt. Coon wrote, "As I rode along the line I found each regiment competing with the others to reach the redoubt. So near the same time did each regiment reach the redoubt that it was difficult for some time to ascertain who was the first to reach the prize. All acted nobly, and are entitled to the highest praise, under the circumstances, for their efforts to be the first."[30]

The small number of Confederate defenders stoutly held their position, firing into the Union lines. Finally, they were simply overwhelmed. The wave of blue-coated soldiers sent the Confederate infantry outside Redoubt No. 4 scurrying to the rear. Lumsden's men implored the retreating men: "Stay and help us! Help us hold!" but the infantry continued moving to the east replying, "It can't be done!" The afternoon duty for the Confederate defenders on the western flank had been impossible. They had been outmatched by the various batteries firing on them but they stubbornly held their position. When the defenders watched their supporting troops withdraw, they turned and saw in front, a hundred yards away, dismounted cavalry and infantry converging on the fort. Sergeant James R. Maxwell, Lumsden's Battery, lamented: "[T]here was nothing they could do but to fire and run." Hatch ordered Coon's men to hold their fire until they were 300 yards away. Then, Coon's cavalry opened fire with concentrated volleys. Hatch, riding to the 7th Illinois Cavalry, encouraged them in the attack, urging: "Go into them, sir, with what you've got." The retreating Confederates left their cannons in the redoubt and they hurried away. After claiming the redoubt, the Union cavalry turned the captured guns 180 degrees and aimed them at the enemy on the hill above.[31]

Some of the Confederate artillerymen stayed with their guns even as the Federal line reached the fort. The dismounted cavalry, members of the 11th Missouri, and even mounted horsemen, "swarmed over, and past our guns at both ends and through the embrasures," wrote one of the artillerymen. Once inside the redoubt, Coon's troopers told the Southern artillerymen, at the point of their sabers, to turn the guns on their retreating comrades, now about 500 yards away. Some accounts reported that the enemy artillerymen complied with this difficult duty. The Union cavalrymen had little sympathy because the guns had been loaded and meant to kill them. However, the accounts from the 9th Illinois Cavalry acknowledged this was too much to ask of anyone. Since the 9th Illinois Cavalry had been equipped with mountain howitzers early in the war, many in the regiments still knew how to fire cannons and they assisted in the firing of the captured guns. The official report of the capture of Redoubt No. 4 confirmed the capture of four 12-pounder guns and 60 prisoners.[32]

The redoubts were placed along the flank in less than an ideal defense. These compact forts had little opportunity for support being placed outside the main infantry line and redoubts 3–5 were spaced so that one fort did not actually provide protection for the other forts. Hood intended that these forts should be self-supporting defenses, but he did not anticipate the intensity of the attacks now taking place.[33]

After the first redoubt was captured, Redoubt No. 5, about 600 yards away on a steep bluff, 200 feet high, with strong defenses, opened fire on the victorious Union cavalry. General Hatch arrived, still mounted and presenting an easy target, and ordered Coon to go after the next redoubt. Again, Hatch advanced with McArthur's First and Second brigades joining the attack. Coon realigned his brigade, moved in the direction of the next redoubt and ordered "charge" again. It took about 20 minutes to reach the next redoubt. This time the 2nd Iowa planted their colors, but Lieutenant John H. Carpenter, 9th Illinois Cavalry, claimed the honor of being the first Union soldier in the redoubt. Sergeant John F. Hartman immediately arrived with the colors and planted them in the redoubt, only to be shot in the stomach as he did so, suffering a mortal wound. "During the charge the enemy kept up a brisk cannonading, accompanied by heavy musketry firing from the infantry within the redoubt. The long march previous, the charge in taking the first redoubt, and the short time given until the charge of the second, rendered it almost impossible for a cavalryman to move faster than a walk," described Coon. During this last mad dash, the effect of the long march and the sprints across the fields filled with cannon and musket fire fatigued many of the men who "fell to the ground exhausted" during the capture of the second redoubt. "Many

Chapter Eleven. The Battle of Nashville—December 15, 1864   243

killed during the attack. Further to the north, IV Corps attacked Redoubt No. 1 which resulted in the capture of the final redoubt.[41]

While the battle on the right was taking place, Wood's corps had advanced and captured the strategically important Montgomery Hill. Thomas ordered Schofield to advance at 1:00 p.m. and around 3:00 p.m. Schofield's XXIII Corps joined in the fight, supporting the flank of XVI Corps. XVI Corps moved toward the Confederate line on the western flank and a line of defenders, behind a stone wall east and parallel to the Hillsboro Pike, greeted the Union line with a furious volley. Facing Reynolds' infantry, Hubbard ordered his men to fire and the defenders "recoiled under our withering fire and fell back in disorder before the steady advance." The first Confederate line was overwhelmed as the Union forces steadily moved forward. Hubbard claimed about 400 prisoners as they moved past the wall. As the brigade moved forward, they also captured two additional cannons that were left unlimbered on a road, but Hubbard prudently decided not to advance further with his flank unprotected. Hubbard formed his line on a crest to meet an approaching Confederate line and brought up the 2nd Iowa Artillery, "whose effective practice checked the movements of the re-enforcing column of the enemy and served to increase the confusion of the retreat." As the Confederate reinforcements hastened to meet the Union attack, the focus of the battle shifted to an intense infantry battle. The Union troops were converging on the angle in the line held by Reynolds. As McArthur's division advanced, General Edward Walthall ordered Reynolds to withdraw from his non-defendable position when he found himself being flanked on both ends of his line.[42]

Schofield's corps reached the right flank of Smith's infantry. Edward Johnson's Confederate infantry division was ordered to the left of Walthall and Loring as the Union lines extended past Hood's left flank. A.J. Smith's infantry continued forward and pushed the Confederate line to the rear. By this time, Schofield's fresh infantry was a "full half mile beyond the Hillsboro Pike and in the rear of both Walthall and Loring," wrote historian Thomas Robson Hay. The two mounted regiments in Hatch's divisions swooped in on several groups of isolated or confused enemy infantry, driving them back toward the Union lines where they were captured.[43]

A.P. Stewart knew he was in trouble as soon as the line of blue moved toward his flank and pushed Ector's brigade and the small number of Chalmers' cavalry rearward. Loring's, Walthall's and French's division were soon "stretched to its utmost tension." Stewart asked Hood for reinforcements to hold the position and Hood responded by sending Manigault's and Deas brigades to bolster the western flank. Later, Hood sent two additional brigades, Jacob Sharp's and William Brantley's, of mostly Mississippi troops to shore up the line, but by the time reinforcements began to arrive the hillside was swarming with Federal troops. Deas' and Manigault's brigades fell into line next to Walthall parallel to the Hillsboro Pike. Walthall's men were securely posted behind a rock wall, but this was only temporary. With Schofield's men hurrying forward, Smith's infantry pushing ahead and two brigades of cavalry advancing, Deas and Manigault withdrew exposing Walthall's left flank. Loring's infantry hastened to fill the gap "arriving just at this moment" and encouraged Deas and Manigault to rally, again moving forward to support the Confederate line. Sharp's and Brantley's men arrived and fell into line, but it was too late. Stewart wrote: "[We] were unable to check the progress of the enemy, who had passed the Hillsborough pike a full half mile, completely turning our flank and gaining the rear of both Walthall and Loring, whose situation was becoming perilous in the extreme. Their positions were maintained to the last possible moment, in the hope that the expected succor would arrive and restore the fight on the left. Deeming it absolutely necessary for them to fall back, orders were dispatched to that effect, when it was found that Walthall had already ordered his line to retire not a moment too soon, and this of itself made it necessary for Loring to withdraw. The latter was directed also to form along the Granny White pike (which would place him nearly at right angles to his former position) to check the anticipated rush of the enemy from his and Walthall's fronts." Captain John Lavender, an Arkansas infantry officer and part of Walthall's division, found that he had been "completely flanked" and the Federals were "on us before any one knew anything about it ... and caught us with our Breaches down."[44]

The Federal troops on the west had barely missed delivering a fatal blow to Hood's army which was saved by the setting sun. Hatch's cavalry ended a tiring but successful day by camping near the captured redoubts, securely on the flank and nearly in the rear of Hood's army. Darkness ended the fighting and the Federal cavalry camped for the night along Hillsboro Pike.[45]

Knipe's Seventh Cavalry Division

Brig. Gen. Joseph F. Knipe	
First Brigade— Brig. Gen. J.H. Hammond	*Second Brigade—* Col. Gilbert M.L. Johnson
9th Indiana, Col. George W. Jackson	12th Indiana, Col. Edward Anderson
10th Indiana, Lt. Col. Benjamin Gresham	13th Indiana, Lt. Col. William T. Pepper
19th Pennsylvania, Lt. Col. Joseph C. Hess	6th Tennessee, Col. Fielding Hurst
2nd Tennessee, Lt. Col. William R. Cook	
4th Tennessee, Lt. Col. Jacob Thornburgh	
Artillery	
Ohio Light, 14th Battery, Lt. William C. Myers	

Finally, Brigadier General Joseph F. Knipe's Seventh Division also began the day on Hardin Pike and as the general attack began, Knipe served as a reserve for Hatch's division. Subsequently, Knipe's cavalry reached Hillsboro Pike after Hatch's successful actions. Then, Knipe crossed the pike at the six-mile post and made its way down a country road to Granny White Pike. Hammond's brigade led the advance and the Second Brigade, dismounted, trudged behind their mounted counterparts. The Second Brigade could not advance farther than Hillsboro Pike, and Hammond's brigade moved "on or near the Granny White pike" where the brigades camped for the night at their final positions. Benjamin Nourse, Chicago Board of Trade Horse Artillery, noted in his journal that his section of artillery did not fire a shot and only ran into enemy pickets at dusk. Still, Nourse observed the aftermath of the battle. "Terrible—death everywhere. Poor troops, poor rebels lay so thick we can hardly drive our horses up the hill without stopping every rod to remove them." While Knipe's division played a small role on the first day of the battle, its position would be critical in the next day's actions, and the ultimate outcome of the battle.[46]

Summary of Chalmers' Actions

Brigadier General James Chalmers	
Col. Edmund Rucker's Brigade	
7th Alabama	12th Tennessee
5th Mississippi	14th Tennessee
7th Tennessee	15th Tennessee
26th Tennessee Battalion (Forrest's Regiment)	
Col. Jacob Biffle's Brigade	
10th Tennessee	

James Chalmers had the unpleasant duty of facing the revitalized Union cavalry alone. With the rest of Forrest's cavalry at Murfreesboro, Chalmers, a reliable and effective commander, had an impossible task. He covered a huge flank with just Rucker's brigade and with only one regiment of Biffle's brigade on the eastern flank. He had the unfortunate position of being on the flank that Thomas' army intended as the major point of attack. Chalmers had his cavalry in front of the advancing Union army and in cooperation with David Coleman, commanding Ector's small brigade of North Carolina and Texas troops, due to a severe wound Matthew Ector received at Atlanta. When the line of blue surged ahead, Coleman withdrew, but he failed to notify Chalmers of this movement. This left Hardin Pike open to a rapid movement by the Union troops which quickly marched and were two miles in the rear of Chalmers' cavalry before he knew it. Chalmers' headquarters and division ordnance train had been placed on Hardin Pike because it was safely behind the infantry and on the pike for ease of movement. The removal of Ector's (Coleman's) Brigade left the train without security, allowing the 12th Tennessee Cavalry an easy capture. Chalmers would have little more to say about the action during the day as he faced gunboats, infantry, artillery, and cavalry. The battle began with Rucker's brigade being shelled in the morning by the gunboats which had little effect according to Chalmers. It was the withdrawal of Ector's brigade that crumbled Chalmers' defense and left the western flank with only a brigade of cavalry to defend it. Once Ector's brigade withdrew, Chalmers "fell back two miles to a cross-road leading from that pike, where we remained until night, when I ordered Colonel Rucker to move across to the Hillsborough pike, leaving the Seventh Alabama Cavalry to hold the position on the Charlotte pike until daylight, which was done. I had attempted several times during the day to communicate with General Hood, but my couriers were either killed or captured and failed to reach him." In an interesting note, Chalmers greatest success came in the defense against Johnson's cavalry at Davidson's house, but Chalmers made almost no comment on this. The grand movement of the Union forces along his flank overwhelmed the success he had on Charlotte Pike.[47]

Closing Events of the Day

The Confederate defenders on the west flank had been roughly handled and only the early darkness of the December night stopped the fighting. After observing the battle and after darkness had fallen, Hood decided to retreat a short distance, shortening and strengthening his lines. At the end of the day, George Thomas sent a telegram to Washington about the day's success. Questions remained about Hood's plans for the next day and whether he would withdraw or stay and fight, but Thomas had successfully dealt with Hood on the first day of the battle. Important decisions were made that evening—Hood felt he had no choice and decided to stay and continue the battle, reasoning that the South needed a victory in Nashville; there was nothing to be gained by retreating and being pursued by a superior force. For Thomas, the success of December 15 convinced him even more that Hood could and would be defeated in the hills north of Brentwood.[48]

The day belonged to the soldiers in blue. The pro–Federal *Nashville Union* printed "The Rebels Driven Back Everywhere." Thomas wrote: "The behavior of the troops was unsurpassed for steadiness and alacrity in every movement, and the original plan of battle, with but few alterations, strictly adhered to." Captain J.C. Van Duzer, Thomas' superintendent of the telegraph office, wrote of the day's efforts. "His center pushed back from one to three miles, with loss, in all, of 17 guns and about 1,500 prisoners, and his whole line of earth-works, except about a mile on his extreme right, where no serious attempt was made to dislodge him.... The whole action of to-day was splendidly successful. The divisions commanded by General Kimball, of the Fourth Corps, by General Garrard, of the command under General A.J. Smith, and the cavalry division under General Knipe, were under my observation, and I have never seen better work."[49]

That evening both Edwin Stanton and Ulysses Grant telegraphed their congratulations for the Union successes of the day. Stanton promised Thomas a 100-gun salute the next morning. Grant wrote to Thomas: "Push the enemy now, and give him no rest until he is entirely destroyed." Perhaps more importantly, Grant was at that moment on his way to Nashville to take charge of the campaign, but he told Thomas he would stop and go no further while encouraging the army at Nashville to crush one of the last two significant Confederate armies.[50]

Hood's withdrawal during the night did not signal a retreat. Hood concentrated and entrenched in front of a group of hills and reinforced his flanks; from west to east Cheatham's Corps, Stewart's Corps and Lee's Corps faced Wilson's Cavalry, Schofield's XXIII, Smith's XVI, Wood's IV, and Steedman's Provisional corps. The new battle line was less than three miles long, and, despite Thomas' optimism, the Confederate army had plenty of fight in it and had the added advantage of excellent defenses and good position. Hood's right had held during Steedman's attack during the day and Lee's forces had scarcely been used. Only Stewart's Corps had been seriously challenged, but Stewart's corps "was left hopelessly broken," wrote historian Thomas Robson Hay. If Hood could claim a solid defensive position, perhaps he could entice Thomas to throw his army away in unsuccessful frontal assaults. In the entire four-month Atlanta Campaign, only one frontal assault was successful. In his mind, Hood faced two possible outcomes the next day: failure, because he marched into Tennessee only to be defeated, or he could stay and fight—and win.[51]

From the Federal point of view, the attack had worked well on the first day of the battle. Hood's left flank had been pushed back and the Confederate army had been saved only because of darkness. The new Confederate line essentially stretched from Orchard Hill on the east flank and to Granny White Pike on the west flank. There was an important salient at Compton's Hill on the western end of the front line. This position formed an angle where the front line of Confederate infantry turned and formed a refused line parallel to Granny White Pike. The Confederate extreme left flank was covered by Chalmers' cavalry division which had been drawn closer to the main army, though Hood positioned it several miles south of the main line again. Hood's line had contracted and was strategically placed in the hills for the best defense.[52]

Wilson communicated with Thomas that evening and told him that the bulk of Forrest's cavalry remained in Murfreesboro. The prisoners collected during the day told Wilson that only Chalmers' division protected the flanks. Wilson planned to put Johnson and Croxton to work on Chalmers the next day and this would leave Hatch and Knipe free to continue to support the Union infantry. Wilson was pleased with what he had seen during the day. "For the first time in our country the horsemen on foot had charged side by side with the infantry, carrying the enemy's entrenchments, taking his field guns, and capturing the detachments told off for their support." As the troopers lay down for the night, their horses remained saddled and they expected to wake early the next morning and continue their work.[53]

For the soldiers on both sides of the line, the night was difficult and, with the promise of more fighting the next day, unpleasant. Ambrose Armitage, 8th Wisconsin Infantry, recorded Hubbard's brigade settled in a muddy spot. "I fired forty three rounds and am a tired chap." Iowa cavalryman Henry Kratzer McVey and his comrades gathered up the wounded after dark in the area of Croxton's brigade and tried to make them comfortable. Some were slightly wounded but some were beyond help. "I saw one man with his head shot clear off but his under jaw. Another a piece of shell had struck him in the back of the head and came out his face. His hair was cut as though some one had struck him in the head with a sharp ax. One poor fellow had been shot with a musket ball clear through his temples. His eyeballs were laying on his cheeks and he was still talking."[54]

In one of the most poignant letters, filled with foreboding about the final result, an unknown Confederate soldier wrote to his father before the end of the battle the next day. The soldier, in the rear on wagon train duty, had the full details of the fighting on December 15. He wrote his father: "I do not know how General Hood intended to protect his flank; I do not see how he could have expected to do so, but I am no general.... I fear the enemy will do him more damage yet, by taking possession of the pike, and cutting him off entirely.... Two men have just come in from the front; they report the Yankees advancing down the pike ... between our position and Franklin. I hope this is not so." These Yankees would have undoubtedly been Wilson's cavalry.[55]

Chapter Twelve

The Battle of Nashville— December 16, 1864

"It was a scene of pandemonium, in which flashing carbines, whistling bullets, bursting shells, and the imprecations of struggling men filled the air."

—James H. Wilson

December 16—The Second Day of the Battle

As Hood realigned his army after the first day of the battle to a position four miles north of Brentwood, Thomas met with his commanding generals. The commanders agreed that the first day's successful attack would continue on December 16. During the night, the Federal army also re-aligned in front of Hood's new position. Facing Hood's east-west line were Steedman's command on the east flank of the Federal army, Wood's IV Corps to the right of that, and Smith's XVI Corps of the right of Wood. Schofield shifted to make his attack perpendicular to Smith's corps, facing east toward Granny White Pike. Wilson's cavalry formed to the right of, and in line with, Schofield's corps.[1]

Hood's men were exhausted by the time the sun rose on December 16. The prior day's battle had been difficult, particularly for Stewart's corps, but Hood ordered his army to the new location and the soldiers worked throughout the night preparing their defenses. There were few shovels and the soil was rocky; a difficult task but all along the Confederate line soldiers dug in. Stewart's corps moved to the center of the newly formed lines and Cheatham's corps took up position on the western flank. Stephen D. Lee held the eastern flank of Hood's army anchored around Peach Orchard Hill (Overton Hill), a high, rocky hill. There would be bloody fighting on all the flanks during the day, but Cheatham had been moved into a particularly difficult position. He anchored the Confederate line, forming a 90-degree angle at Compton's Hill (today referred to as Shy's Hill) and he faced Smith's infantry from the north, and Schofield and Wilson from the west. Texas soldier Benjamin Seaton proudly wrote in his diary, "The Southern flag with its brilent colors floats over the soil of Tennessee," but the soldiers were in for a long day.[2]

Bate's division held the northern position of Cheatham's corps and defended the salient in the Confederate line, forming a right angle with Walthall's division of Stewart's corps after some rearranging during the morning. Bate did not like his position from the time it was assigned to him, but he followed his orders and moved into line. Just south of Bate's infantry on Compton's Hill were Mark Lowrey's and part of James

Chapter Twelve. The Battle of Nashville—December 16, 1864

A. Smith's divisions extending to a large hill even further south about a half mile. Smith refused his west-facing line as his infantry fell into position. The Confederate troops would be re-positioned throughout the day to meet the threat of the larger Union army. Based on the increasing pressure on the western flank and rear of Cheatham's corps, Ector's, Govan's, Maney's, Gist's, and Reynolds' infantry brigades would all, at various times, re-position on the southern part of the Confederate line to meet the threat of Wilson's cavalry. Ultimately, the threat by Wilson's cavalry would fatally weaken Hood's line allowing it to be successfully attacked by the Union infantry.[3]

On the morning of December 16, Smith's XVI Corps moved toward the Confederate breastworks and entrenchments only to come under artillery fire. Smith was reluctant to launch a frontal assault against these strong Confederate defenses. As his infantry moved to within 600 yards of the Confederate line, he ordered his artillery to begin shelling the enemy positions. On Smith's right, Schofield was also reluctant to initiate an attack fearing he did not have the troops to dislodge the enemy infantry. Wood's and Steedman's troops also moved to the front by late morning. Wearying of the delay, Wood's and Steedman's troops initiated the attack on the eastern part of the Confederate line because Wood thought that Orchard Hill (Overton Hill) could be taken and would allow him to turn the Confederate right flank. The attack began at 2:45 p.m., but Wood and Steedman were stopped in separate bloody attacks which decimated many regiments of the United States Colored Troops (USCT). Colonel Charles R. Thompson led a determined attack which ultimately failed and the valiant efforts of the USCT resulted in losses of 80 officers and 388 soldiers in less than 30 minutes.[4]

On the Confederate left, Wilson's cavalry re-positioned during the morning and attacked around noon. The dismounted cavalry made a long movement over a series

Compton's Hill, today called Shy's Hill, viewed from Granny White Pike (courtesy Battle of Nashville Preservation Society).

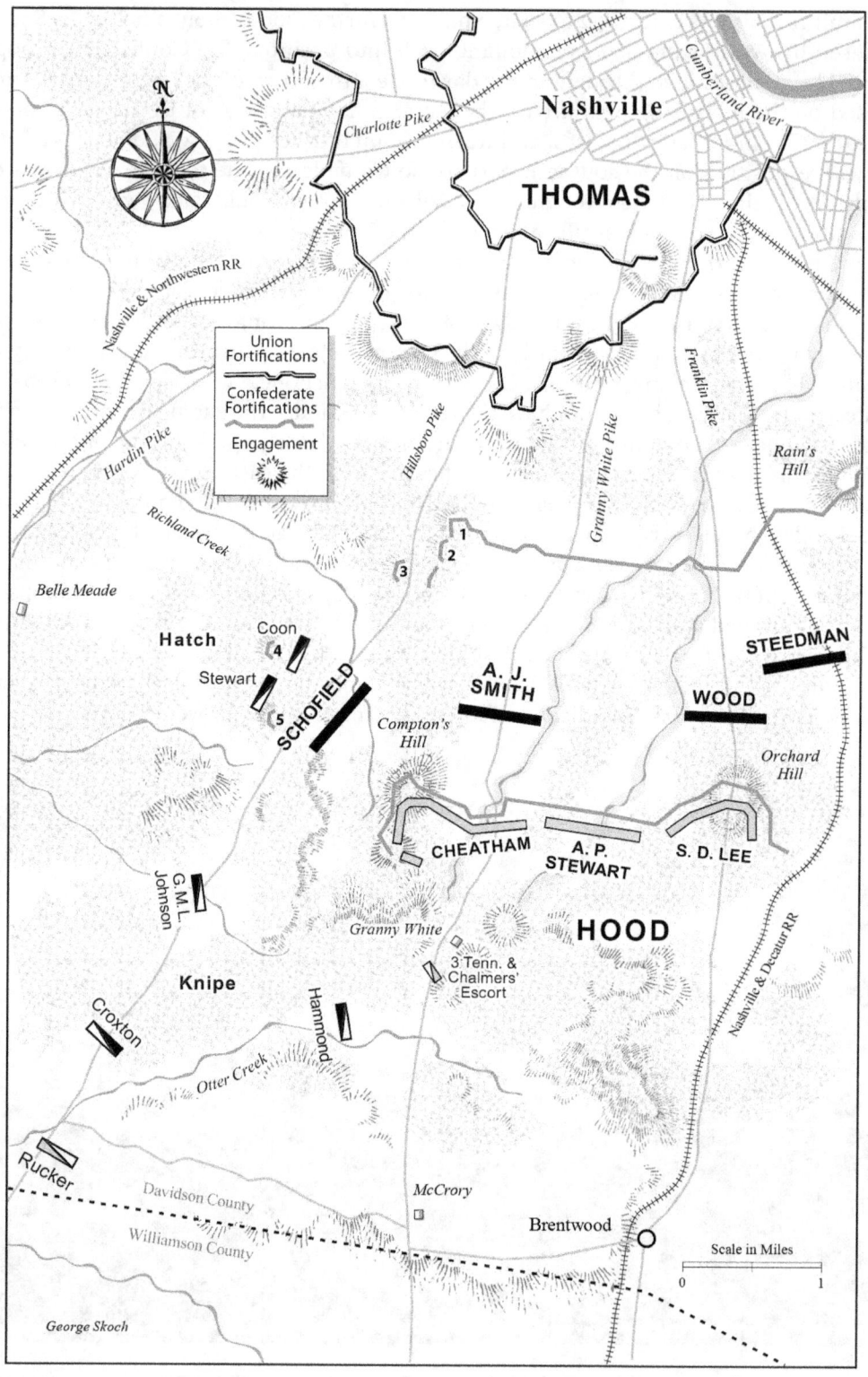

Opposing forces at daybreak, December 16, 1864.

Chapter Twelve. The Battle of Nashville—December 16, 1864

of very high hills but they were able to penetrate the flank and successfully unlimbered their cannons so that they could fire onto the Confederate troops on the western flank.[5]

One of the unsung heroes of the Union Army was General John McArthur. McArthur had an enviable record, successfully leading his commands at Fort Donelson, Shiloh, Corinth, Vicksburg, and now at Nashville, and he was a general who wanted to get in this fight. McArthur replaced the popular Joseph Mower who had been transferred to Sherman's armies in Georgia and, while the men in this division in A.J. Smith's corps would miss Mower, McArthur was "every bit as good a soldier as Mower, and many of his men proudly considered themselves the elite of the army." On the morning of December 16, McArthur felt he had detected a weakness in the Confederate line in his front. McArthur's sharp-eyed aggressiveness observed "that the enemy lines were not heavily defended here and that the enemy gunners could not sufficiently depress the muzzles of their cannons to use them effectively against the attacking infantry." The weakness was the angle at Compton's Hill, a steep rise that looked very formidable to the attacking troops. The Union artillery shelled the Confederate troops at this salient throughout the day. McArthur tried unsuccessfully to convince Major General Darius Couch of Schofield's Corps to coordinate an attack with him, so McArthur stayed in line and told his troops to dig rifle pits for protection from enemy fire, but McArthur was not to be denied and at 2:30 p.m. he convinced Couch to occupy his place in line while McArthur charged the Confederate lines. McArthur was right. Hood could not overcome the vulnerability of this angle which had been exposed to firing throughout the day.[6]

McArthur ordered Colonel William McMillen's First Brigade and Colonel Lucius Hubbard's Second Brigade to charge the hill in their front. McMillen actually marched in front of Couch's position to start his attack. McArthur sent a message to A.J. Smith of his intention to make this attack. Smith passed the message on to Thomas who did not want to start the attack because he was trying to convince Schofield to join in the advance, but before the order was returned, McArthur ordered his men to charge. Of paramount importance in McArthur's attack was Wilson's success by advancing from one hill to another on Hood's left flank and rear, which had caused Hood to order additional support to the left flank. Stewart complied with Hood's orders by sending General Daniel Reynolds infantry brigade to accomplish this. "Not more than fifteen minutes after Reynolds' departure, the entire northern face of Shy's Hill seemed to vanish amid bursting shells," wrote historian Wiley Sword. Ector's, Govan's, Maney's and Gist's brigades had already been shifted to meet the pressure of Wilson's cavalry. Because Hood felt that Compton's Hill was one of his strongest positions, he had pulled these brigades out of the line, thus weakening the position that McArthur planned to attack. This caused Bate's division to stretch to fill in the position most recently vacated by Reynolds. Receiving the order to charge, McArthur's division obeyed amid shouts and yells and the line of blue raced toward the Confederate line. The national and regimental standards flowed in the wind as the Union soldiers ran across 400 yards of open fields, paying a heavy price for the frontal assault on Bate's Division. McMillen's brigade was on the western side of the attack, Hubbard was in the center, and Marshall, while not ordered to attack, attacked on the east. McMillen crashed into General Thomas Smith's Georgia and Tennessee Brigade overwhelming them in fierce hand-to-hand combat. Hood's line was broken.[7]

One of the infantry regiments in Smith's attack was the 57th Indiana. Its historian recorded that the regiment was bolstered by the actions of Wilson's cavalry even though it was a considerable distance away. As McArthur contemplated his attack in a drizzling rain, Hatch's and Knipe's troopers found the rear and flank of Hood's line. The infantrymen heard the "rattle of carbines and the cheers of our cavalry, over beyond the Brentwood Hills, as they pounced on the unguarded flank of the enemy."[8]

Union Cavalry Actions

At the time of McArthur's attack, the Federal cavalry launched an attack of their own along Granny White Pike in the rear of the Confederate line, but much fighting had occurred in the meantime. The second day of the battle would be decisive. Twelve thousand Union cavalry remained virtually unopposed by Forrest's cavalry and this yielded positive results for Thomas' infantry which found itself faced with 20,000 Confederate soldiers in good defensive positions. The cavalry actions on December 16 can be broken down into five parts:

1. Morning Actions (6:00 a.m.—Noon)—approaching Granny White Pike
2. Coon's First Attack and the Movement across Granny White Pike (Noon)
3. The Second Attack 3:00–4:00 p.m.
4. Pursuit Down Granny White Pike 5:00–6:00 p.m.
5. Chalmers' and Richard Johnson's Cavalry Actions

Morning Actions 6:00 a.m. to Noon—Knipe's Division and Rucker's Brigade

The fighting began early on the second day of the battle as Confederate and Union cavalry exchanged volleys. The Northern cavalrymen knew the Southern troops were not defeated and Henry Hempstead, 2nd Michigan Cavalry, recalled a prisoner boldly told them that Hood, who had selected his position well, would repay them for the prior day's losses. For the most part, the Union cavalry, particularly Hatch's division and Croxton's brigade, began the day along Hillsboro Pike. As Wilson prepared for the day's fighting, he ordered Hatch to connect with the right flank of Schofield's infantry. Knipe's division went to the right of Hatch, and Croxton would be held in reserve. Johnson's division would begin the day west of Nashville on Charlotte Pike, some distance away from the main concentration of the forces.[9]

Of particular importance, Hammond's brigade ended the previous day near Granny White Pike and Hammond's pickets had been active overnight, pushing further along the flank of Hood's army. Hammond actually moved his pickets on, or near enough to cover, Granny White Pike on the extreme southern part of both armies. This action would start Wilson's cavalry fighting in the morning because Hood had only two routes leading south from Nashville, should the events of the day turn against him—Granny White Pike and Franklin Pike. By his overnight movements, Hammond had effectively threatened to remove Granny White Pike as one of Hood's potential routes of retreat.[10]

Realizing the importance of Granny White Pike, Wilson wanted Hammond to capture the pike and he moved Hatch's division and Gilbert Johnson's brigade to support him until he could determine Hood's new position. In contrast, Hood needed the pike to remain open, but he had only a few troops to resist Hammond's movements. To prevent this, Chalmers had only a small contingent of cavalry which could secure the road. Chalmers and Rucker reached Hillsboro Pike the prior evening after being guided by a local civilian. Once the Confederate cavalry reached the pike, it slowly and quietly moved northward until Croxton's camp fires could be seen in the darkness. After a brief skirmish, the Confederates moved back some distance and set up a picket line and waited until morning. Rucker moved his brigade onto a hill on the south bank of Otter Creek, set up barricades, and waited to begin fighting the next morning. Overnight, Chalmers received orders from Hood to secure Hillsboro Pike and to open communications with the infantry on the left flank. At daylight, Chalmers dispatched his escort along with David Kelley's 3rd Tennessee to resist the Federal movements along Granny White Pike while the bulk of Rucker's brigade remained in position on Hillsboro Pike near a road leading to Brentwood, so as Hammond tried to claim Granny White Pike, he ran into Kelley's cavalry, which drove Hammond's pickets back (westward) across Granny White Pike. This was a sharp fight and Hammond's brigade gave ground grudgingly.[11]

In addition, only part of Gilbert Johnson's Second Brigade in Knipe's division was active on December 16, but little is known of the actions of this unit. Knipe filed no after-action report, nor did Gilbert Johnson. Wilson's only comment about this brigade was its placement near the Hillsboro Pike the day before, but the 13th Indiana reported seven casualties during the two-day battle. Half of the 13th Indiana, companies B, E, G, K and L (and probably M) which were dismounted, participated in the Battle of Nashville on both days under the command of Lt. Colonel William T. Pepper. The 6th Tennessee Cavalry also participated in the two-day battle, but suffered no casualties. The 12th Indiana and the rest of the 13th Indiana remained at Murfreesboro. In all, Johnson's brigade represented, at most, a regiment and a half during the battle.[12]

The early fighting on December 16 began with Kelley's 3rd Tennessee and Chalmers's escort initially fighting Hammond's brigade, and later when Hammond repositioned, Kelley resisted the movements of Coon's brigade. Kelley had the unenviable task of holding back the Federal cavalry in the early fighting. He held the Federals in check for about three hours, saving Cheatham's ambulances in the process. Just north, General James A. Smith, commanding Cleburne's division, started the day on the west side of Granny White Pike and on the southern end of the Confederate line. He held this position only a short period of time when Hood ordered him to a position near Compton's Hill. When he left, he ordered Daniel Govan's brigade to hold the end of the Confederate line to "check a movement of the enemy on that flank." The move to which Hood referred was Hatch and Knipe advancing toward the Confederate flank.[13]

Hammond's actions during the day are poorly recorded, but Hammond, who had the greatest opportunity to push into the Confederate flank, skirmished with the enemy along Granny White Pike in the early hours of the day. After his pickets were driven in, Hammond counterattacked, but then he was ordered toward Hillsboro Pike to be in position with Hatch and the rest of Knipe's division as Wilson began his advance.[14]

Morning Actions 6:00 a.m. to Noon—Hatch's Division

In the meantime, Wilson ordered Hatch's division, which had camped near Redoubt No. 4 and No. 5, to the right of Schofield's infantry corps. Then at 9:30 a.m., Wilson began his advance on the left flank of Hood's line while gaining control of Granny

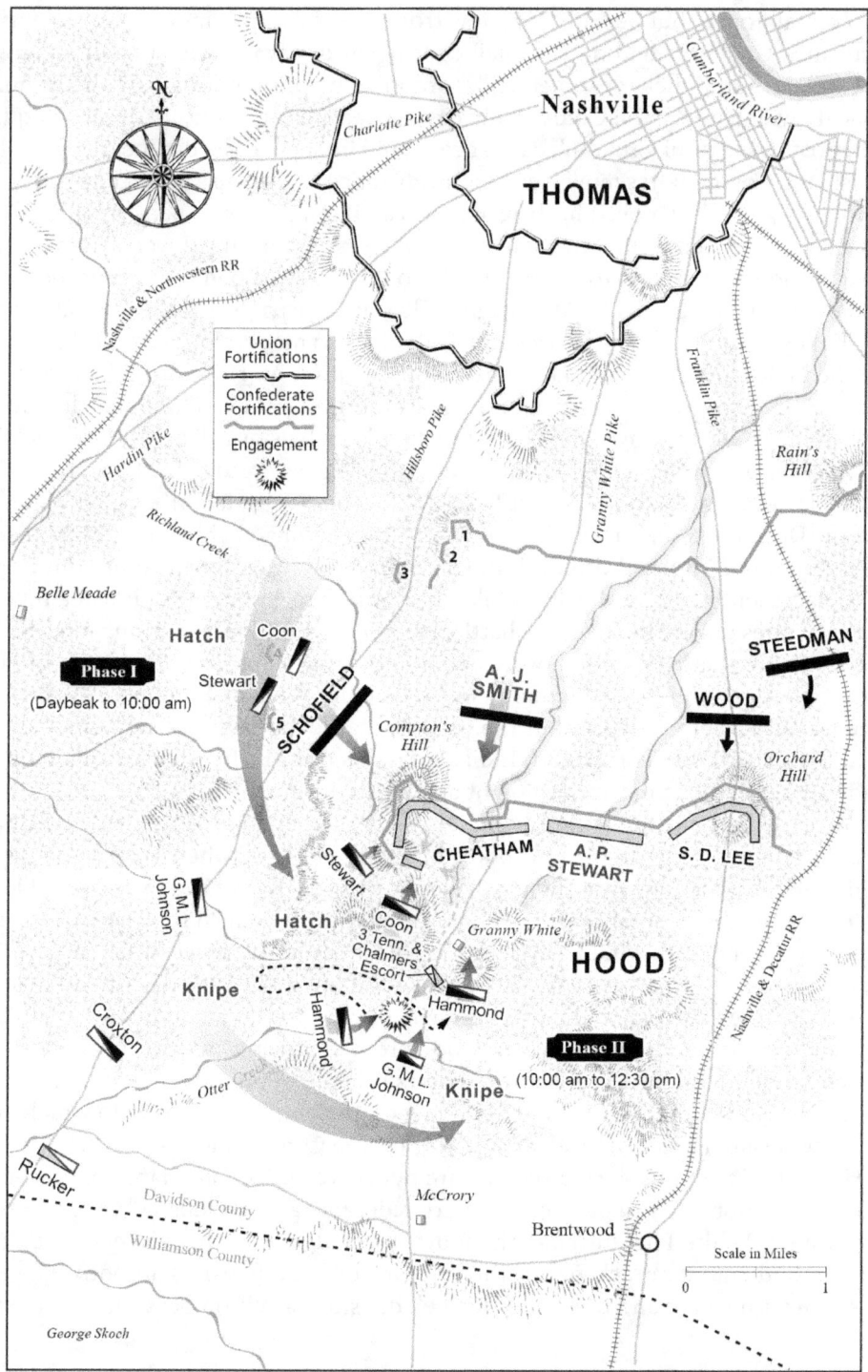

Cavalry actions December 16, 1864–daybreak to 12:30 p.m. *Phase I*: Hammond skirmishes along Granny White Pike and then aligns with Hatch and Johnson; *Phase II*: The unified Union cavalry line moves to and across Granny White Pike, converging on the southern end of the Confederate western flank.

White Pike and he ordered Hatch and Knipe to "drive the enemy from the hills and push them as vigorously as possible in flank and rear..." Hearing the gunfire in the direction of Hammond's brigade along Granny White Pike earlier, Hatch had his division up and moving southward down the Hillsboro Pike. Coon's Second Brigade, receiving his orders at 10:00 a.m., moved to the right of Schofield's infantry and Robert Stewart's First Brigade followed in support, filling the gap between Coon and Schofield's infantry. After moving about a mile south, Coon moved about a mile east into line between Schofield's infantry and Knipe's cavalry which had just realigned. As he advanced, Coon ran into David Kelley's Tennessee cavalry which had shifted its position to meet the new threat. He had little trouble pushing the skirmishers to the rear, but behind them, a strong force of enemy infantry waited in the hills.[15]

Cheatham's Confederate infantry on the western flank was stretched thin, although it had good position. South of Bate's division on Compton's Hill was Mark Perrin Lowrey's division of Strahl's, Vaughn's, Gist's and Maney's brigades, from north to south. The final brigade, and the most southern one in the line, was Daniel Govan's small Arkansas brigade. Govan anchored the line, holding the heights of a hill about a half mile south of Compton's Hill. Cheatham's line was positioned on an impressive set of steep hills. Maney's brigade held the heights on a hill about 900 feet high and Govan refused the Confederate flank on a hill about 800 feet high. The forces of both armies on the southern end of Hood's line would have a difficult day as they battled for control of Granny White Pike bracketed by more hills nearly a thousand feet high, with precipitous slopes. It is important to note that both Hood and A.P. Stewart kept a close watch on the action on the southern end of the western flank. The headquarters of both of these commanders were near the area where Wilson's cavalry advanced. Many of the decisions made in this area of the battlefield resulted from direct observations made by these generals.[16]

Because of the hills and trees, Wilson felt his assigned area was unsuitable for cavalry actions, and Coon explained the dense undergrowth rendered "it almost impossible for the movement of troops even dismounted." Wilson suggested to Thomas that he might have better luck on the other flank, but Thomas wanted Wilson exactly where he was, threatening the west flank and rear of the enemy. Wilson buckled down to his task and the events of the day would confirm that Thomas had just made one of his best decisions of the campaign.[17]

Noon: Coon's First Attack and the Movement Across Granny White Pike

Schofield's infantry had probed the hills east of his line earlier and had been repulsed by Bate and Lowrey. Coon waited about an hour near Hillsboro Pike when he received orders to advance. To the south of Schofield, Coon marched ahead and saw the hills 100–200 feet high with heavy undergrowth. At noon, Coon advanced, steadily pushing the skirmishers from his front toward increasingly steep hills. Coon continued forward about a mile with volleys and counter-volleys being fired along the way. Wilson's line which arced about a mile and a half in length steadily marched past the Confederate flank. This forced Hood to deal with the Union cavalry edging into the rear of his army. Despite meeting stubborn resistance, Wilson explained that the Federals drove the enemy back from "hill to hill all along the line, but particularly in front of General Hatch's left. The positions occupied were heavily wooded and very difficult

After passing through open ground, the steep hills loomed ahead (battlefield looking south from Harding Place, courtesy Battle of Nashville Preservation Society).

of ascent." In this advance Hatch, "with great labor," moved Battery I, 1st Illinois Light Artillery into an advantageous position to enfilade the enemy front and ever "taking in reverse the enemy's line," wrote Wilson. Coon urged his men to press forward to a position opposite the southern-most part of Hood's line occupied by Govan's brigade, which he described as a "high, narrow ridge, thinly wooded, but affording an excellent point to defend." In the meantime, Hammond continued moving east and north. Hammond continued forward in this joint operation and moved his brigade to a large hill, just east of Granny White Pike, now well in the rear of Hood's army.[18]

Coon formed his battle line with the 6th Illinois, 9th Illinois, 2nd Iowa, 7th Illinois, and 12th Tennessee regiments from left to right. His line moved opposite the hill occupied by Govan, a very large hill about 800 feet high which marked the southern end of the Confederate line. Then, Coon ordered "Charge!" and the Union cavalry streamed down the steep incline and up toward Govan's line. James D. Porter, Confederate officer and future governor of Tennessee, described the explosive fight and important Confederate losses, particularly of the top commanders. "There was no panic about it; they overwhelmed him. It was in a little pocket down there. General Cheatham and I were standing together by a big white oak when a ball passed between us, coming from behind. The enemy had gone in there and got behind us. Govan was shot down, the colonel next to him was shot down, and the command devolved on a major. Colonel Field, of the 1st Tennessee, in command of what was formerly Maney's Brigade ... was ordered to retake the position on the extreme left from which Govan had been forced. This he did, being joined immediately by Gist's Brigade..." Govan received a serious wound to his throat in the fight and Colonel Peter Green, 5th Arkansas Infantry, was also wounded in the attack. Importantly, the action drew the next two brigades (Maney's and Gist's) to the south to deal with Coon's attack, and further weakened the Confederate infantry

Chapter Twelve. The Battle of Nashville—December 16, 1864

line which faced A.J. Smith to the north and Schofield's corps waiting to the west. Tennessee infantryman Sam Watkins in Maney's Brigade knew nothing of the plans of the generals and described his movements. "We were continually moving to our left. We would build little temporary breastworks, then we would be moved to another place. Our lines kept on widening out, and stretching further and further apart, until it was not more than a skeleton of a skirmish line from one end to the other."[19]

Lieutenant Elmore Corwin, 7th Illinois, found a secure place to exchange fire with enemy behind a log in the heated fight. Corwin explained that during the first hour along the ridge, "the Seventh Illinois charged the rebel works, driving the enemy away, capturing seventy-five prisoners and a large number of small-arms, bringing the prisoners safely away and destroying the arms." R.W. Surby, 7th Illinois Cavalry, on the right of Coon's line recalled that his regiment had success until about 1:00 p.m. when it attacked Govan's line. During this fight, Coon's cavalrymen faced a combination of a small Arkansas brigade of about 500 men consolidated into three regiments and Kelley's cavalry, and drove them to the rear.

General Daniel Govan's brigade held the southern end of Hood's line (Alabama Department of Archives and History, Montgomery, Alabama).

The 7th Illinois forged ahead, pushing Govan's brigade to the rear, capturing the hill, but the Lowrey sent Gist's and Maney's brigades to counterattack and drove Coon's men off the hill just recently captured. Surby wrote, "the enemy being strongly reinforced ... the 7th was repulsed with heavy loss." Surby lamented that the regiment had not been supported from the other regiments which he believed could have claimed the hill. Gist's and Maney's brigades stabilized the southern flank, just as Ector's brigade (commanded by Colonel David Coleman) arrived on the scene extending the Confederate flank eastward, checking Hammond's advance on the east side of the pike. Gist's South Carolinians and Georgians (commanded by Lieutenant Colonel Zachariah L. Watters) and Maney's Tennessee infantry (commanded by Colonel Hume R. Feild) arrived on the run to hold the hill threatened by Coon. Together, these three new brigades stabilized the south end of Hood's line.[20]

Commanding the part of the Confederate line opposite Wilson was Brigadier General Mark P. Lowrey. The 36-year-old Lowrey, a Southern Baptist minister, lived in Mississippi before the war and had the nickname of the "Preacher General." He had plenty of experience and he knew he was in a difficult position. Lowrey faced a heavy attack on his left flank when Coon's men started their advance. Lowrey wrote, "Soon Govan's brigade was driven from the hill immediately in our rear. I was then compelled to send my strongest brigade to that point; which left me to hold the works with a single rank, thinly scattered along the works. The brigade I sent to the hill in the rear soon regained the hill, but about the same time Bate's division on my right gave way."[21]

As the Federal cavalry advanced, A.P. Stewart observed the fighting and had prudently dispatched Ector's Brigade to bolster the flank to fend off the Federal cavalry. Although Maney and Gist moved into position to meet Coon's attack, more troops were needed. Ector's brigade moved into the hills to halt Hammond's advance, east of the pike. The movement of Ector's Brigade strengthened the rear, but weakened the front line. William Bate explained, "Ector's brigade was withdrawn from its supporting position in rear of the angle, and left me without any support whatever, at which transfer I remonstrated." The Union cavalry's movements were having a profound effect on the Southern infantry positions. Importantly, Hatch's noon attack closed the gap on Granny White Pike and, while stymied by Ector's arrival, still allowed Hammond to move east of the pike.[22]

The added reinforcements by the Southern infantry made any further advance by Coon's and Hammond's brigades a difficult task. Once repulsing Coon, the Confederate infantry made four attacks on Hatch's men trying to drive them away from the rear but each attempt was, in return, repulsed by the stubborn Yankee cavalrymen, who held good defensive positions in the hills opposite the Confederate line. Just to the east, Hammond advanced across Granny White Pike and found it heavily defended by the troops of Ector's Brigade, hurriedly arriving on the scene. Ector's brigade which served as a reserve near Compton's Hill was dispatched by Hood in the late morning to deal with the Union cavalry. Here Hammond had "considerable fighting, the whole brigade being engaged," wrote the historian of the 4th Tennessee Cavalry. Along Granny White Pike, Knipe was greeted with enough resistance to force his division to halt its movements, but the impact of the cavalry operating along this flank had secured the road, effectively cutting one of two potential routes of retreat for the Southern army. Hammond, observing Maney's and Gist's, and now Ector's brigade, noted that "heavy masses of infantry are constantly moving to our left, and have been for nearly an hour."[23]

The arrival of Knipe's and Hatch's men surprised the Confederates. Sam Watkins, 1st Tennessee Infantry of Maney's brigade, described the scene he faced as he moved to strengthen the position along the southern flank: "We could see the Federals advancing, their blue coats and banners flying, and could see their movements and hear them giving their commands. Our regiment was ordered to double quick to the extreme left wing of the army, and we had to pass up a steep hill, and the dead grass was wet and as slick as glass, and it was with the greatest difficulty that we could get up the steep hill side. When we got to the top, we, as skirmishers, were ordered to deploy still further to the left.... While we were deployed as skirmishers, I heard, 'Surrender, surrender,' and on looking around us, I saw that we were right in the midst of a Yankee line of battle. They were lying down in the bushes, and we were not looking for them so close to us."[24]

A member of the 4th Tennessee Cavalry, Alexander Eckel, recalled that his regiment was met by a "storm of lead" from Ector's infantry, but remained in a good defensive position on the east side of the pike. Remarkably, after crossing the pike, a brass band from the 10th Indiana Cavalry on the left of the 9th Indiana began playing a "melancholy" tune. Sergeant Daniel Comstock, 9th Indiana, recalled the music was "not

Chapter Twelve. The Battle of Nashville—December 16, 1864

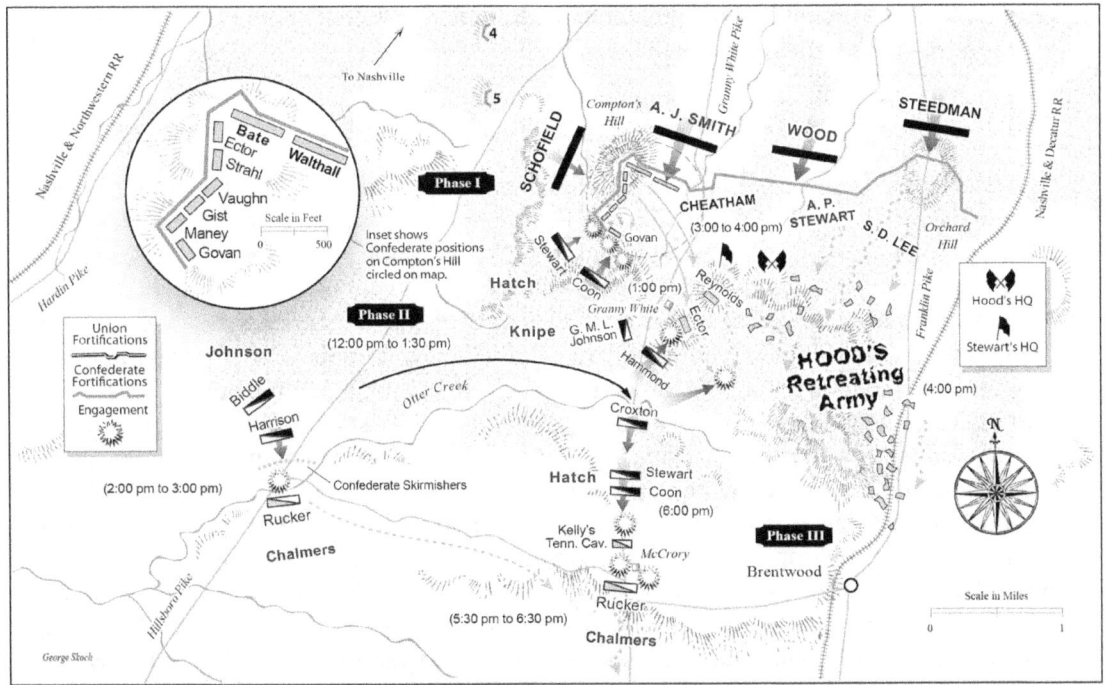

Cavalry actions December 16, 1864–noon to dark. *Phase I*: Hatch and Knipe battle Confederate infantry on the Southern flank; *Phase II*: Ector's, Maney's and Gist's brigades re-position to battle the Union cavalry. Johnson and Rucker battle on Hillsboro Pike; *Phase III*: Reynolds moves to the southern flank while Wilson and A. J. Smith attack Hood's line. Once the Confederate line is broken, Coon, followed by Stewart and Croxton, attacks Rucker's brigade.

inciting an appetite for battle in the hearers." While the Indiana cavalrymen heard one type of music, the 19th Pennsylvania cavalry in Hammond's brigade heard the rousing "Rally Round the Flag." Now, well behind Hood's front line, Hammond's cavalry remained in position for several hours while exchanging fire with the enemy infantry. The 10th Indiana on the left of the 9th Indiana took the brunt of Hammond's losses.[25]

Lieutenant J.T. Tunnell, 14th Texas Cavalry, of Ector's brigade explained: "About noon one (Ector's) brigade was ordered to the left, nearly due south, at a double-quick, to head off a flank movement of the enemy over the range of hills. When we arrived at the place, their skirmish line was in possession of the hill, but we climbed the hill, which was very steep, and drove them off." The difficulty of fighting on the hills occupied by Ector and Hammond cannot be overstated. These hills soared a thousand feet high with extremely steep inclines.[26]

General A.P. Stewart, holding the center of the Confederate line, kept a close eye on the Federal cavalry pushing further into the exposed left flank of the Confederate army. He explained that the addition of new infantry brigades "were strong enough to check the enemy, but not sufficiently so to drive him back and regain the pass by which this pike crosses the ridge, so that retreat was cut off in that direction and greatly endangered even by the Franklin pike, the only route now left open for the entire army. At one time the enemy gained the spurs on the west side of the Granny White pike and occupied by Cheatham's men, some of whom, falling back, formed parallel to Bate's line, on the south side of the hill occupied by his division, but a few hundred yards from his line and fronting in the opposite direction."[27]

The Attack 3:00–4:00 p.m.

The Confederate infantry manning the lines courageously fought the Union forces, seemingly on all sides. Several accounts described the impact of the pressure from Union cavalry along the left flank, including Colonel James L. Cooper, 20th Tennessee Infantry; E.H. Rennolds, 5th Tennessee Infantry; and Colonel W.D. Dale, Leonidas Polk's son-in-law. Dale described that at 2:00–3:00 p.m., Wilson's cavalry had crossed the Granny White Pike and moved further into the rear. Despite initially making good progress, the Federal cavalry advance ground to a halt by mid-afternoon and settled into an exchanges of artillery fire and carbine volleys. Wilson expected the remainder of the Union army to begin its attack at any time, at which point, he would make a concentrated attack. In particular, he needed Schofield, who protected his flank, to advance against Cheatham's infantry line. Throughout the Union lines, the top commanders grew more impatient from Steedman to Wood to Smith and finally, to Wilson. By mid-afternoon, Wilson's cavalry extended from Schofield's XXIII Corps in a curving line finally reaching parallel to Hood's front lines of Stewart's Corps, almost enveloping Cheatham's infantry. Historian Stanley Horn would explain that with Wilson's cavalry in the rear of Hood, this constituted a "lethal weapon aimed directed at Hood's point of greatest weakness." Wilson fumed as he waited for Schofield to initiate an attack to support of the advancing cavalry.[28]

Tiring of the delay, at 3:00 the Federal cavalry began another determined attack on the Confederate infantry in front of their positions. Coon ordered the 6th and 9th Illinois and the 2nd Iowa to open fire on the Confederates behind some earthworks and rough barricades of logs about 500 yards away. Then, he ordered his artillery to fire, from the hills and from the valley, on the infantry facing his brigade. "This, I am satisfied, had the desired effect, for the enemy commenced evacuating in a very few minutes." Coon advanced his entire line with the 12th Tennessee first gaining the hill previously occupied by Govan's brigade, capturing in the process 150 prisoners and three battle flags. After the 12th Tennessee claimed the hill, Coon ordered two field pieces turned on the stubborn defenders in front of the 9th Illinois. This allowed the 9th Illi-

General Daniel Reynolds hurried his brigade to the rear in the late afternoon to fight the cavalry and hold open the route of retreat (*Confederate Veteran*, Vol. 19).

nois, which had been stalled, to push into line with the rest of the brigade, which moved steadily forward. Throughout the afternoon, Hood needed to push the cavalry away from his rear, but he simply did not have men to do it. He already had five brigades dealing with the Federal cavalry, and by moving his infantry away from Compton's Hill, he weakened his front line. Stewart had made several attempts to push the Federal cavalry from his rear but without success. When Smith in front and Wilson in the rear attacked, the Union numbers simply overwhelmed the Confederate forces. Wilson continued to pressure the Confederate flank and timed his attack perfectly. "Coon's brigade charged a large hill in the enemy's rear as McArthur's division assaulted it in front," wrote Wilson.[29]

The Confederate Retreat on the Western Flank

The result of having Wilson's cavalry directly on Granny White Pike placed Cheatham's and part of Stewart's corps in a desperate situation, and threatened the destruction of the Southern army. As those soldiers on the western flank retreated they looked for a route to safety. Many heard the fighting between the infantry brigades and Wilson throughout the day and with Granny White Pike firmly in Union hands, this left only Franklin Pike open for the retreat. The conflagration of the whole Confederate army racing for this road threatened the Army of Tennessee whose retreat became a rout. Those on the western flank had only one way out—passing between Reynolds' and Ector's brigades.

By 3:00 p.m., General Daniel H. Reynolds hurried his brigade to the rear to meet Wilson's latest attack. Reynolds recorded in his diary that the cavalry threatened to turn Hood's left flank. "[T]hey soon succeeded so far as to get in our rear & placing their right across the G. White Pike & still extending their right to the E[ast]." Reynolds was pulled out of the line and moved to the rear and into position on the slope of a hill 300 yards east of the Granny White Pike. Just as he moved his men into position, the entire Federal line appeared to attack. Obviously, the loss of precious daylight boded ill for the Union forces and Wilson had sent three couriers with requests for Thomas to order a general attack. Thomas also wanted to attack, but he had only one corps commander who still felt tentative and was unwilling to attack—Schofield. Even without orders, the entire group of top Union commanders almost at once ordered their respective commands forward. The attacks broke Hood's lines and once the Confederate line crumbled, Wilson ordered Hatch to mount his division and to pursue the enemy down Granny White Pike "for the purpose of striking the enemy again at or beyond Brentwood."[30]

Infantryman Robert Dacus, 1st Arkansas Mounted Rifles of Reynolds' brigade, recalled that upon arriving at the southern end of the line the Union cavalry was driving the Confederate infantry off the hill in front of his position. Pulling Reynolds' out of the front line was a precarious operation and was quietly accomplished, but Dacus believed that A.J. Smith's infantry commanders must have seen the movement. Still, Reynolds' men hurried to the rear to meet the Federal cavalry. Reynolds moved onto a low ridge, or "bench," as described by Dacus, which extended the Confederate line in the rear, but by the time Reynolds reached this position, Wilson and Smith were driving the Confederates from their lines. Reynolds received new orders to hold back the attacking Union troops while the Confederates retreated southward "if it cost every man" in the brigade. Cheatham's corps was at risk of being captured if Knipe and Hatch could thrust their forces to the east, thus cutting off and surrounding Cheatham's troops. Reynolds hurriedly formed a stout defensive line as the other Confederate troops surged toward Franklin Pike, before pulling southward himself.[31]

Lowrey's division, threatened by both Knipe and Hatch in the rear, was nearly surrounded when Bate's division gave way. Lowrey had shifted his line in nearly a right angle to the line to his right while dealing with the cavalry attacks. When Smith's infantry broke the main Confederate line, Lowrey's line had been forced into the shape of a horseshoe and he had only one hope: "I [was] only left the heel to go out at." The general initially thought his entire division had been captured, but some of his men rallied and with Reynolds and Coleman held long enough to allowed the rest of the retreating men to hurry out the closing noose. "[M]ost of my men passed out and joined our broken and discomforted masses."[32]

The Federal cavalry struck Coleman's and Ector's brigades during the rout and whether Hammond or Croxton made the attack remains unclear. When Coon's brigade pushed forward late in the day, Hammond's men also made an attack and "swept the enemy from his position" as the Southern lines crumbled. Hammond received orders from Knipe to charge into the retreating Confederate troops. Hammond reformed his line and attacked the retreating Confederates. Daniel Comstock recalled that as the brigade quickly moved in pursuit, there was a light exchange of fire from the retreating infantry and Hammond's troopers. Comstock explained: "This could scarcely be dignified by the name of 'a charge,' as the enemy practically made no resistance. With fear to lend them speed they were further from us at the end of the race than upon the start.... The charge was along through a cornfield a foot deep in mud, intersected by several ditches and washouts, four to six feet deep, and from three to ten feet wide." By the time Hammond's brigade retrieved their mounts, the enemy was gone and it was dark. The troopers had been dismounted and were unable to reach Franklin Pike before the enemy escaped.[33]

General John McArthur's division charged Bate's position and broke the Confederate line (Library of Congress).

Croxton's brigade also moved eastward gathering up prisoners along the war. Wilson explained: "About 4.30 p.m. the enemy, pressed in front, flank, and rear, broke in disorder. Croxton's brigade, which had been held in reserve on the Hillsborough pike, as soon as the success of these dispositions had become apparent, was ordered to march rapidly across the country to the Granny White Pike and beyond the right flank of Hammond's brigade, but owing to the lateness of the hour and heaviness of the road over which he was compelled to move he secured but few prisoners." It was nearly dark when Croxton received the orders to try to cut off the escape of the retreating Confederate army. W.R. Carter, 1st Tennessee Cavalry, wrote: "Croxton's brigade, which had been in reserve, was now moved to the right of Hammond's brigade of Knipe's division, and in making this move captured several prisoners." The result of keeping the Union cavalry as a dismounted fighting unit cost the Federals a full mounted cavalry attack on a routed foe; however, had Wilson's dismounted cavalry not been on Hood's flank throughout the day, there might never have been this opportunity.[34]

Schofield Hesitated

Schofield spent the day thinking defensively and he worried that Hood planned to attack his position. Just after 10 o'clock, Wilson sent Schofield a message informing him that he was running into some stiff resistance as he moved forward. Wilson also told Schofield that he believed this to be Chalmers' cavalry, but Croxton confirmed that Chalmers had withdrawn in the direction of Brentwood with Richard Johnson's division trailing behind. Two reports from Hammond reporting the arrival of reinforcing enemy infantry near his position could have added to Schofield's distress and one of the messages from the 19th Pennsylvania ominously reported that "heavy masses of infantry" had filled in the Confederate line for the past hour. Based on Hammond's position, these reports could only be descriptions of Maney's, Gist's, and Ector's brigades, well away from Schofield, but these reports from Wilson and Hammond worried Schofield because the terrain in front of his division masked the movements of Cheatham's infantry.[35]

If Wilson was anything, he was aggressive. Wilson continued to move his cavalry into position further in the rear despite the reports of Hood reinforcing the line facing the Union cavalry. Wilson reported to Schofield and Thomas that he was ready to continue the attack, but Schofield still hesitated. Certainly, at this point in the war, the consideration of frontal assaults on heavily defended positions meant heavy casualties. When Wilson spoke with Thomas, the generals surveyed the field ahead and seeing the cavalry troops past Hood's flank, Thomas asked Wilson if he was sure those men were his. Wilson replied, "[D]ead certain of it." Wilson had been waiting for some time for Schofield to begin his push. At 1:00 p.m. while Wilson paced awaiting the order for a coordinated attack by his cavalry, Schofield, who still worried he faced a reinforced line of infantry, requested reinforcements before committing to attack. Thomas sent his chief of staff, Brigadier General William Whipple, to check on the situation and Whipple returned and told Thomas that Schofield did not need any additional reinforcements. In the meantime, Wilson chomped at the bit wanting to start the attack and sent another message urging the attack. Also, wearying of the delay, Steedman and Wood began an attack of their own and then McArthur began his attack, despite Schofield's reluctance to join, without orders. At 3:30 p.m., Thomas arrived at Schofield's headquarters and while he was discussing the matter with him, McArthur's men, adjoining Schofield's position, were racing across the open fields amidst an explosion of artillery and musket fire. Thomas quickly assessed the situation and then looked at Schofield and said, "General Smith is attacking without waiting for you; please advance your entire line." Wilson also began his own attack without waiting for Schofield. Schofield would dispute this account of his hesitation, but he did agree that Wilson's cavalry and Smith's infantry began the attack without orders. Schofield's modern-day biographer decided not to address this issue in his account of Schofield's duty at Nashville, but historian Stanley Horn commented: "One wonders how many troops Schofield would have needed to feel secure from an attack."[36]

Colonel Israel Stiles' 63rd Indiana Infantry served as a link from Schofield's corps to Hatch's cavalry division and he recorded, as the cavalry advanced, his skirmishers had been ordered forward to stay in contact with the cavalry's advance. Stiles' brigade extended further south from the main body of Cox's division and then turned east, remaining in line with Hatch's cavalry, while pushing forward to the hill occupied by the Confederate infantry. When the breakthrough occurred, Jacob Cox ordered Stiles to stay on the flank of the cavalry, but Stiles recorded the cavalry "moving so rapidly that it was impossible for me to operate with it." Clearly, it was the cavalry taking the lead in the attack on the Union right flank, just as McArthur did on Schofield's left flank. Wilson would offer another criticism of Schofield's actions by declaring Schofield's reluctance to attack cost the Federals an hour of daylight which was desperately needed. This was a final act in a rather dismal campaign for Schofield. Wilson's attack began about the same time as McArthur's and, in good-natured competition, Wilson would claim that his cavalry reached the Confederate entrenchments before the infantry did.[37]

Chalmers' Cavalry Actions and Richard Johnson's Cavalry Division

Richard Johnson's division started the day on Charlotte Pike near Sam Davidson's house where he expected to finish the fight he started the day before. Johnson ordered his two brigades to advance, only to find that Chalmers had evacuated during the night. Johnson was rewarded with an abandoned battery of six guns which Chalmers could not remove. Davidson House, the site of the prior day's fight, was described as a large, fine house by Theodore Allen, 7th Ohio. As the sun rose, the devastation of the prior day's fight was visible. The house had been "literally torn to pieces" as the Davidson family of 12 individuals had weathered the storm of shot and shell in the cellar. Allen described trees two feet thick in the yard "shot off like mere stems."[38]

Throughout the day, Richard Johnson suffered from some of the same issues that Chalmers had the previous day by covering a very large exposed flank. Johnson tracked Chalmers back toward Granny White Pike, but he noticed some enemy cavalry still off to his right. Johnson had the responsibility of securing the Union right flank and rear and he wanted no surprises from his Confederate adversaries. To solve this problem, he had Biddle's dismounted cavalry, which had little hope of staying close to Harrison's mounted brigade, check out the enemy cavalry to the west. Biddle's men found little of interest and ultimately reached Hardin Pike, taking charge of the division train, and moved to guard the bridge over the Harpeth River. In a judicious action, Biddle kept pickets posted along the wide western flank of the army.[39]

The day would belong to the Union army, but it still needed to be fought and Chalmers' cavalry gave it their all. Chalmers had communicated with Hood overnight

Chapter Twelve. The Battle of Nashville—December 16, 1864

and received orders that he should work in cooperation with Benjamin Cheatham and to hold Hillsboro Pike. Chalmers explained: "Before daylight I had taken position on that pike, with Rucker's brigade at the point where the road leading from Brentwood intersects it, and was soon engaged in skirmishing with the enemy." Chalmers moved the 3rd Tennessee Cavalry (Kelley's command) and his personal escort across the Granny White Pike intending to stop any movement of the Union cavalry. The rest of Rucker's brigade remained in position on Hillsboro Pike, except for the 7th Tennessee Cavalry (CSA) which was sent to Franklin to guard the supply train. Chalmers placed the rest of his cavalry in a good location south of the main Confederate line because he had little hope of holding the large cavalry force of Hatch, Johnson, Knipe and Croxton. Chalmers stuck with his orders to keep the roads open, but he knew the situation was dire because the movement of Wilson's cavalry "would have placed them entirely in rear of our army, and put them in possession of the road by which it afterward retreated." Chalmers was still being dogged by Johnson's division which had trailed him toward Hillsboro Pike.[40]

Harrison's brigade rode forward on Charlotte Pike that morning while Biddle's dismounted cavalry marched in the rear with four ammunition wagons. They marched about a mile when they found the route of Chalmers' withdrawal in the direction of Hardin Pike. The trail led across country away from the roads. Johnson continued his pursuit of Chalmers along the trail crossing Hardin Pike at mid-morning. Reaching Hardin Pike, Captain R.C. Rankin, 7th Ohio, discovered Chalmers' trail and reported to Harrison: "Chalmers division passed this point this forenoon.... They left some wagons here." Johnson reached Hillsboro Pike at 2:00 p.m. and he found Chalmers' cavalry on some low ridges south of the Murray house in force, supported by artillery. John Johnston, 14th Tennessee Cavalry, recalled that Rucker's brigade remained unmolested in their position until late morning when the enemy moved ahead in a light drizzle. Finding Rucker, Johnson ordered the attack. A "lively skirmish" resulted along Hillsboro Pike for a time, but Rucker withdrew eastward to Granny White Pike along a country lane. J.P. Young, 7th Tennessee (CSA), recalled that his regiment remained on Hillsboro Pike until three o'clock until it was forced to the east. Coming under fire from Confederate artillery, Johnson ordered the 4th U.S. Artillery to unlimber and return fire, and the "first round from Lieutenant Smith's guns, however, silenced their battery." R.C. Rankin explained the 5th Iowa cavalry "'whooped them up' pretty lively" during the fighting. Then, Rucker withdrew while exchanging sporadic fire with the advancing Federal cavalry. Once Johnson reached Hillsboro Pike, his scouts found Knipe's division to the north, securing his flank and rear. Johnson sent couriers asking for orders from either Knipe or Wilson but received no reply until after dark. Meanwhile, Johnson had a difficult decision—continuing the pursuit of Rucker and Chalmers to the east or stop and secure the western flank. Johnson chose to remain on Hillsboro Pike and await orders rather than potentially expose the flank.[41]

Unknown to Johnson, the importance of holding Hillsboro Pike was gone with the successes of Federal army during the day—only Franklin Pike and Granny White Pike needed to remain open as routes of retreat. After the skirmish, Chalmers focused on holding Granny White Pike. Kelley's 3rd Tennessee and Chalmers' escort returned to Rucker's position by mid-afternoon as Hatch and Knipe attacked the Confederate infantry. Hood sent a dispatch telling Chalmers of the necessity of driving Wilson from the rear of the army but Wilson's troopers captured it before noon. Hood's message to Chalmers was reported as: "For God's sake drive the Yankee cavalry from our left and rear, or all is lost." Of course, Hood's decision to keep two cavalry divisions at Murfreesboro made this unlikely. Chalmers would record in his divisional record book a slightly less colorful message from A.P. Mason, Hood's adjutant general, at 3:15 p.m.: "[Y]ou must hold that pike—put in your escort and any available man you can find." No one can criticize James Chalmers who provided exemplary service during the Battle of Nashville, but it was impossible for him to deal with the Union cavalry alone. As Hatch, Croxton, Johnson, and Knipe edged their cavalry into the rear of Hood's army, Chalmers and those in his command regretted Hood's decision to keep Forrest and the two other cavalry divisions at Murfreesboro.[42]

Battle of the Barricades (5:00–6:00 p.m.)

As the day developed, Chalmers faced the dilemma of what to do with Hammond and Hatch to the north and Johnson advancing from the west. Croxton's brigade, in position on Hillsboro Pike, was also placed in reserve to intercept any attempt of Chalmers to move on the flank of the Union cavalry. Then, the Federal attack began across the battlefield and the explosions of artillery and muskets echoed through the hills. Rucker held his position on Granny White Pike as the battle was being decided. As Rucker waited, he received an erroneous message that Forrest was riding hard from Murfreesboro and would arrive at any moment to assist in holding back the Federals. Rucker spread word of this message throughout his brigade. The average trooper of Rucker's brigade did not know what had happened on the battlefield until they saw the Union cavalry "now swooping down the Granny White Pike." Kelley's 3rd Tennessee Cavalry left its earlier position on Cheatham's flank when Wilson began his final attack and realigned with some additional troops from Rucker's brigade on a ridge on Granny White Pike (about a mile south of the Granny White House) in the advance position hoping to slow the Yankee cavalry. The remainder of Rucker's brigade fell into line further south on the pike extending to the right and the left and prepared barricades to stop the Union cavalry. John Johnston wrote: "Here we became immediately engaged."[43]

Edward Davenport, 9th Illinois Cavalry, explained that Coon ordered the brigade to pursue the retreating army and after riding a couple of miles encountered David Kelley's cavalry in line, defending the pike. Kelley had selected his position well behind stone walls, on a ridge with a gradual open slope in the front. The 12th Tennessee (U.S.) advanced on the left, the 9th Illinois moved on the right of the attack, and the 6th Illinois followed in the rear. "[T]his was just at dusk, and the Ninth advanced rapidly, firing as they moved forward; they reached and scaled the stone wall, and carried their position before the Twelfth Tennessee," wrote Davenport. This was the first encounter on the Granny While Pike and Kelley's defenders, which had fought throughout the day, were no match for the Federal cavalry thundering southward. Kelley held out as long as he could, encouraging his men to fire into the approaching Union cavalry. "Pour it into them, boys! Pour it into them!" but Coon's brigade pushed Kelley's troopers rearward.[44]

After Chalmers received Hood's ominous message to hold the pike open, Hood's army streamed south from the battlefield mostly along Franklin Pike. Rucker's brigade prepared for a fight on the next slight ridge line south of Kelley's position as a large body of Coon's Federal cavalry crashed first into Kelley's cavalry which reeled southward and then into Rucker's newly formed line behind barricades. Rucker formed his lines just

Chapter Twelve. The Battle of Nashville—December 16, 1864 267

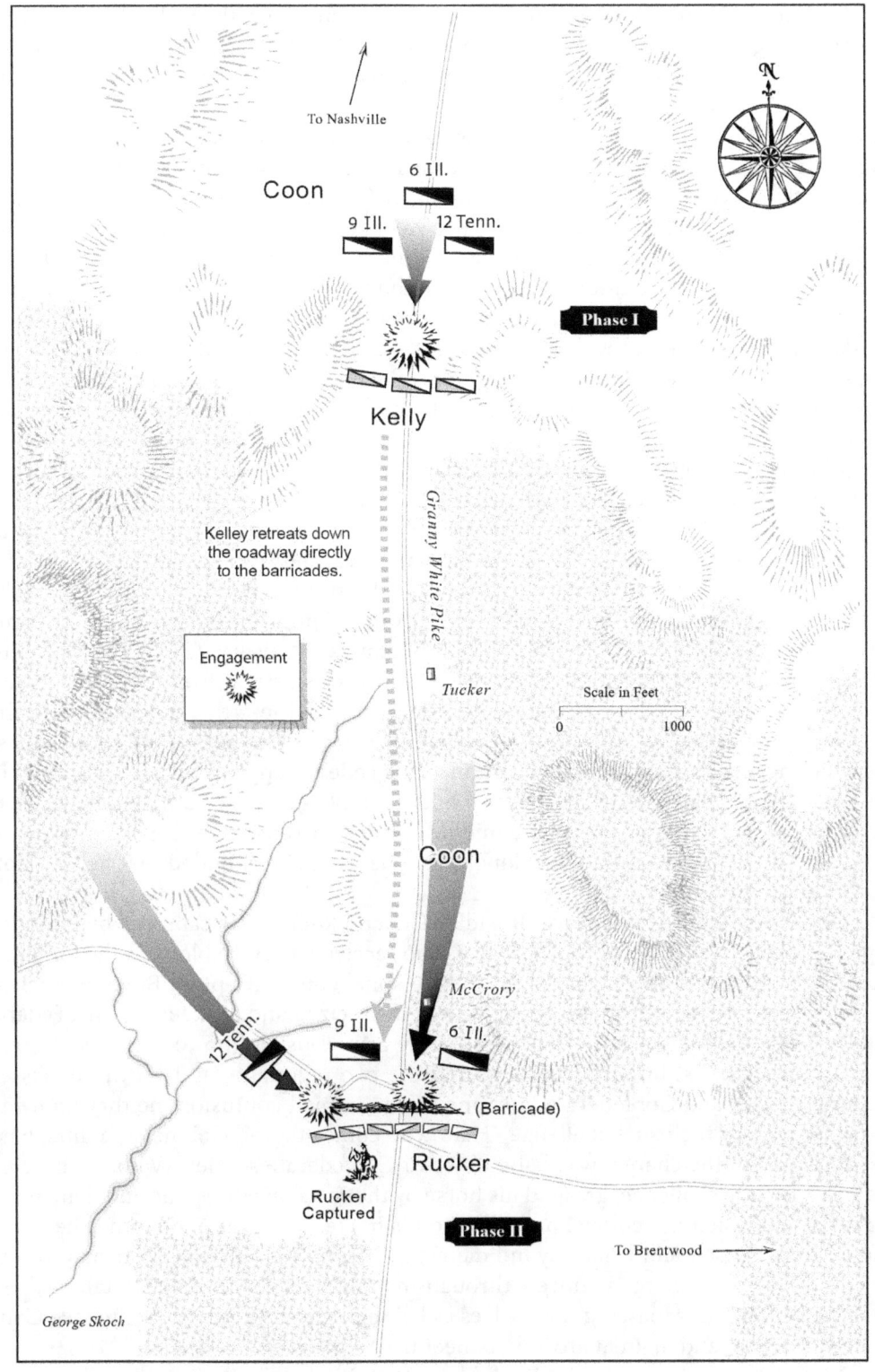

Battle of the Barricades, December 16, 1864.

north of the road leading east to Brentwood, which would keep the Federal cavalry from the retreating mass of the troops on Franklin Pike. The 12th Tennessee Cavalry moved into the center position of the Confederate line just to the left of the pike and the 14th Tennessee moved to its right. Kelley wanted this regiment close and under his direct supervision. Rucker left the overall defense under Kelley's command while he rode and aligned the 7th Alabama to the left of the 12th Tennessee. The Confederate cavalrymen strained their eyes looking for the enemy in the fading light until a man exclaimed, "There they are." Rucker had hardly formed his line, behind barricades, when he met the charging blue-coated cavalry in what Chalmers described as "a sharp struggle" and Rucker "was forced back in some disorder." When the Federal cavalry attacked Rucker's line, the Confederates opened fire from right to left in a "continuous blaze and roar of musketry," but the Union cavalry, at that point, was only a few yards away. "By this time it was so dark that it was impossible to reform the men, or indeed to distinguish friend from foe, so closely were they mingled together, but an irregular firing was kept up for some time until we were compelled to retreat toward the Franklin pike," wrote Chalmers. John Johnson described the Union attack as irresistible. "Instantly, as if by magic, the whole line rose to their feet and began to fall back."[45]

When the Federal cavalry reached Rucker's brigade, a gap had formed in the line as the 12th Tennessee retreated. The cavalry in blue advanced with dismounted regiments on the flanks and the 12th Tennessee Cavalry (U.S.) still mounted and driving into the center of the Confederate line. Rucker rode from his position near the 7th Alabama Cavalry to where he expected to find the 12th Tennessee Cavalry (CSA). The 12th Tennessee had been roughly handled, having been forced to retreat from the earlier fight, and overheard David Kelley talking to the commander of the 14th Tennessee about the enemy passing to the left. This news panicked the nervous troopers of the 12th Tennessee which again retreated from its position as the Federals approached, leaving a gap in the line. Daylight had faded and Rucker, while still looking for the 12th Tennessee, rode a little ahead and found he was in the middle of the 12th Tennessee (U.S.). Expecting to find his men, he asked where the colonel was. The colonel responded that he was Colonel George Spalding.[46]

Coon recorded: "At this place Brigadier-General Rucker was captured by Capt. Joseph C. Boyer, Twelfth Tennessee Cavalry, who received a severe blow on the forehead from the hand of the rebel general. In this personal contest Captain Boyer wrenched the rebel general's saber from his hand, who in turn seized and took his, when a Federal soldier, name unknown, shot the general in the arm, causing him to surrender. It was in this melee, amidst intense darkness, that the two regiments of Twelfth Tennessee Cavalry, Federal and Confederate, met and mixed in mad confusion, neither knowing the other save by the usual challenge, 'Halt, who comes there?' Colonel Spalding, who was foremost in the charge, was halted by two Confederate soldiers, who, on hearing his answer to the challenge, grasped his horse by the reins on either side and demanded his surrender, when the colonel put spurs to his horse, and with one bound the noble animal took himself and rider beyond danger.... Majors Kirwan and Bradshaw, of the Twelfth Tennessee, charged entirely through the rebel lines with their battalions, and afterward returned by passing themselves as belonging to the Twelfth Tennessee Confederate Cavalry, and in great anxiety to meet the Yankees."[47]

There are various accounts of Rucker's capture. James Wilson recorded: "The brunt of the Confederate defense fell upon Colonel Rucker with a small brigade composed

Chapter Twelve. The Battle of Nashville—December 16, 1864

mostly of Tennesseans. As if by design, though it was purely an accident, the leader of Hatch's column was the same Colonel Spalding who broke the Confederate line on the Harding pike the day before. At the first dash, he found himself and his command inextricably mixed up in a hand to hand fight in which no man could distinguish friend from foe. But all did their best with pistol shot and saber stroke to clear the ground they had gained. In the midst of the clash a clear voice rang out: 'Who are you, anyhow?' The answer came back in defiance: 'I am Colonel George Spalding, commanding the Twelfth Tennessee Cavalry,' thereupon, Rucker rushed at Spalding, grabbing at his rein, and calling out fiercely: 'Well, you are my prisoner, for I am Colonel Ed Rucker, commanding the Twelfth Tennessee Rebel Cavalry!' 'Not by a damned sight,' shouted the Union colonel, and giving his horse the spur, with a front cut in the dark, he broke the grip of his antagonist and instantly freed himself."[48]

At that point, Captain Boyer took up the fight with Rucker. Wilson explained Boyer "pushed boldly in to assist his colonel in the blackness of the night, fighting to the front like the hero he was. Without knowing exactly how it came about, Boyer closed in upon Rucker, wresting his saber from his hand, while Rucker, in turn, grabbed Boyer's saber from him. Then occurred one of the most remarkable incidents of the war, for, while the sturdy combatants were whacking each other with exchanged sabers, a pistol shot from an unknown hand broke Rucker's sword arm and thus disabled him, compelling him to surrender at discretion."[49]

Each of the various accounts are slightly different. In James Dinkins' account, Rucker took Spalding's saber. Then, he struck Spalding. "He plunged the spurs into his horse, and forced his way, but he had gone but a short distance when the enemy began to shout, 'Kill the man on the white horse,' and hundreds of shots were fired at him. A man tried to cut him off, but Colonel Rucker struck him with the saber he had taken from the Federal colonel and dismounted him. Just at that moment, however, a ball shattered his left arm above the elbow, and another killed his horse. Both fell, and the enemy rushed on him like wolves."[50]

In the capture of Rucker's colors, Private Berry Watson, 12th Tennessee Cavalry, claimed the prize aided by the increasing darkness. He killed the standard bearer and grabbed the flag just as a Confederate officer rode up and thinking Watson was a Southern trooper said: "Stick to your colors, boys!" Watson replied, "I'll do it" and rode off with the prize.[51]

Despite the drama which surrounded Rucker, the fighting between the two cavalries was an intense hand-to-hand fight. In addition to Rucker's wounding and capture, Colonel Benjamin Gresham, 10th Indiana Cavalry, attacked the enemy cavalry at the barricades and fought hand-to-hand with the defenders. This time it was Gresham's turn to suffer at the hands of his adversaries. He was "struck from his horse and had five ribs broken by a crushing blow from a clubbed rifle in the hands of a sturdy Confederate.... It was a scene of pandemonium, in which flashing carbines, whistling bullets, bursting shells, and the imprecations of struggling men filled the air," described Wilson.[52]

With Rucker wounded and captured and the brigade overwhelmed, Chalmers' men retreated. Fortunately for many in Rucker's brigade, the horse holders had stuck to their positions and the retreating cavalrymen leapt into their saddles, making their escape. In the meantime, Kelley had withdrawn his men to Brentwood. Lieutenant Colonel R.R. White, 14th Tennessee Cavalry, assumed command of the disorganized brigade after Rucker's loss, pulled it together, and moved into a defensive position on Franklin Pike.

Here, White put his own regiment forward as pickets and ordered the reassembled cavalry to attempt to stop the fleeing infantry and artillery, and re-form these into cohesive units. For many in Rucker's brigade, David Kelley and Colonel White were the reliable command figures during this fight and rally. In addition, Colonel Jacob Biffle arrived and also joined in the effort of rallying the troops. It was also lucky for Chalmers and Hood that the Federal troops made no further pursuit that night.[53]

On the eastern side of the line Biffle had his small brigade on duty but at least part of his command had been detached near the Cumberland River on December 15. Lieutenant James Brownlow, Jr., 9th Tennessee (CSA), had been on duty near the river and did not reach the Confederate lines until Hood began his withdrawal on December 15. Brownlow's regiment was deployed on the right flank of Hood's army on December 16 behind a barricade of rails. Brownlow remarked, "We did not have but little fighting that day on our part of the line. We was on the east of our line."[54]

After the battle, Chalmers lamented the losses to his division over the two-day combat which included Rucker. Chalmers had the sole duty of trying to hold back the Federal cavalry and he lost about a third of Rucker's brigade in accomplishing this task. He wrote: "Many others were killed or captured at the same time, and others availed themselves of the opportunity desert and scatter through the country; some of these have now returned to their commands..." A Confederate infantryman merely wrote in his memoirs, "Thus ended one of the most disastirous battles of the western army."[55]

Despite the Federal reports that their cavalry was too late to make a significant impact on the retreating Confederate infantry, some Confederate reports suggested otherwise. Sam Watkins wrote that Hood's army was a "scene of confusion and rout" which was made only worse as "the Federals would dash their cavalry in amongst us." Daniel Reynolds' brigade, which had just been shifted to the rear to meet the threat from Wilson, found itself in position to serve as rearguard, trying to hold off the Federal pursuit, principally Wilson's cavalry, of the routed troops. Reynolds described that just at sunset: "Their cavalry came up on us & we drove them back." For the soldiers of William Bate's division, they expected to retreat through a gap in the rear along Granny White Pike but found Wilson's cavalry in position on the road. Then, they ran southeasterly toward Franklin Pike, hoping to find a path to the rear. Henry Kratzer McVey of Croxton's brigade observed "whole batteries standing in the road with most of the horses hitched to them. The men had run off and left them. It looked like whole brigade had thrown down their guns in their hast to get away." Of the prisoners, McVey saw men in the deplorable condition "entirely barefooted and without coats and bareheaded. One man I remember ... had no coat, no hat, no shoes or stockings. Nothing but a shirt and pants. He had a string tied around his waist and had corn meal inside his shirt next to his skin."[56]

At Murfreesboro, serious concerns about the outcome of the battle resonated at cavalry headquarters when Forrest heard the news of fighting at Nashville on the evening of December 15. Forrest sent orders to William H. Jackson to move his division to Wilkinson Pike at daylight on December 16 on orders from Hood to "concentrate all his force as rapidly as possible, and place it between the garrison at Murfreesborough and Nashville." Buford was still in place near the Cumberland River and Forrest decided to leave him at that location until he received further orders. William Worthington, a 1st Mississippi cavalryman at Murfreesboro, wrote, "We could hear the distant & incessant booming of the cannon, & I confess that I looked forward with great uneasiness to the result."[57]

Chapter Twelve. The Battle of Nashville—December 16, 1864

Doubts became realities. Hood's staff officers arrived at Forrest's headquarters in the evening and told him about the defeat at Nashville. Forrest was ordered to Shelbyville and Pulaski. Forrest recalled Buford from duty on the Cumberland River to protect the rear of Hood's army as it moved south along Franklin Pike. At midnight on December 16, Forrest sent Armstrong's brigade to the same location to bolster the Southern rearguard. Forrest reached Columbia on evening of December 18 to take up duties with the rearguard also.[58]

There would be much criticism over the years about the lack of a more aggressive pursuit of the routed Confederate army on the evening of December 16. Certainly, many Southern accounts sought some solace through criticism of the successful Union cavalry. There were several reasons Wilson did not make a greater impact after the battle. The Federal cavalry was delayed because for the most part it was dismounted during the battle which had contributed greatly to its ability to push into the rear of Hood's army. The early sunset followed by a rain storm which occurred that evening delayed an aggressive pursuit. Sergeant Major Daniel W. Comstock, 9th Indiana Cavalry, would summarize: "Night and Forrest's cavalry alone saved Hood's army from total capture." The impact of Rucker's brigade, while roughly handled, was enough to demonstrate the fool hardiness of riding headlong in the dark upon an enemy's army.[59]

That evening Rucker was treated kindly by the top Federal cavalry officers. He was taken to Tucker's farmhouse, which had been claimed as Wilson's temporary headquarters. He was questioned by Hatch about the Southern forces and he declared: "Forrest has just arrived with all the cavalry, and will give you hell tonight!" Afterward, Rucker, still suffering from his wound, was taken to a room with two beds. Wilson arrived a little later and took the bed opposite Rucker, and Hatch took a position on the floor. Rucker observed that Wilson never slept during the night, but sat cross-legged on the bed writing orders. Hatch took small naps but frequently checked on Rucker's condition, bringing him some much needed water throughout the night. Rucker remarked, referring to Hatch: "(God bless him) got up frequently during the night and gave me water." When Hatch left the next morning, he left Rucker a flask of "good whiskey." Rucker would need it, but it was disheartening that these men who respected each other so much had been placed in such a terrible situation. Rucker would have his arm amputated and remain in a hospital in Nashville for the next two months.[60]

Later that evening, Chalmers searched and found Hood near Brentwood. When Chalmers arrived at Hood's headquarters, Hood asked, "What command is that?" When told it was Chalmers, he told Chalmers to take up a position on the pike securing the flank and putting all the stragglers into line. Chalmers collected about 500 men, but stragglers were joined by the citizens in the area streaming to the rear. The whole scene distressed Hood who said, "They are the people, let them go. Now is the time for soldiers." James Dinkins would write: "There was no occasion during the war that tried men more than that at Nashville."[61]

The Result of the Battle

The next day Hood began sending communications to Richmond to explain the situation at Nashville. He sent a message to Secretary of War James Seddon and Beauregard from Spring Hill on December 17 explaining that a portion of his line gave way on

December 16 and for a few minutes his troops retreated "rapidly" down Franklin Pike. He said his casualties were small and then told Seddon he was marching south of the Duck River. Despite Hood's reluctance to admit defeat to the secretary of war, local citizen Sarah Ridley Trimble, who had several relatives in the Confederate Army, wrote in her journal: "I was satisfied Hood was defeated—but they fought all day Thursday—the soldiers and waggons past rapidly by—such gloom and sorrow in every heart—Nature seems to mourn with us."[62]

Neither Richmond nor Beauregard were fully aware of Hood's plans or his movements during the campaign and after the defeat at Nashville, Beauregard would be quick to criticize Hood for the loss. A few weeks later, he wrote to the War Department: "I am unable yet to express my opinion as to the causes of its failure. It is clear to my mind, however, that after the great loss of life at Franklin the army was no longer in a condition to make a successful attack on Nashville—a strongly fortified city, defended by an army nearly as strong as our own, and which was being re-enforced constantly by river and railroads. From Franklin General Hood should have marched, not on Nashville, but on Murfreesborough, which could doubtless have been captured, with its garrison of about 8,000 men; and after having destroyed the railroad bridges across Duck and Elk Rivers, which would doubtless have caused the evacuation of Bridgeport and Chattanooga, he could have retired, with the prestige of success, into winter quarters behind the Duck or Tennessee Rivers, as circumstances might have dictated." A week later, Beauregard took an opportunity to clarify to Hood that Sherman was not on a "raid" as Hood liked to refer, but instead, Sherman was on a major campaign.[63]

Examining the battle by today's standards, many question the decision to fight where Hood did on December 15–16; however, the battle was anything but a predictable, easy Union victory. Thomas clearly had the numerical advantage but Hood held the Union infantry at bay throughout the day on December 16. Still, the Federal infantry attack occurred very late in the day, and in a rather serendipitous manner by Thomas' various commanders. No one on the Confederate side expected the final attack and Hood was already planning his actions for the next day. He observed that the Union right flank, Schofield and Wilson, "stood in the air." He intended to withdraw overnight and reposition the full might of his army to crush these two corps early the next morning, but the action late in the afternoon put an end to all the hopes of a Confederate victory.[64]

The combined actions of Thomas' concentrated forces resulted in a massive defeat for Hood and despite Hood's description that the rout only lasted a few minutes, his army was in full flight hurrying away from Nashville. Many accounts described the extent of the withdrawal as a nightmare or a terror-stricken mob, but by all accounts, any attempts to rally the defeated Southern army were in vain. Many of the Confederate troops which escaped were not reorganized until they reached Brentwood, and then they marched into the night and many did not stop until they reached Franklin. Fortunately for Hood, darkness stopped any further pursuit and a rain storm arrived by 10:00 p.m., further delaying an aggressive pursuit.[65]

George Thomas met James Wilson on Granny White Pike that evening and said in a delightful tone, "Didn't I tell you we could lick'em? Didn't I tell you we could lick'em, if they would only let us alone!" Thomas congratulated Wilson on the performance of his cavalry and slowly turned and rode into the night. Thomas' method of generalship yielded its fruits as the cavalry, which Thomas insisted needed to be strengthened before he ordered the battle, had moved into the rear of the Confederate army.[66]

Chapter Twelve. The Battle of Nashville—December 16, 1864

The successes of Wilson's cavalry cannot be overlooked. The cavalry attacked as a corps and, while mostly dismounted, worked in combination with the infantry to achieve important results. Had Wilson not been so successful, the Confederate army might not have been weakened to such a point that McArthur's attack would have achieved the breakthrough. In contrast, Hood left his army with minimal cavalry support. The action at Murfreesboro was in itself unsuccessful and left the Confederate army at the mercy of 12,000 Federal cavalry with only Chalmers to fight them. Richard Johnson would write after the war that Thomas' decision to strengthen his cavalry before engaging Hood army was a good one. Disregarding Washington's comments of "Gabriel would blow his horn before Wilson got his cavalry mounted," Johnson stressed the importance of having the cavalry on the flanks on the overall outcome of the battle.[67]

Wilson would remark that all of Thomas' infantry attacks, alone, had failed to penetrate Hood's defenses. The addition of the Union cavalry to the attacks allowed the Federals to successfully flank Hood on both days. If Forrest with Buford and Jackson had been present to assist in dealing with the Federal cavalry, perhaps the outcome of the battle would have been different. Wilson reasoned: "While it cannot be said with certainty that, had Forrest been present with this force united with that of Chalmers…, it may well be claimed that he could have made a better and more stubborn defense than was made by Chalmers and Ector alone." If Forrest had been present and thwarted the movement of the Federal cavalry into the rear of the Army of Tennessee, then the entire second day's success might never have occurred.[68]

At the end of the battle, Thomas had a complete victory and this battle essentially marked the end of the Army of Tennessee. Thomas summarized: "During the two days' operations there were 4,462 prisoners captured, including 287 officers of all grades from that of major-general, 53 pieces of artillery, and thousands of small-arms. The enemy abandoned on the field all his dead and wounded." The wounded were collected and taken to Nashville where a few days later more wounded arrived from Franklin. Greater than 7,000 sick and wounded remained in Nashville, but many others would be shipped by rail to Louisville for treatment.[69]

Chapter Thirteen

Hood Retreats

"You cowardly s—of a b—ch ! why don't you charge?"
—attributed to J.H. Hammond

What began on the evening of December 16 would end on January 7 at Tupelo, Mississippi, as Hood made a general withdrawal over the next three weeks. There was no immediate tally of Confederate losses at Nashville and various numbers have been given, but about 18,000–19,000 men, excluding Confederate cavalry, would be shown on army records a few days after Hood left the Army of Tennessee (at his own request) in mid–January. Historian Wiley Sword estimated that 13,189 Confederate soldiers had been captured, 2,000 men deserted, and 8,600 men killed or wounded during the entire campaign resulting in a total of 23,789 losses to the Army of Tennessee. Sword concluded that about 15,000 men reached Tupelo in mid–January. In the meantime, the immediate task facing Hood was how to save what was left of the once great Army of Tennessee. The Union forces had handily defeated this army over the two-day battle and were now in pursuit.[1]

Overnight, Hood's army slept all along the pike stretching from Brentwood to Franklin, with some of the troops in Franklin proper. Hood established his headquarters near Franklin and considered his next move. He had dispatched a staff officer to Forrest's headquarters carrying his new orders directing him to join the army retreating from Nashville, but heavy rain and flooded streams slowed Forrest's progress and he would not arrive at Columbia until December 18 to take command of the army's rearguard. Sam Dunlap, one of Forrest's soldiers, remarked that they had to take circuitous path over roads so bad it was "impossible to imagine."[2]

The Pursuit of Hood—December 17 (Hollow Tree Gap to Thompson's Station)

As the telegraphs clicked after the previous day's battle, Union supporters were jubilant. George Kryder, 3rd Ohio Cavalry, in Louisville wrote his wife: "I will send you a Louisville Journal and if you read the Telegraphic Dispatches you will see that the rebels did not take the city of Nashville but General Thomas attacked and whipped the rebels and the last account was still driving them." South of Nashville, James Chalmers' division made a gallant stand against the Union cavalry the evening before, and now he joined the rearguard. Hood sent a cryptic message to Chalmers which Wilson's troopers intercepted: "Time is all we want," which many historians interpreted to mean that Forrest would soon arrive to take over the rearguard command. The next morning Hood's army continued southward, and Hood told Chalmers to work in cooperation with Stephen Lee's infantry corps marching at the rear of the Confederate column. Chalmers had the unenviable task of dealing with the Federal cavalry which began its pursuit early. Buford's cavalry division also arrived for rearguard duty on December 17, and Chalmers assumed overall command of the Confederate cavalry—two Confederate cavalry divisions supporting Lee's infantry, against a determined Federal pursuit.[3]

Chalmers and Lee would have a difficult day with four significant skirmishes: Hollow Tree Gap, one just north of Franklin, Winstead Hill, and near the West Harpeth River (just north of Spring Hill). Chalmers recorded: "During the day we were almost constantly engaged with the enemy, who followed us vigorously with a strong force, often in close encounters, and held them in check until nearly nightfall, when by a series of bold charges, they broke the lines of our infantry and cavalry, but were severely punished and driven back by the second line of infantry." The top Confederate cavalry commanders, personally, fought hard during the day's actions. Chalmers, hotly pressed by Wilson's cavalry, killed one of the enemy himself and captured another during one of the exchanges. Abraham Buford also had a hand-to-hand fight with a Union cavalryman. During Buford's combat, he knocked the Federal trooper off his horse with the butt of his pistol and then leapt a ditch to escape the enemy. Private Robert Battle, 9th Tennessee Cavalry, wrote in his diary after reaching the main Confederate column: "[T]he whole army retreating. Troops in awful condition."[4]

Wilson received orders from Thomas at 3:00 a.m. regarding the routes to be used by the cavalry but these didn't agree with Wilson's plans. Thomas wanted Johnson's division to remain on Hillsboro Pike to maintain security on the right flank and then he wanted Wilson to send the remainder of the Federal cavalry down Franklin Pike in pursuit of Hood's army. Wilson had planned also to move down Granny White Pike but shifted the bulk of his command to Franklin Pike in accordance with the new orders; however, he received these orders too late to retain Johnson's division where Thomas wanted it. Hammond's brigade led the Federal advance, followed by Hatch's division, and crashed into the Southern cavalry just south of Brentwood, sending it reeling to the rear. Croxton's brigade rode east of Hammond's column on a parallel route.[5]

The Fight at Hollow Tree Gap

Behind the Confederate cavalry, Brigadier General James T. Holtzclaw's brigade of Alabama infantry in Lee's corps held a rearguard position on Franklin Pike about four miles north of Hollow Tree Gap at 11:00 p.m. on December 16. At 3:00 a.m. the next morning, he moved his brigade into Hollow Tree Gap, joining Brigadier General Edmund Pettus' Alabama brigade and Henry Clayton's other two brigades: Brigadier General Randall Gibson's Louisiana infantry and Brigadier General Marcellus A. Stovall's Georgia infantry. At the gap, Stovall's brigade, supported by Bledsoe's Missouri Artillery set up a defensive position on the right side of the pike, Pettus moved to the left, with Holtzclaw and Gibson in support.[6]

When Buford arrived, he sent Tyree Bell's 19th Tennessee Cavalry a few miles north on Franklin Pike, and the rest of the brigade reached the pike near Hollow Tree Gap at 2:00 a.m. The Tennessee cavalry served as an advanced force buffering Bell's and

Rucker's brigades from a surprise attack; Colonel John Newsom and his regiment paid a high price as the large Federal cavalry forces rode hard after the retreating Confederate army early the next morning. Hammond's brigade slammed into Newsom's regiment and half the regiment was captured in the first action of the day. The remainder of the regiment came streaming toward Bell's position with the Federal cavalry on their heels. The 22nd/2nd Tennessee was the next victim of the onslaught of the cavalry in blue just north of Hollow Tree Gap and the regiment scattered in all directions. Richard Hancock of the 22nd Tennessee recorded in his diary that two regiments (Nixon's and Russell's) were posted at the front of the gap and that the 22nd Tennessee was about 600 yards in the rear. The troopers of the 22nd Tennessee were just checking their powder after the rain overnight when they looked up to see Newsom's regiment riding to the rear without any warning. Newsom's men bolted past and to the surprise of all, Hammond's 19th Pennsylvania Cavalry rode on their heels. With sabers drawn, the Pennsylvanians demanded the 22nd Tennessee to "Halt, and surrender!" Those who could, scattered. Bell hastily prepared a defense at the gap and threw Nixon's Tennessee Cavalry in line, supported by Confederate infantry and a section of Morton's guns. As the Federal cavalry (Hammond's brigade—9th Indiana, 10th Indiana, 19th Pennsylvania, and 2nd and 4th Tennessee) rode ahead, they were greeted with a volley of the unified Confederate rearguard of cavalry and infantry emptying the saddles of the advancing Union troopers. Captain Thomas J. Caper, 9th Indiana, watched as the 19th Pennsylvania and 10th Indiana led the attack into Hollow Tree Gap, with sabers unsheathed, but the Confederates held their fire until the two regiments were in close range, then opened with a blast of grape and canister from the artillery, and the infantry fired a murderous volley into the columns. The attack caused the Federal regiments to "reel and stagger, and finally fall back, leaving the ground literally covered with dead men and horses," wrote Caper.[7]

The rainy morning made marching particularly bad for Lee's Confederate infantry, but the rearguard established a firm position at the gap. At Hollow Tree Gap, Brigadier General James T. Holtzclaw watched at 8:00 a.m. as "our cavalry stampeded, ran through the gap, and formed a mile in the rear." According to Holtzclaw, the Confederate infantry was primarily responsible for the halt of the cavalry pursuit. Despite the losses to the 19th Pennsylvania and 10th Indiana, the mobility of the rest of Hammond's brigade caused any defense at Hollow Tree Gap to be short-lived as it flanked the Confederate position and gained the rear of the defenders in the gap. After meeting the infantry volley, the Federal cavalry also interposed itself between part of Holtzclaw's brigade and the defenders in the gap. Three Confederate infantry regiments, which were attacked by Hammond, had been placed as a first line of defense in the gap, while the remainder of the infantry held a line further south. The revitalized Federal cavalry proved a formidable adversary and it claimed several officers and men in the action. Those captured were "Col. S.E. Hunter, with the greater part of the Fourth and Thirtieth Louisiana Volunteers," wrote Randall Gibson. Henry D. Clayton also disparaged the Confederate cavalry: "About 8 a.m. the enemy's cavalry made their appearance, driving in our own cavalry in a most shameful manner, a few pursuing them even through the line of infantry and cutting with their sabers right and left. A few shots from the infantry, however, drove them back, with the loss of a stand of colors." Holtzclaw reported the fight resulted in the loss of 85 Federal cavalry killed, wounded or captured, but the flanking action by Hammond's cavalry induced Lee to continue a withdrawal toward Franklin.[8]

Chapter Thirteen. Hood Retreats

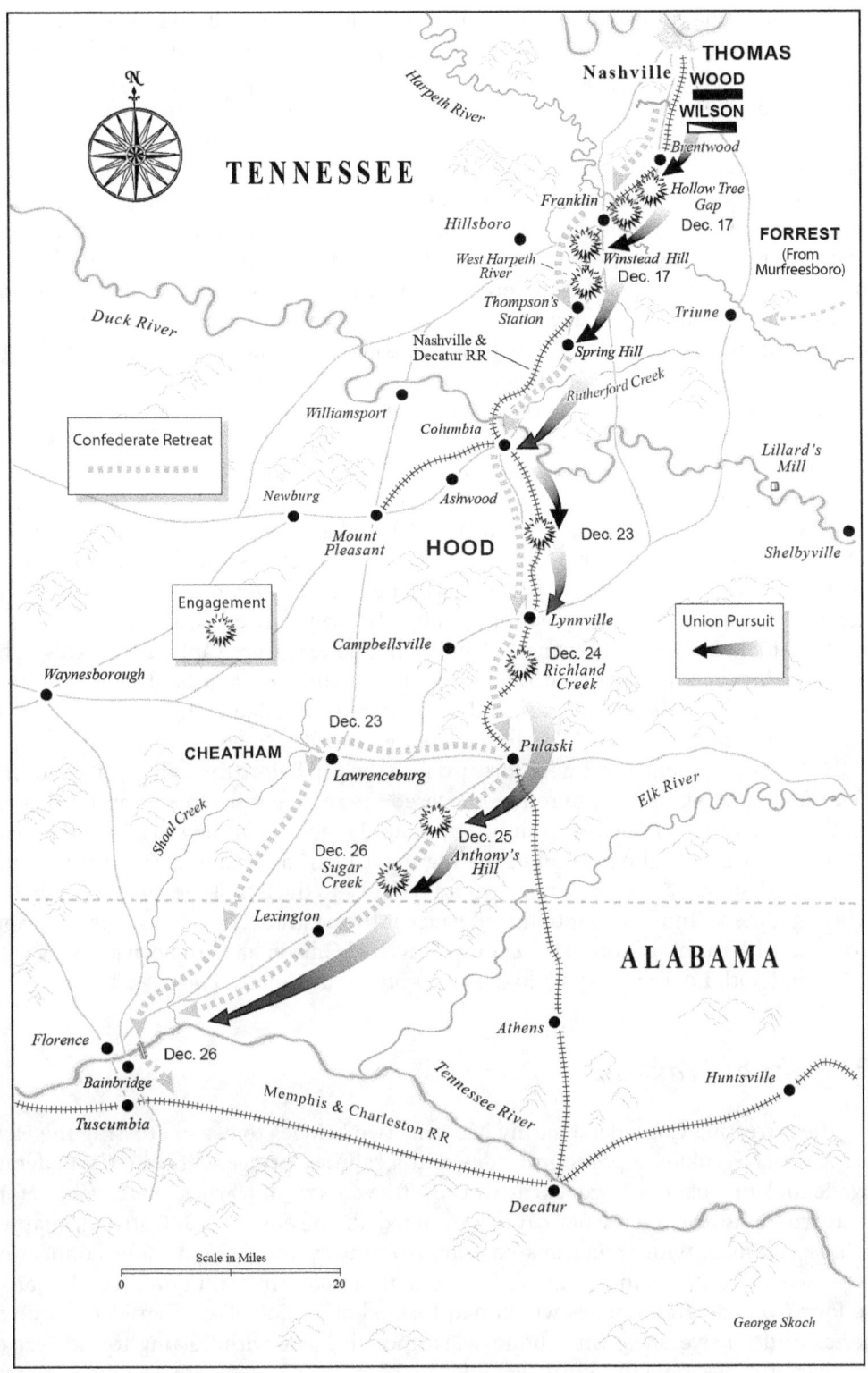

Hood's retreat.

Hammond had good success pushing the Confederate cavalry rearward, but when he encountered the Southern infantry, he quickly realized the situation had turned in favor of the enemy. Hammond saw his regiments come to a standstill, and observing the good position of the enemy infantry, he decided to put his mobility to work. He moved his men through a pass east of the gap and cut Clayton's infantry off from Franklin by securing the road south. Knipe also sent some cavalry around the west side of the gap during the attack. As Hammond executed this maneuver, he sent a message to Knipe asking him to make a strong demonstration in front of the enemy infantry. This allowed Hammond to move into a better position to threaten the enemy but he needed Knipe to send more men to attack the Confederates in the gap. As the Southern commanders saw the unfolding situation, they decided to continue their withdrawal after losing much of their advantage. Hammond, with just his brigade alone, had little hope of stopping a division and brigade of infantry from moving past his position. Hammond had some success and wrote, "[N]o re-enforcement arriving was compelled to return." During the attack the 10th Indiana Cavalry swung into the rear of Confederate infantry in the gap and bagged most of two infantry regiments as prisoners. Once Hammond rejoined the rest of the Federal cavalry, he found that Knipe's attack in the gap had failed, resulting in 22 men being killed and 63 men in the 10th Indiana and 19th Pennsylvania being captured. Wilson recorded the results of Hammond's actions: "After a sharp fight, in which General Hammond with a part of his command passed around the enemy's right and struck them in flank, the position was handsomely carried. Three colors and 413 prisoners, including 2 colonels and 2 lieutenant-colonels, were captured." In this fight, Knipe had direct command of the bulk of Hammond's brigade, at least the 19th Pennsylvania and the 10th Indiana cavalries, and Hammond proceeded with "what men I could collect to the left, by a pass leading to the enemy's rear."[9]

Holtzclaw had sent a regiment forward into the gap before the fighting started, and when the brigade was forced to retire, he feared the regiment had been captured along with the 4th and 30th Louisiana. But he later found the men running to regain the main body of the brigade. "The portion of the regiment I had detached in the morning and could not communicate with passed around the hills to the left of the pike, running five miles to get there. They came into the pike just at the position taken by General Gibson, exhausted with running around the enemy's cavalry." Gibson had not been so lucky with the 4th and 30th Louisiana which had been captured at Hollow Tree Gap.[10]

The Fight at Franklin

The retreating Confederate army had only two bridges to use in crossing the Harpeth River at Franklin, a pontoon bridge and a railroad bridge. Gibson's Confederate brigade took up position "in an earth-work 1,000 yards from Harpeth River, and before any instructions reached me our cavalry stampeded. The enemy, 5,000 strong, charged in three columns, with squadrons covering the intervening ground and connecting them—one in front, one in rear upon the left flank, and one in rear upon the right flank." The four Confederate brigades which had formed at Hollow Tree Gap went through a series of defensive lines, with the forward-most brigade withdrawing to the rear of the other brigades, only to reform again in the rear. The Confederate wagons were just completing the crossing of the river when Wilson's cavalry, about 3,000 men strong and presenting a solid front, struck Buford's cavalry still on the north side of the river. Holtzclaw withdrew his brigade a mile north of Franklin, passing Gibson in the process, and then crossed to the south bank of the river. Holtzclaw explained: "By the time I had formed, the enemy's cavalry pursued Buford's cavalry division, driving it in confusion into the river. They were repulsed by Pettus' brigade, in the works north of the river, and the section of Bledsoe's battery, in my line on the south, not getting in musket-range of my command." Hammond's brigade continued to lead the pursuit with the 9th Indiana leading the advance, the 4th Tennessee and 10th Indiana following in support. The arrival of Hatch's and Knipe's cavalry threw those soldiers on the north side of the river into a panic to get across the pontoon bridge, and after crossing, the bridge was quickly disassembled, preventing the Federals from rushing across the river. Instead, Union horsemen hurried to the nearest fords. Later, the Union engineers quickly assembled a floating bridge of timber and driftwood which enabled the Federal cavalry and infantry to cross at Franklin. In the meantime, Richard Johnson's division arrived from the west and threatened those who had apparently safely reached the southern bank of the river.[11]

Colonel Jacob Biffle declared, "[T]he whole face of the earth is covered with yankees." J.P. Young, 7th Tennessee Cavalry, acknowledged that the whole Confederate force on the Franklin Pike had been driven "headlong into Franklin." North of Franklin, a detachment of the 7th Tennessee Cavalry had the duty of attempting to hold back the pursuing Federals. The rearguard of the 7th Tennessee consisted of men from four companies. Captain W.A. Polk, commanding part of the regiment, recalled the Federal cavalry rode steadily ahead, with sabers drawn, in columns of four. The Confederate artillery at Franklin attempted to delay the Union pursuit but succeeded in shelling the 7th Tennessee as well as the Federals. Polk's company held its position until the enemy was 40 yards away, and then headed for the rear. As he left, he saw Lieutenant Colonel William F. Taylor trying to rally his regiment and Young explained that Taylor was "imploring his men to stand and whip them." Most of the troopers fired a volley and then headed for the river, but Taylor, Lieutenant R.J. Black and two privates were cut off as the Union cavalry overwhelmed the small band of defenders. Taylor and his bodyguard held their ground, emptied their revolvers, spurred their horses, and remarkably, made it across the river.[12]

So aggressive was the Federal pursuit, Randall Gibson exclaimed that he encountered a section of artillery and directed it to fire on the advancing Union cavalry. Gibson hoped the artillery fire would slow Wilson's horsemen, but just the opposite occurred. Gibson explained that it only increased "the speed of his flanking columns, and made no impression upon that one advancing directly upon our front." The battery fired 10 shells and Gibson ordered it to limber and sent it on its way, hoping it would make its escape. Next, Gibson ordered the 16th Louisiana to act as skirmishers, again hoping to slow the pursuit long enough to get the rest of the brigade over the river. The scene was chaos. Gibson described: "The cavalry of the enemy charged all around us. Colonel Campbell broke up, by a well-delivered fire, the column charging down the road, and thus gave time to get the section of artillery to cross the river. The enemy came up within less than 100 yards of the section and fired his revolvers at those about it. My command fought its way to the river, entirely surrounded, with a loss of 10 killed, 25 wounded, and 5 captured." Gibson received some much-needed assistance from the 7th Alabama Cavalry, commanded by Major Eugene Falconett, which charged the Federal cavalry, holding them long enough for Gibson to extract the rest of his infantry. Henry Clayton recorded

"During the day we were almost constantly engaged with the enemy" James Chalmers (Library of Congress).

that Falconett "seeing the enemy charging upon Gibson's brigade, drew his revolver, and gathering less than 100 brave followers, dashed upon the enemy, more than twenty times his number."[13]

Some of Buford's cavalry, being driven into the river, barely made it across at Franklin. Buford rode with Bell's brigade and his acting inspector general, Colonel H.A. Tyler, rode with the Kentucky Brigade. As the Kentuckians hurried to the river at a ford, the Federal cavalry charged them. Tyler tried to avoid having the troops fired upon as they crossed by wheeling the brigade to meet the Union troopers. The two forces clashed amid a melee of hand-to-hand combat, but he got some unanticipated support as Morton's guns opened up on the flank of the Federals. This stalled an overwhelming attack and allowed Tyler time to get the Kentucky cavalry across the river.[14]

Encouraging the Federal cavalry forward, Wilson was heard urging: "Charge them, charge them, sir!" Joseph Knipe rode with Hammond's brigade during the attack. Sergeant Daniel W. Comstock, 9th Indiana Cavalry, recalled Knipe's orders to Hammond: "Take your command and go to Franklin; don't skirmish with the enemy three minutes, but attack him where found and drive him through the town." Knipe wanted to keep the retreating army on the defensive. As Hammond rode ahead, he fell under fire from the artillery on the south of Franklin. Hammond quickly wheeled his brigade in line and gave the order to charge. The right part of the line spurred their horses into a gallop and the center quickly joined in the charge. The left side of the line, 9th Indiana Cavalry, had not heard the order and did not charge. Comstock recalled that Hammond, angered, rode to the regiment and exclaimed: "You cowardly s— of a b—ch! why don't you charge?" Captain Volney Hobson declared: "Boys, we will show who are cowards!" He spurred his horse and led the regiment in the charge. The 9th Indiana had been ordered to charge the fortification occupied by Pettus' infantry. Pettus did not make an after-action report, but James Holtzclaw observed Pettus repulse the initial charge by the Federal horsemen. Captain Thomas J. Caper recalled that the Indiana cavalrymen shuddered as they pursued the enemy toward Franklin. Caper wrote: "The road was choked with dead men and horses, torn and mangled in every conceivable manner."[15]

The defenses around the Confederate-occupied fortifications included an exterior defensive line of posts driven randomly into the ground and wire strung between the posts. "This was unseen by the assaulting party until their horses tumbled over it," described D.W. Comstock. Unable to reach the enemy line, the 9th Indiana fell back in disorder under a hail of musket fire and artillery. Comstock planted the colors and rallied the troops about 200 yards away from the enemy position in a depression out of the line of fire from the infantry in the fort. The Confederate artillery continued lobbing shells and grape near the troopers. The shells took a severe toll on the reorganizing troops, killing men and horses alike. Comstock described: "[A] shell passed through two horses, taking off the leg of one of the riders. Another horse had his head taken off as with a broad-axe. In the charge a horse was struck full in the breast with a cannon ball, passing through and disemboweling him. The rider went headlong in the mud, where he lay stunned until the fight was over. The charge was unwisely ordered, but bravely and brilliantly executed. To ride down in the face of a withering fire on a fort inaccessible to cavalry, defended by artillery and infantry, greatly outnumbering the attacking force, was apparently a ride to death.... No one faltered; none turned back until all that could be done was accomplished." The 4th Tennessee and 10th Indiana followed on the heels of 9th Indiana and Pettus, observing more reinforcements arriving, joined Gibson in the withdrawal over the river.[16]

Once the reinforcements arrived, Hammond gave the order to charge the Southern line on the north side of the Harpeth River and Thomas Caper described: "[I]nstantly the horses were spurred into a dead run, a wall of steel flashed above that line of men, and a chant of defiance that rose above the enemy's guns broke forth from the advancing squadrons that swept along with the force of an avalanche. When half-way up the slope the enemy sought to break the force of the charge by pouring into our ranks a volley from his center line, which was answered by a shout of rage, and the line swept onward, unbroken as before." The Union cavalry clashed into the Confederate line "whooping and yelling, cutting and slashing in every direction." After an intense fight, the Southern lines withdrew with the Union troopers in close pursuit with "flashing sabers" drawn after both Confederate infantry and cavalry crossed to the south side of river. Captain Hobson, Lieutenant James Watts and Lieutenant Burrows of the 9th Indiana were killed in the fight as it moved farther south.[17]

Hammond gave high praise to the 9th Indiana after the fight despite the earlier outburst, but the men of the regiment were angry about how the orders had been given. Daniel Comstock bitterly wrote, "For the regiment, whose heroism converted his blunder into a glorious achievement, this praise is scant enough. For the man, at whom he had but a few minutes before his death, hurled the most opprobrious epithet that can be applied to the brave man who loves his mother, or reveres her memory, this recognition comes too late."[18]

The Confederate rearguard hastily crossed the river, but there promised to be a bloody fight when the Federals tried to cross. The arrival of Richard Johnson's Union division averted a bloody fight and forced the Confederates on the south side of the river to abandon their positions. Johnson had Harrison's brigade riding ahead but Biddle's brigade, still dismounted, began their march in Harrison's trail at 4 a.m. Johnson moved south down Hillsboro Pike, easily pushing aside any enemy pickets they encountered on the way. Johnson forded the Harpeth River west of Franklin and approached along a dirt road on the south side of the river. Johnson slammed into the flank of the enemy trying to form an adequate defense near the river. As Harrison charged, the enemy limbered their guns and marched to the hills a few miles south of Franklin. The 7th Ohio thundered into the town, capturing 50 of the enemy before running into the Confederate rearguard as it made its way south.[19]

Wilson recorded the actions in the first day after the battle: "Knipe crossed by the ford and entered the town almost simultaneously with Harrison's advance.... At Franklin the enemy's hospital with about 2,000 wounded fell into our hands; 200 of our own wounded, left there on the retreat to Nashville, were also recovered, together with 17,000 rations."[20]

The Confederate Stand South of Franklin

Croxton's brigade, missing most of the fighting, advanced ever southward a few miles to the east, crossing the Harpeth River two miles east of Franklin, at the familiar fords they defended a few weeks before. Croxton saw little additional action and crossed the river without resistance. Meanwhile, Richard Johnson reached Franklin and Joseph Knipe, followed by Hatch, crossed the river and continued their pursuit southward. Hatch initially moved down the Lewisburg Pike but was drawn back to the west to the Columbia Pike. Johnson shifted further west and moved down Carter's Creek Pike. Knipe moved southward, parallel to and just west of Hatch.[21]

By all accounts, Wilson's cavalry had dominance over the Southern horsemen throughout the day. Holtzclaw's Alabama infantry brigade continued its march south of Franklin only to be struck again by Wilson's cavalry, forcing it into battle line just outside the entrenchments at Franklin. The Federal cavalry got within 300 yards of Holtzclaw's line which opened on the horsemen. He wrote: "Three or four volleys drove them back." He continued to be harassed by the Federals and this caused him to stop every few hundred yards. Frustrated with the performance of the Southern cavalry, Holtzclaw wrote: "Just after I had formed another of the many cavalry stampedes from Chalmers' division occurred."[22]

Carter Stevenson's division relieved Clayton of the rearguard duty south of the river, although both divisions remained in close proximity. After crossing the Harpeth River at 1:00 p.m., Stephen Lee, commanding the Confederate withdrawal, stopped near Winstead Hill, and Union cavalry soon arrived sending carbine fire into the Southern line. Lee was shot in the foot at this location resulting in several broken bones, but he refused to leave the field. Lee watched the intensity of the Federal attack and, at the same time, placed Chalmers under his command so that he could coordinate a unified defense; however, Stevenson, commanding the rearguard, gained command of Chalmers' cavalry once Lee was wounded. Lee sent the rest of the infantry off toward Spring Hill, and established his rearguard after moving only two or three miles.[23]

James Goodwin, 4th Tennessee in Hammond's brigade, recalled that his regiment swam the river and chased the enemy out of the town. The artillery assigned to Hammond's brigade, moving in the center of the Federal cavalry, was chagrined when it accidentally lobbed a few shells into Hatch's division, mistaking it for enemy cavalry. Hatch had circled back toward the Columbia Pike and took a position on a slight hill facing the enemy. Ironically, as Hammond moved south of Franklin, Hatch's artillery also accidentally sent a few shells in the direction of Hammond's column. Knipe sent a courier to Hatch identifying his column and the shelling immediately stopped.[24]

Wilson reorganized his various commands after crossing the Harpeth River and exchanged volleys with Chalmers' and Buford's cavalry and Lee's infantry as they moved farther south toward the West Harpeth River, which crossed the Columbia Pike just a few miles north of Thompson's Station. Just north of this stream, Wilson sent his cavalry forward in a furious attack. Wilson advanced Hatch's division between the Lewisburg and Columbia pikes while Knipe moved south on Columbia pike. Johnson moved on the far right (west) flank and Croxton continued along the eastern flank. Stevenson's infantry moved south, exchanging shots with the Federal cavalry, until he reached the Johnson House and then he was forced to halt and face the determined Federal attack. He formed a line with about 700 infantry on a ridge with Chalmers on one flank and Buford on the other. He described: "The enemy advanced rapidly upon me, attacking me in front. I found it impossible to control the cavalry and, with the exception of a small force on the left, for a short time, to get them into action. I may as well state that at this point, as soon as the enemy engaged us heavily, the cavalry retired in disorder, leaving my small command to their fate." Stevenson formed his infantry "on a high range of hills crossing the pike at right angles." Still the Union cavalry advanced and pushed the skirmishers back to the main line. Then, the cavalrymen saw "both to the right and left, the crest was fairly bristling with bayonets and artillery." This brought a halt to Hammond's advance and Hammond waited until Wilson arrived shortly thereafter. Wilson arrayed his corps, Hatch joining with Knipe, in preparation for a mounted charge. While the Union cavalry was aligned, the troopers could see the Southern troops hurriedly "piling up logs and rails and building barricades to impede our advance, while the gunners stood beside their pieces, rammers in hand," wrote Thomas Caper.[25]

The array of Wilson's cavalry produced a dramatic sight. Sergeant Major Daniel Comstock observed: "The entire cavalry corps was in sight. The whole face of the country seemed covered with the mighty host." Wilson rode in the center of the two divisions with his own escort of Lieutenant Joseph Hedges' 4th U.S. Cavalry, and he described: "Our own men, well closed up, were ready for the fray. Without an instant's hesitation, I ordered my bugler to sound the charge, sang out for Hatch and Knipe to advance on both flanks, and ordered Lieutenant Hedges, commanding my escort, the Fourth Regular Cavalry two hundred strong, in column of platoons, to charge the enemy's center, head on with drawn sabers." The Chicago Board of Trade Battery answered in reply to the Confederate battery now firing on the advancing lines of blue cavalry. Hatch and Hammond fired away at the Confederate line, driving the Confederates toward the West Harpeth River.[26]

Hatch's and Knipe's cavalry moved across a broad plain with wooded hills in the rear. About a mile ahead, Confederate artillery, positioned on the ridge of a low hill, opened on the Union cavalry. The first shell struck the rear of Hammond's brigade, which incentivized those straggling to quickened their advance. The next salvo of shells struck the rear of the column again as the Confederate artillerymen hastily lowered their guns. On surged the lines of blue cavalry. Hammond's men reached a wooded area in front of the Confederate line and dismounted and advanced again. Hammond's brigade, joined by the 4th U.S. Cavalry, silenced the enemy battery.[27]

James Wilson recorded the actions during the battle from the Union perspective as Stevenson tried to hold off the attack: "The men of General Hatch's advance, by their rapid movements, had become so intermingled with the sullen and disheartened enemy, he began to doubt that the force in his front were really those of the rebel rear guard. The momentary hesitation caused by this uncertainty gave the rebels an opportunity to put their battery in position and reform their line ... the enemy opened a rapid fire from their battery, not over 300 yards from us. Hatch's battery promptly replied. Lieutenant Hedges, thinking that I simply wished him to ascertain the character of the force in our front, hastily moved his regiment about and to the side of the road and out of the range of the rebel guns, but, at my orders as promptly resumed his original formation, in column of fours, in the road, and dashed forward at a gallop with sabers drawn, broke through the enemy's battery; Hatch's division and Hammond's brigade, dismounted, rushed forward at the same moment. The enemy, broken in the center and pressed back on both flanks, fled rapidly from the field, withdrawing his guns at a gallop. Lieutenant Hedges, outstripping his men, was captured three different times, but throwing his hat away and raising the cry 'The Yankees are coming, run for your lives,' succeeded in getting away. The rout was complete, and although it was then very dark everybody pressed rapidly forward, the Fourth U.S. Cavalry and General Hatch, with a handful of men, in advance on the pike, and the Fifth Division on right and left."[28]

Stevenson found he also had too few men to deal with the large number of Union horsemen attacking his vulnerable flanks and rear. Chalmers formed on the left of the Confederate line and Buford formed on the right as the attack began at 4:00 p.m. The Federals closed to within 50 feet of Chalmers' and Buford's defenders, firing their revolvers and John Johnston, 14th Tennessee Cavalry, explained that the Confederate cavalry became "badly scattered and demoralized." It was Stevenson's infantry that saved the day as it stood solidly and fired volleys at the Union horsemen. Lieutenant Preston Sharp, 12th Missouri Cavalry, had not seen much action the day before, but on December 17, the regiment was up early and rode "full speed til (4) four p.m. when we fought them again driving them."[29]

During these fights, Wilson commanded his concentrated cavalry in offensive field actions for the first time. Captain Thomas Caper described: "Hammond's Brigade was assigned the center and ordered to charge in column down the pike, which was done under a galling fire from the rebel artillery. The guns were aimed with deadly precision, and as we swept along many a poor fellow was seen lying where he fell under the horses' feet, covered with mud, waving his hands to keep from being trampled to death with their hoofs. The whole face of the earth seemed to be covered with moving men and horses, sweeping onward with the force of an avalanche. It was a grand sight to see, but many a brave trooper bit the dust before those frowning heights were cleared. The struggle at the crest was desperate beyond description; the fighting was hand to hand. The hill smoked like a volcano, and trembled beneath the shock of battle. It was cavalry

Chapter Thirteen. Hood Retreats

against infantry and artillery; saber against bayonet. Men were cutting and slashing, prodding and stabbing at each other with the energy of desperation.... Men and horse wagons and artillery, pack-mules and ambulances were all crowding together along the highways in inextricable confusion, each trying to outstep the others in getting away from Wilson's pursuing horsemen, who seemed to be everywhere, confronting them on every hand with victorious shouts and gleaming sabers; pressing upon the flanks; crowding the rear; driving them back upon Hood's exhausted and overtaxed trains, struggling through almost impassable roads to get out of the way of their pursuers."[30]

Stephen Lee described the desperate fight: "A more persistent effort was never made to rout the rear guard of a retiring column." The threat was so great that Stevenson formed a three-sided square, a classical defensive formation against cavalry. Stevenson fumed as he tried to extricate his infantry and he placed much of the blame for his predicament on the cavalry, adding, "[T]he shameful example of the cavalry added to the terrible trial..." The square was effective and Stevenson repulsed the Federal attack; he then continued to move farther south and about a half mile to the rear. He reformed his brigades: Brigadier General Edmund Pettus on the east and Colonel Elihu Watkins on the west of the Columbia Pike. Both brigades, sufficiently concerned about the Union cavalry, placed a regiment on each flank, perpendicular to the front line to keep the enemy away from the rear and flanks. With this configuration, Stevenson again marched to the rear. As he began the march, Stevenson found he was enveloped again, with Hammond's attack on the flank and rear. Stevenson described, "[T]hus we moved, driving our way through them, fighting constantly, until within a short distance of Spring Hill." Stevenson was in a dire situation when he received some much-needed assistance as General Henry Clayton advanced to support him. Once Clayton joined in the fight, Stevenson wrote, "While here the enemy made several attacks and opened upon us with artillery but were readily repulsed. This was some time after dark."[31]

The Confederate cavalry had been roughly handled during the morning and the line of infantry, positioned on a low ridge, helped stabilize the withdrawal. From the eastern side of the Confederate line, John Johnston watched the Confederate cavalry, on the west, rapidly riding to the rear with the Union cavalry in hot pursuit. Observing approaching cavalry, Carter Stevenson asked if they were Confederate cavalry and Chalmers replied, "No, they are Yankees." Just as Chalmers answered, the Federal artillery opened fire. The first shell struck one of Confederate guns, disabling it. Then, the opposing cavalry forces were among each other slashing and firing revolvers. James Dinkins watched Buford take two saber slashes on his shoulders when Chalmers arrived firing his revolver, killing Buford's attacker. The Union cavalry divisions were just too strong. Dinkins wrote: "We were overpowered and driven back, but the infantry halted, and we formed again. The enemy, however, did not renew the attack that night. It was a dreadful night, the mud about a foot deep was frozen, but not sufficiently to bear the weight of our horses and the artillery." The temperature was falling so low, Captain John Morton, commanding the battery attached to Buford's division, observed that the soldiers could only cock their revolvers by using both hands.[32]

From Wilson's point of view, Stevenson's square offered only temporary relief and Union cavalry continued to work on the flanks and rear of the retreating outnumbered Confederate division. As darkness fell, the cavalry found what opportunities they could and continued to battle Stevenson's infantry who desperately repulsed the attack. The confusion in the fighting was made worse by the dimming light and the similar uniforms, because many of the Confederates acquired Federal overcoats during the campaign. So desperate was the fighting that the combatants used their weapons as clubs. Alexander Eckel, 4th Tennessee (U.S.), watched two of his comrades unseated from their mounts and sent sprawling into the mud by an angry enemy infantryman during the fight. With the Federal cavalry threatening their rear, the Confederate infantry's only way to safety was to fight its way out. There was nowhere to run. Throughout the fights, Stevenson's infantry continued to edge to the rear until they found Clayton's infantry division, which saved the day for the Confederate rearguard.[33]

Hammond's brigade made the greatest progress during the day of December 17 and he wasn't finished yet. While holding Stevenson's attention in the front, Hammond swung his cavalry around the western flank and attacked the rear of Stevenson's line. This caused an immediate withdrawal of the infantry with "heavy loss" and several prisoners. Unfortunately for the Union cavalry, some of Hammond's men got lost in the darkness allowing many of Stevenson's men to escape, abandoning some artillery in the process. The 10th Indiana led this movement on the enemy's rear supported by the 9th Indiana. Hammond wrote: "Both suffered, but are repaid in the knowledge that this attack caused the abandonment of four cannon by the enemy."[34]

Darkness made movement on the battlefield difficult, and the troopers of the 9th and 10th Indiana edged through the woods on the western flank and discovered a line of enemy when they heard the "ominous click of their guns as they made ready to fire, almost instantly followed by a sheet of flame along their entire front, which for a moment lit up the scene with brightness of day, and revealed their line lying behind a rail fence along the edge of the pike," wrote Thomas Caper. Undaunted the Federal cavalry charged the fence driving the enemy across the pike, and then they rallied and counterattacked. "For a time our men and the Confederates were so intermingled that it was difficult to distinguish friend from foe. First one side and then the other would have possession of the pike." Hearing the fighting, Southern reinforcements arrived, compelling the Indiana cavalry to withdraw. Less than half of the 300 men of the 9th Indiana, which were present for duty that morning, were present at end of the day's action.[35]

Clayton's division served as rearguard earlier in the day and as his division took a short rest, he discovered that Wilson's cavalry threatened to encircle Stevenson's infantry. Clayton immediately placed his division in line, Stovall's brigade on the right, Gibson's in the center and Holtzclaw's on the left. The echo of carbine and musket fire provided evidence of the dire situation. Clayton sent some of his staff to offer assistance to Stevenson and in the meantime, Colonel Bushrod Jones, commanding Holtzclaw's brigade, came under attack on his left from Hammond's Union cavalry. Clayton rode to Jones and positioned his men to repel the attack, and then went to check on Randall Gibson, who was commanding the other two brigades in Clayton's absence. Gibson's left rested on the Columbia Pike and when Clayton reached his brigade, he saw a column of cavalry emerging onto the pike just a few yards in front. An infantryman saw Clayton, hurried to him, and whispered, "They are Yankees." Clayton spurred his horse and rode away only to come under fire from his own infantry as he tried to find Gibson. He survived the ordeal and told Gibson about the Union cavalry, and Gibson wheeled his infantry to face the threat and unleashed a volley into the Union cavalrymen, sending them to the rear. Then, Clayton moved his brigades behind a fence, which offered better protection from a cavalry charge and soon found the enemy cavalry in their front again. In the fading light, someone asked, "Who are they?" Clayton responded, "Federal

Chapter Thirteen. Hood Retreats

troops," and the Southerners opened fire, sending them again to the rear. With Clayton's assistance, Stevenson successfully withdrew his division after nearly being overwhelmed. The performance of the Southern cavalry was assessed by Clayton: "[O]ur cavalry, who, all the day long, behaved in a most cowardly manner."[36]

Despite the disparagement of the Southern cavalry, many believed they offered enough resistance to allow Stevenson to escape destruction. Buford's acting inspector general, Colonel H.A. Tyler, recalled that the Southern cavalry was driven back upon the infantry. Tyler wrote: "The Federals charged in overwhelming numbers, and it seemed that the division of infantry was doomed to capture, as they were on the verge of being surrounded from both flanks." Then, Buford's division charged on one flank and Chalmers' charged on the other, delaying the Federal assault long enough to keep the infantry from being enveloped. As Tyler and Buford reorganized their units, the Union cavalry again charged and in this attack three troopers fought with Buford. In the meantime, Tyler had his own fight. Tyler wrote, "They swarmed around me like a flock of blackbirds. How I got out of it with a whole skin, I do not know. My face was powder-burned and my hair was scorched from a pistol shot thrust in my face at the moment of discharge, and I found myself with two severe bruises on the shoulder from saber strokes." R.W. Surby, 7th Illinois Cavalry, also described the fighting: "Many a brave trooper bit the dust; but on they went, with lines somewhat broken, up to the fence and over it, when a desperate hand-to-hand fight ensued." The daylight was failing so badly that it was difficult to distinguish friend from foe. A Federal cavalryman rode into a body of mounted men and he challenged: "What command?" The reply came: "Nineteenth Tenn., Bell's Brigade, rearguard." The lieutenant spurred his horse away from the group as quickly as he could.[37]

The increasing darkness caused havoc in the exchanges between the opposing forces. Some ambushes were successfully achieved and numerous accounts of running into and away from the enemy were recorded on both sides. During the fighting, the 2nd Iowa Cavalry squared off with some of Ross's Texas Cavalry. Lyman Pierce described one of the best descriptions of the chaotic hand-to-hand struggle for the colors of a Texas regiment: "As the contending forces came together, private Dominic Black, of company K ordered the rebel color bearer to surrender. He refused, when Black, followed by others, rushed upon him. Just as he was in the act of striking the color bearer down with his sabre, one of the color guards shot him through the heart. Sergt. Coulter then seized the flag, wrenching it from the hands of the bearer; the moment Coulter got possession of the flag he was shot through the shoulder by a rebel not three steps distant; though severely wounded he succeeded in escaping with the prize."[38]

The pursuit on December 17 went in favor of the Union cavalry and Wilson had nothing but praise for his commanders. Croxton, while away from the pursuit, reported little in regard to the fights of the day. A trooper of his brigade reported finding many discarded items by the retreating army, ranging from muskets to wagons. Once Croxton reached Franklin, his brigade found every building serving as a hospital and the Union dead still lying on the ground devoid of their clothing. The medical director for the Army of the Cumberland, Dr. George Cooper, also noted that the cavalry advanced so quickly that many wounded men were left in houses beside the road and relied on the infantry surgeons to care for them.[39]

Meanwhile, outside Wilson's immediate attention, Thomas Harrison's brigade of Johnson's division moved down the Carter's Creek Road on the western flank. Johnson's second brigade, James Biddle's, had little work to do in the pursuit, because it was dismounted. Biddle stoutly followed his orders, first securing the crossings over the Harpeth River and then marching toward Franklin reaching there on December 19, only to be ordered to return to Nashville. He reached Nashville on December 21 and he recorded: "The men suffered severely owing to constant rains and the bad condition of the roads."[40]

The fighting along the West Harpeth River lasted well past dark; afterward, the Southern forces retired to Thompson's Station for the night. The end of the battle and the lateness of the day on December 17 caused the Federal cavalry to prudently postpone further pursuit until the next day. Hatch continued southward on December 18 past Spring Hill and encamped at 2:00 p.m., allowing the infantry to catch up. Thomas Wood's IV Corps infantry followed in the trail of the cavalry, observing at different times prisoners captured by the cavalry and discarded equipment and guns from the retreating Confederate column.[41]

December 18–19 (Seven Miles North of Columbia to Rutherford Creek)

The diary of Union soldier William Legg Henderson recorded on December 18, "This day's march was made through mud and slush and a cold, drizzling rain." The Confederate infantry corps also slogged through the mud, and Hood rotated the positions at the rear of the army. This time Benjamin Cheatham's corps assumed rearguard duty. Chalmers moved south on Franklin Turnpike past Spring Hill and crossed Rutherford's Creek a few miles north of Columbia while being tracked by the Federal cavalry, but no significant fights occurred during the day. Only Thomas Harrison's brigade had any important progress as his brigade turned the western flank of the Southern cavalry near Spring Hill, pushing the Southerners further south. The concentration of Federal cavalry ended the day four miles south of Spring Hill after trudging through the mud and rain, gathering stragglers from Hood's army. The pursuit stalled because Rutherford Creek and Duck River were swollen and out of their banks, and Wilson needed to feed the mounts and provide rations for the men.[42]

On December 19, the Union pursuit continued in Hood's tracks on another cloudy and rainy day. The Confederate army held a position along Rutherford's Creek where Forrest, now with the main body of the Army of Tennessee, deployed his cavalry on the south side of the creek, holding the Federal troops on the opposite side of the stream. The arrival of Jackson's cavalry division bolstered the Confederate rear guard. At 3:00 p.m., Hood sent a message telling Forrest that the main Confederate column had moved past the Duck River and he ordered Forrest to withdraw. Chalmers offered a slightly different take on the removal of the Confederate forces. He had taken up position along Rutherford's Creek until 4:00 p.m. when "they having succeeded in crossing a force in front of our infantry pickets, our whole force was withdrawn to the south side of Duck River." The condition of the retreating Confederate troops continued to deteriorate, but the flooded rivers gave the Confederate army time to regroup after the disasters on December 16–17. James O. Walton of Hammond's Union brigade wrote from Spring Hill: "The citizens here say that when the rebels retreated through here, that hundreds of them said they would fight no longer under Hood." Hood had ordered Forrest to march through Shelbyville but instead, Forrest first rode to Triune where his wagon train and wounded were located. He did dispatch Armstrong's brigade to ride to Columbia while Ross' troopers accompanied Forrest. Armstrong arrived at Spring Hill late in the afternoon on December 17 after riding 50 miles in 14 hours. William Worthington, 1st Mississippi Cavalry, wrote that he found the "rear of our army or rather the wreck of it." Worthington found that Chalmers and Buford had been badly beaten and Armstrong's brigade represented the only organized cavalry force at the end of the day. Forrest moved from Triune toward Columbia and crossed the Duck River at Lillard's Mills. It took Forrest two days to reach Hood from Murfreesboro. The poor condition of the roads, livestock, and prisoners delayed his arrival and some of his wagons had to find alternate crossings due to the high water. When he did arrive, Forrest instantly realized the situation and rose to the occasion. It was imperative, despite the condition of the Confederate army, that the men in the rearguard have the will to fight. Chalmers watched Forrest's command style meet this challenge. "At no time in his whole career was the fortitude of General Forrest in adversity and his power of infusing his own cheerfulness into those under his command, more strikingly exhibited than at this crisis."[43]

On December 19, Hatch had his cavalry moving at daylight and he found the Union infantry still along the banks of Rutherford Creek. He moved his cavalry to the west in an attempt to gain the flank of the enemy. He found a potential crossing on Curtis Creek where the enemy held the southern shore. The enemy guard held a railroad bridge which had been burned, and Hatch, not being able to move his mounts over the bridge, advanced his men dismounted, pushing the enemy for about two miles until nightfall. The 6th Illinois crossed the bridge, which collapsed before the other regiments could cross. The rest of the brigade had to move further west, about two miles, to a ford before crossing. In the meantime, the 6th Illinois skirmished with the enemy until dark. Then, Hatch returned to the north side of the creek to re-mount, but the Federal pursuit lingered. It took two days for the engineers to construct an infantry-suitable bridge over the Rutherford Creek which would carry both men and horses. The much-anticipated Federal pontoon bridge was delayed because it was ordered along another road by mistake.[44]

Wilson consolidated the various components of his cavalry corps in the meantime. He ordered Hatch to push back across the creek the next morning, making for Columbia. Both Richard Johnson and Joseph Knipe were ordered back to Nashville to deal with mounting Biddle's and Gilbert Johnson's brigades. Harrison's and Hammond's brigades would continue with the pursuit under Wilson's command which consisted of five brigades over the next week.[45]

The Confederates had withdrawn late in the afternoon with orders to set up a defensive position on the south side of the Duck River. The crossing of the Duck River did not go smoothly for the Confederate forces as the commanders had run out of empathy for each other. Tempers were short and an altercation arose between Cheatham and Forrest regarding whether the cavalry or infantry would cross first. The two generals insisted that their commands cross first and, finally, Forrest drew a revolver and approached Cheatham. Fortunately, cooler minds prevailed as Stephen Lee arrived on the scene and settled the matter, but not before Cheatham's infantrymen prepared to shoot Forrest from his saddle.[46]

December 20–23 Along the Duck River

The next day Hood abandoned his hopes of remaining in Tennessee. Hood intended to move south of the Duck River and set up a strong defensive position, but the condition of the army required him to abandon these plans. The sound of cannonading in the distance, a report from Cheatham that the Federal cavalry was steadily advancing, and Forrest's advice convinced Hood to save his army by marching out of Tennessee. On December 20, he continued his withdrawal to Florence by way of Pulaski. The withdrawal continued under terrible conditions. "Ice, ice, ice—everything is covered with a coating of ice," wrote a Union cavalryman. As the Federal columns crossed Rutherford Creek, there was little or no resistance; by midafternoon some of Wood's infantry reached the north bank of the Duck River, opposite Columbia. Hood left orders for Forrest, with three cavalry divisions and eight brigades of infantry under command of Major General Edward Walthall, to hold the enemy as long as possible. The infantry brigades included: W.S. Featherston's; J.B. Palmer's; Strahl's, commanded by C.W. Heiskell; Smith's, commanded by C.H. Olmstead; Maney's, commanded by H.R. Feild; D.H. Reynolds'; Ector's, commanded by David Coleman; and Quarles', commanded by George D. Johnston.[47]

During the retreat, Sul Ross exhibited an act of kindness which made him one of the most beloved Southern cavalry commanders. While being pressured by the Union forces, a Confederate soldier had been severely wounded and could not keep up with the withdrawal. The soldier had been left beside the muddy road in hopes the Union soldiers would take him to a hospital. Ross was deeply involved in directing his brigade in a rearguard action and the Union cavalry was just to the rear. Ross saw the soldier and dismounted. He asked the soldier if he thought he had the strength to ride behind him on the horse, but he said he was mortally wounded. Then, Ross turned out his pockets looking for some money to give the wounded man and found six dollars. Ross shoved the money into the soldier's pocket reasoning that a prisoner had a better chance of survival if he had some money. The enemy was closing fast, now only 200 yards away. Ross swung up into his saddle and rode away.[48]

Hood continued his withdrawal after leaving Walthall's infantry with Forrest. In all, Forrest had greater than 5,000 men at his disposal including the 2,000 infantry in eight small brigades. The ability of these men to meet the enemy, particularly the infantry which was all but barefooted, revealed the desperate situation. A quagmire of mud remained in place and roads were impeded with wagon trains of all sorts and troops marching to and from the front. The train of the 2nd Michigan Cavalry was only able to move five miles a day due to the poor conditions of the roads. As the rain turned to snow, Hatch's division reached Columbia on the evening of December 20 and began shelling the town, but Forrest sent a message via a flag of truce telling Hatch that the Confederate troops had abandoned the town thus preventing damage to the buildings and injury to the citizens still in residence. Upon receiving the message, Hatch ceased firing.[49]

Wilson reported at midnight on December 20, "Duck River is very high, and therefore cannot be passed at any point without the aid of a bridge train." The Federals awaited the arrival of the pontoon bridge and the supply train before making a general crossing of the swollen rivers and creeks. In the evening, Forrest sent another message under a flag of truce urging an exchange of prisoners. Wilson merely replied that he had no prisoners to exchange. The reply from army headquarters agreed with Wilson's response, and Thomas urged Wilson to try to cross the Duck River, if possible, by the next evening if there was any hope of stopping Hood's further retreat.[50]

On December 21, the 2nd Iowa Cavalry bagged two artillery pieces, six ambulances and several wagons on Lewisburg Pike after skirmishing with Ross' cavalry. Also, Captain R.H. Crowder, 11th Indiana Cavalry, wrote to his wife wearily, "I guess we will follow the Rebs as long as there is any of them to follow," and Wilson issued orders for the line of march for the next day: Hatch's division would begin crossing Duck River as soon as the bridge was completed, Hammond's brigade would follow, Croxton was next, Harrison next and the corps would camp two miles beyond Columbia.[51]

Wilson's cavalry pushed across the Duck River on the morning of December 23 and Forrest withdrew in the direction of Pulaski. The arrival of Forrest and the chance to reorganize after the defeats on December 16 and 17 greatly improved the condition of the rearguard of the Confederate column. Chalmers moved his division south on Campbellsville Pike (in a southwest direction), and he would remain on this road for the day before returning to the main column. Forrest's other two divisions (Jackson's and Buford's) moved directly toward Pulaski in the trail of the infantry. Hood had most of his column at Pulaski and wanted more time to withdraw. He ordered Chalmers, Jackson, and Buford to march in the direction of the Federal pursuit and, then, to delay the enemy. Wilson's cavalry caught the Confederate cavalry rearguard about three miles south of Columbia. Forrest continued screening the withdrawal until he reached two high hills which bracketed the road and made a stand, holding the Federal cavalry in check until nightfall. The next morning many of the Federal regiments took time to draw five days' rations in anticipation of further fighting. Forrest moved south to Lynnville during the day as he tried to hold back the pursuing forces, hoping to allow the Confederate wagon train an opportunity to escape. Walthall's infantry had no participation in the fighting and also continued to march toward Lynnville.[52]

The whole withdrawal of Hood's army was a miserable affair. Soldiers and horses trudged through indescribably wet, cold, and muddy conditions. Once the Confederate infantry started withdrawing from Columbia, the Union pursuit was not far behind. Some of the 20th Tennessee Infantry found a nice farm to spend the night and struggled to fight the chill. The colonel of the regiment, James Cooper, had a single blanket to keep him warm which he credited for keeping him from freezing to death. His men started a fire in an old stump and huddled trying to keep warm. The pleasant scene exploded into a nightmare when a Federal artillery shell landed in the midst of the group. The men scattered with no injuries, but the next morning the men hurried on their way toward the Tennessee River at a "brisk trot."[53]

For the local citizens, the passage of both armies proved an equally unpleasant experience. Nimrod Porter of Maury County found Croxton's headquarters on his farm on the evening of December 23 and he insisted that Croxton provide a provost guard to keep the looting at a minimum. Porter had just experienced the pillaging of a Southern army passing through his farmstead. Now, Porter lamented that the establishment of a provost guard just provided an opportunity for the guard to forage without competition. They stole apples from the cellar, meat from the smokehouse, and stripped weatherboarding off the buildings during their short stay.[54]

Overnight, Wilson again issued marching orders for December 24, Croxton's brigade would lead the column, followed by Hammond, Hatch (Coon and Stewart), and

Harrison in that order. In front of them was the Confederate rearguard that needed to slow the relentless pursuit to give Hood time to move his army across the Tennessee River. The next morning Thomas Wood declared he had never seen so many cavalry troops in a single location. As the Federal horsemen mounted and rode south they passed Wood's infantry and Wilson heard the infantry "splitting their throats with cheer after cheer" for the long columns of Federal horsemen.[55]

Rearguard Resistance Stiffens—December 24–26

Richland Creek

A heated skirmish erupted on the morning of December 24 as Hood's infantry continued it slow march southward. Wilson's cavalry began its pursuit again that morning and after riding three miles, ran into Forrest's line of cavalry about 10 miles north of Pulaski. Forrest spent the night at Pulaski and moved northward early in the morning. Benjamin Nourse, Chicago Board of Trade Horse Artillery, recorded that the Union advance was unimpeded until about noon when it reached a gap in two hills. The Confederate troops held a line in the gap supported by two 12-pound guns; the Union artillery unlimbered and after a few shots, the Confederates withdrew. Then, Nourse's battery advanced in a leap-frog manner—moving two guns forward, while two guns fired. From Nourse's perspective, a half hour artillery duel resulted and the Confederate troops continued their withdrawal, but the troopers faced a determined foe in this hard-fought engagement. Ross's brigade had the rearguard duty and fended off a charge by the Federal cavalry. It appeared the Union horsemen were going to break through the Confederate position when the 6th Texas cavalry "hastily forming, met and hurled them back, administering a most wholesome check to their ardor." This initial skirmish lasted two hours before Forrest pulled his men back another two miles and again fell into position; this time at Richland Creek near Buford's Station on the Nashville & Decatur Railroad about eight miles north of Pulaski. Walthall's infantry marched through the mud into a supporting position, should Forrest be driven from his defensive line.[56]

Walthall's infantry remained at Lynnville the day before and began marching toward Richland Creek on the morning of December 24. Richland Creek proved an important obstacle, described by a Confederate cavalryman as "deep & boggy," which needed to be crossed at a ford or bridge. Forrest settled his cavalry into position on the north side of the creek. Armstrong's brigade, supported by six pieces of artillery, held the forward position on the pike facing the Union cavalry. Ross's brigade held the east flank; Chalmers' and Buford's divisions "formed a junction" and held the west flank. John Morton placed one section of artillery on the north side of the creek and the other section was placed on the south side of the creek covering the road over the bridge. The forward section was unlimbered on the main road and in line with Buford's, Chalmers' and Ross' cavalry. Forrest described: "After severe artillery firing on both sides two pieces of the enemy's artillery were dismounted." As the skirmish developed, Croxton's brigade, leading the attack, moved into position on the west flank and the supporting Union troops filled in the battle line. Coon and Stewart advanced on the eastern flank, pushing forward to the edge of the creek. To meet the Federal movements, Forrest ordered Armstrong and Ross to the south side of the stream to stem the Union advance across the creek on the eastern flank. In the meantime, Buford and Chalmers battled Federal cavalry on the western end of the line. Isaac Rainey, 7th Tennessee Cavalry (CSA), received orders to burn the bridge over the creek as the fight intensified: "We pilled fence rails on both ends and set fire to them. Our cavalry all this time gallopin' over the bridge." With both flanks being turned, Forrest needed to withdraw to the south side of the creek. Then, the Union artillery opened fire on those attempting to burn the bridge, forcing them to the rear. As the groups setting fire to the bridge moved to escape, the Union cavalry rode over the bridge, not 200 yards behind. A counter charge by Armstrong's cavalry brigade stopped the Union pursuit temporarily and allowed the detached Confederates to escape. The rear section of Morton's battery also opened fire on the Federal troops, aiding in halting the pursuit, explained J.P. Young, 7th Tennessee. The battle lasted two hours when the Federal cavalry successfully turned both flanks and Forrest ordered his men to withdraw southward of Richland Creek.[57]

The Confederate withdrawal caused problems for Morton's section on the north side of the creek. The retreating Confederate cavalry began pulling up the boards on the bridge but this stranded Morton's guns which had yet to cross. Fortunately, the Federals were held long enough "to have the flooring replaced with sufficient firmness to allow the guns to be carried over by hand and the horses led across," wrote Morton.[58]

While still on the north side of the creek, three Union troopers descended on Buford, but the Confederate general proved a worthy adversary. He shot one of the approaching enemy cavalrymen with the last shot in his revolver and used the revolver as a club. He successfully clubbed the second man to the ground and grabbed the third man by the hair and threw him off his horse. Later in the fight, Buford received a carbine wound to his leg which ended his participation in the campaign and plagued him for months after the fight. The wound forced Buford from the field and his staff left with him, but this caused more problems for Chalmers who assumed supervisory control of Buford's division in addition to his own. Upon Buford's exit, Tyree Bell directed his own brigade and looked to assist Crossland's brigade still on the field. Bell had no idea where Crossland's brigade, commanded by Lieutenant Colonel Absalom Shacklett, was located, but he soon observed Shacklett racing across the bridge. Bell was not quite so fortunate and he and part of his escort had been cut off, remaining on the north side of the creek.[59]

As Bell looked around for a crossing, a shell burst just by his head, throwing him to the ground. Remarkably, Bell immediately jumped back into the saddle with blood streaming down his face; a piece of shrapnel had permanently damaged his eye in the incident. Then, he continued looking for a way across the creek. Soon, Bell found he was not alone on the north side of the creek when he ran into James Chalmers and part of his escort. This group found they were being pursued by Yankee cavalry, closing in on them as they rode up hills and into valleys trying to get away. At times, the Federal cavalry caught sight of the escaping Confederates, including part of the 7th Tennessee Cavalry. J.P. Young described that the fighting became a hand-to-hand fight on occasion. Eventually, they reached Walthall's infantry behind a barricade of rails. The band of Confederate cavalrymen swam the creek and the infantrymen tore down the rails allowing their mounts to leap safely over the defenses. Walthall's infantry was aghast because when Bell arrived, his face and clothes were covered in blood.[60]

At Richland Creek, the Kentuckians on the opposing sides began the fight, with a clash between Buford's cavalry and Croxton's brigade. Wilson wrote, "With bugles blowing and guidons fluttering in the wind, they rushed bravely at each other and with their followers became engaged in a hand to hand fight which lasted till darkness closed the scene in Croxton's favor." The quick action by the Federals saved the bridge over the creek. The 9th Indiana Cavalry passed over the bridge after the fight and Sergeant Daniel Comstock wrote, "No one will forget the little knot of dead and dying artillerymen and horses by the road-side, maimed and mangled by a bursting shell, a gory, ghastly sight."[61]

Hatch's division marched in the rear of Union cavalry corps and the battle unfolded with Croxton driving the western flank, while Hatch formed a line facing the eastern part of Forrest's cavalry. Hatch began his attack just before dark and Stewart's brigade, on the eastern end of the Union line, was able to cross the creek, turning Ross' right flank. Coon's brigade moved just west of Stewart; Hatch ordered Coon to flank the Confederate line and dislodge the enemy from their position. Coon was unable to accomplish the task because of the "unfordable condition of Richland Creek, when I dismounted my command and engaged the enemy at long range for half an hour. During this skirmish the rebel General Buford was wounded by the Seventh Illinois." Hammond's brigade moved to the west of Croxton and joined the battle, but he did not record any particular action.[62]

During Croxton's attack, Corporal Harrison Collins of the 1st Tennessee Cavalry (U.S.) attacked major who was trying to rally his troops. The major and his standard bearer attempted to hold their position as the Federals closed in. Collins led a group of Tennesseans in the charge, killing the major in the process, and claiming Chalmers' divisional flag in the fight. This attack caused the enemy troops to continue their hasty withdrawal and Collins would be awarded the Medal of Honor for his actions.[63]

Ross recorded: "I was assigned a position on the right of the railroad and in front of the creek. Soon afterward, however, the enemy moving as if to cross above the bridge, I was withdrawn to the south side of the creek, and taking position on the hill near the railroad skirmished with the enemy in my front, holding him in check until our forces had all crossed the creek." Lieutenant George Griscom, 9th Texas, explained that Croxton's cavalry forcing the Confederate line to retreat on the west flank placed Jackson's division into a difficult position. With Chalmers and Buford withdrawing, Jackson was faced with Stewart's brigade pressing from the east and Croxton from the west. This caused Jackson to be "overpowered & enfiladed," forcing the Confederates southward. Forrest was with Walthall during part of the fight and while waiting, an excited courier arrived. The messenger told Forrest: "General the enemy are now in our rear." Forrest looked at the young man and replied, "Well ding it, aint we in theirs?" Seeing the Federals held the better position, Forrest ordered the withdrawal.[64]

Again, Chalmers gave a less than rousing endorsement of the day's action. "On the 24th we moved back toward Columbia, so as to occupy a position on the left flank of our infantry, which had moved back as far as Lynnville. While here we were attacked by a superior force of the enemy and forced back to the main body on the turnpike, when we crossed Richland Creek and moved on to Pulaski." Neither Forrest nor Chalmers recorded the severe wounding of Tyree Bell during this fight, but the fighting resulted in close quarters combat. Chalmers and a Union trooper squared off during the melee, but Chalmers and a Confederate trooper killed the Federal cavalryman in the fight. A member of the cavalry, James H. McNeilly, observed Buford after the battle and described his condition: "His head was tied up.... He was in a bad humor, even profane temper....

Indeed, he called us a pack of infernal idiots, strengthening the term with 'cuss words.'" Not all the injuries occurred in hand-to-hand fights. As the Confederate cavalry withdrew at the end of the day, Lieutenant Henry Watkins decided he wanted to see what an artillery barrage of 6-pound Union guns looked like. Just then, a fragment from a shot from one of the cannons struck his scabbard, driving it into his leg, ultimately causing his death.[65]

Wilson sent a pursing force of Union cavalry after the retreating Confederate column. Forrest, adept at fighting off the enemy, took advantage of the terrain and held off the advance. Further away, Hood's wagon train rumbled ever southward behind a line of Southern cavalry often traveling on dirt, or now muddy, county roads. The hilly, wooded countryside was conducive to rearguard action by Forrest. One trooper of the 1st Mississippi Cavalry recalled the "turnpike itself, threading the valleys, depressions, and gorges, offered many advantageous positions for defense." The Confederate rearguard again withdrew, selecting a new defensive position in the rear. The fight along Richland Creek ended the day's fighting as the main Confederate column ambled southward into Alabama and the Union cavalry prepared to press forward again the next day.[66]

Wilson merely reported the fight at Richland Creek as a minor action in which Croxton forced the enemy to the south side of the creek. Forrest's cavalry made a "short stand" near the creek before withdrawing, according to Wilson. Afterward, Hatch's division rode in the direction of Campbellsville and Mount Pleasant to drive off some lingering Southern cavalry. Not everything had worked well for the Federals and Croxton was clearly displeased with Colonel Joseph Dorr, commanding the 8th Iowa. Dorr had not kept up with the rest of the brigade and he was supposed to be covering the right flank. Croxton repeatedly sent for the regiment to move into the battle, but it did not appear. Croxton fumed: "Had it been up (and I know no good reason why it was not, as the firing indicated clearly the position of the brigade), we would, without doubt, have captured the enemy's artillery and many prisoners." For the cavalrymen on both sides, it was a bitter Christmas Eve and more fighting awaited the next day.[67]

As the retreat continued, Forrest's cavalry provided admirable service, stalling the Federal pursuit; likewise, the Federal cavalry provided equally good service, meeting the enemy and effectively pushing them steadily to the rear. These were two veteran cavalry forces, good at their jobs, and performed accordingly well. However, Wilson worried that he was too slow, but George Thomas told him he was well pleased with the pace and efforts of the Union cavalry. On the Southern side of the field, Hood's main column was making as good progress as could be expected because the head of column was already in Alabama and would camp the next day at Shoal Creek.[68]

Fight at Anthony Hill—December 25

Forrest moved to Pulaski after the fighting at Richland Creek and rested for the night. At daylight, Forrest again moved south after destroying what ammunition Hood could not move past Pulaski with his column the day before. Forrest's command marched through rain and mud which one of his commanders described as "our almost constant companion" during the retreat. Jackson's cavalry division had rearguard duty that day and stayed in Pulaski until the Union cavalry reached the town. Offering only slight resistance, he withdrew southward, hoping to destroy the bridge over Richland Creek as he left, but the Federals followed on his heels and forced him to turn and face his pursuers. "[H]e held him in check for some time, killing and wounding several before retiring," explained Forrest.[69]

The Federal cavalry actions again began a few miles north of Pulaski on December 25. Thomas Harrison's brigade struck the enemy pickets soon after leaving his camp and skirmished with them all the way to Pulaski. The 5th Iowa led Harrison's charge through the town and claimed the bridge across Richland Creek before the enemy could burn it. Harrison resorted to unleashing a section of artillery on Armstrong's cavalry to drive it away from the crossing. George Monlux recalled crossing the creek at Pulaski after an artillery duel and finding Confederate caissons ablaze, pontoons on wagons, and many supply wagons stuck in mud and abandoned. Beyond Pulaski, the Federal and Southern cavalry and infantry moved off a stone pike onto mud roads and the movement became more difficult. As it rode further south, Hammond's brigade followed Harrison while Hatch and Croxton brought up the rear.[70]

Dr. J.W. Worsham, 19th Tennessee Infantry (CSA), recalled that Forrest told Walthall, "Burn the wagons," as the Federal cavalry approached. While Hood's main supply train had moved further south, there remained many straggling wagons and what wagons

The Federal cavalry drove the Confederate rearguard through Pulaski and toward Anthony's Hill ("Driving the Rebs through Strasberg," Library of Congress).

could not be moved on the soft, muddy road were torched. Harrison reported the Southern withdrawal was so rapid "the enemy threw two cannon into the creek, burned a locomotive and train of five cars loaded with arms and ammunition, and it is reported he left near town two locomotives in good order. For six miles below Pulaski the road was strewn with abandoned artillery ammunition, and burning and abandoned wagons. I think he saved some twenty wagons entire." Lieutenant Preston Sharp, 12th Missouri Cavalry, recorded in his diary that as Forrest withdrew "for the next five miles was a stampede of the rebels." Captain Francis Stewart, 49th Ohio Infantry, agreed with Sharp's assessment. Stewart wrote the retreat and fighting of December 25 were heavy at times but the enemy was driven "over the very bad roads which he [enemy] left strewn with abandon stores of all kinds chiefly ordinance and broken wagons and artillery carriages."[71]

There are several accounts of the Union cavalry's actions at Pulaski. James Christy, 4th U.S. Cavalry, recorded in his diary that the Federals gave the Confederates a "good shelling from the town" and then set off in a vigorous pursuit. Captain R.C. Rankin ordered his men of the 7th Ohio Cavalry to dismount as they reached the burning bridge. The dismounted Union cavalry raced through the town, gathering buckets to carry water, and after grabbing some lumber, they were able to knock off the blazing weather boarding on the bridge while the 4th U.S. and 5th Iowa raced across the creek and descended on an ammunition train desperately trying to escape along the muddy road.[72]

Forrest was obliged to move his cavalry into position at Anthony's Hill (seven miles south of Pulaski), alternately called King's Hill and Devil's Gap by others, to hold the enemy cavalry. Again, Forrest chose his position well. Historian J.P. Deupree, member of the 1st Mississippi Cavalry, described the location: "Anthony's Hill for two miles was through a defile formed by two steep high ridges, which united at their common southern extremity to form Anthony's Hill, whose ascent was steep." The ridges were heavily wooded making movement by cavalry difficult and slow. Georgia native and infantry brigade commander Colonel Charles Hart Olmstead recalled: "Here the road, at a steep grade, went straight up the central point of an amphitheater of hills that spread like a great horseshoe directly across the way and here our commanding officer determined to make a stand." Morton's battery was strategically placed on Anthony's Hill and covered the hollow to the north. Forrest ordered Ross' and part of Armstrong's brigades to dismount (Ross to the right and Armstrong to the left) and move to support Featherston's and Palmer's infantry brigades which had been placed on the crest of the hill. Reynolds' and Feild's infantry brigades moved to the rear to serve as reserves. Chalmers' division, now including Buford's division after Forrest gave Chalmers command of both divisions, was ordered about a mile and a half to the east to cover a road which might be used to gain the rear of the Confederate defenders. The Southern troops had not been idle and had constructed defenses of logs and rails. Like so many ants, the skirmishers had been scattered on the hillsides.[73]

When the Union cavalry arrived in the valley in front of Anthony's Hill, the commanders saw this as a potential spot for an ambush. Armstrong's cavalry also performed its duty well, following the fight-retreat-fight method of withdrawal. Harrison, while pursuing Armstrong's cavalry, had driven the Southern cavalry from strong positions and then quickly followed the retreating enemy. When Harrison reached the valley in front of Anthony's Hill, he considered the strong defensive possibilities of the ridge. Harrison observed: "Supposing that the enemy would retire from this position, as he had from others on a flank movement from us, I deployed the Seventh Ohio Cavalry on the right and the Sixteenth Illinois Cavalry on the left of the Fifth Iowa Cavalry, all dismounted. These regiments moved upon the enemy most gallantly."[74]

At one o'clock, the Confederate rearguard closed the trap on their Union pursuers. While withdrawing into the jaws of the ambush, Armstrong's small cavalry detachment pulled Harrison's pursuers toward the awaiting enemy line on the ridge ahead. As the Union troopers moved forward, their officers dismounted the regiments and even placed one piece, a 12-pounder Napoleon, of the 4th U.S. Artillery into position to support the advance. The Confederate rearguard, still in its role as bait, hastened up the road and over the hill, giving the appearance of a detachment riding hard to reach their main column. Walthall's infantry and Jackson's cavalry occupied excellent positions. The hillside was so uneven and heavily wooded that Confederates had no difficulty in concealing the infantry or masking Morton's guns. Walthall presented only a thin line of skirmishers visible to the Union troops in the valley. The advancing Union troopers inched to within 50 yards of the concealed Confederate infantry when Morton's artillery opened with a barrage of canister. Immediately, the skirmishers opened fire on the Union troops. Next, volleys from the lines of Confederate infantry joined in the attack. J.P. Duepree wrote: "The enemy, thoroughly surprised and returning but a feeble and scattering fire, gave way to disorder, when the Confederates sprang forward with a yell and charged down the hill upon them, rushing through the horses of the dismounted men and halting but once to deliver another volley. Thus the enemy were driven in great confusion out of the defile." After chasing the advance force some distance to the rear, the charging Confederates met the concentration of Wilson's cavalry.[75]

Harrison described: "[W]hen suddenly he opened from a masked battery of three guns and charged over his works, in two lines of infantry with a column of cavalry, down the main road. Before this overpowering force my men were obliged to fall back about half a mile." Iowa cavalryman Charles Alley recorded in his journal that his regiment was forced back about 300 yards. Harrison had a gun of the 4th U.S. Artillery unlimbered to support his advance to the ridge and when he was attacked, the gun was lost. Harrison made an off-handed remark in his report: "The battery had been placed

General Edward Walthall's infantry stoutly held back the Federal pursuit of the Army of Tennessee (Alabama Department of Archives and History, Montgomery, Alabama).

in position by General Wilson's order." Others in the Federal cavalry, including a bugler in the 5th Iowa, believed that Harrison had been unhappy about the positioning of the gun.[76]

The Confederate attack pressed through the center of Harrison's brigade and into Hammond's brigade in the rear. Hammond threw his brigade to the right of Harrison's which reeled under the Confederate attack, and the retreating 7th Ohio cut into Hammond's brigade, slamming into the 4th Tennessee which advanced in front of the brigade. This allowed some of the Confederate forces to interpose themselves between Hammond's led horses, his front line, and the remainder of the brigade. Hammond described: "I was obliged to withdraw the Fourth Tennessee to save the horses. When remounted, being joined by part of the Second Tennessee, we attacked the enemy in flank and drove him into his works again, holding the position until ordered away. The remainder of the brigade went into action by order of General Wilson and attacked along with General Hatch's division. The Fourth Tennessee reached the enemy's [works] in time to see him in retreat."[77]

Hatch was third in the column behind Harrison's and Hammond's brigades, and he became aware of the unfolding situation when Harrison's troopers came streaming to the rear. Stewart's brigade was sent on the Union left flank which "checked and drove back" the attack. Next, Coon moved on the right of the road and pushed ahead. Wilson hastened Hatch's division forward and the two generals saw the Confederates moving the gun of the 4th U.S. Artillery up Anthony's Hill. Wilson told Hatch, "There they are; hurry up!" Hatch replied that if Wilson would let him to move by his own discretion he would carry the hill in a short period. Wilson replied, "All right; go ahead." Then, Hatch ordered two regiments dismounted—the 9th Illinois to move up the right of the road directly in front of the enemy position, while sending the 7th Illinois on the left of the road in line with the 9th Illinois. The dismounted 9th Illinois stalled the Confederates still driving the center to the rear. Hatch explained that 9th Illinois moved "to one side to let the flying mass pass, and then with a cheer charged the enemy, driving the enemy back, and forcing him to take shelter under his guns and in the barricades thrown up by the enemy. As soon as my right was well up on the enemy's left flank I ordered the whole division to charge. Then the 2nd Iowa and 12th Tennessee was sent mounted on the right to reach the rear of the enemy and the 6th Illinois, mounted also to the left and rear."[78]

The two dismounted Illinois regiments marched forward but could get no closer due to the defenses as accurate volleys ripped into them. These regiments fired at the enemy behind their defenses for about 20 minutes before the flanking regiments reached the rear of the enemy. This action forced the enemy to withdraw and the 9th and 7th Illinois regiments marched into the enemy works.[79]

James Christy, 4th U.S. Cavalry, played an important role in the flanking movement. Once Hatch and Hammond joined in the fight, the Federals drove the enemy back to the barricades. A heated battle occurred for about an hour, and Christy moved a company around the right flank. He soon found the enemy troops, concluded that he was surrounded by the enemy, and quickly decided to change his "base of operations." He hastened on his new task when a "mischievous reb ... sent a ball whistling by my ear." Christy reported to Hatch that the enemy could be flanked and within 20 minutes the fight was over.[80]

When the concentration of Wilson's forces counterattacked bolstered by a strong flanking movement, the Confederates felt increasingly pressed by the advancing lines of blue-clad soldiers. Battery commander John Morton observed that Frank Armstrong rode to Forrest on three different occasions during the fighting, and told him the Union troops were pressing his brigade and that his men were virtually out of ammunition. Finally, Armstrong had had enough. The last time he approached Forrest, Walthall was present. Instead of addressing Forrest, Armstrong looked at Walthall and asked: "General Walthall, won't you please make that d—d man there on the horse see that my men are forced to retreat?" Forrest, prone to bouts of anger, very quietly told Armstrong he was just trying to give Hood enough time to cross Sugar Creek, a few miles to the rear. Then, he told Armstrong his men did an exemplary job in holding the Union cavalry at bay and then said, "It is about time for us all to get out of here." Walthall ordered his infantry to start marching south at sunset and Forrest kept his cavalry as a rearguard. Despite this setback, by the time Walthall reached Sugar Creek at 11:00 p.m. Forrest told him that the Union cavalry had pushed forward and was no more than a mile behind. At Sugar Creek, Walthall found a part of Hood's ordnance train which had been delayed. The Yankees still closely behind, and a slow train still ahead, meant more fighting the next day along the banks of Sugar Creek.[81]

At Anthony's Hill, the Confederate won the fight, though temporarily. Chalmers would write: "In this fight, which General Thomas treats as a mere skirmish, the Confederates captured fifty prisoners, three hundred cavalry horses, one gun of Company I, Fourth United States artillery, with eight horses, and the killed and wounded were estimated at one hundred and fifty, while the brilliancy and vim of the Confederate charge astonished the Federals so much that they attacked no more that day." Wilson appealed to Thomas Wood for his assistance during the fight which he referred to Thomas as a "slight check" in his pursuit. Facing Forrest's and Walthall's troops at Anthony Hill, Wilson told Wood that he faced eight brigades of infantry behind barricades. He wrote: "Your infantry can materially assist me," but prior to their arrival Wilson successfully forced Forrest to withdraw again. Harrison, despite being roughly handled at Anthony's Hill, reported that he captured one captain, two lieutenants, and 50 or 60 soldiers, leaving another 150 wounded, at Pulaski and his casualties amounted to 26 men—three killed, 18 wounded and five missing. While the fighting was going on at Anthony's Hill, Hood began laying a pontoon bridge over the Tennessee River at Bainbridge. What remained of his command had the opportunity to cross the river to safety if it could make this crossing.[82]

Withdrawing from Anthony's Hill, Forrest wrote: "The enemy made no further demonstrations during the day. I halted my command at Sugar Creek, where it encamped during the night." On the way to Sugar Creek, a Confederate cavalryman noted in his diary—"rains & so muddy." Ross reported that he leisurely withdrew, but Lieutenant S.B. Barron, 3rd Texas, recalled the rearguard action was anything but a picnic. Barron wrote that the rearguard fought to save a "shattered, dispirited, barefooted army from destruction. How well we did our part I will leave the boys in blue who followed us to say." Forrest had reasons for fighting at Anthony's Hill. Harrison correctly surmised that Forrest made this attack because he needed time to move the wagon train he was escorting further south. At least one Southern cavalryman, Newton Cannon, 11th Tennessee Cavalry, heard the rumor that Hood asked Forrest to hold this position until 5:00 p.m. to allow the army's supply train to reach the Tennessee River. Walthall in his after-action report explained the Federal cavalry pressed too closely as the Confederate retreating column. "It was determined to turn upon him, and as an advantageous position for this, a line was selected on Anthony's Hill."[83]

Colonel C.W. Heiskell, 19th Tennessee Infantry, rode along with his regiment as they trudged southward toward Sugar Creek and he humorously asked his men: "[B]oys, how do you like the cavalry." Trooper W.J. Worsham recalled, "Several replied, 'Ah, Colonel, this is not regular cavalry.' Then some one halloed out, 'I think this has been pretty d__d regular for the past forty months.' So when we reached Sugar Creek the foot cavalry waded it, the ice-cold water coming up to our waist."[84]

December 26—Fight at Sugar Creek

John Morton described the withdrawal after the fight at Anthony's Hill as "an all-night race." Forrest withdrew about 10 miles southwest after the previous day's fighting to the banks of Sugar Creek, reaching there at 1:00 a.m. The Confederate soldiers, so ill-clad for the weather, suffered as they marched through mud three feet deep in some places. Many of the infantry were barefooted and had to cross the ice-cold streams as the rain and snow continued to fall. Once they reached Sugar Creek, Forrest's men built fires and tried to warm themselves after the grueling march. Chalmers described: "Having selected an excellent position for his infantry and artillery, and thrown up temporary breastworks of rails, he ordered Colonel Dillon, with the Second Mississippi cavalry, to cross the creek above, mounted ready for a flank attack, and again quietly waited their coming."[85]

Hammond's brigade led the Federal pursuit on December 26 and Forrest prepared to fulfill his task of holding the Federal cavalry away from the retreating Confederate column—this time aided by a dense fog. Walthall's infantry and Ross' brigade were behind fortification at Sugar Creek when Hammond's brigade advanced that morning. Forrest's cavalry served as bait for the pursuing Federals and fought a weak rearguard action until it reached Sugar Creek, just as they had the previous day. Unable to see the enemy due to the dense fog, Hammond rode ahead in pursuit of the enemy. Armstrong's brigade was positioned on the left side of the Confederate line, serving primarily in a reserve role, and Ross was on the right. Forrest explained that two "mounted regiments of Ross' brigade and Ector's and Granbury's brigades of infantry were ordered to charge upon the discomfited foe, which was done, producing a complete rout." Forrest noted the enemy was pursued for two miles, but others described a quite different result. As the Confederates burst through the fog, Chalmers recalled that "the long pent-up Rebel yell burst forth" and the Union cavalry reeled rearward during the attack. Dr. James McNeilly heard Forrest order Jackson to go to the creek and "begin fighting them fellows like the very devil."[86]

Forrest placed most of his command on the west branch of Sugar Creek behind the upper ford. His plan of withdrawal meant he would move over a lower ford which led to the village of Appleton. The gravel-bottomed, tree-lined creek was swollen due to wet weather, and the trees and fog along the creek prevented the Federals from seeing the Confederate line in the field beyond. As the Federals approached, they moved past a bluff on their right flank and on their left was another small stream, Puncheon Branch. Ross had the Texas Legion and 9th Texas Cavalry behind Reynolds' and Ector's brigades (200 yards west of the creek) as the Union cavalry approached in the dense fog. Walthall had Featherston's and Palmer's brigades guarding the lower ford, protecting the route of retreat. The Confederates patiently waited for the Federals to arrive.[87]

Sul Ross described: "When near enough to be seen the infantry fired a volley and charged. At the same time the Legion and Ninth Texas were ordered forward, and passing through our infantry crossed the creek in the face of a terrible fire, overthrew all opposition on the farther side, and pursued the thoroughly routed foe nearly a mile, capturing twelve prisoners and as many horses, besides killing numbers of others. The force opposed to us here and which was so completely whipped, proved, from the statements of the prisoners, to be Hammond's brigade of cavalry." Aiding in the Confederate attack, Morton's battery had been placed in the rear of Ross' cavalry and had the honor of opening the fight by firing the "signal gun and immediately a deadly flood of shot and shell was poured on their backs, with startling effect. As if they had been galvanized by an electric wire, the line broke and rushed madly for the creek" recalled John Morton.[88]

James Goodwin, 4th Tennessee Cavalry, noted that his regiment had crossed the creek when they ran into a barricade of logs, not 50 steps in front. When the Confederates charged, three companies were cut off and had to climb a hill to find their way back to the Federal lines. The intensity of the Southern attack forced the first line of Union cavalry to the rear and into the midst of the horse holders. Sergeant Major Daniel Comstock and Captain Thomas Caper, both of the 9th Indiana Cavalry gave detailed accounts of the action at Sugar Creek. The morning was foggy and a light rain fell. The 2nd Tennessee led the advance of Hammond's brigade, followed by the 4th Tennessee, and the 9th Indiana followed in the rear of the Tennessee cavalry. These regiments followed Forrest's rearguard across a ford narrow enough for only two horses to cross at one time and the crossing was edged with steep banks forming a natural choke point. The roughness of the terrain caused the troopers to dismount, leaving the horses with horse holders. Caper explained, "the enemy charged the two Tennessee regiments with two columns of infantry, with cavalry in the center, and succeeded in driving them a considerable distance to the rear, then, swinging around to the right and left, came up suddenly in the rear of the two detachments of the 9th and made a desperate effort to capture them. Although assailed by greatly superior numbers in front, flank and rear, most of the men succeeded in making their escape." After the Tennessee regiments met the attack, the 9th Indiana split with eight companies moving to the right flank and four companies to the left flank while moving forward to support the Tennesseans. Facing fire from an enemy shrouded by the fog was difficult duty. Soon the 2nd Tennessee edged to the right, allowing the 9th Indiana to form a broader line, adding to the Federal firepower. The 14th Ohio battery unlimbered and shelled the Confederates. The Confederate infantry and cavalry kept up a continual firing. As the fog lifted the Union cavalry saw a log barricade on the other side of the creek which offered good protection for the Confederate infantry.[89]

Hammond's after-action report offered a different account than Forrest's. He explained that the 2nd Tennessee Cavalry had pushed Ross' horsemen to Sugar Creek when they were surprised. "A charge was made in turn by two columns of infantry, with cavalry in the center, driving us back about 300 yards across the creek, where we rallied and drove them back to their works, holding the position until the afternoon, when the Fourteenth Ohio Battery shelled their rear guard out of log-works commanding the road, and pursuit was continued to this place."[90]

After the initial ambush, the Federal lines re-formed. Then, an unidentified Union officer started walking among the firing Union cavalry yelling: "Don't run, boys; for

God's sake, don't run!" Hammond arrived on the scene, silencing the officer who did more to anger the Union cavalrymen than anything else. Hammond, extending his line, was able to move part of his men to the top of a small hill which provided a more direct line of fire into the Confederate infantry behind the log barricades. Hammond shifted some men forward, to prevent a flank attack, and successfully dislodged the Confederate infantry positioned on the extreme left. After a couple of hours of fighting, the Confederates started to withdraw and seeing this, the Union cavalry surged across the creek "wildly yelling, charged the centre of the main line" and pushing them about 300 yards to the rear. At this point, some of the 9th Indiana mounted and rode directly into the midst of the remaining Confederate infantry, but the charge was premature. The Confederates turned to meet the attack and part of the 9th Indiana found itself in the rear of the enemy line. A circuitous route of retreat kept most of the trapped men from being captured. In the meantime, the 14th Ohio artillery hammered away and Hammond's entire brigade fired into the enemy line. Accomplishing what he intended, Forrest decided to continue the withdrawal.[91]

Forrest claimed: "In this engagement he sustained a loss of about 150 in killed and wounded; many prisoners and horses were captured and about 400 horses killed." Chalmers conceded: "The enemy were severely punished, but more frightened than hurt." Forrest remained in line for a couple of hours exchanging gunfire, but being concerned that the Federals might use the fog to their advantage to flank his position, he decided to again head south. This ended the main cavalry events for the campaign and Hood's army moved past the Tennessee River. A member of the 2nd Michigan Cavalry, Josiah B. Smith, wrote a letter at the end of the campaign: "Hood is all used up and he lost 29 thousand ... men in his Campain with us. I think he will not try us on again."[92]

Northern Alabama

As the Army of Tennessee marched out of the state, the Union forces which had contracted to Nashville again marched to claim the territory which had fallen into Confederate hands over the past two months. Major Thomas Williamson commanded a detachment of the 10th Indiana Cavalry and was part of Johnson's Third Brigade (Sixth Cavalry Division) consisting of the 10th Indiana, 2nd Tennessee, and 15th Pennsylvania cavalries. As Hood retreated southward, this brigade became active in attacking the enemy when the opportunity occurred. William Palmer, 15th Pennsylvania, saw action against Hylan Lyon's cavalry and completed the destruction of this command as it reached northern Alabama. This brigade, about 500 men strong, was particularly active from December 28 to January 6 and continued actively reclaiming the territory given up during the Nashville Campaign.[93]

James Steedman's and R.S. Granger's troops also moved back to their positions in Alabama and Georgia securing the territory which had been abandoned. Roddey only became aware of the changing situation after Hood's loss when large bodies of enemy cavalry and infantry arrived and drove the isolated units southward. Near Huntsville, James B. Irvine, a Confederate cavalryman, heard the "shrill whistle of locomotives" which signaled the return of not only cavalry, but Federal infantry. Roddey had not received any messages about Hood's defeat at Nashville before the Union troops began arriving on December 20. Irvine described his first encounter with the returning cavalry. "I saw the bluecoats across the creek [near Huntsville] sabre in hand slashing and cutting at a great rate. Williams Co. having fired their guns & being deserted by the balance had nothing to do but to run of it. But before they could turn their horses the enemy were upon them most of them succeeded however in getting off ... the officers endeavored manfully to check the flight but it was of no use. Go they would." The Union cavalry continued its pursuit, killing and capturing most of the retreating Southern cavalry, including Irvine. By the end of the month, Granger had reestablished his headquarters at Decatur. Federal gunboats, freed up from duty in Nashville, also arrived to assist in the new Union advance into northern Alabama.[94]

Confederate Colonel John R.B. Burtwell, West Point graduate in 1860, commanded a regiment of cavalry in Roddey's brigade. Burtwell rode into Huntsville on the evening of December 20, joined by two companies of Confederates who had recently skirmished with the newly arriving Union troops. These companies had clashed with the Union cavalry brigade which included the 10th, 12th, and 13th Indiana cavalries and the 2nd Tennessee Union Cavalry. The Federal cavalry arrived in Huntsville the next day and was soon joined by the Union infantry; this occupation would last until the end of the war. Burtwell set up defenses along the roads and railroad to try to delay the arrival of the Union troops.[95]

Burtwell, like Roddey, had not received official news of the situation at Nashville but the arrival of so many Federal troops left little to the imagination. Burtwell cobbled together what forces he could, two companies of Lieutenant Colonel F. Windes' 4th Alabama Cavalry, part of the 10th Alabama Cavalry, and Moreland's Cavalry Battalion, about 150–200 men, and hoped for the arrival of reinforcements. Then, he ordered the bridges in the area to be burned and sent his small force to Indian Creek about six miles west of Huntsville. On December 23, an ex-slave, after being poorly treated by the Confederate soldiers, reported the location of Burtwell's troops and the 10th Indiana and 2nd Tennessee cavalries advanced to investigate. At dawn, the Federal troops arrived, with the 10th Indiana in the lead, at the ford at Indian Creek and found Burtwell's troops on the banks of the creek. The Federals routed the Confederate force, effectively dealing with the immediate Confederate threat at Huntsville.[96]

R.S. Granger reported that he was back in possession of Decatur and Huntsville on December 28. All of the territory claimed by Hood's army during his prelude and advance into Middle Tennessee was recaptured by the end of the year.[97]

Richard Johnson's Third Cavalry Brigade dealt one final blow to Hood on December 31 as it moved along the Memphis and Charleston Railroad. On the evening of December 30, the Union cavalry brigade arrived in Leighton, Alabama, having captured only three prisoners in an uneventful day. The next day they moved further south toward Russellville on only a slightly more eventful day, killing one enemy soldier while capturing a lieutenant and six enlisted men. In an unexpected turn of good fortune that night, the Federal horsemen came upon Hood's pontoon train "consisting of eighty pontoons, also forty-five wagons loaded with cordage, equipments, forges, &c. We burned and destroyed the entire train and teams," wrote Major Thomas Williamson. The next day, the fresh Federals found another train—"capturing and destroying the wagons by fire and killing the mules, about 500 in number, dismounted men taking some of the best mules to ride. The train consisted of about 125 wagons (this was Hood's supply train)." The following day, Williamson and the Union cavalry moved back to Decatur. On January 4, the cavalry mop-up continued when the 4th Alabama Cavalry (CSA) was attacked and also lost its supply train. Three of the Alabamans were killed, another 20 wounded and 30 men were taken prisoner. Roddey's headquarters papers were also seized in this attack. The losses of the Confederate trains were probably worse than reported by the Federal cavalry. E.T. Freeman, a staff member in French's division, summarized on January 10: "[T]he enemy's cavalry captured the remains of our pontoon train on this side of the river, near Tuscumbia, and 400 or 500 wagons which had been started to Tuscaloosa without a guard. It is reported that the enemy had only 250 men." Small pockets of Confederate resistance were forced further south in these post campaign actions.[98]

The End of the Nashville Campaign—Confederate Summary

On January 24, Forrest concluded his campaign report: "The campaign was full of trial and suffering, but the troops under my command, both cavalry and infantry, submitted to every hardship with an uncomplaining patriotism; with a single exception, they behaved with commendable gallantry. From the day I left Florence, on the 21st of November, to the 27th of December my cavalry were engaged every day with the enemy." Forrest's losses were not insignificant, but he believed that his command had produced good results. He captured "16 block-houses and stockades, 20 bridges, several hundred horses and mules, 20 yoke of oxen, 4 locomotives, and 100 cars and 10 miles of railroad." He also reported capturing 1,600 enemy soldiers and he ended the campaign with three more field guns than he started. He had nothing but praise for his three division commanders: Chalmers, Buford, and Jackson.[99]

The Confederate cavalry performed well in the campaign and suffered under the adverse weather conditions as did all the Confederate troops. A.W. Sparks, 9th Texas Cavalry, wrote that the days on rearguard duty were particularly difficult ones. Another member of Ross' Texas cavalry stated the campaign was "the severest service experienced during the war." Ross' brigade had 20 fights with Wilson's cavalry and suffered in the cold December nights during the withdrawal from Tennessee. Sparks wrote that Hood's troops were "thinly clad, poorly fed, and dejected and disheartened."[100]

Chalmers gave a slightly more sobering account of the Nashville Campaign. "During the engagements on the march to Nashville, and until after the fight on the Granny White pike on the evening of the 16th of December, the officers and men of this division behaved with great gallantry; but after that time, while there were many who continued to exhibit the same courage and constancy, I regret to say that there were some who so far forgot their duty as to desert their comrades and seek an ignominious safety in flight; some of these have since returned to their colors, but others are still absent." Overall, Chalmers praised those soldiers who remained "faithful to their duty." He also removed a veil of concern regarding the 7th Alabama Cavalry, which had less than a stellar reputation, by stating the regiment performed well during the campaign. It is also important to note the Chalmers reported substantially more casualties than are found in Forrest's casualty report in the *Official Records*. The casualties reported for Forrest's command totaled about 10 percent of the force engaged in the campaign, but these numbers do not accurately tell the losses of the Confederate cavalry.[101]

Casualties in Forrest's Cavalry: November—December, 1864[102]

Buford's Division					
	Officers Killed	Soldiers Killed	Officers Wounded	Soldiers Wounded	Total
Staff & escort	—	2	1	1	4
Bell's Brigade					
Staff	—	—	1	—	1
2nd Tenn.	—	—	4	7	11
19th Tenn.	1	1	—	6	8
20th Tenn.			1	4	5
21st Tenn.	—	5	1	36	42
Nixon's Tenn. Regt.	—	—	1	13	14
BRIGADE TOTAL	*1*	*6*	*8*	*66*	*81*
*Crossland's Brigade**					
3rd Kentucky	—	—	—	8	8
7th Kentucky	—	1	2	15	18
8th Kentucky	—	2	—	8	10
12th Kentucky	—	—	2	9	11
Huey's Kent. Btln.	—	1	0	6	7
BRIGADE TOTAL	*0*	*4*	*4*	*46*	*54*
Buford's Division Total	**1**	**12**	**13**	**113**	**139**

*3rd, 7th and 8th Kentucky regiments designated mounted infantry.

Jackson's Division					
	Officers Killed	Soldiers Killed	Officers Wounded	Soldiers Wounded	Total
Staff & escort	—	—	2	3	5
Armstrong's Brigade					
Staff					
1st Mississippi	1	3	2	45	51
2d Mississippi	—	1	2	3	6
3rd Mississippi	0	1	0	11	12
28th Mississippi	1	9	6	43	59
Ballentine's Regt	—	4	0	15	19
BRIGADE TOTAL	*2*	*18*	*10*	*117*	*147*

Chapter Thirteen. Hood Retreats

Ross's Brigade					
1st Texas Legion	—	—	—	4	4
3d Texas	—	—	2	12	14
6th Texas	—	—	4	5	9
9th Texas	—	1	—	4	5
BRIGADE TOTAL	—	*1*	*6*	*25*	*32*
Jackson's Division Total	**0**	**19**	**18**	**145**	**184**

Chalmers' Division

	Officers Killed	Soldiers Killed	Officers Wounded	Soldiers Wounded	Total
Staff & escort	—	—	—	4	4
Rucker's Brigade					
Staff & escort	—	—	1	—	1
7th Alabama	—	3	7	41	51
5th Mississippi	—	4	—	12	16
7th Tennessee	—	1	3	9	13
12th Tennessee	—	—	—	1	1
14th Tennessee	—	2	2	15	19
15th Tennessee	2	3	—	12	17
Forrest's Regt. Tenn. Cavalry	1	3	3	15	21
BRIGADE TOTAL	*3*	*16*	*16*	*105*	*140*
Biffle's Brigade					
9th Tennessee	—	1	1	6	8
10th Tennessee	—	—	2	8	10
BRIGADE TOTAL	—	*1*	*3*	*14*	*18*
Chalmers' Division Total	**3**	**17**	**19**	**123**	**162**

Miscellaneous Units

	Officers Killed	Soldiers Killed	Soldiers Killed	Soldiers Killed	Total
Forrest's Escort	—	—	1	4	4
Young's (Croft's Georgia) Battery	—	2	—	5	7
Morton's Battery	—	1	—	5	6
Misc. Unit Total	0	3	1	14	17

Chalmers' report of Rucker's November casualties revealed 116 casualties for the dates of November 25 through November 30 alone while Forrest reported only 56 casualties in November for Chalmers' division. Chalmers' report for November plus Forrest's reported losses in December were combined to determine the division's casualties for these two months in the previous table. By all appearances, at least Chalmers' casualties were grossly underestimated in this final report. Forrest's numbers total about 500 casualties but in early January he wrote to Richard Taylor: "My command is greatly reduced in numbers and efficiency by losses in battle and in the worn-down and unserviceable condition of animals. The Army of Tennessee was badly defeated and is greatly demoralized, and to save it during the retreat from Nashville I was compelled almost to sacrifice my command. Aside from the killed, wounded, and captured of my command, many were sent to the rear with barefooted, lame, and unserviceable horses, who have taken advantage of all the confusion and disorder attending the hasty retreat of a beaten army, and are now scattered through the country or have gone to their homes." Certainly, Chalmers' men suffered greatly on the last day of the battle, as did Chalmers' and Buford's men on December 17. Then, another nine days on rearguard duty took a heavy toll on the Southern cavalry.[103]

At the end of the campaign, Forrest sent a message to his troops: "The old campaign is ended, and your commanding general deems this an appropriate occasion to speak of the steadiness, self-denial, and patriotism with which you have borne the hardships of the past year. The marches and labors you have performed during that period will find no parallel in the history of this war.... To sum up, in brief, your triumphs during the past year, you have fought fifty battles, killed and captured 16,000 of the enemy, captured 2,000 horses and mules, 67 pieces of artillery, 4 gun-boats, 14 transports, 20 barges, 300 wagons, 50 ambulances, 10,000 stand of small-arms, 40 blockhouses, destroyed 36 railroad bridges, 200 miles of railroad, 6 engines, 100 cars, and $15,000,000 worth of property. In the accomplishment of this great work you were occasionally sustained by other troops, who joined you in the fight, but your regular number never exceeded 5,000, 2,000 of whom have been killed or wounded, while in prisoners you have lost about 200."[104]

The End of the Nashville Campaign— Union Summary

Somewhat surprisingly, James Wilson made no formal accounting of the casualties for the entire campaign. Wilson reported the Union cavalry casualties related to the Battle of Nashville on December 15–16 in his battle report. These figures do not include the fights between November 19–30 and December 17–26 where the Union cavalry forces had losses, but Wilson mentioned in his final campaign report that he lost "1 gun; 122 officers and men killed, 521 wounded, and 259 missing" during November and December while capturing "enemy 32 guns, 11 caissons, 12 colors, 3,232 prisoners (including 1 general officer), and compelled them to abandon or destroy over 100 wagons, 8 ambulances, and 1,348 mules."[105]

Casualties in Wilson's Cavalry: December 15–16, 1864[106]

	Officers Killed	Soldiers Killed	Officers Wounded	Soldiers Wounded	Total
4th U.S.—escort	—	—	—	—	—
Edward McCook—First Division					
Croxton's Brigade	—	—	—	2	2
Edward Hatch—Fifth Division					
Stewart's Brigade	1	13	7	101	122
Coon's Brigade	0	14	11	87	113*
Division Total	1	27	18	118	235
*Captured: * (1 soldier)*					
Richard Johnson—Sixth Division					
Harrison's Brigade	1	1	0	9	20**
Biddle's Brigade	0	0	0	7	8+
Division Total	1	1	0	16	28
*Captured: ** (one officer and 8 men);+ one soldier*					
Joseph Knipe—Seventh Division					
Hammond's Brigade	0	5	3	39	57++
Johnson's Brigade	0	1	0	4	7^
Division Total	0	6	3	43	64
Captured: ++(10 men); ^2 men					
CORPS TOTAL	**2**	**34**	**21**	**249**	**329**

During the Nashville Campaign, Wilson worked closely with Thomas and the other top commanders in the Union forces, with the notable exception of Schofield who criticized Wilson's actions on November 28 and 29. In Wilson's defense, many of Schofield's remarks were unfair and attempted to mask his own lethargy in withdrawing from Columbia. Wilson made an immediate ally in Thomas and recognized Grant's, his long-term mentor, errors and dismissiveness of Thomas at Nashville. This marked an important step in Wilson's own independence and increased command ability. He saw Thomas command with a steady hand, clear direction, and an ability to win battles without sacrificing his men needlessly. Thomas' selflessness helped Wilson grow as a top-notch commander.[107]

In contrast, Wilson made no small issue of Schofield's corps performance at Nashville where it reported significantly fewer casualties than any actively engaged corps at Nashville, including the cavalry. Wilson's command had about twice the casualties as Schofield's infantry in the battle. Wilson also noted "Schofield's corps met no serious resistance and did no real fighting at Nashville or afterwards is shown beyond doubt or dispute." It was apparent that Schofield's petulance upon reaching Nashville took much of the value of his corps away from the battle.[108]

In contrast, Wilson praised the actions of Thomas Wood, James Steedman and A.J. Smith's infantry during the battle and the pursuit of Hood. Despite nearly losing his command, George Thomas made the right decision in waiting for his cavalry to organize. This decision may have determined the outcome of the battle, and clearly, the rapid retreat of Hood out of Tennessee was forced by Wilson's troopers followed by Thomas' infantry. Perhaps, the greatest compliment to Wilson and Thomas came from Chalmers two weeks later: "To 'learn wisdom from your enemy' is one of the wisest maxims of history. At Nashville our enemy had a large force of cavalry, but instead of wasting its strength in the front, he kept it quietly in the rear of his infantry, resting and recruiting, until the time for action came, and then he moved it out fresh and vigorous with telling effect." Wilson's desire to mass the Union cavalry into a single corps had proved decisive at Nashville and this model would carry forward in the west for the remainder of the war.[109]

Conclusions

[I]n all my experience I have never seen so much suffering.
—James H. Wilson

The cavalry operations in the Nashville Campaign reflected the overall situation in the Civil War of December 1864 perfectly. Forrest's veteran cavalry had a slight numerical advantage on November 21 when the campaign officially began, but by November 30, the Union war machine produced reinforcements, some new units and some veterans, that joined in the fight. By the time the Battle of Nashville was fought, the Federal cavalry had increased from 4,000 troops to three times that number—12,000 cavalry troops on December 15—a remarkable achievement. In many ways, Forrest's effectiveness had caused so much concern that a large cavalry corps was finally organized to deal with his command.

Columbia to Franklin

If the campaign is taken in the various components, the shift in initiative is seen clearly. From November 19 to 29, Forrest's cavalry dominated the cavalry actions. This was true for a variety of reasons, but of prime importance was Sherman's mishandling of his cavalry. Sherman had little confidence in the ability of his cavalry to meet the Confederate cavalry, even though much of Sherman's cavalry problems were of his own making. Of utmost importance, he failed to identify a strong cavalry chief in which he had confidence. The bulk of Sherman's cavalry accompanied his three armies in the Atlanta Campaign where he disregarded Washington Elliott, the chief of cavalry for the Army of the Cumberland, and disliked George Stoneman, who commanded the cavalry division for the Army of the Ohio. He also paid little attention to Grierson's cavalry in Mississippi. As a result, he insisted on directly commanding the four divisions in the Atlanta Campaign, resulting in the virtual destruction of two divisions based on his own poor decisions; with his best division, he so disregarded its commander that it did not operate at its full potential. These decisions left a poorly organized and unprepared mounted arm which had to meet Forrest's cavalry in November. Despite this, the Union cavalry did meet Forrest with some exemplary cavalry commands—particularly Croxton's and Coon's brigades. Stewart's brigade was solid, but Capron's brigade was poorly armed, had low morale, and seemed to have been disregarded by Schofield before Wilson's arrival.

From the Tennessee River to Columbia, ironically, Capron's brigade provided courageous service and demonstrated a remarkable strength of character as it was driven to the rear. Capron had been given confusing orders to move back to the east on some occasions while being told to sacrifice his whole command, if necessary. Despite the fact he was beaten in every fight, he held back the enemy long enough to allow Cox's and Stanley's infantry to reach Columbia in time to take possession of the town and the crossings. Capron's cavalry deserves recognition for preventing Schofield from having his flank turned with the enemy between him and Nashville.

James Chalmers' division faced Capron in the first part of the campaign with complete success. While Chalmers is credited with a division at this disposal, in reality Chalmers operated with Rucker's brigade. Biffle's small brigade was usually performing reconnaissance and security duty during the fights from the Tennessee River to Columbia. Despite the hyperbole of many Civil War reports, Chalmers offered a clear, objective description of the actions of his men throughout the campaign. Chalmers and Rucker successfully kept Capron retreating to Columbia and the most notable actions at Henryville, Fouche Springs and north of Mount Pleasant where the Southern cavalry carried the day.

On the eastern flank, Buford and Jackson had little difficulty in pressing Hatch's division and Croxton's brigade to the rear. Buford and Jackson were experienced and effective commanders and used their divisions well. Still, it was somewhat surprising that Hatch and Croxton, armed with Spencer carbines, were so easily pushed rearward. The fight at Campbellsville provided the most significant action between these two forces; Buford dealt with Oliver Wells' brigade and Jackson dealt with Coon's brigade while Croxton was on security duty.

Once the two armies reached Columbia, the opposing cavalry forces moved along the Duck River on the east side of town. There was little hope that Wilson, now with the Union cavalry in the field, could prevent Forrest from sending a significant force to the north side of the river. There were just too many crossings along 10 to 15 miles of the Duck River for the Federal cavalry to defend. Forrest effectually made the crossings on November 28 and, again, only Capron's brigade stymied Buford for most of the day. Wilson had three brigades (Croxton, Capron/Harrison, and Coon) in place once Forrest crossed the river facing all three of Forrest's divisions.

Once across the river, Forrest made his greatest contribution of the campaign. Wilson had the duty of providing security along Schofield's eastern flank and on November 29, Forrest fought Wilson steadily northward on the Lewisburg Pike, effectively opening up Schofield's flank and rear so that Forrest and Hood could cut off the Union forces still at Columbia. Forrest's action worked so well that Wilson withdrew away from Schofield's flank. Wilson believed that Forrest planned to swing around the eastern flank when, instead, he moved west to Spring Hill. Although Wilson would be criticized by many historians for his actions during the day, he took the actions which he had agreed upon with Schofield. Schofield knew Wilson's plan and Wilson expected Schofield to also be withdrawing on a parallel route throughout the day. Instead, Schofield remained in Columbia and, only by remarkably good luck, Stanley, Wagner, and Hoefling secured Spring Hill until the Union forces could evacuate Columbia. Wilson made some mistakes on November 29, but in light of the understanding with Schofield, small ones.

Forrest clearly won the day on November 29 when he opened up the entire eastern flank of Schofield's infantry. He even placed Jackson's cavalry as far north as Thompson's Station. The timely arrival of Wagner's division was the only thing that kept disaster from the Union infantry. Charles Hoefling and his small band of Union cavalry provided enough time for Wagner's men to secure the town. Again, bad luck struck the Confederate forces. Two of Forrest's divisions ran out of ammunition and were out of action on the evening of November 29. Only Jackson's division had the duty of securing Franklin Pike. The series of events at Spring Hill from a Confederate standpoint has been the subject of controversy for years. The Confederate cavalry actions on that evening should be included in these controversies. The looming question in regard to the cavalry is: if Jackson knew the Union army continued it march to Franklin, why was this not adequately conveyed to army headquarters? Ross had, at least, two fights with the withdrawing Federals and firsthand accounts showed Armstrong was also actively engaged. With five Union divisions and 800 wagons marching past the Southern cavalry, the alarm should have been sounded to deal with such a major event, including rolling the staff of the commanding general out of bed.

The next day the disastrous Battle of Franklin was fought. In regard to the cavalry operations, November 29 would be the last day the Confederate cavalry held the advantage. The Battle of Franklin produced one of the bloodiest and most intensely fought battles of the Civil War. At this point, Wilson had gained Stewart's brigade from the western flank and, importantly, he gained fresh regiments with Hammond's brigade. With the advantage of good position, fresh troops, and effective weapons for his troops, Wilson repulsed Forrest's crossing of the Harpeth River on November 30. This secured the flank and the reputation of the Union cavalry. From the Confederate standpoint, Forrest moved Chalmers' division to the western flank of Hood's army which seemed a good strategy. What we know now is that Chalmers was unable to offer much support in the infantry attack and Forrest probably would have had better luck against Wilson had Chalmers been placed on the eastern flank with the rest of the Southern cavalry. In addition, Forrest was denied permission to cross the Harpeth River, just as he had done on the Duck River, and sweep into the rear of Schofield's infantry.

The Cavalry at Murfreesboro and Nashville

On December 1 the Union withdrawal to Nashville was successfully completed. Then, things began to go dramatically wrong for the Confederates after Hood invested Thomas at Nashville. Wilson continued to gain men and mounts over the next two weeks. Chalmers effectively blockaded the Tennessee River to the chagrin of the Federals. Then, Hood made a serious error by sending, and keeping, Forrest at Murfreesboro. Thomas had 8,000 troops in Murfreesboro, in the rear of Hood, and to be successful Hood needed to pull Thomas from behind his defenses in Nashville. If sending Forrest to pressure Murfreesboro could offer an opportunity to destroy a relieving force from Nashville, this could have been a good decision. The result was just the opposite. Robert Milroy's two brigades handily defeated the Forrest-led troops on December 7, and Hood left two-thirds of his cavalry in place at Murfreesboro thereafter. For security purposes, Hood needed someone to hold the Murfreesboro-based Union troops in place and Hood gave that job to Forrest. This meant Chalmers faced the newly reinforced Union cavalry alone, clearly outmanned. The result of these decisions simply revealed that Hood had too few troops to deal with the situation.

At Nashville, Wilson completed a remarkable task of increasing his command to

12,000 men, albeit with 3,000 dismounted. This made no difference since Wilson and Thomas decided to use most of the cavalry troops, dismounted. During the two-day battle, both Wilson and Chalmers provided effective service. Chalmers stopped Johnson's division the first day and withdrew to Granny White Pike the next day. Wilson's cavalry actions proved just how wise George Thomas was by insisting on improving Wilson's corps. On both days, it was the cavalry which extended past Hood's western flank. On the second day, Wilson's aggressive efforts effectively cut off Granny White Pike as a route of retreat while moving into the rear of the Confederate infantry. This forced Hood to pull desperately needed infantry away from the front lines, critically weakening them. As a result, Hood's lines were crushed an hour before dark. As the Southern troops streamed to the rear, Rucker's brigade bravely defended Granny White Pike in a clash with Coon's brigade which ended the fighting. Wilson would be criticized for not offering a greater pursuit that evening, but this holds little merit. At the end of the day, George Thomas had won the last great battle of the Civil War.[1]

Hood's Retreat

After the battle, the objective of the Federal army was the further destruction of Hood's army and the Union cavalry greatly aided in accomplishing this task. At no time was Wilson's cavalry in jeopardy during the pursuit of Hood's withdrawing army. The challenge for the Federals was how to push forward boldly without being punished by ambushes. The Confederate cavalry provided commendable service during the withdrawal from Nashville. The most notable exception occurred on December 17 when Wilson's cavalry carried the initiative for most of the day. It was totally understandable in light of the overall condition of the Army of Tennessee and the situation which placed Wilson's mounted troops facing Chalmers' and Buford's first line of defense. Once the Army of Tennessee fell behind the swollen rivers on December 18, it had time to regroup and regain its cohesiveness for the remainder of the withdrawal. The soldiers in the Confederate army were rightly proud of the rearguard service beginning at this point. Historians Pryor and Jordan wrote: "At the same time, nothing in the annals of war exceeds in soldierly excellence the conduct of the Confederate rear-guard from Columbia to Shoal creek." Of all the generals of the Army of Tennessee, only Forrest's and Walthall's reputations had been strengthened during the campaign, primarily through the rearguard actions after the battle. Colonel Luke W. Finlay would write of the rearguard action from Nashville to Sugar Creek many years after the war: "They did their duty well in that difficult period under adverse circumstances. May we not hope that they too may deserve for their fidelity to duty in the discharge of life's demands a commendation equally as grand as that with which Thomas spoke of them when he used these remarkable words: 'The rearguard, however, was undaunted and firm, and did its work bravely to the last!'"[2]

On the Union side of the line, the troopers in the pursuit of Hood's army believed they also successfully performed their duty pushing the once proud Army of Tennessee into Mississippi. Joseph Bardwell, Battery I, 1st Illinois Artillery, attached to Hatch's division, wrote: "It has been the hardest trip that we ever made. It was very cold & it either Snowed or rained all the time & we had no tents with us." Bardwell proudly recorded that Hatch's division captured many prisoners and several cannons in the process.[3]

During the pursuit of Hood, the weather conditions took a heavy toll on the cavalry mounts on both sides of line. In the daily actions in the muddy terrain, the horses' legs became covered with mud and at night, the mud froze, softening the hoofs and stripping the hair from the animals' legs. Wilson recalled, "[I]n all my experience I have never seen so much suffering." Wilson own horse was disabled and it took six weeks to recuperate. During the two-week period of the pursuit of Hood, over 5,000 Federal mounts were disabled. Forrest wrote to Richard Taylor about his casualties on January 2: "Aside from the killed, wounded, and captured of my command, many were sent to the rear with barefooted, lame and unserviceable horses..." Forrest also noted that his mules were in terrible condition and unless they were given time to recuperate they would "prove a total loss." Both cavalries needed to rest and recuperate after the campaign, but the initiative now rested with Wilson's cavalry in the west.[4]

Wilson, Forrest and the End of the Campaign

During the Nashville Campaign, John Bell Hood had the services of the best of the Confederate cavalry. Forrest, Buford, Jackson, and Chalmers were all exemplary cavalry commanders, but Hood's management of his cavalry and the increasingly large number of Federal cavalry, many battle-hardened veterans, proved too much. The cavalrymen on both sides stuck by their colors through this grueling campaign and could not have offered more.

So much has been written about Forrest, it would be difficult to add additional meaningful details. Forrest's command style made him a favorite of his men and he is often referred to as a soldier's general. He had no formal military training but he had a string of victories that spoke volumes. He was also a difficult, rough, and violent man which many believe only enhanced his abilities in battles. He issued short and direct orders "laced with curses" and expected them to be carried out to the letter. "The masculine ideal in the South wore two faces. Some leaders were lauded not for their piety and gentility but for their temper, vices, and violent behavior. The purest example of this hyper-masculine, anti-heroic archetype was Nathan Bedford Forrest," described historian Robert Lamar Glaze. Lord Wolseley described Forrest's most notable action during the retreat of Hood's army. "This most trying of duties he discharged with his usual daring, ability and success. No man could have done more than he did with the small force then at his disposal."[5]

Only a few months later, Forrest would join in the surrender of the Confederate troops and he wisely wrote: "I do not think it proper or necessary at this time to refer to causes which have reduced us to this extremity; nor is it now a matter of material consequence to us how such results were brought about. That we are beaten is a self-evident fact, and any further resistance on our part would justly be regarded as the very height of folly and rashness." Despite the persona Forrest carried, this conciliation reflected a mature and honorable act by one who battled to the end.[6]

In regard to Forrest's opposing chief of cavalry, anyone who reads Wilson's autobiography cannot miss its brash, self-congratulatory, and supercilious tone; however, it is important to note that the authors of autobiographies, many times written 30–40 years after the events, are not the same people who experienced those events. In Wilson's case, he wrote his memoirs 48 years after the war. Wilson's leadership during the Nashville Campaign did not reflect the type of personality represented in his autobiography. He was deferential to Sherman when he assumed command of the cavalry and he even chose to align with Thomas, instead of Grant, his mentor. During the campaign in November and December 1864, Wilson showed his collegiality with his fellow officers and quickly gained the respect of his subordinates.

Perhaps his most important accomplishments during the Nashville Campaign were organizational ability as he dealt with his newly forming brigades and his ability to work well with Thomas, resulting in the large number of cavalry troops on December 15. His visions of a large, offensively-minded cavalry corps in the west was his most important legacy. This could not have been accomplished without the support of George Thomas and, more importantly, Grant. Wilson's ability to form alliances with important superior officers was remarkable. During this campaign, the evolution of the Federal cavalry, firmly supported by Grant and Thomas, was finally completed and this significantly contributed to the Union victories in December 1864.

After this campaign, the stage was set for the final months of the Civil War in the west. The model of the Federal cavalry which had assigned cavalry divisions to the various armies was discarded by Wilson who wanted to be thundering into the south in large bodies of blue-coated cavalry troops. John H. Hammond wrote about the changes in the Federal cavalry in Tennessee on February 1, 1865, in a letter to Washington. Hammond wrote that the "new" cavalry under Wilson in the west was "rapidly assuming shape and character. The numerous detached bodies scattered far & wide, too many to lose, too few to effect anything, are by him being drawn together.... The strength of our cavalry acting, as it always should, on the offensive."[7]

The Nashville Campaign concluded over two years of Federal efforts to destroy the Army of Tennessee. The results of this campaign held significant consequences for the war. Despite Jefferson Davis' reservations about the campaign, he did little to limit Hood's decisions because Davis probably felt the irresistible pressure by the Union forces and concluded the situation was desperate enough to allow Hood to proceed. The South was, indeed, in desperate circumstances by the end of 1864. Thomas defeated Hood at Nashville, Sherman marched further into the South, and Grant corralled Lee in Virginia. Many historians would give Sherman credit for destroying the will of the people of the South to continue the fight, but the impact of Thomas' success at Nashville is often overlooked. Historian Bradley R. Clampitt would write: "What is clear is that the bloody defeats in Middle Tennessee crushed the spirit of the people of the western Confederacy." The high hopes of the Southern troops and the Southern sympathizing civilians were destroyed by events in Murfreesboro, Nashville, and the withdrawal of the Army of Tennessee. While the Nashville Campaign did not end the war, from a cavalry standpoint, it set the stage for the campaigns over the next four months and the ultimate surrender of Forrest in April 1865.[8]

Chapter Notes

Chapter One

1. Stanley Horn, *The Decisive Battle of Nashville* (Knoxville: University of Tennessee Press, 1986), xiii, 166 (Horn's italics).
2. Philip L. Secrist, *Sherman's 1864 Trail of Battle to Atlanta* (Macon: Mercer University Press, 2006), 165–167.
3. Wiley Sword, *Embrace an Angry Wind: The Confederacy's Last Hurrah: Spring Hill, Franklin and Nashville* (New York: Harper Collins Publishers, 1992), 6–13; Stanley Horn, *Decisive Battle of Nashville*, 5; Henry Cist, *The Army of the Cumberland* (New York: Charles Scribner's Sons, 1882), 72–173.
4. Wiley Sword, *The Confederacy's Last Hurrah: Spring Hill, Franklin, and Nashville* (Topeka: University of Kansas Press, 1992), 28–29; John B. Hood, *Advance and Retreat* (New Orleans: G. T. Beauregard, 1880), 140, 183, 210; Thomas L. Connelly, *Autumn of Glory: The Army of Tennessee, 1862–1865* (Baton Rouge: Louisiana State University Press, 1971), 322–323, 411–416; Richard McMurry, *John Bell Hood and the War for Southern Independence* (Lexington: University Press of Kentucky, 1982), 152; R. W. Banks, *The Battle of Franklin: November 30, 1864* (New York and Washington: The Neale Publishing Company, 1908), 18–19.
5. Abraham Lincoln, *Official Records*, Series 1, Volume 38, Part 1, 87; Ulysses Grant, *Official Records*, Series 1, Volume 38, Part 1, 87.
6. Albert Castel, *Decision in the West: The Atlanta Campaign of 1864* (Lawrence: University Press of Kansas, 1992), 542; William Sherman, *Personal Memoirs of Gen. W. T. Sherman*, Vol. 2 (New York: Charles L. Webster & Co., 1890), 109–110.
7. William Sherman, *Official Records*, Series 1, Volume 38, Part 1, 115–117; J. B. Hood, *Official Records*, Series 1, Volume 38, Part 3, 642–643.
8. Robert B. Leach, "The Role of Union Cavalry During the Atlanta Campaign," Master's Thesis, U.S. Army Command and General Staff College, Fort Leavenworth, Kansas, 1994, pp. 15, 37; George Thomas, *Official Records*, Series 1, Volume 38, Part 5, 311; Ben Fuller Fordney, *George Stoneman: A Biography of the Union General* (Jefferson, NC: McFarland, 2008), 92–93; Albert E. Castel, *Articles of War: Winners, Losers, and Some who Were Both in the Civil War* (Mechanicsburg, PA: Stackpole Books, 2001), 123–124; William Sherman, *Official Records*, Series 1, Volume 39, Part 2, 80.
9. Robert B. Leach, "The Role of Union Cavalry During the Atlanta Campaign," 95; Edward G. Longacre, *A Soldier to the Last: Maj. Gen. Joseph Wheeler in Blue and Gray* (Washington: Potomac Books Inc., 2007), 55–60; J. P. Dyer, "The Civil War Career of General Joseph Wheeler," *The Georgia Historical Quarterly*, Vol. 19, No. 1 (Mar. 1935), pp. 17–46; William Brooksher and David Snider, "The War Child Rides: Joe Wheeler at Stones River," *Civil War Times Illustrated*, Vol. 14 (1976): 4–10; James Arthur Schaefer, "The Tactical and Strategic Evolution of Cavalry During the American Civil War," Ph.D. Dissertation, University of Toledo, 1982, 173; George Walsh, *Those Damn Horse Soldiers* (New York: A Tom Doherty Associates Book, 2006), 235; David A. Powell, *Failure in the Saddle* (New York and California: Savas Beatie, 2010), 213–219.
10. J. B. Hood, *Official Records*, Series 1, Volume 38, Part 3, 957; Joseph Wheeler, *Official Records*, Series 1, Volume 38, Part 3, 957; Robert Black, *Cavalry Raids of the Civil War* (Mechanicsburg, Pennsylvania: Stackpole Books, 2004), 65–66; Edward G. Longacre, *A Soldier to the Last*, 172–175; W. T. Sherman *Official Records*, Series 1, Volume 38, Part 1, 83; Joseph Wheeler, *Official Records*, Series 1, Volume 38, Part 5, 1031 [Message in Hood's dispatch].
11. Edward G. Longacre, *A Soldier to the Last*, 174–5; Robert Black, *Cavalry Raids of the Civil War*, 68; John Franklin Culver, Letter to wife September 13, 1864, Joseph Franklin Culver papers, MSC0373, Special Collections Dept., University of Iowa Libraries, Iowa City; N. B. Forrest, *Official Records*, Series 1, Volume 39, Part 2, 859; Joseph Wheeler, *Official Records*, Series 1, Volume 38, Part 3, 960–961.
12. W. C. Dodson, *Campaigns of Wheeler and His Cavalry, 1862–1865* (Atlanta: Hudgins Publishing, 1899), 287–288; John Witherspoon Dubose, *General Joseph Wheeler and the Army of Tennessee* (New York: The Neale Publishing Company, 1912), 405–408; W. L. Elliot, *Official Records*, Series 1, Volume 39, Part 1, 724.

13. David Powell, *Failure in the Saddle*, 212.
14. J. P. Strange, *Official Records*, Series 1, Volume 32, Part 2, 614; N. B. Forrest, *Official Records*, Series 1, Volume 32, Part 2, 617; John A. Wyeth, *Life of Lieutenant-General Nathan Bedford Forrest* (New York and London: Harper & Brothers, Publishers, 1900), 403.
15. Westley F. Busbee, Jr., *Mississippi: A History* (Malden, MA: Wiley Blackwell, 2015), 144–145.
16. John A. Wyeth, *Life of Lieutenant-General Nathan Bedford Forrest*, 416; Edward F. Winslow papers, September 1862-August 1864, Edward F. Winslow papers, MSC0424, Special Collections, University of Iowa.
17. Charles Treadway, "The Letters of Charles Wesley Treadway," In *Foot Prints: Past and Present*, Vol. 9, Richland County Genealogical Society, Olney, IL, 140–141; A. J. Smith, *Official Records*, Series 1, Volume 39, Part 1, 250–254; Michael Ballard, *The Battle of Tupelo, Mississippi: July 14–15* (Tupelo: Northeast Mississippi Historical and Genealogical Society, 2009), 10–28.
18. Stephen Enzweiler, "Union Memoir Details Day Oxford Burned," August 22, 2014, *Oxford Citizen*; John A. Wyeth, *Life of Lieutenant-General Nathan Bedford Forrest*, 525, 529, 539–540; Jack D. L. Holmes, "Forrest's 1864 Raid on Memphis," *Tennessee Historical Quarterly*, Vol. 18, No. 4 (December, 1959), pp. 298, 300, 317; W. T. Sherman, *Official Records*, Series 1, Volume 39, Part 2, 296.
19. Jack Hurst, *Nathan Bedford Forrest: A Biography* (New York: Vintage Press, 1993), 211–215.
20. Ulysses Grant, *Official Records*, Series 1, Volume 31, Part 3, 123; Stephen Z. Starr, *The Union Cavalry in the Civil War: The War in the West*, Volume III (Baton Rouge: Louisiana State University, 2007), 368–369.
21. W. T. Sherman, *Official Records*, Series 1, Volume 32, Part 1, 171–172; Lloyd Lewis, *Sherman: Fighting Prophet* (Lincoln: University of Nebraska Press, 1993), 336; A. C. McClurg, *Official Records*, Series 1, Volume 38, Part 5, 628; Richard W. Johnson, *A Soldier's Reminiscences in Peace and War* (Philadelphia: Press of J. B. Lippincott Company, 1886), 279, 283; Buck T. Foster, *Sherman's Mississippi Campaign* (Tuscaloosa: University of Alabama Press, 2006), 19–21.
22. Dennis Peterson, *Confederate Cabinet Departments and Secretaries* (Jefferson, NC: McFarland, 2016), 127.
23. S. D. Lee, *Official Records*, Series 1, Volume 32, Part 3, 864; S. D. Lee, *Official Records*, Series 1, Volume 39, Part 2, 675.

Chapter Two

1. Gideon Welles, *The Civil War Diary of Gideon Welles, Lincoln's Secretary of the Navy: The Original Manuscript Edition*, William E. Gienapp and Erica L. Gienapp, editors (Champaign: University of Illinois Press, 2014), 459–531.
2. John B. Hood, *Official Records*, Series 1, Volume 38, Part 3, 636; Joseph Johnston *Official Records*, Series 1, Volume 38, Part 3, 637; Samuel W. Melton, *Official Records*, Series 1, Volume 38, Part 5, 965; John B. Hood, *Official Records*, Series 1, Volume 38, Part 5, 1021, 1023; L. S. Ross, *Personal Civil War Letters of General Lawrence Sullivan Ross with other letters*, transcribed and compiled by Perry Wayne Shelton, edited by Shelly Morrison (Austin: Shelly and Richard Morrison, 1994), 68; Thomas L. Livermore, *Numbers and Losses in the Civil War in America, 1861–1865* (Boston and New York: Houghton, Mifflin and Co., 1901), 47; Eric Jacobson and Richard Rupp, *For Cause, For Country: A Study of the Affair at Spring Hill and the Battle of Franklin* (Franklin, Tennessee: O'More Publishing, 2007), 19.
3. William T. Sherman, *Official Records*, Series 1, Volume 38, Part 5, 794; James M. Calhoun, *Official Records*, Series 1, Volume 38, Part 5, 838; Brooks D. Simpson and Jean V. Berlin, *Sherman's Civil War: Selected Correspondence of William T. Sherman, 1860–1865* (Chapel Hill: University of North Carolina Press, 1999), 719; Henry Halleck, *Official Records*, Series 1, Volume 38, Part 5, 857.
4. William Sherman, *Personal Memoirs of Gen. W. T. Sherman*, Vol. 2 (New York: Charles L. Webster & Co., 1890), 134; Christopher N. Schloemer, "General John Bell Hood: His Leadership During the 1864 Tennessee Campaign," *Saber and Scroll*, Vol. 5: Issue 2 (2016), p. 24.
5. John B. Hood, *Official Records*, Series 1, Volume 38, Part 1, 801; John B. Hood, "The Invasion of Tennessee, In *Battles and Leaders of the Civil War*, Volume IV (New York: The Century Co., 1888), 427.
6. John B. Hood, *Advance and Retreat* (New Orleans: G. T. Beauregard, 1880), 254; John B. Hood, *Official Records*, Series 1, Volume 39, Part 1, 801.
7. Samuel Watkins, *Co. Aytch* (Chattanooga, TN: Times Printing Company, 1900), 194; John B. Hood, *Advance and Retreat*, 249, 253; Jefferson Davis, *Official Records*, Series 1, Volume 39, Part 2, 879; Sam Davis Elliott, *Soldier of Tennessee: General Alexander P. Stewart and the Civil War in the West* (Baton Rouge: Louisiana State University Press, 1999), 218; Jefferson Davis, *The Papers of Jefferson Davis*, Volume 11, Lynda Lasswell Crist, Barbara J. Rozek, Kenneth H. Williams, editors (Baton Rouge: Louisiana State University Press, 2003), 61–63; The Papers of Jefferson Davis, Rice University, Transcribed from the *Macon Telegraph*, September 24, 1864.
8. William Sherman, *Personal Memoirs*, 114–115; William T. Sherman, *Official Records*, Series 1, Volume 39, Part 2, 411–412.
9. William T. Sherman, *Official Records*, Series 1, Volume 39, Part 2, 464, 480; William Sherman, *Personal Memoirs*, 141; Ulysses Grant, *Official Records*, Series 1, Volume 39, Part 2, 478.
10. John B. Hood, *Official Records*, Series 1,

Volume 39, Part 2, 860; Braxton Bragg, *Official Records*, Series 1, Volume 39, Part 2, 867; Richard Taylor, *Official Records*, Series 1, Volume 39, Part 2, 873; James Chalmers, *Official Records*, Series 1, Volume 39, Part 2, 876.

11. William Sherman, *Personal Memoirs*, 144; Mark A. Smith, "Sherman's Unexpected Companions: Marching Through Georgia With Jomini and Clausewitz," *The Georgia Historical Quarterly*, Vol. 81, No. 1 (Spring 1997), pp. 10–14.

12. William Sherman, *Official Records*, Series 1, Volume 39, Part 2, 442; Ulysses Grant, *Official Records*, Series 1, Volume 39, Part 2, 438; Richard Johnson, *Official Records*, Series 1, Volume 39, Part 2, 438–439.

13. Jefferson Davis, *Official Records*, Series 1, Volume 39, Part 2, 818; Richard Taylor, *Official Records*, Series 1, Volume 39, Part 2, 818–819.

14. N. B. Forrest, *Official Records*, Series 1, Volume 39, Part 2, 886.

15. Richard Taylor, *Official Records*, Series 1, Volume 39, Part 2, 888.

16. N. B. Forrest, *Official Records*, Series 1, Volume 39, Part 1, 543; Edward Hatch, *Official Records*, Series 1, Volume 39, Part 2, 438; J. P. Strange, *Official Records*, Series 1, Volume 39, Part 2, 835; Nathaniel Cheairs Hughes, Jr., *Brigadier General Tyree H. Bell, CSA* (Knoxville: University of Tennessee Press, 2004), 170.

17. George Spalding, *Official Records*, Series 1, Volume 39, Part 1, 536; Michael Bradley, *They Rode with Forrest* (Gretna, LA: Pelican Publishing Company, 2012), 99; John Starkweather, *Official Records*, Series 1, Volume 39, Part 1, 530–531; John Starkweather, *Official Records*, Series 1, Volume 39, Part 2, 435; Robert Granger, *Official Records*, Series 1, Volume 39, Part 2, 435; William T. Sherman, *Official Records*, Series 1, Volume 38, Part 5, 792.

18. George Thomas, *Official Records*, Series 1, Volume 39, Part 2, 544–551; Pocket Journal of Joseph Vincent Hinchman, Co. B, 9th Indiana Cavalry, Private, Private collection of J. Griffing, Batavia, Illinois.

19. George Thomas, *Official Records*, Series 1, Volume 39, Part 2, 560–562.

20. W. B. Emmons, October 1, 1864, diary entry, W. B. Emmons diary, 1864–185, MSC0010, Special Collections Dept. at the University of Iowa; Letter to wife, October 4, 1864, John J. Pribble Letter, S1934, Rare Books and Manuscripts, Indiana State Library, Indianapolis; Charles A. Harper, Diary—October 6, 1864, F84 N & P, Indiana Historical Society; Abraham Buford, Letter from Buford to Col., September 30, 1864, Folder 2, Edward F. Reid Papers, 1863–1888 (Bulk 1864–1865), Indiana Historical Society; R. S. Granger, *Official Records*, Series 1, Volume 39, Part 1, 515–517.

21. Samuel Agnew, September 29, 1864 diary entry (Samuel Agnew Diary, 1851–1902), Collection Number: 00923, Southern Historical Collection, The Wilson Library, University of North Carolina at Chapel Hill; C. C. Washburn *Official Records*, Series 1, Volume 39, Part 3, 42; George Thomas, *Official Records*, Series 1, Volume 39, Part 3, 81–82.

22. N. B. Forrest, Official Records, Series 1, Volume 39, Part 1, 548.

23. N. B. Forrest, *Official Records*, Series 1, Volume 39, Part 1, 548; "Battle of Eastport," *Confederate Veteran*, Vol. 5, No. 1 (January 1897), p. 13.

24. George B. Hoge, *Official Records*, Series 1, Volume 39, Part 1, 541; David Dixon Porter, *The Naval History of the Civil War* (New York: The Sherman Publishing Co, 1886), 564–564; Myron J. Smith Jr., *Tinclads in the Civil War: Union Light-Draught Gunboat Operations on Western Waters, 1862–1865* (Jefferson, NC: McFarland, 2010), 269–270.

25. N. B. Forrest, *Official Records*, Series 1, Volume 39, Part 3, 807, 812; N. B. Forrest, *Official Records*, Series 1, Volume 39, Part 1, 548–549.

26. D. C. McCallum, *Official Records*, Series 1, Volume 39, Part 1, 507; George Kryder, Letter to wife—October 17, 1864; MS 163—George Kryder Papers, Bowling Green University.

27. W. T. Sherman, *Official Records*, Series 1, Volume 39, Part 3, 191; George Thomas, *Official Records*, Series 1, Volume 39, Part 3, 199; C. C. Washburn, *Official Records*, Series 1, Volume 39, Part 3, 384; Lovell Rousseau, *Official Records*, Series 1, Volume 39, Part 1, 506–507; Lovell Rousseau, *Official Records*, Series 1, Volume 39, Part 3, 141–142.

28. George P. Buell, *Official Records*, Series 1, Volume 39, Part 3, 15; William T. Sherman, *Official Records*, Series 1, Volume 39, Part 3, 203.

29. John B. Hood, *Official Records*, Series 1, Volume 39, Part 1, 801–802; Jefferson Davis, *Official Records*, Series 1, Volume 39, Part 3, 782; C. K. Stribling, "Letter, October 16, 1864," In *Batchelor-Turner letters, 1861–1864*, written by two of Terry's Texas Rangers, Annotated by H. J. H. Rugeley (Austin, TX: The Steck Company, 1961), 86–87; Lawrence Sul Ross, Letter, October 23, 1864, Ross Family Papers, Manuscript #0014, The Texas Collection, Baylor University, Waco, TX; Lawrence Sullivan Ross, "Personal Civil War letters of General Lawrence Sullivan Ross: with other letters," transcribed and compiled by Perry Wayne Shelton, Master's Thesis, Baylor University, 1938, pp. 68–69; Richard McMurry, *John Bell Hood and the War for Southern Independence* (Lexington: The University Press of Kentucky, 1982), 158; Daniel Prickitt, Diary—October 13, 1864, Daniel Prickitt, 3rd Ohio Cavalry, Diary, ed. Edwin Stoltz, Bowling Green State University; W. B. Corbitt, Diary—October 31, 1864, Civil War-era documents, 1860–1865, Box 2, Folder 37, Emory University.

30. William Sherman, *Personal Memoirs*, 136; W. T. Sherman, *Official Records*, Series 1, Volume 38, Part 3, 115–117.

31. William Sherman, *Official Records*, Series 1, Volume 39, Part 1, 581; Stewart Bennett, "The Storm Broke in All Its Fury: The Struggle for Alla-

toona Pass," In *The Tennessee Campaign of 1864*, edit. Steven Woodworth and Charles Grear (Carbondale: Southern Illinois University Press, 2016), 45; Samuel French, *Official Records*, Series 1, Volume 39, Part 1, 813.

32. N. B. Forrest, *Official Records*, Series 1, Volume 39, Part 3, 812, 815–817.

33. John B. Hood, *Official Records*, Series 1, Volume 39, Part 1, 802–803; N. B. Forrest, *Official Records*, Series 1, Volume 39, Part 3, 837–838; Richard McMurry, *John Bell Hood*, 162; James McDonough, *Nashville: The Western Confederacy's Final Gamble* (Knoxville: University of Tennessee Press, 2004), 29; Alfred Roman, *The Military Operations of General Beauregard* (New York: Harper & Brothers, Franklin Square, 1884), 279; T. Harry Williams, *P. G. T. Beauregard: Napoleon in Gray* (Baton Rouge: Louisiana State University Press, 1991), 241.

34. William T. Sherman, *Official Records*, Series 1, Volume 39, Part 1, 581–582; Willard Warner, *Official Records*, Series 1, Volume 39, Part 3, 324; John Crittenden, Diary—October 22, 1864, John Crittenden Papers, Auburn University Libraries, Special Collections and Archives.

35. George Thomas, *Official Records*, Series 1, Volume 39, Part 3, 318–319; John Croxton, *Official Records*, Series 1, Volume 39, Part 3, 318; L. M. Dayton, *Official Records*, Series 1, Volume 39, Part 3, 325; W. L. Elliott, *Official Records*, Series 1, Volume 39, Part 3, 327.

36. J. P. Strange, *Official Records*, Series 1, Volume 39, Part 3, 819; George H. Thomas, *Official Records*, Series 1, Volume 39, Part 3, 368; Michael Thomas Smith, *The 1864 Franklin-Nashville Campaign: The Finishing Stroke* (Santa Barbara: ABC-CLIO, 2014), 80.

37. George H. Thomas, *Official Records*, Series 1, Volume 39, Part 3, 390–391, 431.

38. William T. Sherman, *Official Records*, Series 1, Volume 39, Part 1, 582–583; William T. Sherman, *Official Records*, Series 1, Volume 39, Part 3, 333; L. M. Dayton, *Official Records*, Series 1, Volume 39, Part 3, 511; G. T. Beauregard, *Official Records*, Series 1, Volume 39, Part 3, 841; Robert Winn, Letter to Sister, October 21, 1864, Winn—Cook Family Papers, 1861–1875, Mss. A W776, Filson Historical Society, Louisville, Kentucky; George Healy, Letter to Mother et. al., October 18, 1864, George Healey Papers, State Historical Society of Iowa, Des Moines, 1F 006: F22 N14/3/4B/HU.

39. Richard Taylor, *Official Records*, Series 1, Volume 39, Part 3, 844; W. F. Bullock, Jr., *Official Records*, Series 1, Volume 39, Part 3, 847; George Thomas, *Official Records*, Series 1, Volume 39, Part 3, 449; W. T. Sherman, *Official Records*, Series 1, Volume 39, Part 3, 448–449; R. S. Granger, *Official Records*, Series 1, Volume 39, Part 3, 488; P. G. T. Beauregard, *Official Records*, Series 1, Volume 39, Part 3, 843; J. P. Strange, *Official Records*, Series 1, Volume 39, Part 3, 843; John Andes and Will McTeer, *Loyal Mountain Troopers: The Second and Third Tennessee Volunteer Cavalry in the Civil War* (Maryville, TN: Blount County Genealogical and Historical Society, 1992), 163–173; James C. Bates, *A Texas Cavalry Officer's Civil: The Diary and Letters of James C. Bates*, Richard Lowe, ed. (Baton Rouge: Louisiana State University Press, 1999), 326.

40. J. H. Wilson, *Official Records*, Series 1, Volume 39, Part 3, 449–460; George Thomas, *Official Records*, Series 1, Volume 39, Part 3, 466; James O. Walton letter to wife, October 31, 1864, S1355, Rare Books and Manuscripts, Indiana State Library, Indianapolis; Charles A. Harper, Diary—October 28, 1864, F84 N & P, Indiana Historical Society; George Clark, Letter to My dear Mother, October 23, 1864, Collection Number—GLC0616713, Gilder Lehrman Institute of American History.

41. W. T. Sherman, *Official Records*, Series 1, Volume 39, Part 3, 7; J. C. Van Duzer, *Official Records*, Series 1, Volume 39, Part 3, 467.

42. John Croxton, *Official Records*, Series 1, Volume 39, Part 3, 490, 507, 524; A. P. Mason, *Official Records*, Series 1, Volume 39, Part 3, 866; George Thomas, *Official Records*, Series 1, Volume 39, Part 3, 497, 508; W. H. Sinclair, *Official Records*, Series 1, Volume 39, Part 3, 502; P. G. T. Beauregard, *Official Records*, Series 1, Volume 39, Part 3, 870; John B. Hood, *Official Records*, Series 1, Volume 39, Part 3, 870; William E. Crane, "William E. Crane's Daily Journal of Life in the Field during the War of the Rebellion," October 18–26, 1864 entry, Mss. 980, Cincinnati Historical Society, Cincinnati Museum Center.

43. William T. Sherman, *Official Records*, Series 1, Volume 39, Part 3, 365; William T. Sherman, *Official Records*, Series 1, Volume 39, Part 1, 583–584; James A. Connolly, *Three Years in the Army of the Cumberland: The Letters and Diary of Major James A. Connolly*, Paul M. Angle, ed. (Bloomington, IN: Indiana University Press, 1990), 288.

44. John B. Hood, *Official Records*, Series 1, Volume 39, Part 1, 803; P. G. T. Beauregard, *Official Records*, Series 1, Volume 39, Part 3, 797; Eric Jacobson and Richard Rupp, *For Cause, For Country: A Study of the Affair at Spring Hill and the Battle of Franklin* (Franklin, TN: O' More Publishing, 2007), 45; Alfred Roman, *The Military Operations of General Beauregard*, 292–293.

45. Miranda Becker, *A Southerner for the Union: Major General George Henry Thomas—A Brief Biographical Sketch and Analysis of the Causes and Effects of His Decision for the North*, Liberty University (2014), 5; Ernest B. Furguson, "Catching up with 'Old Slow Trot,'" *Smithsonian*, March 2007, Vol. 37, Issue 12, pp. 50–57; Christopher J. Einolf, *George Thomas: Virginian for the Union* (Norman: University of Oklahoma Press, 2007), 62–63.

46. Benson Bobrick, *Master of War: The Life of George H. Thomas* (New York: Simon and Schuster, 2009), 265; Don Piatt, *General George H. Thomas: A Critical Biography* (Cincinnati: Robert Clarke and Co, 1893), 502; George Thomas, *Official Records*, Series 1, Volume 38, Part 5, 311.

47. Thomas Budd Van Horne, *The Life of Major-General George H. Thomas* (New York: Charles Scribner's Sons, 1882), 256–257; William T. Sherman, *Official Records*, Series 1, Volume 39, Part 3, 335; George Thomas, *Official Records*, Series 1, Volume 39, Part 3, 352; Ephraim Otis, "The Nashville Campaign," In *Military Essays and Recollections*, Vol. III (Chicago: The Dial Press, 1899), 269.

48. George H. Thomas, *Official Records*, Series 1, Volume 39, Part 3, 535.

Chapter Three

1. J. H. Wilson, *Official Records*, Series 1, Volume 39, Part 3, 87; Ulysses Grant, *Official Records*, Series 1, Volume 39, Part 3, 64.

2. William T. Sherman, *Official Records*, Series 1, Volume 39, Part 3, 127; Washington L. Elliott, *Official Records*, Series 1, Volume 39, Part 3, 127.

3. James H. Wilson, *Official Records*, Series 1, Volume 39, Part 3, 574.

4. James H. Wilson, *Official Records*, Series 1, Volume 39, Part 3, 443; John Schofield, *Official Records*, Series 1, Volume 39, Part 3, 573; Stephen Starr, *The Union Cavalry in the Civil War*, Volume III (Baton Rouge and London: Louisiana State University Press, 1985), 535.

5. James H. Wilson, *Official Records*, Series 1, Volume 39, Part 3, 444.

6. James H. Wilson, *Official Records*, Series 1, Volume 39, Part 3, 444; Richard Johnson, *Official Records*, Series 1, Volume 39, Part 3, 301, 440–442; T. G. Baylor, *Official Records*, Series 1, Volume 39, Part 3, 414; William T. Sherman, *Memoirs of General William T. Sherman, Volume II* (New York: D. Appleton & Co., 1904), 159–160.

7. Benjamin Grierson, *Official Records*, Series 1, Volume 39, Part 3, 528–529; James Wilson, *Official Records*, Series 1, Volume 39, Part 3, 444.

8. James Wilson, Official Records, Series 1, Volume 39, Part 3, 444.

9. Henry Stone, "Repelling Hood's Invasion of Tennessee," In *Battles and Leaders* Vol. 4 (New York: The Century Company, 1884), 456; Edwin Stuart, "The Federal Cavalry with the Armies in the West: 1861–186," *Journal of the United States Cavalry Association*, Vol XVII (July 1906), No. 62, pp. 251–252.

10. James Wilson, *Official Records*, Series 1, Volume 39, Part 3, 425.

11. James H. Wilson, *Official Records*, Series 1, Volume 39, Part 3, 574.

12. James H. Wilson, *Under the Old Flag*, Volume II (New York and London: D. Appleton And Company, 1912), 168–169; Aldice G. Warren, editor, *Catalogue of the Delta Kappa Epsilon Fraternity* (New York: Published by the Delta Kappa Epsilon Council, 1910), 103; Rex Miller, "John Thomas Croxton: Scholar, Lawyer, Soldier, Military Governor, Newspaperman, Diplomat, and Mason," *The Register of the Kentucky Historical Society*, Volume 74, No. 4 (October 1976), 281–299.

13. Rex Miller, "John Thomas Croxton," 283–287.

14. Rex Miller, "John Thomas Croxton," 288; Thomas Speed, *Union Regiments of Kentucky Volume I* (Louisville: The Courier Journal Job Printing, Co., 1897), 72, 309–311.

15. William Perrin, *The History of Bourbon, Scott, Harrison and Nicholas Counties, Kentucky* (Chicago: O. L. Baskin & Co., 1882), 457–458; John Croxton, *Official Records*, Series 1, Volume 38, Part 2, 770; Edward McCook, *Official Records*, Series 1, Volume 38, Part 2, 762–764, 768; W. R. Carter, *History of the First Regiment of Tennessee Volunteer Cavalry* (Knoxville: Gaut-Ogden Co., Printers and Binders, 1902), 183; August 2, 1862 letter, Joshua Breyfogle family papers, ms 3124, Hargrett Rare Book and Manuscript Library, The University of Georgia Libraries, Athens.

16. Shawn J. Coakley, *Norwich University: Citizen Soldiers in the Civil War*, Master's Thesis, United States Marine Corps Command and Staff College, Quantico, Virginia, 2002, p. 28; Richard Surby, *Grierson Raids, Hatch's Sixty-Four Days March* (Chicago: Rounds and James, Steam Book and Job Printers, 1866), 191–194; W. T. Sherman, *Official Records*, Series 1, Volume 30, Part 4, 405; Charles L. Kenner, *Buffalo Soldiers and Officers of the Ninth Cavalry, 1867–1898* (Norman: University of Oklahoma Press, 1999), 30–34.

17. Robert Stevens, *The Bracken Rangers: Company K, 28th Regiment, 1st Indiana Cavalry* (Miami and Los Angeles: Three Stars Press, 2011), 103; Charles Cochran Oakey, *Greater Terre Haute and Vigo County: Closing the First Century's History of City and County* (Chicago and New York: The Lewis Publishing Co., 1908), 303; George Thomas, *Official Records*, Series 1, Volume 39, Part 2, 327.

18. Benjamin F. Gue, *History of Iowa: From the Earliest Times to the Beginning of the Twentieth Century*, Vol. IV (New York: Century History Co., 1903), 59–60; Lyman Pierce, *History of the Second Iowa Cavalry* (Burlington, Iowa: Hawkeye Steam Book and Job Printing Establishment, 1865), 10.

19. George Cullum, *Biographical Register of the Officers and Graduates of the U.S. Military Academy, 1841–1867*, Vol. II (New York: D. Van Nostrand, 1868) 391–393; Richard Johnson, *A Soldier's Reminiscences in Peace and War* (Philadelphia: Press of J. B. Lippincott Company, 1886), 10–19, 38–40, 57, 212–214, 275–279; Ezra J. Warner, *Generals in Blue: Lives of Union Commanders* (Baton Rouge: Louisiana State University Press, 1992), 253–254.

20. George Thomas, *Official Records*, Series 1, Volume 39, Part 3, 302; John Schofield, *Official Records*, Series 1, Volume 39, Part 3, 302, 322; R. W. Johnson, *Official Records*, Series 1, Volume 16, Part 1, 871–872.

21. Merritt Starr, "General Horace Capron, 1804–1885," *Journal of the Illinois State Historical*

Society, Vol. XVIII, No. 2, pp. 262–276; Horace Capron, *Official Records*, Series 1, Volume 38, Part 2, 928–929; H. Niles, editor, "Baltimore and Washington Rail Road," November 29, 1834 and December 20, 1834, In *Niles Weekly Register* (Baltimore: Published by editor, bound editions covering September, 1834 to March, 1835), 197–198, 272.

22. Jacob Piatt Dunn, *Memorial and Genealogical Record of Representative Citizens of Indiana* (Indianapolis: B. F. Brown Publisher, 1912), 657–661; Robert Black, *Cavalry Raids of the Civil War* (Mechanicsburg, PA: Stackpole Books, 2004), 183.

23. Mahlon Manson, *Official Records*, Series 1, Volume 16, Part 1, 915–916; George Thomas, *Official Records*, Series 1, Volume 45, Part 1, 90; William H. Powell, ed., *Officers of the Volunteer Army and Navy who served in the Civil War* (Philadelphia: L.R. Hamersly & Co., 1893), 16; Francis B. Heitman, *Historical Register and Dictionary of the United States Army*, Vol. 1 (Washington: Govt. Printing Office, 1903), 217; Wm. C. Rawolle, *Official Records*, Series 1, Volume 32, Part 3, 303.

24. Ezra J. Warner, *Generals in Blue*, 272–273.

25. Samuel P. Bates, *History of the Pennsylvania Volunteers, 1861–65*, Volume I (Harrisburg: B. Singerly, State Printer 1868–1871), 1110–1117; "Brig. General Joseph F. Knipe at Camp Curtin," *The Bugle, Quarterly Journal of the Camp Curtin Historical Society*, Summer 2007 and Civil War Round Table, Inc., Volume 17, Number 2, pp. 1–2; Joseph Hooker, *Official Records*, Series 1, Volume 25, Part 1, 184.

26. James L. Selfridge, *Official Records*, Series 1, Volume 39, Part 1, 654; L. M. Dayton, *Official Records*, Series 1, Volume 39, Part 2, 400; James H. Wilson, *Official Records*, Series 1, Volume 39, Part 3, 442; E. B. Beaumont, *Official Records*, Series 1, Volume 45, Part 1, 909.

27. *Commemorative Biographical Record of the Upper Lake Region* (Chicago: J. H. Beers & Co. 1905), 5; John Henry Hammond Papers, Wisconsin Historical Society, Superior Mss R, Box 1, Folder 1; John Y. Simon, ed., *The Papers of Ulysses S. Grant: June 1–August 15, 1864*, Volume 11 (Carbondale and Edwardsville: Southern Illinois University Press, 1984), 266–267.

28. William T. Sherman, *Official Records*, Series 1, Volume 10, Part 1, 254, 744; R. R. Townes, *Official Records*, Series 1, Volume 32, Part 2, 7; T. S. Bowers, *Official Records*, Series 1, Volume 32, Part 3, 15; John Y. Simon, ed., *The Papers of Ulysses S. Grant: June 1–August 15, 1864*, Volume 11, 266–267.

29. John Rison Jones, Jr, "Do We Purposely Forget? The Unknown Generals in Our Midst," *Huntsville Historical Review*, Volume 18 (Fall-Summer 1991), No. 2, pp. 3–4; John H. Eicher and David Eicher, *Civil War High Commands* (Stanford: Stanford University Press, 2001), 321.

30. James H. Wilson, *Under the Old Flag*, Vol. 1, 1–6; James Pickett Jones, *Yankee Blitzkrieg: Wilson's Raid through Alabama and Georgia* (Lexington: University Press of Kentucky, 1976), 3–4.

31. James H. Wilson, *Under the Old Flag*, Vol. 1, 7; Doug Gelbert, *Civil War Sites, Memorials, Museums and Library Collections: A State-by-State Guidebook* (Jefferson, NC: McFarland, 2005), 4.

32. James H. Wilson, *Under the Old Flag*, Vol. 1, 23, 31, 41–42, 70–95, 99–100, 118–119, 128–129, 148, 265–267.

33. James H. Wilson, *Under the Old Flag*, Vol. 1, 329–333; George Thomas, *Official Records*, Series 1, Volume 32, Part 2, 154; Charles Dana, *Official Records*, Series 1, Volume 32, Part 2, 115–116.

34. James H. Wilson, *Under the Old Flag*, Vol. 1, v–vi, 385–401, 517, 537–8; E. D. Townsend, *Official Records*, Series 1, Volume 33, 816; James P. Jones, "Wilson's Raiders Reach Georgia: The Fall of Columbus, 1865," *The Georgia Historical Quarterly*, Vol. 59, No. 3 (Fall, 1975), pp. 313–314; James P. Jones, "Your Left Arm: James H. Wilson's Letters to Adam Badeau," *Civil War History*, Volume 12, Number 3 (September 1966), pp. 230–231.

35. James H. Wilson, *Under the Old Flag*, Vol. 2, 7–8.

36. James H. Wilson, *Under the Old Flag*, Vol. 2, 14, 20, 21.

37. Benjamin Grierson, *A Just and Righteous Cause*, Bruce Dinces and Shirley Leckie, eds. (Carbondale: Southern Illinois University Press, 2008), 287–293.

38. Edward Longacre, *Lincoln's Cavalrymen: A History of the Mounted Forces of The Army of the Potomac* (Mechanicsburg, PA: Stackpole Books, 2000), 252.

Chapter Four

1. T. M. Jack, *Official Records*, Series 1, Volume 32, Part 2, 550; Leonidas Polk, *Official Records*, Series 1, Volume 32, Part 3, 825; Dabney Maury, *Official Records*, Series 1, Volume 39, Part 2, 773–774.

2. Clement A. Evans, editor, *Confederate Military History*, Volume I (Atlanta: Confederate Publishing Co., 1899), 699–702; Michael Bradley, *Nathan Bedford Forrest's Escort and Staff* (Gretna, LA: Pelican Publishing Co., 2006), 22–26.

3. John R. Sanders, "Operational Leadership of Nathan Bedford Forrest," Monograph, Naval War College, Newport, RI, 1994, p. 23; James Chalmers, "Forrest and His Campaigns," *Southern Historical Society Papers*, Volume 7, Number 10 (October 1879), p. 454; Jac Weller, "Nathan Bedford Forrest: An Analysis of Untutored Military Genius," *Tennessee Historical Quarterly*, 18 (1959), pp. 214–223.

4. Braxton Bragg, *Official Records*, Series 1, Volume 6, 779; Richard Anderson, *Official Records*, Series 1, Volume 6, 461; J. P. Benjamin, *Official Records*, Series 1, Volume 6, 824; Willie D. Halsell, "James R. Chalmers and 'Mahoneism' in Mississippi," *Journal of Southern History*, Volume 10 (February 1944), 37–58.

5. James Chalmers, *Official Records*, Series 1, Volume 10, Part 1, 553; Braxton Bragg, *Official Records*, Series 1, Volume 10, Part 1, 468; Thomas Jordan, *Official Records*, Series 1, Volume 17, Part 2, 650; Braxton Bragg, *Official Records*, Series 1, Volume 20, Part 1, 658, 670, 674; J. R. Chalmers, *Official Records*, Series 1, Volume 7, 883.

6. James R. Chalmers, *Official Records*, Series 1, Volume 24, Part 1, 471; E. R. Bennett, *Official Records*, Series 1, Volume 24, Part 3, 663; Michael L. Godfrey, *Reflections of a Confederate Soldier: Duty—Honor—Courage* (Rockport, TX: All American Historical Publishing Co., 2006), 62; Ulysses Grant, *Official Records*, Series 1, Volume 24, Part 1, 25–26.

7. S. D. Lee, *Official Records*, Series 1, Volume 31, Part 3, 732; James Chalmers, *Official Records*, Series 1, Volume 31, Part 3, 829–831; N. B. Forrest, *Official Records*, Series 1, Volume 32, Part 3, 610; S. D. Lee, *Official Records*, Series 1, Volume 31, Part 3, 858, 864; N. B. Forrest, *Official Records*, Series 1, Volume 31, Part 3, 858–859; N. B. Forrest, *Official Records*, Series 1, Volume 32, Part 1, 610; James M. Houry, "Citizen, as Well as Brig. General Chalmers, Broadside by Oxford, Mississippi Resident," Archives and Special Collections, The University of Mississippi, Oxford, MS.

8. Bruce S. Allardice, *More Generals in Gray* (Baton Rouge: Louisiana State University Press, 1995), 202–203; V. Sheliha, *Official Records*, Series 1, Volume 8, 810–811; Edmund Rucker, *Official Records*, Series 1, Volume 8, 159–160; John P. McCown, *Official Records*, Series 1, Volume 8, 129.

9. Bruce S. Allardice, *ibid.*.; Thomas McAdory Owen, *History of Alabama and Dictionary of Alabama Biography*, Volume IV (Chicago: The S. J. Clarke Publishing Company, 1921), 472; Clement Evans, *Confederate Military History*, Vol. VIII (Atlanta, GA: Confederate Publishing Company 1899), 30–31, 235–237, 239; E. Kirby Smith, *Official Records*, Series 1, Volume 16, Part 2, 984; Braxton Bragg, *Official Records*, Series 1, Volume 31, Part 2, 663; "Gen. Edmund W. Rucker," *Confederate Veteran*, Vol. XXXII (May 1924), No, 5, 163–164; James Chalmers, *Official Records*, Series 1, Volume 39, Part 1, 328; S. D. Lee, *Official Records*, Series 1, Volume 39, Part 2, 677; W. H. Brand, *Official Records*, Series 1, Volume 39, Part 2, 717; David Powell, *Failure in the Saddle* (New York and California: Savas Beatie, 2010), 249.

10. "Gen. Edmund W. Rucker" *Confederate Veteran*, 163–164; N. B. Forrest, *Official Records*, Series 1, Volume 39, Part 2, 805.

11. Braxton Bragg, *Official Records*, Series 1, Volume 20, Part 2, 20; Isaac R. Hamilton, Letter, August 9, 1863 and footnote, In *The Papers of Andrew Johnson*, Volume 6, LeRoy P. Graf and Ralph Haskins, eds. (Knoxville: University of Tennessee Press, 1983), 322–323; Michael R. Bradley, *They Rode with Forrest* (Gretna, LA: Pelican Publishing Co., 2012), 99–100; Brent A. Cox, *Born to Fight* (n.p.: Sons of the South Publications, 1991), 7–17.

12. N. B. Forest, *Official Records*, Series 1, Volume 39, Part 1, 530; N. B. Forrest, *Official Records*, Series 1, Volume 45, Part 1, 752; Clement Evans, *Confederate Military History*, Vol. 8: Tennessee (Atlanta, GA: Confederate Publishing Co., 1899), 94, 222–228, 242; John B. Lindsley, *The Military Annals of Tennessee: Confederate* (Nashville, TN: Lindsley, 1886), 687–697; Darrell L. Collins, *The Army of Tennessee: Organization, Strength, Casualties, 1862–1865* (Jefferson, NC: McFarland, 2017), 23, 29, 133; Michael Bradley, *They Rode with Forrest*, 99–100; Braxton Bragg, *Official Records*, Series 1, Volume 31, Part 2, 663; Braxton Bragg, *Official Records*, Series 1, Volume 32, Part 2, 642; Joseph Johnston, *Official Records*, Series 1, Volume 38, Part 3, 642.

13. Michael Cotton, *The Williamson County Cavalry: A History of Company F, Fourth Tennessee Cavalry Regiment, C.S. A.* (Goodlettsville: D.M. Cotton, 1994), 187.

14. Marcus Bainbridge Buford, *A Genealogy of the Buford Family in America* (San Francisco: n. p., 1903), 235; Byron Farwell, *The Encyclopedia of Nineteenth-century Land Warfare: An Illustrated World View* (New York, London: W. W. Norton & Co, 2001), 139.

15. Braxton Bragg, *Official Records*, Series 1, Volume 23, Part 2, 656–657; Leonidas Polk, *Official Records*, Series 1, Volume 16, Part 2, 963; Abraham Buford, *Official Records*, Series 1, Volume 20, Part 1, 970; Spencer C. Tucker, ed., *American Civil War: The Definitive Encyclopedia and Document Collection* (Santa Barbara: ABC—Clio LLC, 2013), 251; Bruce Allardice and Lawrence Lee Hewitt, *Kentuckians in Gray: Confederate Generals and Field Officers of the Bluegrass State* (Lexington: University of Kentucky Press, 2008), 51–52.

16. Leonidas Polk, *Official Records*, Series 1, Volume 23, Part 3, 865–866; Thomas M. Jack, *Official Records*, Series 1, Volume 32, Part 2, 578; Abraham Buford, *Official Records*, Series 1, Volume 39, Part 1, 329–335; Marcus B. Buford, *History and Genealogy of the Buford Family in America With Records of a Number of Allied Families* (La Belle, MO: Mildred B. Minter, 1924), 236–237.

17. Randy Bishop, *Civil War Generals of Tennessee* (Gretna, LA: Pelican Publishing Co., 2013), 32–33; Nathaniel Cheairs Hughes, Jr., *Brigadier General Tyree H. Bell, CSA* (Knoxville: UT Press, 2004), 1–11; Bruce S. Allardice and Lawrence Lee Hewitt, editors, *Kentuckians in Gray*, 29–30.

18. Randy Bishop, *ibid.*; Michael B. Ballard, *The Civil War in Mississippi: Major Campaigns and Battles* (Jackson: University Press of Mississippi, 2011), 228–229; Abraham Buford, *Official Records*, Series 1, Volume 39, Part 1, 335; Tyree Bell, *Official Records*, Series 1, Volume 39, Part 1, 348; Nathaniel Cheairs Hughes, Jr., *Brigadier General Tyree H. Bell*, 12–13, 24–27, 39, 42–43, 81–88, 126, 140–149, 154–156, 162; Bruce S. Allardice and Lawrence Lee Hewitt, *Kentuckians in Gray*, 29–35;

"Gen. Tyree H. Bell," *Confederate Veteran*, Vol. 10 (October 1902), p. 464.

19. "Col. Edward Crossland, of Kentucky," *Confederate Veteran*, Volume 19, No. 8 (August 1911), 366.

20. Edward DeVries, *Glory in Gray*, Volume 1 (n.p.: Dixie Heritage Press, 2004), 447.

21. Randy Bishop, *Civil War Generals of Tennessee*, 111–112; Vic Currier, *Good-bye, Lord, I'm Going To New York: The Secret Life of Belle Meade's William Harding Jackson* (Bloomington, IN: Xlibris Corp, 2015), 13–14; J. P. Young, *The Seventh Tennessee Cavalry: A History* (Nashville: M. E. Church, South, 1890), 30; Jack Welsh, *Medical Histories of Confederate Generals* (Kent, Ohio: Kent State University Press, 1995), 113–114.

22. David Evans, *Sherman's Horsemen* (Bloomington: Indiana University Press, 1996), 224; *The National Cyclopaedia of American Biography*, Vol. IX (New York: James T. White & Co., 1907), 212; Jim Woodrick, *The Civil War Siege of Jackson Mississippi* (Charleston, SC: The History Press, 2016), 131; W. H. Jackson, *Official Records*, Series 1, Volume 24, Part 2, 659; J. C. Pemberton, *Official Records*, Series 1, Volume 24, Part 3, 743; Joseph Johnston, *Official Records*, Series 1, Volume 30, Part 4, 517; W. H. Jackson, *Official Records*, Series 1, Volume 30, Part 4, 656; William H. Jackson, *Official Records*, Series 1, Volume 32, Part 1, 371.

23. Carolyn Thomas Foreman, "The Armstrongs of Indian Territory: General Frank Crawford Armstrong, Part III," *Chronicles of Oklahoma*, Vol. 31, No. 1 (1953), 56–65; Ezra Warner, *Generals in Gray* (Baton Rouge: Louisiana State University Press, 1959), 12–13.

24. Clement Evans, ed. *Confederate Military History*, Vol. VIII (Atlanta: Confederate Publishing Company, 1899), 288–292; David Powell, *Failure in the Saddle*, xxiii–xxiv.

25. Braxton Bragg, *Official Records*, Series 1, Volume 30, Part 2, 20; James Longstreet, *Official Records*, Series 1, Volume 31, Part 1, 453; James Longstreet, *Official Records*, Series 1, Volume 32, Part 2, 682; Joseph Johnston, *Official Records*, Series 1, Volume 38, Part 3, 660; N. B. Forrest, *Official Records*, Series 1, Volume 32, Part 3, 616; William Mason Worthington, Letter to "My Dear sister," November 8, 1864, Worthington Family Papers, MS Z/0658.000/S, Box 1, Mississippi Department of History and Archives.

26. Judith Ann Benner, *Sul Ross: Soldier, Statesman, Educator* (College Station: Texas A&M University Press, 1983), 3–7, 14, 18, 25–26, 30–31.

27. "General and Governor Ross, of Texas," *Confederate Veteran*, Volume 2 (June, 1894) No. 6, p. 169; Judith Ann Benner, *Sul Ross*, 36–42, 68.

28. Peter Cozzens, *The Darkest Days of the War: The Battles of Iuka and Corinth* (Chapel Hill & London: University of North Carolina Press, 1997), 266, 286; Judith Ann Benner, *Sul Ross*, 69, 72, 76–79, 82–88; L. S. Ross, *Personal Civil War Letters of General Lawrence Sullivan Ross with other letters*, transcribed and compiled by Perry Wayne Shelton, edited by Shelly Morrison (Austin: Shelly and Richard Morrison, 1994), IX–X.

29. Judith Ann Benner, *Sul Ross*, 89–90, 99, 102–106; Lawrence Ross, *Personal Civil War Letters of General Lawrence Sullivan Ross: With Other Letters, ibid.*; Perry Wayne Shelton, "Personal Letters Written by Lawrence Sullivan Ross," M.A. thesis, Baylor University, 1938, Ross Family Papers #0014.

30. Hyland B. Lyon, "Memoirs of Hylan B. Lyon Brigadier General, CSA," Edward M. Coffman ed., *Tennessee Historical Quarterly*, Volume 18, No. 1 (March, 1959), pp. 35–39.

31. J.P. Strange, *Official Records*, Series 1, Volume 39, Part 2, 806; Hyland B. Lyon, "Memoirs of Hylan B. Lyon Brigadier General," 39–47; Bruce S. Allardice and Lawrence Lee Hewitt, eds., *Kentuckians in Gray*, 180–183.

32. Clement Evans, editor, *Confederate Military History, Alabama*, Vol. VII (Cartersville, GA: Eastern Digital Resources, 2014), 440–441; P. D. Roddey, *Official Records*, Series 1, Volume 30, Part 2, 729; Ezra Warner, *Generals in Gray*, p. 262; Arley H. McCormick, "The Defender of North Alabama," In *North Alabama Civil War Generals: 13 Wore Gray, the Rest Blue*, Huntsville History Collection, Tennessee Valley Civil War Roundtable, pp. 83–85.

33. Joseph Johnson, *Official Records*, Series 1, Volume 32, Part 1, 477; Arley H. McCormick, *Ibid.*; Joseph Johnston, *Official Records*, Series 1, Volume 32, Part 3, 739; Francis A. Shoup, "Journal of the Army of Tennessee," *Official Records*, Series 1, Volume 38, Part 3, 989.

Chapter Five

1. Abraham Lot, November 9, 1864—diary entry, Lot Abraham diary, 1864, Special Collections, The University of Iowa Libraries.

2. G. T. Beauregard, *Official Records*, Series 1, Volume 39, Part 3, 843; George Wm. Brent, *Official Records*, Series 1, Volume 39, Part 3, 845; Richard Taylor, *Official Records*, Series 1, Volume 39, Part 3, 845.

3. N. B. Forrest, *Official Records*, Series 1, Volume 39, Part 3, 815–816; William Brooksher, *Glory at a Gallop: Tales of the Confederate Cavalry* (Gretna, LA: Pelican Publishing Co., 1993), 226; Edward F. Williams, III, "The Johnsonville Raid and Nathan Bedford Forrest State Park," *Tennessee Historical Quarterly*, Vol. 28, No. 3 (Fall 1969): 225–251, p. 229; W. H. Jackson, Orders—October 27, 1864, Capt. George Moorman Papers, RG 109, entry 130, National Archives, Washington.

4. Timothy A. Parsons, "Rivers and Rifles: The Role of Fort Heiman in the Western Theater of the Civil War,"
Journal of Kentucky Archaeology, 1, No. 2 (Winter 2012): 16–38, pp. 16–24.

5. Dan Lee, *The Civil War in the Jackson Pur-

chase, 1861–1862: The Pro-Confederate Struggle and Defeat in Southwest Kentucky (Jefferson, NC: McFarland, 2014), 207–208; N. B. Forrest, *Official Records*, Series 1, Volume 39, Part 1, 870; Jerry T. Wooten, "Johnsonville: The Evolution, Defense, and Demise of the Union's Tennessee River Supply Depot, 1790–1890," Ph.D. dissertation, Middle Tennessee State University December 2015, 162–164; William L. Clark, *Official Records*, Series 1, Volume 39, Part 1, 877; John Morton, *The Artillery of Nathan Bedford Forrest's Cavalry* (Nashville and Dallas: Publishing House of the M. E. Church, South Smith & Lamar, Agents, 1909), 247–248; James Chalmers, *Official Records*, Series 1, Volume 39, Part 1, 872; Jerry T. Wooten, "Johnsonville," 165; James Dinkins, "Destroying Military Stores and Gunboats," *Confederate Veteran*, Volume 34, No. 5 (May 1926), 176–178; Nathaniel Cheairs Hughes, Jr., *Brigadier General Tyree H. Bell, CSA* (Knoxville: UT Press, 2004), 182–183; Andrew Nelson Lytle, *Bedford Forrest: and His Critter Company* (Nashville: J. S. Sanders & Co., 1992), 347; James Chalmers, *Official Records*, Series 1, Volume 39, Part 1, 873.

6. N. B. Forrest, *Official Records*, Series 1, Volume 39, Part 1, 869; James Chalmers, *Official Records*, Series 1, Volume 39, Part 1, 874; William Sinclair, *Official Records*, Series 1, Volume 39, Part 1, 861; Jerry T. Wooten, "Johnsonville," 172; "Capture of the Mazeppa," *Confederate Veteran*, Volume VIII, No. 12 (December 1905): 566–570, p. 568; John Morton, *The Artillery of Nathan Bedford Forrest's Cavalry*, 248–50; Edward F. Williams, III, "The Johnsonville Raid and Nathan Bedford Forrest State Park," p. 239.

7. Jerry T. Wooten, "Johnsonville," 174; William Sinclair, *Official Records*, Series 1, Volume 39, Part 1, 861.

8. N. B. Forrest, *Official Records*, Series 1, Volume 39, Part 1, 869; Samuel D. Smith, Benjamin C. Nance and Fred M. Prouty, "A Survey of Civil War Era Military Sites in Tennessee," Tennessee Department of Environment and Conservation, Division of Archaeology, Research Series No. 14, 2003, pp. 30, 44, 56, 205.

9. James Dinkins, "Destroying Military Stores and Gunboats," 178; Jerry T. Wooten, "Johnsonville," 177, 180, 184; Michael Bradley, *They Rode with Forrest* (Gretna, Louisiana: Pelican Publishing Company, 2012), 37; N. B. Forrest, *Official Records*, Series 1, Volume 39, Part 1, 871; John W. Morton, "Battle of Johnsonville," *Southern Historical Society Papers*, Volume 10: 480–481.

10. N. B. Forrest, *Official Records*, Series 1, Volume 39, Part 1, 871–872.

11. William Sinclair, *Official Records*, Series 1, Volume 39, Part 1, 862; George Thomas, *Official Records*, Series 1, Volume 39, Part 1, 859; Alfred H. Guernsey and Henry H. Alden, "Battle of Nashville," In *Harper's Pictorial History of the Great Rebellion*, Vol. 2 (Chicago: McDonnell Brothers, 1868), 675.

12. Jerry T. Wooten, "Johnsonville,"198–200; W. H. Henderson, Letter to wife—November 18, 1864, William Henry Henderson letters: 2003—L501, Pearce Museum at Navarro College, Corsicana, Texas.

13. Christopher Lyle McIlwain, *Civil War Alabama* (Tuscaloosa: University of Alabama Press, 2016), 230–235; *The Opelousas Courier* (Opelousas, LA), "The Teachings of Lincoln's Reelection," Dec. 17, 1864, p. 1; John B. Hood *Official Records*, Series 1, Volume 45, Part 1, 657; J. N. and Virginia Adkins Coleman Papers, Letter—December 6, 1865, The Texas Collection, Baylor University, Waco, Texas; James C. Bates, Letter—November 8, 1864, In *A Texas Cavalry Officer's Civil: The Diary and Letters of James C. Bates*, Richard Lowe, ed. (Baton Rouge: Louisiana State University Press, 1999), 327–328; Thomas Robson Hay, *Hood's Tennessee Campaign* (New York: Press of Morningside Books, 1976), 69; Alexander Jackson, Letter to son—November 16, 1864, Jackson, William Hicks (1835–1903) Papers 1766–1978, Box 1, Folder 26, Tennessee State Library and Archives.

14. Henry Kratzer McVey, *A Writ of My Civil War Experiences* (Jefferson County, Iowa: n.p. 2001), 15; Orr Kelly and Mary Davies Kelly, *Dream's End: Two Iowa Brothers in the Civil War* (New York: Kodansha America, Inc., 1998), 243; Sid Champion, *My Dear Wife: Letters to Matilda, The Civil War Letters of Sid and Matilda Champion of Champion Hill*, edited by Rebecca Blackwell Drake and Margie Riddle Bearss, ed. (n.p.:Self-published, 2005), 240.

15. P. G. T. Beauregard, *Official Records*, Series 1, Volume 45, Part 1, 648; Thomas Robson Hay, *Hood's Tennessee Campaign*, 65; David Rey Moody, "'The Best Move of My Career': Spring Hill and the Failure of Confederate Command in the West," San Jose: Ph.D. Dissertation, San Jose State University, 1993, 48.

16. A. P. Mason, *Official Records*, Series 1, Volume 45, Part 1, 663.

17. P. G. T. Beauregard, *Official Records*, Series 1, Volume 45, Part 1, 649; George Wm. Brent, *Official Records*, Series 1, Volume 45, Part 1, 1207; John Morton, *The Artillery of Nathan Bedford Forrest's Cavalry* (Nashville and Dallas: Publishing House of the M. E. Church, South Smith & Lamar, Agents, 1909), 267; William Mason Worthington, Letter to "My Dear sister," November 8, 1864, Worthington Family Papers, MS Z/0658.000/S, Box 1, Mississippi Department of History and Archives.

18. P. G. T. Beauregard, *Official Records*, Series 1, Volume 45, Part 1, 648; Joseph Wheeler, *Official Records*, Series 1, Volume 45, Part 1, 1206.

19. N. B. Forrest, *Official Records*, Series 1, Volume 45, Part 1, 751–752; Francis A. Shoup, *Official Records*, Series 1, Volume 39, Part 1, 808; Daniel Harris Reynolds, Diary entry, November 17, 1864, Daniel Harris Reynolds Papers (MS R32), University of Arkansas, Special Collections; N. B. Forrest, *Official Records*, Series 1, Volume 39, Part 3, 915.

20. Francis A. Shoup, *Official Records*, Series 1, Volume 39, Part 1, 808; G. P. T. Beauregard, *Official Records*, Series 1, Volume 45, Part 1, 1207.

21. G. T. Beauregard, *Official Records*, Series 1, Volume 45, Part 1, 1213, 1216; George Wm. Brent, *Official Records*, Series 1, Volume 45, Part 1, 1215; John B. Hood, *Official Records*, Series 1, Volume 45, Part 1, 1215–6, 1219–20.

22. A. P. Mason, *Official Records*, Series 1, Volume 45, Part 1, 1227; Thomas Smyrl, Letter to wife, November 20, 1864, Thomas Smyrl Civil War letters, 1861–1865 (SPR382), Alabama Department of Archives and History; W. O. Dodd, "Reminiscences of Hood's Tennessee Campaign," *Southern Historical Society Papers*, Vol. 9, No. 10–12 (October-December 1881): 518–524, p. 518; Enoch L. Mitchell, "Letters of a Confederate Surgeon in the Army of Tennessee to His Wife," *Tennessee Historical Quarterly*, Vol. 5, No. 2 (June, 1946), pp. 176–177.

Chapter Six

1. J. H. Martin, *Official Records*, Series 1, Volume 45, Part 1, 1228; W. H. Jackson, *Official Records*, Series 1, Volume 45, Part 1, 1228; A. P. Mason, *Official Records*, Series 1, Volume 45, Part 1, 1227–1228; E. H. Rennolds, Diary November 17 and 18, 1864, E. H. Rennolds Diaries, MS.0170, The Special Collections Library of the University of Tennessee, Knoxville; William H. Young letter to his wife, Susan Young, 14 November 1864, MS—008: The Papers of William H. Young, Special Collections, Gettysburg College.

2. Richard Taylor, *Official Records*, Series 1, Volume 45, Part 1, 1232–1235.

3. David Stanley, *An American General: The Memoirs of David Sloan Stanley* (Santa Barbara, CA: The Narrative Press, 2003), 192–194.

4. George Thomas, *Official Records*, Series 1, Volume 45, Part 1, 52–53.

5. Ibid.

6. George Thomas, *Official Records*, Series 1, Volume 45, Part 1, 52; Robert Shields, Letter to wife November 21, 1864, Robert D. Shields Papers, 1862–1865, [MSS 1473], Ohio Historical Society; James H. Wilson, "The Union Cavalry in the Hood Campaign, In *Battles and Leaders of the Civil War*, Vol. IV (New York: The Century Co., 1888), 465; Thomas A. Wigginton, "Cavalry Operations," *Civil War Times Illustrated Magazine*, Volume 3, Number 8 (December 1964), 40–43 (In Tennessee State Library Printed Material Collection).

7. John Schofield, *Forty-Six Years in the Army* (New York: The Century Co., 1897), 156–157; David Stanley, *Official Records*, Series 1, Volume 38, Part 1, 214.

8. Ulysses Grant, *Official Records*, Series 1, Volume 39, Part 3, 684; David Stanley, *Official Records*, Series 1, Volume 45, Part 1, 960; Southard Hoffman, *Official Records*, Series 1, Volume 39, Part 2, 638.

9. Robt. H. Ramsey, *Official Records*, Series 1, Volume 45, Part 1, 953; E. B. Beaumont, *Official Records*, Series 1, Volume 45, Part 1, 952; W. P. Chambliss, *Official Records*, Series 1, Volume 45, Part 1, 908.

10. John W. Leonard, *Who's Who in Pennsylvania: A Biographical Dictionary of Contemporaries*, Volume 2 (New York: John W. Hamersly & Co., 1908), 50.

11. James H. Wilson, *Official Records*, Series 1, Volume 45, Part 1, 954–955, 961.

12. David Stanley, *An American General*, 193–194.

13. James H. Wilson, *Official Records*, Series 1, Volume 45, Part 1, 555–556.

14. James H. Wilson, *Official Records*, Series 1, Volume 45, Part 1, 556–557; Benjamin Franklin Cooling, *To the Battles of Franklin and Nashville and Beyond* (Knoxville: University of Tennessee Press, 2011), 284; W. R. Carter, *History of the First Regiment of Tennessee Volunteer Cavalry* (Knoxville, TN.: Gaut-Ogden Co., Printers and Binders, 1902) 202–203; Garrison Wright, Letter to sister, November 4, 1864, Garrison H. Wright Correspondence, Bentley Historical Library, University of Michigan; George Monlux, "To My Comrades Co. I, 8th Iowa Cavalry," Personal narrative, State Historical Library & Archives, p. 47; Jerry Keenan, *Wilson's Cavalry Corps* (Jefferson, NC: McFarland, 1998), 30.

15. Edward Hatch, *Official Records*, Series 1, Volume 45, Part 1, 887; George Thomas, *Official Records*, Series 1, Volume 45, Part 1, 85–87; E. H. Rennolds Diary—November 9, 1864, E. H. Rennolds Diaries, MS.0170, The Special Collections Library of the University of Tennessee, Knoxville.

16. George Thomas, *Official Records*, Series 1, Volume 45, Part 1, 888; John Schofield, *Official Records*, Series 1, Volume 45, Part 1, 899, 907; Horace Capron, *Official Records*, Series 1, Volume 45, Part 1, 909; Edward Hatch, *Official Records*, Series 1, Volume 45, Part 1, 910.

17. Edward Hatch, *Official Records*, Series 1, Volume 45, Part 1, 911–912.

18. Edward Hatch, *Official Records*, Series 1, Volume 45, Part 1, 928.

19. Edward Hatch, *Official Records*, Series 1, Volume 45, Part 1, 942; Alonzo Aulsbro, Letter to parents, November 18, 1864, Martin Barnhart collection, 1861–1920, Alma MMS ID 9920181483802436, Western Michigan State University, Kalamazoo.

20. Horace Capron, *Official Records*, Series 1, Volume 45, Part 1, 936–937; W. L. Sanford, *History of Fourteenth Illinois Cavalry and the Brigades to Which It Belonged* (Chicago: R. R. Donnelley & Sons Company, 1898), 232; Wright Garrison, Letter to sister, November 16, 1864, Grace Edmonds collection, 1860–1932, Alma MMS ID 9920545023802436, Western Michigan State University, Kalamazoo.

21. Edward Hatch, *Official Records*, Series 1, Volume 45, Part 1, 942–943.

22. George H. Thomas, *Official Records*, Series 1, Volume 45, Part 1, 944–945.

23. John B. Hood, *Official Records*, Series 1, Volume 45, Part 1, 652, 669–670; A. P. Mason, *Official Records*, Series 1, Volume 45, Part 1, 1211; F. H. Wigfall, *Official Records*, Series 1, Volume 45, Part 1, 1217; Nathaniel Cheairs Hughes, Jr., *Brigadier General Tyree H. Bell, CSA* (Knoxville: UT Press, 2004), 194; John Bell Hood letter to soldiers, November 21, 1864, General Orders and Circulars, Army of Tennessee, December 1863—January 1865; and General Orders, Gen. J.E. Johnston's Headquarters, March—April 1865, RG 109 Chapter Volume 2–350, National Archives; Martha L. Crabb, *All Afire to Fight: The Untold Tale of the Civil War's Ninth Texas Cavalry* (New York: Avon Books, 2000), 262.

24. Edward Hatch, *Official Records*, Series 1, Volume 45, Part 1, 945; Nathaniel Cheairs Hughes, Jr., *Brigadier General Tyree H. Bell, CSA*, 192–193; J. G. Deupree, "The Noxubee Squadron of the First Mississippi Cavalry, C. S. A. 1861–1865," In *Publications of the Mississippi Historical Society*, Volume II, Dunbar Rowland, ed. (Jackson, MS: Democrat Printing Co., 1918), 109; Edward A. Davenport, editor, *History of the Ninth Regiment Illinois Cavalry Volunteers* (Chicago: Donohue & Henneberry, Printers and Binders, 1888), 135–137; Lyman Pierce, *History of the Second Iowa Cavalry* (Burlington, IA: Hawkeye Steam Book and Job Printing Establishment, 1865), 127.

25. J. G. Deupree, "The Noxubee Squadron," 109; Thomas Jordan and J. P. Pryor, *The Campaigns of Lieut.-Gen. N. B. Forrest* (New Orleans, Memphis and New York: Blelock & Company, 1868), 613; Richard R. Hancock, *Hancock's Diary: Or, A History of the Second Tennessee Confederate Cavalry* (Nashville: Brandon Printing Company, 1887), 511.

26. Datus Coon, *Official Records*, Series 1, Volume 45, Part 1, 585; Lyman Pierce, *History of the Second Iowa Cavalry*, 127–129.

27. Coon, *Ibid.*; W. R. Carter, *History of the First Regiment of Tennessee Volunteer Cavalry* (Knoxville: Gaut-Ogden Co., Printers and Binders, 1902), 205; Lyman Pierce, *History of the Second Iowa Cavalry*, 129; George L. Griscom, *Fighting with Ross' Texas Cavalry Brigade, C.S. A.: The Diary of George L. Griscom, adjutant, 9th Texas Cavalry Regiment*, edited by Homer L. Kerr (Hillsboro, TX: Hill Junior College Press, 1976), 189.

28. John Schofield, *Official Records*, Series 1, Volume 45, Part 1, 946; Edward Hatch, *Official Records*, Series 1, Volume 45, Part 1, 945; Nathaniel Cheairs Hughes, Jr., *Brigadier General Tyree H. Bell, CSA*, 192–193.

29. Edward Hatch, *Official Records*, Series 1, Volume 45, Part 1, 954.

30. Edward Hatch, *Official Records*, Series 1, Volume 45, Part 1, 962.

31. George Thomas, *Official Records*, Series 1, Volume 45, Part 1, 957; John Schofield, *Official Records*, Series 1, Volume 45, Part 1, 955–956, 959, 963.

32. James Dinkins, *1861 to 1865: Personal Reminiscences and Experiences in the Confederate Army* (Cincinnati: Robert Clarke Co., 1897), 223–224; Datus Coon, *Official Records*, Series 1, Volume 45, Part 1, 586.

33. Edward A. Davenport, *History of the Ninth Regiment Illinois Cavalry*, 140.

34. N. B. Forrest, *Official Records*, Series 1, Volume 45, Part 1, 752; J. P. Young, *Seventh Tennessee Cavalry (Confederate): A History* (Nashville: M.E. Church South, 1890), 117.

35. L. S. Ross, *Official Records*, Series 1, Volume 45, Part 1, 769.

36. Edward Hatch, *Official Records*, Series 1, Volume 45, Part 1, 963, 970; S. A. Strickland, *Official Records*, Series 1, Volume 45, Part 1, 964; John Schofield, *Official Records*, Series 1, Volume 45, Part 1, 964; Henry M. Hempstead, Journal—November 21, 184, Bentley Historical Library, University of Michigan; Datus Coon, *Official Records*, Series 1, Volume 45, Part 1, 585–586; Marshall P. Thatcher, *A Hundred Battles in the West: The Second Michigan Cavalry* (Detroit: L. F. Kilroy, Printer, 1884), 198; Edward A. Davenport, *History of the Ninth Regiment Illinois Cavalry*, 138–140; Edward Hatch, *Official Records*, Series 1, Volume 45, Part 1, 970; Nathaniel Cheairs Hughes, Jr., *Brigadier General Tyree H. Bell, CSA*, 193.

37. J. A. Bigger, Diary, November 21, 1864, J. A. Bigger Diary, April 30, 1862-Mary 12, 1865, Small Manuscripts 76–3 (4 folders), Archives and Special Collections, The University of Mississippi, Oxford, MS.

38. J. M. Schofield, *Official Records*, Series 1, Volume 45, Part 1, 971; Edward Hatch, *Official Records*, Series 1, Volume 45, Part 1, 970–971; George Thomas, *Official Records*, Series 1, Volume 45, Part 1, 970–971.

39. Edward Hatch, *Official Records*, Series 1, Volume 45, Part 1, 989; W. L. Sanford, *History of Fourteenth Illinois Cavalry*, 236.

40. J. M. Schofield, *Official Records*, Series 1, Volume 45, Part 1, 974; George Thomas, *Official Records*, Series 1, Volume 45, Part 1, 971–973; E. B. Beaumont, *Official Records*, Series 1, Volume 45, Part 1, 988.

41. Datus Coon, *Official Records*, Series 1, Volume 45, Part 1, 586.

42. L. S. Ross, *Official Records*, Series 1, Volume 45, Part 1, 768–769; George L. Griscom, *Fighting with Ross' Texas Cavalry Brigade*, 189.

43. Thomas Jordan and J. P. Pryor, *The Campaigns of Lieut.-Gen. N. B. Forrest*, 613; John Berrien Lindsley, *Military Annals of Tennessee: Confederate* (Nashville: J. M. Lindsley & Co., Publishers, 1886), 745; Henry George, *History of the 3d, 7th, 8th and 12th Kentucky Cavalry, CSA* (Lyndon, KY: Mull-Wathen Historic Press, 1911), 131–134; Datus Coon, *Official Records*, Series 1, Volume 45, Part 1, 586; George Thomas, *Official Records*,

Series 1, Volume 45, Part 1, 88–89; Edward A. Davenport, *History of the Ninth Regiment Illinois Cavalry*, 145.

44. Edward Hatch, *Official Records*, Series 1, Volume 45, Part 1, 994–995.

45. Henry M. Hempstead, Journal—November 22, 184, Bentley Historical Library, University of Michigan.

46. William Mason Worthington, Letter to "My Dear sister," November 8, 1864, Worthington Family Papers, MS Z/0658.000/S, Box 1, Mississippi Department of History and Archives.

47. R. S. Granger, *Official Records*, Series 1, Volume 45, Part 1, 1028; J. M. Schofield, *Official Records*, Series 1, Volume 45, Part 1, 996; George Thomas, *Official Records*, Series 1, Volume 45, Part 1, 994–995; Jacob Cox, *Official Records*, Series 1, Volume 45, Part 1, 356.

48. J. C. Van Duzer, *Official Records*, Series 1, Volume 45, Part 1, 996; Henry M. Hempstead, Journal—November 23, 184, Bentley Historical Library, University of Michigan; Edward Hatch, *Official Records*, Series 1, Volume 45, Part 1, 576.

49. J. M. Schofield, *Official Records*, Series 1, Volume 45, Part 1, 998; S. A. Strickland, *Official Records*, Series 1, Volume 45, Part 1, 997; Datus Coon, *Official Records*, Series 1, Volume 45, Part 1, 586.

50. Lyman Pierce, *History of the Second Iowa Cavalry*, 134; Edward Hatch, *Official Records*, Series 1, Volume 45, Part 1, 576; David B. Van Dyke, *The Devil's Whirlwind: the Battle of Campbellsville, November 24, 1864* (Campbellsville, TN:, David Van Dyke, 2011), 17–18.

51. William T. Shaver, "Reminiscences," Shaver, William Thompson (1840–1893) papers, A0286–00559, Missouri History Museum, St. Louis, MO; J. M. Hubbard, Letter, December 8, 1864 to Gen. Gray, 12th Regiment Cavalry, Personnel correspondence, RG 133 Adjutant General Records, Box 32, Folder 73, Missouri State Archives; Compiled records showing service of military units in volunteer Union organizations—Missouri, company history cards, National Archives Record Administration, RG 94, M594, Washington, D. C.; Richard R. Hancock, *Hancock's Diary: Or, A History of the Second Tennessee Confederate Cavalry* (Nashville: Brandon Printing Company, 1887), 512–513.

52. Datus Coon, *Official Records*, Series 1, Volume 45, Part 1, 586–587; Edward Hatch, *Official Records*, Series 1, Volume 45, Part 1, 575–576; Nathaniel Cheairs Hughes, Jr., *Brigadier General Tyree H. Bell*, CSA, 194; J. G. Deupree, "The Noxubee Squadron of the First Mississippi Cavalry, C. S. A. 1861–1865," In *Publications of the Mississippi Historical Society*, Volume II, Dunbar Rowland, ed. (Jackson, MS: Democrat Printing Co., 1918), 110; Edward A. Davenport, *History of the Ninth Regiment Illinois Cavalry*, 145.

53. Datus Coon, *Official Records*, Series 1, Volume 45, Part 1, 586–588; Edward Hatch, Official Records, Series 1, Volume 45, Part 1, 575–576; Lyman Pierce, *History of the Second Iowa Cavalry*, 135; David B. Van Dyke, *The Devil's Whirlwind*, 23.

54. L. S. Ross, *Official Records*, Series 1, Volume 45, Part 1, 768–769; I. N. Rainey, "Experiences of I. N. Rainey in the Confederate Army," Southern History Collection, University of North Carolina.

55. George L. Griscom, *Fighting with Ross' Texas Cavalry Brigade, C.S. A.: The Diary of George L. Griscom, adjutant, 9th Texas Cavalry Regiment*, 189–190.

56. Datus Coon, *Official Records*, Series 1, Volume 45, Part 1, 586–588; Edward Hatch, Official Records, Series 1, Volume 45, Part 1, 575–576; Lyman Pierce, *History of the Second Iowa Cavalry*, 135.

57. Edward Hatch, Official Records, Series 1, Volume 45, Part 1, 575–576; Edward A. Davenport, *History of the Ninth Regiment Illinois Cavalry*, 147–148.

58. Datus Coon, *Official Records*, Series 1, Volume 45, Part 1, 586–588; Edward Hatch, *Official Records*, Series 1, Volume 45, Part 1, 575–576.

59. Edward Hatch, *Official Records*, Series 1, Volume 45, Part 1, 575–576; N. B. Forrest, *Official Records*, Series 1, Volume 45, Part 1, 752; J. G. Deupree, "The Noxubee Squadron," 100; Henry M. Hempstead, Journal—November 24, 184, Bentley Historical Library, University of Michigan; David B. Van Dyke, *The Devil's Whirlwind*, 25.

60. J. M. Schofield, *Official Records*, Series 1, Volume 45, Part 1, 1018.

61. Francis Stewart, Diary, November 25, 1865 MS 744—Francis Stewart Papers, Bowling Green University.

62. L. S. Ross, *Official Records*, Series 1, Volume 45, Part 1, 768–769; I. N. Rainey, "Experiences of I. N. Rainey in the Confederate Army," Southern History Collection, University of North Carolina.

63. John Schofield, *Official Records*, Series 1, Volume 45, Part 1, 963.

64. J. M. Schofield, *Official Records*, Series 1, Volume 45, Part 1, 961; Horace Capron, *Official Records*, Series 1, Volume 45, Part 1, 964–965.

65. W. L. Sanford, *History of Fourteenth Illinois Cavalry*, 232–33; John Schofield, *Official Records*, Series 1, Volume 45, Part 1, 964; Horace Capron, *Official Records*, Series 1, Volume 45, Part 1, 965–966.

66. Ibid.

67. John B. Hood, *Official Records*, Series 1, Volume 45, Part 1, 669–670; W. L. Sanford, *History of Fourteenth Illinois Cavalry*, 234–235.

68. W. L. Sanford, *History of Fourteenth Illinois Cavalry*, 236; H. C. Connelly, "From Nashville to the Tennessee," *National Tribune*, July 11, 1895, p. 1.

69. S. A. Strickland, *Official Records*, Series 1, Volume 45, Part 1, 973; John Schofield, *Official Records*, Series 1, Volume 45, Part 1, 975–976; James A. Strong, *Official Records*, Series 1, Volume 45, Part 1, 973.

Notes—Chapter Six

70. Horace Capron, *Official Records*, Series 1, Volume 45, Part 1, 976–977, 1005–1006, 1011.

71. W. L. Sanford, *History of Fourteenth Illinois Cavalry*, 236–237.

72. Thomas Jordan and J. P. Pryor, *The Campaigns of Lieut.-Gen. N. B. Forrest*, 614; John Johnston, Diaries and Memoirs, Confederate Collection, Box 13, Folder 6, Tennessee State Library and Archives, p. 133; H. C. Connelly, "From Nashville to the Tennessee."

73. W. L. Sanford, *History of Fourteenth Illinois Cavalry*, 237–238.

74. W. L. Sanford, *Ibid.*; I. N. Rainey, "Experiences of I. N. Rainey in the Confederate Army," Southern History Collection, University of North Carolina; J. Harvey Mathes, *Great Commanders: General Forrest* (New York; D. Appleton and Company, 1902), 307; H. C. Connelly, "From Nashville to the Tennessee."

75. Thomas Jordan and J. P. Pryor, *The Campaigns of Lieut.-Gen. N. B. Forrest*, 615; N. B. Forrest, *Official Records*, Series 1, Volume 45, Part 1, 752; James Chalmers, *Official Records*, Series 1, Volume 45, Part 1, 763; N. B. Forrest Special Order, November 22, 1864, Military Departments—Special Orders, Letters, Telegrams, Orders and Circulars Received, Brig. Gen. James R. Chalmers, August 1864-March 1865, RG 109 Chapter Volume 2–294, National Archives; Michael R. Bradley, *Nathan Bedford Forrest's Escort and Staff* (Gretna, LA: Pelican Publishing Co., 2006), 126.

76. W. L. Sanford, *History of Fourteenth Illinois Cavalry*, 239–240; Thomas Jordan and J. P. Pryor, *The Campaigns of Lieut.-Gen. N. B. Forrest*, 615–616; H. C. Connelly, "From Nashville to the Tennessee."

77. I. N. Rainey, "Experiences of I. N. Rainey in the Confederate Army," Southern History Collection, University of North Carolina; Michael Cotton, *The Williamson County Cavalry: A History of Company F, Fourth Tennessee Cavalry Regiment, C.S. A.* (Goodlettsville: D.M. Cotton, 1994), 189.

78. W. L. Sanford, *History of Fourteenth Illinois Cavalry*, 242–243.

79. James Chalmers, *Official Records*, Series 1, Volume 45, Part 1, 763; J. P. Young, *The Seventh Tennessee Cavalry: A History* (Nashville: M. E. Church, South, 1890), 117–118.

80. Michael R. Bradley, *Nathan Bedford Forrest's Escort and Staff*, 126; James Dinkins, *1861 to 1865: Personal Reminiscences*, 224–225.

81. N. B. Forrest, *Official Records*, Series 1, Volume 45, Part 1, 752; W. L. Sanford, *History of Fourteenth Illinois Cavalry*, 241.

82. W. L. Sanford, *History of Fourteenth Illinois Cavalry*, 242–243.

83. W. L. Sanford, *History of Fourteenth Illinois Cavalry*, 243.

84. W. L. Sanford, *History of Fourteenth Illinois Cavalry*, 244–245.

85. John Schofield, *Official Records*, Series 1, Volume 45, Part 1, 341; David Stanley, *Official Records*, Series 1, Volume 45, Part 1, 112.

86. Horace Capron, *Official Records*, Series 1, Volume 45, Part 1, 1005–1006; Joseph Jones, letter to dear companion, November 24, 1864, Collection Number—GLC02739.144, Gilder Lehrman Institute of American History.

87. Datus Coon, *Official Records*, Series 1, Volume 45, Part 1, 586; W. L. Sanford, *History of Fourteenth Illinois Cavalry*, 245–6.

88. W. L. Sanford, *History of Fourteenth Illinois Cavalry*, 246–247; N. B. Forrest, *Official Records*, Series 1, Volume 45, Part 1, 752; I. N. Rainey, "Experiences of I. N. Rainey in the Confederate Army"; N. B. Forrest, Official Records, Series 1, Volume 45, Part 1, 752; Campbell H. Brown, "To Rescue the Confederacy," *Civil War Times Illustrated Magazine*, Volume 3, Number 8 (December 1964), 13–15, 44–48 (In Tennessee State Library Printed Material Collection).

89. W. L. Sanford, *History of Fourteenth Illinois Cavalry*, 246–247.

90. W. L. Sanford, *History of Fourteenth Illinois Cavalry*, 248.

91. W. L. Sanford, *History of Fourteenth Illinois Cavalry*, 249; James Chalmers, *Official Records*, Series 1, Volume 45, Part 1, 763.

92. Harold S. Russell, *Time to Become Barbarian: The Extraordinary Life of General Horace Capron* (Lanham, MD: University Press of America, 2007), 74–75.

93. Theo Cox, *Official Records*, Series 1, Volume 45, Part 1, 1021; John Schofield, *Official Records*, Series 1, Volume 45, Part 1, 1020; Henry Stone, "Repelling Hood's Invasion of Tennessee," In *Battles and Leaders of the Civil War*, Vol. IV (New York: The Century Co., 1888), 440–465.

94. W. L. Sanford, *History of Fourteenth Illinois Cavalry*, 249–250; Jacob Cox, *Official Records*, Series 1, Volume 45, Part 1, 401; Thomas Connelly, *Autumn of Glory: The Army of Tennessee, 1862–1865* (Baton Rouge: Louisiana State University Press, 1971), 491; Edwin Lewis Hayes, Diary and Memoirs, Federal Collection, Box 25, Folder 4, Tennessee State Library and Archives.

95. James Chalmers, *Official Records*, Series 1, Volume 45, Part 1, 763.

96. James Cooper, Diaries and Memoirs, Confederate Collection, Box 12, Folder 11, Tennessee State Library and Archives, p. 50.

97. John Schofield, *Official Records*, Series 1, Volume 45, Part 1, 341; John B. Hood, *Official Records*, Series 1, Volume 45, Part 1, 669–670.

98. J. M. Schofield, *Official Records*, Series 1, Volume 45, Part 1, 1016–1017; George H. Thomas, *Official Records*, Series 1, Volume 45, Part 1, 1015–1016.

99. E. B. Beaumont, *Official Records*, Series 1, Volume 45, Part 1, 1001–1002; James H. Wilson, *Official Records*, Series 1, Volume 45, Part 1, 1027.

100. John Schofield, *Official Records*, Series 1, Volume 45, Part 1, 885, 1000; Richard Johnson, *Official Records*, Series 1, Volume 45, Part 1, 597; Guy E. Logan, ed., *Roster and Record of Iowa*

Soldiers in the War of the Rebellion: 1st-9th Regiments of Cavalry (Des Moines: Emory H. English State Printer, 1910), 859; E. B. Beaumont, *Official Records*, Series 1, Volume 45, Part 1, 927.

101. E. B. Beaumont, *Official Records*, Series 1, Volume 45, Part 1, 1001–1002.

102. George H. Thomas, *Official Records*, Series 1, Volume 45, Part 1, 1001; Edward McCook, *Official Records*, Series 1, Volume 45, Part 1, 988; E. B. Beaumont, *Official Records*, Series 1, Volume 45, Part 1, 987; J. H. Wilson, *Official Records*, Series 1, Volume 45, Part 1, 987.

103. W. H. Morgan, *Official Records*, Series 1, Volume 45, Part 1, 1033; J. M. Schofield, *Official Records*, Series 1, Volume 45, Part 1, 1017–1018; C. C. Washburn, *Official Records*, Series 1, Volume 45, Part 1, 1024.

Chapter Seven

1. A. P. Mason, *Official Records*, Series 1, Volume 45, Part 1, 1245; J. B. Hood, *Official Records*, Series 1, Volume 45, Part 1, 1245.

2. George H. Thomas, *Official Records*, Series 1, Volume 45, Part 1, 1034; David M. Lamborn, "Operational Risk Preparedness: General George H. Thomas and the Franklin and Nashville Campaign," Monograph, School of Advanced Military Studies United States Army Command and General Staff College Fort Leavenworth, Kansas, 2014, p. 35.

3. George H. Thomas, *Official Records*, Series 1, Volume 45, Part 1, 1036.

4. W. H. Sinclair, *Official Records*, Series 1, Volume 45, Part 1, 1038; Thomas Wood, *Official Records*, Series 1, Volume 45, Part 1, 1039; J. A. Campbell, *Official Records*, Series 1, Volume 45, Part 1, 1039; Jacob Cox, *Official Records*, Series 1, Volume 45, Part 1, 1040.

5. J. H. Wilson, *Official Records*, Series 1, Volume 45, Part 1, 1040, 1061–1064, 1092; E. B. Beaumont, *Official Records*, Series 1, Volume 45, Part 1, 1041; J. N. Andrews, *Official Records*, Series 1, Volume 45, Part 1, 1042; Edward Hatch, *Official Records*, Series 1, Volume 45, Part 1, 1064; J. H. Hammond, *Official Records*, Series 1, Volume 45, Part 1, 1046; Alexander Eckel, *History of the Fourth Tennessee Cavalry* (Johnson City, TN: Overmountain Press, 2001), 70; James Alex Baggett, *Homegrown Yankees: Tennessee's Union Cavalry in the Civil War* (Baton Rouge: Louisiana State University, 2009), 293.

6. J. H. Wilson, *Official Records*, Series 1, Volume 45, Part 1, 1037–1038, 1042–1043; E. T. Wells, *Official Records*, Series 1, Volume 45, Part 1, 1043–1045.

7. P. G. T. Beauregard, *Official Records*, Series 1, Volume 45, Part 1, 1251; John V. Du Bois, *Official Records*, Series 1, Volume 45, Part 1, 1058; Southard Hoffman, *Official Records*, Series 1, Volume 45, Part 1, 1057–1058; James Steedman, *Official Records*, Series 1, Volume 45, Part 1, 1050; George H. Thomas, *Official Records*, Series 1, Volume 45, Part 1, 1050; R. S. Granger, *Official Records*, Series 1, Volume 45, Part 1, 1046–1047; B. H. Polk, *Official Records*, Series 1, Volume 45, Part 1, 1048.

8. John V. Du Bois, *Official Records*, Series 1, Volume 45, Part 1, 1057; E. J. Wilson, *Official Records*, Series 1, Volume 45, Part 1, 1057; George Thomas, *Official Records*, Series 1, Volume 45, Part 1, 1056; W. H. Sinclair, *Official Records*, Series 1, Volume 45, Part 1, 1059; John Schofield, *Official Records*, Series 1, Volume 45, Part 1, 1058.

9. James H. Wilson, *Official Records*, Series 1, Volume 45, Part 1, 1059; Jacob Cox, *Official Records*, Series 1, Volume 45, Part 1, 1059–1061; John N. Andrews, *Official Records*, Series 1, Volume 45, Part 1, 1062–1063; Jerry Keenan, *Wilson's Cavalry Corps* (Jefferson, NC: McFarland, 1998), 44.

10. Richard Johnson, *Official Records*, Series 1, Volume 45, Part 1, 1064–1065; W. B. Smith, *Official Records*, Series 1, Volume 45, Part 1, 1068.

11. R. W. Johnson, *Official Records*, Series 1, Volume 45, Part 1, 1066.

12. James H. Wilson, *Official Records*, Series 1, Volume 45, Part 1, 1064–1065; John N. Andrews, *Official Records*, Series 1, Volume 45, Part 1, 1065–1066; Richard Johnson, *Official Records*, Series 1, Volume 45, Part 1, 1065.

13. E. T. Wells, *Official Records*, Series 1, Volume 45, Part 1, 1067–1068, 1097; James Wilson, *Official Records*, Series 1, Volume 45, Part 1, 1096–1097; J. H. Hammond, *Official Records*, Series 1, Volume 45, Part 1, 1069; John Croxton, *Official Records*, Series 1, Volume 45, Part 1, 1069.

14. E. B. Beaumont, *Official Records*, Series 1, Volume 45, Part 1, 1061–1062; Robt. H. Ramsey, *Official Records*, Series 1, Volume 45, Part 1, 1061; George H. Thomas, *Official Records*, Series 1, Volume 45, Part 1, 1070; A. V. Matzdorff, *Official Records*, Series 1, Volume 45, Part 1, 1070; T. B. Springer, F. C. Phillips, D. M. Burns, "A Brief History of the Eleventh Indiana Cavalry," Indiana Historical Society (Indianapolis: Baker and Randolph Printers, 1890), 1–5.

15. J. H. Martin, *Official Records*, Series 1, Volume 45, Part 1, 1249; E. H. Rennolds, Diary—November 25, 1864, E. H. Rennolds Diaries, MS.0170, The Special Collections Library of the University of Tennessee, Knoxville.

16. Douglas John Cater, *As It Was: Reminiscences of a Soldier of the Third Texas Cavalry and the Nineteenth Louisiana Infantry* (Austin: State House Press, 1990), 198.

17. J. H. Wilson, *Official Records*, Series 1, Volume 45, Part 1, 1089–1090, 1096; John Schofield, *Official Records*, Series 1, Volume 45, Part 1, 1086–1087; J. A. Campbell, *Official Records*, Series 1, Volume 45, Part 1, 1086; William M. Wherry, *Official Records*, Series 1, Volume 45, Part 1, 1089.

18. Clinton A. Cilley, *Official Records*, Series 1, Volume 45, Part 1, 1092; J. A. Campbell, *Official*

Records, Series 1, Volume 45, Part 1, 1090; James H. Wilson, *Official Records*, Series 1, Volume 45, Part 1, 1090–1091; Theodore Allen, November 26 entry, 1842–1919, Diary, 1864–1865, Mss. A A431 1, Filson Historical Society, Louisville.

19. R. W. Johnson, *Official Records*, Series 1, Volume 45, Part 1, 597–598, 1093–1094; James H. Wilson, *Official Records*, Series 1, Volume 45, Part 1, 1093–1094; John T. Croxton, *Official Records*, Series 1, Volume 45, Part 1, 1093.

20. Horace Capron, *Official Records*, Series 1, Volume 45, Part 1, 1096–99; E. T. Wells, *Official Records*, Series 1, Volume 45, Part 1, 1098; J. H. Wilson, *Official Records*, Series 1, Volume 45, Part 1, 1095.

21. Israel Garrard, *Official Records*, Series 1, Volume 45, Part 1, 1099; Theodore Allen, November 11 and 27 entries, 1842–1919, Diary.

22. R. H. Milroy, *Official Records*, Series 1, Volume 45, Part 1, 1101.

23. Jno. O. Cravens, *Official Records*, Series 1, Volume 45, Part 1, 1101–1102.

Chapter Eight

1. G. T. Beauregard, *Official Records*, Series 1, Volume 45, Part 1, 1254; Albert Lee, *Official Records*, Series 1, Volume 45, Part 1, 2–3; George Wm. Brent, *Official Records*, Series 1, Volume 45, Part 1, 1242, 1257; Dabney Maury, *Official Records*, Series 1, Volume 45, Part 1, 1244–1246; Edward Canby, *Official Records*, Series 1, Volume 45, Part 1, 777–778; Jason Niles, November 28–29 diary entries, Diary of Jason Niles, Southern Historical Collection, University of North Carolina at Chapel Hill.

2. A. P. Mason, *Official Records*, Series 1, Volume 45, Part 1, 1221; P. G. T. Beauregard, *Official Records*, Series 1, Volume 45, Part 1, 1242–1243.

3. Thomas Robson Hay, "The Cavalry at Spring Hill," *Tennessee Historical Magazine*, Vol. 8, No. 1 (April, 1924), p. 9; Jordan Pryor, *Official Records*, Series 1, Volume 45, Part 1, 619; Winston Groom, *Shrouds of Glory: From Atlanta to Nashville, The Last Great Campaign of the Civil War* (New York: Atlantic Monthly Press, 1995), 133; Thomas Jordan and J. P. Pryor, *The Campaigns of Lieut.-Gen. N. B. Forrest* (New Orleans, Memphis and New York: Blelock & Company, 1868), 619–620; George L. Griscom, *Fighting with Ross' Texas Cavalry Brigade, C.S.A.: The Diary of George L. Griscom, adjutant, 9th Texas Cavalry Regiment*, edited by Homer L. Kerr (Hillsboro, TX: Hill Junior College Press, 1976), 190; N. B. Forrest, *Official Records*, Series 1, Volume 45, Part 1, 752; L. S. Ross, *Official Records*, Series 1, Volume 45, Part 1, 769; James R. Chalmers, *Official Records*, Series 1, Volume 45, Part 1, 764; Wiley Sword, *The Confederacy's Last Hurrah: Spring Hill, Franklin, and Nashville* (Topeka: University of Kansas Press, 1992), 97; W. L. Sanford, "Holding Duck River," *National Tribune*, March 16, 1899; J. P. Young, "Hood's Failure at Spring Hill," *Confederate Veteran*, Vol. XVI, No. 1 (Jan. 1908), p. 25; James Dinkins, *1861 to 1865: Personal Reminiscences*, 228; J. Harvey Mathes, *Great Commanders: General Forrest* (New York; D. Appleton and Company, 1902), 310; Richard R. Hancock, *Hancock's Diary: Or, A History of the Second Tennessee Confederate Cavalry* (Nashville: Brandon Printing Company, 1887), 514.

4. Thomas Robson Hay, "The Cavalry at Spring Hill," pp. 9–10.

5. George Thomas, *Official Records*, Series 1, Volume 45, Part 1, 1104; William C. Davis, *Breckinridge: Statesman, Soldier, Symbol* (Lexington: University Press of Kentucky, 2010), 464–469.

6. Jno. M. Schofield, *Official Records*, Series 1, Volume 45, Part 1, 1105–1107.

7. A. P. Mason, *Official Records*, Series 1, Volume 45, Part 1, 1255; J. B. Hood, *Official Records*, Series 1, Volume 45, Part 1, 1254.

8. George Thomas, *Official Records*, Series 1, Volume 45, Part 1, 1107; J. M. Schofield, *Official Records*, Series 1, Volume 45, Part 1, 1107.

9. George H. Thomas, *Official Records*, Series 1, Volume 45, Part 1, 1108; J. M. Schofield, *Official Records*, Series 1, Volume 45, Part 1, 1108.

10. N. B. Forrest, *Official Records*, Series 1, Volume 45, Part 1, 752; George Thomas, *Official Records*, Series 1, Volume 45, Part 1, 52–53, 95–96.

11. J. H. Wilson, *Official Records*, Series 1, Volume 45, Part 1, 1109.

12. Richard Johnson, *Official Records*, Series 1, Volume 45, Part 1, 1110; James H. Wilson, *Official Records*, Series 1, Volume 45, Part 1, 558; E. T. Wells, *Official Records*, Series 1, Volume 45, Part 1, 1109; Don Treichler, *Cold Steel—Raw Courage: Major John Dance and the 8th Iowa Cavalry* (Charleston, SC: Don Treichler, 2012), 112.

13. James McDonough, *Nashville: The Western Confederacy's Final Gamble* (Knoxville: University of Tennessee Press, 2004), 57–58; John Croxton, *Official Records*, Series 1, Volume 45, Part 1, 1110–1111; J. H. Wilson, *Official Records*, Series 1, Volume 45, Part 1, 1110–1111.

14. Henry M. Hempstead, Journal—November 28, 1864, Bentley Historical Library, University of Michigan; Wm. M. Wherry, *Official Records*, Series 1, Volume 45, Part 1, 1112; James H. Wilson, *Official Records*, Series 1, Volume 45, Part 1, 1111; Thomas Robson Hay, "The Cavalry at Spring Hill," p. 11; John Johnston, Diaries and Memoirs, Confederate Collection, Box 13, Folder 6, Tennessee State Library and Archives, p. 138; J. A. Bigger, Diary, November 29, 1864, J.A. Bigger Diary, April 30, 1862-Mary 12, 1865, Small Manuscripts 76–3 (4 folders), Archives and Special Collections, The University of Mississippi, Oxford, MS.

15. J. P. Metcalf, *Official Records*, Series 1, Volume 45, Part 1, 1120.

16. J. H. Wilson, *Official Records*, Series 1, Volume 45, Part 1, 1119.

17. J. H. Wilson, *Official Records*, Series 1, Volume 45, Part 1, 1120.

18. J. H. Wilson, *Official Records*, Series 1, Volume 45, Part 1, 550; Datus Coon, *Official Records*, Series 1, Volume 45, Part 1, 588.

19. R. W. Johnson, *Official Records*, Series 1, Volume 45, Part 1, 1123; Guy E. Logan, ed., *Roster and Record of Iowa Soldiers in the War of the Rebellion: 1st-9th Regiments of Cavalry* (Des Moines: Emory H. English State Printer, 1910), 858; John Croxton, *Official Records*, Series 1, Volume 45, Part 1, 573; George Thomas, *Official Records*, Series 1, Volume 45, Part 1, 96.

20. R. Thornburg, *Official Records*, Series 1, Volume 45, Part 1, 1121; John Croxton, *Official Records*, Series 1, Volume 45, Part 1, 1121; Richard Johnson, *Official Records*, Series 1, Volume 45, Part 1, 598; Jacob Cox, *The March to the Sea: Franklin and Nashville* (New York: Charles Scribner's Sons, 1882), 69.

21. L. H. Patten, *Official Records*, Series 1, Volume 45, Part 1, 1124–1125; W. L. Sanford, *History of Fourteenth Illinois Cavalry and the Brigades to Which It Belonged* (Chicago: R. R. Donnelley & Sons Company, 1898), 250.

22. R. W. Johnson, *Official Records*, Series 1, Volume 45, Part 1, 1121; W. L. Sanford, *History of Fourteenth Illinois Cavalry*, 256–257; J. H. Wilson, *Official Records*, Series 1, Volume 45, Part 1, 1122.

23. Horace Capron, *Official Records*, Series 1, Volume 45, Part 1, 1122–1124.

24. E. T. Wells, *Official Records*, Series 1, Volume 45, Part 1, 1123; W. L. Sanford, *History of Fourteenth Illinois Cavalry*, 262.

25. W. L. Sanford, *History of Fourteenth Illinois Cavalry*, 263–267; Lawrence Ross, *Official Records*, Series 1, Volume 45, Part 1, 769; R. C. Rankin, "In the Saddle," *National Tribune*, November 18, 1886, p. 1.

26. Ross, *Ibid.*; George L. Griscom, *Fighting with Ross' Texas Cavalry Brigade, C.S. A.*, 190.

27. R. C. Rankin, *History of the Seventh Ohio Volunteer Cavalry* (Ripley, OH: J.C. Newcomb, Printer, 1881), 20.

28. W. L. Sanford, *History of Fourteenth Illinois Cavalry*, 268–270; Theodore Allen, November 28 entry, 1842–1919, Diary, 1864–1865, Mss. A A431 1, Filson Historical Society, Louisville.

29. R. C. Rankin, *History of the Seventh Ohio Volunteer Cavalry*, 20.

30. W. L. Sanford, *History of Fourteenth Illinois Cavalry*, 258–260; "Capron's Cavalry," *National Tribune*, March 29, 1883, p. 1.

31. J. Morris Young, *Official Records*, Series 1, Volume 45, Part 1, 604; Thomas Robson Hay, "The Cavalry at Spring Hill," p. 12; Guy E. Logan, ed., *Roster and Record of Iowa Soldiers in the War of the Rebellion: 1st-9th Regiments of Cavalry* (Des Moines: Emory H. English State Printer, 1910), 860.

32. L. S. Ross, *Official Records*, Series 1, Volume 45, Part 1, 769; George L. Griscom, *Fighting with Ross' Texas Cavalry Brigade, C.S. A.*, 190–191; E. T. Wells, *Official Records*, Series 1, Volume 45, Part 1, 605; J. Morris Young, *Official Records*, Series 1, Volume 45, Part 1, 604; Charles Alley, Diary entry—November 28, 1864, Alley, Charles. Diary, 1861–1865, University of Oklahoma Libraries, Western History Collections; Elisha Mix, Letter to wife, December 12, 1864, Elisha Mix Papers, Bentley Historical Library, University of Michigan; George Garrison, Letter to Sister, December 1864, Grace Edmonds collection, 1860–1932, Alma MMS ID 9920545023802436, Western Michigan State University, Kalamazoo.

33. Nathaniel Cheairs Hughes, Jr., *Brigadier General Tyree H. Bell, CSA* (Knoxville: UT Press, 2004), 196; Richard R. Hancock, *Hancock's Diary: Or, A History of the Second Tennessee Confederate Cavalry* (Nashville: Brandon Printing Company, 1887), 515; Robert Lewis Bliss, Letter to mother, December 1, 1864, Robert Lewis Bliss papers, 1861–1865 (SPR614), Alabama Department of Archives and History.

34. J. M. Schofield, *Official Records*, Series 1, Volume 45, Part 1, 1112; James H. Wilson, *Official Records*, Series 1, Volume 45, Part 1, 1112; W. L. Sanford, "Holding the Duck River," *National Tribune*, March 16, 1899, p. 7.

35. N. B. Forrest, *Official Records*, Series 1, Volume 45, Part 1, 752–753; Thomas Robson Hay, "The Cavalry at Spring Hill," *Tennessee Historical Magazine*, Vol. 8, No. 1 (April, 1924), p. 11; J. G. Deupree, "The Noxubee Squadron of the First Mississippi Cavalry, C. S. A. 1861–1865," In *Publications of the Mississippi Historical Society*, Volume II, Dunbar Rowland, ed. (Jackson, MS: Democrat Printing Co., 1918), 111.

36. Thomas Wood, *Official Records*, Series 1, Volume 45, Part 1, 1115.

37. John Schofield, *Official Records*, Series 1, Volume 45, Part 1, 1116; J. A. Campbell, *Official Records*, Series 1, Volume 45, Part 1, 1117; Jacob Cox, *Official Records*, Series 1, Volume 45, Part 1, 1115–1116.

38. John N. Andrews, *Official Records*, Series 1, Volume 45, Part 1, 1125; J. M. Schofield, *Official Records*, Series 1, Volume 45, Part 1, 1125; J. H. Wilson, *Official Records*, Series 1, Volume 45, Part 1, 1145–1146.

39. Thomas Robson Hay, "The Cavalry at Spring Hill," p. 13; James H. Wilson, *Under the Old Flag*, Volume II (New York and London: D. Appleton And Company, 1912), 40; James H. Wilson *Official Records*, Series 1, Volume 45, Part 1, 1145–1146; Jacob Cox, *The March to the Sea: Franklin and Nashville* (New York: Charles Scribner's Sons, 1882), 73.

40. John K. Shellenberger, *The Battle of Spring Hill, Tennessee, November 29, 1864* (Cleveland: Arthur H. Clark Company, 1913), 17; W. W. Gist, "The Battle of Franklin," *Tennessee Historical Magazine*, Vol. 6, No. 3 (October 1920), p. 217.

41. J. H. Wilson, *Official Records*, Series 1, Volume 45, Part 1, 1113; H. C. Wharton, *Official Records*, Series 1, Volume 45, Part 1, 1113; Thomas Robson Hay, "The Cavalry at Spring Hill,"

pp. 11–12; Edward Longacre, *Grant's Cavalryman: The Life and Wars of General James H. Wilson* (Mechanicsburg, PA: Stackpole Books, 2000), 169.

42. Charles T. Quintard, *Doctor Quintard: Chaplain C. S. A. and Second Bishop of Tennessee*, edited by Arthur Howell Noll (Sewanee, TN: University Press of Sewanee, Tennessee, 1905), 108–109.

Chapter Nine

1. John Schofield, *Official Records*, Series 1, Volume 45, Part 1, 1137–1138; George H. Thomas, *Official Records*, Series 1, Volume 45, Part 1, 1137; Jacob Cox, *The Army in the Civil War: The March to the Sea: Franklin and Nashville*, Vol. 10 (New York: Charles Scribner's Sons, 1885), 235.

2. W. H. Sinclair, *Official Records*, Series 1, Volume 45, Part 1, 1141–1142; Wm. M. Wherry, *Official Records*, Series 1, Volume 45, Part 1, 1141.

3. John Schofield, *Official Records*, Series 1, Volume 45, Part 1, 1141, 1144; J. H. Wilson, *Official Records*, Series 1, Volume 45, Part 1, 1143; Stephen A. Jordan, "Diary of Stephen A. Jordan," In *The Civil War in Maury County, Tennessee*, Jill K. Garrett and Marise P. Lightfoot, ed. (Columbia, TN.: n. p., 1966), 35.

4. J. M. Schofield, *Official Records*, Series 1, Volume 45, Part 1, 1141; James L. McDonough, "West Point Classmates--Eleven Years Later: Some Observations on the Spring Hill-Franklin Campaign," *Tennessee Historical Quarterly*, Vol. 28, No. 2 (Summer 1969), p. 189.

5. J. H. Wilson, *Official Records*, Series 1, Volume 45, Part 1, 1144–1145; John N. Andrews, *Official Records*, Series 1, Volume 45, Part 1, 1144; David Rey Moody, "'The Best Move of My Career': Spring Hill and the Failure of Confederate Command in the West," San Jose: Ph.D. Dissertation, San Jose State University, 1993, p. 236.

6. James H. Wilson, *Under the Old Flag*, Volume II (New York and London: D. Appleton And Company, 1912), 46; Ron Seymour, *The Life of Col. Joseph B. Dorr and his 8th Iowa Cavalry* (self-published eBook, www.8thIowaCav.com, 2012), 145.

7. W. R. Carter, *History of the First Regiment of Tennessee Volunteer Cavalry* (Knoxville: Gaut-Ogden Co., Printers and Binders, 1902), 209; Richard Johnson, *Official Records*, Series 1, Volume 45, Part 1, 598; N. B. Forrest, *Official Records*, Series 1, Volume 45, Part 1, 753; James Chalmers, *Official Records*, Series 1, Volume 45, Part 1, 763–764; Thomas Harrison, Letter to wife, December 13, 1864, Thomas Harrison Letters, Howard County Historical Society, Kokomo; J. A. Bigger, Diary, November 30, 1864, J. A. Bigger Diary, April 30, 1862-Mary 12, 1865, Small Manuscripts 76–3 (4 folders), Archives and Special Collections, The University of Mississippi, Oxford, MS.

8. Richard Johnson, *Official Records*, Series 1, Volume 45, Part 1, 598; Datus Coon, *Official Records*, Series 1, Volume 45, Part 1, 588; Edward Hatch, *Official Records*, Series 1, Volume 45, Part 1, 576; W. R. Carter, *History of the First Regiment of Tennessee Volunteer Cavalry*, 209; Wiley Sword, *The Confederacy's Last Hurrah: Spring Hill, Franklin, and Nashville* (Topeka: University of Kansas Press, 1992), 113; Michael Cotton, *The Williamson County Cavalry: A History of Company F, Fourth Tennessee Cavalry Regiment, C.S. A.* (Goodlettsville: D.M. Cotton, 1994), 191.

9. Thomas Jordan and J. P. Pryor, *The Campaigns of Lieut.-Gen. N. B. Forrest* (New Orleans, Memphis and New York: Blelock & Company, 1868), 621.

10. E. A. Gibson, "The Flag of the Twenty-Eighth Mississippi," *The Clarion* (Jackson, MS), October 1, 1884.

11. Datus Coon, *Official Records*, Series 1, Volume 45, Part 1, 588; Lyman Pierce, *History of the Second Iowa Cavalry* (Burlington, IA: Hawkeye Steam Book and Job Printing Establishment, 1865), 137.

12. N. B. Forrest, *Official Records*, Series 1, Volume 45, Part 1, 753; O. D. Brown, diary, Confederate Collection, Box 6, Folder 4, Tennessee State Library and Archives; George L. Griscom, *Fighting with Ross' Texas Cavalry Brigade, C.S. A.: The Diary of George L. Griscom, adjutant, 9th Texas Cavalry Regiment*, edited by Homer L. Kerr (Hillsboro, TX: Hill Junior College Press, 1976), 191.

13. Thomas Robson Hay, "The Cavalry at Spring Hill," *Tennessee Historical Magazine*, Vol. 8, No. 1 (April, 1924), p. 18.

14. Chas. C. Hoefling, *Official Records*, Series 1, Volume 45, Part 1, 1152; James Alex Baggett, *Homegrown Yankees: Tennessee's Union Cavalry in the Civil War* (Baton Rouge: Louisiana State University, 2009), 295; Myers E. Brown, II, *Tennessee's Union Cavalrymen* (Charleston, Chicago, Portsmouth, San Francisco: Arcadia Publishing, 2008), 107.

15. Thomas Robson Hay, "The Cavalry at Spring Hill," 16; Joseph Fullerton, *Official Records*, Series 1, Volume 45, Part 1, 148; Philip Langer and Robert Pois, *Command Failure in War: Psychology and Leadership* (Bloomington and Indianapolis: Indiana University Press, 2004), 112–113; James Alex Baggett, *Homegrown Yankees: Tennessee's Union Cavalry in the Civil War*, 295; Wiley Sword, *The Confederacy's Last Hurrah*, 118–119; John B. Hood, *Advance and Retreat* (New Orleans: G. T. Beauregard, 1880), 288; Henry M. Hempstead, Journal—November 29, 1864, Bentley Historical Library, University of Michigan; Eric Jacobson and Richard Rupp, *For Cause, For Country: A Study of the Affair at Spring Hill and the Battle of Franklin* (Franklin, Tennessee: O' More Publishing, 2007), 88–89; N. B. Forrest, *Official Records*, Series 1, Volume 45, Part 1, 753; Wilson Burroughs, *Official Records*, Series 1, Volume 45, Part 1, 248.

16. J. P. Young, "Hood's Failure at Spring Hill," *Confederate Veteran*, Vol. XVI, No. 1 (Jan. 1908)p.

30; Emery Pratt, Letter to Friend Frank, December 29, 1864, Collection Number—GLC06728.080, Gilder Lehrman Institute of American History.

17. J. P. Young, "Hood's Failure at Spring Hill," 30–31; James Dinkins, *1861 to 1865: Personal Reminiscences*, 231; John Johnston, Diaries and Memoirs, Confederate Collection, Box 13, Folder 6, Tennessee State Library and Archives, p. 158–159; Emerson Opdycke, *Official Records*, Series 1, Volume 45, Part 1, 239.

18. Nathaniel Cheairs Hughes, Jr., *Brigadier General Tyree H. Bell, CSA* (Knoxville: UT Press, 2004), 198; Tyree Bell, "Autobiography," typeset manuscript, David M. Rubenstein Rare Book & Manuscript Library, Duke University, p. 118; James Dinkins, *1861 to 1865: Personal Reminiscences and Experiences in the Confederate Army* (Cincinnati: Robert Clarke Co., 1897), 229–230; George A. Williams, Letter from Capt. Geo A. Williams to Capt. Irving A. Buck. Dec. 14, 1864, Stones River Technical Information Center, Murfreesboro; Margaret Bell Harrell Farnham, "Brig. Gen. Tyree H. Bell," In *South to West*, Robert Selph Henry Papers, 1861–1971, Ms1989–020, Box-folder 1–3 Bell, n.d., pp. 20–21, Special Collections, Virginia Tech University Libraries; N. B. Forrest, *Official Records*, Series 1, Volume 45, Part 1, 753; Wilson Burroughs, *Official Records*, Series 1, Volume 45, Part 1, 248; Robert J. Fryman, and Laura B. Reidy, *They was There Sure Enough: A Limited Archaeological Assessment of the 1864 Civil War Battle at Spring Hill, Tennessee* (Atlanta: Garrow and Associates, 1995), 8.

19. Henry George, *History of the 3d, 7th, 8th and 12th Kentucky Cavalry, CSA* (Lyndon, KY: Mull-Wathen Historic Press, 1911), 132; John Johnston, Diaries and Memoirs, Confederate Collection, Box 13, Folder 6, Tennessee State Library and Archives, p. 159; David Rey Moody, "The Best Move of My Career," 81; Park Marshall and H. A. Tyler, "Hood's Failure at Spring Hill," *Confederate Veteran*, Volume 22, No. 1 (January 1914), p. 15; Jill Knight Garrett, ed. "Hood's Failure at Spring Hill-Rebuttals," *Historic Maury* Vol. 12, No. 3 (1976), 115.

20. Thomas Connelly, *Autumn of Glory: The Army of Tennessee, 1862–1865* (Baton Rouge: Louisiana State University Press, 1971), 492.

21. N. B. Forrest, *Official Records*, Series 1, Volume 45, Part 1, 753; Nathaniel Cheairs Hughes, Jr., *Brigadier General Tyree H. Bell*, CSA, 199; Tyree Bell, "Autobiography," p. 118; Robert C. Brown, *Official Records*, Series 1, Volume 45, Part 1, 283–284; James R. Knight, *Hood's Tennessee Campaign* (Charleston: The History Press, 2014), 42–43; Jamie Gillum, *Twenty-Five Hours to Tragedy: The Battle of Spring Hill and Operations on November 29, 1864* (n. d.: n.p. 2004), 37.

22. L. S. Ross, *Official Records*, Series 1, Volume 45, Part 1, 769–770; James Alex Baggett, *Homegrown Yankees*, 295.

23. F. M. Postgate, "Battle of Franklin: The Gallant Part Taken by the 175th Ohio," *News-Herald* (Hillsboro, OH), April 25, 1889, p. 1.

24. Thomas Robson Hay, "The Cavalry at Spring Hill," 17–18; John Schofield, *Official Records*, Series 1, Volume 45, Part 1, 1141; Jack H. Lepa, *Breaking the Confederacy: The Georgia and Tennessee Campaigns of 1864* (Jefferson, NC: McFarland, 2005), 178.

25. David Stanley, *Official Records*, Series 1, Volume 45, Part 1, 113; David Stanley, *David Stanley, An American General—The Memoirs of David Sloan Stanley*, Samuel W. Fordyce IV, ed. (Santa Barbara, California: The Narrative Press, 2004), 194.

26. David Stanley, *Official Records*, Series 1, Volume 45, Part 1, 113–114; David S. Stanley, *Address of General Stanley, Reunion of the Society of the Army of the Cumberland: Twenty-sixth Reunion* (Cincinnati: The Robert Clarke Company, 1897), 53; J. A. Campbell, *Official Records*, Series 1, Volume 45, Part 1, 1139–1140.

27. J. P. Young, "Hood's Failure at Spring Hill," 34.

28. *Ibid.*; James Dinkins, *1861 to 1865: Personal Reminiscences*, 232.

29. David Stanley, *Official Records*, Series 1, Volume 45, Part 1, 114.

30. David Stanley, *Official Records*, Series 1, Volume 45, Part 1, 114–115; John Schofield, *Forty-Six Years in the Army* (New York: The Century Company, 1897), 217.

31. Wiley Sword, *The Confederacy's Last Hurrah*, 151; John Schofield, *Official Records*, Series 1, Volume 45, Part 1, 342, David Stanley, *Official Records*, Series 1, Volume 45, Part 1, 114–115.

32. N. B. Forrest, *Official Records*, Series 1, Volume 45, Part 1, 753; Thomas Robson Hay, "The Cavalry at Spring Hill," 20; Thomas Robson Hay, *Hood's Tennessee Campaign* (New York: Press of Morningside Books, 1976), 113–114; Douglas Hale, *The Third Texas Cavalry in the Civil War* (Norman: University of Oklahoma Press, 1993), 259; Eddy Davison and Daniel Fox, *Nathan Bedford Forrest: In Search of the Enigma* (Gretna, LA: Pelican Publishing Co., 2007), 357; Henry M. Field, *Bright Skies and Dark Shadows* (New York: Charles Scribner's Sons, 1890), 216; Terry L. Jones, *Campbell Brown's Civil War: With Ewell and the Army of Northern Virginia* (Baton Rouge: Louisiana State University Press, 2001), 166.

33. Stanley F. Horn, *The Army of Tennessee* (Norman: University of Oklahoma Press, 1952), 393; Benjamin Cheatham, "The Lost Opportunity at Spring Hill, Tenn. General Cheatham's Reply to General Hood," *Southern Historical Society Papers*, Vol. 9, No. 10–12 (October-December 1881), p. 541; Bruce H. Stewart, *Invisible Hero: Patrick R. Cleburne* (Macon: Mercer University Press, 2009), 325.

34. L. S. Ross, *Official Records*, Series 1, Volume 45, Part 1, 769–770; John Schofield, *Official Records*, Series 1, Volume 45, Part 1, 342; J. Har-

vey Mathes, *Great Commanders: General Forrest* (New York; D. Appleton and Company, 1902), 311; Thomas Jordan and J. P. Pryor, *The Campaigns of Lieut.-Gen. N. B. Forrest*, 624; Benjamin Smith, *Private Smith's Journal*, Clyde C. Walton, ed. (Chicago: R. R. Donnelley & Sons Company, 1963), 186; P. B. Simmons, "The Correction Cheerfully Made," *Confederate Veteran*, Vol. 1, No. 6 (June 1893), 163; Christopher Losson, *Tennessee's Forgotten Warriors* (Knoxville: University of Tennessee Press, 1989), 208–209; George L. Griscom, *Fighting with Ross' Texas Cavalry Brigade, C.S. A.*, 191; James R. Knight, *Hood's Tennessee Campaign*, 51; B. F. Thompson, *History of the 112th Regiment of Illinois Volunteer Infantry* (Toulon, IL: Stark County News Office, 1885), 265.

35. Diary, November 30, 1864, J.A. Bigger Diary, April 30, 1862-May 12, 1865, Small Manuscripts 76-3 (4 folders), Archives and Special Collections, The University of Mississippi, Oxford, MS.

36. Samuel G. French, *Two Wars: An Autobiography of General Samuel G. French* (Nashville: Confederate Veteran, 1901), 291; Thomas John Brown, "John Bell Hood: Extracting Truth from History," (2011), Master's Thesis, Paper 4040, San Jose State University, p. 97; J. D. Porter, ed., *Confederate Military History*, Vol. VIII (Atlanta: Confederate Publishing Co., 1899), 158; David Rey Moody, "The Best Move of My Career,"131; G. Campbell Brown, Manuscript, Hood's Campaign, Middle Tenn., Transcript of Conversation, 1868, May 5, 1868, Box 1, Folder 23, Robert Selph Henry Papers, 1861–1971, Ms1989-020, Special Collections, Virginia Tech, Blacksburg, VA.; Stanley F. Horn, *The Army of Tennessee*, 393; W. O. Dodd, "Reminiscences of Hood's Tennessee Campaign," *Southern Historical Society Papers*, Vol. 9, No. 10–12 (October-December 1881), 521.

37. David Rey Moody, "The Best Move of My Career," 88–89; Ellison Capers, *Official Records*, Series 1, Volume 45, Part 1, 737; Tyree Bell, "Autobiography," p. 119.

38. David Stanley, *David Stanley, An American General*, 199; Thomas Robson Hay, *Hood's Tennessee Campaign*, 96.

39. James McDonough, *Nashville: The Western Confederacy's Final Gamble* (Knoxville: University of Tennessee Press, 2004), 75; John Johnston, Diaries and Memoirs, Confederate Collection, Box 13, Folder 6, Tennessee State Library and Archives, p. 139.

40. J. H. Wilson, *Official Records*, Series 1, Volume 45, Part 1, 1146; Chris Perello, *The Quest for Annihilation: The Role & Mechanics of Battle in the American Civil War* (Bakersfield, CA: Strategy & Tactics Press, 2009), 253.

41. J. H. Hammond, *Official Records*, Series 1, Volume 45, Part 1, 1150–1151; Alexander Eckel, *Alexander Eckel, History of the Fourth Tennessee Cavalry* (Johnson City, TN: Overmountain Press, 2001), 71.

42. E. B. Beaumont, *Official Records*, Series 1, Volume 45, Part 1, 1151–1152; John N. Andrews, *Official Records*, Series 1, Volume 45, Part 1, 1151.

43. J. H. Wilson, *Official Records*, Series 1, Volume 45, Part 1, 1145; Edward Hatch, *Official Records*, Series 1, Volume 45, Part 1, 1149.

44. James H. Wilson, *Official Records*, Series 1, Volume 45, Part 1, 550; John E. Fisher, *They Rode with Forrest and Wheeler* (Jefferson, NC: McFarland, 1995), 152–153.

45. N. B. Forrest, *Official Records*, Series 1, Volume 45, Part 1, 753; Thomas Robson Hay, "The Cavalry at Spring Hill," 18–19; Nathaniel Cheairs Hughes, Jr., *Brigadier General Tyree H. Bell, CSA*, 197; Thomas Budd Van Horne, *The Life of Major-General George H. Thomas* (New York: Charles Scribner's Sons, 1882), 287; James H. Wilson, *Under the Old Flag*, Volume II (New York and London: D. Appleton And Company, 1912), 45.

46. Edward Longacre, *From Union Stars to Top Hat: A Biography of the Extraordinary General James Harrison Wilson* (Harrisburg, PA: Stackpole Books, 1972), 169; Daniel Harris Reynolds, Diary entry, November 29, 1864, Daniel Harris Reynolds Papers (MS R32), University of Arkansas, Special Collections.

47. John A. Wyeth, *Life of Lieutenant-General Nathan Bedford Forrest* (New York and London: Harper & Brothers, Publishers, 1900), 541.

48. Wiley Sword, *The Confederacy's Last Hurrah*, 167.

49. J. M. Schofield, *Official Records*, Series 1, Volume 45, Part 1, 1171.

50. Wiley Sword, *The Confederacy's Last Hurrah*, 167.

51. David Stanley, *David Stanley, An American General*, 201.

52. Joseph Conrad, *Official Records*, Series 1, Volume 45, Part 1, 271; Wiley Sword, *The Confederacy's Last Hurrah*, 189.

53. David Stanley, *Official Records*, Series 1, Volume 45, Part 1, 117; L. G. Bennett and William M. Haigh, *History of the Thirty-Sixth Regiment Illinois Volunteers, during the War of the Rebellion* (Aurora, Illinois: Knickerbocker & Hodder, Printers and Binders, 1876), 652; Joseph Conrad, *Official Records*, Series 1, Volume 45, Part 1, 271.

54. Stanley Horn, *The Decisive Battle of Nashville* (Knoxville: University of Tennessee Press, 1986), 32; Thomas Taylor, Letter to Sister, December 15, 1864, Letter to Sister, Civil War-era documents, 1860–1865, Taylor, Thomas, letters (typescripts), Box 6, Folder 47, Emory University.

55. J. M. Schofield, *Official Records*, Series 1, Volume 45, Part 1, 1169.

56. Geo. H. Thomas, *Official Records*, Series 1, Volume 45, Part 1, 1170–1171; John Schofield, *Official Records*, Series 1, Volume 45, Part 1, 1170.

57. J. A. Campbell, *Official Records*, Series 1, Volume 45, Part 1, 1173.

58. James H. Wilson, *Official Records*, Series 1, Volume 45, Part 1, 1183; J. A. Campbell, *Official Records*, Series 1, Volume 45, Part 1, 1173; John A.

Davis, *Official Records*, Series 1, Volume 45, Part 1, 1180; Marshall P. Thatcher, *A Hundred Battles in the West: The Second Michigan Cavalry* (Detroit: L. F. Kilroy, Printer, 1884), 202–203.

59. J. M. Schofield, *Official Records*, Series 1, Volume 45, Part 1, 1177; J. H. Wilson, *Official Records*, Series 1, Volume 45, Part 1, 1177; Thomas Robson Hay, *Hood's Tennessee Campaign*, 120; Eddy Davison and Daniel Fox, *Nathan Bedford Forrest: In Search of the Enigma* (Gretna, LA: Pelican Publishing Co., 2007), 359; Eric Jacobson and Richard Rupp, *For Cause, For Country*, 237–238.

60. "At Sunset Gen. Forrest Called on Mrs. Peters at Spring Hill," *Nashville Tennessean*, December 6, 1964; John M. Copley, *A Sketch of the Battle of Franklin, Tenn.; with Reminiscences of Camp Douglas* (Austin, TX: Eugene Von Boeckmann, Printer, 1893), 34; James Adams Tillman, *A Palmetto Boy: Civil War-Era Diaries and Letters of James Adams Tillman* (Columbia: University of South Carolina Press 2010), 125.

61. James Dinkins, *1861 to 1865: Personal Reminiscences and Experiences in the Confederate Army* (Cincinnati: Robert Clarke Co., 1897), 234–235; N. B. Forrest, *Official Records*, Series 1, Volume 45, Part 1, 753–754; A. P. Stewart, *Official Records*, Series 1, Volume 45, Part 1, 708; John B. Hood, *Advance and Retreat* (New Orleans: G. T. Beauregard, 1880), 293; James R. Knight, *Hood's Tennessee Campaign*, 64; Gus F. Smith, "The Battle of Franklin," In *War Papers*, MOLLUS, MI, Vol. 2 (Detroit: James H. Stone & Co., 1898), 254; Eric Jacobson and Richard Rupp, *For Cause, For Country*, 190.

62. Thomas Robson Hay, *Hood's Tennessee Campaign*, 125; James Chalmers, *Official Records*, Series 1, Volume 45, Part 1, 764; Winston Groom, *Shrouds of Glory: From Atlanta to Nashville, The Last Great Campaign of the Civil War* (New York: Atlantic Monthly Press, 1995), 205; James Lee McDonough and Thomas L. Connelly, *Five Tragic Hours*, 143; Jacob Cox, *Battle Of Franklin*, 83–84; James Dinkins, *1861 to 1865: Personal Reminiscences*, 235; Jacob Cox, *Battle of Franklin* (New York: Charles Scribner's Sons, 1897), 139–140; Sims Crownover, "The Battle of Franklin," *Tennessee Historical Quarterly* Vol. 14, No. 4 (December, 1955), pp. 291–322; James Dinkins, "The Battle of Spring Hill, Tennessee: Personal Recollections and Experiences in the Confederate Army," *Historic Maury*, 31:3 (1995), p. 111.

63. James Brownlow, Jr., "Autobiography of James Polk Brownlow, Jr.," 1994, From the private collection of John A. Hastings of Austin, Texas; James Chalmers, *Official Records*, Series I, Number 45, Part 1, 764.

64. N. B. Forrest, *Official Records*, Series 1, Volume 45, Part 1, 753–754; A. P. Stewart, *Official Records*, Series 1, Volume 45, Part 1, 708; John B. Hood, *Advance and Retreat* (New Orleans: G. T. Beauregard, 1880), 293; Ridley Wills, "The Military Experiences of William Hicks 'Red' Jackson, 1852–1865," *Tennessee Historical Quarterly* Vol. 70, No. 3 (Fall 2011), p. 222.

65. Marshall P. Thatcher, *A Hundred Battles in the West*, 202–203, 305; John Croxton, *Official Records*, Series 1, Volume 45, Part 1, 573; W. R. Carter, *History of the First Regiment of Tennessee Volunteer Cavalry* (Knoxville: Gaut-Ogden Co., Printers and Binders, 1902), 214–215.

66. Lucy Henderson Horton, "Reminiscences of the War Between the States," In *Williamson County and the Civil War*, Rick Warwick, compiler (Franklin: Williamson County Historical Society, 2008), 71; Marshall P. Thatcher, *A Hundred Battles in the West*, 203–204, 307; Henry M. Hempstead, Journal—November 30, 184, Bentley Historical Library, University of Michigan.

67. John Croxton, *Official Records*, Series 1, Volume 45, Part 1, 573; W. R. Carter, *History of the First Regiment of Tennessee Volunteer Cavalry*, 1902), 214–215; David R. Logsdon, *Eyewitnesses at the Battle of Franklin* (Nashville: published by author, 1988), 6.

68. Marshall P. Thatcher, *A Hundred Battles in the West*, 204–206; A. P. Stewart, *Official Records*, Series 1, Volume 45, Part 1, 708; Henry M. Hempstead, "Dr. Cannon's Story: Indorses Cannon's Statements," *National Tribune*, February 24, 1864, p. 10; Henry M. Hempstead, Journal—November 30, 1864, Bentley Historical Library, University of Michigan.

69. Henry George, *History of the 3d, 7th, 8th and 12th Kentucky Cavalry, CSA* (Lyndon, KY: Mull-Wathen Historic Press, 1911), 132–133; Nathaniel Cheairs Hughes, Jr., *Brigadier General Tyree H. Bell, CSA*, 202; Tyree Bell, "Autobiography," p. 121.

70. J. H. Wilson, *Official Records*, Series 1, Volume 45, Part 1, 1178–1179; J. H. Hammond, *Official Records*, Series 1, Volume 45, Part 1, 1183; J. A. Campbell, *Official Records*, Series 1, Volume 45, Part 1, 1178.

71. R. W. Johnson, *Official Records*, Series 1, Volume 45, Part 1, 1181; J. H. Wilson, *Official Records*, Series 1, Volume 45, Part 1, 1181; George Monlux, "To My Comrades Co. I, 8th Iowa Cavalry," Personal narrative, State Historical Library & Archives, p. 54; Theodore Allen, November 30 entry, 1842–1919, Diary, 1864–1865, Mss. A A431 1, Filson Historical Society, Louisville; Ron Seymour, *The Life of Col. Joseph B. Dorr and his 8th Iowa Cavalry* (self-published eBook, www.8thIowaCav.com, 2012), 147.

72. John Croxton, *Official Records*, Series 1, Volume 45, Part 1, 573; W. R. Carter, *History of the First Regiment of Tennessee Volunteer Cavalry*, 214–215; George Monlux, "To My Comrades Co. I, 8th Iowa Cavalry," p. 55.

73. Marshall P. Thatcher, *A Hundred Battles in the West*, 210–211.

74. Edward Hatch, *Official Records*, Series 1, Volume 45, Part 1, 576; Eugene Bruce Read Diary, Volume 4, November 27, 1864, Special Collections,

Newberry Library; Datus Coon, *Official Records*, Series 1, Volume 45, Part 1, 589.

75. N. B. Forrest, *Official Records*, Series 1, Volume 45, Part 1, 753–754; Albert Fout, *The Darkest Days of the Civil War, 1864 and 1865* (Bailey's Harbor, WI: Philip Graupner, 2014), 112–113; Jacob Cox, *Battle of Franklin*, 175.

76. James Lee McDonough and Thomas L. Connelly, *Five Tragic Hours: The Battle of Franklin* (Knoxville: University of Tennessee Press, 1983), 154; John Croxton, *Official Records*, Series 1, Volume 45, Part 1, 573; Robert Selph Henry, *Forrest: First with the Most* (n.p.: Pickle Partners Publishing, 2015), 441–444; Nathaniel Cheairs Hughes, Jr., *Brigadier General Tyree H. Bell, CSA*, 202; Tennessee State Library, Map of the Battle of Franklin, Printed Materials Collections, Box 2, maps folder.

77. Edward Hatch, *Official Records*, Series 1, Volume 45, Part 1, 576.

78. George L. Griscom, *Fighting with Ross' Texas Cavalry Brigade, C.S.A.: The Diary of George L. Griscom, adjutant, 9th Texas Cavalry Regiment*, edited by Homer L. Kerr (Hillsboro, TX: Hill Junior College Press, 1976), 192; Sidney Smith Johnson, *Texans Who Wore the Gray*, Volume 1 (Tyler: TX: Author, 1907), 230; Martha L. Crabb, *All Afire to Fight: The Untold Tale of the Civil War's Ninth Texas Cavalry* (New York: Avon Books, 2000), 268; Stephen S. Kirk, *Line of Battle: Sul Ross' Brigade* (Harrisonville, MO: Burnt District Publishing, 2012), 187.

79. L. S. Ross, *Official Records*, Series 1, Volume 45, Part 1, 771; Edward Hatch, *Official Records*, Series 1, Volume 45, Part 1, 576; Elizabeth Clarke, "Narrative," Elizabeth Clarke Papers (Box 2J143), page 110, University of Texas at Austin, Briscoe Center for American History; Douglas Hale, *The Third Texas Cavalry in the Civil War*, 260; R. W. Surby, "A 64-Days March," *National Tribune*, June 5, 1884, p. 3; Sul Ross, Nashville Campaign Report, William Hicks Jackson Papers, RG 109, National Archives Record Administration.

80. Birney McClean, "Sabers to the Front," *National Tribune*, October 8, 1896, p. 2; D. B. Spencer, "At Franklin and Afterwards," *National Tribune*, January 27, 1898, p. 7.

81. A. W. Sparks, *The War Between the States: As I Saw It* (Tyler: Lee & Burnett, Printers, 1901), 283–284.

82. William Mason Worthington, Letter to "Sam," December 11, 1864, Worthington Family Papers, MS Z/0658.000/S, Box 1, Mississippi Department of History and Archives.

83. J. P. Strange, *Official Records*, Series 1, Volume 45, Part 1, 1260.

84. Samuel Watkins, *"Co. Aytch"* (Chattanooga, TN., Times Printing Company, 1900), 208.

85. Richard Johnson, *Official Records*, Series 1, Volume 45, Part 1, 598; J. N. Andrews, *Official Records*, Series 1, Volume 45, Part 1, 1180; G. M. L. Johnson, *Official Records*, Series 1, Volume 45, Part 1, 1181; J. H. Wilson, *Official Records*, Series 1, Volume 45, Part 1, 1184–1185; J. H. Hammond, *Official Records*, Series 1, Volume 45, Part 1, 1184; James Goodwin, "The Fourth Tennessee Cavalry," Box F25, folder 3, Federal Collection, Tennessee State Library and Archives, 38.

86. John N. Andrews, *Official Records*, Series 1, Volume 45, Part 1, 1179; Wm. M. Wherry, *Official Records*, Series 1, Volume 45, Part 1, 1179; James H. Wilson, *Official Records*, Series 1, Volume 45, Part 1, 550.

87. Nathaniel Cheairs Hughes, Jr., *Brigadier General Tyree H. Bell, CSA*, 202; John N. Andrews, *Official Records*, Series 1, Volume 45, Part 1, 1180.

88. Thomas Robson Hay, *Hood's Tennessee Campaign*, 126–127; Donald M. Lynn, "Wilson's Cavalry at Nashville," *Civil War History*, Volume 1, No. 2 (June 1955), p. 147.

89. John Schofield, *Official Records*, Series 1, Volume 45, Part 1, 343.

90. James H. Wilson, *Under the Old Flag*, Volume II (New York and London: D. Appleton And Company, 1912), 52.

91. Thomas Robson Hay, *Hood's Tennessee Campaign*, 130; James H. Wilson, "The Union Cavalry in the Hood Campaign," In *Battles and Leaders of the Civil War*, Vol. IV (New York: The Century Co., 1888), 466.

92. John Allan Wyeth, *That Devil Forrest: The Life of General Nathan Bedford Forrest* (Baton Rouge: Louisiana State University Press, 1989), 480; Thomas John Brown, "John Bell Hood: Extracting Truth from History," pp. 104–106.

93. Thomas Robson Hay, *Hood's Tennessee Campaign*, 146; O. A. Abbott, "The Last Battle of Nashville" In *Civil War Sketches and Incidents* (Omaha: Nebraska, Military Order of the Loyal Legion of the United States, 1902), 237.

94. Robt. H. Ramsey, *Official Records*, Series 1, Volume 45, Part 1, 1167–1168; J. M. Schofield, *Official Records*, Series 1, Volume 45, Part 1, 1167; J. C. Van Duzer, *Official Records*, Series 1, Volume 45, Part 1, 1168.

95. George H. Thomas, *Official Records*, Series 1, Volume 45, Part 1, 1167.

96. A. P. Mason, *Official Records*, Series 1, Volume 45, Part 2, 628–629; E. H. Rennolds, December 1, 1864, E. H. Rennolds Diaries, MS.0170, The Special Collections Library of the University of Tennessee, Knoxville; Robert Lewis Bliss, Letter to mother, December 1, 1864, Robert Lewis Bliss papers, 1861–1865 (SPR614), Alabama Department of Archives and History; John B. Hood, *Advance and Retreat*, 297; Mamie Yeary, *Reminiscences of the Boys in Gray: 1861–1865* (Dallas: Publishing House M. E. Church, South, 1912), 66; Alice Nichol, "What an Old Lady Remembers about the Battle of Franklin," Confederate Collection, Sketches, Box 4, Folder 1, Tennessee State Library and Archives; James I. Robertson, Jr., "The Human Battle of Franklin," *Tennessee Historical Quarterly* Vol. 24, No. 1 (Spring 1965), p. 24; Benjamin R. Harris, "Diary," In *The Civil War in Maury County*,

Tennessee, Jill K. Garrett and Marise P. Lightfoot, ed. (Columbia, TN.: n. p., 1966), 165; *Chicago Tribune*, "The Battle Begun Below Nashville," December 1, 1864, p. 1, col. 3; *Abingdon Virginian*, "The Fight Near Franklin," December 9, 1864, p. 2, col. 1.

97. R. H. Milroy, September 16, 1864 Letter, R. H. Milroy Letters, Jasper County Public Library, Rensselaer, Indiana; Michael R. Bradley, *With Blood and Fire: Life Behind Union Lines in Middle Tennessee, 1863–1865* (Shippensburg, PA: Burd Street Press, 2003), 121.

98. Geo. H. Thomas, *Official Records*, Series 1, Volume 45, Part 1, 1153; Lovell H. Rousseau, *Official Records*, Series 1, Volume 45, Part 1, 1153; Mary Jane Chadick, *Incidents Of The War: The Civil War Journal of Mary Jane Chadick*, Nancy Rohr, ed. (Huntsville: SilverThreads Publishing, 2005), 227.

Chapter Ten

1. George H. Thomas, *Official Records*, Series 1, Volume 45, Part 2, 3; Benjamin Nourse, Diary, November 29, 1864, David M. Rubenstein Rare Book & Manuscript Library, Duke University; Milton Barnes, Letter to wife—December 1, 1864, Milton Barnes papers, Collection #C0065, Box 2 Folder 32, Special Collections Research Center, George Mason University Libraries.

2. J. B. Hood, *Official Records*, Series 1, Volume 45, Part 2, 643–44, 650; A. P. Mason, *Official Records*, Series 1, Volume 45, Part 2, 630; J. C. Van Duzer, *Official Records*, Series 1, Volume 45, Part 2, 4; Alex Hall, Letter to mother—December 3, 1864, Alexander K. Hall family papers, 1839–1917 (LPR58), Alabama Department of Archives and History.

3. A. P. Mason, *Official Records*, Series 1, Volume 45, Part 2, 652, 655; John B. Hood, *Official Records*, Series 1, Volume 45, Part 2, 657; P. G. T. Beauregard, *Official Records*, Series 1, Volume 45, Part 2, 636; James O. Walton letter to wife, November 29, 1864; S1355, Rare Books and Manuscripts, Indiana State Library, Indianapolis; Letter to wife, November 29, 1864, Walton, James Orvin, 1843-Letters, 1864–1865, 1 vol., Mss. A W239, Filson Historical Society.

4. Wm. M. Wherry, *Official Records*, Series 1, Volume 45, Part 2, 5; J. H. Wilson, *Official Records*, Series 1, Volume 45, Part 2, 6; John N. Andrews, *Official Records*, Series 1, Volume 45, Part 2, 5.

5. James Dinkins, *1861 to 1865: Personal Reminiscences and Experiences in the Confederate Army* (Cincinnati: Robert Clarke Co., 1897), 238–239.

6. G. M. L. Johnson, *Official Records*, Series 1, Volume 45, Part 2, 10–11; J. Morris Young, *Official Records*, Series 1, Volume 45, Part 2, 10; N. B. Forrest, *Official Records*, Series 1, Volume 45, Part 1, 754; Frederick H. Dyer, *A Compendium of the War of the Rebellion*, Part 2 (Des Moines: The Dyer Publishing Company, 1908), 875; William Black, Letter to friends—December 14, 1864, Civil War Letters of William Black, Vigo County Public Library, Terre Haute, Indiana; Nathaniel Cheairs Hughes, Jr., *Brigadier General Tyree H. Bell, CSA* (Knoxville: UT Press, 2004), 304; Alexis Cope, *The Fifteenth Ohio Volunteers and Its Campaigns: 1861–1865* (Columbus, OH: By author, 1916), 621; J. G. Deupree, "The Noxubee Squadron of the First Mississippi Cavalry, C. S. A. 1861–1865," In *Publications of the Mississippi Historical Society*, Volume II, Dunbar Rowland, ed. (Jackson, MS: Democrat Printing Co., 1918), 111; T. B. Springer, F. C. Phillips, D. M. Burns, "A Brief History of the Eleventh Indiana Cavalry," pamphlet, Indiana Historical Society, Indianapolis. David Stanley, *Official Records*, Series 1, Volume 45, Part 1, 113.

7. J. H. Wilson, *Official Records*, Series 1, Volume 45, Part 2, 6–7; J. H. Wilson, *Official Records*, Series 1, Volume 45, Part 1, 550; W. R. Carter, *History of the First Regiment of Tennessee Volunteer Cavalry* (Knoxville: Gaut-Ogden Co., Printers and Binders, 1902), 221; James Goodwin, "The Fourth Tennessee Cavalry," Box F25, folder 3, Federal Collection, Tennessee State Library and Archives. 38.

8. R. H. Crowder, Letter, December 4, 1864, R. H. Crowder papers, 1859–1908, 0208, Box 1, Folder 12, Indiana Historical Society; Addison McKee, Casualty report, December 5, 1864, Crowder-Bose Papers, M0671, Box 1, Folder 7, Indiana Historical Society.

9. D. W. Comstock, *Ninth Cavalry: One Hundred and Twenty-first Regiment Indiana Volunteers* (Richmond, IN.: Published By J. M. Coe, 1890), 28–30; Richard Carlton Fulcher, *Civil War Battles and Skirmishes in Williamson County, Tennessee* (Brentwood, TN: Richard Carlton Fulcher, 2000), 17; Stephen A. Jordan, "Diary of Stephen A. Jordan," In *The Civil War in Maury County*, Tennessee, Jill K. Garrett and Marise P. Lightfoot, ed. (Columbia, TN.: n. p., 1966), 37.

10. James Chalmers, *Official Records*, Series 1, Volume 45, Part 1, 764; N. B. Forrest, *Official Records*, Series 1, Volume 45, Part 1, 754; Richard R. Hancock, *Hancock's Diary: Or, A History of the Second Tennessee Confederate Cavalry* (Nashville: Brandon Printing Company, 1887), 522; Martha L. Crabb, *All Afire to Fight: The Untold Tale of the Civil War's Ninth Texas Cavalry* (New York: Avon Books, 2000), 271.

11. J. H. Wilson, *Official Records*, Series 1, Volume 45, Part 2, 6–7; James Chalmers, *Official Records*, Series 1, Volume 45, Part 1, 551–552; John Andrews, *Official Records*, Series 1, Volume 45, Part 2, 6–7.

12. John N. Andrews, *Official Records*, Series 1, Volume 45, Part 2, 8; Edwin Bearss, "The History of Fortress Rosecrans," United States Department of Interior, Research Report, Stones River National Military Park, 1960.

13. E. M. Stanton, *Official Records*, Series 1, Volume 45, Part 2, 15–16.

14. U.S. Grant, *Official Records*, Series 1, Vol-

ume 45, Part 2, 16–17; Edwin Stanton, *Official Records*, Series 1, Volume 45, Part 2, 18.

15. George H. Thomas, *Official Records*, Series 1, Volume 45, Part 2, 17–18.

16. J. P. Strange, *Official Records*, Series 1, Volume 45, Part 2, 641; A P. Mason, *Official Records*, Series 1, Volume 45, Part 2, 641.

17. N. B. Forrest, *Official Records*, Series 1, Volume 45, Part 1, 754; Edwin Bearss, "The History of Fortress Rosecrans"; A. P. Mason, December 2, 1984, dispatch to A. P. Stewart from Army of Tennessee Headquarters, RG 109, National Archives Record Administration.

18. Nathaniel Cheairs Hughes, Jr., *Brigadier General Tyree H. Bell, CSA* (Knoxville: University of Tennessee Press, 2004), 206.

19. J. H. Wilson, *Official Records*, Series 1, Volume 45, Part 2, 23; E. B. Beaumont, *Official Records*, Series 1, Volume 45, Part 2, 24; John T. Croxton, *Official Records*, Series 1, Volume 45, Part 2, 24.

20. James Chalmers, *Official Records*, Series 1, Volume 45, Part 2, 764; Benjamin Franklin Cooling, *To the Battles of Franklin and Nashville and Beyond* (Knoxville, University of Tennessee Press, 2011), 311; Marion Elias Lazenby, *The History of Methodism in Alabama and West North Florida* (Nashville: North Alabama Conference and Alabama-West Florida Conference, 1960), 459; John Morton, *The Artillery of Nathan Bedford Forrest's Cavalry* (Nashville and Dallas: Publishing House of the M. E. Church, South Smith & Lamar, Agents, 1909), 279.

21. LeRoy Fitch, *Official Records of the Union and Confederate Navies in the War of the Rebellion*, Series I, Volume 26, 641–643; Israel Garrard, *Official Records*, Series 1, Volume 45, Part 2, 37.

22. David R. Logsdon, *Eyewitnesses at the Battle of Nashville* (Nashville: Kettle Mill Press, 2004), 12.

23. R. W. Johnson, *Official Records*, Series 1, Volume 45, Part 2, 48–49; LeRoy Fitch, *Official Records*, Series 1, Volume 45, Part 2, 44.

24. James Chalmers, *Official Records*, Series 1, Volume 45, Part 1, 764; A. P. Mason, *Official Records*, Series 1, Volume 45, Part 2, 648.

25. LeRoy Fitch, *Official Records of the Union and Confederate Navies in the War of the Rebellion*, Series I, Volume 26, 649.

26. LeRoy Fitch, *Official Records of the Union and Confederate Navies in the War of the Rebellion*, Series I, Volume 26, 649–650; Michael R. Bradly, *Forrest's Fighting Preacher: David Campbell Kelley of Tennessee* (Charleston: The History Press, 2011), 85.

27. James Chalmers, *Official Records*, Series 1, Volume 45, Part 1, 764; LeRoy Fitch, *Official Records of the Union and Confederate Navies in the War of the Rebellion*, Series I, Volume 26, 650.

28. J. H. Wilson, *Official Records*, Series 1, Volume 45, Part 2, 36; E. B. Beaumont, *Official Records*, Series 1, Volume 45, Part 2, 35; A. J. Alexander, *Official Records*, Series 1, Volume 45, Part 2, 35; Edson Washburn diary, December 3, 1864, Edson Washburn diaries, 1863–1865, P2244, Minnesota Historical Society, St. Paul.

29. J. H. Hammond, *Official Records*, Series 1, Volume 45, Part 2, 37–38, 49, 60, 63; Israel Garrard, *Official Records*, Series 1, Volume 45, Part 2, 37; Robert H. Ramsey, *Official Records*, Series 1, Volume 45, Part 2, 60.

30. G. T. Beauregard, *Official Records*, Series 1, Volume 45, Part 2, 636–638; J. B. Hood, *Official Records*, Series 1, Volume 45, Part 2, 653.

31. Charles T. Quintard, *Doctor Quintard: Chaplain C. S. A. and Second Bishop of Tennessee*, edited by Arthur Howell Noll (Sewanee, TN: University Press of Sewanee, Tennessee, 1905), 119; *Cleveland Morning Leader*, "From Nashville," December 6, 1864, p. 1, col. 7.

32. U.S. Grant, *Official Records*, Series 1, Volume 45, Part 2, 55; H. W. Halleck, *Official Records*, Series 1, Volume 45, Part 2, 29, 54–55; George Thomas, *Official Records*, Series 1, Volume 45, Part 2, 29, 71.

33. H. W. Halleck, *Official Records*, Series 1, Volume 45, Part 2, 82; George H. Thomas, *Official Records*, Series 1, Volume 45, Part 2, 55; Edwin M. Stanton, *Official Records*, Series 1, Volume 45, Part 2, 84; William Lamers, *The Edge of Glory: A Biography of General William S. Rosecrans, U.S. A.* (New York: Harcourt, Brace & World, Inc.,1961), 437–438; W. S. Rosecrans, *Official Records*, Series 1, Volume 45, Part 2, 56; Francis Audsley, Letter to wife, December 7, 1864, Francis Fairbank (1835–1922) and Harriet Elizabeth Audsley (1840–1924), Papers, 1862–1912, n.d. (C2374), The State Historical Society of Missouri; Alonzo Aulsbro, Letter to parents, December 6, 1864, Martin Barnhart collection, 1861–1920, Alma MMS ID 9920181483802436, Western Michigan State University, Kalamazoo.

34. Henry E. Noyes, *Official Records*, Series 1, Volume 45, Part 2, 61–62.

35. John B. Hood, *Official Records*, Series 1, Volume 45, Part 1, 658; Edwin Bearss, "The History of Fortress Rosecrans"; J. P. Young, "Notes," John Preston Young Collection, 1862–1930, Box 1–2, MUM01699, University of Mississippi, Department of Archives and Special Collections. University, MS.

36. N. B. Forrest, *Official Records*, Series 1, Volume 45, Part 1, 754–755; John B. Hood, *Official Records*, Series 1, Volume 45, Part 1, 660; Thomas C. Boone, *Official Records*, Series 1, Volume 45, Part 1, 631; Richard R. Hancock, *Hancock's Diary: Or, A History of the Second Tennessee Confederate Cavalry* (Nashville: Brandon Printing Company, 1887), 523–524; William M. Worthington, Letter to "Sam," December 11, Worthington Family Papers, MS Z/0658.000/S, Box 1, Mississippi Department of History and Archives.

37. William B. Bate, *Official Records*, Series 1, Volume 45, Part 1, 745; H. Milo Torrence, *Official Records*, Series 1, Volume 45, Part 1, 635; Fred-

erick H. Dyer, *A Compendium of the War of the Rebellion* (Des Moines, The Dyer Publishing Company, 1908), 1110; Gilbert Johnson *Official Records*, Series 1, Volume 45, Part 1, 631; John Powell, *The History of the Thirteenth Indiana Cavalry Regiment: 1863–1865* (Utica, KY.: McDowell Publications, 1987), 119.

38. Minor T. Thomas *Official Records*, Series 1, Volume 45, Part 1, 622; R. H. Milroy, *Official Records*, Series 1, Volume 45, Part 1, 615–616.

39. *Ibid.*

40. William B. Bate, *Official Records*, Series 1, Volume 45, Part 1, 745.

41. J. A. Chalaron, "Hood's Campaign Murfreesboro," *Confederate Veteran*, Volume 11, pp. 439–440.

42. Nathaniel Chairs Hughes, Jr., *The Pride of the Confederate Artillery: The Washington Artillery in the Army of Tennessee* (Baton Rouge: LSU Press, 1997), 235.

43. G. M. L. Johnson, *Official Records*, Series 1, Volume 45, Part 1, 630–631.

44. Minor T. Thomas, *Official Records*, Series 1, Volume 45, Part 1, 622; Milroy *Official Records*, Series 1, Volume 45, Part 1, 615–616.

45. R. H. Milroy *Official Records*, Series 1, Volume 45, Part 1, 616.

46. William B. Bate, *Official Records*, Series 1, Volume 45, Part 1, 745.

47. H. R. Jackson, Letter to Cheatham, December 10, 1864, Benjamin Cheatham Papers (1834–1893), Folder 5, General Correspondence, Tennessee State Library and Archives.

48. Lovell Rousseau *Official Records*, Series 1, Volume 45, Part 1, 610; R. H. Milroy, *Official Records*, Series 1, Volume 45, Part 1, 612–613.

49. Edwin Bearss, "The History of Fortress Rosecrans"; Lenard E. Brown, "Fortress Rosecrans: A History, 1865–1990," *Tennessee Historical Quarterly*, Vol. 50, No. 3 (Fall 1991), p. 138.

50. E. A. Otis, *Official Records*, Series 1, Volume 45, Part 2, 64–65; George H. Thomas *Official Records*, Series 1, Volume 45, Part 2, 64; Edwin Bearss, "The History of Fortress Rosecrans"; Ira B. Conine, Letter to Jennie, December 8, 1864, MS 673—Ira Conine Papers (November–December 1864), Bowling Green University.

51. N. B. Forrest, *Official Records*, Series 1, Volume 45, Part 1, 755.

52. William Bate, *Official Records*, Series 1, Volume 45, Part 1, 746; Thomas C. Boone *Official Records*, Series 1, Volume 45, Part 1, 632; A. P. Mason, *Official Records*, Series 1, Volume 45, Part 2, 652.

53. H. M. Torrence, *Official Records*, Series 1, Volume 45, Part 1, 635–636; Gilbert Johnson, *Official Records*, Series 1, Volume 45, Part 1, 631; Lovell Rousseau, *Official Records*, Series 1, Volume 45, Part 1, 612.

54. William Bate, *Official Records*, Series 1, Volume 45, Part 1, 746; N. B. Forrest, *Official Records*, Series 1, Volume 45, Part 1, 756.

55. John Berrien Lindsley, *Military Annals of Tennessee,* Confederate (Nashville: J. M. Lindsley & Co., Publishers, 1886), 622; Richard R. Hancock, *Hancock's Diary*, 526; Robert Milroy letter to wife Mary, January 1, 1865, Jasper County Public Library, Rensselaer.

56. N. B. Forrest, *Official Records*, Series 1, Volume 45, Part 1, 756; Sam Dunlap, Journal, Dunlap Family, Papers, 1780–2002, C4004, Missouri Historical Society, Columbia; R. H. Milroy, *Official Records*, Series 1, Volume 45, Part 1, 617.

57. *Ibid.*

58. William Bate, *Official Records*, Series 1, Volume 45, Part 1, 746–747.

59. William Velie, Letter—December 22, 1864, William Veile Papers, MS.3211, University of Tennessee, Knoxville.

60. William Bate, *Official Records*, Series 1, Volume 45, Part 1, 746–747; James Cooper, Diaries and Memoirs, Confederate Collection, Box 12, Folder 11, Tennessee State Library and Archives, p. 52–53; John A. Wyeth, *Life of Lieutenant-General Nathan Bedford Forrest* (New York and London: Harper & Brothers, Publishers, 1900), 551.

61. N. B. Forrest, *Official Records*, Series 1, Volume 45, Part 1, 756; Sam Dunlap, Journal, Dunlap Family, Papers.

62. Sam B. Dunlap, "Hard Times on Hood's Retreat," *Confederate Veteran*, Volume 7, No. 6 (June 1899), p. 266; Sam Dunlap, Journal; J. G. Deupree, "The Noxubee Squadron of the First Mississippi Cavalry, C. S. A. 1861–1865," In *Publications of the Mississippi Historical Society*, Volume II, Dunbar Rowland, ed. (Jackson, MS: Democrat Printing Co., 1918), 115.

63. Richard R. Hancock, *Hancock's Diary*, 527; William M. Worthington, Letter to "Sam," December 11, 1864, Worthington Family Papers, MS Z/0658.000/S, Box 1, Mississippi Department of History and Archives.

64. R. H. Milroy, *Official Records*, Series 1, Volume 45, Part 1, 617–618.

65. Edward Anderson, *Official Records*, Series 1, Volume 45, Part 1, 610–611; Alfred Reed, *Official Records*, Series 1, Volume 45, Part 1, 629; Jonathan A. Noyalas, *"My Will is Absolute Law": A Biography of Union General Robert H. Milroy* (Jefferson, NC: McFarland, 2006), 152.

66. *Ibid.*; Alfred Reed, Casualty list, Murfreesboro, Battle of, Murfreesboro, Tenn., 1864, Registers of dead, Jasper County Public Library, Rensselaer; William Smith Carson, Letter—December 19, 1864, Carson family papers, 1851–1932, #1978–0009M15, Georgia Archives.

67. Nathaniel Cheairs Hughes, Jr., *Brigadier General Tyree H. Bell, CSA* (Knoxville: University of Tennessee Press, 2004), 208; Richard R. Hancock, *Hancock's Diary*, 528; John C. Spence, *A Diary of the Civil War* (Murfreesboro: Rutherford County Historical Society, 1993), 152.

68. Wm. B. Bate, *Official Records*, Series 1, Vol-

ume 45, Part 1, 747; Richard R. Hancock, *Hancock's Diary*, 527.

69. N. B. Forrest, *Official Records*, Series 1, Volume 45, Part 1, 754; Stanley Horn, *The Decisive Battle of Nashville* (Knoxville: University of Tennessee Press, 1968), 39; Charles W. Anderson, *Official Records*, Series 1, Volume 45, Part 2, 693; Martha L. Crabb, *All Afire to Fight: The Untold Tale of the Civil War's Ninth Texas Cavalry* (New York: Avon Books, 2000), 274.

70. A. P. Mason, *Official Records*, Series 1, Volume 45, Part 2, 654; John Morton, *The Artillery of Nathan Bedford Forrest's Cavalry* (Nashville and Dallas: Publishing House of the M. E. Church, South Smith & Lamar, Agents, 1909), 290.

71. Hylan Lyon, *Official Records*, Series 1, Volume 45, Part 1, 803; A. P. Mason, *Official Records*, Series 1, Volume 45, Part 1, 1221.

72. Hylan Lyon, *Official Records*, Series 1, Volume 45, Part 1, 803–804.

73. Hylan Lyon, *Official Records*, Series 1, Volume 45, Part 1, 804; Edward M. Coffman, ed., "Memoirs of Hylan B. Lyon, Brigadier General, CSA," *Tennessee Historical Quarterly*, Vol. XVIII (March 1959), 44.

74. George Thomas, *Official Records*, Series 1, Volume 45, Part 2, 154; S. F. Johnson, *Official Records*, Series 1, Volume 45, Part 2, 154; Wm. Forbes, *Official Records*, Series 1, Volume 45, Part 2, 140; I. P. Williams, *Official Records*, Series 1, Volume 45, Part 2, 145; S. Meredith. *Official Records*, Series 1, Volume 45, Part 2, 154.

75. Hylan Lyon, *Official Records*, Series 1, Volume 45, Part 1, 804; S. F. Johnson, *Official Records*, Series 1, Volume 45, Part 2, 176; Edward McCook, *Official Records*, Series 1, Volume 45, Part 2, 176; Eugene Bruce Read Diary, Volume 5, December 23, 1864, Special Collections, Newberry Library.

76. E. M. McCook, *Official Records*, Series 1, Volume 45, Part 1, 791–792; George Thomas, *Official Records*, Series 1, Volume 45, Part 1, 1204.

77. E. M. McCook, *Official Records*, Series 1, Volume 45, Part 1, 792; Bruce S. Allardice, *More Generals in Gray* (Baton Rouge: Louisiana State University Press, 1995), 201–202; Louis Watkins, *Official Records*, Series 1, Volume 45, Part 1, 796–797; C. H. Sowle, Military Record of C. H. Sowle, unpublished, Manuscript C. S., undated, Filson Historical Society, Louisville, Kentucky; Robert S. Merrill, Diary, December 16, 1864 (Cedarburg, WI: MSG, 2007), 199.

78. E. M. McCook, *Official Records*, Series 1, Volume 45, Part 1, 792.

79. O. H. La Grange, *Official Records*, Series 1, Volume 45, Part 1, 794–795; Edward M. Coffman, ed., "Memoirs of Hylan B. Lyon, Brigadier General, CSA," 45; Perry Goodrich, Letter to Frankie, December 27, 1864, Letters Home from the 1st Wisconsin Cavalry, typeset, State Historical Society of Wisconsin, Madison.

80. Louis Watkins, *Official Records*, Series 1, Volume 45, Part 1, 796–797; Hylan Lyon, *Official Records*, Series 1, Volume 45, Part 1, 805; Joseph Fuquay, Letter to Delia December 22, 1864, Folklife and Manuscripts Archives, Hopkins County, Kentucky—Letters, SC 59, 2012.205.1, Western Kentucky State University.

81. O. H. La Grange, *Official Records*, Series 1, Volume 45, Part 1, 794–795; Homer Carpenter, Letter to Mary January 1, 1865, Homer C. Carpenter papers, 1851–1897, M0694, Box 1, Folder 12, Indiana Historical Society.

82. Hylan Lyon, *Official Records*, Series 1, Volume 45, Part 1, 805; Adrastus Newell, Letter, 26–27 December 1864, Adrastus Newell Papers, Filson Historical Society, Louisville.

83. William Palmer, *Official Records*, Series 1, Volume 45, Part 1, 799–800; Edward M. Coffman, ed., "Memoirs of Hylan B. Lyon, Brigadier General, CSA," 47–48; Charles H. Kirk, "The Last Blow at Hood's Army," In *History of the Fifteenth Pennsylvania Volunteer Cavalry*, Charles Kirk, ed. (Philadelphia: Society of the Fifteenth Pennsylvania Cavalry, 1906), 442–443.

84. Hylan Lyon, *Official Records*, Series 1, Volume 45, Part 1, 805; James Wiswell, Letter to sister, January 6, 1865, James Wiswell Papers (1861–1867), David M. Rubenstein Rare Book & Manuscript Library, Duke University.

85. O. H. La Grange, *Official Records*, Series 1, Volume 45, Part 1, 795; William Palmer, *Official Records*, Series 1, Volume 45, Part 1, 800; Hylan Lyon, *Official Records*, Series 1, Volume 45, Part 1, 806; James Hughes, Letter—December 30, 1864, Hughes, James L. Letters, 1864–1865, Filson Historical Society, Louisville.

86. Edward McCook, *Official Records*, Series 1, Volume 45, Part 1, 793.

87. George H. Thomas, *Official Records*, Series 1, Volume 45, Part 2, 70; U.S. Grant, *Official Records*, Series 1, Volume 45, Part 2, 70; Franklin Hammond, Letter to sister December 16, 1864, Franklin J. Hammond letters, 1861–1865, Iowa State Historical Library & Archives (MS1998.8).

88. George H. Thomas, *Official Records*, Series 1, Volume 45, Part 2, 85; U.S. Grant, *Official Records*, Series 1, Volume 45, Part 2, 84.

89. G. T. Beauregard, *Official Records*, Series 1, Volume 44, Part 1, 932–933; Henry M. Cist, *Official Records*, Series 1, Volume 45, Part 2, 73; Thomas Wood, *Official Records*, Series 1, Volume 45, Part 2, 72; A. J. Smith, *Official Records*, Series 1, Volume 45, Part 2, 73.

90. William Dudley Gale, Letter to wife—December 9, 1864, Gale and Polk Family Papers, 1815–1940, #266, Southern Historical Collection, The Wilson Library, University of North Carolina at Chapel Hill.

91. J. H. Wilson, *Official Records*, Series 1, Volume 45, Part 2, 76; A. J. Alexander, *Official Records*, Series 1, Volume 45, Part 2, 75; J. H. Wilson, *Official Records*, Series 1, Volume 45, Part 2, 75; A. J. Alexander, *Official Records*, Series 1, Volume 45,

Part 2, 74; Jas. F. Rusling, *Official Records*, Series 1, Volume 45, Part 2, 74, 89.

92. E. B. Beaumont, *Official Records*, Series 1, Volume 45, Part 2, 89–90; Henry Stone, *Official Records*, Series 1, Volume 45, Part 2, 89; A. J. Alexander, *Official Records*, Series 1, Volume 45, Part 2, 76; E. T. Wells, *Official Records*, Series 1, Volume 45, Part 2, 77; Edson Washburn, Diary—December 9; B. H. Grierson, *Official Records*, Series 1, Volume 45, Part 2, 90; T. H. Harris, *Official Records*, Series 1, Volume 45, Part 2, 106–107; Gilbert Johnson, *Official Records*, Series 1, Volume 45, Part 1, 611; W. H. Terrell, G. L. M. Johnson, G.M. L. Johnson to Commanding officer, Detachment 4th Tennessee Cavalry from Edgefield—December 6, 1864, Edward F. Reid Papers, 1863–1888 (Bulk 1864–1865), Indiana Historical Society.

93. J. H. Hammond, *Official Records*, Series 1, Volume 45, Part 2, 107; J. H. Wilson, *Official Records*, Series 1, Volume 45, Part 2, 106.

94. E. T. Wells, *Official Records*, Series 1, Volume 45, Part 2, 125.

95. J. H. Hammond, *Official Records*, Series 1, Volume 45, Part 2, 126; E. B. Beaumont, *Official Records*, Series 1, Volume 45, Part 2, 135.

96. Geo. H. Thomas, *Official Records*, Series 1, Volume 45, Part 2, 97; Ulysses Grant, *Official Records*, Series 1, Volume 45, Part 2, 96–97; H. W. Halleck, *Official Records*, Series 1, Volume 45, Part 2, 96.

97. Geo. H. Thomas, *Official Records*, Series 1, Volume 45, Part 2, 114–115; Ulysses Grant *Official Records*, Series 1, Volume 45, Part 2, 115.

98. Geo. H. Thomas, *Official Records*, Series 1, Volume 45, Part 2, 118; Thomas Wood, *Official Records*, Series 1, Volume 45, Part 2, 118; John Schofield, *Official Records*, Series 1, Volume 45, Part 2, 121; A. J. Smith, *Official Records*, Series 1, Volume 45, Part 2, 122; James Steedman *Official Records*, Series 1, Volume 45, Part 2, 123; Robt. Ramsey, *Official Records*, Series 1, Volume 45, Part 2, 124; A. P. Mason, *Official Records*, Series 1, Volume 45, Part 2, 666, 669–670.

99. Thomas Wood, *Official Records*, Series 1, Volume 45, Part 2, 132–133; George Thomas, *Official Records*, Series 1, Volume 45, Part 2, 131; Robert Ramsey, *Official Records*, Series 1, Volume 45, Part 2, 132; John Schofield, *Official Records*, Series 1, Volume 45, Part 2, 133; James Steedman, *Official Records*, Series 1, Volume 45, Part 2, 133; Edson Washburn diary, December 11, 1864; Wirt A. Cate, ed., *Two Soldiers: The Campaign Diaries of Thomas J. Key and Robert J. Campbell* (Chapel Hill: University of North Carolina Press, 1938), 166.

100. Geo. H. Thomas, *Official Records*, Series 1, Volume 45, Part 2, 143; Ulysses Grant, *Official Records*, Series 1, Volume 45, Part 2, 143; John Schofield, *Forty-Six Years in the Army* (New York: The Century Co., 1897), 296–297; Winston Groom, *Shrouds of Glory: From Atlanta to Nashville, The Last Great Campaign of the Civil War* (New York: Atlantic Monthly Press, 1995), 233–234; Freeman Cleaves, *Rock of Chickamauga: The Life of General George H. Thomas* (Norman: University of Oklahoma Press, 1986), 259–260; James H. Wilson, *Under the Old Flag*, Volume II (New York and London: D. Appleton And Company, 1912), 101–102.

101. Don Piatt, *General George H. Thomas: A Critical Biography* (Cincinnati: Robert Clarke and Co, 1893), 585; James H. Wilson, "The Union Cavalry in the Hood Campaign, In *Battles and Leaders of the Civil War*, Vol. IV (New York: The Century Co., 1888), 467.

102. Maggie Lindsley, *"'Maggie!' Maggie Lindsley's Journal*, Muriel Davies Mackenzie, ed. (Southbury, CT: privately printed, 1977), 37.

103. Henry Halleck, *Official Records*, Series 1, Volume 45, Part 2, 142; E. F. Winslow, *Official Records*, Series 1, Volume 45, Part 2, 204; Henry Halleck, *Official Records*, Series 1, Volume 45, Part 2, 136–137; George H. Thomas, *Official Records*, Series 1, Volume 45, Part 2, 141.

104. E. B. Beaumont, *Official Records*, Series 1, Volume 45, Part 2, 173; E. F. Winslow, *Official Records*, Series 1, Volume 45, Part 2, 204; Stephen Z. Starr, *The Union Cavalry in the Civil War: The War in the West*, Volume III (Baton Rouge: Louisiana State University, 2007), 543.

105. E. B. Beaumont, *Official Records*, Series 1, Volume 45, Part 2, 135–136; J. F. Speed and Bland Ballard, *Official Records*, Series 1, Volume 45, Part 2, 139; Richard Johnson, *Official Records*, Series 1, Volume 45, Part 2, 139; Eli Russell, Letter to wife, December 23, 1864, Russell, Eli, 1834–1865 Papers, Bentley Historical Library, University of Michigan; Elisha Mix, Letter to wife, December 23, 1864, Elisha Mix Papers, Bentley Historical Library, University of Michigan; Don Piatt, *General George H. Thomas: A Critical Biography* (Cincinnati: Robert Clarke and Co, 1893), 583.

106. A. P. Mason *Official Records*, Series 1, Volume 45, Part 2, 673; Jams H. Wilson, *Under the Old Flag*, Volume II (New York and London: D. Appleton And Company, 1912), 33.

107. Henry Kratzer McVey, *A Writ of My Civil War Experiences* (Jefferson County, Iowa: n.p. 2001), 19; Joseph Rabb, Letter to sister, December 5, 1864, Joseph M. Rabb papers, 1860–1925, M0557, Box 1, Folder 6, Indiana Historical Society; Robt. H. Ramsey, *Official Records*, Series 1, Volume 45, Part 2, 148; E. B. Beaumont, *Official Records*, Series 1, Volume 45, Part 2, 148–149; J. H. Wilson, *Official Records*, Series 1, Volume 45, Part 2, 149; A. J. Alexander, *Official Records*, Series 1, Volume 45, Part 2, 149.

108. James H. Wilson, *Official Records*, Series 1, Volume 45, Part 2, 150; John Croxton, *Official Records*, Series 1, Volume 45, Part 2, 150; Edward McCook, *Official Records*, Series 1, Volume 45, Part 2, 150; R. W. Johnson, *Official Records*, Series 1, Volume 45, Part 2, 151; Edward Hatch, *Official Records*, Series 1, Volume 45, Part 2, 151; Eben Ellison, Letter to father, December 12, 1864, Col-

lection Number—GLC03523.10, Gilder Lehrman Institute of American History.

109. T. S. Bowers, *Official Records*, Series 1, Volume 45, Part 2, 171; James Steedman, *Official Records*, Series 1, Volume 45, Part 2, 173; Thomas J. Wood, *Official Records*, Series 1, Volume 45, Part 2, 172; A. J. Smith, *Official Records*, Series 1, Volume 45, Part 2, 173; J. D. Cox, *Official Records*, Series 1, Volume 45, Part 2, 172; Geo. H. Thomas, *Official Records*, Series 1, Volume 45, Part 2, 170–171; George Thomas, *Official Records*, Series 1, Volume 45, Part 2, 168; Geo. H. Thomas, *Official Records*, Series 1, Volume 45, Part 2, 155; Thomas Wood, *Official Records*, Series 1, Volume 45, Part 2, 155; A. J. Smith, *Official Records*, Series 1, Volume 45, Part 2, 159; A. P. Mason, *Official Records*, Series 1, Volume 45, Part 2, 676.

110. Richard Taylor, *Official Records*, Series 1, Volume 45, Part 2, 689; Robert S. Hudson, *Official Records*, Series 1, Volume 45, Part 2, 1247; Dabney Maury, *Official Records*, Series 1, Volume 45, Part 2, 1257; George Brent, *Official Records*, Series 1, Volume 45, Part 2, 658–659; Sul Ross, *Official Records*, Series 1, Volume 45, Part 2, 682, 771; William F. Miller, *Official Records*, Series 1, Volume 45, Part 2, 685; J. B. Nulton, *Official Records*, Series 1, Volume 45, Part 1, 620–621.

111. James Brownlow, Jr., "Autobiography of James Polk Brownlow, Jr.," C. Brownlow Hastings, 1994. From the private collection of John A. Hastings of Austin, Texas.

112. A. J. Alexander, *Official Records*, Series 1, Volume 45, Part 2, 160; E. B. Beaumont, *Official Records*, Series 1, Volume 45, Part 2, 160; A. P. Mason, *Official Records*, Series 1, Volume 45, Part 2, 686; Stanley Horn, *The Decisive Battle of Nashville* (Knoxville: University of Tennessee Press, 1986), 40; John B. Hood, *Official Records*, Series 1, Volume 45, Part 2, 680.

113. A. J. Alexander, *Official Records*, Series 1, Volume 45, Part 2, 188–189; Geo. H. Thomas, *Official Records*, Series 1, Volume 45, Part 2, 180; H. W. Halleck, *Official Records*, Series 1, Volume 45, Part 2, 180.

114. A. J. Alexander, *Official Records*, Series 1, Volume 45, Part 2, 190–191; Hervey A. Colvin, *Official Records*, Series 1, Volume 45, Part 2, 190; Green Raum, "The Battle of Nashville," *National Tribune*, August 27, 1903, p. 1.

115. Francis Stewart, Diary—December 14, 1864, 1865, MS 744—Francis Stewart Papers, Bowling Green University; Henry Boynton, *Was General Thomas Slow at Nashville?* (New York: Francis P. Harper, 1896), 38–39.

116. James Chalmers, *Official Records*, Series 1, Volume 45, Part 2, 764–765; William J. Wood, *Civil War Generalship: The Art of Command* (Westport, CT: Praeger, 1997), 221; Stanley F. Horn, *Tennessee's War: 1861–1865* (Nashville: Tennessee Civil War Centennial Commission, 1965), 323.

117. William Black, Letter to friends—December 14, 1864, Civil War Letters of William Black, Vigo County Public Library, Terre Haute, Indiana; George Monlux, "To My Comrades Co. I, 8th Iowa Cavalry," Personal narrative, State Historical Library & Archives, p. 57; Dwight Fraser, Letter, December 14, 1864, Dwight Fraser Letters, M0591, Folder 3, Indiana Historical Society.

Chapter Eleven

1. Thomas Robson Hay, *Hood's Tennessee Campaign* (New York: Press of Morningside Books, 1976), 148–149; Wiley Sword, *Embrace an Angry Wind: The Confederacy's Last Hurrah: Spring Hill, Franklin and Nashville* (New York: Harper Collins Publishers, 1992), 280; J. W. Harmon, Diaries and Memoirs, Confederate Collection, Box 13, Folder 6, Tennessee State Library and Archives, p. 60; Harry W. Houchens, "The Making of General John B. Hood: A Study of Command," Study project for the U.S. Army War College, Carlisle Barracks, Pennsylvania, 1993, 34.

2. Thomas Robson Hay, *Hood's Tennessee Campaign*, 149–150; Henry M. Kendall, *The Battles of Franklin and Nashville, In the War of the Sixties* (New York, The Neale Publishing Company, 1912), 130; Susan K. Parman, "The Battle of Nashville," Master's Thesis, George Peabody College for Teachers, 1932, p. 10.

3. Thomas Robson Hay, *Hood's Tennessee Campaign*, 149–151.

4. Wiley Sword, *Embrace an Angry Wind*, 316; Stanley F. Horn, *Tennessee's War: 1861–1865* (Nashville: Tennessee Civil War Centennial Commission, 1965), 417; George Little and James R. Maxwell, *A History of Lumsden's Battery, C.S.A.* (Tuscaloosa, AL : R.E. Rhodes Chapter, United Daughters of the Confederacy, 1905), 93.

5. Eli Russell, Letter to wife, December 23, 1864, Russell, Eli, 1834–1865 Papers, Bentley Historical Library, University of Michigan.

6. James H. Wilson, *Official Records*, Series 1, Volume 45, Part 1, 551.

7. Thomas Robson Hay, *Hood's Tennessee Campaign*, 152; George Monlux, "To My Comrades Co. I, 8th Iowa Cavalry," Personal narrative, State Historical Library & Archives, p. 57; Stanley Horn, *The Decisive Battle of Nashville* (Knoxville: University of Tennessee Press, 1986), 77; Paul H. Stockdale, *The Death of an Army: The Battle of Nashville and Hood's Retreat* (Murfreesboro: Southern Heritage Press, 1992), 39–40; Susan K. Parman, "The Battle of Nashville," 24.

8. Jerry Keenan, *Wilson's Cavalry Corps* (Jefferson, NC: McFarland, 1998), 98; James H. Wilson, *Under the Old Flag*, Volume II (New York and London: D. Appleton And Company, 1912), 107; Lucius F. Hubbard, "Minnesota in the Battles of Nashville, December 15–16, 1864." In *Glimpses of the Nation's Struggle* (MOLLUS, MN, Vol. 6 (Minneapolis: Davis, 1909), 271.

9. W. H. Gilliard, "The First Shot at Nashville," *National Tribune*, September 28, 1911.

10. Stanley Horn, *The Decisive Battle of Nashville*, 82; John Johnston, "The Civil War Reminiscences of John Johnston, 1861–1865," William T. Alderson, editor, *Tennessee Historical Quarterly*, Vol. 14, No. 1 (March, 1955), p. 80; John A. Wyeth, *Life of Lieutenant-General Nathan Bedford Forrest* (New York and London: Harper & Brothers, Publishers, 1900), 554; Ben H. Severance, *Portraits of Conflict: A Photographic History of Alabama in the Civil War* (Fayetteville: University of Arkansas Press, 2012), 227.

11. Richard Johnson, *Official Records*, Series 1, Volume 45, Part 1, 599; James McDonough, *Nashville: The Western Confederacy's Final Gamble* (Knoxville: University of Tennessee Press, 2004), 175; W. L. Sanford, *History of Fourteenth Illinois Cavalry and the Brigades to Which It Belonged* (Chicago: R. R. Donnelley & Sons Company, 1898), 284; Henry Stone, *Official Records*, Series 1, Volume 45, Part 2, 200; Zealous B. Tower, letter to Secretary of Treasury, December 25, 1864, Collection Number—GLC00849.001, Gilder Lehrman Institute for American History; Michael R. Bradley, *Forrest's Fighting Preacher: David Campbell Kelley of Tennessee* (Charleston: The History Press, 2011), 86; David R. Logsdon, *Eyewitnesses at the Battle of Nashville* (Nashville: Kettle Mill Press, 2004), 45.

12. Elisha Mix, Letter to wife, December 8, 1864, Elisha Mix Papers, Bentley Historical Library, University of Michigan.

13. John Johnston, Diaries and Memoirs, Confederate Collection, Box 13, Folder 6, Tennessee State Library and Archives, p. 148; John Johnston, "Cavalry of Hood's Left at Nashville," *Confederate Veteran*, Volume 13, p. 28.

14. W. R. Carter, *History of the First Regiment of Tennessee Volunteer Cavalry* (Knoxville: Gaut-Ogden Co., Printers and Binders, 1902), 226; W. L. Sanford, *History of Fourteenth Illinois Cavalry*, 286; John Johnston, Diaries and Memoirs, p. 110.

15. Richard Johnson, *Official Records*, Series 1, Volume 45, Part 1, 600; John Johnston, Diaries and Memoirs, 150; Theodore Allen, December 15 entry, 1842–1919, Diary, 1864–1865, Mss. A A431 1, Filson Historical Society, Louisville.

16. J. P. Young, *The Seventh Tennessee Cavalry: A History* (Nashville: M. E. Church, South, 1890), 124; Jerry Keenan, *Wilson's Cavalry Corps*, 99.

17. Richard Johnson, *Official Records*, Series 1, Volume 45, Part 1, 600; James McDonough, *Nashville: The Western Confederacy's Final Gamble*, 175; W. L. Sanford, *History of Fourteenth Illinois Cavalry*, 287; Richard Johnson, *Official Records*, Series 1, Volume 45, Part 2, 206; Theodore Allen, December 15 diary entry; R. C. Rankin, "In the Saddle," *National Tribune*, November 18, 1886.

18. James Dinkins, *1861 to 1865: Personal Reminiscences and Experiences in the Confederate Army* (Cincinnati: Robert Clarke Co., 1897), 245–246.

19. John Johnston, Diaries and Memoirs, p. 149.

20. Richard Johnson, *Official Records*, Series 1, Volume 45, Part 1, 600–601; Richard Johnson, *Official Records*, Series 1, Volume 45, Part 2, 206; Theodore Allen, December 15 diary entry; W. L. Sanford, *History of Fourteenth Illinois Cavalry*, 286; Johnston, *Ibid*.

21. John Johnston, Diaries and Memoirs, 151; Stanley Horn, *The Decisive Battle of Nashville*, 84; James Chalmers, *Official Records*, Series 1, Volume 45, Part 1, 765; James Dinkins, *1861 to 1865: Personal Reminiscences*, 247; Waldon Loving, *Coming Like Hell!: The Story of the 12th Tennessee Cavalry* (San Jose, New York, Lincoln and Shanghai: Writer's Club Press, 2002), 131; John Johnston, Diaries and Memoirs, p. 147.

22. James Biddle, *Official Records*, Series 1, Volume 45, Part 1, 606; Theodore Allen, December 15 diary entry.

23. W. R. Carter, *History of the First Regiment of Tennessee Volunteer Cavalry*, 228; Isaac R Sherwood, *Memoirs of the War* (Toledo: The H. J. Crittenden, Co., 1923), 149; James Chalmers, *Official Records*, Series 1, Volume 45, Part 1, 765; George Monlux, "To My Comrades Co. I, 8th Iowa Cavalry," p. 58.

24. Henry M. Hempstead, Journal—December 15, 1864, Bentley Historical Library, University of Michigan.

25. John Croxton, *Official Records*, Series 1, Volume 45, Part 1, 572; W. R. Carter, *History of the First Regiment of Tennessee Volunteer Cavalry*, 227; George Monlux, "To My Comrades Co. I, 8th Iowa Cavalry," p. 58; Homer Mead, *The Eighth Iowa Cavalry in the Civil War* (Carthage, IL: S. C. Davidson, Publisher, 1927), 44; David R. Logsdon, *Eyewitnesses at the Battle of Nashville*, 46; J. T. Tunnell, "Ector's Brigade in the Battle of Nashville," *Confederate Veteran*, Volume 12, p. 348.

26. W. R. Carter, *History of the First Regiment of Tennessee Volunteer Cavalry*, 230; John Johnston, Diaries and Memoirs, 151; James H. Wilson, *Official Records*, Series 1, Volume 45, Part 1, 551; Guy E. Logan, ed., *Roster and Record of Iowa Soldiers in the War of the Rebellion: 1st-9th Regiments of Cavalry* (Des Moines: Emory H. English State Printer, 1910), 1517; George Monlux, "To My Comrades Co. I, 8th Iowa Cavalry," p. 58.

27. James H. Wilson, *Official Records*, Series 1, Volume 45, Part 1, 552; James H. Wilson, *Official Records*, Series 1, Volume 45, Part 2, 200; Reid Smith, *Majestic Middle Tennessee* (Gretna, LA: Pelican Publishing Co, 1998), 118; Edward A. Davenport, editor, *History of the Ninth Regiment Illinois Cavalry Volunteers* (Chicago: Donohue & Henneberry, Printers and Binders, 1888), 157; James Wilson, *Under the Old Flag*, Volume II (New York and London: D. Appleton And Company, 1912), 110; Datus Coon, *Official Records*, Series 1, Volume 45, Part 1, 590–591; Thomas Wood, *Official Records*, Series 1, Volume 45, Part 1, 128; A. J. Smith, *Official Records*, Series 1, Volume 45, Part 1, 433; Susan K. Parman, "The Battle of Nashville," 27–28.

28. Lucius Hubbard, *Official Records*, Series 1, Volume 45, Part 1, 445–447; Stanley Horn, *The Decisive Battle of Nashville*, 183; Edwin Huddleston, *The Civil War in Middle Tennessee* (Nashville: The Parthenon Press, 1965), 143.

29. Edward Hatch, *Official Records*, Series 1, Volume 45, Part 1, 577; James Christy, December 15, 1864 entry, Journal of Sgt. James Christy, 4th Regiment, U.S. Cavalry, Company F., Des Moines Historical Library Manuscripts (N14/3/4 Box 6 Folder 2); R. H. Crowder, Letter, December 21, 1864, R. H. Crowder papers, 1859–1908, M0208, Box 1, Folder 12, Indiana Historical Society; T. Springer, Invoice of ordnance, Crowder-Bose Papers, M0671, Box 1, Folder 7, Indiana Historical Society; M. D. Price, "Two Mooted Questions," *National Tribune*, August 7, 1890, p. 3; R. W. Surby, "Hatch's Hard Riders"; Preston Sharp, Diary entry—December 15, 1864, Sharp, Preston T. Collection, R1204, Missouri Historical Society, Columbia.

30. Datus Coon, *Official Records*, Series 1, Volume 45, Part 1, 590–591; Sidney O. Roberts, *Official Records*, Series 1, Volume 45, Part 1, 594–595; O. A. Abbott, "The Last Battle of Nashville" In *Civil War Sketches and Incidents* (Omaha: Nebraska, Military Order of the Loyal Legion of the United States, 1902), 239.

31. Edward Hatch, *Official Records*, Series 1, Volume 45, Part 1, 577; James Christy, December 15, 1864 entry, Journal of Sgt. James Christy, 4th Regiment, U.S. Cavalry, Company F.; R. H. Crowder, Letter, December 21, 1864; M. D. Price, "Two Mooted Questions"; R. W. Surby, "Hatch's Hard Riders"; Stanley Horn, *The Decisive Battle of Nashville*, 183; Edwin Huddleston, *The Civil War in Middle Tennessee*, 143; David R. Logsdon, *Eyewitnesses at the Battle of Nashville*, 55.

32. Datus Coon, *Official Records*, Series 1, Volume 45, Part 1, 590–591; Sidney O. Roberts, *Official Records*, Series 1, Volume 45, Part 1, 594–595; O. A. Abbott, "The Last Battle of Nashville," 239; R. W. Surby, "Hatch's Hard Riders"; Edward A. Davenport, *History of the Ninth Regiment Illinois Cavalry*, 158; George Little and James R. Maxwell, *A History of Lumsden's Battery, C.S. A.*, 95.

33. James McDonough, *Nashville: The Western Confederacy's Final Gamble*, 182.

34. Datus Coon, *Official Records*, Series 1, Volume 45, Part 1, 590–591; Sidney O. Roberts, *Official Records*, Series 1, Volume 45, Part 1, 594–595; Lyman Pierce, *History of the Second Iowa Cavalry* (Burlington, IA: Hawkeye Steam Book and Job Printing Establishment, 1865), 144; R. W. Surby, "Hatch's Hard Riders"; John McArthur, *Official Records*, Series 1, Volume 45, Part 1, 437–438.

35. Datus Coon, *Official Records*, Series 1, Volume 45, Part 1, 590–591; Sidney O. Roberts, *Official Records*, Series 1, Volume 45, Part 1, 594–595; Lyman Pierce, *History of the Second Iowa Cavalry*, 144–145.

36. Edward Hatch, *Official Records*, Series 1, Volume 45, Part 1, 577; James Christy, December 15, 1864 entry, Journal of Sgt. James Christy, 4th Regiment, U.S. Cavalry, Company F; R. H. Crowder, Letter, December 21, 1864; M. D. Price, "Two Mooted Questions"; R. W. Surby, "Hatch's Hard Riders."

37. J. T. Tunnell, "Ector's Brigade in the Battle of Nashville," p. 348.

38. Christy, *ibid.*.

39. Edward Hatch, *Official Records*, Series 1, Volume 45, Part 1, 577; James Christy, December 15, 1864 entry, Journal of Sgt. James Christy; R. H. Crowder, Letter, December 21, 1864; M. D. Price, "Two Mooted Questions"; R. W. Surby, "Hatch's Hard Riders."

40. Datus Coon, *Official Records*, Series 1, Volume 45, Part 1, 590–591; Sidney O. Roberts, *Official Records*, Series 1, Volume 45, Part 1, 594–595; James H. Wilson, *Official Records*, Series 1, Volume 45, Part 1, 552; Preston Sharp, Diary entry—December 15, 1864; *History of Tennessee* (Nashville: The Goodspeed Publishing Company, 1886), 508; *Report of the Adjutant General of the State of Tennessee, of the Military Forces of the State, from 1861 to 1866* (Nashville: Office of the Adjutant General, S. C. Mercer printer, 1866), 554, 574; R. W. Surby, "Hatch's Hard Riders."

41. *Ibid.*; Henry R. Pippitt, December 15, 1864, Diary, 1862 September 18–1863 May 19, The Special Collections Library of the University of Tennessee, Knoxville.

42. *Ibid.*; Thomas Hawley, *"This Terrible Struggle for Life": The Civil War Letters of a Union Regimental Surgeon* (Jefferson, NC: McFarland, 2012), 218–219.

43. Thomas Robson Hay, *Hood's Tennessee Campaign*, 153; Lyman Pierce, *History of the Second Iowa Cavalry*, 144–145.

44. A. O. Stewart, *Official Records*, Series 1, Volume 45, Part 1, 710–711; James McDonough, *Nashville: The Western Confederacy's Final Gamble*, 193; John Lavender, *The War Memoirs of Captain John W. Lavender, CSA*, Ted R. Worley, ed. (Pine Bluff, AR: The Southern Press, 1956), 113.

45. Edward Hatch, *Official Records*, Series 1, Volume 45, Part 1, 577.

46. J. H. Hammond, *Official Records*, Series 1, Volume 45, Part 1, 606–607; James H. Wilson, *Official Records*, Series 1, Volume 45, Part 1, 551–552; Benjamin Nourse, Diary, December 15, 1864, David M. Rubenstein Rare Book & Manuscript Library, Duke University; Alexander Eckel, *History of the Fourth Tennessee Cavalry* (Johnson City, TN: Overmountain Press, 2001), 74.

47. James Chalmers, *Official Records*, Series 1, Volume 45, Part 1, 765; Stanley Horn, *The Decisive Battle of Nashville* (Knoxville: University of Tennessee Press, 1986), 40; James McDonough, *Nashville: The Western Confederacy's Final Gamble*, 174–175; Chris Perello, *The Quest for Annihilation* (Bakersfield, CA: Strategy & Tactics Press, 2009), 262; John R. Lundberg, *The Finishing Stroke:*

Texans in the 1864 Tennessee Campaign (Abilene, TX: McWhiney Foundation Press, 2003), 108.

48. George Thomas, *Official Records*, Series 1, Volume 45, Part 2, 194.

49. J. C. Van Duzer, *Official Records*, Series 1, Volume 45, Part 2, 196; George Thomas, *Official Records*, Series 1, Volume 45, Part 1, 39; *Nashville Union,* "The Great Battle Yesterday!" December 16, 1864, p. 2.

50. Edwin Stanton, *Official Records*, Series 1, Volume 45, Part 2, 195; George Thomas, *Official Records*, Series 1, Volume 45, Part 2, 195.

51. Thomas Robson Hay, *Hood's Tennessee Campaign,* 154–155.

52. Thomas Robson Hay, *Hood's Tennessee Campaign,* 156–157.

53. James H. Wilson, *Official Records*, Series 1, Volume 45, Part 2, 202–203; James H. Wilson, *Under the Old Flag,* Volume II (New York and London: D. Appleton And Company, 1912), 113.

54. Ambrose Armitage, *Brother to the Eagle: The Civil War Journal of Sgt. Ambrose Armitage, 8th Wisconsin Infantry*, Alden Carter, ed. (United States: Booklocker, Inc, 2006), 519: Henry Kratzer McVey, *A Writ of My Civil War Experiences* (Jefferson County, Iowa: n.p. 2001), 19–20.

55. Stanley F. Horn, *Tennessee's War: 1861–1865* (Nashville: Tennessee Civil War Centennial Commission, 1965), 335; Kate Cumming, *The Journal of Hospital Life in the Confederate Army* (Louisville: John P. Morton & Company, 1866), 162–163.

Chapter Twelve

1. George Thomas, *Official Records*, Series 1, Volume 45, Part 1, 39; Stanley Horn, *The Decisive Battle of Nashville* (Knoxville: University of Tennessee Press, 1986), 108.

2. Stanley Horn, *The Decisive Battle of Nashville,* 109–110; Benjamin M. Seaton, *The Bugle Softly Blows: The Confederate Diary of Benjamin M. Seaton,* Harold Simpson, ed. (Waco: Texian Press, 1965), 65; Walter T. Durham, "The Battle of Nashville," *Confederate History*, Volume 1, No. (Summer 1888): 119–151, p. 131.

3. Wiley Sword, *Embrace an Angry Wind: The Confederacy's Last Hurrah: Spring Hill, Franklin and Nashville* (New York: Harper Collins Publishers, 1992), 369–372; Stanley Horn, *The Decisive Battle of Nashville,* 110–112; James A. Smith, *Official Records*, Series 1, Volume 45, Part 1, 740; Christopher Losson, *Tennessee's Forgotten Warriors* (Knoxville: University of Tennessee Press,1989), 236–237.

4. Robert Dobak, *Freedom by the Sword: The U.S. Colored Troops, 1862–1867* (Washington, D. C.: Center of Military History, 2011), 291–292; Stanley Horn, *The Decisive Battle of Nashville,* 225–230.

5. James H. Wilson, *Official Records*, Series 1, Volume 45, Part 1, 552.

6. Wiley Sword, *Embrace an Angry Wind: The Confederacy's Last Hurrah: Spring Hill, Franklin and Nashville,* 365; W. W. Clayton, *History of Davidson County, Tennessee, with Illustrations and Biographical Sketches of Its Prominent Men and Pioneers* (Philadelphia, PA: J. W. Lewis & Co., 1880), 179.

7. Wiley Sword, *Embrace an Angry Wind,* 369.

8. Ashby L. Kerwood, *Annals of the Fifty-Seventh Regiment Indiana Volunteers* (Dayton: O. W. J. Shuey, 1868), 303.

9. Henry M. Hempstead, Journal—December 16, 1864, Bentley Historical Library, University of Michigan; James H. Wilson, *Official Records*, Series 1, Volume 45, Part 1, 551–552; Bruce Catton, *This Hallowed Ground: A History of the Civil War* (New York: Vintage Books, 2012), 367.

10. James H. Wilson, *Official Records*, Series 1, Volume 45, Part 1, 552.

11. James Chalmers, *Official Records*, Series 1, Volume 45, Part 1, 765; James H. Wilson, *Official Records*, Series 1, Volume 45, Part 1, 551–552; Michael R. Bradley, *Forrest's Fighting Preacher: David Campbell Kelley of Tennessee* (Charleston: The History Press, 2011), 87–88.

12. Compiled records showing service of military units in volunteer Union organizations, Indiana- Eighth Cavalry through Thirteenth Cavalry, and Sixth Tennessee Cavalry, company and regiment history cards, RG 94, National Archives Record Administration Reel 0035 and 188—Washington, D. C.; Kevin D. McCann, *Hurst's Wurst: Colonel Fielding Hurst and the Sixth Tennessee Cavalry U.S. A.* (Dickson, TN: McCann Publications, 2007), 78; Edward Hatch, *Official Records*, Series 1, Volume 45, Part 1, 578; Datus Coon, *Official Records*, Series 1, Volume 45, Part 1, 591; Michael R. Bradley, *Forrest's Fighting Preacher*, 87–88; James Chalmers, *Official Records*, Series 1, Volume 45, Part 1, 765; Paul E. Vandor, *History of Fresno County, California: With Biographical Sketches, Volume 2* (Los Angeles: Historic Record Company, 1919), 1974. [The role of Johnson's 2nd Brigade is not well understood during the battle, but records indicate the 6th Tennessee and about half of the 13th Indiana (commanded by Lieutenant Colonel William Pepper) were involved in the battle. The 12th Indiana and the other half of the 13th Indiana remained near Murfreesboro as evidenced by company records in the Compiled Service Records of these two regiments and by correspondence from Rousseau to Johnson. See Edward F. Reid Papers, 1863–1888 (Bulk 1864–1865) at the Indiana Historical Society. Alexander Eckel, 4th Tennessee, who participated in the battle, observed Gilbert Johnson commanding the brigade at Nashville on December 16.]

13. Edward Hatch, *Official Records*, Series 1, Volume 45, Part 1, 578; Datus Coon, *Official Records*, Series 1, Volume 45, Part 1, 591; Michael R. Bradley, *Forrest's Fighting Preacher,* 87–88; James Chalmers, *Official Records*, Series 1, Volume 45, Part 1, 765.

14. James H. Wilson, *Official Records*, Series 1, Volume 45, Part 1, 551–552; Marshall P. Thatcher, *A Hundred Battles in the West: The Second Michigan Cavalry* (Detroit: L. F. Kilroy, Printer, 1884), 232; William Titus Rigby, Letter, March 24, 1865, William Titus Rigby letters, 1864–1865, Special Collections Dept., University of Iowa; Jerry Keenan, *Wilson's Cavalry Corps* (Jefferson, NC: McFarland, 1998), 108; James A. Smith, Letter to Cheatham, January 23, 1865, Benjamin Cheatham Papers (1834–1893), Folder 5, General Correspondence, Tennessee State Library and Archives.

15. Edward Hatch, *Official Records*, Series 1, Volume 45, Part 1, 578; Datus Coon, *Official Records*, Series 1, Volume 45, Part 1, 591; James H. Wilson, *Official Records*, Series 1, Volume 45, Part 1, 552; J. H. Hammond, *Official Records*, Series 1, Volume 45, Part 1, 607; Gary Blankinship, "Colonel Fielding Hurst and the Hurst Nation," *Western Tennessee Historical Society Papers*, Volume 24 (1980), p. 85.

16. M. B. Morton, "The Battle of Nashville," *Confederate Veteran*, Volume XVII, No. 1 (Jan. 1909), p. 19; Wiley Sword, *The Confederacy's Last Hurrah*, 370–372.

17. James Wilson, *Under the Old Flag*, Volume II (New York and London: D. Appleton And Company, 1912), 114; Patrick Brennan, "Early Winter Sunset," *The Civil War Monitor*, Vol. 4, No. 3 (Fall 2014), p. 46; Datus Coon, *Official Records*, Series 1, Volume 45, Part 1, 591.

18. Edward Hatch, *Official Records*, Series 1, Volume 45, Part 1, 578; Datus Coon, *Official Records*, Series 1, Volume 45, Part 1, 591; Michael R. Bradley, *Forrest's Fighting Preacher: David Campbell Kelley of Tennessee* (Charleston: The History Press, 2011), 87–88; James H. Wilson, *Official Records*, Series 1, Volume 45, Part 1, 551–552; J. H. Hammond, Official Records, Series 1, Volume 45, Part 1, 607; James H. Wilson, *Official Records*, Series 1, Volume 45, Part 2, 216; Henry M. Hempstead, Journal—December 16, 1864, Bentley Historical Library, University of Michigan; James Wilson, *Under the Old Flag*, Volume II (New York and London: D. Appleton And Company, 1912), 114; Patrick Brennan, "Early Winter Sunset," p. 46.

19. Sam Watkins, *Co. Aytch* (Chattanooga, TN: Times Printing Company, 1900), 213; Daniel E. Sutherland, "No Better Officer in the Confederacy: The Wartime Career of Daniel C. Govan," in *Confederate Generals in the Western Theater: Classic Essays on the American Civil War*, Lawrence Lee Hewitt and Arthur W. Bergeron, Jr., ed. (Knoxville: University of Tennessee Press, 2010), 247.

20. Jerry Keenan, *Wilson's Cavalry Corps*, 109; Datus Coon, *Official Records*, Series 1, Volume 45, Part 1, 591; R. W. Surby, "Hatch's Hard Riders," *National Tribune*, September 9, 1886, p. 1; Edward A. Davenport, editor, *History of the Ninth Regiment Illinois Cavalry Volunteers* (Chicago: Donohue & Henneberry, Printers and Binders, 1888), 160; Daniel E. Sutherland, "No Better Officer in the Confederacy: The Wartime Career of Daniel C. Govan," *The Arkansas Historical Quarterly*, Vol. 54, No. 3 (Autumn, 1995), p. 298; David R. Logsdon, *Eyewitnesses at the Battle of Nashville* (Nashville: Kettle Mill Press, 2004), 81. [Colonel Hume R. Feild is often spelled as Field.]

21. Mark Perrin Lowrey, Autobiographical Essay, M49, Historical Manuscripts, Special Collections, The University of Southern Mississippi Libraries. 7.

22. M. B. Morton, "The Battle of Nashville," p. 19; Daniel E. Sutherland, "No Better Officer in the Confederacy: The Wartime Career of Daniel C. Govan," p. 298; William Bate, *Official Records*, Series 1, Volume 45, Part 1, 749.

23. Alexander Eckel, *History of the Fourth Tennessee Cavalry* (Johnson City, TN: Overmountain Press, 2001), 74–75; J. H. Wilson, *Official Records*, Series 1, Volume 45, Part 1, 552; J. H. Hammond, *Official Records*, Series 1, Volume 45, Part 2, 223–224.

24. Samuel Watkins, *Co. Aytch*, 214–215; Bromfield L. Ridley, *Battles and Sketches of the Army of Tennessee* (Mexico, MO: Missouri Printing, 1906), 431.

25. D. W. Comstock, *Ninth Cavalry: One Hundred and Twenty-first Regiment Indiana Volunteers* (Richmond, IN: Published by J. M. Coe, 1890), 33; Alexander Eckel, *History of the Fourth Tennessee Cavalry*, 74.

26. J. T. Tunnell, "Ector's Brigade in the Battle of Nashville," *Confederate Veteran*, Volume 12, p. 349.

27. A. P. Stewart, *Official Records*, Series 1, Volume 45, Part 1, 711.

28. Stanley Horn, *The Decisive Battle of Nashville*, 125; Edwin Huddleston, *The Civil War in Middle Tennessee* (Nashville: The Parthenon Press, 1965), 150; Benjamin Nourse, Diary, December 16, 1864, David M. Rubenstein Rare Book & Manuscript Library, Duke University; E. H. Rennolds, *A History of the Henry County Commands Which Served in the Confederate States of America* (Kennesaw, GA: Continental Book Company, 1961), 111; *A Military Record of Battery D First Ohio Veteran Volunteers Light Artillery* (Oil City, PA: The Derrick Publishing Company, 1908), 168–169; James Cooper, Diaries and Memoirs, Confederate Collection, Box 12, Folder 11, Tennessee State Library and Archives, p. 57; W. D. Dale, "The Disaster at Nashville: Another Letter From Col. W. D. Dale to His Wife After Hood's Defeat Before Nashville," *Confederate Veteran*, Vol. 2, No. 2 (Feb. 1894), p. 47.

29. Datus Coon, *Official Records*, Series 1, Volume 45, Part 1, 591; R. W. Surby, "Hatch's Hard Riders," *National Tribune*, September 9, 1886, p. 1; Edward A. Davenport, editor *History of the Ninth Regiment Illinois Cavalry Volunteers*, 160; James Wilson, *Under the Old Flag*, 115; Orange Jackson, *The History of Orange Jackson's War Life as Related by Himself* (n.p: n. p., 1865), 26–27; James H. Wilson, *Official Records*, Series 1, Volume 45, Part 1,

551–552; J. H. Hammond, *Official Records*, Series 1, Volume 45, Part 1, 607; A. P. Stewart, *Official Records*, Series 1, Volume 45, Part 1, 711.

30. James H. Wilson, *Official Records*, Series 1, Volume 45, Part 1, 551–552; Marshall P. Thatcher, *A Hundred Battles in the West*, 232; William Titus Rigby, Letter, March 24, 1865, William Titus Rigby letters, 1864–1865, Special Collections Dept., University of Iowa; Jerry Keenan, *Wilson's Cavalry Corps*, 108; Daniel Harris Reynolds, Diary entry, December 16, 1864, Daniel Harris Reynolds Papers (MS R32), University of Arkansas, Special Collections; Edwin Huddleston, *The Civil War in Middle Tennessee*, 150; Daniel Harris Reynolds, *Worthy of the Cause for Which They Fight: The Civil War Diary of Brigadier General Daniel Harris Reynolds, 1861–1865*, Robert Patrick Bender, ed. (Fayetteville: University of Arkansas Press, 2011), 162.

31. Robert H. Dacus, *Reminiscences of Company H, First Arkansas Mounted Rifles* (Dardanelle, AR: Post-Dispatch Print, 1897), 20–22.

32. Mark Perrin Lowrey Autobiographical Essay, 7–8.

33. J. H. Hammond, *Official Records*, Series 1, Volume 45, Part 1, 607; D. W. Comstock, *Ninth Cavalry*, 34.

34. John Croxton, *Official Records*, Series 1, Volume 45, Part 1, 573; James H. Wilson, *Official Records*, Series 1, Volume 45, Part 1, 551–552; J. H. Hammond, *Official Records*, Series 1, Volume 45, Part 1, 607; W. R. Carter, *History of the First Regiment of Tennessee Volunteer Cavalry* (Knoxville: Gaut-Ogden Co., Printers and Binders, 1902), 232; *A Military Record off Battery D First Ohio Veteran Volunteers Light Artillery*, 168–169.

35. James H. Wilson, *Official Records*, Series 1, Volume 45, Part 2, 215–216; J. H. Hammond, *Official Records*, Series 1, Volume 45, Part 2, 223–224; Stanley Horn, *The Decisive Battle of Nashville*, 245; Samuel P. Bates, *History of Pennsylvania volunteers, 1861–5*, Volume 5 (Harrisburg: B. Singerly, State Printer, 1871), 3.

36. Thomas Budd Van Horne, *The Life of Major-General George H. Thomas* (New York: Charles Scribner's Sons, 1882), 331–332; Stanley Horn, *The Decisive Battle of Nashville*, 133, 245; Donald B. Connelly, *John Schofield & The Politics of Generalship* (Chapel Hill: University of North Carolina Press, 2006), 144; A. J. Bradford, "Hood's Lines Broken," *National Tribune*, April 23, 1896, p. 2; Patrick Brennan, "Early Winter Sunset," *The Civil War Monitor*, Vol. 4, No. 3 (Fall 2014), p. 51.

37. James Wilson, *Under the Old Flag*, 117–118; Israel Stiles, *Official Records*, Series 1, Volume 45, Part 1, 431; B. F. Thompson, *History of the 112th Regiment of Illinois Volunteer Infantry* (Toulon, IL: Stark County News Office, 1885), 287.

38. Theodore Allen, December 16 entry, 1842–1919, Diary, 1864–1865, Mss. A A431 1, Filson Historical Society, Louisville.

39. James Biddle, *Official Records*, Series 1, Volume 45, Part 1, 606; Richard Johnson, *Official Records*, Series 1, Volume 45, Part 2, 221.

40. James Chalmers, *Official Records*, Series 1, Volume 45, Part 1, 765; W. R. Carter, *History of the First Regiment of Tennessee Volunteer Cavalry*, 232; T. W. Lippincott, "Hatch's Division at Nashville," *National Tribune*, January 10, 1884, p.7.

41. Richard Johnson, *Official Records*, Series 1, Volume 45, Part 1, 601; J. P. Young, *The Seventh Tennessee Cavalry: A History* (Nashville: M. E. Church, South, 1890), 124; W. L. Sanford, *History of Fourteenth Illinois Cavalry and the Brigades to Which It Belonged* (Chicago: R. R. Donnelley & Sons Company, 1898), 289; John Johnston, Diaries and Memoirs, Confederate Collection, Box 13, Folder 6, Tennessee State Library and Archives, p. 152; R. C. Rankin, "In the Saddle," *National Tribune*, November 18, 1886, p. 2.

42. Thomas Budd Van Horne, *The Life of Major-General George H. Thomas* (New York: Charles Scribner's Sons, 1882), 334; A. P. Mason message to James Chalmers, December 16, 1864, Military Departments—Special Orders, Letters, Telegrams, Orders and Circulars Received, Brig. Gen. James R. Chalmers, August 1864-March 1865, RG 109 Chapter Volume 2–294, National Archives; James Arthur Schaefer, "The Tactical And Strategic Evolution Of Cavalry During The American Civil War," Ph.D. Dissertation, The University of Toledo, 1982, p. 186.

43. James Chalmers, *Official Records*, Series 1, Volume 45, Part 1, 765; W. R. Carter, *History of the First Regiment of Tennessee Volunteer Cavalry*, 232; T. W. Lippincott, "Hatch's Division at Nashville," p. 7; John Johnston, Diaries and Memoirs, 152–153; John A. Wyeth, *Life of Lieutenant-General Nathan Bedford Forrest* (New York and London: Harper & Brothers, Publishers, 1900), 558; Thomas Jordan and J. P. Pryor, *The Campaigns of Lieut.-Gen. N. B. Forrest* (New Orleans, Memphis and New York: Blelock & Company, 1868), 660–641; David C. Kelley, "More on the Confederate Cavalry at Nashville," In *The Battle Of Nashville: Recollections Of Confederate & Union Soldiers*, Lochlainn Seabrook (Nashville: Sea Raven Press, 2018), 44–45.

44. Edward A. Davenport, *History of the Ninth Regiment Illinois Cavalry*, 160; John Johnston, "Cavalry of Hood's Left at Nashville," *Confederate Veteran*, Volume 13, p. 29.

45. James Chalmers, *Official Records*, Series 1, Volume 45, Part 1, 766; John Johnston, Diaries and Memoirs, 153–154; Thomas Jordan and J. P. Pryor, *The Campaigns of Lieut.-Gen. N. B. Forrest*, 660–641; David C. Kelley, "More on the Confederate Cavalry at Nashville," 44–45.

46. James Dinkins, *1861 to 1865: Personal Reminiscences and Experiences in the Confederate Army* (Cincinnati: Robert Clarke Co., 1897), 249; Thomas Jordan and J. P. Pryor, *The Campaigns of Lieut.-Gen. N. B. Forrest*, 641; David C. Kelley, "More on the Confederate Cavalry at Nashville," 45.

47. Datus Coon, *Official Records*, Series 1, Volume 45, Part 1, 591–592.
48. James Wilson, *Under the Old Flag*, Volume II (New York and London: D. Appleton And Company, 1912), 122.
49. James Wilson, *Under the Old Flag*, 122–123.
50. James Dinkins, *1861 to 1865: Personal Reminiscences*, 249; James Wilson, *Under the Old Flag*, 122; Charles S. O. Rice, "Reminiscences of a Confederate Soldier" and articles from *The Enterprise*, MS.1263, University of Tennessee Special Collections, Knoxville.
51. Sidney O. Roberts, *Official Records*, Series 1, Volume 45, Part 1, 595.
52. James Wilson, *Under the Old Flag*, 123–124.
53. James Chalmers, *Official Records*, Series 1, Volume 45, Part 1, 765–766; John Johnston, Diaries and Memoirs, pp. 155–156.
54. James Brownlow, Jr., "Autobiography of James Polk Brownlow, Jr.," C. Brownlow Hastings, 1994. From the private collection of John A. Hastings of Austin, Texas; James P. Brownlow, Autobiography, Small Collections, Box 7, Ac. No., 1074, Tennessee State Library and Archives; Michael Cotton, *The Williamson County Cavalry: A History of Company F, Fourth Tennessee Cavalry Regiment, C.S. A.* (Goodlettsville: D.M. Cotton, 1994), 197.
55. James Chalmers, *Official Records*, Series 1, Volume 45, Part 1, 766; MS-0124: T. J. Walker, "Reminiscences," MS-0124, p. 30, The Special Collections Library of the University of Tennessee, Knoxville; James R. Chalmers, Letter to major, August 27, 1866, Pearce Museum at Navarro College, Corsicana, Texas.
56. Henry Kratzer McVey, *A Writ of My Civil War Experiences* (Jefferson County, Iowa: n.p. 2001), 20; Samuel Watkins, *"Co. Aytch"* (Chattanooga, TN., Times Printing Company, 1900), 216; Daniel Harris Reynolds, Diary entry, December 16, 1864, Daniel Harris Reynolds Papers (MS R32), University of Arkansas, Special Collections; William Josiah McMurray, *History of the Twentieth Tennessee Regiment Volunteer Infantry, C. S. A.* (Nashville, TN: The Publication Committee, consisting of W.J. McMurray, D.J. Roberts, and R.J. Neal, 1904), 541.
57. Charles Anderson, *Official Records*, Series 1, Volume 45, Part 2, 693; William Worthington, Letter to "My Dear Mother," January 15, 1865, Worthington Family Papers, MS Z/0658.000/S, Box 1, Mississippi Department of History and Archives.
58. N. B. Forrest, *Official Records*, Series 1, Volume 45, Part 1, 756; Allen G. Hatley, *The First Texas Legion during the American Civil War* (East Lake, TX: Centex Press, 2004), 134.
59. D. W. Comstock, *Ninth Cavalry*, 34.
60. John Allan Wyeth, *Life of General Nathan Bedford Forrest* (New York and London: Harper & Brothers Publishers, 1899), 559; Michael P. Rucker, *The Meanest and 'Damnest Job': Being the Civil War Exploits and Civilian Accomplishments of Colonel Edmund Winchester Rucker During and After the War* (Montgomery: NewSouth Books, 2019), 204.
61. James Dinkins, *1861 to 1865: Personal Reminiscences*, 248.
62. John B. Hood, *Official Records*, Series 1, Volume 45, Part 2, 699; Sarah Ridley Trimble, "Behind The Lines In Middle Tennessee, 1863–1865: The Journal of Bettie Ridley Blackmore," *Tennessee Historical Quarterly*, Vol. 12, No. 1 (March, 1953): 48–80, p. 78.
63. G. P. T. Beauregard, *Official Records*, Series 1, Volume 45, Part 1, 662; Richard McMurry, *John Bell Hood and the War for Southern Independence* (Lexington: The University Press of Kentucky, 1982), 183; Brian Craig Miller, *John Bell Hood and the Fight for Civil War Memory* (Knoxville: University of Tennessee Press, 2010), 170; G. T. Beauregard, *Official Records*, Series 1, Volume 45, Part 2, 726.
64. John B. Hood, *Advance and Retreat* (New Orleans: G. T. Beauregard, 1880), 303.
65. John Hood, *Official Records*, Series 1, Volume 45, Part 1, 660–661; Wiley Sword, *Embrace an Angry Wind*, 393–394.
66. James H. Wilson, "The Union Cavalry in the Hood Campaign, In *Battles and Leaders of the Civil War*, Vol. IV (New York: The Century Co., 1888), 470.
67. Thomas Robson Hay, *Hood's Tennessee Campaign* (New York: Press of Morningside Books, 1976), 164–169; Richard Johnson, *Memoir of Maj.-Gen. George H. Thomas* (Philadelphia: J. B. Lippincott and Co., 1881), 205.
68. James Wilson, *Under the Old Flag*, 120.
69. George Thomas, *Official Records*, Series 1, Volume 45, Part 1, 40; Walter T. Durham, *Reluctant Partners: Nashville and the Union* (Nashville: The Nashville Historical Society, 1987), 263.

Chapter Thirteen

1. Wiley Sword, *Embrace an Angry Wind: The Confederacy's Last Hurrah: Spring Hill, Franklin and Nashville* (New York: Harper Collins Publishers, 1992), 426; Francis A. Shoup, "Journal of the Army of Tennessee," *Official Records*, Series 1, Volume 45, Part 1, 673–674; A. P. Mason, *Official Records*, Series 1, Volume 45, Part 1, 663–664; *Daily Clarion*, "Gen. Hood Relieved at His Own Request," January 19, 1865, p. 2, col. 5.
2. John B. Hood, *Official Records*, Series 1, Volume 45, Part 1, 661; Francis A. Shoup, *Official Records*, Series 1, Volume 45, Part 1, 673; Sam Dunlap, Journal, Dunlap Family, Papers, 1780–2002, C4004, Missouri Historical Society, Columbia.
3. George Kryder, Letter to wife, December 17, 1864, MS 163—George Kryder Papers, Bowling Green University; James R. Chalmers, Letter to major, August 27, 1866, Pearce Museum at Navarro College, Corsicana, Texas; J. P. Young, *Seventh Tennessee Cavalry (Confederate): A History* (Nash-

ville: M.E. Church South, 1890), 124; Tyree Bell, "Autobiography," typeset manuscript, David M. Rubenstein Rare Book & Manuscript Library, Duke University, p. 127; Thomas John Brown, "John Bell Hood: Extracting Truth from History," (2011), Master's Thesis, San Jose State University, 159.

4. James Chalmers, *Official Records*, Series 1, Volume 45, Part 1, 766; Robert I. Battle, Diary—December 17, 1864, Smith, Elvin, Jr.—Collector (MSS 534), Special Collections, Western Kentucky State University.

5. Robert H. Ramsey, *Official Records*, Series 1, Volume 45, Part 2, 218–219; James Wilson, *Official Records*, Series 1, Volume 45, Part 2, 237.

6. D. W. Sanders, "The Battle of Nashville," *Southern Bivouac*, Volume 1 (Louisville, Ky: B. F. Avery and Sons, Publishers, 1886), 176; Derek Smith, *In the Lion's Mouth: Hood's Tragic Retreat from Nashville, 1864* (Mechanicsburg, PA: Stackpole Books, 2011), 107.

7. Nathaniel Cheairs Hughes, Jr., *Brigadier General Tyree H. Bell, CSA* (Knoxville: UT Press, 2004), 210–211; Richard R. Hancock, *Hancock's Diary: Or, A History of the Second Tennessee Confederate Cavalry* (Nashville: Brandon Printing Company, 1887), 532–534; Thomas J. Caper, "Chasing Hood," *National Tribune*, March 22, 1888, p. 1.

[Note: Lindsley refers to Nixon's and Russell's regiments both as the 20th Tennessee.]

8. James Holtzclaw, *Official Records*, Series 1, Volume 45, Part 1, 706; Henry D. Clayton, *Official Records*, Series 1, Volume 45, Part 1, 699; M. Jane Johansson, "Gibson's Louisiana Brigade During the 1864 Tennessee Campaign," *Tennessee Historical Quarterly*, Vol. 64, No. 3 (Fall 2005), p. 193.

9. John H. Hammond, *Official Records*, Series 1, Volume 45, Part 1, 607; James Wilson, *Official Records*, Series 1, Volume 45, Part 1, 565; Stephen Lee, *Official Records*, Series 1, Volume 45, Part 1, 690.

10. James Holtzclaw, *Official Records*, Series 1, Volume 45, Part 1, 706; Randall Gibson, *Official Records*, Series 1, Volume 45, Part 1, 703.

11. James Holtzclaw, *Official Records*, Series 1, Volume 45, Part 1, 706; Randall Gibson, *Official Records*, Series 1, Volume 45, Part 1, 703; Henry D. Clayton, *Official Records*, Series 1, Volume 45, Part 1, 699; Henry Stone, "The Battle of Nashville, Tennessee: December 15 and 16, 1864," In *Campaigns in Kentucky and Tennessee Including the Battle of Chickamauga: 1862–1864, Papers of the Military Historical Society of Massachusetts*, Vol. VII (Boston: Military Historical Society of Massachusetts, 1908), 536; George E. Brewer, "Incidents of the Retreat from Nashville," *Confederate Veteran*, Volume 18, No. 7 (July 1910), p. 327.

12. J. P. Young, *Seventh Tennessee Cavalry (Confederate): A History*, 124–125; W. A. Polk, "Gallant Col. William F. Taylor," *Confederate Veteran*, Volume 16, No. 3 (March 1908), 124–125; R. J. Black, "How Three Men Held an Army in Check," *Confederate Veteran*, Volume 16, No. 6 (June 1908), 268; Brent A. Cox, *Colonel Jacob Barnett Biffle: Born to Fight* (n.p.: Sons of the South Publications, 1991), 44.

13. Randall Gibson, *Official Records*, Series 1, Volume 45, Part 1, 703; Henry Clayton, *Official Records*, Series 1, Volume 45, Part 1, 699; Derek Smith, *In the Lion's Mouth*, 113.

14. H. A. Tyler, "Forrest Covers Hood's Retreat," *Confederate Veteran*, Vol. 12, No. 9 (Sept. 1904), p. 436.

15. D. W. Comstock, *Ninth Cavalry: One Hundred and Twenty-first Regiment Indiana Volunteers* (Richmond, IN.: Published by J. M. Coe, 1890), 35–37; Thomas J. Caper, "Chasing Hood," *National Tribune*, March 22, 1888, p. 1; Ashby L. Kerwood, *Annals of the Fifty-Seventh Regiment Indiana Volunteers* (Dayton, O. W. J. Shuey, 1868), 304; James Holtzclaw, *Official Records*, Series 1, Volume 45, Part 1, 707.

16. D. W. Comstock, Ninth Cavalry, 37–38.

17. Ibid.

18. D. W. Comstock, *Ninth Cavalry*, 38.

19. Richard Johnson, *Official Records*, Series 1, Volume 45, Part 1, 601; Theodore Allen, December 17 entry, 1842–1919, Diary, 1864–1865, Mss. A A431 1, Filson Historical Society, Louisville.

20. James Wilson, *Official Records*, Series 1, Volume 45, Part 1, 565.

21. W. R. Carter, *History of the First Regiment of Tennessee Volunteer Cavalry* (Knoxville: Gaut-Ogden Co., Printers and Binders, 1902), 235–236; James H. Wilson, *Official Records*, Series 1, Volume 45, Part 1, 553; Derek Smith, *In the Lion's Mouth*, 118–119.

22. James Holtzclaw, *Official Records*, Series 1, Volume 45, Part 1, 707.

23. Carter Stevenson, *Official Records*, Series 1, Volume 45, Part 1, 696; Stephen D. Lee, *Official Records*, Series 1, Volume 45, Part 1, 690.

24. James Goodwin, "The Fourth Tennessee Cavalry," Box F25, folder 3, Federal Collection, Tennessee State Library and Archives. 40.

25. Thomas J. Caper, "Chasing Hood," p. 1; Carter Stevenson, *Official Records*, Series 1, Volume 45, Part 1, 696; James Wilson, *Official Records*, Series 1, Volume 45, Part 1, 565–566.

26. Ibid.; James Wilson, *Under the Old Flag*, 132–133.

27. Ibid.

28. James Wilson, *Official Records*, Series 1, Volume 45, Part 1, 565–566.

29. Preston Sharp, Diary entry—December 17, 1864, Sharp, Preston T. Collection, R1204, Missouri Historical Society, Columbia; John Johnston, Diaries and Memoirs, 159–160.

30. Thomas J. Caper, "Chasing Hood."

31. Carter Stevenson, *Official Records*, Series 1, Volume 45, Part 1, 696; S. D. Lee, *Official Records*, Series 1, Volume 45, Part 1, 690.

32. James Dinkins, *1861 to 1865: Personal Reminiscences and Experiences in the Confederate Army* (Cincinnati: Robert Clarke Co., 1897),

251; J. Harvey Mathes, *Great Commanders: General Forrest* (New York; D. Appleton and Company, 1902), 322; John Morton, *The Artillery of Nathan Bedford Forrest's Cavalry* (Nashville and Dallas: Publishing House of the M. E. Church, South Smith & Lamar, Agents, 1909), 287; John Johnston, Diaries and Memoirs, p. 158; James H. Wilson, *Official Records*, Series 1, Volume 45, Part 2, 237–238.

33. Derek Smith, *In the Lion's Mouth*, 123; Alexander Eckel, *History of the Fourth Tennessee Cavalry* (Johnson City, TN: Overmountain Press, 2001), 76.

34. J. H. Hammond, *Official Records*, Series 1, Volume 45, Part 1, 607.

35. Thomas J. Caper, "Chasing Hood," *National Tribune*, March 22, 1888, p. 1.

36. Henry Clayton, *Official Records*, Series 1, Volume 45, Part 1, 699–700.

37. R. W. Surby, "Hatch's Hard Riders," *National Tribune*, September 9, 1886, p. 1; H. A. Tyler, "Forrest Covers Hood's Retreat," 436.

38. Lyman Pierce, *History of the Second Iowa cavalry* (Burlington, Iowa: Hawkeye Steam Book and Job Printing Establishment, 1865), 150–151.

39. George Monlux, "To My Comrades Co. I, 8th Iowa Cavalry," Personal narrative, State Historical Library & Archives, p. 61; James H. Wilson, *Official Records*, Series 1, Volume 45, Part 2, 238–239; George E. Cooper, *Official Records*, Series 1, Volume 45, Part 1, 110.

40. James Biddle, *Official Records*, Series 1, Volume 45, Part 1, 606.

41. Edward Hatch, *Official Records*, Series 1, Volume 45, Part 1, 578; Francis Stewart, Diary, December 17, 1864, MS 744—Francis Stewart Papers Transcripts, Bowling Green University; Alexis Cope, *The Fifteenth Ohio Volunteers and Its Campaigns: 1861–1865* (Columbus, OH: By author, 1916), 662.

42. W. R. Carter, *History of the First Tennessee Volunteer Cavalry*, 236; William Legg Henderson, Journal entry—December 18, 1864, William Legg Henderson Civil War Diaries, MSC0926, Special Collections, University of Iowa; James H. Wilson, *Official Records*, Series 1, Volume 45, Part 2, 253; Richard Johnson, *Official Records*, Series 1, Volume 45, Part 2, 602.

43. James Chalmers, *Official Records*, Series 1, Volume 45, Part 1, 766; Nathan B. Forrest, *Official Records*, Series 1, Volume 45, Part 1, 756–767; James O. Walton letter to Mary Ann, no date, from Spring Hill, S1355, Rare Books and Manuscripts, Indiana State Library, Indianapolis; Sam Dunlap, Journal; James Chalmers, "Forrest and His Campaigns," *Southern Historical Society Papers*, Volume 7, Number 10 (October 1879), 482; December 19—diary entry, John Quincy Adams Baker Papers, 1862–1865, 1892 [VFM 2956], Ohio Historical Society; Derek Smith, *In the Lion's Mouth*, 141; William M. Worthington, Letter to "My Dear Mother," January 15, 1865, Worthington Family Papers, MS Z/0658.000/S, Box 1, Mississippi Department of History and Archives.

44. Edward Hatch, *Official Records*, Series 1, Volume 45, Part 1, 578; James Wilson, *Under the Old Flag*, 135; Datus Coon, *Official Records*, Series 1, Volume 45, Part 1, 592–593.

45. A. J. Alexander, *Official Records*, Series 1, Volume 45, Part 2, 277.

46. "An Incident in Hood's Campaign," *Southern Bivouac* (Nov. 1884), 131–132; Christopher Losson, *Tennessee's Forgotten Warriors* (Knoxville: University of Tennessee Press, 1989), 240.

47. Francis A. Shoup, "Journal of the Army of Tennessee," *Official Records*, Series 1, Volume 45, Part 1, 673; John B. Hood, *Official Records*, Series 1, Volume 45, Part 1, 655; Benjamin Nourse, Diary, December 20, 1864, David M. Rubenstein Rare Book & Manuscript Library, Duke University; Edward Walthall, *Official Records*, Series 1, Volume 45, Part 1, 730–731; T. J. Wood, *Official Records*, Series 1, Volume 45, Part 2, 287; Christopher Losson, *Tennessee's Forgotten Warriors*, 240–241.

48. John Henry Brown, *Indian Wars and Pioneers of Texas* (Austin: L. E. Daniell, Publisher, 1890), 318.

49. N. B. Forrest, *Official Records*, Series 1, Volume 45, Part 1, 757; Sam Dunlap, Journal; Henry M. Hempstead, Journal—December 20, 1864, Bentley Historical Library, University of Michigan.

50. James H. Wilson, *Official Records*, Series 1, Volume 45, Part 2, 291; Robert Ramsey, *Official Records*, Series 1, Volume 45, Part 2, 291.

51. E. B. Beaumont, *Official Records*, Series 1, Volume 45, Part 2, 314; James H. Wilson, *Official Records*, Series 1, Volume 45, Part 2, 302; R. H. Crowder, Letter, December 21, 1864, R. H. Crowder papers, 1859–1908, M0208, Box 1, Folder 12, Indiana Historical Society.

52. N. B. Forrest, *Official Records*, Series 1, Volume 45, Part 1, 757; James Chalmers, *Official Records*, Series 1, Volume 45, Part 1, 766; Edward Walthall, *Official Records*, Series 1, Volume 45, Part 1, 727; Preston Sharp, Diary entry—December 23, 1864; W. R. Carter, *History of the First Tennessee Volunteer Cavalry*, 237; James H. Wilson, *Official Records*, Series 1, Volume 45, Part 2, 291; J. P. Strange, *Official Records*, Series 1, Volume 45, Part 2, 726.

53. James Cooper, Diaries and Memoirs, Confederate Collection, Box 12, Folder 11, Tennessee State Library and Archives, p. 58.

54. Nimrod Porter, Diary entry—December 24, 1864, Nimrod Porter Papers #01094, Southern Historical Collection, The Wilson Library, University of North Carolina at Chapel Hill.

55. E. B. Beaumont, *Official Records*, Series 1, Volume 45, Part 2, 324–325; James Wilson, *Under the Old Flag*, 136.

56. Benjamin Nourse, Diary, December 24, 1864, David M. Rubenstein Rare Book & Manuscript Library, Duke University; J. A. Creager,

"Ross's Brigade of Cavalry," *Confederate Veteran*, Volume 28, No. 8 (August 1920), 292; Scott Walker, *Hell's Broke Loose in Georgia* (Athens & London: University of Georgia Press, 2005), 213.

57. N. B. Forrest, *Official Records*, Series 1, Volume 45, Part 1, 757–758; J. G. Deupree, "The Noxubee Squadron of the First Mississippi Cavalry, C. S. A. 1861–1865," In *Publications of the Mississippi Historical Society*, Volume II, Dunbar Rowland, ed. (Jackson, MS: Democrat Printing Co., 1918), 117–118; J. Harvey Mathes, *Great Commanders: General Forrest* (New York; D. Appleton and Company, 1902), 326; Derek Smith, *In the Lion's Mouth*, 189; D. W. Sanders, "Hood's Tennessee Campaign," *Confederate Veteran*, Volume 15, No. 9 (September 1907), p. 403; John Morton, *The Artillery of Nathan Bedford Forrest's Cavalry* (Nashville and Dallas: Publishing House of the M. E. Church, South Smith & Lamar, Agents, 1909), 294.

58. John Morton, *The Artillery of Nathan Bedford Forrest's Cavalry*, 294.

59. Eddy Davison and Daniel Fox, *Nathan Bedford Forrest: In Search of the Enigma* (Gretna, LA: Pelican Publishing Co., 2007), 373; Jack Welsh, *Medical Histories of Confederate Generals* (Kent, OH: Kent State University Press, 1995), 31.

60. Nathaniel Cheairs Hughes, Jr., *Brigadier General Tyree H. Bell, CSA*, 214–215; J. P. Young, *Seventh Tennessee Cavalry (Confederate): A History* (Nashville: M.E. Church South, 1890), 128.

61. James Wilson, *Under the Old Flag*, 140; D. W. Comstock, *Ninth Cavalry*, 40.

62. Datus Coon, *Official Records*, Series 1, Volume 45, Part 1, 593; Edward Hatch, *Official Records*, Series 1, Volume 45, Part 1, 578.

63. *The Soldier's Casket*, Volume 1 (Philadelphia: C. W. Alexander, 1865), 135; Tim Hashaw, *Children of Perdition: Melungeons and the Struggle of Mixed America* (Macon: Mercer University Press, 2006), 47; James Alex Baggett, *Homegrown Yankees: Tennessee's Union Cavalry in the Civil War* (Baton Rouge: Louisiana State University, 2009), 310.

64. L. S. Ross, *Official Records*, Series 1, Volume 45, Part 1, 772; Douglas Hale, *The Third Texas Cavalry in the Civil War* (Norman: University of Oklahoma Press, 1993), 264–265; George L. Griscom, *Fighting with Ross' Texas Cavalry Brigade, C.S.A.: The Diary of George L. Griscom, adjutant, 9th Texas Cavalry Regiment*, edited by Homer L. Kerr (Hillsboro, TX: Hill Junior College Press, 1976), 197; William Johnson Worsham, *The Old 19th Tennessee Regiment, C.S. A. June 1861-April 1865* (Knoxville, TN: Press of Paragon Printing company, 1902), 259; Stephen S. Kirk, *Sul Ross' Sixth Texas Cavalry: Six Shooters & Bowie Knives* (Independence, MO: Two Trails, 2008), 113.

65. James Chalmers, *Official Records*, Series 1, Volume 45, Part 1, 767; James R. Chalmers, Letter to major, August 27, 1866, Pearce Museum at Navarro College, Corsicana, Texas; I. N. Rainey, "Experiences of I. N. Rainey in the Confederate Army," Southern History Collection, University of North Carolina; James H. McNeilly, "With the Rear Guard," *Confederate Veteran*, Volume 26, No. 8 (August 1981), p. 338.

66. J. G. Deupree, "The Noxubee Squadron of the First Mississippi Cavalry, C. S. A. 1861–1865," 118.

67. James H. Wilson, *Official Records*, Series 1, Volume 45, Part 2, 334; John Croxton, *Official Records*, Series 1, Volume 45, Part 1, 574.

68. J. H. Wilson, *Official Records*, Series 1, Volume 45, Part 1, 335; Robert Ramsay, *Official Records*, Series 1, Volume 45, Part 1, 335; Derek Smith, *In the Lion's Mouth*, 194–195.

69. N. B. Forrest, *Official Records*, Series 1, Volume 45, Part 1, 758; J. G. Deupree, "The Noxubee Squadron of the First Mississippi Cavalry, C. S. A. 1861–1865."

70. George Monlux, "To My Comrades Co. I, 8th Iowa Cavalry," Personal narrative, State Historical Library & Archives, p. 63; Thomas Harrison, *Official Records*, Series 1, Volume 45, Part 1, 603; Charles Alley, Diary entry—December 25, 1864, Alley, Charles. Diary, 1861–1865, University of Oklahoma Libraries, Western History Collections.

71. Thomas Harrison, *Official Records*, Series 1, Volume 45, Part 1, 603; J. A. Bigger, Diary, November 25, 1864, J.A. Bigger Diary, April 30, 1862-Mary 12, 1865, Small Manuscripts 76–3 (4 folders), Archives and Special Collections, The University of Mississippi, Oxford, MS; J. W. Worsham, *Old Nineteenth Tennessee Regiment, C.S. A. June, 1861-April, 1865* (Knoxville, TN: Press of Paragon Printing Company, 1902), 159; Preston Sharp, Diary entry—December 25, 1864; Francis Stewart, Diary December 25, 1864.

72. R. C. Rankin, "Dr. Cannon's Story: With the 7th Ohio Cavalry," *National Tribune*, February 17, 1898, p. 8; James Christy, December 25, 1864 entry, Journal of Sgt. James Christy, 4th Regiment, U.S. Cavalry, Company F., Des Moines Historical Library Manuscripts (N14/3/4 Box 6 Folder 2).

73. J. G. Deupree, "The Noxubee Squadron of the First Mississippi Cavalry, C. S. A. 1861–1865," 119; Edward Walthall, *Official Records*, Series 1, Volume 45, Part 1, 727; Charles Hart Olmstead, "Rear Guard Service in Tennessee," Charles Hart Olmstead papers, MS 599, Georgia Historical Society, Savannah, Georgia; Martha L. Crabb, *All Afire to Fight: The Untold Tale of the Civil War's Ninth Texas Cavalry* (New York: Avon Books, 2000), 279.

74. Thomas Harrison, *Official Records*, Series 1, Volume 45, Part 1, 603; J. A. Bigger, Diary, December 26, 1864.

75. Edward Walthall, *Official Records*, Series 1, Volume 45, Part 1, 727; J. G. Deupree, "The Noxubee Squadron of the First Mississippi Cavalry, C. S. A. 1861–1865," 119; John Morton, *The Artillery of Nathan Bedford Forrest's Cavalry*, 295.

76. Thomas Harrison, *Official Records*, Series 1, Volume 45, Part 1, 603; Edward Walthall, *Official Records*, Series 1, Volume 45, Part 1, 727; Newton

Cannon, *The Reminiscences of Sergeant Newton Cannon*, Samuel Fleming, Jr., editor (Franklin, TN: Carter House Assoc., 1963), 59–60; O. B. Hayden, "Disagreeing Troopers," *National Tribune*, October 28, 1886, p. 4; Charles Alley, diary, December 25, 1865.

77. J. H. Hammond, *Official Records*, Series 1, Volume 45, Part 1, 607–608; D. W. Comstock, *Ninth Cavalry*, 41.

78. Edward A. Davenport, editor, *History of the Ninth Regiment Illinois Cavalry Volunteers* (Chicago: Donohue & Henneberry, Printers and Binders, 1888), 164–165; Edward Hatch, *Official Records*, Series 1, Volume 45, Part 1, 578–579; Eugene Bruce Read Diary, Volume 5, December 25, 1864, Special Collections, Newberry Library.

79. *Ibid.*

80. James Christy, December 25, 1864 entry, Journal of Sgt. James Christy.

81. John Morton, *The Artillery of Nathan Bedford Forrest's Cavalry*, 297; Edward Walthall, Official Records, Series 1, Volume 45, Part 1, 727.

82. James Chalmers, "Forrest and His Campaigns," 483; Thomas Harrison, *Official Records*, Series 1, Volume 45, Part 1, 603; James H. Wilson, *Official Records*, Series 1, Volume 45, Part 2, 348; John B. Hood, *Official Records*, Series 1, Volume 45, Part 2, 731.

83. N. B. Forrest, *Official Records*, Series 1, Volume 45, Part 1, 758; Sam Dunlap, Journal; Jack Hurst, *Nathan Bedford Forrest: A Biography* (New York: Vintage Press, 1993), 244; S. B. Barron, *The Lone Star Defenders: A Chronicle of the Third Texas Cavalry, Ross' Brigade* (New York and Washington: The Neale Publishing Company, 1908), 252–253; L. S. Ross, *Official Records*, Series 1, Volume 45, Part 1, 771; George L. Griscom, *Fighting with Ross' Texas Cavalry Brigade, C.S. A.*, 198; S. B. Barron, "From The Other Side: Confederate Cavalry Officer Tells of Hood's Rearguard after Nashville," *National Tribune*, June 2, 1887, p. 5; Thomas Harrison, *Official Records*, Series 1, Volume 45, Part 1, 603; Edward Walthall, *Official Records*, Series 1, Volume 45, Part 1, 727; Newton Cannon, *The Reminiscences of Sergeant Newton Cannon*, Samuel Fleming, Jr., editor (Franklin, TN: Carter House Assoc., 1963), 59–60; O. B. Hayden, "Disagreeing Troopers," 4; Charles Alley, diary, December 25, 1865.

84. W. J. Worsham, *Old Nineteenth Tennessee Regiment*, 160.

85. *Ibid.*, J. G. Deupree, "The Noxubee Squadron of the First Mississippi Cavalry, C. S. A. 1861–1865," 121; John Morton, *The Artillery of Nathan Bedford Forrest's Cavalry*, 297.

86. N. B. Forrest, *Official Records*, Series 1, Volume 45, Part 1, 758; James Chalmers, "Forrest and His Campaigns," 484; George L. Griscom, *Fighting with Ross' Texas Cavalry Brigade, C.S. A.*, 198; J. A. Bigger, Diary, December 26 1864: Thomas Jordan and J. P. Pryor, *The Campaigns of Lieut.-Gen. N. B. Forrest* (New Orleans, Memphis and New York: Blelock & Company, 1868), 652; James H. McNeilly, "With the Rear Guard," *Confederate Veteran*, Volume 26, No. 8 (August 1981), p. 339.

87. L. S. Ross, *Official Records*, Series 1, Volume 45, Part 1, 772; John Morton, *The Artillery of Nathan Bedford Forrest's Cavalry*, 299; Edward Walthall, *Official Records*, Series 1, Volume 45, Part 1, 727–728.

88. L. S. Ross, *Official Records*, Series 1, Volume 45, Part 1, 772; John Morton, *The Artillery of Nathan Bedford Forrest's Cavalry*, 299.

89. D. W. Comstock, *Ninth Cavalry*, 42–43; Thomas J. Caper, "Chasing Hood," *National Tribune*, March 22, 1888, p. 1; James Goodwin, "The Fourth Tennessee Cavalry," Box F25, folder 3, Federal Collection, Tennessee State Library and Archives, 42–43; Thomas Jordan and J. P. Pryor, *The Campaigns of Lieut.-Gen. N. B. Forrest*, 653.

90. J. H. Hammond, *Official Records*, Series 1, Volume 45, Part 1, 608.

91. D. W. Comstock, *Ninth Cavalry*, 42–43.

92. N. B. Forrest, *Official Records*, Series 1, Volume 45, Part 1, 758; James Chalmers, "Forrest and His Campaigns," 484; George L. Griscom, *Fighting with Ross' Texas Cavalry Brigade, C.S. A.*, 198; J. A. Bigger, Diary, December 26 1864: Thomas Jordan and J. P. Pryor, *The Campaigns of Lieut.-Gen. N. B. Forrest*, 652; James H. McNeilly, "With the Rear Guard," *Confederate Veteran*, Volume 26, No. 8 (August 1981), p. 339; Edward Hatch, *Official Records*, Series 1, Volume 45, Part 1, 579; Josiah B. Smith, Letter to wife -January 27, 1865, Smith and Carpenter Families papers, 1864–1913, c.00301, Michigan State University Archives & Historical Collections.

93. Thos. G. Williamson, *Official Records*, Series 1, Volume 45, Part 1, 609; Charles H. Kirk, "The Last Blow at Hood's Army," 441–442.

94. James B. Irvine, The Civil War Diary of James Bennington Irvine (SPR323), Alabama Department of Archives and History; James Steedman, *Official Records*, Series 1, Volume 45, Part 1, 506; R. S. Granger, *Official Records*, Series 1, Volume 45, Part 2, 401; William Lyon, *Official Records*, Series 1, Volume 45, Part 1, 638.

95. Ben Hoksbergen and Brian Hogan, "The Affair at Indian Creek Ford: The Archaeology of a Small Civil War Battle," *The Huntsville Historical Review*, Vol. 37, No. 1 (Fall 2013- Winter 2014), pp. 23–25

96. Ben Hoksbergen and Brian Hogan, "The Affair at Indian Creek Ford," 26–28.

97. R. S. Granger, *Official Records*, Series 1, Volume 45, Part 2, 401.

98. Thos. G. Williamson, *Official Records*, Series 1, Volume 45, Part 1, 609; Charles H. Kirk, "The Last Blow at Hood's Army," In *History of the Fifteenth Pennsylvania Volunteer Cavalry*, Charles Kirk, ed. (Philadelphia: Society of the Fifteenth Pennsylvania Cavalry, 1906), 441–442; E. T. Freeman, *Official Records*, Series 1, Volume 45, Part 2, 775.

99. N. B. Forrest, *Official Records*, Series 1, Volume 45, Part 1, 758.

100. A. W. Sparks, *The War Between the States: As I Saw It* (Tyler, TX: Lee & Burnett, Printers, 1901), 285.
101. James Chalmers, *Official Records*, Series 1, Volume 45, Part 1, 767.
102. N. B. Forrest, *Official Records*, Series 1, Volume 45, Part 1, 761–762.
103. N. B. Forrest, *Official Records*, Series 1, Volume 45, Part 2, 757; James Chalmers, *Official Records*, Series 1, Volume 45, Part 2, 764–767 (In Chalmers' after action report he wrote he had 116 casualties by the end of the November and he also attached an addendum to his report showing 116 casualties from November 25 through December 6. Chalmers was essentially unengaged during this time period after November 30. So for some reason Forrest reported sixty fewer casualties for Chalmers just for November alone.)
104. N. B. Forrest, *Official Records*, Series 1, Volume 45, Part 1, 759–760.
105. James Wilson, *Official Records*, Series 1, Volume 45, Part 1, 568.
106. James Wilson, *Official Records*, Series 1, Volume 45, Part 1, 568; George Thomas, *Official Records*, Series 1, Volume 45, Part 1, 104–105.
107. James H. Wilson, *Under the Old Flag*, Vol. II, 72–74.
108. George Thomas, *Official Records*, Series 1, Volume 45, Part 1, 104–105; Wilson, *ibid.*.
109. James Chalmers, *Official Records*, Series 1, Volume 45, Part 2, 758.

Conclusions

1. Ebert Watson, "John Bell Hood's Tennessee Campaign," Sketches, Box 4, Folder 1, Tennessee State Library and Archives, p. 26.
2. Alexis Cope, *The Fifteenth Ohio Volunteers and Its Campaigns*, 668–672; Luke W. Finlay, "Another Report of Hood's Campaign," *Confederate Veteran*, Volume 15, No. 9 (September 1907), p. 407; Thomas Jordan and J. P. Pryor, *The Campaigns of Lieut.-Gen. N. B. Forrest* (New Orleans, Memphis and New York: Blelock & Company, 1868), 564; Eric William Sheppard, *Bedford Forrest: The Confederacy's Greatest Cavalryman* (Dayton, OH: Morningside House, Inc., 1988), 260.
3. Joseph Bardwell letter—February 12, 1865, Charles Butler correspondence, Bentley Historical Library, University of Michigan
4. N. B. Forrest, *Official Records*, Series 1, Volume 45, Part 2, 756; James H. Wilson, *Under the Old Flag*, , Volume II (New York and London: D. Appleton And Company, 1912), 143.
5. "Lieutenant-General N. B. Forrest," *Southern Historical Society Papers*, Volume 20 (1892): 325–335, p. 332; Robert Lamar Glaze, "Experiencing Defeat, Remembering Victory: The Army of Tennessee in War and Memory, 1861–1930," Ph.D. Dissertation, The University of Tennessee, Knoxville, 2016, p. 92; Walter E. Pittman, Jr, "General Nathan Bedford Forrest and Military Leadership," *West Tennessee Historical Society Papers*, Vol. 35 (1981), pp. 56–59; Williams III, Edward F., *Fustest with the Mostest; The Military Career of Confederate General Nathan Bedford Forrest* (Memphis: Historical Hiking Trails, Inc., 1973), 30.
6. N. B. Forrest, *Official Records*, Series 1, Volume 49, Part 2, 1290.
7. J. H. Hammond, Letter to Henry Wilson, February 1, 1865, John Henry Hammond, Papers, 1860–1890, Mss. A H226 3, Filson Historical Society.
8. Bradley R. Clampitt, *The Confederate Heartland: Military and Civilian Morale in the Western Confederacy* (Baton Rouge: Louisiana State University Press, 2011), 126; Steven E. Woodworth, *Jefferson Davis and his Generals: The Failure of Confederate Command in the West* (Lawrence: University of Kansas Press, 1990), 304.

Bibliography

Primary Sources—Published

Andes, John, and Will McTeer. *Loyal Mountain Troopers: The Second and Third Tennessee Volunteer Cavalry in the Civil War.* Maryville, Tennessee: Blount County Genealogical and Historical Society, 1992.

Armitage, Ambrose. *Brother to the Eagle: The Civil War Journal of Sgt. Ambrose Armitage, 8th Wisconsin Infantry,* Alden Carter, ed. United States: Booklocker, Inc, 2006.

Bates, James C. *A Texas Cavalry Officer's Civil: The Diary and Letters of James C. Bates,* Richard Lowe, ed. Baton Rouge: Louisiana State University Press, 1999.

Cate, Wirt A., ed. *Two Soldiers: The Campaign Diaries of Thomas J. Key and Robert J. Campbell.* Chapel Hill: University of North Carolina Press, 1938.

Chadick, Mary Jane. *Incidents of the War: The Civil War Journal of Mary Jane Chadick,* Nancy Rohr, ed. Huntsville: SilverThreads Publishing, 2005.

Champion, Sid. *My Dear Wife: Letters to Matilda, The Civil War Letters of Sid and Matilda Champion of Champion Hill,* Rebecca Blackwell Drake and Margie Riddle Bearss, ed. Self-published, 2005.

Connolly, James A. *Three Years in the Army of the Cumberland: The Letters and Diary of Major James A. Connolly,* Paul M. Angle, ed. Bloomington, IN: Indiana University Press, 1990.

Cumming, Kate. *The Journal of Hospital Life in the Confederate Army.* Louisville: John P. Morton & Company, 1866.

Dale, W. D. "The Disaster at Nashville: Another Letter From Col. W. D. Dale to His Wife After Hood's Defeat Before Nashville," *Confederate Veteran,* Vol. 2, No. 2 (Feb. 1894): 47.

Davis, Jefferson. *The Papers of Jefferson Davis,* Volume 11, Lynda Lasswell Crist, Barbara J. Rozek, Kenneth H. Williams, editors. Baton Rouge: Louisiana State University Press, 2003.

Graf, Leroy, and Ralph Haskins, editors. *Papers of Andrew Johnson,* Volume 6. Knoxville: University of Tennessee Press, 1983.

Griscom, George L. *Fighting with Ross' Texas Cavalry Brigade, C.S.A.: The Diary of George L. Griscom, Adjutant, 9th Texas Cavalry Regiment,* edited by Homer L. Kerr. Hillsboro, TX: Hill Junior College Press, 1976.

Hamilton, Isaac R. Letter, *The Papers of Andrew Johnson,* Volume 6, LeRoy P. Graf and Ralph Haskins, eds. Knoxville: University of Tennessee Press, 1983.

Hancock, Richard R. *Hancock's Diary: Or, A History of the Second Tennessee Confederate Cavalry.* Nashville: Brandon Printing Company, 1887.

Harris, Benjamin R. "Diary," In *The Civil War in Maury County,* Tennessee, Jill K. Garrett and Marise P. Lightfoot, ed. Columbia, TN.: n. p., 1966.

Hawley, Thomas. *"This Terrible Struggle for Life": The Civil War Letters of a Union Regimental Surgeon,* Dennis W Belcher, ed. Jefferson, NC: McFarland, 2012.

Jordan, Stephen A. "Diary of Stephen A. Jordan." In *The Civil War in Maury County, Tennessee,* Jill K. Garrett and Marise P. Lightfoot, ed. Columbia, TN.: n. p., 1966.

Lindsley, Maggie. *"Maggie!" Maggie Lindsley's Journal,* Muriel Davies Mackenzie, ed. Southbury, CT: privately printed, 1977.

Logsdon, David R., ed. *Eyewitnesses at the Battle of Franklin.* Nashville: published by author, 1988.

Merrill, Robert S. *Robert S. Merrill, Diary.* Cedarburg, WI: MSG, 2007.

Mitchell, Enoch L. "Letters of a Confederate Surgeon in the Army of Tennessee to His Wife," *Tennessee Historical Quarterly,* Vol. 5, No. 2 (June, 1946): 142–181.

Reynolds, Daniel Harris. *Worthy of the Cause for Which They Fight: The Civil War Diary of Brigadier General Daniel Harris Reynolds, 1861–1865,* Robert Patrick Bender, ed. Fayetteville: University of Arkansas Press, 2011.

Robins, Glenn. *They Have Left Us Here to Die: The Civil War Prison Diary of Sgt. Lyle Adair, 111th U.S. Colored Infantry.* Kent: Kent State University Press, 2011.

Ross, L. S. *Personal Civil War Letters of General Lawrence Sullivan Ross with other letters,* transcribed and compiled by Perry Wayne Shelton, edited by Shelly Morrison. Austin: Shelly and Richard Morrison, 1994.

Seaton, Benjamin M. *The Bugle Softly Blows: The*

Confederate Diary of Benjamin M. Seaton. Harold Simpson, ed. Waco: Texian Press, 1965.
Simon, John Y., ed. *The Papers of Ulysses S. Grant: June 1-August 15, 1864,* Volume 11. Carbondale and Edwardsville: Southern Illinois University Press, 1984.
Simpson, Brooks D., and Jean V. Berlin. *Sherman's Civil War: Selected Correspondence of William T. Sherman, 1860–1865.* Chapel Hill: University of North Carolina Press, 1999.
Smith, Benjamin. *Private Smith's Journal,* Clyde C. Walton, ed. Chicago: R. R. Donnelley & Sons Company, 1963.
Spence, John C. *A Diary of the Civil War.* Murfreesboro: Rutherford County Historical Society, 1993.
Stribling, C. K. "Letter, October 16, 1864," In *Batchelor-Turner letters, 1861–1864, written by two of Terry's Texas Rangers,* annotated by H. J. H. Rugeley. Austin, TX: The Steck Company, 1961.
Tillman, James Adams. *A Palmetto Boy: Civil War-Era Diaries and Letters of James Adams Tillman,* Bobbie Swearingen Smith, ed. Columbia: University of South Carolina Press 2010.
Treadway, Charles. "The Letters of Charles Wesley Treadway," In *Foot Prints: Past and Present,* Vol. 9, Richland County Genealogical Society, Olney, IL.
Trimble, Sarah Ridley. "Behind the Lines in Middle Tennessee, 1863–1865: The Journal of Bettie Ridley Blackmore." *Tennessee Historical Quarterly,* Vol. 12, No. 1 (March, 1953): 48–80.
Watkins, Samuel. *Co. Aytch.* Chattanooga: Times Printing Company, 1900.
Wells, Gideon. *The Civil War Diary of Gideon Welles, Lincoln's Secretary of the Navy: The Original Manuscript Edition,* William E. Gienapp and Erica L. Gienapp, editors. Champaign: University of Illinois Press, 2014.

Primary Sources—Unpublished

Alabama Department of Archives and History
Robert Lewis Bliss Papers
Alexander K. Hall Family Papers
James Bennington Irvine Diary
Thomas Smyrl Papers

Arlington Heights Historical Museum
Charles Sigwalt Diaries

Auburn University—Special Collections and Archives
John Crittenden Papers

Baylor University
J. N. and Virginia Adkins Coleman Papers, The Texas Collection
Ross Family Papers, The Texas Collection

Bowling Green State University, William T. Jerome Library
Ira Conine Papers
George Kryder Papers
Daniel Prickitt Papers
Francis Stewart Papers

Private Collection of John A. Hastings, Austin, Texas
James Brownlow, Jr., Papers

Cincinnati Historical Society, Cincinnati Museum Center
William E. Crane, "William E. Crane's Daily Journal of Life in the Field during the War of the Rebellion"

Duke University, David M. Rubenstein Rare Book and Manuscript Library
Tyree Harris Bell Autobiography
Benjamin Nourse Journal
James Wiswell Letters

Emory University, Manuscript, Archives and Rare Book Library
W. B. Corbitt Diary
Thomas Taylor Letters

Filson Historical Society
Theodore Allen Diary, 1864–1865
John Henry Hammond Papers, 1860–1890
James L. Hughes Letters, 1864–1865
Adrastus Newell Papers, 1831–1912
C. H. Sowle Manuscript
Winn–Cook Family Papers

Georgia Historical Society
Charles Hart Olmstead Papers

Georgia Archives
Carson Family Papers

Gettysburg College
William H. Young Papers

George Mason University
Milton Barnes Papers

Gilder Leheman Institute of American History
George Clark Letters
Eben Ellison Papers
Joseph Jones Papers
Emery Pratt Papers
Zealous B. Tower Papers

W. J. Griffing—Private Collection, Batavia, IL

Pocket Journal of Joseph Vincent Hinchman

Howard Country Historical Society, Kokomo, Indiana

Thomas J. Harrison Letters

Indiana Historical Society, Indianapolis

"A Brief History of the Eleventh Indiana Cavalry," pamphlet
Homer Carpenter Papers
R. H. Crowder Papers
Crowder-Bose Papers
Dwight Fraser Letters
Charles A. Harper Diary
Joseph Rabb Papers
Edward Reid Papers

Indiana State Library

John J. Pribble Letter
James O. Walton Letters

Jasper County Indiana Public Library (used with permission from the special collections of the Jasper County Public Library)

Robert H. Milroy Letters
Alfred Reed Papers

Michigan State University Archives & Historical Collections

Smith and Carpenter Family Papers

Minnesota Historical Society

Edson Washburn Diary

Mississippi Department of Archives and History

Vertical Regimental Files
Worthington Family Papers

Missouri Historical Society

Dunlap Family Papers
Preston T. Sharp Collection

Missouri History Museum (St. Louis)

Francis Fairbank and Harriet Elizabeth Audsley Papers
Thomas Hawley Letters
William Thompson Shaver Papers

Missouri State Archives

12th Regiment Cavalry, RG 133 Adjutant General Records

National Archives Records Administration, Washington, D.C. (NARA—RG 109)

Army of Tennessee Headquarters letters sent
Capt. George Moorman Papers, Jackson's Cavalry Division
Orders and Circulars, General N. B. Forrest's Cavalry
Special Orders, Letters, Telegrams, Orders Received, Brig. Gen. James R. Chalmers
Special Orders, Letters, Telegrams, Orders Received, Brig. Gen. William Hicks Jackson

(NARA—RG 94)

Compiled Service Records—Illinois, Indiana, Missouri, Tennessee regiments

Navarro College, Pearce Civil War Collection

James R. Chalmers Letter
William Henry Henderson Letter

Newberry Independent Research Library

Eugene Bruce Read Diary

Ohio Historical Society

John Quincy Adams Baker Papers
Robert D. Shields Papers

Rice University

The Papers of Jefferson Davis

State Historical Library & Archives (Iowa)

James Christy Journal
Franklin Hammond Letters
George Healy Papers
George Monlux Personal Narrative

Stones River National Park, Technical Information Center

George A. Williams Letter

Tennessee State Library and Archives

O. D. Brown Papers
James P. Brownlow Papers
Benjamin Cheatham Papers
James L. Cooper Papers
James W. Goodwin diaries and memoirs
J. W. Harmon diaries and memoirs
Edwin Lewis Hayes diaries and memoirs
William Hicks Jackson Papers
John Johnston diaries and memoirs
Printed material—Confederate Collection, Box 2, Folder 12
Printed material—Confederate Collection, maps collection, Box 2

Sketches of the Battle of Franklin, Alice Nichol
Sketches of the Nashville Campaign, Elbert Watson

University of Arkansas
Daniel Harris Reynolds Diary

University of Georgia, Hargrett Rare Book and Manuscript Library
Breyfogle Family Papers

University of Iowa
Lot Abraham Diary, 1864
Joseph Franklin Culver Papers
W.B. Emmons Diary, 1864–1865
William Legg Henderson Civil War Diaries
William Titus Rigby Letters
Edward F. Winslow Papers

University of Michigan, Bentley Historical Library
Charles Butler Correspondence
Wright H. Garrison Correspondence
Henry Mortimer Hempstead Journal
Elisha Mix Papers
Eli Russell Papers

University of Mississippi, Archives and Special Collections, J. D. Williams Library
J. A. Bigger Diary
James M. Houry
John Preston Young Collection

University of North Carolina, Louis Round Wilson Special Collections Library
Samuel Agnew Diary
Gale and Polk Family Papers
Jason Niles Diary
Nimrod Porter Diary
Isaac N. Rainey Papers

University of Oklahoma
Charles Alley Diary, 1861–1865, Western History Collection

The University of Southern Mississippi
Mark P. Lowrey Collection

University of Tennessee
Henry R. Pippitt Diary
E. H. Rennolds Diary
Charles S.O. Rice Papers
Julius E. Thomas Collection
William Velie Letter
T. J. Walker Reminiscences

University of Texas at Austin, Briscoe Center for American History
Elizabeth Clarke Narrative

Vigo County Public Library
Civil War Letters of William Black

Virginia Tech University Libraries
Robert Selph Henry Papers

Western Kentucky State University
Folklife and Manuscripts Archives, Hopkins County, Kentucky, Letters
Robert I. Battle Diary

Western Michigan University
Martin Barnhart Collection
Grace Edmonds Collection

Wisconsin Historical Society Archives
Perry Goodrich Letters
J. H. Hammond Papers

Government Documents

The War of the Rebellion: A Compilation of the Official Records of the Union and Confederate Armies, the Official Records are compiled in 127 volumes, plus a General Index and accompanying Atlas. [Hereafter referred to as *Official Records*]

Official Records of the Union and Confederate Navies in the War of the Rebellion

Articles

Barron, S. B. "From the Other Side: Confederate Cavalry Officer Tells of Hood's Rearguard after Nashville," *National Tribune*, June 2, 1887: 5.

"Battle of Eastport," *Confederate Veteran*, Vol. 5, No. 1 (January 1897): 13.

Black, R. J. "How Three Men Held an Army in Check," *Confederate Veteran*, Volume 16, No. 6 (June 1908): 268.

Blankinship, Gary. "Colonel Fielding Hurst and the Hurst Nation," *Western Tennessee Historical Society Papers*, Volume 24 (1980): 71–87.

Bradford, A. J. "Hood's Lines Broken," *National Tribune*, April 23, 1896: 2.

Brennan, Patrick. "Early Winter Sunset," *The Civil War Monitor*, Vol. 4, No. 3 (Fall 2014): 40–51,73.

Brewer, George E. "Incidents of the Retreat from Nashville," *Confederate Veteran*, Volume 18, No. 7 (July 1910): 327–329.

"Brig. General Joseph F. Knipe at Camp Curtin," *The Bugle, Quarterly Journal of the Camp Curtin Historical Society and Civil War Round Table.* Volume 17, No. 2 (Summer 2007): 1–2.

Brooksher, William, and David Snider. "The War

Child Rides: Joe Wheeler at Stones River," *Civil War Times Illustrated*, Volume 14 (1976): 4–10.

Brown, Campbell H. "To Rescue the Confederacy," *Civil War Times Illustrated Magazine*, Volume 3, Number 8 (December 1964): 13–15, 44–48.

Brown, Lenard E. "Fortress Rosecrans: A History, 1865–1990," *Tennessee Historical Quarterly*, Vol. 50, No. 3 (Fall 1991): 135–141.

Caper, Thomas J. "Chasing Hood," *National Tribune*, March 22, 1888: 1.

"Capron's Cavalry," *National Tribune*, March 29, 1883: 1.

"Capture of the Mazeppa," *Confederate Veteran*, Volume VIII, No. 12 (December 1905): 566–570.

Chalaron, J. A. "Hood's Campaign Murfreesboro," *Confederate Veteran*, Volume 11, Number 10 (October 1903): 438–440.

Chalmers, James. "Forrest and His Campaigns," *Southern Historical Society Papers*, Volume 7, Number 10 (October 1879): 449–488.

Connelly, H. C. "From Nashville to the Tennessee," *National Tribune*, July 11, 1895: 1.

Crownover, Sims. "The Battle of Franklin," *Tennessee Historical Quarterly*, Vol. 14, No. 4 (December, 1955): 291–322.

Dinkins, James. "The Battle of Spring Hill, Tennessee: Personal Recollections and Experiences in the Confederate Army," *Historic Maury*, Volume 31, 3 (1995): 108–111.

Dinkins, James. "Destroying Military Stores and Gunboats," *Confederate Veteran*, Volume 34, No. 5 (May 1926): 176–178.

Dodd, W. O. "Reminiscences of Hood's Tennessee Campaign," *Southern Historical Society Papers*, Vol. 9, No. 10–12 (October-December 1881): 518–524.

Dunlap, Sam B. "Hard Times on Hood's Retreat," *Confederate Veteran*, Volume 7, No. 6 (June 1899): 266.

Durham, Walter T. "The Battle of Nashville," *Journal of Confederate History*, Volume 1, No. 1 (Summer 1888): 118–151.

Dyer, J. P. "The Civil War Career of General Joseph Wheeler," *The Georgia Historical Quarterly*, Vol. 19 No. 1 (Mar. 1935): 17-46.

Foreman, Carolyn Thomas. "The Armstrongs of Indian Territory: General Frank Crawford Armstrong, Part III," *Chronicles of Oklahoma*, Vol. 31, No. 1 (1953): 56–65.

Furgurson, Ernest B. "Catching up with 'Old Slow Trot,'" *Smithsonian*, March 2007, Vol. 37 (Issue 12): 50–57.

Garrett, Jill Knight, ed. "Hood's Failure at Spring Hill-Rebuttals," *Historic Maury*, Volume 12, 3 (1976): 112–119.

"Gen. Edmund W. Rucker," *Confederate Veteran*, Vol. XXXII (May 1924), No. 5: 163–164.

"Gen. Tyree H. Bell," *Confederate Veteran*, Vol. X, No. 10 (October 1902): 464.

"General and Governor Ross of Texas," *Confederate Veteran*, Volume 2, No. 6 (June, 1894): 169.

Gilliard, W. H. "The First Shot at Nashville," *National Tribune*, September 28, 1911.

Gist, W. W. "The Battle of Franklin," *Tennessee Historical Magazine*, Vol. 6, No. 3 (October 1920): 213–265.

Halsell, Willie D. "James R. Chalmers and 'Mahoneism' in Mississippi," *Journal of Southern History*, Volume 10, No. 1 (February 1944): 37–58.

Hay, Thomas Robson. "The Cavalry at Spring Hill," *Tennessee Historical Magazine*, Vol. 8, No. 1 (April, 1924): 7–23.

Hayden, O. B. "Disagreeing Troopers," *National Tribune*, October 28, 1886: 4.

Hempstead, Henry M. "Dr. Cannon's Story: Indorses Cannon's Statements," *National Tribune*, February 24, 1864: 10.

Hoksbergen, Ben, and Brian Hogan, "The Affair at Indian Creek Ford: The Archaeology of a Small Civil War Battle," *The Huntsville Historical Review*, Vol. 37, No. 1 (Fall 2013-Winter 2014): 23–66.

Holmes, Jack D. L. "Forrest's 1864 Raid on Memphis," *Tennessee Historical Quarterly*, Vol. 18, No. 4 (December, 1959): 295–321.

Johansson, M. Jane. "Gibson's Louisiana Brigade During the 1864 Tennessee Campaign," *Tennessee Historical Quarterly*, Vol. 64, No. 3 (Fall 2005): 186–195.

Johnston, John. "The Civil War Reminiscences of John Johnston, 1861–1865," William T. Alderson, editor, *Tennessee Historical Quarterly*, Vol. 14, No. 1 (March, 1955): 43–81.

Jones, James P. "Wilson's Raiders Reach Georgia: The Fall of Columbus, 1865," *The Georgia Historical Quarterly*, Vol. 59, No. 3 (Fall, 1975): 313–329.

Jones, James P. "Your Left Arm: James H. Wilson's Letters to Adam Badeau," *Civil War History*, Volume 12, Number 3 (September 1966): 230–245.

Jones, John Rison, Jr. "Do We Purposely Forget? The Unknown Generals in Our Midst," *Huntsville Historical Review*, Volume 18, No. 2 (Fall-Summer 1991): 3–4.

"Lieutenant-General N. B. Forrest," *Southern Historical Society Papers*, Volume 20 (1892): 325–335.

Lippincott, T. W. "Hatch's Division at Nashville," *National Tribune*, January 10, 1884: 7.

Lynn, Donald M. "Wilson's Cavalry at Nashville," *Civil War History*, Volume 1, No. 2 (June 1955): 141–159.

Lyon, Hyland B. "Memoirs of Hylan B. Lyon Brigadier General, CSA," Edward M. Coffman ed., *Tennessee Historical Quarterly*, Volume 18, No. 1 (March, 1959): 35–53.

Marshall, Park. "Hood's Failure at Spring Hill," *Confederate Veteran*, Volume 22, No. 1 (January 1914): 14–15.

McClean, Birney. "Sabers to the Front," *National Tribune*, October 8, 1896: 2.

McDonough, James L. "West Point Classmates— Eleven Years Later: Some Observations on the Spring Hill-Franklin Campaign," *Tennessee Historical Quarterly*, Vol. 28, No. 2 (Summer 1969): 182–196.

Miller, Rex. "John Thomas Croxton: Scholar, Law-

yer, Soldier, Military Governor, Newspaperman, Diplomat, and Mason," *The Register of the Kentucky Historical Society,* Volume 74, No. 4 (October 1976): 281–299.
Morton, John W. "Battle of Johnsonville," *Southern Historical Society Papers,* Volume 10 (Oct-Nov. 1882): 471–488.
Morton, M. B. "The Battle of Nashville," *Confederate Veteran,* Volume XVII, No. 1 (Jan. 1909): 17–20.
Parsons, Timothy A. "Rivers and Rifles: The Role of Fort Heiman in the Western Theater of the Civil War," *Journal of Kentucky Archaeology,* 1, No. 2 (Winter 2012): 16–38.
Pittman, Walter E., Jr. "General Nathan Bedford Forrest and Military Leadership," *West Tennessee Historical Society Papers,* Vol. 35 (1981): 51–62.
Polk, W. A. "Gallant Col. William F. Taylor," *Confederate Veteran,* Volume 16, No. 3 (March 1908): 124–125.
Price, M. D. "Two Mooted Questions," *National Tribune,* August 7, 1890: 3.
Rankin, R. C. "Dr. Cannon's Story: With the 7th Ohio Cavalry," *National Tribune,* February 17, 1898: 8.
Raum, Green. "The Battle of Nashville," *National Tribune,* August 27, 1903: 1.
Robertson, James I., Jr. "The Human Battle of Franklin," *Tennessee Historical Quarterly,* Vol. 24, No. 1 (Spring 1965): 20–30.
Sanders, D. W. "Hood's Tennessee Campaign," *Confederate Veteran,* Volume 15, No. 9 (September 1907): 401–404.
Sanford, W. L. "Holding Duck River," *National Tribune,* March 16, 1899.
Schloemer, Christopher N. "General John Bell Hood: His Leadership During the 1864 Tennessee Campaign," *Saber and Scroll,* Vol. 5, Issue 2 (2016): 23–35.
Simmons, P. B. "The Correction Cheerfully Made," *Confederate Veteran,* Vol. 1, No. 6 (June 1893): 163.
Smith, Mark A. "Sherman's Unexpected Companions: Marching Through Georgia With Jomini and Clausewitz," *The Georgia Historical Quarterly,* Vol. 81, No. 1 (Spring 1997): 1–24.
Spencer, D. B. "At Franklin and Afterwards," *National Tribune,* January 27, 1898: 7.
Starr, Merritt. "General Horace Capron, 1804–1885," *Journal of the Illinois State Historical Society,* Vol. XVIII, No. 2 (April-June 1925): 259–349.
Stuart, Edwin. "The Federal Cavalry with the Armies in the West: 1861–1865," *Journal of the United States Cavalry Association,* Vol. XVII, No. 62 (July 1906):195–259.
Surby, R. W. "A 64-Days March," *National Tribune,* June 5, 1884: 3.
Sutherland, Daniel E. "No Better Officer in the Confederacy: The Wartime Career of Daniel C. Govan," *The Arkansas Historical Quarterly,* Vol. 54, No. 3 (Autumn, 1995): 269–303.
Tunnell, J. T. "Ector's Brigade in the Battle of Nashville," *Confederate Veteran,* Volume 12: 348–349.
Tyler, H. A. "Forrest Covers Hood's Retreat," *Confederate Veteran,* Vol. 12, No. 9 (Sept. 1904): 436.
Weller, Jac. "Nathan Bedford Forrest: An Analysis of Untutored Military Genius," *Tennessee Historical Quarterly,* 18 (1959): 213–251.
Wigginton, Thomas A. "Cavalry Operations," *Civil War Times Illustrated Magazine,* Volume 3, Number 8 (December 1964): 40–43.
Williams, Edward F., III. "The Johnsonville Raid and Nathan Bedford Forrest State Park," *Tennessee Historical Quarterly,* Volume 28, No. 3 (Fall 1969): 225–251.
Wills, Ridley. "The Military Experiences of William Hicks 'Red' Jackson, 1852–1865," *Tennessee Historical Quarterly,* Vol. 70, No. 3 (Fall 2011): 212–227.
Young, J. P. "Hood's Failure at Spring Hill," *Confederate Veteran,* Vol. XVI, No. 1 (Jan. 1908): 25–41.

Newspapers

Abingdon Virginian
Chicago Tribune
The Clarion (Jackson, MS)
Cleveland Morning Leader
Daily Clarion (Meridian, MS)
Nashville Tennessean
Nashville Union
National Tribune (Washington)
News-Herald (Hillsboro, OH)
The Opelousas Courier (Opelousas, LA)
Oxford Citizen (Mississippi)

Regimental Histories

Barron, S. B. *The Lone Star Defenders: A Chronicle of the Third Texas Cavalry, Ross' Brigade.* New York and Washington: The Neale Publishing Company, 1908.
Bennett, L. G., and William M. Haigh. *History of the Thirty-Sixth Regiment Illinois Volunteers, during the War of the Rebellion.* Aurora, Illinois: Knickerbocker & Hodder, Printers and Binders, 1876.
Cannon, Newton. *The Reminiscences of Sergeant Newton Cannon,* Samuel Fleming, Jr., editor. Franklin, TN: Carter House Assoc., 1963.
Carter, W. R. *History of the First Regiment of Tennessee Volunteer Cavalry.* Knoxville: Gaut-Ogden Co., Printers and Binders, 1902.
Comstock, D. W. *Ninth Cavalry: One Hundred and Twenty-first Regiment Indiana Volunteers.* Richmond, IN: Published by J. M. Coe, 1890.
Cope, Alexis. *The Fifteenth Ohio Volunteers and Its Campaigns: 1861–1865.* Columbus, OH: author, 1916.
Crabb, Martha L. *All Afire to Fight: The Untold Tale of the Civil War's Ninth Texas Cavalry.* New York: Avon Books, 2000.
Davenport, Edward A., editor. *History of the Ninth Regiment Illinois Cavalry Volunteers.* Chicago: Donohue & Henneberry, Printers and Binders, 1888.
Deupree, J. G. "The Noxubee Squadron of the First Mississippi Cavalry, C.S.A. 1861–1865," In *Publications of the Mississippi Historical Society,*

Volume II, Dunbar Rowland, ed. Jackson, MS: Democrat Printing Co., 1918.

Eckel, Alexander. *History of the Fourth Tennessee Cavalry.* Johnson City, TN: Overmountain Press, 2001.

George, Henry. *History of the 3d, 7th, 8th and 12th Kentucky Cavalry, CSA.* Lyndon, KY: Mull-Wathen Historic Press, 1911.

Hale, Douglas. *The Third Texas Cavalry in the Civil War.* Norman: University of Oklahoma Press, 1993.

Kerwood, Ashby L. *Annals of the Fifty-Seventh Regiment Indiana Volunteers.* Dayton, O. W. J. Shuey, 1868.

Kirk, Stephen S. *Sul Ross' Sixth Texas Cavalry: Six Shooters & Bowie Knives.* Independence, MO: Two Trails, 2008.

Loving, Waldon. *Coming Like Hell!: The Story of the 12th Tennessee Cavalry.* San Jose, New York, Lincoln and Shanghai: Writer's Club Press, 2002.

McMurray, William Josiah. *History of the Twentieth Tennessee Regiment Volunteer Infantry, C.S.A.* Nashville, TN: The Publication Committee, consisting of W.J. McMurray, D.J. Roberts, and R.J. Neal, 1904.

Mead, Homer. *The Eighth Iowa Cavalry in the Civil War.* Carthage, IL: S. C. Davidson, Publisher, 1927.

A Military Record off Battery D First Ohio Veteran Volunteers Light Artillery. Oil City, PA: The Derrick Publishing Company, 1908.

Pierce, Lyman. *History of the Second Iowa Cavalry.* Burlington, Iowa: Hawkeye Steam Book and Job Printing Establishment, 1865.

Powell, John. *The History of the Thirteenth Indiana Cavalry Regiment: 1863–1865.* Utica, KY: McDowell Publications, 1987.

Rankin, R. C. *History of the Seventh Ohio Volunteer Cavalry.* Ripley, OH: J. C. Newcomb, Printer, 1881.

Sanford, W. L. *History of Fourteenth Illinois Cavalry and the Brigades to Which It Belonged.* Chicago: R. R. Donnelley & Sons Company, 1898.

Springer, T. B., F. C. Phillips, and D. M. Burns. "A Brief History of the Eleventh Indiana Cavalry," pamphlet, Indiana Historical Society. Indianapolis: Baker and Randolph Printers, 1890.

Stevens, Robert. *The Bracken Rangers: Company K, 28th Regiment, 1st Indiana Cavalry.* Miami and Los Angles: Three Stars Press, 2011.

Thompson, B. F. *History of the 112th Regiment of Illinois Volunteer Infantry.* Toulon, IL: Stark County News Office, 1885.

Worsham, William Johnson. *The Old 19th Tennessee Regiment, C.S.A. June 1861–April 1865.* Knoxville, TN: Press of Paragon Printing company, 1902.

Young, J. P. *The Seventh Tennessee Cavalry: A History.* Nashville: M. E. Church, South, 1890.

Other

Abbott, O. A. "The Last Battle of Nashville" In *Civil War Sketches and Incidents.* Omaha: Military Order of the Loyal Legion of the United States, 1902.

Allardice, Bruce, and Lawrence Lee Hewitt. *Kentuckians in Gray: Confederate Generals and Field Officers of the Bluegrass State.* Lexington: University of Kentucky Press, 2008.

Allardice, Bruce S. *More Generals in Gray.* Baton Rouge: Louisiana State University Press, 1995.

Baggett, James Alex. *Homegrown Yankees: Tennessee's Union Cavalry in the Civil War.* Baton Rouge: Louisiana State University, 2009.

Ballard, Michael. *The Battle of Tupelo, Mississippi: July 14–15.* Tupelo: Northeast Mississippi Historical and Genealogical Society, 2009.

Ballard, Michael B. *The Civil War in Mississippi: Major Campaigns and Battles.* Jackson: University Press of Mississippi, 2011.

Banks, R. W. *The Battle of Franklin: November 30, 1864.* New York and Washington: The Neale Publishing Company, 1908.

Bates, Samuel P. *History of the Pennsylvania Volunteers, 1861–65,* Volume I and V. Harrisburg: B. Singerly, State Printer 1868–1871.

Bearss, Edwin. "The History of Fortress Rosecrans," United States Department of Interior, Research Report, Stones River National Military Park.

Becker, Miranda. "A Southerner for the Union: Major General George Henry Thomas—A Brief Biographical Sketch and Analysis of the Causes and Effects of His Decision for the North," Master's Thesis, Liberty University, 2014.

Benner, Judith Ann. *Sul Ross: Soldier, Statesman, Educator.* College Station: Texas A&M University Press, 1983.

Bennett, Stewart. "The Storm Broke in All Its Fury: The Struggle for Allatoona Pass," In *The Tennessee Campaign of 1864,* Steven Woodworth and Charles Grear, editors. Carbondale: Southern Illinois University Press, 2016.

Bishop, Randy. *Civil War Generals of Tennessee.* Gretna, LA: Pelican Publishing Co., 2013.

Black, Robert. *Cavalry Raids of the Civil War.* Mechanicsburg, Pennsylvania: Stackpole Books, 2004.

Bobrick, Benson. *Master of War: The Life of George H. Thomas.* New York: Simon & Schuster, 2009.

Boynton, Henry. *Was General Thomas Slow at Nashville?* New York: Francis P. Harper, 1896.

Bradley, Michael R. *Forrest's Fighting Preacher: David Campbell Kelley of Tennessee.* Charleston: The History Press, 2011.

Bradley, Michael R. *Nathan Bedford Forrest's Escort and Staff.* Gretna, LA: Pelican Publishing Co., 2006.

Bradley, Michael R. *They Rode with Forrest.* Gretna, Louisiana: Pelican Publishing Company, 2012.

Bradley, Michael R. *With Blood and Fire: Life Behind Union Lines in Middle Tennessee, 1863–1865.* Shippensburg, PA: Burd Street Press, 2003

Brooksher, William. *Glory at a Gallop: Tales of the Confederate Cavalry.* Gretna, LA: Pelican Publishing Co., 1993.

Brown, Myers E., III. *Tennessee's Union Cavalrymen.* Charleston, Chicago, Portsmouth, San Francisco: Arcadia Publishing, 2008.

Brown, Thomas John. "John Bell Hood: Extract-

ing Truth from History," Master's Thesis, Paper 4040, San Jose State University, 2011.
Brownlow, James Polk. *Autobiography of James Polk Brownlow, Jr.* (non-published) in private collection of Abigail Hastings.
Buford, Marcus B. *History and Genealogy of the Buford Family in America With Records of a Number of Allied Families.* La Belle, MO: Mildred B. Minter, 1924.
Buford, Marcus Bainbridge. *A Genealogy of the Buford Family in America.* San Francisco: n. p., 1903.
Busbee, Westley F., Jr. *Mississippi: A History.* Malden, MA: Wiley Blackwell, 2015.
Castel, Albert. *Articles of War: Winners, Losers, and Some Who Were Both in the Civil War.* Mechanicsburg, PA: Stackpole Books, 2001.
Castel, Albert. *Decision in the West: The Atlanta Campaign of 1864.* Lawrence: University Press of Kansas, 1992.
Cater, Douglas John. *As It Was: Reminiscences of a Soldier of the Third Texas Cavalry and the Nineteenth Louisiana Infantry.* Austin: State House Press, 1990.
Catton, Bruce. *This Hallowed Ground: A History of the Civil War.* New York: Vintage Books, 2012.
Cist, Henry. *The Army of the Cumberland.* New York: Charles Scribner's Sons, 1882.
Clampitt, Bradley R. *The Confederate Heartland: Military and Civilian Morale in the Western Confederacy.* Baton Rouge: Louisiana State University Press, 2011.
Clayton, W. W. *History of Davidson County, Tennessee, with Illustrations and Biographical Sketches of Its Prominent Men and Pioneers.* Philadelphia, PA: J. W. Lewis & Co., 1880.
Cleaves, Freeman. *Rock of Chickamauga: The Life of General George H. Thomas.* Norman: University of Oklahoma Press, 1986.
Coakley, Shawn J. "Norwich University: Citizen Soldiers in the Civil War," Master's Thesis, United States Marine Corps Command and Staff College, Quantico, Virginia, 2002.
Collins, Darrell L. *The Army of Tennessee: Organization, Strength, Casualties, 1862–1865.* Jefferson, NC: McFarland, 2017.
Commemorative Biographical Record of the Upper Lake Region. Chicago: J. H. Beers & Co., 1905.
Connelly, Donald B. *John Schofield & The Politics of Generalship.* Chapel Hill: University of North Carolina Press, 2006.
Connelly, Thomas L. *Autumn of Glory: The Army of Tennessee, 1862–1865.* Baton Rouge: Louisiana State University Press, 1971.
Connolly, James A. *Three Years in the Army of the Cumberland: The Letters and Diary of Major James A. Connolly,* Paul M. Angle, ed. Bloomington, IN: Indiana University Press, 1990.
Cooling, Benjamin Franklin. *To the Battles of Franklin and Nashville and Beyond.* Knoxville, University of Tennessee Press, 2011.
Copley, John M. *A Sketch of the Battle of Franklin, Tenn.; with Reminiscences of Camp Douglas.* Austin, Texas: Eugene Von Boeckmann, Printer, 1893.

Cotton, Michael. *The Williamson County Cavalry: A History of Company F, Fourth Tennessee Cavalry Regiment, C.S.A.* Goodlettsville: D.M. Cotton, 1994.
Cox, Brent A. *Colonel Jacob Barnett Biffle: Born to Fight.* Sons of the South Publications, 1991.
Cox, Jacob. *The Army in the Civil War: The March to the Sea: Franklin and Nashville,* Vol. 10. New York: Charles Scribner's Sons, 1885.
Cox, Jacob. *Battle of Franklin.* New York: Charles Scribner's Sons, 1897.
Cox, Jacob. *The March to the Sea: Franklin and Nashville.* New York: Charles Scribner's Sons, 1882.
Cozzens, Peter. *The Darkest Days of the War: The Battles of Iuka and Corinth.* Chapel Hill & London: University of North Carolina Press, 1997.
Crute, Joseph H., Jr. *Units of the Confederate States Army.* Midlothian, VA: Derwent Books, 1987.
Cullum, George. *Biographical Register of the Officers and Graduates of the U. S. Military Academy, 1841–1867,* Vol. II. New York: D. Van Nostrand, 1868.
Currier, Vic. *"Good-bye, Lord, I'm Going To New York": The Secret Life of Belle Meade's William Harding Jackson.* Bloomington, IN: Xlibris Corp, 2015.
Dacus, Robert H. *Reminiscences of Company H, First Arkansas Mounted Rifles.* Dardanelle, AR: Post-Dispatch Print, 1897.
Davis, William C. *Breckinridge: Statesman, Soldier, Symbol.* Lexington: University Press of Kentucky, 2010.
Davison, Eddy, and Daniel Fox. *Nathan Bedford Forrest: In Search of the Enigma.* Gretna, LA: Pelican Publishing Co., 2007.
DeVries, Edward. *Glory in Gray,* Volume 1. Dixie Heritage Press, 2004.
Dinkins, James. *1861 to 1865: Personal Reminiscences and Experiences in the Confederate Army.* Cincinnati: Robert Clarke Co., 1897.
Dobak, Robert. *Freedom by the Sword: The U. S. Colored Troops, 1862–1867.* Washington, D.C.: Center of Military History, 2011.
Dodson, W. C. *Campaigns of Wheeler and His Cavalry, 1862–1865.* Atlanta: Hudgins Publishing, 1899.
Dubose, John Witherspoon. *General Joseph Wheeler and the Army of Tennessee.* New York: The Neale Publishing Company, 1912.
Dunn, Jacob Piatt. *Memorial and Genealogical Record of Representative Citizens of Indiana.* Indianapolis: B. F. Brown Publisher, 1912.
Durham, Walter T. *Reluctant Partners: Nashville and the Union.* Nashville: The Nashville Historical Society, 1987.
Dyer, Frederick H. *A Compendium of the War of the Rebellion.* Des Moines: The Dyer Publishing Company, 1908.
Eicher, John H., and David Eicher. *Civil War High Commands.* Stanford: Stanford University Press, 2001.
Einolf, Christopher J. *George Thomas: Virginian for the Union.* Norman: University of Oklahoma Press, 2007.
Elliott, Sam Davis. *Soldier of Tennessee: General*

Alexander P. Stewart and the Civil War in the West. Baton Rouge: Louisiana State University Press, 1999.

Evans, Clement A., editor. *Confederate Military History,* Volume I, VII, VIII. Atlanta: Confederate Publishing Co., 1899.

Evans, David. *Sherman's Horsemen.* Bloomington: Indiana University Press, 1996.

Farwell, Byron. *The Encyclopedia of Nineteenth-century Land Warfare: An Illustrated World View.* New York, London: W. W. Norton & Co., 2001.

Field, Henry M. *Bright Skies and Dark Shadows.* New York: Charles Scribner's Sons, 1890.

Fisher, John. *They Rode with Forrest: The Chronicle of Five Tennessee Brothers' Service in the Western Cavalry.* Jefferson, NC: McFarland, 1995.

Fordney, Ben Fuller. *George Stoneman: A Biography of the Union General.* Jefferson, NC: McFarland, 2008.

Foster, Buck T. *Sherman's Mississippi Campaign.* Tuscaloosa: University of Alabama Press, 2006.

Fout, Albert. *The Darkest Days of the Civil War, 1864 and 1865.* Bailey's Harbor, WI: Philip Graupner, 2014.

French, Samuel G. *Two Wars: An Autobiography of General Samuel G. French.* Nashville: Confederate Veteran, 1901.

Fryman, Robert J., and Laura B. Reidy. *They Was There Sure Enough: A Limited Archaeological Assessment of the 1864 Civil War Battle at Spring Hill, Tennessee.* Atlanta: Garrow and Associates, 1995.

Fulcher, Richard Carlton. *Civil War Battles and Skirmishes in Williamson County, Tennessee.* Brentwood, TN: Richard Carlton Fulcher, 2000.

Gelbert, Doug. *Civil War Sites, Memorials, Museums and Library Collections: A State-by-State Guidebook.* Jefferson, NC: McFarland, 2005.

Gillum, Jamie. *Twenty-Five Hours to Tragedy: The Battle of Spring Hill and Operations on November 29, 1864.* n. d.: n. p. 2004.

Glaze, Robert Lamar. "Experiencing Defeat, Remembering Victory: The Army of Tennessee in War and Memory, 1861–1930," Ph. D. Dissertation, University of Tennessee, Knoxville, 2016.

Godfrey, Michael L. *Reflections of a Confederate Soldier: Duty—Honor—Courage.* Rockport, TX: All American Historical Publishing Co., 2006.

Grierson, Benjamin. *A Just and Righteous Cause,* Bruce Dinces and Shirley Leckie, eds. Carbondale: Southern Illinois University Press, 2008.

Groom, Winston. *Shrouds of Glory: From Atlanta to Nashville, The Last Great Campaign of the Civil War.* New York: Atlantic Monthly Press, 1995.

Gue, Benjamin F. *History of Iowa: From the Earliest Times to the Beginning of the Twentieth Century,* Vol. IV. New York: Century History Co., 1903.

Guernsey, Alfred H., and Henry H. Alden. "Battle of Nashville," In *Harper's Pictorial History of the Great Rebellion,* Vol. 2. Chicago: McDonnell Brothers, 1868.

Hashaw, Tim. *Children of Perdition: Melungeons and the Struggle of Mixed America.* Macon: Mercer University Press, 2006.

Hatley, Allen G. *The First Texas Legion during the American Civil War.* East Lake, TX: Centex Press, 2004.

Hay, Thomas Robson. *Hood's Tennessee Campaign.* New York: Press of Morningside Books, 1976.

Heitman, Francis B. *Historical Register and Dictionary of the United States Army,* Vol. 1. Washington: Govt. Printing Office, 1903.

Henry, Robert Selph. *Forrest: First with the Most.* n.p.: Pickle Partners Publishing, 2015.

History of Tennessee. Nashville: The Goodspeed Publishing Company, 1886.

Hood, John B. *Advance and Retreat.* New Orleans: G. T. Beauregard, 1880.

Hood, John B. "The Invasion of Tennessee." In *Battles and Leaders of the Civil War,* Volume IV. New York: The Century Co., 1888.

Horn, Stanley F. *The Army of Tennessee.* Norman: University of Oklahoma Press, 1952.

Horn, Stanley F. *The Decisive Battle of Nashville.* Knoxville: University of Tennessee Press, 1986.

Horn, Stanley F. *Tennessee's War: 1861–1865.* Nashville: Tennessee Civil War Centennial Commission, 1965.

Horton, Lucy Henderson. "Reminiscences of the War Between the States," In *Williamson County and the Civil War,* Rick Warwick, compiler. Franklin: Williamson County Historical Society, 2008.

Houchens, Harry W. "The Making of General John B. Hood: A Study of Command," Study project for the U. S. Army War College, Carlisle Barracks, Pennsylvania.

Hubbard, Lucius F. "Minnesota in the Battles of Nashville, December 15–16, 1864." In *Glimpses of the Nation's Struggle,* MOLLUS, MN, Vol. 6. Minneapolis: Davis, 1909.

Huddleston, Edwin. *The Civil War in Middle Tennessee.* Nashville: The Parthenon Press, 1965.

Hughes, Nathaniel Cheairs, Jr. *Brigadier General Tyree H. Bell, CSA.* Knoxville: UT Press, 2004.

Hughes, Nathaniel Cheairs, Jr. *The Pride of the Confederate Artillery: The Washington Artillery in the Army of Tennessee.* Baton Rouge: LSU Press, 1997.

Hurst, Jack. *Nathan Bedford Forrest: A Biography.* New York: Vintage Press, 1993.

Jackson, Orange. *The History of Orange Jackson's War Life as Related by Himself.* n.p: n. p., 1865.

Jacobson, Eric, and Richard Rupp. *For Cause, For Country: A Study of the Affair at Spring Hill and the Battle of Franklin.* Franklin, TN: O'More Publishing, 2007.

Johnson, Richard. *Memoir of Maj.-Gen. George H. Thomas.* Philadelphia: J. B. Lippincott and Co., 1881.

Johnson, Richard W. *A Soldier's Reminiscences in Peace and War.* Philadelphia: Press of J. B. Lippincott Company, 1886.

Johnson, Sidney Smith. *Texans Who Wore the Gray,* Volume 1. Tyler, TX: Author, 1907.

Jones, James Pickett. *Yankee Blitzkrieg: Wilson's Raid through Alabama and Georgia.* Lexington: University Press of Kentucky, 1976.

Jones, Terry L. *Campbell Brown's Civil War: With*

Ewell and the Army of Northern Virginia. Baton Rouge: Louisiana State University Press, 2001.

Jordan, Thomas, and J. P. Pryor. *The Campaigns of Lieut.-Gen. N. B. Forrest.* New Orleans, Memphis and New York: Blelock & Company, 1868.

Keenan, Jerry. *Wilson's Cavalry Corps.* Jefferson, NC: McFarland, 1998.

Kelley, David C. "More on the Confederate Cavalry at Nashville," In *The Battle Of Nashville: Recollections of Confederate & Union Soldiers,* by Lochlainn Seabrook. Nashville: Sea Raven Press, 2018.

Kelly, Orr, and Mary Davies Kelly. *Dream's End: Two Iowa Brothers in the Civil War.* New York: Kodansha America, Inc., 1998.

Kendall, Henry M. "The Battles of Franklin and Nashville," In *The War of the Sixties.* New York, The Neale Publishing Company, 1912.

Kenner, Charles L. *Buffalo Soldiers and Officers of the Ninth Cavalry, 1867–1898.* Norman: University of Oklahoma Press, 1999.

Kirk, Charles H. "The Last Blow at Hood's Army," In *History of the Fifteenth Pennsylvania Volunteer Cavalry,* Charles Kirk, ed. Philadelphia: Society of the Fifteenth Pennsylvania Cavalry, 1906.

Kirk, Stephen S. *Line of Battle: Sul Ross' Brigade.* Harrisonville, MO: Burnt District Publishing, 2012.

Knight, James R. *Hood's Tennessee Campaign.* Charleston: The History Press, 2014.

Lamborn, David M. "Operational Risk Preparedness: General George H. Thomas and the Franklin and Nashville Campaign," Monograph, School of Advanced Military Studies United States Army Command and General Staff College Fort Leavenworth, KS, 2014.

Lamers, William. *The Edge of Glory: A Biography of General William S. Rosecrans, U.S.A.* New York: Harcourt, Brace & World, Inc., 1961.

Langer, Philip, and Robert Pois. *Command Failure in War: Psychology and Leadership.* Bloomington and Indianapolis: Indiana University Press, 2004.

Lavender, John. *The War Memoirs of Captain John W. Lavender, CSA,* Ted R. Worley, ed. Pine Bluff, AR: The Southern Press, 1956.

Lazenby, Marion Elias. *The History of Methodism in Alabama and West North Florida.* Nashville: North Alabama Conference and Alabama-West Florida Conference, 1960.

Leach, Robert B. "The Role of Union Cavalry During the Atlanta Campaign." Master's Thesis, U.S. Army Command and General Staff College, Fort Leavenworth, Kansas, 1994.

Lee, Dan. *The Civil War in the Jackson Purchase, 1861–1862: The Pro-Confederate Struggle and Defeat in Southwest Kentucky.* Jefferson, NC: McFarland, 2014.

Leonard, John W. *Who's Who in Pennsylvania: A Biographical Dictionary of Contemporaries, Volume 2.* New York: John W. Hamersly & Co., 1908.

Lepa, Jack H. *Breaking the Confederacy: The Georgia and Tennessee Campaigns of 1864.* Jefferson, NC: McFarland, 2005.

Lewis, Lloyd. *Sherman: Fighting Prophet.* Lincoln: University of Nebraska Press, 1993.

Lindsley, John B. *The Military Annals of Tennessee: Confederate.* Nashville, TN: Lindsley, 1886.

Little, George, and James R. Maxwell. *A History of Lumsden's Battery, C.S.A.* Tuscaloosa, AL: R.E. Rhodes Chapter, United Daughters of the Confederacy, 1905.

Livermore, Thomas L. *Numbers and Losses in the Civil War in America, 1861–1865.* Boston and New York: Houghton, Mifflin and Co., 1901.

Logan, Guy E., ed. *Roster and Record of Iowa Soldiers in the War of the Rebellion: 1st-9th Regiments of Cavalry.* Des Moines: Emory H. English State Printer, 1910.

Logsdon, David R. *Eyewitnesses at the Battle of Franklin.* Nashville: published by author, 1988.

Logsdon, David R. *Eyewitnesses at the Battle of Nashville.* Nashville: Kettle Mill Press, 2004.

Longacre, Edward. *From Union Stars to Top Hat: A Biography of the Extraordinary General James Harrison Wilson.* Harrisburg, PA: Stackpole Books, 1972.

Longacre, Edward. *Lincoln's Cavalrymen: A History of the Mounted Forces of the Army of the Potomac.* Mechanicsburg, PA: Stackpole Books, 2000.

Longacre, Edward. *A Soldier to the Last: Maj. Gen. Joseph Wheeler in Blue and Gray.* Washington: Potomac Books Inc., 2007.

Losson, Christopher. *Tennessee's Forgotten Warriors.* Knoxville: University of Tennessee Press, 1989.

Lundberg, John R. *The Finishing Stroke: Texans in the 1864 Tennessee Campaign.* Abilene, TX: McWhiney Foundation Press, 2003.

Lytle, Andrew Nelson. *Bedford Forrest and His Critter Company.* Nashville: J. S. Sanders & Co., 1992.

Mathes, J. Harvey. *Great Commanders: General Forrest.* New York; D. Appleton and Company, 1902.

McCann, Kevin D. *Hurst's Wurst: Colonel Fielding Hurst and the Sixth Tennessee Cavalry U.S.A.* Dickson, TN: McCann Publications, 2007.

McCormick, Arley H. "The Defender of North Alabama," In *North Alabama Civil War Generals: 13 Wore Gray, the Rest Blue,* Huntsville History Collection, Tennessee Valley Civil War Roundtable.

McDonough, James. *Nashville: The Western Confederacy's Final Gamble.* Knoxville: University of Tennessee Press, 2004.

McDonough, James Lee, and Thomas L. Connelly. *Five Tragic Hours: The Battle of Franklin.* Knoxville: University of Tennessee Press, 1983.

McIlwain, Christopher Lyle. *Civil War Alabama.* Tuscaloosa: University of Alabama Press, 2016.

McMurry, Richard. *John Bell Hood and the War for Southern Independence.* Lexington: The University Press of Kentucky, 1982.

McVey, Henry Kratzer. *A Writ of My Civil War Experiences.* Jefferson County, Iowa: n.p. 2001.

Miller, Brian Craig. *John Bell Hood and the Fight for Civil War Memory.* Knoxville: University of Tennessee Press, 2010.

Moody, David Rey. "'The Best Move of My Career': Spring Hill and the Failure of Confederate Command in the West." San Jose: Ph. D. Dissertation, San Jose State University, 1993.

Morton, John. *The Artillery of Nathan Bedford Forrest's Cavalry.* Nashville and Dallas: Publishing House of the M. E. Church, South Smith & Lamar, Agents, 1909.

The National Cyclopaedia of American Biography. Vol. IX. New York: James T. White & Co., 1907.

Niles, H. editor. "Baltimore and Washington Rail Road—November 29, 1834 and December 20, 1834," In *Niles Weekly Register.* Baltimore: Published by editor, bound editions covering September 1834 to March 1835.

Noyalas, Jonathan A. *"My Will is Absolute Law": A Biography of Union General Robert H. Milroy.* Jefferson, NC: McFarland, 2006.

Oakey, Charles Cochran. *Greater Terre Haute and Vigo County: Closing the First Century's History of City and County.* Chicago and New York: The Lewis Publishing Co., 1908.

Otis, Ephraim. "The Nashville Campaign," In *Military Essays and Recollections,* Vol. III. Chicago: The Dial Press, 1899.

Owen, Thomas McAdory. *History of Alabama and Dictionary of Alabama Biography,* Volume IV. Chicago: The S. J. Clarke Publishing Company, 1921.

Parman, Susan K. "The Battle of Nashville," Master's Thesis, George Peabody College for Teachers, Nashville, 1932.

Perello, Chris. *The Quest for Annihilation: The Role & Mechanics of Battle in the American Civil War.* Bakersfield, CA: Strategy & Tactics Press, 2009.

Perrin, William. *The History of Bourbon, Scott, Harrison and Nicholas Counties, Kentucky.* Chicago: O. L. Baskin & Co., 1882.

Peterson, Dennis. *Confederate Cabinet Departments and Secretaries.* Jefferson, NC: McFarland, 2016.

Piatt, Don. *General George H. Thomas: A Critical Biography.* Cincinnati: Robert Clarke and Co., 1893.

Porter, David Dixon. *The Naval History of the Civil War.* New York: The Sherman Publishing Co., 1886.

Powell, David A. *Failure in the Saddle.* New York and California: Savas Beatie, 2010.

Powell, William H., ed. *Officers of the Volunteer Army and Navy who served in the Civil War.* Philadelphia: L.R. Hamersly & Co., 1893.

Rennolds, E. H. *A History of the Henry County Commands Which Served in the Confederate States of America.* Kennesaw, GA: Continental Book Company, 1961.

Report of the Adjutant General of the State of Tennessee, of the Military Forces of the State, from 1861 to 1866. Nashville: Office of the Adjutant General; Mercer, S. C. (Samuel C.), printer, 1866.

Ridley, Bromfield L. *Battles and Sketches of the Army of Tennessee.* Mexico, MO: Missouri Printing, 1906.

Roman, Alfred. *The Military Operations of General Beauregard.* New York: Harper & Brothers, Franklin Square, 1884.

Ross, L. S. *Personal Civil War Letters of General Lawrence Sullivan Ross with other letters,* transcribed and compiled by Perry Wayne Shelton, edited by Shelly Morrison. Austin: Shelly and Richard Morrison, 1994.

Ross, Lawrence Sullivan. "Personal Civil War letters of General Lawrence Sullivan Ross: with other letters," transcribed and compiled by Perry Wayne Shelton, Master's Thesis, Baylor University, 1938.

Rucker, Michael P. *The Meanest and 'Damnest Job': Being the Civil War Exploits and Civilian Accomplishments of Colonel Edmund Winchester Rucker During and After the War.* Montgomery: NewSouth Books, 2019.

Russell, Harold S. *Time to Become Barbarian: The Extraordinary Life of General Horace Capron.* Lanham, MD: University Press of America, 2007.

Sanders, D. W. "The Battle of Nashville," *Southern Bivouac,* Volume 1. Louisville, Ky: B. F. Avery and Sons, Publishers, 1886.

Sanders, John R. "Operational Leadership of Nathan Bedford Forrest." Monograph, Naval War College, Newport, RI, 1994.

Schaefer, James Arthur. "The Tactical and Strategic Evolution of Cavalry During the American Civil War," Ph. D. Dissertation, The University of Toledo, 1982.

Schofield, John. *Forty-Six Years in the Army.* New York: The Century Co., 1897.

Secrist, Philip L. *Sherman's 1864 Trail of Battle to Atlanta.* Macon: Mercer University Press, 2006.

Severance, Ben H. *Portraits of Conflict: A Photographic History of Alabama in the Civil War.* Fayetteville: University of Arkansas Press, 2012.

Seymour, Ron. *The Life of Col. Joseph B. Dorr and his 8th Iowa Cavalry.* self-published eBook, www.8thIowaCav.com, 2012.

Sheppard, Eric William. *Bedford Forrest: The Confederacy's Greatest Cavalryman.* Dayton, OH: Morningside House, Inc., 1988.

Sherman, William. *Personal Memoirs of Gen. W. T. Sherman,* Vol. 2. New York: Charles L. Webster & Co., 1890.

Sherwood, Isaac R. *Memoirs of the War.* Toledo: The H. J. Crittenden, Co., 1923.

Smith, Derek. *In the Lion's Mouth: Hood's Tragic Retreat from Nashville, 1864.* Mechanicsburg, PA: Stackpole Books, 2011.

Smith, Gus F. "The Battle of Franklin," In *War Papers* (MOLLUS, MI, Vol. 2). Detroit: James H. Stone & Co., 1898.

Smith, Michael Thomas. *The 1864 Franklin-Nashville Campaign: The Finishing Stroke.* Santa Barbara: ABC-CLIO, 2014.

Smith, Myron J., Jr. *Tinclads in the Civil War: Union Light-Draught Gunboat Operations on Western Waters, 1862–1865.* Jefferson, NC: McFarland, 2010.

Smith, Reid. *Majestic Middle Tennessee.* Gretna, LA: Pelican Publishing Co., 1998.

Smith, Samuel D., Benjamin C. Nance, and Fred M. Prouty. "A Survey of Civil War Era Military Sites in Tennessee." Tennessee Department of

Environment and Conservation, Division of Archaeology, Research Series No. 14, 2003.

The Soldier's Casket, Volume 1. Philadelphia: C. W. Alexander, 1865.

Sparks, A. W. *The War Between the States: As I Saw It.* Tyler: Lee & Burnett, Printers, 1901.

Speed, Thomas. *Union Regiments of Kentucky,* Volume I. Louisville: The Courier Journal Job Printing, Co., 1897.

Stanley, David S. *Address of General Stanley, Reunion of the Society of the Army of the Cumberland: Twenty-sixth Reunion.* Cincinnati: The Robert Clarke Company, 1897.

Stanley, David S. *An American General: The Memoirs of David Sloan Stanley.* Santa Barbara, CA: The Narrative Press, 2003.

Starr, Stephen Z. *The Union Cavalry in the Civil War: The War in the West,* Volume III. Baton Rouge: Louisiana State University, 2007.

Stewart, Bruce H. *Invisible Hero: Patrick R. Cleburne.* Macon: Mercer University Press, 2009.

Stockdale, Paul H. *The Death of an Army: The Battle of Nashville and Hood's Retreat.* Murfreesboro: Southern Heritage Press, 1992.

Stone, Henry. "The Battle of Nashville, Tennessee: December 15 and 16, 1864," In *Campaigns in Kentucky and Tennessee Including the Battle of Chickamauga: 1862–1864, Papers of the Military Historical Society of Massachusetts,* Vol. VII. Boston: Military Historical Society of Massachusetts, 1908.

Stone, Henry. "Repelling Hood's Invasion of Tennessee," In *Battles and Leaders of the Civil War,* Vol. 4. New York: The Century Company, 1884.

Surby, Richard. *Grierson Raids, Hatch's Sixty-Four Days March.* Chicago: Rounds and James, Steam Book and Job Printers, 1866.

Sutherland, Daniel E. "No Better Officer in the Confederacy: The Wartime Career of Daniel C. Govan," in *Confederate Generals in the Western Theater: Classic Essays on the American Civil War,* Lawrence Lee Hewitt and Arthur W. Bergeron, Jr., ed. Knoxville: University of Tennessee Press, 2010.

Sword, Wiley. *The Confederacy's Last Hurrah: Spring Hill, Franklin, and Nashville.* Topeka: University of Kansas Press, 1992.

Sword, Wiley. *Embrace an Angry Wind: The Confederacy's Last Hurrah: Spring Hill, Franklin and Nashville.* New York: HarperCollins Publishers, 1992.

Thatcher, Marshall P. *A Hundred Battles in the West: The Second Michigan Cavalry.* Detroit: L. F. Kilroy, Printer, 1884.

Treichler, Don. *Cold Steel—Raw Courage: Major John Dance and the 8th Iowa Cavalry.* Charleston, SC: Don Treichler, 2012.

Tucker, Spencer C., editor. *American Civil War: The Definitive Encyclopedia and Document Collection.* Santa Barbara: ABC—Clio LLC, 2013.

Vandor, Paul E. *History of Fresno County, California: With Biographical Sketches,* Volume 2. Los Angeles: Historic Record Company, 1919, 1974.

Van Dyke, David B. *The Devil's Whirlwind: the Battle of Campbellsville, November 24, 1864.* Campbellsville, TN: David Van Dyke, 2011.

Van Horne, Thomas Budd. *The Life of Major-General George H. Thomas.* New York: Charles Scribner's Sons, 1882.

Walker, Scott. *Hell's Broke Loose in Georgia.* Athens & London: University of Georgia Press, 2005.

Walsh, George. *Those Damn Horse Soldiers.* New York: A Tom Doherty Associates Book, 2006.

Warner, Ezra J. *Generals in Blue: Lives of Union Commanders.* Baton Rouge: Louisiana State University Press, 1992.

Warner, Ezra J. *Generals in Gray.* Baton Rouge: Louisiana State University Press, 1959.

Warren, Aldice G., editor. *Catalogue of the Delta Kappa Epsilon Fraternity.* New York: Published by the Delta Kappa Epsilon Council, 1910.

Welsh, Jack. *Medical Histories of Confederate Generals.* Kent, Ohio: Kent State University Press, 1995.

Williams, Edward F., III. *Fustest with the Mostest; The Military Career of Confederate General Nathan Bedford Forrest.* Memphis: Historical Hiking Trails, Inc., 1973.

Williams, T. Harry. *P. G. T. Beauregard: Napoleon in Gray.* Baton Rouge: Louisiana State University Press, 1991.

Wills, Brian Steel. *A Battle from the Start: The Life of Nathan Bedford Forrest.* New York: HarperCollins Publishers, 1992.

Wilson, James H. *Under the Old Flag,* Volumes I & II. New York and London: D. Appleton And Company, 1912.

Wilson, James H. "The Union Cavalry in the Hood Campaign," In *Battles and Leaders of the Civil War,* Vol. IV. New York: The Century Co., 1888.

Wood, William J. *Civil War Generalship: The Art of Command.* Westport, CT: Praeger, 1997.

Woodrick, Jim. *The Civil War Siege of Jackson Mississippi.* Charleston, SC: The History Press, 2016.

Woodworth, Steven E. *Jefferson Davis and his Generals: The Failure of Confederate Command in the West.* Lawrence: University of Kansas Press, 1990.

Wooten, Jerry T. "Johnsonville: The Evolution, Defense, and Demise of the Union's Tennessee River Supply Depot, 1790–1890," Ph. D. dissertation, Middle Tennessee State University December 2015.

Wyeth, John A. *Life of Lieutenant-General Nathan Bedford Forrest.* New York and London: Harper & Brothers, Publishers, 1899/1900.

Wyeth, John Allan. *That Devil Forrest: The Life of General Nathan Bedford Forrest.* Baton Rouge: Louisiana State University Press, 1989.

Yeary, Mamie. *Reminiscences of the Boys in Gray: 1861–1865.* Dallas: Publishing House M. E. Church, South, 1912.

Index

Numbers in ***bold italics*** indicate pages with illustrations

Abbott, Lt. O.A. 189, 239
Abernathy, Maj. James T. 46, 237, 242
Adams, Gen. Wirt 58, 128
Alabama Troops: 4th Cavalry 24, 26, 85, 304–305; 5th Cavalry 73, 85; 7th Cavalry 223, 227, 229, 234, 245, 268, 279, 305; 10th Cavalry 85, 304; 35th Infantry 226; 53rd Cavalry 73; Burtwell's Cavalry 85, 304; Lumsden's Artillery 239–240; Moreland's Cavalry 85, Roddey's Cavalry 21, 24, 30, 32, 71–73, 80, 120, 184, 304–305; Stuart's Cavalry 85
Albritten, James 99
Allatoona, attack at 29
Allen, Capt. Theodore 126, 139, 232, 234–235, 264
Alley, Charles 298
Anderson, Col. Edward 25, 53, 203, 207, 244
Andersonville Prison 11, 40
Anna 76
Anthony's Hill, attack at 296–301
Antietam, Battle of 9, 52
Arkansas Troops: 1st Mounted Rifles 242, 261; 2nd Mounted Rifles 242; 4th Infantry 242; 5th Infantry 256; 9th Infantry 242; 25th Infantry 242; "Arkansas Braves" 77; "Arkansas Rats" 77; Thrall's Battery 23, 77, 85
Armitage, Sgt. Ambrose 247
Armstrong, Gen. Frank 29, 63 ***68***-69, 81–82, 85, 91, 94–96, 99, 103, 105–106, 138, 141, 143, 150, 152, 159–160, 175–177, 196, 202, 204–207, 271, 289, 292–293, 296–298, 300–301, 303, 306, 313
Armstrong, Maj. John F. 25, 127
Army Corps: IV Corps 22, 29, 31–34, 39, 81, 86–90, 117, 121, 123, 142, 161, 165, 180, 183, 187, 226, 237, 243, 246, 248, 288; IX Corps 51; XI Corps 52; XII Corps 52; XIV Corps 29; XV Corps 29; XVI Corps 4, 14, 21, 34–35, 75, 83, 93, 121, 123, 130, 165, 187, 226–228, 243, 246, 248–249; XVII Corps 29; XX Corps 29, 52; XXIII Corps 22, 29, 30, 32, 34, 49, 79, 81, 86–89, 92, 121, 126, 133, 158, 161, 183, 187, 226, 243, 246, 260
Army of Northern Virginia 9
Army of Tennessee 3, 5, 8–11, 13, 16, 19, 21–22, 32, 34, 36, 58, 69, 71, 80, 83, 86, 94, 100, 180, 261, 273–274, 288, 303, 308, 314, 316
Army of the Cumberland 10, 15–16, 24, 34, 36, 40, 52, 55, 181, 287, 311
Army of the Ohio 10, 12, 15, 36, 39, 41, 49, 51, 87–88, 133, 311
Athens, siege of 24–25, 27
Atlanta Campaign 8–13, 15–22, 36, 38, 40, 44, 48–49, 51–52, 58, 63, 68–69, 71, 73, 75, 80–81, 86, 109, 133, 246, 311
Aulsbro, Alonzo 92
Aurora 26–27
Ayres, Gen. Romeyn B. 22

Baird, Lt. Col. Harlon 48, 219, 229
Baker, Capt. D.W. 25
Baltimore & Washington Railroad 49
Bardwell, Joseph 314
Barricades, Battle of the 266–271
Barteau, Col. Clark R. 23, 85, 141, 202
Bate, Gen. William 159–160, 169, 197-***198***, 200–202; Battle of Nashville 248, 255, 258; Battle of the Cedars 202–205, 208
Battle, Pvt. Robert 275
Battle of the Cedars *see* Murfreesboro, the Third Battle of
Beaumont, Col. E.B. 4, 88–89, 119, 121,125, 187
Beauregard, Gen. Pierre G.T. 28, 30, 32, 34, 80–82, 120, 128–129, 183, 194, 215, 272
Beck, Capt. Moses M. 43
Beeres, Maj. Charles H. 48, 93, 229, 232
Bell, Col. Tyree H. 23, 64-***65***, 66, 76, 85, 101, 104, 153, 155, 157, 160–161, 173, 175, 178, 189, 194, 197, 204, 208, 275–276, 280, 287, 293–294, 306

Belle Meade 234–235, 238
Bell's Mill, Confederate blockade at 190–193, 223, 225, 229
Belmont, Battle of 65, 67
Bethel, Tennie 208
Biddle, Col. James 48, ***50***-51, 216, 229–230, 234–235, 264, 288
Biffle, Col. Jacob 24, 61–63, 82, 85–86, 93, 110–111, 141, 171, 189, 216, 222, 227, 245, 270, 279, 307, 312
Bigger, Cpl. J.A. 99, 132, 150, 159–160
Black, Pvt. Dominic 287
Black, Lt. R.J. 98, 279
Black, Trooper William 225
Black River Bridge 128
blacksmith(s) 51, 187, 221
Bliss, Robert Lewis 181
blockhouses 156, ***196***-198, 200–202
Boonville fight at 45
Boyer, Capt. Joseph C. 268–269
Boynton, Gen. Henry 225
Bradley, Gen. Luther 152–154
Bragg, Gen. Braxton 9, 13, 59, 63–64, 71, 73
Brantley, Gen. William F. 243
Breckinridge, Gen. John C. 130, 194
Brice's Crossroads, Battle of 13–14, 16, 24, 62, 66, 72
Bridges, Lt. Col. G.W. 121
Britton's Lane, attack at 67, 69
Brown, G. Campbell 160
Brown, Gen. John 157, 160
Brown, Lt. Col. Robert C. 155
Brownlow, Lt. James, Jr. 171, 222, 270
Buckner, Gen. Simon B. 71
Buford, Gen. Abraham 13, 23, 25, 31, 53, 58, 63-***64***, 66, 73, 76, 77–78, 81, 94–96, 98, 101, 104–105, 108, 111, 129, 131–133, 136–144, 147, 150–153, 155, 159, 162, 164, 168, 169, 171–175, 177–180, 184–189, 201, 204–205, 207–208, 270–271, 273, 275, 279–280, 283–287, 289, 291, 305–306, 308, 312314–315
Bull Run, First Battle of 68, 88
Bull Run, Second Battle of 9

367

Index

Bullock, Col. Robert 200
Bull's Gap 51, 130
Burbridge, Gen. Stephen 130
Burnside, Gen. Ambrose 49, 88, 122
Burtwell, Col. John R.B. 85, 304
Butler, Col. R.J. 64
Butler Creek, skirmish at 95–96, 99

Campbell's Station, Battle of 51
Campbellsville, cavalry fight at 104–108, 312
Canby, Gen. Edward 21, 82, 128
Cannon, Newton 300
Caper, Capt. Thomas J. 276, 281, 283–284, 286, 302
Capers, Col. Ellison 160
Capron, Col. Horace 39, 48-**49**, 87, 91–93, 95, 97, 99–100, 103, 108–118, 122–127, 131, 133, 135–140, 312
carbines: 162, 173, 236, 252, 269; Burnside 122; Maynard 119, 122, 186; replacements (Springfield muskets) 109, 111, 113, 230; Sharps 41; Spencer 31, 41, 96, 112, 119, 312
Carnahan, Lt. Col. Robert H. 46, 237
Carondelet 191, 193
Carpenter, Homer 212
Carpenter, Lt. John H. 240
Carson, William 207
Carter, W.R. 150, 263
Cater, Douglas 125
Cedar Mountain, Battle of 51
Chadick, Mary Jane 182
Chalmers, Gen. James R. 13–14, 21, 23–24, 30, 32, 58–59, **60**-62, 69, 73, 76–78, 81, 83–86, 94–95, 98, 108–113, 117–118, 129, 131–133, 135, 141, 150, 152–153, 155, 157, 159–160, 168–169, 171, 178–179, 184, 187–190, 192–193, 196, 208, 215, 222–223, 225, 227, 229–230, 232–238, 243, 245, 247, 252–253, 263–266, 268–271, 273–275, 280, 283–285, 287–289, 291–294, 297, 300–301, 303, 305, 307–308, 312–315
Champion, Sid 80
Champion Hill, Battle of 64
Chancellorsville, Battle of 52
Charlaron, Joseph A. 199
Cheatham, Gen. Benjamin 2, 82, **94**, 99, 104, 109–110, 118, 126, 147, 160–161, 188, 194, 200, 208, 222, 226–227, 246, 248–249, 253, 256, 259–263, 265–266, 288–291
Chenoweth, Col. James Q. 209–211
Chickamauga, Battle of 8–9, 35–36, 44, 48, 50, 72
Chickamauga Campaign 1, 13, 16, 60, 62–63, 69, 73

Christy, James 241, 297, 299
City of Pekin 26
Clark, George 33
Clayton, Gen. Henry 276, 279, 282, 285–287
Cleburne, Gen. Patrick 155–157, 161, 166, 168, 253
Coleman, Col. David 2, 223, 229, 232, 235–238, 241, 245, 257, 262, 290; *see also* Ector's Brigade
Coleman, Maj. John N. 80
Collins, Corp. Harrison 294
Compton's Hill 4, 241, 246, 248–249, 251, 253, 255, 258, 261
Comstock, Daniel W. 186, 258, 262, 271, 280–281, 283, 294, 302
Connelly, Capt. H.C. 112–114, 116
Connelly, Thomas 155
Conrad, Col. Joseph 166
Cook, Lt. Col. William R. 53, 244
Coon, Col. Datus 14, 46-**47**, 95–98, 101, 103–108, 131–133, 139, 141, 148–151, 175–176, 225, 237–242, 252–253, 255–262, 266, 268, 291–292, 294, 299, 209, 311–312, 314
Cooper, Dr. George 287
Cooper, Col. James 117, 260, 291
Copley, John M. 168
Corinth, Battle of 45, 47, 67, 69, 71, 76
Corwin, Lt. Elmore 257
Couch, Gen. Darius 251
couriers 97, 109–111, 115, 117, 127, 159, 172–173, 197, 229, 234, 245, 261, 265, 283, 294
Cox, Gen. Jacob 97, 100, 103, 115, 117–118, 121, 123, 125, 130, 142–143, 158, 161, 165, 171, 264, 312
Crittenden, John 31
Crook, Gen. George 54
Crossland, Col. Edward 23, 64, **66**-67, 85, 95, 204
Crowder, Capt. R.H. 185–186, 241, 291
Croxton, Gen. John 25, 31–34, 36, 41–42, **43**-44, 75, 87, 90–91, 95, 97, 99, 101, 104, 108, 110, 118–119, 122, 124, 126, 131–133, 135–141, 149–150, 163–164, 167–168, 171–175, 177–179, 190, 221, 223, 229, 232, 234–238, 247, 252–253, 259, 262–263, 265–266, 270, 275, 282–283, 287, 291–296, 309, 311–312
Cunningham, Maj. Benjamin 48, 229
Cunningham, Capt. John 54

Dacus, Robert 261
Dale, Col. W.D. 260
Dalton garrison 11, 29, 31, 72–73
Dana, Asst. Sec. of War Charles 54–55

Dana, Gen. Napoleon 195, 218–219
Davenport, Edward 266
Davidson, Gen. Henry B. 62
Davidson's house 223, 225, 231–233, 235, 245, 264
Davis, Pres. Jefferson 10, 16, 20–22, 28, 53, 93, 215, 316; visit to Palmetto 20
Davis Bridge, Battle at 71
Davis' Ford 129, 133, 148, 177
Dawson, Lt. Col. William Azariah 117
D.B. Campbell 212
Deas, Gen. Zachariah C. 243
Deupree, J.G. 108, 297
Dibrell, Col. George 63
Dinkins, James 98, 113, 153, 169, 171, 184, 235, 269, 271, 285
discipline 15, 30, 45–46, 55, 59, 63, 121, 181, 213, 218
District of Tennessee 24–25, 35, 39, 86–87
District of the Etowah 35, 86–87, 180, 187, 196, 216, 226
Dodd, Capt. W.O. 83, 160
Dodge, Gen. Grenville M. 45, 72, 195
Doolittle, Col. Charles C. 25
Dorr, Col. Joseph B. 43, 172, 174, 235, 295
Duff, Col. William L. 85
Dunlap, Sam 202, 206, 223
Dyer, Lt. Col. Calvin M. 43, 235–236

Early, Gen. Jubal 18
Eastport, attack at 26–27
Eaton, Joe 208
Eckel, Alexander 258, 286
Ector's Brigade 2, 223, 225, 229, 243, 245, 257–259, 261–263, 301; *see also* Coleman, Col. David
Elliott, Gen. Washington L. 11, 38–39, 41–42, 47, 54, 57, 311
Ellison, Eben 221

Fairplay 191
Falconett, Maj. Eugene 279–280
Farmington, Battle at 45, 47, 73
Faulkner, Col. W.W. 23, 85, 153, 211
Featherston, Col. W.S. 297, 301
Feild, Col. Hume 257
Ferrell, Capt. Coleman B. 85
Finlay, Col. Luke W. 314
Fitch, Lt. Cmdr. Le Roy 190–193
Florida troops: 197–198, 300
Forbes, Col. William 209
Forrest, Lt. Col. Jesse A. 27
Forrest, Gen. Nathan Bedford 3–5, 8, 12-**13**, 14–17, 20–31, 34, 41–42, 44, 49, 58–66, 69, 71–73, 75–79, 81–82, 84–85, 89–91, 93–96, 97–100, 103, 106–116, 119–120, 122, 124–127, 129–131, 133–134,

136, 139, 141–143, 146–155, 159–165, 167–171, 173, 175, 177–181, 183–184, 187–190, 194, 196–197, 200–206, 208, 214–215, 217, 266, 270–271, 273, 289–297, 300–301, 303, 305–308, 311–315
Forrest's Cavalry Department 13
Forrest's Raid (Sept. 1864) 25–28
Fort Donelson 24, 59, 72, 76, 87, 209, 251
Fort Heiman 75–76
Fort Henry 76
Fort Pillow 13, 61, 64, 66
Fort Pulaski, Battle of 54
Fort Vancouver 54
Fortress Rosecrans 195, 197, 201–203, 207, 215
Fouche Springs, cavalry fight at 111–115
Franklin, Battle of 165–181; cavalry fight (Dec. 17) 278–288; Chalmers' attack 168, 171; Hughes' Ford battle 171–178
Fredericksburg, Battle of 9
Freeman, E.T. 305
French, Gen. Samuel 29, 160. 204, 229, 243, 305
Fry, Col. Speed 43–44
Fuquay, Joseph 212

Gaines Mill, Battle of 9
Garrard, Col. Israel 39–40, 48–49, 119, 125–126, 133, 138–139, 190, 229, 233
Garrard, Gen. Kenner 11, 30, 36, 38–41, 55, 57, 246
Garrison, George 140
Georgia troops 275; Ferrell's Battery 73, 85; Young's (Croft's) Battery 61, 101, 105–106, 307
Gettysburg, Battle of 9, 53, 89
Gibson, Gen. Randall 275–276, 278–279, 280, 286
Gillem, Gen. Alvan 10–12, 130
Gilliard, William H. 229
Gist, Gen. States Rights 160, 249, 255–259, 263
Gist's Brigade 249, 251, 255–259, 263
Goodwin, James 177, 283, 302
Govan, Gen. Daniel 255–256
Govan's brigade 255-*257*
Graham, Maj. John M. 46, 237
Granger, Gen. Robert 24–25, 31–33, 100, 119, 122, 124, 181, 304
Grant, Gen. Ulysses 10, 15, 21–22, 36, 38–39, 41, 52–56, 67, 120, 128–129, 183, 187–188, 194–195, *214*-218, 246, 316
Green, Col. John U. 23
Green, Col. Peter 256
Gregg, Gen. David 22
Gresham, Lt. Col. Benjamin 53, 244, 269
Grierson, Gen. Benjamin 13, 16, 32, 39, 40-*42*, 52, 57, 88–89,

190, 195; relieved of command 219
Griscom, Lt. George 101, 106, 176, 294
gunboats 26–27, 75–77, 79, 123, 191, 212, 225, 229, 231, 234–235, 245, 304
Halleck, Gen. Henry 19, 22, 28, 31, 36, 54, 89, 99, 180, 183, 188, 194–195, 216-*217*, 219, 221, 223
Hall's Mill 129
Hammond, Gen. John H. 52–53, 119,121-*122*, 124, 144, 147, 162, 167, 174, 184–186, 193–194, 216, 244, 252–254, 256, 258–259, 262–263, 266, 276, 278–281, 285–286, 291, 299, 301, 303, 309
Hancock, Richard 206, 208, 276
Hannum, Maj. Jehu 185
Hardee, Gen. William 18
Harding, Seline 235
Hardison, Calvin 136
Hardison, Sam 126
Hardison's Mill, cavalry fight at 123–124, 126, 129, 131–132, 135–141
Harmon, Col. M.W. 73
Harper, Capt. Joseph W. 46, 96, 237
Harpers Ferry 51
Harris, Gov. Isham 160
Harrison, Col. Thomas 48, 50, 121, 133, 135-*136*, 149–150, 163–164, 174, 177–178, 215, 221, 230, 232, 234–235, 264–265, 282, 287–289, 296, 298–299, 309
Hartman, Sgt. John F. 240
Hartsville, Battle of 46
Hatch, Gen. Edward 25–26, 33, 39, 41, *45*-47, 75, 86–87, 90–93, 95–106, 108–111, 115–116, 118–120, 131–133, 137–139, 163, 175–176, 178–179, 184, 216, 221, 223–225, 231, 236–238, 240–242, 247, 252–256, 261–262, 265–266, 271, 282–284, 288–289, 290–291, 294, 299, 309, 312
Hattery, Capt. John 113
Hawkins, Col. Edwin 138, 140
Hay, Thomas Robson 1, 80, 129, 143, 151, 178, 180, 243, 246
Hedges, Lt. Joseph 283–284
Heiskell, Col. C.W. 290, 301
Hempstead, Henry Mortimer 103, 107, 173, 236, 252
Henderson, William Legg 288
Henryville, cavalry fight 111–115
Hess, Col. Joseph C. 53, 244
Hill, Col. Sylvester 237, 242
Hobson, Capt. Volney 281
Hodgson, Col. Joseph 85, 229
Hoefling, Lt. Col. Charles C. 151–153, 155, 312–313

Hoge, Col. George 26–27
Holland's Ford 129, 135
Hollow Tree Gap. fight at 275–278
Holt, Col. Gustavus 23, 85
Holtzclaw, Gen. James T. 275–279, 281, 283
Hood, Gen. John Bell 3–4, 8-*9*, 10–12, 18–22, 28–38, 49, 75–77, 79–84, 86–87, 90–94, 97–100, 104, 108–110, 115–118, 120, 122, 125, 127–131, 139, 142–144, 147, 155–156, 159–161, 163, 165–171, 177, 179–181, 183–184, 188, 192, 194–196, 201, 208, 214–215, 217, 219–229, 240–241, 243, 245–248, 251–255, 258, 260–261, 263–265, 270–275, 288–292, 296, 300, 303–304, 310, 312–316
Hooker, Gen. Joseph 19
Horton, Maj. Charles C. 46, 237
Horton, Lucy Henderson 172
Howard, Gen. O.O. 33, 35, 57
Howland, Capt. Henry 79
Hubbard, Col. Lucius F. 228, 237, 239, 242–243, 247, 251
Huey's Mill 104, 124, 126, 129, 131–132, 135–136
Hughes' Ford, Battle at 171–177
Humes, William Y.C. 10–11, 63
Hunter, Col. S.E. 276
Hurst, Col. Fielding 53, 244
Hurt's Crossroads 133, 135, 137–138, 141–143, 146–148, 150

Illinois troops: 1st Artillery 314; 3rd Cavalry 132, 211; 6th Cavalry 96, 132, 221; 7th Cavalry 176, 240, 257, 287; 9th Cavalry 95, 98, 107, 132, 151, 180, 239–240, 266; 14th Cavalry 49, 114, 135, 137, 230, 235; 16th Cavalry 93, 135, 231, 298; 61st Infantry 203, 208; 72nd Infantry 159; 73rd Infantry 152; 113th Infantry 26; 114th Infantry 238; 120th Infantry 26; Chicago Board of Trade Horse Artillery 183, 216, 221, 237, 244, 283, 292, Cogswell's Battery 238
Indiana troops: 1st Cavalry 46; 2nd Cavalry 46, 53, 197; 4th Cavalry 212; 5th Cavalry 216; 6th Cavalry 51, 216, 221; 8th Cavalry 50, 122; 9th Cavalry 122, 186, 271, 280–281, 286, 294, 302; 10th Cavalry 25, 32–33, 52, 119, 122, 184, 258–259, 269, 278, 286, 303; 11th Cavalry 47, 53, 119, 122, 132, 175, 185, 227, 235, 241–242, 291; 12th Cavalry 25, 122, 202–203, 207; 13th Cavalry 53, 124, 185, 197–202, 216; 18th Artillery 43, 210; 39th Infantry 50; 57th Infantry 251; 63rd Infantry 264;

Index

71st Infantry 51; 91st Infantry 118; 123rd Infantry 118
Iowa troops: 2nd Cavalry 45–47, 95–96, 101, 104–107, 132, 175–176, 237–238, 240–241, 243, 256, 260, 287, 291; 5th Cavalry 48, 116, 118, 131, 133, 135, 140, 164, 177, 216, 219, 221, 229, 231, 233, 265, 296–297, 299; 8th Cavalry 131, 172, 174, 225, 235–236, 295
Irvine, James B. 303–304
Island No. 10; *see also* New Madrid and Island No. 10, Siege of
Iuka, Battle of 45, 47, 69
Iverson, Gen. Alfred 20, 28

Jackson, Col. George W. 25, 53, 244
Jackson, Gen. Henry 200
Jackson, Gen. Stonewall 51–52
Jackson, William "Red" Hicks 10, 12, 20, 28, 30, 32, 34–35, 58, 67-*68*, 69, 71–73, 75, 79–85, 90–91, 94–96, 98–99, 101, 104–106, 108, 111, 116, 125, 129, 132, 135, 138, 141, 144, 150, 158–161, 163, 168–169, 171–180, 187–189, 196–198, 200–201, 203–206, 208, 270, 273, 288, 291, 294–295, 298, 301, 305–307, 312–313, 315
Jackson, Battle of 45, 72
Jefferson Barracks 48
Johnson, Gov. Andrew 55
Johnson, Col. Gilbert M.L. 25, 53, 185, 197, *199*, 202, 215, 244, 252–253, 289
Johnson, Gen. Richard W. 16, 22, 40–42, 47-*48*, 55, 87, 118–124, 126–127, 131, 133, 135–140, 148, 164, 174, 177–178, 184–185, 192, 213, 215–216, 221–223, 225, 229–236, 242, 247, 264–266, 273, 282–283, 289, 309
Johnson, Lt. Col. Samuel F. 209
Johnson, Col. William A. 24
Johnsonville supply depot, attack on 75-*78*, 79
Johnston, Gen. Albert Sidney 53
Johnston, Col. George D. 290
Johnston, John 153, 162, 229–232, 234–236, 265–266, 284–285
Johnston, Gen. Joseph 8–10, 18–19, 21, 53, 60
Jones, Col. Bushrod 286
Jones, Col. Dudley 94, 106, 176
Jonesborough, Battle of 8, 18, 88
Jordan, Stephen 187
Julian, Capt. W.R. 73
J.W. Cheesman 76
Kelley, Lt. Col. David 23, 26–27, 85, 112–114, *190*-193, 223, 229, 253, 255, 257, 265–266, 268–270
Kelly, Gen. John H. 10–11

Kelly, Lt. Col. Robert M. 43, 235
Kennesaw Mountain, Battle of 36
Kenton 26–27
Kentucky troops (CSA): 3rd Mounted Infantry 23, 64, 85, 306; 7th Mounted Infantry 23, 64, 66–67, 85, 306; 8th Mounted Infantry 23, 64, 85, 306; 12th Cavalry 23, 64, 85, 306; Chenoweth's Cavalry 209–211; Cobb's Battery 71; Huey's Cavalry Battalion 64
Kentucky troops (US): 3rd Cavalry 32, 48; 4th Cavalry 210; 4th Infantry 43–44; 4th Mounted Infantry 43–44, 170, 221, 235, 237; 6th Cavalry 210; 7th Cavalry 210–211; 52nd Infantry 209
Key West 26–27
Kilpatrick, Gen. Hugh Judson 11–12, 29, 34, 36, 38–39, 40–41, 57, 120, 126
Kimball, Gen. Nathan 146, 158, 161, 169, 246
King, Lt. Edward M. 27, 76, 78–80
Kirwan, Maj. John S. 25, 268
Knipe, Gen. Joseph 41–42, *51*-53, 57, 87, 215–216, 219, 221, 223, 244–247, 252–253, 255, 258, 262–263, 265–266, 278–280, 282–283, 289, 309
Knoxville Campaign 49, 51
Kryder, George 28, 274

La Grange, Oscar 42, 210, *211*-212, 215
Lane, Col. John Q. 166
Lash, Maj. Jacob A. 204
Lavender, Capt. John 244
Lawrenceburg, cavalry fight at 101–104
Lee, Gen. Albert 128
Lee, Gen. Fitzhugh 35, 67, 71
Lee, Gen. Robert E. 35, 160
Lee, Gen. Stephen D. 13–14, 58, 61, 94, *100*, 110 118, 227, 248, 275–276, 282–283, 285, 289
Lillard's Mills 129, 289
Lincoln, Pres. Abraham 10, 35, 44, 54, 79–80, 218
Lindsley, Margaret "Maggie" 218
Linsday, Judge Nathaniel 50
Logan, Gen. John 52–53, 221
Long, Gen. Eli 41, 86–87, 89, 215
Loring, Gen. William W. 64, 171, 173, 243–244
Louisiana troops: 3rd Infantry 69; 4th Infantry 276, 278; 16th Infantry 279; 30th Infantry 276, 278; Slocomb's Battery 68
Louisville & Nashville Railroad 129, 189, 194, 212, 215
Lovejoy's Station, attack at 36, 42, 44, 71
Lowrey, Gen. Mark 248, 255, 257, 262

Lumsden, Capt. John 238–240
Lynch, Lt. Col. John 46, 237
Lyon, Sgt. Arthur P. 213
Lyon, Gen. Hylan B. 23, 71–72; Hylan's Raid 129, 209–214
Lyon, Maj. Virgil 186

Mabry, Col. Hinchie P. 76
Macon & Western Railroad 8
Magnet 190
Maney's Brigade 251, 255–259
Manigault, Gen. Arthur 243
Mansfield, Gen. Joseph 52
Martin, Gen. William T. 11–12
Matthews' House 163, 168, 171, 175
Matzdorff, Col. Alvin 124
Maury, Gen. Dabney 58, 128
Mazeppa 76
McArthur, Gen. John 227, 235, 237–238, 240, 242–243, 251–252, 261-*262*, 263–264, 273
McCallum, Gen. D.C. 27
McCarthey, Lt. Joseph A. 46, 237
McClean, Sgt. Birney 176
McClellan, George 54, 188; presidential election 10, 79–80, 103
McCook, Gen. Alexander 35
McCook, Gen. Edward 10–11, 38–43, 44, 46, 86–87, 209-*210*, 211, 213, 309
McCook's Raid 12, 36, 44, 50, 71
McCown, Gen. John P. 61
McCulloch, Gen. Ben 68
McCulloch, Col. Robert 23, 60, 76, 85–86
McGavock's Ford 171–172, 174–175, 178–179
McIntosh, Col. James 68
McLeary, A.C. 191
McMillen, Col. William L. 237–238, 242, 251
McNeilly, James H. 294
McPherson, Gen. James 35
McVey, Henry Kratzer 80, 220–221, 247, 270
Memphis Raid 14
Meridian Campaign 13, 16, 47, 61, 64, 66–68, 71, 80
Metamora 215
Michigan troops: 2nd Cavalry 43, 92, 103, 107, 150, 152, 171–175, 227, 235–236, 252, 290, 303; 8th Cavalry 48–49, 93, 109, 111, 113, 118, 123–124, 135–136, 140, 200, 216, 219, 221, 229–230
Mill Springs, Battle of 35, 44
Milroy, Gen. Robert H. 127, 181, 195, 197–200, 202-*203*, 204–207, 217
Minnesota troops: 8th Infantry 197–198; 10th Infantry 238
Missionary Ridge, Battle of 36, 44
Mississippi Central Railroad 45, 128

Mississippi troops: 1st Cavalry 68–69, 103, 108, 177, 270, 289, 295, 297, 306; 2nd Cavalry 68, 99, 132, 152, 159; 5th Cavalry 61, 236, 245, 307; 7th Cavalry 23; 8th Cavalry 23, 62; 18th Cavalry 23, 62; 28th Cavalry 68, 80, 91, 150, 306; Ballentine's Cavalry 68, 306; Duff's Cavalry 85; Hudson's Battery 23, 77
Missouri troops (CSA): 1st Artillery 202, 206; 2nd Cavalry 23, 26; Bledsoe's Battery 275
Missouri troops (US): 11th Infantry 229, 240–241; 12th Cavalry 46–47, 104, 132–133, 237, 242, 284, 297; 42nd Infantry 209
Mix, Col. Elisha 48, 140, 219, 229–230
Mobile & Ohio Railroad 13, 75, 219
Mobile Campaign 18, 21, 75
Mock, Capt. Anthony E. 96, 98, 107
Monlux, George 90, 174, 225, 236, 296
Montgomery Hill 243
Moore, Col. O.H. 97
Moose 191
Moreland, Lt. Col. M.D. 85, 304
Morgan, Gen. James D. 22
Morgan, Gen. John Hunt 49, 51, 194
Morris, Lt. Robert 101
Morris' Ford 136–137
Morton, Lt. Col. George 202
Morton, Capt. John W. 208, 276, 280, 285, 293, 297–298, 300–302, 307
Mount Pleasant, Capron's retreat from 115–118
Mower, Gen. Joseph 14, 45, 251
Murfreesboro, the Third Battle of 195–208
Murry, Joseph 112
muskets, Springfield *see* carbines
Myers, Lt. William 53, 244

Nashville & Chattanooga Railroad 25, 148
Nashville & Decatur Railroad 61, 292
Nashville & Northwestern Railroad 25, 76, 235
Nashville, Battle of : Day 1 (the battle of the barricades *see* Barricades, Battle of the Chalmers' defense 244; Chalmers' supply train captured 238; Croxton's Attack 235–237; Hatch's Attack 237–242; Johnson's attack 229–235); Day 2 (Chalmers' defense 264–271; Confederate retreat 261–263; Hammond's early morning action 252; Hatch's attack 253–261; Johnson's attack 264–266; Knipe's attack 258–259; Schofield hesitates 263)
Nelson, Gen. William "Bull" 45
Neosho **191**, 193
New Hope Church, Battle of 48
New Madrid and Island No. 10, Siege of 45, 47, 61
New York troops: 10th Infantry 50; 13th Artillery 198, 202–204, 206–207
Newsom, Col. John F. 23, 85, 141, 276
Nourse, Benjamin 183, 221, 244, 292
Noyes, Lt. Col. Henry E. 195

Ohio troops: 3rd Cavalry 28, 274; 7th Cavalry 119, 125, 133, 140, 190, 297–298; 12th Artillery 202–203; 14th Artillery 221, 302–303; 49th Infantry 108, 225, 297; 64th Infantry 155; 72nd Infantry 238; 95th Infantry 238; 111th Infantry 238; 174th Infantry 198, 200, 203, 207; 177th Infantry 203, 207; 178th Infantry 203, 207; 181st Infantry 203
Olmstead, Col. Charles H. 208, 290, 297
Opdyke, Col. Emerson 154, 156, 166, 168
Orr's Crossroad, cavalry fight at 137–141
Osband, Col. Embury 128
Overton Hill *see* Peach Orchard Hill
Oxford, Mississippi expedition 14, 16, 45, 64

Pace, Col. Thomas N. 25
Palmer, Gen. Joseph 204–205
Palmer, Col. William 213, 215, 303
Patten, Lt. L.H. 124, 136
Patterson, Col. Josiah 73
Pea Ridge, Battle of 70
Peach Orchard Hill 4, 248–249
Pemberton, Gen. John C. 60, 68
Peninsula Campaign 54
Pennsylvania troops: 15th Cavalry 39, 87, 213, 216, 303; 19th Cavalry 53, 119, 244, 259, 263, 276, 278; 46th Infantry 51
Pepper, Lt. Col. W.T. 244, 253
Perryville, Battle of 35–36, 44, 63, 77
Peters, Jessie 156, 162
Pettus, Gen. Edmund 275, 279, 281, 285
Phifer's Brigade 71
Phillips, Dr. G.C. 172
Pickett. Col. Richard O. 85
Pierce, Sgt. Lyman 96, 104, 106, 241, 287
Pillow, Gen. Gideon 65, 67
Polk, Gen. Leonidas 13, 58

Polk, Capt. W.A. 279, 260
Port Royal Expedition 54
Porter, James D. 256
Porter, Nimrod 291
Post, Col. P. Sidney 147
Postgate, F.M. 156
Prairie State 190
presidential election (1864) 10, 79–80
Price, Gen. Sterling, Missouri Raid 18, 21, 34, 40, 69, 75, 120
Prima Donna 190
Prosser, Lt. Col. Wm. F. 25
Pulaski, cavalry fight at 295–297

Quintard, the Rev. Charles Todd 144, 194

Rabb, Joseph 221
Rainey, Isaac N. 112–113, 293
Rally Hill 123–124, 126, 131–133, 139, 141, 143, 147, 151, 153
Rankin, Capt. Richard C. 138–139, 232–233, 265, 297
Ransom, Gen. Thomas E.G. 45
Raum, Gen. Green B. 31
Rawlins, John 54
Read, Sgt. Eugene 209
Red River Campaign 22
Redoubts 1, 77, 201, 227, 229, 238–244, 253
Reed, Lt. Col. Alfred 207
Reindeer 191
Rennolds, E.H. 125, 181, 260
Resaca garrison 29, 31
Reynolds, Gen. Daniel Harris 164, 242–243, 249, 251, 256, 259, **260**-262, 270, 290, 297, 301
Rice, Capt. T.W. 23, 85
Richland Creek, cavalry fight at 292–295
Richmond (KY), Battle of 50, 65
Ridge Meeting House 147–148, 150–151, 162, 168
Roddey, Gen. Philip 21, 24, 28, 30, 32, 71-**72**, 73, 80, 85, 120, 122, 184, 303–305
Rosecrans, Gen. William S. 36, 52, 54, 69, 188, 194, 197
Ross, Gen. Lawrence "Sul" 18, 68-**70**, 71 85, 91, 94, 99, 101, 105–106, 108, 137–141, 144, 151, 155–156, 159–160, 176–177, 204–206, 287, 289, 290–292, 294, 297, 300–302, 305, 307, 313
Ross, Col. Reuben 211
Rousseau, Gen. Lovell 24–26, 28, 35, 180–181, 195, 197, 200–202, 207, 217
Rousseau's Raid 50
Rucker, Col. Edmund W. 23, 61-**62**, 76, 81, 91, 97–98, 111–113, 153, 190–192, 223, 225, 227, 229, 230–232, 234, 236–237, 245, 252–253, 259, 265–271, 276, 307–308, 312, 314

Ruger, Gen. Thomas 97, 118, 130, 142, 158, 161, 169
Russell, Eli 227
Russell, Col. Robert M. 23, 65, 85

Sale, Lt. T. Sanders 23, 85
Sanford, W.L. 110, 112, 114–119, 137, 139, 230–231
Schofield, Gen. John 3–4, 19, 22, 28, 32, 35–36, 49, 75, 81, 86–89, 91-*92*, 93, 95, 97, 99–103, 108–110, 114–118, 120–125, 129–132, 138–139, 141–144, 146–148, 151, 156–168, 171, 173–174, 178–184, 188, 214, 216, 218, 226, 242–243, 246, 248, 251–256, 260, 262–264, 272, 309, 311–313
Scott, Gen. Winfield 53
Sears, Gen. Claudius W. 201–202, 204–205, 217
Seddon, J.A. 33, 130, 183, 222, 271–272
Sedgwick, Gen. John 88–89
Shacklett, Lt. Col. Absalom 23, 85, 293
Sharp, Gen. Jacob H. 243
Sharp, Lt. Preston 237, 284, 297
Sharra, Lt. Col. Abram 46, 237
Shaver, Lieutenant William 104
Shellenberger, John 143
Sheridan, Gen. Phil 55, 117
Sherman, Gen. William T. 3–4, 10–17, *19*-22, 24, 28–36, 38, 41–42, 53, 56–57, 59, 76, 80–82, 89–90, 120, 128, 187–188, 215, 222, 272, 311, 316
Sherwood, Lt. Col. Isaac R. 235
Shiloh, Battle of 35, 52, 59, 65, 72, 157, 251
Shoal Creek 73, 80, 90, 95–98, 295, 314
Shy's Hill *see* Compton's Hill
Silver Lake 191
Simmons, P.B. 159
Sipes, Col. William B. 25
Smith, Gen. Andrew J. 4, 14, 21, 34–35, 64, 66, 75, 83, 93, 99, 121, *123*, 165, 181, 183, 187–188, 199, 223, 225–229, 236–237, 241, 243, 246, 248–249, 251, 257, 260–262, 264
Smith, Lt. Col. Benjamin 43, 172, 235
Smith, Pvt. Benjamin 159
Smith, Lt. Frank G. 48, 229, 233
Smith, Gus 168
Smith, Gen. James A. 253
Smith, Josiah B. 303
Smith, Gen. Thomas B. 197, 204–205, 208
Smith, Capt. W.B. 123
Smith, Gen. William Sooy 13–14, *15*-16
South Carolina troops: 24th Infantry 160
Spalding, Col. George 24, 46, 237–238, 268–269

Sparks, A.W. "Tuck" 177, 305
Spencer, D.B. 176
Spencer carbines/rifles *see* carbines
Spring Hill: Confederate cavalry 148–156; night action 158–162; Union cavalry 146, 151–152; Union withdrawal 148–155
Stanley, Gen. David 11, 22, 28, 32–33, 75, 81, 86, 88–*90*, 91, 97, 100, 103, 115, 117–118, 121, 123, 130, 141, 146–148, 151–153, 156–158, 160, 165–167, 312
Starkweather, Gen. John 34–25
Steedman, Gen. James 24, 122, 183, 188, 218, 227, 249, 260, 263, 310
Stephens, Maj. Jacob S. Stephens 49, 229
Stephens, Maj. Meshack 25
Stevenson, Gen. Carter 204, 283–287
Stewart, Gen. A.P. 29, 82, 92–94, 99-*100*, 110, 118, 129, 147, 159–160, 172, 183, 188, 192, 217, 222–223, 227–229, 238, 243, 246, 248, 251, 255, 258–259, 260–261
Stewart, Lt. Francis 108
Stewart, Col. Francis M. 23, 62
Stewart, Col. James 46
Stewart, Col. Robert R. *46*-47, 104, 131–133, 135, 141–143, 147, 150, 162, 167–168, 175, 178, 184–185, 225, 237–238, 242, 291–292, 294, 299, 309, 311, 313
Stiles, Col. Israel 264
Stoneman, Gen. George 10–12, 36, 49, 57, 130, 311
Stoneman's Raid 36, 49, 51
Stones River, Battle of 16, 35, 44, 60, 64, 204
Stones River Campaign 48, 60, 189, 201
Story, Maj. William P. 46, 237, 242
Stovall, Gen. Marcellus A. 275, 286
Strahl, Gen. Otho 160, 255, 290
Strange, Maj. John P. 113
Streight's raid 72
Strickland, Col. Silas 97, 99, 103, 109–110
Strong, Capt. James 109–110
Stuart, Maj. James H. 85
Stuart, Gen. J.E.B. 35
Sturgis, Gen. Samuel 13, 41
Sugar Creek, attack at 301–303
Sulfur Creek railroad trestle 25
Surby, Sgt. Richard 45, 176, 257, 287
Swallow, Maj. G.R. 25

Taylor, Gen. Richard 21–23, 28–29, 32, 77, 81–82, 84, 308, 315

Taylor, Lt. Col. William F. 23, 85, 232, 279
Taylor, Pres. Zachary 22, 53
Tennessee, Army of (CSA) *see* Army of Tennessee
Tennessee forces (CSA): 1st Infantry 177, 258; 2nd Cavalry 23, 64, 85, 206; 3rd Cavalry 114, 190, 255, 265–267; 4th Cavalry 61; 5th Infantry 125, 181, 260; 7th Cavalry 23, 61–62, 67, 76, 85, 92, 98, 112, 157, 169, 232, 245, 265, 279, 293; 9th Cavalry 24, 61–62, 171, 187, 222, 275; 10th Cavalry 61, 245; 11th Cavalry 131; 12th Cavalry 23, 61–62, 85, 92, 245, 268; 12th Infantry 65; 14th Cavalry 23, 61, 85, 111, 152–153, 229, 245, 265, 269, 284; 15th Cavalry 23, 61, 85, 92, 117, 245; 16th Cavalry 23, 85; 18th Cavalry 23, 141; 19th Cavalry 62, 64, 104,-105, 275; 19th Infantry 296, 301; 20th Cavalry 23, 64, 197; 20th Infantry 260, 291; 21st Cavalry 64, 101; 22th Cavalry 141, 155, 202, 208; 26th Cavalry Battalion 23, 61–62, 85, 92, 114; 30th Infantry 209; 49th Infantry 168; Morton's Battery 23, 68, 77, 85, 184–185, 197, 207, 276, 280, 293, 297–298, 302, 307; Neeley's Cavalry 62; Newsom's Cavalry 85, 141, 276; Nixon's Cavalry 64, 155, 276, 306; Rice's Battery 23, 85, 190
Tennessee forces (US): 1st Cavalry 135, 150, 263, 294; 2nd Cavalry 25, 31–32, 302; 3rd Cavalry 24–25, 32, 177; 4th Cavalry 25, 32, 119, 127, 258, 302; 5th Cavalry 25, 127, 197, 202–203; 6th Cavalry 119, 253; 10th Cavalry 24–25, 90, 103, 132–133, 162, 167, 242; 11th Cavalry 112, 126, 300; 12th Cavalry 24, 90, 112, 126, 132, 151, 245, 268–269
Texas troops: 3rd Cavalry 68, 80, 99, 101, 116, 137–138, 156, 159, 176–177, 300, 307; 4th Infantry 9; 6th Cavalry 68, 70–71, 99, 106, 138, 156, 159, 176–177, 292, 307; 8th Cavalry 29; 9th Cavalry 68, 94, 99, 101, 106, 138, 156, 176–177, 294, 301–302, 305, 307; 14th Cavalry (Dismounted) 241, 259; 27th Cavalry (1st Texas Legion) 68, 99, 101, 106, 138, 140, 156, 159, 177, 301–302, 307; Willis' (Texas) Cavalry battalion 23
Thatcher, Marshall 171, 173, 175
Thomas, Gen. George 3–5, 8, 11, 19, 22, 26, 28–29, 31-*36*, 37, 41, 44, 48–49, 54, 57, 75–76, 78,

81, 86, 88–91, 93, 97, 99–101, 103, 118–126, 128–131, 133, 135, 142–143, 146, 162–163, 165–167, 179–181, 183, 187–188, 191–192, 194–195, 197, 214–218, 221–226, 228–229, 242, 245–248, 251–252, 255, 261, 263, 272–275, 291, 295, 300, 309–310, 313–314, 316
Thomas, Col. Minor T. 200, 203
Thompson, Col. Charles R. 78–79, 249
Thompson's Station 63, 68–69, 71, 133, 143, 147–148, 150–151, 155–156, 158–159, 162–163, 172, 274, 283, 288, 312
Thornburg, Russell 135
Thornburgh, Lt. Col. Jacob 24–25, 39, 53, 132, 244
Thrall, Capt. James C. 23, 85, 76–77
Tilghman, Col. Lloyd 71
Tompkins, Maj. Haviland 48, 229
Treadway, Charles 14
Tullahoma Campaign 11, 16, 24, 44, 46, 48, 69
Tunnell, Lt. J.T. 241, 259
Tupelo, Battle of 14, 16, 62, 66–67, 72
Turner, Col. James J. 209
Tyler, H.A. 155, 280, 287

Undine 26–27, 76–77
United States Cavalry Bureau 41, 55–56, 188
United States (U.S.) forces: 1st Cavalry 88; 1st Dragoons 68; 1st Infantry 48; 2nd Artillery 71; 2nd Cavalry 9, 48; 3rd Artillery 71; 3rd Cavalry 67; 3rd Colored Cavalry 128; 4th Artillery 48, 216, 230, 233, 265, 298–299; 4th Cavalry 119, 152, 187, 213, 241, 283–284, 297, 309; 4th Infantry 9; 14th Colored Infantry 196; 44th Colored Infantry 196; 61st Colored Infantry 26; Mounted Rifles 67
United States Military Academy 9, 35, 45, 47, 54, 67, 71, 88
Upton, Gen. Emory 41, 48, 219
USS see specific boat name

Van Dorn, Gen. Earl 68, 70–71, 162
Van Duzer, Capt. J.C. 33, 246
Venus 76–77
Vicksburg Campaign 54, 56, 60, 64, 67–68, 71–72, 251

Wagner, Gen. George 97, 104, 115, 147–148, 151–157, 161, 165–166, 168–169, 312–313
Walker, Lt. Col. William 85
Wallace's Mill 129, 135
Walthall, Gen. Edward 238, 243, 248, 290–294, 296, **298**, 300–303, 314
Walton, Lt. Edwin S. 23, 85
Walton, James O. 33, 184, 298
Warren, Lt. Col. James M. 85
Washburn, Gen. Cadwallader C. 14, 17, 28–29, 119–120, 195, 218
Watkins, Col. Elihu 285
Watkins, Lt. Henry 295
Watkins, Gen. Louis 31, 42, 187, 210–211, 215, 218
Watkins, Sam 177, 257–258, 270
Watson, Pvt. Berry 269
Watters, Lt. Col. Zachariah L. 257
Wells, Col. Oliver 46–47, 95, 103–108, 121, 126, 237, 312
Wester, Lt. George W. 25
Wheeler, Col. James T. 62
Wheeler's Raid 11–12, 16, 20–22, 44
Whipple, Gen. William 263
White, Lt. Col. Raleigh R. 23, 85, 111, 269–270
Wilder's brigade 50
Williams, Gen. Alpheus 52

Williamson, Maj. Thomas 303–304
Wilson, Col. Andrew 23, 85, 153
Wilson, Gen. James Harrison 3–5; 8, 23, 33–35, **40**-42, 53-**56**, 57, 86–89, 99, 103, 109, 118–119, 121–127, 129–139, 141–144, 146–151, 153, 162–164, 167–168, 171, 173–175, 177–179, 183–185, 187–190, 193–194, 214–216, 218–221, 223, 227–228, 230, 234, 248, 252–257, 260–266, 268–273, 275, 278, 280, 282–284, 287–293, 295, 299–300, 308,-316
Wilson's Crossroads, cavalry fight at 184–187
Winchester, First Battle of 51
Windes, Lt. Col. Frances M. 26, 85, 304
Winn, Robert 32
Winslow, Col. Edward 14, 39–41, 57, 75, 88, 119–121, 195, 218–219
Winstead Hill, fight at (Dec. 17) 282–288
Wisconsin troops: 1st Cavalry 210; 8th Infantry 247
Wiswell, James 213
Withers, Gen. Jones M. 59
Wood, Gen. Thomas 121, 141–142, 167, 175, 186, 217, 237, 248–249, 260, 263, 292, 300, 310
Woodward, Capt. S.L. 88–89
Worsham, Dr. J.W. 296, 301
Worthington, William Mason 177, 206, 270, 289
Wright, Garrison 93
Wyeth, John Allan 164, 179

Yazoo River Campaign 46
Young, Maj. J. Morris 118, 135–136; charge at Orr's Crossroads 139–140
Young, J.P. 113, 157, 230, 232, 265, 279, 293–294

www.ingramcontent.com/pod-product-compliance
Lightning Source LLC
Chambersburg PA
CBHW080755300426
44114CB00020B/2735